ASIATISCHE FORSCHUNGEN

MONOGRAPHIENREIHE
ZUR GESCHICHTE, KULTUR UND SPRACHE
DER VÖLKER OST- UND ZENTRALASIENS

Begründet von Walther Heissig

Herausgegeben von Thomas O. Höllmann

Band 160

2020

Harrassowitz Verlag · Wiesbaden

Moritz Huber

Lives of Sogdians in Medieval China

2020
Harrassowitz Verlag · Wiesbaden

Zugl. Diss. an der Ludwig-Maximilians-Universität München, 2020.

Bibliografische Information der Deutschen Nationalbibliothek
Die Deutsche Nationalbibliothek verzeichnet diese Publikation in der Deutschen Nationalbibliografie; detaillierte bibliografische Daten sind im Internet über http://dnb.de abrufbar.

Bibliographic information published by the Deutsche Nationalbibliothek
The Deutsche Nationalbibliothek lists this publication in the Deutsche Nationalbibliografie; detailed bibliographic data are available in the internet at http://dnb.de.

For further information about our publishing program consult our website http://www.harrassowitz-verlag.de

Printing and binding: BoD - Books on Demand, Norderstedt
Printed in Germany

ISSN 0571-320X
ISBN 978-3-447-11380-9

To those who strive to “play gracefully with ideas” instead of “[arriving] at the violence of opinion merely”.[1]

1 Small, *De Profundis*, 39.

Table of Contents

Appendices online at https://www.harrassowitz-verlag.de/titel_6520.ahtml

Preface and Acknowledgements

A thesis does not arise in a vacuum. Long in the making, they can be traced far back along the academic career of the researcher, a role that can further be situated in the more complex life of the individual, who again can be situated in a cultural background and history or even further in the fundaments of human nature. Without getting into the psychological abysses of deeper motivations behind why a person would write the book that you happened to open, some words may be helpful to understand the genesis and present state of this project.

After returning from a stay in China in 2010 to continue my Magister studies, I visited a course on the Silk Roads. Pursuing my interests, I minored in the Science of Religion and Chinese Art and Archaeology. For these courses I chose to present a short introduction into Zoroastrianism on the Silk Roads, which resulted in a paper on the *sabao* and my first encounter with Sogdians in China. Little did I know that I had retraced the same path that Sinologists had ventured on over 150 years prior. I became more and more interested in the exchange between cultures and people in the following years, especially in how to frame these contacts, and eventually stumbled upon epitaphs and the fascinating possibilities they promised to offer for many of my questions. I decided to write a dissertation project in late 2013 about how to use these underestimated but challenging sources to produce biographies of Sogdians in China. One of the main motivations was to show that they were not only active as merchants and exotic foreigners searching profit in China or desiring to become assimilated – to dramatically polemise two of the main perspectives current in scholarship. It was only after digging deeper into the topic and realising the true complexity of its intertwining discourses and objects that the magnitude of the task at hand presented itself., Due to the additional pressures of funding and the ambitious time constraint I set myself of composing and defending the thesis within 3 years, my thesis ended quite differently from what I expected. While I met my time frame, the object and the meta-questions were thus never to satisfyingly covered. I realised in the process, however, that the driving force behind this thesis was never to publish, but simply to engage in fascinating research.

The resulting book that emerges from the unrewarding task of publication is thus a compromise. While I am responsible for and defend every one of the many points of controversy that are made in this thesis – a danger, to polemicise again, quite often avoided in scholarship due to sinological self-censorship and the related self-preservationist and careerist desire of publishing instead of perishing – it is written with the best of intentions to instigate academic debate. To let another far wiser than I phrase the gist of my inner conflicts in this regard: "(…) and you Think of Things, you find sometimes that a Thing which seemed very Thingish inside you is quite different when it gets out into the open and has other people looking at it."[1]

Part of such a compromise are shortcomings such as discoveries made too late, i.e. mainly the two important publications of Bi Bo and Fukushima Megumi, which could distressingly not be considered in this thesis.[2] I must also apologise for any poor English style and formulations.

For their support and criticism of my endeavours, I want to thank my supervisors Thomas O. Höllmann and Dr. Hans van Ess. After their encouragement to enter the Promotionsprogramm Altertumswissenschaften (PAW) of the Ludwigs-Maximilians-Universität München (LMU), from which I profited greatly, they supported my application to the Graduate School Distant Worlds (GSDW). The Graduate School and its members, the associated institutions, as well as the Deutsche Forschungsgemeinschaft also deserve a special place in this list. Among the various conferences, I am specially indebted to Martin Lehnert for his friendly invitation to an inspiring symposium on Buddhism and the Formation of Authority in East Asia, for his insights and wisdom, and Sabrina Rastelli for a wonderful conference on Sogdians in China in Venice, and last but not least, the productive exchange I was allowed to have with Albert Dien through letters and in Stanford. Among my former teachers and later colleagues in the Institute of Sinology of the LMU, aside from my supervisors and the support of Armin Selbitschka, I am most indebted to Soong Shing Müller whose patience with me seems to have no limits, for her insights and hints, and for her unwavering and friendly encouragement. Academic life is, however, empty without dear colleagues from neighbouring fields, among which my warmest thoughts go to Henry Albery, Lauren Morris, and Constanze Pabst von Ohain. Last but not least, I have to thank my friends and family, and most importantly my wife, for their unconditional support.

Munich, 18.12.2019

Moritz Huber

1 Milne, *Winnie-the-Pooh*, 196.
2 Bi Bo, *Zhonggu*; Fukushima Megumi, *Tōbu*.

Style Sheet

The following formatting and transcription methods are based on the consistent and much more elaborate style sheet of Wilkinson.[1]

In this paper, Chinese characters are generally standardised in traditional characters *zhengti* 正體,[2] the font being KaiTi, resembling the regular script (*kaishu* 楷書), which was mostly used on the epitaphs during the Tang.[3] Chinese characters in the English text are not put between quotation marks, as they are obviously distinguishable.

Transcription

The characters are from Chinese into *pinyin* 拼音, the latter being the most common transcription method in use today. The characters from the manuscripts are transcribed into *zhengzi* 正字. This means that a character written in a manuscript with a simplified version which is part of the official *jianhuazi* 簡化字 is still transcribed into a *zhengzi* 正字, such as *wu* 无 into *wu* 無. As most of the characters transcribed were pronounced with different phonemic tones (as well as vowels and consonants, which would lead even further) in different ages and different places – to put it simply – intonation marks are not added. Some transcriptions that have found in one way or another their common use in English are kept (e.g., Shanxi for 山西, and Shaanxi for 陝西). Proper names and titles that are part of proper names are capitalised, including dynasties and historical periods, whereas modern author's Chinese names are not written both in Chinese characters and *pinyin* 拼音 in the text, as they can be found in the bibliography. If not being part of a name, titles of offices are in lower case (e.g., 將軍 *jiangjun,* general). Titles are translated by mostly relying on Hucker for the English part, in the explanation in the footnote referring to more accurate and/or

1 Wilkinson, *Chinese History*, xvii–xxiii.

2 Following by this choice of characters the policy of the Ministry of Education of the RoC, as proclaimed in August 1935, and not the misleading term *fantizi* 繁體字 (complicated characters), being used since the *Hanzi jianhua fang'an* 漢子字简化方案 passed in the PRC in 1956. The term is actually simply the continuation of the term *zhengtizi* 正體字 (sometimes omitting the *ti* 體) used before this time. Some people prefer to use the term *chuantong hanzi* 傳統漢字 to circumvent the issue. It seems, however, that the nature of the debate has become rather political than linguistic, which shouldn't afflict a correct nomenclature.

3 Every font has its own deficiencies in character display, PmingLiU being among the most correct, but also the most unattractive fonts.

extensive reference works and sources.[4] Toponyms are capitalised in *pinyin*. However, 州 *zhou* is understood as part of toponyms (Yangzhou 揚州), whereas *guo* 國 (state), *jun* 郡 (commandery), *fu* 府 (prefecture), *xian* 縣 (district; present-day: county), *xiang* 鄉 (town), *li* 里 (hamlet), etc., are translated. For the sake of consistency, even the Chinese or Sanskrit terms being common in English are italicised (*sūtra*; an exception being those words understood as proper names, e.g., Buddha, actually the *buddha*).

The ranks (*pin* 品/*ming* 命) are transcribed in the usual manner (e.g. *zheng san pin xia* 正三品下 to 3a2) except for the Northern Zhou, which worked with an inversed nine rank system. For the sake of comparability, for these ranks, an equivalency in the usual rank system is given, with the official rank of the Northern Zhou in brackets, e.g. "*zheng san ming* 正三命" to "equivalent to rank 7a (*zheng san ming* 正三命)". If the title was honorary, it is marked by an asterisk in the tables with biographic data (e.g.: rank 7*). If the person was noble, it is additionally marked by a plus (e.g., rank 4^{+}), and if the title of nobility is of a foreign state, it is marked by an asterisk (noble*).[5]

Book titles are capitalized and written in cursive (e.g. *Hanshu*). Chinese characters are never italicised. Book titles are not translated from Chinese or Japanese to English for the classical works (e.g. *Hanshu*).

Relying on the conversion tool of the Academia Sinica Department of Information Technology Services (http://sinocal.sinica.edu.tw, last access 11/2016), the Chinese lunisolar dates are transcribed and then translated into the Gregorian calendar in the following way:

Nianhao # [*ganzhi*]/#month [*ganzhi*]/#day [*ganzhi*] (#day.#month.#year CE).

E.g.:

咸亨元年歲次庚午十二月庚午朔十三日壬午

Xianheng 咸亨 1 [*gengwu*]/12 [*gengwu*]/13 [*renwu*] (29.1.671 CE).

If a Chinese epitaph states that the person passed away at the age of 63, in Western counting it translates to the age of 62, as the pregnancy is not included.

The reconstructions of Early Middle Chinese (EMC*) are reproduced from Pulleyblank's dictionary, except the ə-breve, which does not have a unicode point and is thus – in accordance to an older version of his dictionary – rendered as an a-breve (ă).[6]

4 Hucker, *Dictionary*. *Cishi* 刺史 is to be noted as one of the extraordinary cases, being translated to English with two different terms: as "regional inspector" for before the Sui and as "prefect" since the Sui, due to changes in the bureaucratic organisation.

5 For more information, see: Johnson, *The Medieval Chinese Oligarchy*, 19–31; and: Miyazaki Ichisada, *Kyūhin kanjin hō*; Yang Yunru, *Jiu pin zhongzheng*; Miyakawa Hisayuki, *Rikuchō shi kenkyū*, 238–63; Holzman, "Débuts du système".

6 Pulleyblank, *Lexicon*.

Translation of biological terms

The translation of biological terms from ancient Chinese sources is a challenge. The translations are as precise as possible, except for *niu* 牛, translated as "cattle" which may refer to various animals of the subfamily *Bovinae*, and *yang* 羊, translated as "sheep", which may refer to various animals of the subfamily *Caprinae*.

Bibliography and footnotes

The footnotes and bibliography are formatted based on the Chicago Style Manual[7] and supplemented with the necessary changes required for East Asian Studies (e.g., Chinese names are always written in full, together with their transcription in *pinyin* 拼音, or *rōmaji* for Japanese etc.), with the exception of the primary works, which are quoted by title and listed alphabetically (with the exception of Dunhuang 敦煌 documents from the International Dunhuang Project website). The Chinese characters (*jianti* 簡體 or *zhengti* 正體) used for the authors and titles in the bibliography correspond to the usage in the publication.

Abbreviations

Apart from the standard abbreviations (e.g., m, kg, CE, etc.), some of the lesser known are listed below, mostly used in Vol. 2:

S-N	south-north	L	length	Thk	thickness
T-B	top-bottom	W	width	Wt	weight
H	height	Dia	diameter	D	depth

Format of the Chinese texts

For the transcriptions made by the author (and thus excluding any quotes from other publications), *lacunae* on the epitaphs are marked in the transcribed text with a blank square inside square brackets "[□]" for which the number of squares mark the number of characters being assumed to make the *lacuna*),[8] and column-breaks with a dash "/". A character being reconstructed or exchanged according to the original character – mostly due to its poor legibility, or some contextual or external knowledge –

7 Chicago University, *Chicago Manual.*

8 For the transcriptions filled into the tables, reproducing the epitaph, the characters of a *lacuna* are marked with an "◇", to be able to format the table.

is marked with square brackets “[ ]” and, if needed, a footnote supplies the argumentation behind the reconstruction. A character reconstructed from external material or knowledge is marked with round brackets “( )”. Left out passages are marked with six ellipsis points “……”. Chinese punctuation marks are used: “ ， ” marking a comma, “ 、 ” marking an enumerating comma, “ 。 ” marking a full stop, “ ！ ” marking an exclamation mark, and “ 『』 ” and “ 「」 ” marking the single and double quotation marks. Book titles are not rendered with Chinese styled brackets “ 《》 ”. For the tables in the chapter on epitaphs, the information is divided by a dash “/”: first the information from the Chinese side, then from the Sogdian side.

Formatting of the illustrations

Most of the Chinese captions, legends, annotations, etc., have been translated into English. For some, major changes have been made, e.g., a rearrangement, mirroring, or additions. The latter are detailed below the figure.

Introduction

Sogdians, a group of Central Asians based between the Amu Darya and the Syr Darya, played a significant historical role at the crossroads of the Silk Roads. Travelling the world as caravan leaders, organised in trading networks, they were found from Byzantium to the Chinese heartland. Their language was a candidate for the *lingua franca* of the Silk Roads for some hundred years and they became famous as polyglot mediators at courts and prominent as translators of Buddhist texts. In the Chinese capitals, fire temples were erected for their use and the products they imported were cherished by the people and the court.

Forschungsgeschichte – a closer look

The beginning of the interest on Sogdians in China may be traced to the literary studies of the 1830s. Rémusat, Landresse, and Shen Dacheng 沈大成 studied references to the *safu* 薩甫/*sabo* 薩薄/*sabao* 薩保/薩寶 in written sources, and concluded that it must have been some sort of leader of the Sogdians, maybe related to religious functions.[1] Some 70 years later, several, now famous, expeditions of Western powers were conducted into what is today Xinjiang and the Silk Roads, a term coined by von Richthofen in 1877, transporting home such a substantial amount of material that its study is still far from completion.[2] Pelliot, one of the leading scholars of the time, reiterated the debate on the *sabao* in 1903, followed by an article on Manichaeism by Chavannes, another eminent French scholar, in 1912, and a second article by Pelliot on the Dunhuang documents and Sogdians around lake Lop Nor in 1916.[3] To my knowledge, this is the first article specifically mentioning Sogdians in China in its title. A great step forward was made by Laufer in his pioneering and encyclopaedic study on Sino-Iranian exchange in 1919.[4] In China, the first influential article in this area was published in 1923 by Chen Yuan who gathered material on Zoroastrianism in China. At this time, two Japanese scholars ventured into the topic, namely Fujita Toyohachi, writing about the *sabao* and on the Western Regions in 1925, and Kuwabara in 1926, more generally discussing immigration from the West to China.[5] Shiratori Kurakichi then followed with his impressive study on Sogdiana in 1928.[6]

1 See p. 240 fn. 1.

2 See: Waugh, "Richthofen's 'Silk Roads'".

3 Pelliot, "Le sa-pao"; Chavannes and Pelliot, "Traité Manichéen I" ; Pelliot, "Cha tcheou tou fou t'ou king". In 1903, Chavannes had already made an important contribution to the field with his study on the Tujue 突厥 (Chavannes, *Documents*).

4 Laufer, *Sino-Iranica.*

5 Fujita Toyohachi, "Saiiki kenkyū"; Fujita Toyohachi, *Xiyu yanjiu*; Kuwabara Jitsuzō, "Zui Tō jidai".

6 Shiratori Kurakichi, "Study on Su-t'ê".

In 1931, Reichelt made a pioneering edition of the "Ancient Sogdian Letters", found during an expedition of Stein in a watchtower near Dunhuang 敦煌.[7] Besides Chen Yuan, a second Chinese scholar, Xiang Da, also published an article in 1933, discussing different foreign influences in the Tang, especially in the capital Chang'an 長安.[8]

In the 35 years after the second World War, few articles were written. First came Pulleyblank in 1952, publishing his article on the Six Garrisons in Inner Mongolia, dominated by Sogdians, followed by his dissertation in 1955 on the background of the An Lushan 安祿山 Rebellion, the latter allegedly being of Turco-Sogdian descent.[9] This was followed shortly thereafter by three articles concerned with Zoroastrianism in China: Dien in 1957, laying the foundation for future studies, followed by a short comment by Eichhorn in 1959, and crowned by far the most extensive study on the *sabao* by Dien then published in 1962, which was unchallenged until his own article in 2006.[10] In 1963, Schafer came forward with a tribute to Laufer, writing the second magisterial study focused on Tang exotica from the west, especially from Iran.[11] Finally, the lifework of Boyce on Zoroastrianism, with the first of three volumes published in 1975, amply provided for the Iranian part of the picture.[12] All the research done until then, put together, covered the vast majority of the classical historical sources, and not much has been, nor indeed can be added to this.

Another field also resurfaced after the wars: so-called Dunhuang 敦煌 Studies, with its material now stored around the globe. Although associated publications are far too numerous to all be listed here, some, to digress slightly from the direction of our narration untill now, deserve particular mention. Waley published on the Iranian temples in Dunhuang 敦煌 in 1957, followed by Ikeda On, writing several important articles concerning, among others, Sogdians in Dunhuang 敦煌 in 1965, 1975, 1981, and 1999.[13] Japanese scholars started a series of editions in 1978, concerning the social and economic history of Dunhuang 敦煌 and Turfan 吐魯番, the last volume published in 2001.[14] These were supplemented by the similarly exhaustive studies in

7 Reichelt, *Die soghdischen Handschriftenreste*.

8 Xiang Da, *Tangdai Chang'an*.

9 Pulleyblank, "Sogdian Colony"; Pulleyblank, *Rebellion of An Lu-Shan*.

10 Dien, "A Note on Hsien 祆"; Eichhorn, "Materialien"; Dien, "Sa-Pao Problem"; Dien, "Further Thoughts". Among others, Jiang Boqin and Rong Xinjiang published some articles of interest on the topic, as discussed p. 240 fn. 1.

11 Schafer, *Golden Peaches*.

12 Boyce, *A History of Zoroastrianism*.

13 Waley, "Some References to Iranian Temples"; Ikeda On, "Hasseiki chūyō"; Ikeda On, "Sashū zukei ryakkō"; Ikeda On, "Marchands sogdiens"; Ikeda On, "Dunhuang de Suteren juluo".

14 Arranged chronologically: Yamamoto Tatsuro, Okano Makoto and Ikeda On, *Tun-huang, Legal Texts*; Yamamoto Tatsuro and Dohi Yoshikazu, *Tun-Huang, Census Registers (B)*; Yamamoto Tatsuro and Dohi Yoshikazu, *Tun-Huang, Census Registers (A)*; Yamamoto Tatsuro and Ikeda On, *Tun-huang, Contracts*; Yamamoto Tatsuro, Dohi Yoshikazu and Ishida Yusaku, *Tun-Huang, She Associations*; Yamamoto Tatsuro et al., *Tun-huang, Supplement*.

six volumes on the material stored in China, published between 1981 and 1991.[15] Besides that, several articles were written on Dunhuang 敦煌 and Turfan 吐魯番, concerning the temple system,[16] Turco-Sogdian documents,[17] Zoroastrianism,[18] re-editions of and comments on the Ancient Sogdian Letters,[19] a Sogdian slave contract,[20] and some articles presenting overviews.[21] Another small and specialised field is that of numismatics, which, besides some material analysis on individual finds has been scarcely worked on. To name are the studies of Xia Nai in 1974, Thierry in 1993, 1994, and 2005, Lin Ying in 2003, and a smaller study of Luo Feng in 2005.[22]

Returning to the above interrupted chronology, starting from the 1980s, three altered factors changed the field radically, although mostly from a quantitative perspective. First, in the midst of the Cultural Revolution, the trajectory of Chinese politics shifted towards the study of ancient culture, orchestrated inside the limits of ideological policy and Marxist history. Second, and as a consequence of the former, Chinese archaeology and literary studies received extensive state sponsorship, artefacts were displayed worldwide, and thus Chinese academia connected increasingly with the outside world. Although hundreds of the graves and epitaphs in China were by then already destroyed or taken out of context, a series of extraordinary finds related to Sogdians provided fresh material. As a third factor, the number of students and thus the competition between scholars suddenly rocketed, resulting in a never-ending flow of publications.

On the archaeological side, the first grave attributed to a Sogdian was excavated in 1982, succinctly followed by eleven others, until the most recent publication of 2014: the grave of Shi Daode 史道德,[23] the Tang graves in Yanchi 鹽池, Ningxia Province,[24] the grave of Shi Shewu 史射勿,[25] the graves of Shi Daode 史道德 and Shi Shewu 史射勿, combined with the other graves of the Shi 史 families in Guyuan

15 Guojia wenwuju guwenxian yanjiu shi, *Tulufan chutu wenshu*.
16 Jiang Boqin, *Dunhuang sihu zhidu*.
17 Sims-Williams and Hamilton, *Documents turco-sogdiens*.
18 Grenet and Zhang Guangda, "Last Refuge"; Zhang Guangda, "Iranian Religious Evidence".
19 Grenet, Sims-Williams and Vaissière, "Sogdian Ancient Letter V"; Sims-Williams, "Sogdian Ancient Letter II"; Sims-Williams: Silk Road Seattle Website, "Sogdian Ancient Letters".
20 Yoshida Yutaka, Moriyasu Takao and Xinjiang Uyghur Autonomous Museum, "Sogudo bun baibai monjo"; Lin Meicun, "Sutewen mai bi qi"; Yoshida Yutaka, "Translation".
21 Jiang Boqin, *Dunhuang Tulufan wenshu*; Hansen, "Introduction: Turfan"; Jonathan K. Skaff, "La documentation"; Skaff, "Sogdian Trade Diaspora".
22 Xia Nai, "Zongshu Sanshanchao yinbi"; Thierry, "Monnaies Sassanides"; François Thierry, "La monétarisation"; Thierry and Morrison, "Monnaies Byzantines"; Luo Feng, "Bei Zhou Shi jun mu"; Lin Ying, "Sogdians".
23 Ningxia Guyuan bowuguan, "Ningxia Shi Daode mu".
24 Ningxia huizu zizhiqu bowuguan, "Ningxia Yanchi mu".
25 Luo Feng et al., "Ningxia Shi Shewu mu".

固原, Ningxia Province,[26] the grave of An Jia 安伽,[27] the grave of master Shi 史,[28] the grave of Yu Hong 虞弘,[29] the grave of Kang Ye 康業,[30] and the grave of Shi Daoluo 史道洛.[31] Most of the ensuing archaeological articles to engage with these finds updated their own theories with the new input. In 2005, the first overview about funerary practices and furnishings of Central Asians (mostly Sogdians) was published by Lerner.[32] This was followed on the Chinese side by a study on Sogdians in mediaeval Chang'an 長安 by Bi Bo.[33] The publication of de la Vaissière's seminal study in the same year presented a new economical perspective on the growing corpus of sources.[34] In 2015, Wertmann published his overview on archaeological sources on Sogdians in China, and finally, Fukushima Megumi presented her study focused on epitaphs of Sogdians in Chines in 2017.[35]

On the side of Zoroastrianism, Manichaeism, and Nestorianism, papers were published by Leslie in 1981, dealing with mentions of foreign temples in China, by Lieu on Manichaeism in 1985 and 1998, by Chen Guocan on Zoroastrianism in 1988, followed by Lin Wushu in 1992 and 1995, Zhang Guangda in 1994, Lin Meicun in 1998, more focused on the archaeological material, Rong Xinjiang in 2003, Riboud in 2005, Grenet in 2007, from a broader perspective, and Zhang Naizhu on *the* Nestorian Pillar in 2013.[36]

As some of the excavated graves included epitaphs that mention the *sabao*, this topic was revived through the publications by Arakawa in 1998, Jiang Boqin in 1998, Luo Feng in 1998, Forte in 1999, Rui Zhuanming and Rong Xinjiang in 2003 and 2005, Su Hang in 2005, Dien in 2005 and 2006, supplemented by some transcriptions of epitaphs of Sogdians by Iwami Kiyohiro.[37]

26 Luo Feng, *Guyuan nanjiao Sui Tang mudi.*

27 Shaanxi sheng kaogu yanjiusuo, "Xi'an beijiao An Jia mu"; Shaanxi sheng kaogu yanjiusuo, "Xi'an faxian de Bei Zhou An Jia mu"; Shaanxi sheng kaogu yanjiusuo, *Xi'an Bei Zhou An Jia mu.*

28 Xi'an shi wenwu baohu kaogusuo, "Xi'an Bei Zhou Shijun".

29 Shanxi sheng kaogu yanjiusuo, Taiyuan shi wenwu kaogu yanjiusuo and Taiyuan shi Jinyuan qu wenwu lüyouju, "Taiyuan Suidai Yu Hong mu".

30 Xi'an shi wenwu baohu kaogusuo, "Xi'an Bei Zhou Kang Ye".

31 Yuanzhou lianhe kaogudui, *Tang Shi Daoluo mu.*

32 Lerner, "Aspects of Assimilation".

33 Bi Bo, *Zhonggu.*

34 Vaissière, *Histoire des marchands sogdiens*; in English: Vaissière, *Sogdian Traders.*

35 Wertmann, *Sogdians in China*; Fukushima Megumi, *Tōbu.*

36 Leslie, "Persian Temples"; Lieu, Samuel N. C., *Manichaeism in the Later Roman (1992)*, 219–62; Lieu, Samuel N. C., *Manichaeism in Central Asia*; Chen Guocan, "Wei"; Lin Wushu, "Discussion Heaven-God"; Lin Wushu, *Bosi baihuojiao*; Zhang Guangda, "Trois exemples"; Lin Meicun, "Cong kaogu faxian"; Rong Xinjiang, "Beichao Sui Tang huren"; Pénélope Riboud, "Réflexions sur *xian* 祆"; Grenet, "Religious Diversity"; Zhang Naizhu, "Luoyang Nestorian Pillar".

37 Rong Xinjiang, "*Sabao* or *Sabo*"; Rong Xinjiang, "Sabao yu Sabo"; Su Hang, "Beichao moqi de sabao pinwei," ; Albert E. Dien, "Caravans and Caravan Leaders"; Dien, "Further Thoughts"; Arakawa Masaharu, "'Sappō' no sēkaku"; Jiang Boqin, "Sabaofu zhidu," ; Luo Feng, "Sabao: Zai kaocha"; Forte, "Sabao 薩寶 Question"; Rui Chuanming, "Sabao de zai renshi"; Rong Xinjiang, "Sabao yu Sabo: Beichao"; Iwami Kiyohiro, *Sogudo jin boshi kenkyū*; the transcriptions

Apart from these studies, a few remain that discussed the material in larger contexts. These include such articles on material culture, as the publication by Rawson in 1982, Lin Meicun in 1997 on inscribed silverware Iran and Central Asia found in China, Carter and Wu Hung on funerary stone beds in 2002, Compareti on pearl roundels in 2003, and Müller on chin straps in a broader historical and geographical context in 2003 and 2016.[38] On the side of literary sources, the article of Dien in 1990 on military in the Northern Wei is to be mentioned, Forte on An Shigao 安世高 and his Iranian family, Cheng Xilin in 2000 on passports in the Tang, followed by Arakawa in 2001, de la Vaissière about Sogdian militia in China, Yoshida in 2006 on Sogdian personal names in Chinese sources, followed by Xu Xuya in 2007, and Zhao Zhenhua in 2012 on Sogdian craftsmen in China.[39]

Methodological approach

To open with the most basic approach on how to set about studying Sogdians in China, a first step is to investigate who Sogdians are, i.e. how they were identified and how they identified themselves, and to then explain what "China" refers to. In the studies laid out above, Sogdians were mostly identified in the primary sources by means of their family names. These sources provide information about their presence in the territory of present-day China, which, during the ca. 600 years between the fourth and ninth century in which they are mainly mentioned, was a tumultuous place over which dozens of dynasties of various ethnic and cultural backgrounds vied for supremacy, not to mention the conflicts with their neighbours and the outbreak of major rebellions. In Chinese sources on Sogdians, they are mostly called *hu* 胡,[40] an *exonym,* which during the Han, derogatorily referred to various northern neighbours from the steppe and thence came to be more commonly applied to Iranian and Central Asian people,

were made in Japanese *kanji* 漢子 and originally published from 2004 to 2008 in *Shiteki.*

38 Rawson, *Ornament on Chinese Silver*; Lin Meicun, "Zhongguo jingnei chutu"; Carter, "Notes"; Wu Hung, "A Case of Cultural Interaction"; Matteo Compareti, "The Role of the Sogdian Colonies"; Müller, "Chin-Straps"; Müller, "Zhongguo jinshu xia'etuo".

39 Albert E. Dien, "The Role of the Military"; Forte, *Hostage An Shigao*; Cheng Xilin, *Tangdai guosuo yanjiu*; Arakawa Masaharu, "Transit Permit System"; Vaissière, "Sute"; Yoshida Yutaka, "Personal Names, Sogdian"; Xu Xuya, "Sute"; Zhao Zhenhua, "Tangdai Zheng Yan".

40 In the following, the term *hu* 胡 will mostly not be translated due to the term's ambiguity when used in certain collocations. It can often unambiguously be translated into English as a noun (as in *jiuxing hu* 九姓胡 'Westerners of the Nine Names'). However, it is sometimes problematic to determine what 'Westerner' refers to. In addition, the 'Nine Names' are not clearly defined (see p. 89; 1.15.13). A similar change in meaning occurred for the *Xiyu* 西域. Whereas during the Han it referred to areas mostly located in present-day Xinjiang Uyghur Autonomous Region, it later more commonly meant Central Asia.
In contrast, some ambiguity remains in certain instances as to whether *hu* 胡 should be translated as a possessive noun or a proper adjective. While for the *Liu hu zhou* 六胡州, for example, it is clear from the context that it means 'Six Western Prefectures' instead of 'Six Prefectures of the Westerners' (discarding the options 'Prefectures of the Six Westerners' and 'Prefectures of the Six Western [Tribes]'), in the case of the *hu zhu* 胡祝 office, it could either mean 'Precentor of the Westerners' or 'Western Precentor'.

still conceivably connotated with exoticism and Otherness. Thus, while Sogdiana was not a unified state but a composite of fairly independent and disparate oasis cities with differing cultural identities connected under the rule of Samarqand, immigrants from these states were defined as a group in China under this term. In consequence, Sogdians in China themselves refer to their state of origin and not to Sogdiana.

Having set the basic scene and its apparent problems, in a next step the content of the various sources needs to be investigated. Pre-emptively, a first choice is to divide as far as possible literary and material evidence, as these require different heuristic approaches. In regard to literary sources, it is the description of Sogdian states in Sogdiana found in transmitted historical accounts that provide the basis for the identification of Sogdians in China, i.e. the family names. Deriving from the results of this step is that if these identifications turn out to be problematic, any further statement about the so-identified Sogdians needs to be questioned. The first chapter will thus present and translate a selection of relevant sources and analyse them critically to understand which countries were described and how they were named as well as serve as a source book for future research. Due to the nature of transmitted records, the critical analysis shall aim to differentiate between descriptions that may reflect a recorded observation, hearsay, and conflated or erroneously related statements. To achieve such distinction, it is necessary to retrace the compilation process, which includes the separation of information copied from older accounts and newly gathered information to further compare these to other sources external to this compilation. If possible, another analytical step consists in the isolation of judgements from informative description. Through this process, patterns, *topoi* and opinions may be identified.

The second chapter will then proceed to use the information gathered about the identification of Sogdians to engage with the sources on Sogdians in China. As already mentioned above, there are nearly no sources on Sogdians as a distinct group in China. Most information is gained through contemporary literary sources that mention individuals with the above identified family names and which may refer to their country of origin. Nonetheless there are several problems that come with this means of identification. The majority of these sources can be divided into two groups: on the one hand there are excavated manuscripts, such as registers, gazetteers, and letters, and on the other, epitaphs. These two source groups differ greatly in style and content. The registers, gazetteers, and letters are mostly informational and bureaucratic and appended with few judgements. Epitaphs, however, present quite the opposite state of affairs; while these too are highly standardised, their goal is to stress the importance of the tomb owner and his or her standing in society, placing overt emphasis on their career. Albeit standardised as they are, they do uniquely provide a self-defined portrait of Sogdians in China.

Material evidence from archaeological context represents a third group of sources. This mostly comes from graves and as most of the graves and their contents have been commented on rather extensively, this book presents a detailed case-study of the underrepresented graves of the Shi 史 in Guyuan 固原, Ningxia Province. In the analysis and final synthesis, all other relevant excavated sources on Sogdians in China will be used, including, e.g. ossuaries.

What should have been achieved by this stage is careful dissection of the selected material. To now further problematise the above-described approach and evaluate where to place the next step, consider the two images devised by Frankl to visualise his concept of Dimensional Ontology.

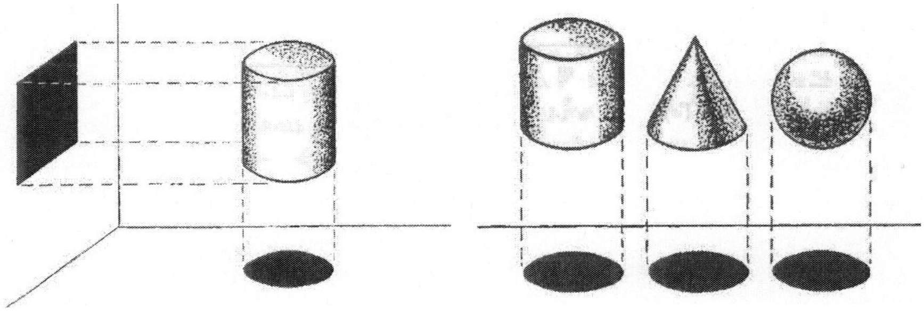

Figure 1a and b: Illustrations of the concept of Dimensional Ontology by Frankl
Source: Frankl, "Pluralismus," 24, figs. 24–25; *apud*: Frankl, "Revolutionierung"

According to him, there are two laws of Dimensional Ontology (referring to Figure 1a and b). The first law is:[41]

> The same thing projected from its dimension into different dimensions that are lower than its own is reproduced in such a way that the images contradict each other. If, for example, I project the drinking glass here, geometrically a cylinder, from the three-dimensional space into the two-dimensional levels of the horizontal and vertical section, the result is in one case a circle, however, in the other a rectangle. Furthermore, the projection results in a contradiction in the sense that in any case it will be a closed figure, whereas the drinking glass is an open receptacle.
>
> The second law of Dimensional Ontology is: (Not the same thing, but) different things, projected from their dimension (not into different dimensions, but) into the same dimension that is lower than itself, are reproduced in such a way that the images (do not contradict each other, but) are ambiguous. If, for example, I project a cylinder, a cone, and a sphere from their three-dimensional space into the two-dimensional space of the horizontal section, the result is in any case a circle. On the assumption that the cylinder, the cone, and the sphere cast

41 Frankl, "Pluralismus," 24; author's translation.

> a shadow, the shadows are ambiguous in the sense that I cannot infer from these, as they are the same, if it is a cylinder, a cone, or a sphere that casts them.

Frankl went on:[42]

> Science not only has the right, but even the duty to factor out the multidimensionality of reality, to blind out reality, to filter a frequency from the spectrum of reality. The projection is thus more than legitimate. It is obligatory. The scientist has to maintain the fiction of dealing with a unidimensional reality. But he also has to know what he does, and that means that he must know the sources of error around which he has to guide research.

Whereas Frankl applied these ideas to the problem of psychophysicality, in the following it shall be used as a simple metaphor for problems in historic studies, consciously chosen here to avoid conventionally used heuristics and their broadly threaded paths and pits. What is indeed interesting about the shadows cast upon the wall is that each of them is true. As he pointed out, the combination of these contradictory truths would, in the case of the cup, result in a three-dimensional cylinder, and still miss an important aspect of the object. At the same time, different objects of study may produce the same shadows. As scientists, we are, however, reduced to approach the object from the sections and their combinations. Indeed, only a new perspective, such as combined views or a three-quarter view from the top, would aid in discerning that the object in Figure 1a is a receptacle. However, we can be made aware that we do not know certain aspects of the object, and to state a tautology, we do not know what we do not know.[43] What may, however, occur to the person gathering these projections is an idea of the cylinder being a receptable, an educated guess based on the scrupulous study of such projections and experience in heuristic problems. Einstein wrote to this effect: [44]

> A new idea comes suddenly and in a rather intuitive way. That means it is not reached by conscious logical conclusions. But, thinking it through afterwards, you can always discover the reasons which have led you unconsciously to your guess and you will find a logical way to justify it. Intuition is nothing but the outcome of earlier intellectual experience.

Strikingly honest, this exposes what many a scholar desires to obscure by post-engineered introductions to their research process: research motivation starts with an intuition derived from personal experience and not from logical conclusions. In the field of historic studies, as the projections of the object are not accessible, the scholar is dissociated even further from the object. Even the access is limited to records of the object which are edited, or transmitted by a purposeful or even random choice, and

42 Ibid., 28; author's translation.

43 As banal as such a statement seems, the thought behind was once famously used by Rumsfeld in 2002 before invading a foreign country on a false pretence (U.S. Department of Defense, "DoD").

44 Einstein and Gordon, "My opinion".

even these records are often themselves second-hand information or compiled from earlier sources. Further, there is no possibility to go beyond the projections and look at it with from new perspectives to produce new shadows. Even material evidence is by the choice of a study subject projected as a phenomenon of a larger topic and includes source-specific biases; for example, most excavated artefacts pertain to high society or derive from graves. In the search for truth, the historian's effort was, however, a quest for the same approximation to the object. Another capitulation is the presentation of atomistic and positivistic listings and translations without a problematising perspective. However, what became apparent after several paradigm shifts is that the accounts and the material available to the present scholar are inextricably embedded in their own *Zeitgeist's* discourse. It was the problems that emerged out of this realisation that drove deconstructivists and post-modernists to eventually abandon the study of the object and sail in the seemingly safe haven of discourse analysis and its relativistic pitfalls.

It is, however, entirely possible to search to know for the sources of error, as Frankl put it, and continue with the careful dissection and understanding of the objects through its facets. After the dissection of the second chapter, the third thus aims to construct a synthesis of the gained information organised in categories. To define the categories in which to describe the object is the dilemma of knowing where to put the knife to slice the horizontal and vertical sections of knowledge, being aware that these slices derive from a personal opinion and experience while guiding the research around the traps of teleological research goals. The path chosen in this study is to avoid imposing classical Western categories of etic knowledge such as economy, politics, or religion on the material. The study of the religion of Sogdians, for example, is a category strongly influenced by a monotheistic and exclusivist mindset. To artificially introduce the framework of *religion* in the ancient Chinese context may result in the study of the competition between politics and religion, whereas a functionalistic study of *rituals*, for example, could result in an analysis of actors of power in society. The use of such a category may well create various conflicts needing to be solved within the self-inflicted discourse and thus result in the distancing from the object of the study.

To avoid these implications as far as possible, the categories that emerged from analysis of etic Chinese accounts on Sogdians in Sogdiana provide a structure that is probably closer to the object and thus less prone to anachronism. However, due to the nature of the letters, gazetteers, and epitaphs, no categories emerged from the sources on Sogdians in China that would lend themselves to an overview of their social situation, defined as the large frame of study. As a compromise, the aforementioned categories from the first chapter, such as *ritual*, were used to organise the information. Although these are etic in the sense that they were defined by Chinese authors in the description on foreign countries and people, they were chosen in place of even further removed etic modern categories and circumvent my own categorical blindness. As a side effect, the divergence between the information gathered on Sogdians in Sogdiana and China can be observed, which may produce new ideas and further questions to engage with.

The thesis concludes by presenting some thoughts on the results of the synthesis in order that the guiding meta-questions of this study may be addressed, some of which may already be patent in light of the above considerations regarding categorical implications: What can be gained by scrutinising the sources on Sogdians in China from the above-outlined definition of multiple facets? How do these insights compare to previous research questions? And, most importantly, what perspectives may be ventured from these divergences? Beyond any findings that result from the synthesis, the conclusion aims at transcending the positivistic presentations criticised above and rather presents ideas that originated during the research process – educated guesses peppered with theoretically consolidated inferences that need to be separated from the results "strictly" derived from the material.

At the end of this volume are a list of dynasties and the references. The second volume, to be found online at the address indicated below the table of contents, includes the appendices which include excavations reports, case studies of epitaphs, tables listing information from the epitaphs, the great majority of illustrations and glossaries of toponyms and office names.

Chapter 1: Historically transmitted Chinese accounts about Sogdiana

傳自遠國	[The accounts] came from distant countries
夷語訛舛	barbarian language is mistakable
年代綿邈	[from] times far away
莫知根實	nobody knows the truth.

Tongdian 193.5260

1.1 Introduction

The following pages provide an overview of the historically transmitted Chinese accounts related to Sogdians in Sogdiana, from the *Shiji* to the *Xin Tangshu*.

1.2 *Shiji*

1.2.1 Zhang Qian's 張騫 missions

The first available information concerning the Western Regions comes from Zhang Qian's 張騫 adventurous expeditions which were recorded in the *Shiji*, in the *liezhuan* 列傳 concerning Dayuan 大宛 (Ferghana) and its neighbouring regions.[1] Zhang Qian 張騫 was dispatched in 138 BCE to form an alliance with the Da Yuezhi 大月氏 but came to be captured by the Xiongnu 匈奴 while trying to reach them. After more than ten years, he was then able to move on. On his road, he came by Kangju 康居,[2] which

1 *Shiji* 123.3157–80. The information is reproduced nearly identically in the *Hanshu* 61.2687–98, and the *Hanshu* 96a.3894–96.
For a short overview of the discussion about the genesis of *Shiji* 123, i.e. if it is reconstructed based on the *Hanshu*, or rather not, see: Vaissière, *Sogdian Traders*, 25, fn. 30. See also: Pulleyblank, "Han," 281–86. For the argument, based on numismatics, that the passage of the *Shiji* was written earlier, see p. 17.

2 大宛以為然，遣騫，為發導繹，抵康居，康居傳致大月氏。 "The king of Dayuan trusted his words and sent him on his way, giving him guides and interpreters to take him to the state of Kangju (Trans-Oxania). From there he was able to make his way to the land of the Great Yuezhi." *Shiji* 123.3158. Translation: Watson, *Records*, 232.

was conflated in later accounts with the state of Kang 康, the latter identified as Samarqand in Sogdiana.[3] Concerning the state itself, the record says:[4]

> 康居在大宛西北可二千里。……與大宛鄰國。國小。
>
> Kangju is situated about 2,000 *li* north-west of Dayuan 大宛. (…) [It] is a neighbouring state of Dayuan 大宛. [The] state is small.

As the Da Yuezhi 大月氏 were themselves said to be located ca. 1,000–1,500 km west of Dayuan 大宛,[5] it can be gathered that his route first took him from Dayuan 大宛 north-west to Kangju 康居 and then south-west to the Da Yuezhi 大月氏. Only relying on this description, Kangju 康居 can, however, not be identified as Sogdiana.[6]

1.2.2 Suxie 蘇薤

A later passage includes the name Suxie 蘇薤, which was in later accounts connected to Shi 史 (Kesh). While returning from Anxi 安息 (Parthia) somewhat after 105 BCE,[7] a party of Chinese envoys apparently received some company:[8]

> 及宛西小國驩潛、大益，宛東姑師、扜冞、蘇薤之屬，皆隨漢使獻見天子。天子大悅。
>
> In addition, the smaller states west of Dayuan, such Huanqian and Dayi, as well as those east of Dayuan, such as Gushi, Wumi, and Suxie, all sent parties to accompany the Han envoys back to China and present gifts at court. The emperor was delighted at this.

The recently excavated bamboo slips in Xuanquanzhi 懸泉置 indeed corroborate that the king of Suxie 蘇薤, together with the king of Kangju 康居, sent envoys to China.[9]

3 See the *Weishu* p. 28 (1.7.12), the *Tongdian* p. 47 (1.12.1), and the *Jiu Tangshu* p. 50 (1.13.1).
4 *Shiji* 123.3161.
5 大月氏在大宛西可二三千里，居媯水北。 "The Great Yuezhi are ca. 2,000 or 3,000 *li* west of Dayuan 大宛, living north of the Gui 媯 River (Amu Darya)." *Shiji* 123.3161.
6 As de la Vaissière pointed out (Vaissière, *Sogdian Traders*, 27, fns. 36, 37). For further arguments on the topic, see: Shiratori Kurakichi, "Study on Su-t'ê," 84–90; Haloun, "Zur Üe-tṣï-Frage," 252; Daffinà, *L'immigrazione*, 48–63; Pulleyblank, "Wusun and Sakas"; and: Bernard, "Marcanda-Afrasiab," 345–46.
7 The *Hanshu* states that Emperor Wu 武 sent the embassy (96a.3859). Sima Guang 司馬光 dates these events to 105 BCE (*Zizhi tongjian* 21.695).
8 *Shiji* 123.3173; translation: Watson, *Records*, 243.
9 This information is to be found on excavated material and thus technically belongs to another chapter, but has no meaningful place there. The slips themselves have not been dated but among the 17,915 slips, 2086 are inscribed with dates, ranging from 111 BCE to 218 CE (Hao Shusheng and Zhang Defang, *Xuanquan*, 37). They were excavated ca. three kilometres south-east of present-day Tianshuijing 甜水井, Dunhuang 敦煌, Gansu Province. The two relevant passages are on the slips II90DXT0216②877 and II90DXT0216②882. The entire document goes from slip four to ten, i.e. II90DXT0216②877 to slip II90DXT0216②883. Slightly problematic are the different characters which were used in the available editions. In the earliest publication, Wu Rengzhou transcribed the passage concerning the king as Susheng wang 苏圣王 (Wu Rengzhou,

Further, while the *Shiji* proposes that there must be at least 10,000 *li* (ca. 5,000 km) from Dayuan 大宛 to the Han, the *Hanshu* states that it is 12,550 *li* (ca. 6,275 km) from the seat of government of the Dayuan 大宛 to the Han, and 4,310 *li* (ca. 2,155 km) from it to the seat of the protector general.[10] If the *Hanshu* is correct in stating that the distance is 5,776 *li* (ca. 2,888 km; actually 5,766 *li*, ca. 2,883 km)[11] from the Suxie 蘇䪥 Fort to the seat of the protector general, Suxie 蘇薤 must have been *west* of Dayuan 大宛 and not *east*, as was stated in the quote above. If at this time, Dayuan 大宛 is indeed to be identified as Ferghana, it could mean that Suxie 蘇薤 may have referred to a place in Sogdiana.

1.2.3 Around Dayuan 大宛, and between Dayuan 大宛 and Anxi 安息

The *Shiji* goes on to describe the region around Dayuan 大宛, which may already partly apply to Sogdiana:[12]

> 宛左右以蒲陶為酒，富人藏酒至萬餘石，久者數十歲不敗。俗嗜酒，馬嗜苜蓿。漢使取其實來，於是天子始種苜蓿、蒲陶肥饒地。及天馬多，外國使來，則離宮別觀旁盡種蒲萄、苜蓿極望。
>
> The regions around Dayuan 大宛 make wine out of grapes, the wealthier inhabitants keeping as much as 10,000 or more piculs stored away. It can be kept for as long as 20 or 30 years without spoiling. The people love their wine and the horses love their alfalfa. The Han envoys brought back grape and alfalfa seeds to China and the emperor for the first time tried growing these plants in areas of rich soil. Later, when the Han acquired large numbers of the "heavenly horses" and the envoys from foreign states began to arrive with their retinues, the lands on all sides of the emperor's summer palaces and pleasure towers were planted with grapes and alfalfa for as far as the eye could see.

More importantly, there follows a short description of the countries that lie between Dayuan 大宛 and Anxi 安息 (Parthia), a space that, geographically speaking, refers to Sogdiana:[13]

"Dunhuang," 105), while Li Jinyun read Subie wang 苏鼈王 (Gansu sheng wenwu kaogu yanjiusuo, "Dunhuang,"), Hu Pingsheng and Zhang Defang proposed to read Suxie wang 蘇韰王 (Hu Pingsheng and Zhang Defang, *Dunhuang*, 118; Hao Shusheng and Zhang Defang, *Xuanquan*, 197), and Wang Su read Suxie wang 苏薤王 (Wang Su, "Xuanquan," 155). The only facsimile available to me is of insufficient quality to make a definitive judgement on the identification: Hao Shusheng and Zhang Defang, *Xuanquan*, in the preface.

10 *Shiji* 123.3160, *Hanshu* 96a.3895.

11 See the discussion on the distances between the kingdoms of the petty kings of Kangju 康居 in the *Hanshu* p. 16 (1.3.1).

12 *Shiji* 123.3173–74; translation: Watson, *Records*, 244–45.

13 *Shiji* 123.3173. Although there is much debate about what and whom the Chinese sources are actually referring to, I do agree with de la Vaissière on the issue of this identification based on a geographic space, although I am sceptical about the veracity of the content. In the description of the travels of Zhang Qian 張騫, geographic data, stereotypes, and beliefs (e.g., it is reported that

自大宛以西至安息，國雖頗異言，然大同俗，相知言。其人皆深眼，多鬚，善市賈，爭分銖。俗貴女子，女子所言而丈夫乃決正。其地皆無絲漆，不知鑄錢器。及漢使亡卒降，教鑄作他兵器。得漢黃白金，輒以為器，不用為幣。

Although the countries from west of Dayuan 大宛 to Anxi 安息 speak rather different languages, their customs are generally similar and their languages mutually understandable. The men all have deep-set eyes and profuse beards and whiskers. They are skilful at commerce and will haggle over a fraction of a cent. Women are held in great respect, and the men make decisions on the advice of their women. No silk or lacquer is produced anywhere in the region, and the casting of coins and vessels was formerly unknown. Later, however, when some of the Chinese soldiers attached to the Han embassies deserted and surrendered to the people of the area, they taught them how to cast and manufacture [other kinds of] weapons.[14] Now, whenever people of the region lay their hands on any Han gold or silver they immediately make it into vessels and do not use it for currency.

1.2.4 The Chinese invasion of Central Asia

Furthermore, the *Shiji* includes the impression Zhang Qian's 張騫 report made on the emperor after his return:[15]

天子既聞大宛及大夏、安息之屬皆大國，多奇物，土著，頗與中國同業，而兵弱，貴漢財物；其北有大月氏、康居之屬，兵彊，可以賂遺設利朝也。且誠得而以義屬之，則廣地萬里，重九譯，致殊俗，威德徧於四海。

Thus, the emperor learned of Dayuan, Daxia, Anxi, and the others, all great states rich in unusual products whose people cultivated the land and made their living in much the same way as the Chinese. All these states, he was told, were militarily weak and prized Han goods and wealth. He also learned that to the north of them lived the Yuezhi and Kangju people who were strong in arms but who could be persuaded by gifts and the prospect of gain to acknowledge allegiance to the Han court. If it were only possible to win over these states by [righteous][16] means, the emperor thought, he could then extend his domain 10,000 *li* (ca. 5,000 km), [make nine translations to reach [people of] strange customs],[17] and his might would become known to all the lands within the four seas.

the Queen Mother of the West was not seen), are mixed together (Vaissière, *Sogdian Traders*, 26–28); translation: Watson, *Records*, 245.

14 The brackets are additions by the author. Watson did not translate the *ta* 他. I propose to understand it as referring to the new weapons they were taught to produce by casting.

15 *Shiji* 123.3161; translation: Watson, *Records*, 236.

16 Watson translated "peaceful".

17 Watson translated "attract to his court men of strange customs who would come translating and

However, the account goes on to say that the men of Dayuan 大宛 used to plot together. They observed that the Han envoys often were short of food and half of the men died on the journey, and concluded that the Han were too far away and would never succeed in sending a large army, and thus chose not to trade their precious and coveted horses to the Han. The Han envoys cursed at them and smashed their golden horse with a mallet, which resulted in the nobles of Dayuan 大宛 killing them and seizing their goods. As a result, the Han emperor sent two campaigns against the Dayuan 大宛 that established the control over these regions. The Han also sent parties west of Dayuan 大宛 with the goal of seeking for rare objects and informing the other people of their "might and moral virtue" (*weide* 威德), as evidenced by the conquest of Dayuan 大宛.[18]

1.3 *Hanshu*

The narration of the contact between the Han and the Western Regions in the *Hanshu* starts from the reign of Emperor Wu 武 (141–87 BCE), when the Han led campaigns against the "Four Barbarians" with the goal of spreading "might and moral virtue" (*weide* 威德).[19] After subjugating Dayuan 大宛, the rulers of polities in the Western Regions sent princes as hostages and envoys with tribute to the Han while the Chinese envoys that were sent to the Western Regions were prone to be appointed as officers in compensation for their hardship. Progressing west, they installed commanderies and under Emperor Xuan 宣, in 59 BCE, a "protector-general" of the Western Regions

retranslating their languages". I believe he translated the first part in accordance with the part on the translations. My understanding of the *chong jiu yi* 重九譯 (lit. multiple nine translations), derives from my reading of a passage in the *Shangshu dazhuan* 尚書大傳 4 (*da gao* 大誥; as quoted in the *Hanyu da cidian* under *chong yi* 重譯; or in the *Gujing jiehuihan* 古經解彙函 2.215a; author's translation): 成王之時，越裳重譯而來朝，曰道路悠遠，山川阻深，恐使之不通，故重三譯而朝也。"During the time of King Cheng 成, [envoys from] Yuecheng 越裳 [had to] make several translations to come to court. [They] said that the road was long, [with] mountains high and rivers deep. Because [they] feared that the envoys would not reach [the court], [they] translated (their documents) three times to [come to] court." Although we do not know what they translated exactly, we may presume that these were travel documents. The "because" makes clear that they prepared the translations beforehand, as it is not possible that "because" they were afraid of not reaching China, they made three translations on the road. Whereas I slightly disagree with the translation of Watson, I disagree with Sinor, Li Jinxiu, and Wang Zijin that the passage in the *Shiji* refers to the number of interpreters or consecutive interpretations (Sinor, "Pray," 177; Wang Zijin, "Chongyi"; Li Jinxiu, "Tangdai de fanshu," 35). It is clear, however, that the "multiple translations" became synonymous with cultural and geographical distance, with nine representing the maximum.

18 *Shiji* 123.3174–79; for a translation, see: Watson, *Records*, 245–52. For a commentary on these events, see: Hulsewé and Loewe, *China*, 54–59.

19 *Hanshu* 96a.3871–74.

was eventually installed. His task was to inspect the countries with his political strategy being:[20]

> 可安輯，安輯之；可擊，擊之。
>
> If the situation was suitable for peaceful settlement, he settled it peacefully; if it was suitable for launching and attack, he attacked.

It is quite possible that this follows a maxim of the *Zuozhuan*, in which Cang Ce 蒼葛 differentiates between suitable approaches to rule the Chinese and the Barbarians:[21]

> 德以柔中國，形以威四夷。
>
> To appease the Central Lands, use moral [power], to spread might [among] the Four Barbarians, punish [with military power].

1.3.1 Kangju 康居 and Sogdiana

After the reproduction of the information concerning Dayuan 大宛 in the *Shiji* 史記, which was presented above, ensues the description of various regions, including a passage on the state of Kangju 康居, of which the relevant information is paraphrased hereafter.[22] This state was located ca. 12,300 *li* (ca. 6,150 km) west of Chang'an 長安,[23] with a population of ca. 120,000 households, that is 600,000 people (probably not counting women and children), and with ca. 120,000 men able to bear arms. During the reign of Emperor Xuan 宣 (r. 91–48 BCE), it is said that one group of the Xiongnu 匈奴 held power over Kangju 康居. Then, during the reign of Emperor Yuan 元, in 36 BCE, the Han came with an army raised in the Western Regions and conquered Kangju 康居. Under Emperor Cheng 成 (r. 33–7 BCE), the king of Kangju 康居 sent his son to attend the Han court with gifts, thereby defined as subjects by the Han Empire. The responsible officer for the Western Regions was, however, upset by their lack of etiquette and criticised them as barbaric and arrogant. To the question why they would still send their sons to China, he answered that they intended to keep up good relations due to their desire for trade and lied about their motives[24] – a statement that stands in contrast to the *Shiji's* description of the people of Dayuan 大宛 plotting against the Han to avoid selling their precious horses.[25] Generally speaking, this may quite well have been a trend, as Han authorities admonished envoys from Jibin 罽賓 as being merchants in disguise, meaning they only wished to trade.[26]

20 *Hanshu* 96a.3874. Translation: Hulsewé and Loewe, *China*, 79.

21 *Chunqiu Zuozhuan* 16.428; author's translation.

22 *Hanshu* 96a.3891–94. For a short discussion of earlier accounts mentioning Kangju 康居, see: Hulsewé and Loewe, *China*, 123–24, fn. 298.

23 For a discussion of the corrupted numbers, see: Hulsewé and Loewe, *China*, 124–25, fn. 299.

24 *Hanshu* 96a.3892–93. I therefore agree with the translation of Hulsewé from 1979, and not those from Yang Shuda (1955), Jian Bozan (1958), or Loewe (1963). See: Hulsewé and Loewe, *China*, 128, and 128, fn. 312.

25 See p. 14 (1.2.4).

26 *Hanshu* 94a.3886.

How is Kangju 康居, however, connected to the Sogdians? Whereas on the basis of the *Shiji*, it is impossible to relate Sogdiana to Kangju 康居, the *Hanshu* provides new geographic information, including a passage on Dayuan 大宛:[27]

> 北與康居、南與大月氏接。
>
> It adjoins Kangju 康居 in the north and the Da Yuezhi 大月氏 in the south.

And Anxi 安息:[28]

> 北與康居……接。
>
> It adjoins Kangju 康居 in the north.

A piece of information about the coinage of Anxi 安息 provides further valuable numismatic information, which can be used for dating:[29]

> 亦以銀為錢，文獨為王面，幕為夫人面。
>
> Likewise, they use silver to make coin, the obverse decorated exclusively with the [image] of the king's face and the reverse with that of his consort.

All coins matching this description were minted after the time the *Shiji* was compiled.[30] Further, whereas in the *Shiji*, the Da Yuezhi 大月氏 were located between Anxi 安息 and Kangju 康居, the *Hanshu* tells us that Anxi 安息 had a common border with Kangju 康居. Both discrepancies put together, it is probable that the description of the *Hanshu* describes a political change and not a conflict of information. If that is

27 *Hanshu* 96a.3894; translation: Hulsewé and Loewe, *China*, 132. The Chinese characters are added and the transcription is changed into *pinyin*.

28 *Hanshu* 96a.3889; translation: Hulsewé and Loewe, *China*, 116. The Chinese characters are added and the transcription is changed into *pinyin*.

29 *Hanshu* 96a.3889; translation: Hulsewé and Loewe, *China*, 116.

30 The *Shiji* already included the first part of this description, leaving out, however, the consort (以銀為錢，錢如其王面。*Shiji* 123.3161). Although there are multiple coins that match the description of the *Hanshu* which were found in this area, there is an agreement in that all were minted after the time the *Shiji* was compiled. This which reinforces the conclusion that the passage of the *Shiji* was written earlier. For the general debate about the genesis of these texts, see p. 11 fn. 1.
The debate on possible matching coins can be traced back to the article of Daffinà in 1967. He argued that later coins matched the description, as for example the coins of Phraatēs V (Phratakēs, 2 BCE–4 CE), or even later, of Gōtarzēs II (ca. 36–51 CE; Daffinà, *L'immigrazione*, 72). Loewe reproduced in 1979 this information in his introduction, although he pointed out that a precise dating is difficult (Hulsewé and Loewe, *China*, 42, fn. 90). Leslie and Gardiner retraced in 1982 the different arguments and came to the conclusion that the coins of Phraatēs V were the closest to the description, "and one cannot exclude the possibility that the reference is to coins of the Seleucia mint" (Leslie and Gardiner, "Chinese Knowledge," 280–81, fn. 51). Finally, in 2005 de la Vaissière came to the conclusion that the coins can only have been, in the Parthian Empire, those of Phraatēs V (he does not – while in the footnote solely referring to the article of Leslie and Gardiner – however, explain why he excluded the possibility of the Seleucia mint: Vaissière, *Sogdian Traders*, 38).

true, the Da Yuezhi 大月氏 were not at the same location anymore, and either Kangju 康居 or Anxi 安息 now were the rulers of Sogdiana. As laid out in the corresponding passage below, the *Hou Hanshu* contains a passage which helps to clarify who of these two may have been the ruler of Sogdiana.

Further, the *Hanshu* includes one passage in which five petty kings of Kangju 康居 are mentioned:[31]

> 康居有小王五：一曰蘇䪥[32]王，治蘇䪥城，去都護五千七百七十六里，去陽關八千二十五里；二曰附墨王，治附墨城，去都護五千七百六十七里，去陽關八千二十五里；三曰窳匿王，治窳匿城，去都護五千二百六十六里，去陽關七千五百二十五里；四曰罽王，治罽城，去都護六千二百九十六里，去陽關八千五百五十五里；五曰奧鞬王，治奧鞬城，去都護六千九百六里，去陽關八千三百五十五里。凡五王，屬康居。

> In Kangju 康居 there are five petty kings.
> The first is called the Suxie 蘇䪥 King, governing [from] the Suxie 蘇䪥 Fort. It is 5,776 *li* (ca. 2,888 km) to the [seat of the] protector general (of the Western Regions) and 8,025 *li* (ca. 4,013 km) to the Yang 陽 Barrier.
> The second is called the Fumo 附墨 King, governing [from] the Fumo 附墨 Fort. It is 5,767 *li* (ca. 2,884 km) to the [seat of the] protector general (of the Western Regions) and 8,025 *li* (ca. 4,013 km) to the Yang 陽 Barrier.
> The third is called the Yuni 窳匿 King, governing [from] the Yuni 窳匿 Fort. It is 5,266 *li* (ca. 2,633 km) to the [seat of the] protector general (of the Western Regions) and 7,525 *li* (ca. 3,763 km) to the Yang 陽 Barrier.
> The fourth is called the Ji 罽 King, governing [from] the Ji 罽 Fort. It is 6,296 *li* (ca. 3,148 km) to the [seat of the] protector general (of the Western Regions) and 8,555 *li* (ca. 4,278 km) to the Yang 陽 Barrier.
> The fifth is called the Aojian 奧鞬 King, governing [from] the Aojian 奧鞬 Fort. It is 6,906 *li* (ca. 4,453 km) to the [seat of the] protector general (of the Western Regions) and 8,355 *li* (ca. 4,178 km) to the Yang 陽 Barrier.
> All five kings are subject to Kangju 康居.

Parenthetically, the distances are not only exaggerated but obviously erroneous, as the distance between the Yang 陽 Barrier and the seat of the protector general should always be the same. If the distance from the Ji 罽 Fort to the seat of the protector general of the Western Regions is 6,296 *li* and the distance to the Yang 陽 Barrier is 8,555 *li*, the distance between the Yang 陽 Barrier and the seat of the protector general is (8,555 – 6,296 =) 2,259 *li*. If, however, the distance from the Aojian 奧鞬 Fort to the Yang 陽 Barrier is 8,355 *li*, the distance from the Aojian 奧鞬 Fort to the seat of the protector general should be (8,355 – 2,259 =) 6,096 *li* and not 6,906 *li*, as mentioned in the account. The simplest explanation for this discrepancy is that the

31 *Hanshu* 96a.3894; based on the translation of: Hulsewé and Loewe, *China*, 130–31.
32 A variant of *xie* 薤.

number 9 was moved from the third to the second digit. This conclusion is supported by the matching distances given for the Yuni 寙匿 Fort: (7,525 – 5,266 =) 2,259 *li*. Continuing in the same logic of misplaced digits, the distances to the seat of the protector general from the Suxie 蘇䪥 Fort and Fumo 附墨 Fort should both be 5,766 *li* (changing respectively 5,776 into 5,766 and 5,767 into 5,766), to arrive at the common difference of 2,259 *li*.[33]

1.4 *Hou Hanshu*

The introduction to the Accounts of the Western Regions of the *Hou Hanshu* explains that after the interregnum of Wang Mang 王莽, the relationship with the Western Regions was interrupted, resulting in their occupation by the Xiongnu 匈奴, who imposed heavy taxes.[34] As a consequence, they asked for Chinese support:[35]

> 建武中，皆遣使求內屬，願請都護。光武以天下初定，未遑外事，竟不許之。
>
> In the middle of the Jianwu period (25–56 CE), they each (Shanshan and Yarkand in 38 CE, and 18 kingdoms in 45 CE), sent envoys to ask if they could submit to the Interior (China), and to express their desire for a Protector General. Emperor Guangwu, decided that because the Empire was not yet settled (after a long period of civil war), he had no time for outside affairs, and in the end refused his consent (in 45 CE).

In 73 CE, Emperor Ming 明 then attacked the Xiongnu 匈奴 and re-established the connection to the Western Regions. Some countries sent their sons as hostages, and generally, the Han were present again in the politics of the Western Regions.[36]

1.4.1 Liyi 栗弋

The *Hou Hanshu* also contains a new paragraph concerning Liyi 栗弋 (*li* 栗 certainly referring to what later was written as *su* 粟, and therefore to "Suyi", i.e. Sogdiana), including information about the state of Yan 嚴, Yan 奄, and Yancai 奄蔡:[37]

> 栗弋國屬康居。出名馬牛羊、蒲萄眾果，其土水美，故蒲萄酒特有名焉。嚴國在奄蔡北，屬康居，出鼠皮以輸之。奄蔡國改名阿蘭聊國，居地城，屬康居。土氣溫和，多楨松、白草。民俗衣服與康居同。

33 Yu Taishan proposed similar calculations (Yu Taishan, "Saka History," 102). He further referred to different, but as he says, equally possible proposals of: Matsuda Hisao, *Kodai*, 71–72; and: Cen Zhongmian, *Hanshu*, 237–65.

34 *Hou Hanshu* 88.2909–15.

35 *Hou Hanshu* 88.2909; translation, brackets adjusted: Hill, *Through*, 3.

36 *Hou Hanshu* 88.2909.

37 *Hou Hanshu* 88.2922–23; translation: Hill, *Through*, 33.

> The kingdom of Liyi (read Suyi=Sogdiana) is a dependency of Kangju (the Talas basin, Tashkent and Sogdiana). It produces famous horses, cattle, sheep, grapes,38 and all sorts of fruits. The water and soil of this state are excellent, which is why its grape wine is so well known.
> The kingdom of Yan is to the north of Yancai (= "Alan (and) Liao") and is a dependency of Kangju (the Talas basin, Tashkent and Sogdiana). It produces small animal pelts,[39] which it uses to pay its tribute to that state [Kangju]. The Kingdom of Yancai (lit. "Vast Steppe") has changed its name to the kingdoms of Alan [and] Liao. They occupy the country and the towns.[40] They are dependencies of Kangju (the Talas basin, Tashkent and Sogdiana). The climate is mild. Wax trees, pines, and "white grass" (aconite)[41] are plentiful. Their way of life and dress are the same as those of Kangju.

This is the first time Sogdiana is identifiably mentioned. It states that Kangju 康居 ruled over the state of Liyi 栗弋 (Sogdiana), the state of Yan 嚴, and the state of Yancai 奄蔡, i.e. Alan 阿蘭 and Liao 聊. If, as proposed above, the differences between the *Shiji* and the *Hanshu* are to be interpreted as political changes, the information provided by the *Hou Hanshu* supports the theory that 1) the passage of the *Hanshu* is posterior to the *Shiji*, and 2), it was Kangju 康居, and not Anxi 安息, that later ruled over Sogdiana.

1.5 *Sanguozhi*

The *Sanguozhi* states:[42]

> 魏興，西域雖不能盡至，其大國龜茲、于寘、康居、烏孫、疏勒、月氏、鄯善、車師之屬，無歲不奉朝貢，略如漢氏故事。
>
> Although [since] the rise of Wei the Western Region could not entirely be reached [by Chinese influence], yet the largest states such as Qiuci 龜茲

38 See: Laufer, *Sino-Iranica*, 220–45.

39 Hill opts for "small animals", which is slightly misleading, although he recognises that "it is not clear what pelts they traded with Kangju.". I would, however, tend to translate it as "marten felt". See: Schafer, *Golden Peaches*, 107–8. Fire-marten is mentioned as export product of the state of Shi 史 (Kesh) in the *Suishu* (see p. 35; 1.9.6) and the *Jiu Tangshu* reports that marten fell from Iran was used as dance carpets (see p. 66 fn. 330).

40 Chavannes commented: "there is no indication in the Chinese text of any such capital" and therefore concluded that it should be read as translated above (Chavannes, "Wei Lio," 195) translated "it has as capital the city of Di". Hill (Hill, *Through*, 399). I would add to this comment that the passage is likely corrupted.

41 See: ibid., 207–10.

42 *Sanguozhi* 30.840. For the compilation history, see: Dien, "Historiography," 520–23. Translation: Zürcher, "Yüeh-chih and Kaniṣka," 371. *Pinyin* and the Chinese characters have been added to the translation, the comments removed, translations added, and the formatting adjusted.

> (Kucha), Yutian 于寘 (Khotan), Kangju 康居 (Sogdia [sic]),[43] Wusun 烏孫, Shule 疎勒 (Kashgar), Yuezhi 月氏, Shanshan 鄯善 (Cherchen) and Jushi 車師 every year sent tribute to the court, more or less as had been the custom in Han times.

There was thus a connection between the Wei and different countries in the Western Regions, although Sogdiana is not explicitly mentioned.[44]

1.5.1 Zhuyao 屬繇

The commentary to this passage of the *Sanguozhi*, that is the passage on the Xirong 西戎,[45] is from the now lost *Weilüe* 魏略 (written 239–65 CE), provides further information on the furthest Western Regions:[46]

> 大秦西有海水，海水西有河水，河水西南北行有大山，西有赤水，赤水西有白玉山，白玉山有西王母，西王母西有脩流沙，流沙西有大夏國、堅沙國、屬繇國、月氏國、四國西有黑水，所傳聞西之極矣。

> West of Daqin 大秦 there is sea water. West of the sea water there is the river water. West of the river water there are large mountains going from the south to the north. West [of this] there is Red River (Chishui 赤水). To the west of Red River there are the White Jade Mountains. In the White Jade Mountains is *Xi wangmu* 西王母.[47] West of the *Xi wangmu* 西王母 there are the large[48] Shifting Sands. West of the Shifting Sands are the countries of Daxia 大夏, Jiansha 堅沙,[49] Zhuyao 屬繇, Yuezhi 月氏 (Kushans?). To the west of [these] four countries is Black River (Heishui 黑水), which is the furthest west heard of.

Although the geographic information makes little sense and seems to be a conflation of mythological concepts with shreds of hearsay, the mentioned names speak of the state of (dis)information of the Chinese authors and do provide us with further transcriptions of toponyms.[50] To supplement this passage, as Haloun already pointed out in 1926, the *Shanhaijing* 山海經 includes a passage listing the "countries outside the Moving Sands":[51]

43 Kangju 康居 is not Sogdiana and not Samarqand. See the discussion above about Kangju 康居 and Sogdiana.
44 See footnote above.
45 Another term for "Western Barbarians".
46 *Sanguozhi* 30.862; author's translation.
47 The White Jade Mountains are the abode of the mythological "Queen Mother of the West". I prefer to keep the transcribed term as the possible English translations – be it (traditionally) "Queen Mother of the West" or "Spirit-Mother of the West" (Goldin, "On the Meaning," 83) – are slightly misleading, as the term basically refers to a female (lit. grandmother) deity.
48 Hirth translated "rectified": Hirth, *China*, 77.
49 Hill translated the term Jiansha 堅沙 in a parenthesis as "Stable Sands" as it follows the term Liusha 流沙 (lit. shifting sands) and is unknown in other sources (Hill, *Through*, 316).
50 For a commentary on this confusion, see: Pulleyblank, "Review: The Roman Empire," 78.
51 *Shanhaijing* 8.328; author's translation. Haloun, *Seit wann*, 146–47.

> 國在流沙外者，大夏、豎沙、居繇、月支之國。
>
> Countries outside of the Moving Sands: the countries Daxia 大夏, Shusha 豎沙, Juyao 居繇, Yuezhi 月支.

By comparing the two lists, it becomes obvious that they describe the same places. Two differences are to be noted however: first, instead of "Jiansha 堅沙" the *Shanhaijing* 山海經 mentions "Shusha 豎沙" and second, instead of "Zhuyao 屬繇" it lists "Juyao 居繇". The first change is most likely to be explained by the similarity of the name's first character, whereas in the second case, the first character of the names was once homophonic. As Shiratori points out, the second character *yao* 繇, could well have been pronounced "*do*", thus reading *Šuk-do*.[52] This, combined with the supposed approximate geographic region, may lead us to assume that the texts refer to Sogdiana.

1.6 *Jinshu*

1.6.1 Kangju 康居

The *Jinshu* also includes a short passage concerning the state of Kangju 康居:[53]

> 康居國在大宛西北可二千里，與粟弋、伊列鄰接。其王居蘇薤城。風俗及人貌、衣服略同大宛。地和暖，饒桐柳蒲陶，多牛羊，出好馬。泰始中，其王那鼻遣使上封事，并獻善馬。
>
> The state of Kangju 康居 is located about 2,000 *li* (ca. 1,000 km) north-west of Dayuan 大宛 [and] adjoins Suyi 粟弋 (Sogdiana) and Yili 伊列. Its king resides in the Suxie 蘇薤 Fort. The customs, people's appearance, and clothing are somewhat similar to Dayuan's 大宛. The land's [climate] is mild. [There are] many paulownias, willows, grapes, many sheep and cattle [and they] bring forth fine horses. During the Taishi 泰始 (era, 265–74 CE), their king Nabi 那鼻 sent envoys to present a memorial and offer excellent horses.

Among some confusing information that will be discussed below, it provides the novelty that during the Taishi 泰始 era (265–74 CE), their king sent embassies to present a memorial and fine horses.

1.7 *Weishu*

Concerning the contact with the Western Regions, we read that at the beginning of the reign of Emperor Taizu 太祖 (r. 386–98 CE), an official requested that the connection

52 Shiratori Kurakichi, "Study on Su-t'ê," 100.
53 *Jinshu* 97.2544; author's translation.

to the Western Regions may be re-established, to "spread might and moral virtue to remote places", as already stated in the *Hanshu*, "but also to be able to send their precious goods to the court", which was however not granted.[54] During the Taiyan 太延 era (435–40 CE), as "Wei's moral virtue [was] more and more heard of [in] far away [places]",[55] many states of the Western Regions, including the country of Sute 粟特 (Sogdiana), sent envoys to present tribute.[56] After 437 CE, the countries were reorganised into four sections of altogether 16 states, Sogdiana being included in the second section.[57] The emperor was, however, apparently not utterly pleased with the general situation:[58]

> 世祖以西域漢世雖通，有求則卑辭而來，無欲則驕慢王命，此其自知絕遠，大兵不可至故也。若報使往來，終無所益，欲不遣使。有司奏九國不憚遐嶮，遠貢方物，當與其進，安可豫抑後來，乃從之。
>
> Although the emperor's [realm] had reached the Han's Western Regions, they humbled themselves and came when in need, [but] neglected the orders of the emperor when not in need. This is because they know themselves cut off and far away [and] that no large army can reach them. If envoys are sent forth and back, in the end there is no benefit [to be gained], [so] there was no desire to send envoys. An official presented a memorial [stating that] "the nine countries neither fearing distance nor danger [and] have come from afar [to] present regional goods [as] tribute. [We] should allow them to come close. How could [we] restrict their future coming?" Only then did [the emperor] accept [this petition].

As the *Weishu* goes on, the emperor then sent envoys to different countries, which increased their respective number of envoys and eventually submitted to Chinese domination. The Western Regions were then divided into four districts and the roads number of roads leading to it being augmented from two to four.[59] The account provides the description of various new countries, including states in Sogdiana, listed below.

1.7.1 The state of Mimi 迷密 (Māymurgh)[60]

> 迷密國，都迷密城，在者至拔西，去代一萬二千六百里。正平元年，遣使獻一峯黑橐駝。其國東有山，名郁悉滿，山出金玉，亦多鐵。

54 *Weishu* 102.2259; author's translation.
55 Id.
56 *Weishu* 102.2259–60.
57 See: *Weishu* 102.2261; and: Enoki Kazuo, "Sogdiana," 53–58.
58 *Weishu* 102.2260; author's translation.
59 The details are to be found in: *Weishu* 102.2261.
60 *Weishu* 102.2269; author's translation.

The state of Mimi 迷密[61] (Māymurgh). [Its] capital is the Mimi 迷密 Fort. [It is] located west of Zhezhiba 者至拔 (?),[62] 12,600 *li*[63] (ca. 6,300 km) to Dai 代. In Zhengping 正平 1 (451 CE), [they] sent an envoy to present a black camel as gift. East of its state lie mountains called Yuximan 郁悉滿. The mountains bring forth gold and jade, as well as much iron.

1.7.2 The state of Xiwanjin 悉萬斤 (Samarqand)[64]

悉萬斤國，都悉萬斤城，在迷密西，去代一萬二千七百二十里。其國南有山，名伽色那，山出師子。每使朝貢。

The state of Xiwanjin 悉萬斤 (Samarqand). [Its] capital is the Xiwanjin 悉萬斤 Fort. [It is] located west of Mimi 迷密 (Māymurgh), 12,720 *li* (ca. 6,360 km) from Dai 代. South of this state lie mountains called Jiasena 伽色那, in which lions are to be found. [They] regularly send envoys to present tribute to the court.

1.7.3 The state of Niumi 忸密 (Bukhārā)[65]

忸密國，都忸密城，在悉萬斤西，去代二萬二千八百二十八里。

The state of Niumi 忸密 (Bukhārā). [Its] capital is the Niumi 忸密 Fort (Numijkath). [It is] located west of Xiwanjin 悉萬斤 (Samarqand), 22,728 *li* (ca. 11,364 km) from Dai 代.

1.7.4 The state of (Po)luona (破)洛那 (Ferghana)[66]

洛那國，故大宛國也。都貴山城，在疏勒西北，去代萬四千四百五十里。太和三年，遣使獻汗血馬，自此每使朝貢。

The state of (Po)luona (破)洛那 (Ferghana).[67] [It] is the ancient territory of the state of Dayuan 大宛. [Its] capital is the Guishan 貴山 Fort. [It is] located northwest of Shule 疏勒 (Kashgar), 14,450 *li* (ca. 7,225 km) from Dai 代. In Taihe

61 Mimi 迷密 was corrected from Ximi 悉密 in the passage of the *Weishu* 102.2269–70 in the present Zhonghua shuju edition due to: 1) the passage concerning the state of Mimi 迷密 in the *Weishu* 102.2269, 2) the parallel passage in the *Beishi* 97.3221, which originally also stated Ximi 悉密, but was corrected due to two passages, in the 3) *Tongzhi* 41.559b and 196.3154.2a. It is also written Ximi 悉蜜 in the *Cefu yuangui* 961.10a.11306a.

62 Probably corrupt, maybe referring to Ferghana.

63 In the *Beishi* 97.3221, the distance is given as 12,100 *li* (ca. 6,050 km), the number six (*liu* 六) or one (*yi* 一) probably being corrupted in the copying process, as Ma Yong proposed (Ma Yong, "Chinese," 146).

64 *Weishu* 102.2269–70; author's translation.

65 *Weishu* 102.2270; author's translation.

66 Id.

67 The *po* 破 is added according to the passage on the state of Zheshe 者舌 (Chach, see p. 41; 1.11.3).

太和 3 (479 CE; actually Taiyan 太延 3, 437 CE),[68] [they] sent envoys to offer "blood-sweating" horses.[69] Since then, [they] regularly send envoys to present tribute to the court.

1.7.5 The state of Sute 粟特 (Sogdiana)

It is also the first time a passage concerning the state of Sute 粟特 (Sogdiana) is to be found:[70]

粟特國，在葱嶺之西，古之奄蔡，一名溫那沙。居於大澤，在康居西北，去代一萬六千里。先是，匈奴殺其王而有其國，至王忽倪已三世矣。其國商人先多詣涼土販貨，及克姑臧，悉見虜。高宗初，粟特王遣使請贖之，詔聽焉。自後無使朝獻。

The state of Sute 粟特 (Sogdiana): West of the Congling 葱嶺 (Pamirs), the Yancai 奄蔡 (Alan 阿蘭 and Liao 聊) of the antiquity,[71] also called Wennasha 溫那沙.[72] [It is] located on the Great Marsh, north-west of Kangju 康居, 16,000 *li* (ca. 8,000 km) from Dai 代. Since the time the Xiongnu 匈奴 killed

68 This can be corrected with help of the parallel passages of the *Weishu*. In the passage listing the events of Emperor Xiaowen 孝文 (r. 467–99 CE) there is no mention of sending envoys with horses (see: *Weishu* 7a.146–47). In the passage narrating the events of the reign of Emperor Taiwu 太武 (r. 408–52 CE), it is written that the countries of Poluona 破洛那 (Ferghana) and Zheshe 者舌 (Chach) sent said "blood-sweating" horses (*Weishu* 4a.88; on the "blood-sweat" see footnote below). This embassy is also mentioned in the passage on Zheshe 者舌 (see p. 41; 1.11.3).

69 One of the important products traded with China. See: Laufer, *Sino-Iranica*, 210; Schafer, *Golden Peaches*, 58–70. Schafer was informed by R. N. Frye that one of another name, used in story told at the beginning of the 11th century (*Qin Zaisi* 秦再思 3.6b), for them (*chibo* 叱撥) is related to the Sogdian word for quadruped, used specifically for "horse" (Schafer, *Golden Peaches*, 61, 295, no. 29). Epstein, *apud* a private communication by T. Young of the Commonwealth Bureau of Helminthology in 1966, proposed that the "blood-sweat" may be caused by the parasitic nematode Parafilaria multipapillosa: "The presence of the parasite under the skin causes slight bleeding when the animal is active (but only during the summer), the foamy sweat being pink from the tiny amounts of blood oozing through the skin." Epstein, *Domestic*, 96. Falk recently proposed to alternatively explain this phenomenon by the habit of certain horses biting themselves, as observed by Filchner (Falk, "Five Yabghus," 3; (Filchner, *Ritt*, 38). The theory published by Epstein is, however, presently commonly accepted.

70 *Weishu* 102.2270; author's translation. For two other translations, see: Enoki Kazuo, "Sogdiana," 44; and: Hirth, "Mr. Kingsmill," 33, 43.

71 For an analysis of the misleading assertion that Yancai 奄蔡 (referring to Alan 阿蘭 and Liao 聊, as seen above) and Sogdiana were identical, see: Shiratori Kurakichi, "Study on Su-t'ê," 98–100; and: Enoki Kazuo, "Sogdiana," 47–50, 57–58. This erroneous equivalence most probably led the authors of the *Weishu* to state that Sogdiana lay in extensive marshes, as the passage on Yancai 奄蔡 of the *Hanshu* informs (96a.3893). This information is reproduced in the *Zhoushu* (p. 31; 1.8.1), although the latter added that it is "presumably the Yancai 奄蔡 of antiquity".

72 This is the short version of the name of the king of Kang 康, also to be found in the description of Sute 粟特 in the *Zhoushu* below. See also the passage on the state of Kang 康 (Samarqand), later copied in the *Jiu Tangshu* and *Xin Tangshu*. For a discussion, see: Livšic, "Sogdian," 61–62, 62, fn. 1; Shiratori Kurakichi, "Study on Su-t'ê," 138–39; Haussig, "Theophylakts," 417–18; and: Miller, *Accounts*, 34–35, no. 94.

the king [of Sute 粟特] and took his state, three generations have elapsed until King Huni 忽倪.[73] Before, most of their state's merchants went to Liangzhou 涼州 [for] commerce, [but] when Guzang 姑臧 was conquered (by the Wei in 439 CE), all [were] taken hostage. At the beginning of [the reign of] Gaozong 高宗 (of the Wei, r. 452–65 CE, in 457 CE?),[74] the king of Sute 粟特 sent envoys bidding to ransom them, which was accorded. From then on, no envoys were sent to court to present gifts.[75]

1.7.6 The state of Sezhixian 色知顯 (Ishitikhan)[76]

色知顯國，都色知顯城，在悉萬斤西北，去代一萬二千九百四十里，土平，多五果。

The state of Sezhixian 色知顯 (Ishitikhan). [Its] capital is the Sezhixian 色知顯 Fort. [It is] located north-west of Xiwanjin 悉萬斤 (Samarqand), 12,940 *li* (ca. 6,470 km) from Dai 代. The soil is flat. [There are] many of the Five Fruits.[77]

1.7.7 The state of Muzhi 牟知 (Vardana?)[78]

牟知國，都牟知城，在忸密西南，去代二萬二千九百二十里。土平，禽獸草木類中國。

The state of Muzhi 牟知 (Vardana?). [Its] capital is the Muzhi 牟知 Fort. [It is] located south-west of Niumi 忸密 (Bukhārā), 22,920 *li* (ca. 11,460 km) to Dai 代. The soil is flat. The beasts of the air and ground and the vegetation are similar to China's.

73 For a discussion regarding whether this statement can be considered to be "uncontested proof" of identification of the Xiongnu 匈奴, discussed here, with the Huns, see: Enoki Kazuo, "Gisho," 44–45.

74 The *Beishi* states it was at the beginning of the Wencheng 文成 era (*Beishi* 97.3221). The *Weishu* further mentions that in Tai'an 太安 3 (457 CE) Sute 粟特 sent an envoy in the first month (*Weishu* 5.116).

75 Both translations (Enoki's: "the king (of Su-t'ê) sent embassies to ask for their ransom", Enoki Kazuo, "Sogdiana," 44; and Hirth's first: "the king of Suk-tak sent ambassadors to ask for their ransom", Hirth, "Mr. Kingsmill," 33) are, however, wrongly worded. It was the king of Sute 粟特 who actually sought to ransom the merchants instead of asking the Wei for ransom (as Hirth correctly translated in his second translation: ibid., 43). Unlike Enoki, I further propose that it probably was a single embassy (although maybe with multiple envoys/ambassadors, as Hirth translated), not multiple embassies. I thus fully agree with the translation of Shiratori: Shiratori Kurakichi, "Study on Su-t'ê," 98.

76 *Weishu* 102.2272; author's translation.

77 Peach, plum, apricot, chestnut, and date.

78 *Weishu* 102.2272; author's translation.

1.7.8 The state of Husimi 呼似密 (Khwārizmik)[79]

呼似密國，都呼似密城，在阿弗太汗西，去代二萬四千七百里。土平，出銀、琥珀，有師子，多五果。

The state of Husimi 呼似密 (Khwārizmik). [Its] capital is the Husimi 呼似密 Fort. [It is] located west of Afutaihan 阿弗太汗 (?), 24,700 *li* (ca. 12,450 km) from Dai 代. The soil is flat. [It] brings forth silver and amber. There are lions [and] many of the Five Fruits.[80]

1.7.9 The state of Jiabudan 伽不單 (Kapūtānā)[81]

伽不單國，都伽不單城，在悉萬斤西北，去代一萬二千七百八十里。土平，宜稻麥，有五果。

The state of Jiabudan 伽不單 (Kapūtānā). [Its] capital is the Jiabudan 伽不單 Fort. [It is] located north-west of Xiwanjin 悉萬斤 (Samarqand), 12,780 *li* (ca. 6,490 km) from Dai 代. The soil is flat [and] favourable for [growing] millet and wheat. [They] have the Five Fruits.[82]

1.7.10 The state of Zheshe 者舌 (Chach)[83]

者舌國，故康居國，在破洛那西北，去代一萬五千四百五十里。太延三年，遣使朝貢，自是不絕。

The state of Zheshe 者舌 (Chach) [was part of] the ancient state of Kangju 康居.[84] [It is] located north-west of Poluona 破洛那 (Ferghana), 15,450 *li* (ca. 7,725 km) from Dai 代. In Taiyan 太延 3 (437 CE),[85] [they] sent envoys to present tribute. Since then, this has not been discontinued.

1.7.11 The state of Fuhuo 副貨 (Bukhārā?)[86]

副貨國，去代一萬七千里。東至阿副使且國，西至沒誰國，中間相去一千里；南有連山，不知名；北至奇沙國，相去一千五百里。國中有副貨城，周帀[87]七十里。宜五穀、葡桃，唯有馬、駝、騾。國王有黃金殿，殿下金駝七頭，各高三尺。其王遣使朝貢。

79 *Weishu* 102.2273; author's translation.

80 See p. 26 fn. 77.

81 *Weishu* 102.2274; author's translation.

82 See p. 26 fn. 77.

83 *Weishu* 102.2274; author's translation.

84 Interestingly, this is the only state said to have been related to the ancient "state" and not the ancient "territory" of Kangju 康居. The phrasing "ancient state of" is also used in the description of the state of An 安, referring to Anxi 安息.

85 See the passage on Poluona 破洛那 (p. 24; 1.7.4).

86 *Weishu* 102.2277–78; author's translation.

87 This is another character for *za* 匝.

The state of Fuhuo 副貨 (Bukhārā?). [It] is located 17,000 *li* (ca. 8,500 km) from Dai. To the east, [one] arrives at the state of Afushiqie 阿副使且 (?).[88] To the (south-)west,[89] [one] arrives at the state of Moshui 沒誰 (Vardana?). [It takes] 1,000 *li* (ca. 500 km) to go to each from the centre. In the south, there is a mountain range. [Its] name is unknown. [Going] north, [one] arrives at the state of Qisha 奇沙 (Chach), at a distance of 1,500 *li* (ca. 750 km). In the state [of Fuhuo 副貨] lies the Fuhuo 副貨 Fort, [which is] 70 *li* (ca. 35 km) in circuit. [The climate is] favourable for [growing] the Five Crops[90] [and] grapes. [They] have horses, camels, [and] mules. The state's king has a golden palace under which are seven golden camels, each three *chi* high (ca. one m). Its king sends envoys to present tribute.

1.7.12 The state of Kang 康 (Samarqand)[91]

康國者，康居之後也。遷徙無常，不恒故地，自漢以來，相承不絕。其王本姓溫，月氏人也。舊居祁連山北昭武城，因被匈奴所破，西踰葱嶺，遂有其國。枝庶各分王，故康國左右諸國，並以昭武為姓，示不忘本也。王字世夫畢，為人寬厚，甚得眾心。其妻突厥達度可汗女也。

The state of Kang 康 (Samarqand) is the successor [state] of Kangju 康居. [They] continually moved around without taking up abode. There lineage is unbroken since the Han. Their kings' surname was originally Wen 溫, of the Yuezhi 月氏.[92] They once lived north of the Qilian 祁連 range in the city of Zhaowu 昭武. As [they] were defeated by the Xiongnu 匈奴, [they moved] west and crossed the Congling 葱嶺 (Pamirs), whereupon [they] had their kingdom. The descendants of the cadet brothers all [became] separate kings. [This is] why [in] all countries around the state of Kang 康 all have the surname Zhaowu 昭武, to show that [they] do not forget [their] origin. The courtesy name of the king is Shifubi 世夫畢 (Shishibi).[93] [He is] generous, of gentle

88 Written Afushiqie 阿富使且 in the *Beishi* 97.3229.

89 See the passage on Muzhi 牟知 (p. 26; 1.7.7). On the conflicting information, see the glossary.

90 Different listings exist, all referring to crops commonly planted in China.

91 *Weishu* 102.2281; author's translation.

92 Pulleyblank decided to add a period mark and change the subject in his translation of the parallel passage in the *Suishu*: Pulleyblank, "Sogdian Colony," 320, fn. 1.

93 Daishibi 代失畢 in the *Suishu* 83.1848. The version of the *Weishu* and *Beishi* (Shifubi 世夫畢; 97.3233) were probably copied from the *Suishu*, *dai* 代 replacing *shi* 世 due to a taboo and *shi* 失 and *fu* 夫 being only one stroke apart. Shishibi 世失畢 is thus another possible reconstruction, sounding and fitting temporally with the king Šyšpyr (*MLK'*). See: Okamoto Takashi, "Sogudo," 73–75, 79, 80–83, 90; who comments on the foundational work of: Smirnova, *Sogdiiskikh monet*, 423–31. Okamoto believes, however, that Šyšpyr is not Shasebi 沙瑟畢 of Shi 史, as mentioned in the *Xin Tangshu* (see p. 68; 1.14.13).
Indeed, we are confronted with several problems. For Kang 康, we know precise dates for Qushuzhi 屈术支 (for other names, see p. 52, fn. 222), of which we know that he married the daughter of the Yehu 葉護 Khagan during the reign of Emperor Yang 煬 (r. 604–618 CE) and

character [and] deeply appreciated by the people. His wife [is] the daughter of Khagan Tardu 達度[94] of the Tujue 突厥.

都於薩寶水上阿祿迪城，多人居。大臣三人共掌國事。其王索髮，冠七寶金花，衣綾、羅、錦、繡、白疊；其妻有髻，幪以皂巾。丈夫翦髮，錦袍。名為強國，西域諸國多歸之。米國、史國、曹國、何國、安國、小安國、那色波國、烏那曷國、穆國皆歸附之。

The capital was on the Sabao 薩寶 River (Zerafshan), the city of Aludi 阿祿迪, [in which] many people live. Three chancellors handle the politics of the state together. Their king [has] plated hair, a crown with all kind of jewellery [and] golden flowers, [and wears] garments of thin silk, silk gaze, brocade, embroidered cloth, [and] white cotton cloth. His wife[95] has [her hair in a] topknot, veiled by a black cloth. Men [have their] hair cropped short [and clothe in] brocade robes. Famous as a mighty state, most of the countries of the Western Regions are subject to it. The states of Mi 米 (Māymurgh), of Shi 史 (Kesh), of Cao 曹 (Ishitikhan), of He 何 (Kushaniyya), of An 安 (Bukhārā), of Lesser An 小安 (Kharghān), of Nasebo 那色波 (Nakhshab), of Wunahe 烏那曷 (Balkh?), [and] of Mu 穆 (Amul?), all are their subjects.

sent horses in Wude 武德 10. As I explain in p. 52 fn. 224, this information is already corrupt, as there is no Wude 武德 10, which therefore is probably Wude 武德 9/11 (629 CE). Previous scholars determined the last known date related to him to have been 637 CE, as there is mention of subsequent envoys until then. I do not categorically object to that date but would like to add that it could also have been envoys sent by "them" and not by "him", as the subject of the sentences is not specified. The consequent envoys were thus not necessarily sent by him, pushing the date back to 629 CE.
As Shifubi 世夫畢 is said to have married the daughter of Khagan Tardu 達度, who died in 603 CE, he must have been a predecessor of Qushuzhi 屈术支. Shasebi 沙瑟畢 of Shi 史 (see *Xin Tangshu*, p. 68; 1.14.13), however, is mentioned as having sent gifts in Zhenguan 貞觀 16 (642 CE). It follows that Shasebi 沙瑟畢 and Shifubi 世夫畢 are two different individuals.
The major problematic, however, presents itself to the numismatist. Coins attributed to Šyšpyr have been found both in Samarqand and Kesh, while they are apparently more typical for Samarqand (Naymark, "O date," 218), dated to the beginning to the middle of the seventh century. Smirnova thought that Shasebi 沙瑟畢 is Šyšpyr, whereas Okamoto Takashi believes Shifubi 世夫畢 (possibly also Shishibi) is Šyšpyr.
If the Chinese records are not completely mistaken (which is a possibility), it may actually be that two kings with this name existed, one in Kang 康 and one in Shi 史, both living in the first half of the seventh century. To add to the confusion, I would like to advance the idea that it is possible that both kings may have minted coins with similar *thamgas* on them during this time in their respective polities.

94 D. 603 CE, second *yabgu* and first *khagan* of the Western Turkic Khaganate. Mentioned as Datou 達頭 in the *Suishu* 83.1848.

95 For the discrepancies between the *Weishu*, *Beishi*, *Suishu* (*qi qi* 其妻), *Jiu Tangshu* (*furen* 婦人, see p. 51) and *Xin Tangshu* (see p. 55: *nüzi* 女子) see p. 55, fn. 245.

有胡律，置於[祆][96]祠，將決罰，則取而斷之。重者族，次罪者死，賊盜截其足。人皆深目、高鼻、多髯。善商賈，諸夷交易多湊其國。有大小鼓、琵琶、五弦箜篌。婚姻喪制與突厥同。國立祖廟，以六月祭之，諸國皆助祭。奉佛為胡書。氣候溫，宜五穀，勤修園蔬，樹木滋茂。出馬、駝、驢、犎牛、黃金、硇沙、[97]賵香、阿薛那香、瑟瑟、麞皮、[98]氍毹、錦、疊。多蒲萄酒，富家或致十石，連年不敗。太延中，始遣使貢方物，後遂絕焉。

There is a [code of] law of the hu 胡, placed in the Zoroastrian temple. To pass sentence, [they] retrieve [it] and decide the penalty. [The sanction for] heavy criminals [is] collective family [punishment], next [comes] the death [penalty], [and] thieves and robbers [have their] feet cut off. All people have deep-set eyes, high noses, [and] profuse beards. [They are] excellent merchants. Many among the barbarians come to their state [for] commerce. [They] have large [and] small drums, the *pipa* 琵琶,[99] the five-stringed lute, and the harp.[100] Weddings and mourning are similar to [those of] the Tujue 突厥.[101] [In their] state are erected ancestral temples, [in which] sacrifices are offered to the ancestors in the sixth month.[102] Every state contributes to [these] sacrifices. [They] believe in Buddha, [and] write in hu 胡 scripts.[103] The climate [is] warm [and] favourable [for growing] the Five Crops.[104] [They] diligently keep vegetable gardens and trees [are] luxuriant. [They] bring forth horses, camels, mules, bumped cattle,[105] gold, sal ammoniac, true spikenard scent,[106] asana scent,[107] precious stones, roebuck skin, woollen rugs,[108] brocades,[109] [and] cotton.[110] Wine is cherished.[111] [Among] rich families, some [store] up to ten

96 Originally *yao* 祆, see p. 270, fn. 170.
97 Read *naosha* 硇砂. See: Laufer, *Sino-Iranica*, 503–8.
98 Read *zhangpi* 獐皮. See: Schafer, *Golden Peaches*, 106–7.
99 A lute of Western origin.
100 The *Suishu* 83.1849 adds here *di* 笛, a flute.
101 See below.
102 This is referring to the *Fravardīgān*.
103 In the *Suishu* 83.1849, the parallel passage reads 俗奉佛，為胡書。I therefore propose to read the passage of the *Weishu* as two separate units of meaning.
104 There are different listings, all referring to crops commonly planted in China.
105 Probably zebus. See: Schafer, *Golden Peaches*, 73–75.
106 See fn. below.
107 In the *Suishu* 83.1849, this item is specified as *kanxiang* 賵香. As Laufer points out, a parallel in the *Taiping huanyu ji* 183.4 equally lists the products of Kang 康, referring to these two as *gansong xiang* 甘松香 and *asana xiang* 阿薩那香. The first is to be identified as true spikenard, whereas the second is unknown (Laufer, *Sino-Iranica*, 455–56).
108 See: ibid., 492–93; Schafer, *Golden Peaches*, 198–99.
109 See: Laufer, *Sino-Iranica*, 488–92.
110 For the cotton, see fn. above. In the *Suishu* 83.1849, *luo* 騾, the donkey or rather mule, is added to this list of products.
111 See: Laufer, *Sino-Iranica*, 220–45.

pecks, [which] do not spoil for years.[112] During the Taiyan 太延 era (435–40 CE), [they] first sent envoys to present regional goods [as] tribute, which [was] later discontinued.

史臣曰：西域雖通魏氏，而中原始平，天子方以混一為心，未遑征伐。其信使往來，深得羈縻勿絕之道耳。

The historiographer said: Although the Western Regions were reached by the Wei Clan, when peace [was] just [established in] the Central Plains, the Son of Heaven was preoccupied with the unification, [and] did not have time to lead an expedition (to the Western Regions and the state of Kang 康). His messengers were coming and going, deeply concerned about keeping a loose rein[113] [and] an uninterrupted road.

1.8 *Zhoushu*

1.8.1 Sute 粟特

The *Zhoushu* contains information about the state of Sute 粟特 (Sogdiana):[114]

粟特國在葱嶺之西，蓋古之庵蔡，一名溫那沙。治於大澤，在康居西北。保定四年，其王遣使獻方物。

The state of Sute 粟特 (Sogdiana) [is] west of the Congling 葱嶺 (Pamirs), presumably the Yancai 奄蔡 (Alan 阿蘭 and Liao 聊) of antiquity, also called Wennasha 溫那沙.[115] [It is] ruled from the Great Marsh,[116] north-west of Kangju 康居. In Baoding 保定 4 (of the Northern Zhou, 564 CE) its king sent envoys to offer regional goods as gifts.

1.8.2 The envoy An Nuopantuo 安諾槃陀

Another passage has further caught the eye of Sogdian studies due to the name of an envoy sent by the Chinese emperor to the Tujue 突厥:[117]

大統十一年，太祖遣酒泉胡安諾槃陀使焉。

112 This is a reproduction of the passage concerning the states "around Dayuan 大宛" above in the *Shiji* and *Hanshu*.

113 A phrase stemming from husbandry. It was later used when the *jimi zhou* 羈縻州 were installed in 679 CE by the Tang, often translated as "loose rein prefecture/department", which were fairly self-governing districts. For more information, see the glossary.

114 *Zhoushu* 50.918; author's translation.

115 See p. 26 fn. 72.

116 On this confusing statement, see the glossary.

117 *Zhoushu* 50.908; author's translation.

In Datong 大統 11 (545 CE), the Founding Emperor (of the Western Wei, Wen 文) sent the envoy An Nuopantuo 安諾槃陀, a *hu* 胡 from Jiuquan 酒泉, to him (i.e. Tumen 土門).

1.9 *Suishu*

With the second emperor of the Sui, the contact with the Western Regions was re-established:[118]

煬帝時，遣侍御史韋節、司隸從事杜行滿使於西蕃諸國。至罽賓，得碼碯杯；王舍城，得佛經；史國，得十儛女、師子皮、火鼠毛而還。

During the reign of Emperor Yang 煬 (604–18 CE), the assistant censor-general Wei Jie 韋節 and assistant inspector Du Xingman 杜行滿 were sent to all countries in the Western Regions.[119] In Jibin 罽賓, [they] received agate bowls; in the city of Wangshe 王舍, [they] obtained Buddhist *sutras;* and in the state of Shi 史 (Kesh), [they] acquired ten female dancers, lion skin, and fur of the fire-marten.[120]

In relation to Sogdiana and Sogdians, there is (in the order of the volume) mention of the state Kang 康, An 安, Shi 石, Mi 米, Shi 史, Cao 曹, He 何, Cao 漕,[121] the Tujue 突厥 and the Western Tujue 突厥. In the following, a selection of the relevant passages for the present study is provided.

1.9.1 The state of Kang 康 (Samarqand)

The passage on the state of Kang 康 (Samarqand)[122] is nearly identical to that of the *Weishu* – as the latter is reconstructed relying on it[123] – and will therefore not be reproduced here. The only difference is the mention of an envoy being sent during the Daye 大業 era, instead of the Taiyan 太延 era:[124]

118 *Suishu* 83.1841–42; author's translation.

119 In this case referred to as Xifan 西蕃 and not Xiyu 西域.

120 From the *Hou Hanshu* (see above), we know about the state of Yan 嚴 exporting marten felt.

121 Also referred to as Jiaseni 伽色尼 (*Weishu* 102.2272); and later as Xieyu 謝颶, Caojuzha 漕矩吒, or Caoju 漕矩, with the Hexina 鶴悉那 Fort as capital (*Xin Tangshu* 221b.6253) and saying that it was the earlier Jibin 罽賓 (*Xin Tangshu* 221a.6241). This is referring to Kāpiśī (Yoshida Yutaka, "On the Origin," 38), or Zāblistān, which is located in present-day Ghazni, Afghanistan (Wang Shangshou and Ji Chengjia, *Sichou zhi lu*, 83). The passage is therefore not reproduced below. In the passages of the *Weishu*, *Suishu* and *Beishi*, the king of the state is also said to be of the Zhaowu 昭武 clan of the state of Kang 康. Why it is said to be related is unclear.

122 *Suishu* 83.1848–49. For an English translation of most of the passage, see: Pulleyblank, "Sogdian Colony," 320, fn. 1; and for a full translation: Shiratori Kurakichi, "Study on Su-t'ê," 101.

123 See p. 75 (1.15.5).

124 *Suishu* 83.1849; author's translation.

大業中，始遣使貢方物，後遂絕焉。

During the Daye 大業 era (605–18 CE), [the state of Kang 康 (Samarqand)] first sent envoys to present regional goods [as] tribute. Later, this was discontinued.

1.9.2 The state of An 安 (Bukhārā)[125]

安國，漢時安息國也。王姓昭武氏，與康國王同族，字設力登。妻，康國王女也。都在那密水南，城有五重，環以流水。宮殿皆為平頭。王坐金駝座，高七八尺。每聽政，與妻相對，大臣三人評理國事。風俗同於康國，唯妻其姊妹，及母子遞相禽獸，此為異也。煬帝即位之後，遣司隸從事杜行滿使於西域，至其國，得五色鹽而返。

The state of An 安 (Bukhārā). During the Han, [it was] the state of Anxi 安息 (Parthia).[126] The king's name is Zhaowu 昭武. [He is] of the same clan as the king of the state of Kang 康 (Samarqand), [his] courtesy name is Shelideng 設力登. [His] wife is the daughter of the king of the state of Kang 康. The capital is located south of the Nami 那密 River (Zerafshan). The city wall has five stories and is surrounded by a stream. The entire palace has flat roofs. The king is seated on a golden camel throne [that is] seven to eight *chi* (ca. 207–36 cm) high. Every time [he] attends to governmental affairs, [he sits] opposite his wife. Three chancellors decide on the national affairs. The customs are similar to those of the state of Kang 康. [The] only difference is that [they] marry their older or younger sister, and mother and son do to each other like the beasts of the air and ground do. After Emperor Yang 煬 ascended the throne (605 CE), the Retainer Commandant Du Xingman 杜行滿 was sent as an envoy to the Western Regions. Arriving at their state, [he] received multicoloured salt[127] and returned.

1.9.3 The state of Bi 畢 (Paykand?)[128]

國之西百餘里有畢國，可千餘家。其國無君長，安國統之。大業五年，遣使貢獻，後遂絕焉。

Over 100 *li* (ca. 50 km) (south-) west[129] is the state of Bi 畢 (Paykand?), [with] about over 1,000 families. Its state has no ruler. The state of An 安 governs it. In Daye 大業 5 (609 CE), [they] sent envoys to offer tribute, [which was] later discontinued.

125 *Suishu* 83.1849; author's translation.
126 For this misleading conflation, see the glossary.
127 See: Laufer, *Sino-Iranica*, 511.
128 *Suishu* 83.1849; author's translation.
129 See the passage on An 安 in the *Xin Tangshu*, which fits the identification with Paykand (p. 58; 1.14.2).

1.9.4 The state of Shi 石 (Chach)[130]

石國，居於藥殺水，都城方十餘里。其王姓石，名涅。國城之東南立屋，置座於中，正月六日、七月十五日以王父母燒餘之骨，金甕盛之，置于牀上，巡遶而行，散以花香雜果，王率臣下設祭焉。禮終，王與夫人出就別帳，臣下以次列坐，享宴而罷。

The state of Shi 石 (Chach) [is] located on the Yaosha 藥殺 River (Yaxartes, Syr Darya). The capital is over ten square *li* (ca. five km^2) [large]. Their king's family name is Shi 石, [his] given name [is] Nie 涅. South-east of the capital stands a house in [which] is installed a seat.[131] On the sixth day of the first month, and the 15th day of the seventh month, the bones that remain [after] cremating the king's parents are placed [in] a golden urn, and [then] placed on a bed.[132] [They] circle around [it], disperse flowers' scent [and] various fruits. The king [then] gives the officials the order to offer to them. At the end of the ritual, the king and [his] wife go out into different tents, [and] the officials sit in [hierarchical] order and feast until finished.

有粟麥，多良馬。其俗善戰，曾貳於突厥，射匱可汗興兵滅之，令特勤甸職攝其國事。南去鏺汗六百里，東南去瓜州六千里。甸職以大業五年遣使朝貢，其後不復至。

[They] have millet [and] wheat, [and] many fine horses. They traditionally excel in fighting. In the past, [they] parted [from a Chinese dominion] for the Tujue 突厥. Shegui 射匱 Khagan (of the Western Turkic Khaganate) levied troops and subjugated them, [and] ordered Dianzhi 甸職[133] Tegin to supervise their national affairs. To the south [one] goes 600 *li* (ca. 300 km) to Pohan 鏺汗 (Ferghana). To the south-east, [one] goes 6,000 *li* (ca. 3,000 km) to Guazhou 瓜州. Dianzhi 甸職 sent envoys to the court [to present] tribute in Daye 大業 5 (609 CE); after him, [they] did not visit again.

1.9.5 The state of Mi 米 (Māymurgh)[134]

米國，都那密水西，舊康居之地也。無王。其城主姓昭武，康國王之支庶，字閉拙。都城方二里。勝兵數百人。西北去康國百里，東去蘇對沙

130 *Suishu* 83.1850; author's translation.

131 A throne?

132 Marshak proposed that the ritual on the sixth day of the first month could have been a reminder of the destruction of mausoleums as prescribed by Jam/Yima, and thus the temporary abolition of death on New Year. He also proposed to understand both dates as maybe referring to different festivals (the *Beishi* provides only the first date, including a commentary, explaining that the omission is due to the belief of the authors that the accounts of the *Suishu* and *Tongdian* are corrupt; *Beishi* 97.3235; *Tongdian* 193.5275; Marshak, "Historico-Cultural," 151, 154, fn. 60).

133 Replaced by Fuzhi 匐職 in the description of the state of Shi 石 (Chach) in the *Xin Tangshu*. The first character conceivably is a variant (see also: Chavannes, *Documents*, 141, fn. 1).

134 *Suishu* 83.1854; author's translation.

那國五百里，西南去史國二百里，東去瓜州六千四百里。大業中，頻貢方物。

The state of Mi 米 (Māymurgh). The capital [is] west of the Nami 那密 River (Zerafshan). [It was part of] the ancient territory of Kangju 康居. [It] has no king. Their city's lord is surnamed Zhaowu 昭武, a descendant of the cadet brother of the king of the state of Kang 康 (Samarqand), [his] courtesy name is Bizhuo 閉拙.[135] The capital [measures] two square *li* (ca. one km^2). [They have] hundreds of elite soldiers. To the north-west, [one] goes 100 *li* (ca. 50 km) to the state of Kang 康. To the east, [one] goes 6,400 *li* (ca. 3,200 km) to Guazhou 瓜州. During the Daye 大業 era (605–18 CE), local goods [were] repeatedly offered as tribute.

1.9.6 The state of Shi 史 (Kesh)[136]

史國，都獨莫水南十里，舊康居之地也。其王姓昭武，字逖遮，亦康國王之支庶也。都城方二里。勝兵千餘人。俗同康國。北去康國二百四十里，南去吐火羅五百里，西去那色波國二百里，東北去米國二百里，東去瓜州六千五百里。大業中，遣使貢方物。

The state of Shi 史 (Kesh). The capital [is located] 10 *li* (ca. five km) south of the Dumo 獨莫 River (Kashka Darya?). [It was part of] the ancient territory of Kangju 康居. Their king is surnamed Zhaowu 昭武, [his] courtesy name is Tizhe 逖遮, also a descendant of the cadet brother of the king of the state of Kang 康 (Samarqand). The capital city [measures] two square *li* (ca. one km^2). [They have] over 1,000 elite soldiers. [Their] customs are similar [to] the state of Kang 康. To the north, [one] goes 240 *li* (ca. 120 km) to the state of Kang 康. South, [one] goes 500 *li* (ca. 250 km) to Tuhuoluo 吐火羅 (Tokharistan). To the west, [one] goes 200 *li* (ca. 100 km) to the state of Nasebo 那色波. To the north-west, [one] goes 300 *li* (ca. 150 km) to the state of Mi 米 (Bukhārā). To the east, [one] goes 6,500 *li* (ca. 3,250 km) to Guazhou 瓜州. During the Daye 大業 era (605–18 CE), [they] sent envoys [to] offer regional goods as tribute.

1.9.7 The state of Cao 曹 (Ishitikhan)[137]

曹國，都那密水南數里，舊是康居之地也。國無主，康國王令子烏建領之。都城方三里。勝兵千餘人。國中有得悉神，自西海以東諸國並敬事之。其神有金人焉，金破羅闊丈有五尺，高下相稱。每日以駝五頭、馬

135 According to Yoshida the ruler of Panjikant, *c'yn cwr βyδk''* (r. ? – 709 CE), Middle Iranian **piei tsi̯wät* (Yoshida Yutaka, "On the Origin," 60; see also: Yoshida Yutaka, "Review," 254). Marshak provided additional numismatic information, questioning this hypothesis: Marshak, "Panjikant".

136 *Suishu* 83.1854; author's translation.

137 *Suishu* 83.1855; author's translation.

十四、羊一百口祭之，常有千人食之不盡。東南去康國百里，西去何國百五十里，東去瓜州六千六百里。大業中，遣使貢方物。

The state of Cao 曹 (Ishitikhan). The capital [is] several *li* south of the Nami 那密 River (Zerafshan). [It was part of] the ancient territory of Kangju 康居. [It] has no ruler. The king of the state of Kang 康 ordered [his] son Wujian 烏建 to rule it. The capital [measures] three square *li* (ca. 1.5 km²). [They have] over a 1,000 elite soldiers. Inside the state, [they] have the deity Dexi 得悉[138] which is worshipped by all countries east of the Western Sea. Their deity has a gold human [statue to represent] it. [There is also a] gold *poluo* 破羅 (*piyāla?*)[139] [which] is one *zhang* and five *chi* in diameter (ca. 4.6 m).[140] The [gold statue on the] top and [the gold *poluo* 破羅 (*piyāla?*)] below are matching. Every day, five camels, ten horses, [and] 100 sheep are offered to it. Often there are a 1,000 people eating it, not [being able to] finish. To the south-east, [one] goes 100 *li* (ca. 50 km) to the state of Kang 康 (Samarqand). To the

138 As Shiratori laid out, Tomaschek started the debate about the identification of this deity (Shiratori Kurakichi, "Study on Su-t'ê," 112–13; Tomaschek, *Centralasiatische*, 152; *apud*: Spiegel, *Erânische Altertumskunde*, 70). He proposed to connect *Dexi* with *Tištrya*, whereas Hirth thought it was referring to *Tös* (plural *Töstör*; Hirth, *Über fremde Einflüsse*, 33). Chavannes was not satisfied with the conclusions and declared the question as open to further debate (Chavannes, *Documents*, 139, fn. 3). Henning proposed to identify the deity as *Taxsīč* (Henning, "Sogdian," 253, fn. 71). This name is also known as a personal name from the Ancient Sogdian letter II (line 53 and 59, *txs'yc-βntk*; *Takhsich-vandak*; see: Sims-Williams, "Sogdian Ancient Letter II," 270–73) and Upper-Indus inscriptions (see: Sims-Williams, *Sogdian*, 74). In a more recent publication, Ma Xiaohe also favoured *Tištrya* (Ma Xiaohe, "Suoluoyaside"). Concerning *Tištrya*, an Old Iranian astral divine being, see: Panaino, "Tištrya". The *Tang hui yao* 98.1754 and *Xin Tangshu* (see below p. 61; 1.14.5) provide the name of the city in which the temple is to be found: Yueyudi 越於底. According to its description in the *Tang hui yao*, Stark proposed to identify this location as Kurgantepe, north-east of present-day Ishitikan and north-west of Kišlak Orlat: Stark, *Transoxanien*, 21–22, fn. 31.

139 Chavannes was not quite sure what object this refers to, proposing an honorific distinction awarded in the Nanzhao kingdom. He rejected *poluo* 破羅 as basket, as Bushell translated in a passage of the *Xin Tangshu* 216a.6075, in which Tibetan envoys of 658 CE presented "a gold basin and a gold basket" (*jin ang jin poluo* 金盎金頗羅) (Chavannes, *Documents*, 119, fn. 2). The latter *po* 頗 is a different character, used in the same description of the state of Cao 曹 in the *Tang hui yao* 98.1754. The episode of the Tibetan envoys is also to be found in the *Cefu yuangui* 970.11402a with the same characters (apart from the basin being a *jin weng* 金甕, more a jar than a basin).
Henning proposed to identify it as a golden banner (*palā*) (Henning, "Sogdian," 253, fn. 70).
If one accepts that *jin poluo* 金叵羅 is another variation of the same term, dozens of quotes provide more context of the use, referring to a vessel used for alcohol and wine, perhaps related to the Persian *piyāla*, cognate with Greek *phialē* (see, among others, the quote from the *Bei Qishu* 39.514: 後為神武中外府功曹，神武宴僚屬，於坐失金叵羅，竇泰令飲酒者皆脫帽，於珽髻上得之，神武不能罪也。 For a short essay supporting such an idea, see: Cai Hongsheng, *Tangdai*, 11–14. In the analysis below concerning the *Xin Tangshu*, I provide new ideas on this passage.

140 See: Qiu Guangming, *Zhongguo gudai jiliang shi*; and: Wilkinson, *Chinese History*, 554–64.

west, [one] goes 150 *li* (ca. 75 km) to the state of He 何 (Kušaniyya). To the east, [one] goes 6,600 *li* (ca. 3,300 km) to Guazhou 瓜州. During the Daye 大業 era (605–18 CE), [they] sent envoys [to] offer regional goods [as] tribute.

1.9.8 The state of He 何 (Kušaniyya)[141]

何國，都那密水南數里，舊是康居之地也。其王姓昭武，亦康國王之族類，字敦。都城方二里。勝兵千人。其王坐金羊座。東去曹國百五十里，西去小安國三百里，東去瓜州六千七百五十里。大業中，遣使貢方物。

The state of He 何 (Kušaniyya). The capital [is] several *li* south of the Nami 那密 River (Zerafshan). [It was part of] the ancient territory of Kangju 康居. Their king is surnamed Zhaowu 昭武, also from the clan of the king of the state of Kang 康, [his] courtesy name is Dun 敦. The capital [measures] two square *li* (ca. 1.5 km^2). [They have] a 1,000 elite soldiers. Their king is seated [on a] golden sheep throne. To the east, [one] goes 150 *li* (ca. 75 km) to the state of Cao 曹 (Ishitikhan). To the west, [one] goes 300 *li* (ca. 150 km) to the state of Lesser An 安 (Kharghān). To the east, [one] goes 6,750 *li* (ca. 3,375 km) to Guazhou 瓜州. During the Daye 大業 era (605–18 CE), [they] sent an envoy [to] offer regional goods [as] tribute.

1.10 *Beishi*

The *Beishi*, a rather privately organised compilation during the Tang, does not offer much additional information in its Account of the Western Regions. This is due to the "earlier" accounts of the *Weishu* being supplemented with information of the *Beishi* while the latter relied on the *Suishu*.[142]

1.10.1 The state of Mu 穆 (Amul?)

A novelty is a separate passage dedicated to the state of Mu 穆 (Amul?), which is allegedly subject to the state of Kang 康, as already mentioned in the *Weishu*. However, it is most certainly not related to what is commonly defined as Sogdiana:[143]

穆國，都烏滸河之西，亦安息之故地，與烏那遏為隣。其王姓昭武，亦康國王之種類也，字阿濫密。都城方三里，勝兵二千人。東北去安國五百里，東去烏那遏二百餘里，西去波斯國四千餘里，東去瓜州七千七百里。大業中，遣使貢方物。

The state of Mu 穆. The capital [is] west of the Wuxu 烏滸 River (Amu Darya). [It] also is [part of] the ancient territory of Anxi 安息 and adjoins Wuna'e

141 *Suishu* 83.1855; author's translation.

142 See p. 75 (1.15.5).

143 *Beishi* 99.3238; author's translation.

烏那遏 (Balkh?). Their king is surnamed Zhaowu 昭武, also from the clan of the king of the state of Kang 康, [his] courtesy name is Alanmi 阿濫密.[144] The capital [measures] three square *li* (ca. 1.5 km²). [They] have 2,000 elite soldiers. To the north-east, [one] goes 500 *li* (ca. 250 km) to the state of An 安 (Bukhārā). To the east, [one] goes over 200 *li* (ca. 100 km) to Wuna'e 烏那遏. To the west, [one] goes over 4,000 *li* (ca. 2,000 km) to Bosi 波斯 (Iran). To the east, [one] goes 7,700 *li* (ca. 3,850 km) to Guazhou 瓜州. During the Daye 大業 era (605–18 CE), [they] sent envoys [to] offer regional goods [as] tribute.

1.11 Addendum: *Da Tang Xiyu ji* and other Buddhist texts

The Account of the Western Regions of Xuanzang 玄奘 is added to this list of material, as it is one of the sources used in later official historiographies. The quality of the information visibly surpasses the hearsay on which much of the earlier sources were based. While travelling to Northern India and back, the monk and his fellowship passed through Sogdiana, then controlled by the Tujue 突厥. In the following, a selection of the information is provided.

1.11.1 The Suye 素葉 River Fort (Ak-Beshim Sūyāb)

Xuanzang's 玄奘 first description of a place that is located in Sogdiana is the Suye 素葉 River Fort (Ak-Beshim Sūyāb):[145]

> 清池西北行五百餘里，至素葉水城。城周六七里，諸國商胡雜居也。土宜糜、麥、蒲萄，林樹稀疎。氣序風寒，人衣氈褐。素葉已西數十孤城，城皆立長，雖不相稟命，然皆役屬突厥。
>
> Going over 500 *li* (ca. 250 km) north-west from the Blue Lake (Issyk Kul), [one] arrives at the Suye 素葉 River Fort (Ak-Beshim Sūyāb). The fort is six to seven *li* (ca. 3–3,5 km) in circuit. [Here,] the *hu* 胡 merchants of all countries live together.[146] The agricultural products [are] millet, wheat, and grapes. Forests are few and scattered. The climate is windy and cold. The people wear

144 Actually referring to Rīyāmithan. See the glossary.

145 All passages from the *Da Tang Xiyu ji* are taken with their punctuation out of the *Da Tang Xiyu ji jiaozhu*. The author's translation is based on Beal's translation (Beal, *Buddhist Records I*, 26–28, 30–38), the comments of the *Taishō* (T51.871a06–18, 871b11–872a20), and the comments of the *Da Tang Xiyu ji jiaozhu* (71–76, 82–99).
The following passage is to be found in: T51.871a06–10 and the *Da Tang Xiyu ji jiaozhu* (71–72); see also: Beal, *Buddhist Records I*, 26.

146 This same statement is made for the Taluosi 呾邏私 (Talas) River Fort. T51.871a26; *Da Tang Xiyu ji jiaozhu* (77); see also: Beal, *Buddhist Records I*, 28.

clothes of wool.[147] West of Suye 素葉 are several dozen independent forts.[148] All forts have an [own] ruler. Although [they] do not take orders from each other, they are all subject to the Tujue 突厥.

1.11.2 Suli 窣利 (Sogdiana)

The account then continues with an overview of Suli 窣利 (Sogdiana). Besides Suli 窣利 of the *Da Tang Xiyu ji*, the *Nanhai qigui neifa zhuan* 南海寄歸內法傳[149] and the *Da Tang Xiyu qiufa gaoseng zhuan* 大唐西域求法高僧傳[150] use "Suli 速利", the *Fanyu qianzi wen* 梵語千字文 uses "Sunlin 孫鄰",[151] and the *Fanyu zaming* 梵語雜名 uses "Suli 蘇哩"[152] to refer to Sogdiana. The passage reads as follows:[153]

> 自素葉水城至羯霜那國，地名窣利，人亦謂焉。文字語言，即隨稱矣。字源簡略，本二十餘言，轉而相生，其流浸廣。粗有書記，竪[154]讀其文，遞相傳授，師資無替。
>
> From the Suye 素葉 River Fort (Ak-Beshim Sūyāb) to the state of Jieshuangna 羯霜那 (Kesh), the land is called Suli 窣利 (Sogdiana). The people are also called this way. The script and spoken language are also called accordingly. The primary characters are simple and few, originally 20 or so.[155] [Words] are produced [by their] alignment. [From this] the derivations further diversify. [They] have some literature, the script is read vertically. The teaching method is handed down from one teacher to another, [so that there is] no loss.
>
> 服氈褐，衣皮氈，裳服褊急，齊髮露頂，或總剪剃，繒綵絡額。形容偉大，志性恇怯。風俗澆訛，多行詭詐，大抵貪求，父子計利，財多爲貴，良賤無差。雖富巨萬，服食麁[156]弊，力田逐利者雜半矣。

147 Beal translated here "twilled wool" although just a page later, he translates the same two characters as "fine hair-cloth (linen)" (see also the description of Suli 窣利 just below; ibid., 26).

148 Beal translated "deserted towns", which is more interpretation than translation and further seems to contradict his own subsequent translation (ibid.).

149 T54.215b13, b19, b25.

150 T51.1c04, 2c13.

151 [illegible], explained as *hu* 胡 (Western). T54.1216a03.

152 [illegible], explained as *hu* 胡 (Western). T54.1236a12.

153 *Taishō* (T51.871a10–18), *Da Tang Xiyu ji jiaozhu* (72–76). For the basis of this translation, see p. 39 fn. 145.

154 A variant of *shu* 豎. Beal translated: "which the common sort read together" (Beal, *Buddhist Records I*, 27). The meaning of the word he is referring to is however not "the common sort" but either "children" or "servants", which does not make much sense in this context, I believe. His Chinese text was probably corrupt in this instance.

155 According to different editions, the number of the characters varies from twenty to thirty; based to the statement that there were few characters, the *Da Tang Xiyu ji jiaozhu* (73, fn. 1) concludes it should be 20.

156 A variant of *cu* 麤.

[Their] clothes [are made of] woollen cloth,[157] [their] upper garments [are] of leather and felt, [and their] lower garments short [and] tight. They adjust [their] hair [so as to] reveal the top of the head, or shave [it] all off. [They] bind a coloured silk band around [their] foreheads. [Of] large stature, [they are but] coward of will. As a rule treacherous, [they] often swindle. [They are] highly covetous, [so that even between] father and son [they] seek profit.[158] It is highly regarded if [someone] possesses much wealth, [in this respect] the good or the lowly are no different.[159] Even when immensely rich, [they] clothe and eat meanly and lowly. Half work the fields [and] half seek profit (i.e. engage in trade).

1.11.3 The state of Zheshi 赭時 (Chach)

After that follows a description of all the countries in between the Suye 素葉 River Fort (Ak-Beshim Sūyāb) and the state of Jieshuangna 羯霜那 (Kesh). The state of Zheshi 赭時 (Chach), the first in the account, is described as follows:[160]

赭時國周千餘里，西臨葉河，東西狹，南北長。土宜氣序，同笯赤建國。城邑數十，各別君長，既無總主，役屬突厥。

The state of Zheshi 赭時 (Chach) is over 1,000 *li* (ca. 500 km) in circuit. In the west, [it] borders on the Ye 葉 River (Jaxartes, Syr Darya). [It is] narrow from east to west [and] broad from south to north. The agricultural products [and] climate are similar to [those of] the state of Nuchijian 笯赤建 (Nujikath). There are dozens of forts and towns,[161] each with a separate lord. There is no common ruler, they serve [and] are subject to the Tujue 突厥.

從此東南千餘里，至怖數發反。捍國。

From here, [going] 1,000 *li* (ca. 500 km) south-east, [one] arrives at the state of Fei- 怖 (pronounced *fu* 數 + *fa/fei* 發: *fa/fei*) han 捍 (Ferghana).

157 Beal understood this as "fine hair-cloth (linen)" (see p. 39 fn. 147) (Beal, *Buddhist Records I*, 27).

158 Beal translated: "Both parent and child plan how to get wealth". It is, however, father and son, excluding females. Furthermore, I believe that the relationship between father and son is especially addressed (ibid.).

159 Beal translated: "but the well-to-do and the poor are not distinguished". The text is written in a two-sentence structure, in which the second sentence clarifies the first – as is common practice in Chinese. I therefore believe that this sentence is adding further information to the preceding statement and not to be seen as a separate statement (ibid.).

160 T51.871b11–14. *Da Tang Xiyu ji jiaozhu* (82–84); see also: Beal, *Buddhist Records I*, 30. For the basis of this translation, see p. 39 fn. 145.

161 Beal translated *cheng yi* 城邑 as the combined expression "towns", which in my opinion, should be separated into forts/cities and towns (ibid.).

1.11.4 The state of Feihan 怖捍 (Ferghana)

The description of this state is included below due to its lying between the Suye 素葉 River Fort (Ak-Beshim Sūyāb) and the state of Jieshuangna 羯霜那 (Kesh), and because it includes references to neighbouring Sogdian countries:[162]

怖捍國周四千餘里，山周四境。土地膏腴，稼穡滋盛。多花菓，宜羊馬。氣序風寒，人性剛勇，語異諸國，形貌醜弊。自數十年無大君長，酋豪力競，不相賓伏，依川據險，畫野分都。

The state of Feihan 怖捍 (Ferghana) is over 1,000 *li* (ca. 500 km) in circuit. Mountains surround [it] on four sides. The soil is fat and rich, harvest is plentiful [and] there are many flowers and fruits. [It is] favourable for sheep and horses. The climate is windy and cold [and] the people [are] of firm and courageous character. [Their] language differs from all other countries. [Their people's][163] appearance [is] ugly and mean. Since dozens of years, [they] have had no supreme lord. Chiefs and leaders compete for power [and] do not submit or subject to each other. Land and cities[164] are divided according to rivers and ridges.

從此西行千餘里，至窣堵利瑟那國。

From here, going 1,000 *li* (ca. 500 km) west, [one] arrives at the state of Sudulisena 窣堵利瑟那 (Sutrūshana, Ushrusana).

1.11.5 The state of Sudulisena 窣堵利瑟那 (Sutrūshana/Ushrusana)[165]

窣堵利瑟那國周千四五百里，東臨葉河。葉河出葱嶺北原，西北而流，浩汗渾濁，汩淴[166]漂急。土宜風俗，同赭時國。自有王，附突厥。

The state of Sudulisena 窣堵利瑟那 (Sutrūshana/Ushrusana) measures 1,400–1,500 *li* (ca. 700–750 km) in circuit. In the east, [it] borders on the Ye 葉 River (Jaxartes, Syr Darya). The Ye 葉 River comes from the northern plateau of the Congling 葱嶺 (Pamirs) and flows north-west. [Its water] is [sometimes] large and turbid [and sometimes] rapid and torrential. [Its] agricultural products and

162 T51.871b11–20. *Da Tang Xiyu ji jiaozhu* (84–85). For a discussion about different transcriptions, see the glossary. For the basis of this translation, see p. 39 fn. 145.

163 Beal translated "Their form is rather poor and mean", i.e. reading this as a description of the script (Beal, *Buddhist Records I*, 31).

164 The character *du* 都 was ignored in Beal's translation ("their separate possessions"; ibid.). The *Quan Tang wen* 328.3326a includes a similar passage: 山川不可以不守。於是開分都野。 "Mountains and valleys cannot be ignored. According to this, cities and land are divided."

165 T51.871b21–27. *Da Tang Xiyu ji jiaozhu* (85–87); see also: Beal, *Buddhist Records I*, 31–32. For the basis of this translation, see p. 39 fn. 145.

166 The *Da Tang Xiyu ji jiaozhu* (85) uses here the character *hu* 淴, whereas the *Taishō* has *se*/*yi* 澺, which means "torrent". T51.871b22. The *Da Tang Xiyu ji jiaozhu* (86, fn. 5) further explains that an earlier volume had *cong* 潨 (a variant of *cong* 潀) but was corrected for this edition.

customs are similar to those of the state of Zheshi 赭時 (Chach). Although [they] have a king, [they] are subject to the Tujue 突厥.[167]

從此西北，入大沙磧，絕無水草，途路彌漫，疆境難測，望大山，尋遺骨，以知所指，以記經途。

From here, [going] north-west, [one] enters the Great Sand Desert (Kyzylkum?) [with] absolutely no water nor grass. The paths [are] widespread[168] [and the desert's] limits are difficult to gauge. To know the direction [to take and] mark the travelled course, [one] looks at the great mountains [and] searches for left over carcasses.[169]

行五百餘里，至颯秣建國。唐言康國。

Travelling for over 500 *li* (ca. 250 km), [one] arrives at the state of Samojian 颯秣建 (Samarqand). Called state of Kang 康 [in] the *Tang*(*shu*) 唐(書).

1.11.6 The state of Samojian 颯秣建 (Samarqand)[170]

颯秣建國周千六七百里，東西長，南北狹。國大都城周二十餘里，極險固，多居人。異方寶貨，多聚此國。土地沃壤，稼穡備植，林樹蓊欝[171]，花菓滋茂。多出善馬。機巧之技[172]，特工[173]諸國。氣序和暢，風俗猛烈。凡諸胡國，此爲其中，進止威儀，近遠取則。其王豪勇，隣國承命，兵馬強盛，多諸[174]赭羯。赭羯之人，其性勇烈，視死如歸，戰無前敵。

The state of Samojian 颯秣建 (Samarqand) is about 1,600–1,700 *li* (ca. 800–850 km) in circuit, broad from east to west [and] narrow from south to north. The capital of the state is over 20 *li* (ca. ten km) in circuit. [Although the land

167 Beal translated: "Since it has had a king, it has been under the rule of the Turks", translating *zi* 自 with "since" instead of "although" (Beal, *Buddhist Records I*, 32).

168 The roads are described as "widespread" in that they are too many and long and thus of no use to the traveller without knowledge. Beal thus translated: "The road is lost in the waste" (ibid.). The *Xinyi Da Tang Xiyu ji*'s footnote (23, fn. 1) for *miman* 瀰漫 says that in this case it means "unsteady" without, however, providing an explanation.

169 Beal translated: "and only by looking in the direction of some great mountain, and following the guidance of bones which lie scattered about, can we know the way in which we ought to go" (Beal, *Buddhist Records I*, 32). I believe that *yi ji jing tu* 以記經途 "to mark the travelled course" should be translated as active. Carcasses and bones were and are still indeed used to mark desert roads.

170 T51.871b28–c06. *Da Tang Xiyu ji jiaozhu* (87–89); see also: Beal, *Buddhist Records I*, 32–33. For the basis of this translation, see p. 39 fn. 145.

171 A variant of *yu* 鬱.

172 The character *ji* 技 is used in the *Taishō* and in the *Da Tang Xiyu ji jiaozhu* (87). The *Taishō* indicates, however, that in other editions this character is rendered as *ji* 伎 (T51.871c02, fn. 28).

173 In other editions *gong* 工 is rendered as *shang* 上. See: *Da Tang Xiyu ji jiaozhu* (88, fn. 5) and T51.871c02.

174 The *Taishō* provides a footnote stating that in other editions, the character is rendered as *shi* 是 (T51.871c05, fn. 30).

is] extremely rugged, many people live [there]. Many precious goods of foreign countries are amassed inside this state.[175] [Its] soil is fertile [and] harvest plentiful. Forests are dense, flowers and fruits luxuriant. Many excellent horses are bred [here]. [With their] skill in ingenious crafts[176] [they are highly regarded] as artisans in all countries. [Although] the climate is moderate, the customs are fierce. All *hu* 胡 countries consider it as [their] centre. [Their] behaviour in virtue and propriety is copied near and far. Their king is brave, the neighbouring countries obey [his] orders. Soldiers and horses are mighty and magnificent, many are *zhejie* 赭羯 (*čākar*). The *zhejie* 赭羯 people are by nature courageous [and] fierce, [they] see death as a return home.[177] No enemy [withstands] their attack.

從此東南至弭秣賀國。唐言米國。

From here, [going] 1,000 *li* (ca. 500 km) south-east, [one] arrives at the state of Mimohe 弭秣賀 (Māymurgh). Called state of Mi 米 [in] the *Tang*(*shu*) 唐(書).

1.11.7 The state of Mimohe 弭秣賀 (Māymurgh)[178]

弭秣賀國，周四五百里。據川中。東西狹，南北長。土宜風俗，同颯秣建國。

The state of Mimohe 弭秣賀 (Māymurgh) measures 400–500 *li* (ca. 200–250 km) in circuit. [It lies] in a valley. [The state is] narrow from east to west [and] broad from south to north. [Its] agricultural products and customs are similar to those of the state of Samojian 颯秣建 (Samarqand).

從此北至劫布呾那國。唐言曹國。

From here, [going] north, [one] arrives at the state of Jiebudanna 劫布呾那 (Kapūtānā). Called state of Cao 曹 [in] the *Tang*(*shu*) 唐(書).

1.11.8 The state of Jiebudanna 劫布呾那 (Kapūtānā)[179]

劫布呾那國周千四五百里，東西長，南北狹。土宜風俗同颯秣建國。

175 Beal translated: "The precious merchandise of many foreign countries is stored up here." I believe that *duo* 多 (many, much) is qualifying the goods, and not the countries (Beal, *Buddhist Records I*, 32).

176 Beal translated: "The inhabitants are skilful in the arts and trades" (ibid.).

177 It seems that these *čākar* came from Sogdiana and where used as mercenaries or elite units by different leaders and armies. At the time of the An Lushan 安祿山 Rebellion, the meaning may however have already changed, referring to Western people generally. For two discussions of the term, see: Vaissière, "Sute"; and the answer to this article: Wang Rui, "Zai lun". For a more linguistic approach to the term *jie* 羯, see: Vovin, Vajda and Vaissière, "Who Were the *Kjet".

178 T51.871c08–10. *Da Tang Xiyu ji jiaozhu* (89–91); see also: Beal, *Buddhist Records I*, 33. For the basis of this translation, see p. 39 fn. 145.

179 T51.871c11–13. *Da Tang Xiyu ji jiaozhu* (91–92); see also: Beal, *Buddhist Records I*, 33–34.

The state of Jiebudanna (Kapūtānā) measures 1,400–1,500 *li* (ca. 700–750 km) in circuit, broad from east to west [and] narrow from south to north. [Its] agricultural products and customs are similar to those of the state of Samojian 颯秣建 (Samarqand).

從此國西三百餘里，至屈居勿反。霜去聲。你[180]迦國。唐言何國。

From this state, [going] west for over 300 *li* (ca. 150 km), [one] arrives at the state of Qu 屈 (pronounced *ju* 居+ *hu* 勿 = *ju*) xiang 霜 (fourth tone) nijia 你迦 (Kushaniyya). Called state of He 何 [in] the *Tang*(*shu*) 唐(書).

1.11.9 The state of Qushuangnijia 屈霜你迦 (Kushaniyya)[181]

屈霜你[182]迦國周千四五百里，東西狹，南北長。土宜風俗同颯秣建國。

The state of Qushuangnijia 屈霜你迦 (Kushaniyya) measures 1,400–1,500 *li* (ca. 700–750 km) in circuit, narrow from west to east [and] broad from south to north. [Its] agricultural products and customs are similar to those of the state of Samojian 颯秣建 (Samarqand).

從此國西二百餘里，至喝捍國。唐言東安國。

From this state, [going] west for over 200 *li* (ca. 100 km), [one] arrives at the state of Hehan 喝捍 (Kharghān). Called state of Eastern An 安 [in] the *Tang*(*shu*) 唐(書).

1.11.10 The state of Hehan 喝捍 (Kharghān)[183]

喝捍國周千餘里。土宜風俗同颯秣建國。從此國西四百餘里，至捕喝國。唐言(中)[184]安國。

The state of Hehan 喝捍 (Kharghān) measures over 1,000 *li* (ca. 500 km) in circuit. [Its] agricultural products and customs are similar to those of the state of Samojian 颯秣建 (Samarqand). From this state, [going] west for over 400 *li* (ca. 200 km), [one] arrives at the state of Buhe 捕喝 (Bukhārā). Called state of (Middle) An 安 [in] the *Tang*(*shu*) 唐(書).

For the basis of this translation, see p. 39 fn. 145.

180 The *Taishō* erroneously gives the character *er* 爾: T51.871c13.

181 T51.871c14–16. *Da Tang Xiyu ji jiaozhu* (92–93); see also: Beal, *Buddhist Records I*, 34. For the basis of this translation, see p. 39 fn. 145.

182 The *Taishō* erroneously gives the character *er* 爾: T51.871c14.

183 T51.871c17–18. *Da Tang Xiyu ji jiaozhu* (93–94); see also: Beal, *Buddhist Records I*, 34. For the basis of this translation, see p. 39 fn. 145.

184 Originally *shou* 守, corrected by the *Da Tang Xiyu ji jiaozhu* edition according to various other editions (for details, see the edition, 93, fn. 3). The round brackets were added to fit the present formatting style.

1.11.11 The state of Buhe 捕喝 (Bukhārā)[185]

捕喝國周千六七百里，東西長南北狹。土宜風俗同颯秣建國。

The state of Buhe 捕喝 (Bukhārā) measures 1,600–1,700 *li* (ca. 800–850 km) in circuit, broad from east to west [and] narrow from south to north. [Its] agricultural products and customs are similar to those of the state of Samojian 颯秣建 (Samarqand).

從此國西四百餘里，至伐地國。唐言西安國。

From this state, [going] west for over 400 (100?)[186] *li* (ca. 200 km, or ca. 50 km), [one] arrives at the state of Fadi 伐地 (Vardana?). Called state of Western An 安 [in] the *Tang*(*shu*) 唐(書).

1.11.12 The state of Fadi 伐地 (Vardana?)[187]

伐地國周四百餘里。土宜風俗同颯秣建國。

The state of Fadi 伐地 (Vardana?) measures over 400 *li* (ca. 200 km) in circuit. [Its] agricultural products and customs are similar to those of the state of Samojian 颯秣建 (Samarqand).

從此西(南)[188]五百餘里，至貨利習彌伽[189]國。

From here, [going] west[190] for over 500 *li* (ca. 250 km), [one] arrives at the state of Huoliximijia 貨利習彌伽 (Khwārizmik).

1.11.13 The state of Huoliximijia 貨利習彌伽 (Khwārizmik)[191]

貨利習彌伽國順縛芻河兩[192]岸，東西二三十里，南北五百餘里。土宜風俗同伐地國，語言少異。

185 T51.871c19–21. *Da Tang Xiyu ji jiaozhu* (94–95); see also: Beal, *Buddhist Records I*, 34. For the basis of this translation, see p. 39 fn. 145.

186 As the *Da Tang Xiyu ji jiaozhu* (94, fn. 2) indicates, the *Da Tang da ci'en si sanzang fashi zhuan xu* 大唐大慈恩寺三藏法師傳序 (T50.227c24–25) of Huili 慧立 says instead: 又西百餘里至伐地國。 "Then, after over 100 *li*, [one] arrives at the state of Fadi 伐地." On the conflicting information, see the glossary.

187 T51.871c22–23. *Da Tang Xiyu ji jiaozhu* (95–96); see also: Beal, *Buddhist Records I*, 35. For the basis of this translation, see p. 39 fn. 145.

188 As the *Da Tang Xiyu ji jiaozhu* (96, fn. 1) indicates, the *Da Tang da ci'en si sanzang fashi zhuan xu* 大唐大慈恩寺三藏法師傳序 (T50.227c25–26) does not include the character *nan* 南 (south).

189 As the *Da Tang Xiyu ji jiaozhu* (96, fn. 2) indicates, the character *jia* 伽 is not included in the *Shijia fangzhi* 釋伽方志 (T51.953a12) and the *Xin Tangshu* (see the description of Huoxun 火尋 p. 67; 1.14.12).

190 On the conflicting information concerning Fadi 伐地, see the glossary.

191 T51.871c24–27. *Da Tang Xiyu ji jiaozhu* (96–97); see also: Beal, *Buddhist Records I*, 35.

192 As the *Da Tang Xiyu ji jiaozhu* (97, fn. 1) indicates, the annotated version (of the *Jing da ben*

The state of Huoliximijia 貨利習彌伽 (Khwārizmik) follows the west bank of the Fuchu 縛芻 River (Skt. *Vakṣu*; Oxus, Amu Darya). [It] measures 200–300 *li* (ca. 100–150 km) from east to west [and] over 500 *li* (ca. 250 km) from south to north. [Its] agricultural products and customs are similar to those of the state of Fadi 伐地 (Vardana?), [although] the language is slightly different.

從颯秣建國西南行三百餘里，至羯霜。去聲。那國。唐言史國。

From the state of Samojian 颯秣建 (Samarqand), going south-west for over 300 *li* (ca. 150 km), [one] arrives at the state of Jieshuang 羯霜 (fourth tone) na 那 (Kesh). Called state of Shi 史 [in] the *Tang(shu)* 唐(書).

1.11.14 The state of Jieshuangna 羯霜那 (Kesh)[193]

羯霜那國周千四五百里。土宜風俗同颯秣建國。

The state of Jieshuangna 羯霜那 (Kesh) measures 1,400–1,500 *li* (ca. 700–750 km) in circuit. [Its] agricultural products and customs are similar to those of the state of Samojian 颯秣建 (Samarqand).

從此西南行二百餘里入山，山路崎嶇[194]，谿徑危險，既絕人里，又少水草。東南山行三[195]百餘里入鐵門。

From here, going south-west for over 200 *li* (ca. 100 km), [one] enters the mountains. The mountains and roads are steep and rugged and the passes and paths are high and dangerous. It is not only devoid of humans and towns, but scarce in water and vegetation. Going south-east for over 300 *li* (ca. 150 km), [one] enters the Iron Gates (Dar-i Āhanīn).

京大本; see the edition, 145, for further explanations) suggested the idea that *liang* 兩 (both) should actually be *xi* 西 (west), which is the conclusion Beal (Beal, *Buddhist Records I*, 35, fn. 115) also reached after reading that Huili 慧立 said it bounded on the east by the Amu Darya.

193 T51.871c28–872a02. *Da Tang Xiyu ji jiaozhu* (97–98); see also: Beal, *Buddhist Records I*, 36. For the basis of this translation, see p. 39 fn. 145.

194 As the *Da Tang Xiyu ji jiaozhu* (98, fn. 2) indicates, that the *Dunhuang jia ben* 敦煌甲本 (S.2659 and S.958, not yet digitised on the International Dunhuang Probject Website) gives *xian* 嶮 instead of *qu* 嶇.

195 As the *Da Tang Xiyu ji jiaozhu* (98, fn. 3) indicates, that the *Dunhuang jia ben* 敦煌甲本 (see footnote above) lacks these three characters, meaning that the passage reads: 東南百餘里入鐵門。 "South-east, after over 100 *li* (ca. 50 km), [one] enters the Iron Gates." This seems, however, too short.

1.12 *Tongdian*[196]

1.12.1 Kangju 康居 and the state of Kang 康 (Samarqand)

The *Tongdian*, an encyclopedic work of the late Tang, also contains some information pertaining to Sogdians. In the description of the state of Kangju 康居, after information is provided on Kangju 康居 since the Han directly ensues the state of Kang 康. This contextualisation and the following passage propose that the state of Kang 康 was the successor of the Kangju 康居:[197]

> 至隋時，謂之康國。
>
> Since the Sui it was called the state of Kang 康.

Besides reproducing the already mentioned information, the information of the surrounding countries – which was previously given at the end of the section – is now conflated with the beginning:[198]

> 枝庶各分王，故康國左右諸國，米國、史國、曹國、何國、安國、小安國、那色波國、烏那曷國、穆國凡九國，皆其種類，並以昭武為姓，示不忘本也。
>
> The descendants of the cadet brothers all [became] kings. [This is] why all nine states around the state of Kang 康, [i.e.] the state of Mi 米 (Māymurgh), of Shi 史 (Kesh), of Cao 曹 (Kapūtānā), of He 何 (Kušaniyya), of An 安 (Bukhārā), of Lesser An 小安 (Kharghān), of Nasebo 那色波 (Nakhshab), of Wunahe 烏那曷 (Balkh?), [and] of Mu 穆 (Amul?) are of their clan [and thus] all have the surname Zhaowu 昭武, showing that [they] did not forget [their] origin.

The *Tongdian* also includes some new details. These were probably gathered from the travels of Wei Jie 韋節 during the Sui,[199] who is said to have recorded information about the state of Kang 康 in his *Xifan ji*, listed in the *Tongdian* under the description of Kangju 康居:[200]

> 康國人並善賈，男年五歲則令學書，少解則遣學賈，以得利多為善。其人好音聲。以六月一日為歲首，至此日，王及人庶並服新衣，翦髮鬚。在國城東林下七日馬射，至欲罷日，置一金錢於帖上，射中者則得一日為王。
>
> The people of the state of Kang 康 (Samarqand) [are] all excellent merchants. Once a boy turns five, [they] make him learn writing. After having grasped [it]

196 The *Tongzhi* is not included as separate source in this list. The little information that it provides concerning Sogdiana is referred to in the footnotes.
197 *Tongdian* 193.5255; author's translation.
198 *Tongdian* 193.5255; author's translation.
199 See: Yu Taishan, "Sui Dynasty," 20–21; and: Yoshida Yutaka, "On the Origin," 37, fn. 5.
200 *Tongdian* 193.5256; author's translation.

a little,[201] he is sent off to learn commerce. Obtaining larger profits is considered positive.[202] They are fond of music. The first day of the sixth month is the beginning of the year. On this day, the king and the people all dress in new clothes, cut [their] hair [and shave their] beards. In the woods east of the capital, [they] shoot [arrows from] horses for seven days. [When] the last day arrives, [they] fix a golden coin on a sign. Who hits [it] becomes king for one day.[203]

俗事天神，崇敬甚重。云神兒七月死，失骸骨，事神之人每至其月，俱著黑疊衣，徒跣撫胸號哭，涕淚交流。丈夫婦女三五百人散在草野，求天兒骸骨，七日便止。國城外別有二百餘戶，專知喪事，別築一院，院內養狗。每有人死，即往取屍，置此院內，令狗食之，肉盡收骸骨，埋殯無棺槨。

[They] traditionally make offerings to the heaven deity [with] deep reverence. [They] say that the deity's son died in the seventh month [and his] bones were lost. Every time this month comes, the people who serve the deity dress in black cotton clothes, go barefooted, wail, and strike their chests, [while their] tears run. Three to five hundred men and women scatter in the outdoors [and] search for the bones of the celestial son.[204] On the seventh day [they] stop. Secluded outside of the capital's wall there are over 200 households, specialised in burial practices. [There they have] an isolated court, in which dogs are held. Every time someone dies, [they] go to get the corpse, put [it] in this court, [and] let the dogs eat it. [When] the flesh is gone, [they] collect the bones, [which are] buried without coffins.

201 The passage on the state of Kang 康 in the *Jiu Tangshu* (see p. 50; 1.13.1) says that when they turn twenty, they go abroad for commerce. The reliability of this information may, however, be called into question, as the passages concerning the beginning of the year contradict each other.

202 A similar comment is also made in the *Da Tang Xiyu ji* (see the description of Suli 窣利 p. 39; 1.11.2), which may have relied on this earlier source.

203 Marshak proposed to correlate this to the new-year festivity of Iran, lasting six days from the (lesser) Nau Rūz until the greater Nau Rūz (Marshak, "Historico-Cultural," 151, 154, fn. 60).

204 As Marshak stated (ibid., 151, 154, fn. 58), "A. N. Belenitskij rightly compared this agricultural-seasonal un-Zoroastrian calendar festival with the Mesopotamian summer ceremony of mourning for Tammuz, whose bones were ground in a mill and scattered to the wind." He quotes: Belenitskyi, "Voprosy," 77; and: Henning, "Sogdian," 252. Henning wrote: "This is a fair description of Adonia, which took place at the height of the summer: the seventh (Chinese) month began at the end of July or in August. The possibility that 'Kūyūne, the son of Ahriman, was a Sogdian version of Adonis should now be considered." He further provides quotes on the topics of sacrificing on a bridge, cutting of ears, and the laceration of faces (ibid., 252, fn. 67).

A quote from Du Huan's 杜環 *Jing xing ji* is further provided in the commentary of this passage:[205]

> 康國在米國西南三百餘里，一名薩末建。土沃，人富，國小。有神祠名[祆][206]，諸[207]國事者，本出於此。
>
> The state of Kang 康 (Samarqand) is located over 300 *li* (ca. 150 km) south-west of the state of Mi 米 (Māymurgh). [It is] also called Samojian 薩末建. The soil [is] fertile, the people rich, [and] the state small. They have a temple of a deity called *xian* 祆. All state affairs originate here.[208]

This last sentence implies that before going to war or attending to matters of state, offerings would have to be made at the Zoroastrian temple. If this is an observation, hearsay, or a projection related to Chinese traditions is difficult to say.[209]

1.12.2 Suyi 粟弋 (Sogdiana)

Interestingly, a description of Suyi 粟弋 (Sogdiana) is also provided in the list of countries:[210]

> 粟弋，後魏通焉。在葱嶺西，大國。一名粟特，一名特拘夢。出好馬、牛、羊、蒲萄諸果。出美蒲萄酒，其土地水美故也。出大禾，高丈餘，子如胡豆。在安息北五千里。附庸小國四百餘城。至太武帝時，遣使來朝獻。
>
> The contact to Suyi 粟弋 (Sogdiana) was established during the Later Wei (Northern Wei). [It is] located west of the Congling 葱嶺 (Pamirs) [and is] a great state. [It is] also called Sute 粟特 or Tejumeng 特拘夢. [They] bring forth fine horses, cattle, sheep, grapes, and all kind of fruits. [They] produce choice wine, as their soil and water are good, and large grain, over a *zhang* (ca. 30 cm) high, [with] seeds like broad beans.[211] [It is] located 5,000 *li* (ca. 2,500 km) north of Anxi 安息 (Parthia). [It] is sovereign over more than 400 forts of smaller countries. During the [reign of] Emperor Taiwu 太武 (423–52 CE), [they] sent envoys to offer gifts to the court.

205 *Tongdian* 193.5256; author's translation.

206 Originally *ba* 祓. Already annotated in the version of Wang Jing'an 王靜安. See also p. 270 fn. 170.

207 Originally *zhi* 諳 (in another – obviously corrupted – version *zhu* 誅). Annotated and corrected in the Zhonghua shuju edition.

208 As commentaries have stated before, this passage may be corrupted (Zhang Yi and Zhang Yichun, *Wang*, 10). I am grateful to Hans van Ess who pointed out to me that this passage conceivably refers to the custom of first performing rituals before going to war or attending to matters of state, as first mentioned in the *Chunqiu Zuozhuan* 27.867: 國之大事，在祀與戎。

209 See fn. above.

210 *Tongdian* 193.5273–74; author's translation.

211 See p. 37 fn. 140.

1.13 *Jiu Tangshu*

The *Jiu Tangshu* only includes a passage on the state of Kang 康.

1.13.1 The state of Kang 康 (Samarqand)

This passage partly reproduces the information as seen before, with, however, some interesting changes, and further adds new information and observations:[212]

> 康國，即漢康居之國也。其王姓溫，月氏人。先居張掖祁連山北昭武城，為突厥所破，南依葱嶺，遂有其地。枝庶皆以昭武為姓氏，不忘本也。其人皆深目高鼻，多鬚髯。丈夫翦髮或辮髮。其王冠氈[213]帽，飾以金寶。婦人盤髻，幪以皁巾，飾以金花。
>
> The state of Kang 康, that is the state of Kangju 康居 of the Han. [Their] kings are surnamed Wen 溫,[214] of the Yuezhi 月氏. Once, [they] lived [in] the city of Zhaowu 昭武 north of the Qilian 祁連 range [of] Zhangye 張掖. Subjugated by the Tujue 突厥, [they moved] south along the Congling 葱嶺 (Pamirs) and then had their place. The descendants of the cadet brothers all have the family and clan name of Zhaowu 昭武 – not forgetting their origins. All have deep-set eyes and high noses, and profuse beards. Men cut their hair or [wear] them plaited. Their king's crown [is] a felt hat, decorated with gold and jewellery. Women[215] wind [their hair in a] topknot, use a black cloth to cover [it], [and] decorate [it] with gold flowers.[216]
>
> 人多嗜酒，好歌舞於道路。生子必以石蜜納口中，明膠置掌內，欲其成長口常甘言，掌持錢如膠之黏物。俗習胡書。善商賈，爭分銖之利。男子年二十，即遠之旁國，來適中夏，利之所在，無所不到。以十二月為歲首。有婆羅門為之占星候氣，以定吉凶。頗有佛法。至十一月，鼓舞乞寒，以水相潑，盛為戲樂。
>
> People are very fond of wine, [and] like to sing and dance on the street. [When] a son is born, hard honey[217] must be put into his mouth, [and] glue[218] put on the palm [of his hands], [as they] hope that [when] he grows up, [his] mouth

212 *Jiu Tangshu* 198.5310–11; author's translation.

213 A variant of *zhan* 氈.

214 The short version of Wennasha 溫那沙. See the description of Sute 粟特 in the *Weishu* p. 25 (1.7.5) and especially p. 75 (1.15.5).

215 For the discrepancies between the *Weishu* , *Beishi*, *Suishu* (see p. 29: *qi qi* 其妻), *Jiu Tangshu* (*furen* 婦人, see p. 51) and *Xin Tangshu* (see p. 55: *nüzi* 女子) see p. 55 fn . 245.

216 Or, as the parallel construction may be hinting at: "with gold and flowers".

217 See: Laufer, *Sino-Iranica*, 376–77; and: Schafer, *Golden Peaches*, 152–54. Skaff translates this as muscovado sugar (Skaff, "Sogdian Trade Diaspora," 511).

218 Literally gelatine, in sources of the Tang and Song mostly referred to as *huang mingjiao* 黃明膠. See the *Waitai miyao* 27.744b of the Tang, of the Song, among others, the *Weisheng jiabao chanke beiyao* 6.83 and 6.87, and 12 times in the *Taiping sheng'en fang*.

[may] ever [utter] sweet talk, [and his] palm grasp money, as if sticking to glue. Customarily, [they] learn how to write the *hu* 胡 script. [They are] excellent merchants, disputing for the profit [of every] *fen* 分 [and] *zhu* 銖.[219] When [their] sons turn 20, although [being] from a far away state, they come to China. Wherever profit lies, they have gone.[220] The twelfth month is the beginning of the year. There are Brahmin that study the stars and seasons to determine fortune and misfortune. The Buddhist *dharma* is widespread. In the eleventh month, [they] play the drums [and] dance [and celebrate] the "Winter-Prayers".[221] [They] use water to splash each other in a great entertainment.

隋煬帝時，其王屈术支娶西突厥葉護可汗女，遂臣於西突厥。武德十年，屈术支遣使獻名馬。貞觀九年，又遣使貢獅子，太宗嘉其遠至，命祕書監虞世南為之賦，自此朝貢歲至。十一年，又獻金桃、銀桃，詔令植之於苑囿。萬歲通天年，則天封其大首領篤娑鉢提為康國王，仍拜左驍衛大將軍。鉢提尋卒，又冊其子泥涅師師為康國王。師師以神龍中卒，國人又立突昏為王。

During [they reign] of Emperor Yang 煬帝 (r. 604–18 CE), their king Qushuzhi 屈术支[222] married the daughter of Yehu 葉護 (Yabğu)[223] Khagan of

219 Meaning small amounts of money. This expression is already to be found in the account of the countries west of Dayuan 大宛 in the *Shiji* (see p. 14; 1.2.4) and later in other works, as in the *Jinshu* 97.2543–44 or in the description of the state of Anxi 安息 in the *Cefu yuangui* 960.15b.11298a.

220 An early and striking parallel to this statement is to be found in *Guanzi* 53.849, thematising merchants and profit, however, in another context: 其商人通賈，倍道兼行，夜以續日，千里而不遠者，利在前也。漁人之入海，海深萬仞，就彼逆流，乘危百里，宿夜不出者，利在水也。故利之所在，雖千仞之山，無所不上；深源之下，無所不入焉。"When the merchant engages in trade and travels twice the ordinary distance in a day uses the night to extend the day, and covers a thousand *li* without considering it too far, it is because profit lies ahead. When the fisherman puts out to sea, the sea may be ten thousand-*ren* 仞 deep, and when he heads into the waves and struggles against its tides, raises his small mast and sails out a hundred li, never leaving the water from morning to night, it is because profit lies in the water. Thus, wherever profit lies, even though it be atop a thousand-ren peak, there is no place people will not climb. Even though it is at the bottom of the deepest depths, there is no place people will not enter." Translation: Rickett, *Guanzi*, 220.

221 Cristoforeti believes it recalls *Bahārjašn* of the 1st of *Āḏar* (with the custom of *Rukūb al-kawsaj* = *Kūsa*), which is however not attested for Sogdiana. She proposed that the author may have confused customs of Persian and Samarqand and refers to the accounts of al-Bīrūnī (see: Sachau, *Chronologie*, 235). This celebration is reportedly held in different parts of the Western Regions. See e.g. mentions and similar descriptions in: *Zhoushu* 7.122; *Jiu Tangshu* 7.149; *Xin Tangshu* 118.4273, 125.4407, 221b.6244; *Tongdian* 146.3724–25.

222 The name is transcribed with different characters in the following works: as Qumuzhi 屈木支 in the *Xin Tangshu* 221b.6244, as Qumuyou 屈木友 in the *Cefu yuangui* 970.5b.11397a, as Wubenzhi 屋本支 in the *Cefu yuangui* 966.16b.11365b. Yoshida proposed to identify his Sogdian name as *'wkkwrtcm'wkt(')*, which is attested for two Sogdian kings (Yoshida Yutaka, "On the Origin," 50–51). See also: Okamoto Takashi, "Sogudo," 90.

223 Concerning the title and its origins, see: Humbach, *Baktrische Sprachdenkmäler*, 24–28;

the Western Tujue 突厥 [and] in consequence [became] subject of the Western Tujue 突厥. In Wude 武德 10 (629 CE?), Qushuzhi 屈术支 sent fine horses as a gift.[224] In Zhenguan 貞觀 9 (635 CE), [they] sent envoys that presented a lion as tribute.[225] Taizong 太宗 was delighted by the remote arrival [and] ordered the Director of the Palace Library Yu Shinan 虞世南 to compose a *fu* 賦 for it.[226] From then on, tribute missions arrived yearly. In [Zhenguan 貞觀] 11 (637 CE?), [they] offered golden [and] silver peaches.[227] [They were] ordered by decree to be planted in the imperial garden. In Wansuitongtian 萬歲通天 (696–97 CE), [Wu 武] Zetian 則天 ennobled their great chief Dupo Boti 篤婆鉢提 (Tūkspādak) as king of the state of Kang 康 [and] further appointed [him] as courageous guard general-in-chief on the left.[228] [When] Boti 鉢提 (Tūkspādak) passed away, she ennobled his son Ninieshishi 泥涅師師 (Ninišyše/Nnyšyrč) as king of the state of Kang 康.[229] [When] Shishi 師師

Clauson, *Etymological Dictionary*, 873–74.

224 There is no Wude 武德 10, the era lasted only nine years. As the *Xin Tangshu* reproduces the information, the editors added a footnote that explains that there was no tenth year and the *Cefu yuangui* 970.5b.11397a changed the date into Wude 武德 9/11.

225 On the history of lions in China, see: Schafer, *Golden Peaches*, 84–87.

226 Often translated as rhapsody, a famous category of poetry in the Tang.

227 The metals describe the colour of the peaches. There are different dates recorded for that event in various works:
1) *Feng shi wen jian ji* 7.1b. Without exact date. The last date mentioned is the Taizong 太宗 era (626–49 CE).
2) *Cefu yuangui* 970.8b.11398b: Zhenguan 貞觀 11 (637 CE).
3) *Jiu Tangshu*, as seen above: Zhenguan 貞觀 11 (637 CE).
4) *Xin Tangshu* 221b.6244: Zhenguan 貞觀 5 (631 CE).
5) *Tongdian* 193.5256 (however, from Kangju 康居): Zhenguan 貞觀 21 (647 CE), described as large as goose eggs and of golden colour.
6) *Tang hui yao* 99.1774: Zhenguan 貞觀 21/11 (647 CE).
7) *Tang hui yao* 100.1796: Zhenguan 貞觀 21/3/11 (647 CE), also described as large as goose eggs and of golden colour.
It seems as if the editors of these different sources were rather sure of the reading of the characters *shi yi* 十一 (11), as it occurs in the passages 2), 3), 6), and 7). It is, however, in 2) and 3) correlated with the year, in 6) correlated with the month, and in 7) correlated with the day. Nevertheless, all agree that the present happened during the Zhenguan 貞觀 era (627–649 CE) of Tang Taizong 唐太宗.
Laufer mentioned the occurrences in 1), 2), and 6–7), with an erroneous date for the *Cefu yuangui* (625 CE), placing it under Emperor Gaozu 高祖. I cannot, however, confirm his quote of the *Taiping huanyu ji*: "Ch. 183, p. 3" (Laufer, *Sino-Iranica*, 379); Schafer translates *yuanyou* 苑囿 as "Tabooed Park" (Schafer, *Golden Peaches*, 121).

228 In the *Xin Tangshu* (see p. 54; 1.14.1), his name is given as Dusuo Boti 篤娑鉢提. Smirnova proposed to identify him as the Iḫšīd Tūkspādak known to numismatists (Smirnova, *Sogdiiskikh monet*, 40–42, 423); see also: Okamoto Takashi, "Sogudo"; and: Chavannes, *Documents*, 138, 294.

229 In the *Cefu yuangui* 964.10b.11341b his name is given as Nijushihi 泥沮師師 and in 966.16b.11365b as Nishishishi 泥濕師師. It is the transcription of the King Ninišyše/Nnyšyrč (r. 698–705/707 CE), which means "those who are close to the Goddess Nana" (Kljaštornyj

(Ninišyše/Nnyšyrč) passed away during the Shenlong 神龍 era (705–7 CE), the state's people[230] installed Tuhun 突昏 (Tarxūn)[231] as [their] king.

開元六年，遣使貢獻鎖子甲、水精杯、馬腦瓶、駝鳥卵及越諾之類。十九年，其王烏勒上表，請封其子咄曷為曹國王，默啜為米國王，許之。二十七年，烏勒卒，遣使冊咄曷襲父位。天寶三年，又封為欽化王，其母可敦封為郡夫人。十一載、十三載，並遣使朝貢。

In Kaiyuan 開元 6 (718 CE), [they] sent envoys to offer as tribute coats of mail, crystal bowls, agate jars, ostrich eggs, and precious cloth as tribute.[232] [In Kaiyuan 開元] 19 (731 CE), their king Wule 烏勒 (*wr'kk*/Ġūrak)[233] made a request, asking to ennoble his son Duohe 咄曷 (Tūrγār)[234] as king of the state of Cao 曹 (Kapūtānā), and his son Mochuo 默啜 (?)[235] as king of the state of Mi 米 (Māymurgh), which was granted. [As in Kaiyuan 開元] 27 (739 CE), Wule 烏勒 (Wr'kk/Ġūrak) passed away, [they] sent envoys with a decree that Duohe 咄曷 (Tūrγār) [should] take [his] father's throne. In Tianbao 天寶 3 (744 CE), [he was] enfeoffed "naturalised king"[236] [and] his mother Kedun 可敦[237]

and Livšic, "Sogdijskaja," 238). See also: Okamoto Takashi, "Sogudo".

230 *Guo ren* 國人. A rather singular expression. Shenlong 神龍 was the last era of Wu Zetian 武則天, reigning together with emperor Zhongzong 中宗. He restored the Tang in the second month of the first year. The formulation may be related to this temporary loss of power.

231 He is referred to on Sogdian coins and documents from Qalʿa-i Mūġ as Tarxūn (*trxwn*), and in the Arabic sources as Ṭarḫūn (r. ca. 707–18 CE). See: Livshits, *Iuridicheskie dokumenty*, 62–70; Smirnova, *Sogdiiskikh monet*, 41, 424; and: Okamoto Takashi, "Sogudo".

232 Maybe a translation of the Iranian *barnu vala* (Sichou zhi lu da cidian bianweihui, Zhou Weizhou, Ding Jingtai, *Sichou zhi lu*, 217).

233 In the *Xin Tangshu* 221b.6244, his name is given as Wulejia 烏勒伽. Interestingly, in the *Tang hui yao* 99.1775, he is first mentioned as Wulejia 烏勒伽 and then, 23 characters later, as Wule 烏勒. He can be identified as the Iḫšīd *'wr'kk*, or, in the Arabic sources as "Ġūrak" (r. ca. 744–754). See: Marquart, *Chronologie*, 36; Smirnova, *Sogdiiskikh monet*, 42–43, 424; and: Okamoto Takashi, "Sogudo".

234 He can be identified as Iḫšīd Tūrγār (*twrγ'r*) (r. ca. 744–50 CE, mentioned in connection to an embassy sent to the Tang (see: Chavannes, *Documents*, 136, fn. 6). See also, for his coins: Smirnova, *Sogdiiskikh monet*, 44–45.

235 Unclear: As Stark (Stark, *Transoxanien*, 42, fn. 133) mentioned (the quotes in square brackets were added by the author), "this name or title is identical to the Eastern Turkic Qapaγan Qaγan's before his enthronement. He was earlier interpreted as '*Bäg Čor'*; in contrast see Beckwith 1987 [(Beckwith, *Tibetan*, 58, no. 28)]. Rybatzki recently proposed **Bügü Čor* as underlying original [(Rybatzki, "Titles," 223)]."

236 I propose to read *qinhua* 欽化 as *guihua* 歸化, which is based on parallel passages, e.g. *Songshi* 496.14225: 詔授漢王堯寧遠大將軍，封歸化王。 Or as it was similarly changed and commented on in the *Zizhi tongjian* 209.6636: 秋，七月，突騎施娑葛遣使請降；騎，奇寄翻。娑，素何翻。使，疏吏翻。降，戶江翻。庚辰，拜欽化【嚴：「欽化」改「歸化」。】可汗，賜名守忠。

237 A name/title. Sogdian: *xwt'ynh* (see: Smirnova, *Sogdiiskikh monet*, 58), and in the Arabic-Persian as "*Ḫatūn*": (Stark, *Transoxanien*, 42–43, fn. 136). The same as the one mentioned in the description of the state of Kang 康 (Samarqand, see p. 54; 1.14.1), Eastern An 安 (Kharghān, see p. 59; 1.14.359), and Mi 米 (Māymurgh, see p. 65; 1.14.10). For more

was enfeoffed as "commandery mistress".[238] In both [Tianbao 天寶] 11 (752 CE) and 13 (754 CE), envoys were sent to offer tribute to the court.

1.14 *Xin Tangshu*

1.14.1 Kang 康 (Samarqand)[239]

康者，一曰薩末鞬，亦曰颯秣建，元魏所謂悉萬斤者。其南距史百五十里，西北距西曹百餘里，東南屬米百里，北中曹五十里。在那密水南，大城三十，小堡三百。君姓溫，本月氏人。枝庶分王，曰安，曰曹，曰石，曰米，曰何，曰火尋，曰戊地，曰史，世謂「九姓」，皆氏昭武。

Kang 康 (Samarqand), also called Samojian 薩末鞬 or Samojian 颯秣建, [during] the Yuan Wei 元魏 (Northern Wei) called Xiwanjin 悉萬斤. To its south, [it] adjoins Shi 史 [after] 150 *li* (ca. 75 km). To the north-west [it] adjoins Western Cao 曹 (Ishitikhan) [after] over 100 *li* (ca. 50 km). To the south-east, [it] adjoins Mi 米 (Māymurgh) [after] 100 *li* (ca. 50 km) [and] to the north, Cao 曹 (Kapūtānā) [after] 50 *li* (ca. 25 km). [It] is located south of the Nami 那密 River (Zerafshan). [It counts] 30 large forts, [and] 300 smaller fortifications.[240] [Their] rulers are surnamed Wen 溫[241] [and] stem from the Yuezhi 月氏. The cadet sons became kings, called An 安, Cao 曹, Shi 石, Mi 米, He 何, Huoxun 火尋, Wudi 戊地, Shi 史, later called the "Nine Surnames"; all have the clan name of Zhaowu 昭武.

土沃宜禾，出善馬，兵彊諸國。人嗜酒，好歌舞于道。王帽氈，飾金雜寶。女子盤髻，幪黑巾，綴金蘤。生兒以石蜜啖之，置膠於掌，欲長而甘言，持珤若黏云。習旁行書。善商賈，好利，丈夫年二十，去傍國，利所在無不至。以十二月為歲首，尚浮圖法，祠[祆][242]神，出機巧技。十一月鼓舞乞寒，以水交潑為樂。

The soil is fertile [and] favourable for [growing] crops. [It] brings forth excellent horses. [Its] troops are mightier [than] of all the [surrounding] countries.[243] People are very fond of wine, [and] like to sing and dance on the

information, see: Stark, *Transoxanien,* 42–43, fn. 136.

238 Mostly *jun taifuren* 郡太夫人, the *tai* 太 missing in this case. See the glossary.

239 *Xin Tangshu* 221b.6243–44. The author's translation is based on the extant translations in French and English (Chavannes, *Documents*, 132–36; Pulleyblank, "Sogdian Colony," 320, fn. 1; Pulleyblank only translated the beginning of the passage).

240 If the punctuation of the Zhonghua shuju edition above wants to insinuate that it is the forts that are described by the statement "[…] located south of the Nami 那密 River (Zerafshan)", I have to disagree (and thus concur with Chavannes: Chavannes, *Documents*, 133).

241 See the description of Sute 粟特 in the *Weishu* (p. 26 and especially fn. 72).

242 Originally *yao* 祆; see p. 270 fn. 170.

243 Chavannes did instead connect *zhu guo* 諸國 (all countries) to the next unit of meaning,

street.[244] [The] king's hat is [made of] felt [and] decorated with gold and diverse jewellery. The women[245] wind [their hair in a] topknot, [use] a black cloth to cover [it], [and] decorate [it] with gold flowers.[246] [When] a son is born, hard honey[247] is fed to him, [and] glue[248] put on the palm [of his hands], hoping that [when] he grows up, [he shall utter] sweet talk [and] grasp treasures as if sticking [to glue]. [They] write horizontally. [They are] excellent merchants [and] treasure profit. When a man turns 20, [he] goes to neighbouring countries. Wherever profit lies, they have gone.[249] The twelfth month is the beginning of the year. [People] revere Buddhism [and] offer to the Zoroastrian Deity. [They] make ingenious crafts. In the eleventh month, [they] play the drums [and] dance [and celebrate] the "Winter-Prayers".[250] [They] use water to splash each other in a great entertainment.

隋時，其王屈木支娶西突厥女，遂臣突厥。武德十年，始遣使來獻。貞觀五年，遂請臣。太宗曰：「朕惡取虛名，害百姓，且康臣我，緩急當同其憂。師行萬里，寧朕志邪？」卻不受。俄又遣使獻師子獸，帝珍其遠，命秘書監虞世南作賦。自是歲入貢，致金桃、銀桃，詔令植苑中。

During the Sui (i.e. the reign of Emperor Yang 煬, 604–18 CE),[251] their king Qumuzhi 屈木支[252] married the daughter of (Yehu 葉護, i.e. Yabğu[253] Khagan of)[254] the Western Tujue 突厥, [and] in consequence [became] subject of the Western Tujue 突厥. In Wude 武德 10 (629 CE?),[255] [they] sent envoys to offer gifts for the first time. In Zhenguan 貞觀 5 (631 CE), [they] then requested to become vassals. Taizong 太宗 declared: "We despise to obtain empty names and hurt the common people. Furthermore, [if] Kang 康 subjects to us, [and there is] distress, [We] have to share their worries. [Our] military [would have to] travel 10,000 *li* (ca. 5,000 km). How could that be Our wish?"

resulting in the translation "people from these various principalities cherish wine"; author's translation from the French: Chavannes, *Documents*, 134. I believe the Zhonghua shuju's punctuation and understanding to be correct.

244 At this place, the *Tang hui yao* 99.1774 adds: 勝兵三千人。 "[They have] 3,000 elite soldiers."

245 While in the *Jiu Tangshu* (*furen* 婦人, p. 51) and the *Xin Tangshu* (*nüzi* 女子), women in general are the subject, the *Weishu* (see p. 29: *qi qi* 其妻) – and in consequence also the *Beishi* and *Suishu* – refers to the king's wife. The editors of the *Jiu Tangshu* and *Xin Tangshu* probably choose to understand the *qi qi* 其妻 of the earlier works as "their women".

246 See p. 51 fn. 216.

247 See p. 51 fn. 217.

248 See p. 51, fn. 218.

249 See p. 51 fn. 220.

250 See p. 52 fn. 221.

251 See the parallel passage in the *Jiu Tangshu* p. 52.

252 See p. 52 fn. 222.

253 See p. 52 fn. 223.

254 See the parallel passage in the *Jiu Tangshu* p. 52.

255 See p. 52 fn. 224.

So [the request was] refused. Soon (i.e. in 635 CE),[256] [they] again sent envoys to offer a lion as a gift.[257] The emperor was delighted by its remoteness [and] ordered the Director of the Palace Library Yu Shinan 虞世南 to compose a *fu* 賦.[258] From then on tribute missions arrived yearly. (In Zhenguan 貞觀 11, 637 CE?)[259] [they] offered golden [and] silver peaches.[260] [They were] ordered by decree to be planted in the imperial garden.

高宗永徽時，以其地為康居都督府，即授其王拂呼縵為都督。萬歲通天中，以大首領篤娑鉢提為王。死，子泥涅師師立。死，國人立突昏為王。開元初，貢鎖子鎧、水精杯、碼碯瓶、駝鳥卵及越諾、侏儒、胡旋女子。其王烏勒伽與大食亟戰不勝，來乞師，天子不許。久之，請封其子咄曷為曹王，默啜為米王，詔許。烏勒伽死，遣使立咄曷，封欽化王，以其母可敦為郡夫人。

During Gaozong's 高宗 Yonghui 永徽 (era, 650–55 CE), their land was changed into "Kangju 康居 Area Command", and their king Fuhuman 拂呼縵 ((A)varxumān) was appointed as commander-in-chief.[261] In Wansuitongtian 萬歲通天 (696–97 CE), Dusuo Boti 篤娑鉢提 (Tūkspādak) was made king of the state of Kang 康.[262] [When he] passed away, [his] son Ninieshishi 泥涅師師 (Ninišyše/Nnyšyrč) was installed.[263] [When he] died (during the Shenlong 神龍 era, 705–7 CE),[264] the state's people[265] installed Tuhun 突昏 (Tarxūn)[266] as king. At the beginning of the Kaiyuan 開元 (era, 713–41 CE, in Kaiyuan 開元 6, 718 CE),[267] [they] presented coats of mail, crystal bowls, agate jars, ostrich eggs, precious cloth,[268] dwarves, [and] *hu* 胡 twirl (-dance)[269] women as tribute. [As] their king Wulejia 烏勒伽 (Wr'kk/Ġūrak)[270] often went to war with the Arabs[271] without victory, [he] requested support. The Son of Heaven

256 See the parallel passage in the *Jiu Tangshu* p. 52.
257 See p. 52 fn. 225.
258 See p. 52 fn. 226.
259 See parallel passage in the *Jiu Tangshu* p. 52.
260 Id.
261 This is the Iẖšīd (A)varxumān (['']*βrxwm'n*). (Smirnova, *Sogdiiskikh monet*, 38–40, 423).
262 In the *Jiu Tangshu* mentioned as Dupo Boti 篤婆鉢提 (see p. 50; 1.13.1).
263 See p. 53 fn. 229.
264 See parallel passage in the *Jiu Tangshu* p. 53.
265 See p. 53 fn. 230.
266 See p. 53 fn. 231.
267 See parallel passage in the *Jiu Tangshu* p. 53.
268 *Barnu vala*? See 53 fn. 232.
269 Referring to the famous *huxuanwu* 胡旋舞, the Western twirling dance, which is to be found both represented in the material culture (since the Northern Wei), and in literature (since the Tang), with the related dance, the *hutengwu* 胡騰舞, literally the Western jumping dance. For an overview, see: Müller, "Sogdier in China," 124–25, fn. 25. See also: Zhang Qingjie, "*Hutengwu* and *Huxuanwu*"; Trombert, *Les Sogdiens en Chine*.
270 See p. 54 fn. 233.
271 *Dashi* 大食, a transcription from the Persian Tazi, also written *duoshi* 多食 or *dashi* 大寔,

did not consent [to it]. Much later (in Kaiyuan 開元 19, 731 CE), [he] requested that his son Duohe 咄曷 (Tūrγār) may be enfeoffed as king of Cao 曹 (Kapūtānā), [and] Mochuo 默啜 (?) as king of Mi 米 (Māymurgh), [which was] granted by imperial decree.[272] (As in Kaiyuan 開元 27, 739 CE) Wule 烏勒 (Wr'kk/Ġūrak) passed away, [they] sent envoys to [ask for the] enthronement of Duohe 咄曷 (Tūrγār).[273] (In Tianbao 天寶 3, 744 CE)[274] [he was] enfeoffed as "naturalised king" [275] [and] his mother Kedun 可敦 [276] was made "commandery mistress".[277]

1.14.2 An 安 (Bukhārā)[278]

安者，一曰布豁，又曰捕喝，元魏謂忸蜜者。東北至東安，西南至畢，皆百里所。西瀕烏滸河，治阿濫謐城，即康居小君長罽王故地。大城四十，小堡千餘。募勇健者為柘羯。柘羯，猶中國言戰士也。武德時，遣使入朝。貞觀初，獻方物，太宗厚尉其使曰：「西突厥已降，商旅可行矣。」諸胡大悅。其王訶陵迦又獻名馬，自言一姓相承二十二世云。是歲，東安國亦入獻，言子姓相承十世云。

An 安 (Bukhārā), also called Buhua 布豁 or Buhe 捕喝, called Niumi 忸蜜 [during] the Yuan Wei 元魏 (Northern Wei). To the north-east, [one] arrives at Eastern An 安 (Kharghān). To the south-west, [one] arrives at Bi 畢 (Paykand?). Both [are] at a distance of 100 *li* (ca. 50 km). To the west, [An 安] lies on the bank of the Wuxu 烏滸 River (Amu Darya), governed from the Alanmi 阿濫謐 Fort (Rīyāmithan). This was the ancient territory of a petty ruler of Kangju 康居, the King of Ji 罽.[279] [They have] 40 large forts, [and] over 1,000 smaller fortifications. [They] recruit[280] the brave [and] strong as *zhejie* 柘羯 (*čākar*).[281] The *zhejie* 柘羯 are what is called "warrior" in Chinese. In Wude 武德 5 (622 CE), [they] sent envoys to the court. At the beginning of the Zhenguan 貞觀 (era, 627–49 CE), [they] offered regional goods. Taizong 太宗 reassured their envoys, saying: "The Western Tujue 突厥 have already surrendered, merchants can travel [again]!" All *hu* 胡 [were] overjoyed. Their

refers to the ethnic Arabian group of the Tayyi' living at the western frontier of the Parthian Empire in the first century CE. In Persian, it is used as a denomination for Arabs. From the Tang and Song on, it was used to refer to the Abbasid Caliphat (Jin Yijiu, *Yisilanjiao cidian*, 343).

272 See parallel passage in the *Jiu Tangshu* p. 54.

273 Id.

274 Id.

275 See p. 54 fn. 236.

276 A name/title. See p. 54 fn. 237.

277 See p. 54 fn. 238.

278 *Xin Tangshu* 221b.6244–45. The author's translation is based on the translation by Chavannes: Chavannes, *Documents*, 136–37.

279 See the passage in the *Hanshu* concerning the petty kings of Kangju 康居 (p. 16; 1.3.1).

280 Probably as mercenaries.

281 See p. 43 fn. 177.

king Helingjia 訶陵迦 offered fine horses as gift. [He] said himself that for 22 generations they succeeded each other in the family. In this year, the state of Eastern An 安 (Kharghān) also sent in presents, [and] said that the family's sons succeeded each other for 10 generations.

1.14.3 Eastern An 安 (Kharghān)[282]

東安，或曰小(安)國，[283]曰喝汗，在那密水之陽，東距何二百里許，西南至大安四百里。治喝汗城，亦曰[illegible]斤。[284]金城二十，小堡百。顯慶時，以阿濫為安息州，即以其王昭武殺為刺史；[illegible]斤為木鹿州，以其王昭武閉息為刺史。開元十四年，其王篤薩波提遣弟阿悉爛達拂耽發黎來朝，納馬豹。後八年，獻波斯二，拂菻繡氍毬一，鬱金香、石蜜等，其妻可敦獻柘辟大氍毬二、繡氍毬一，丐賜袍帶、鎧仗及可敦袿襆澤。

Eastern An 安 (Kharghān), also called state of Lesser (An 安) or Hehan 喝汗. [It] is located on the north side of the Nami 那密 River (Zerafshan). To the east, it adjoins He 何 (Kušaniyya) [after] about 200 *li* (ca. 100 km). To the south-west, [one] goes 400 *li* (ca. 200 km) to Greater An 安 (Bukhārā). Governed from the Hehan 喝汗 Fort, [which is] also called Houjin [illegible]斤. [They have] 20 large forts [and] 100 smaller fortifications. During the Xianqing 顯慶 (era, 656–61 CE), Alan(mi) 阿濫(謐)[285] (Rīyāmithan) was changed into Anxi 安息 District, [and] their king Zhaowu Sha 昭武殺[286] was appointed as governor; Houjin [illegible]斤 was changed into Mulu 木鹿 District, [and] their king Zhaowu Bixi 昭武閉息 made governor. In Kaiyuan 開元 14 (726 CE), the cadet brother of their king Dusa Boti 篤薩波提 (Toγšāda),[287]

282 *Xin Tangshu* 221b.6245. The author's translation is based on the translation by Chavannes: Chavannes, *Documents*, 137–38.

283 As the commentary also states, the original text is probably mistaken. In the *Beishi*'s passage concerning the state of Kang 康, a state of Lesser An 安 is listed, which is taken here to correct the passage.

284 After thorough research, I must agree with Chavannes that the character is – oddly enough for such a canonical text – not to be found in any other source or dictionary (ibid., 137, fn. 5). Chavannes, however, searched for the character having as lower part *si* 俟 instead of *hou* 侯, the latter to be found in all the editions available to me. This lead him to preliminarily transcribe it as *Sijin*. As the pronunciation does indeed probably depend on the lower part of the character, which is *hou* 侯, I propose to instead preliminarily transcribe it as *Houjin*. This is also quite similar to the conclusion Marquart must have reached, transcribing it as "*Jo-kin*" (Marquart, *Chronologie*, 61).

285 Added according to the description of An 安, see p. 58 (1.14.2).

286 Given as Zhaowu Shi'ahe 昭武失阿喝 in the description of the state of Shi 史 (Kesh), see p. 68 (1.14.13). The identification of this individual is unclear. For an overview of the current state of research, see: Stark, *Transoxanien*, 44–45, fn. 144.

287 In the *Cefu yuangui* 971.11408a, he is mentioned with another version of his name, Boboti 波婆提: 五月安國王波婆提遣其弟…… "In the fifth month, the king of the state of An 安, Boboti 波婆提, sent his cadet brother (…)". As Chavannes mentioned, Marquart proposed to identify this king, relying on the "Dusa 篤薩", as the King of Bukhārā Toghshada (Chavannes,

Axilanda 阿悉爛達 (Arslan Tarkhan) Fudanfali 拂耽發黎,[288] came to the court to present horses and a *panthera*[289] as gifts. Eight years later, [they] offered as present two Persian and one Byzantine embroidered carpet,[290] tulip scent, [and] hard honey.[291] His wife Kedun 可敦[292] offered two large carpets[293] [and] one embroidered carpet from Zhepi 柘辟[294] as presents, [and] got conferred with robes, armours and weapons, and Kedun 可敦 [received] a long dress.

1.14.4 Eastern Cao 曹 (Sutrūshana, Ushrusana)[295]

東曹，或曰率都沙那，蘇對沙那，劫布呾那，蘇都識匿，凡四名。居波悉山之陰，漢貳師城地也。東北距俱戰提二百里，北至石，西至康，東北寧遠，皆四百里許，南至吐火羅五百里。有野叉城，城有巨窟，嚴以關鑰，歲再祭，人向窟立，中即煙出，先觸者死。武德中，與康同遣使入朝，其使曰：「本國以臣為健兒，聞秦王神武，欲隸麾下。」高祖大悅。

Documents, 138, fn. 2; Marquart, *Ērānšahr*, 309; for a new annotated translation, see: Daryaee, *Šahrestānīhā*). He is mentioned by Tabarī (II., 7., 7) in correlation with the date 738–39 CE, and mentioned by Naršaxī as Toγšāda (1.1.v,12,8.,17,2.). Marquart was, however, mistaken to conflate him with Dupo Boti 篤婆鉢提, also called Dusuo Boti 篤娑鉢提 in the description of the state of Kang 康 (see p. 54, 1.14.1; Marquart, *Ērānšahr*, 309, fn. 1).
In 719 CE, Toghshada already sent a request to China, asking for military support against the Arabs (*Cefu yuangui* 999.11721a–b. See: Chavannes, *Documents*, 203–205, 292).

288 This is the same person also mentioned as King of Ferghana (Bahanna 拔汗那) Axilan Dagan 阿悉爛達干, who was given Princess Heyi 和義 in 744 CE in marriage. See: *Cefu yuangui* 358.4246a, 971.11410b, 11411b, 11412a, 11413a, 11413b, 999.11724a, *Zizhi tongjian* 215.6862. The authors of the *Cefu yuangui* understood it demonstrably this way, as the same passage is written in one occurrence (971.11408a) as: 五月安國王波婆提遣其弟可悉爛達千拂耽發黎來朝獻馬及豹。 "In the fifth month, the king of the state of An 安, Boboti 波婆提, sent his cadet brother Kexilan Daqian 可悉爛達千 Fudandali 拂耽發黎 to the court to present as gifts horses and a *panthera*." (This is another version of his name. The *ke* 可 is most probably to be understood as a corruption of *he* 何, whereas the *qian* 千 certainly is a corruption of *gan* 干.
According to the Chinese records, he then sent envoys to request his state to be named the state of Ningyuan 寧遠 (lit. appeased far region) in 744 CE. This version of the account, however, seems a bit far-fetched, even for Chinese records, as the Tang reaffirmed their sovereignty over these regions by conferring new names. See: Chavannes, *Documents*, 294–95.

289 Zhang Guangda proposed that it may also be read as a "horsed leopard", i.e. a leopard on a horse (Zhang Guangda, "Tangdai," 181).

290 In the *Weishu*, the term *qushu* 氍毹 is used in the list of goods from the state of Kang 康, and in the *Suishu* only *qu* 氍, for the state of Cao 曹. I suppose the same is meant here.

291 See p. 51 fn. 217.

292 A name/title, see p. 54 fn. 237.

293 On other carpets, see p. 66 fn. 330.

294 It is unclear where this is supposed to be.

295 *Xin Tangshu* 221b.6245. The author's translation is based on the translation by Chavannes: Chavannes, *Documents*, 138–39.

Eastern Cao 曹 (Sutrūshana, Ushrusana), also called by the four names Shuaidushana 率都沙那, Suduishana 蘇對沙那, Jiebudanna 劫布呾那,[296] and Sudushini 蘇都識匿. [It] is located north of the Boxi 波悉 Mountains. [It is] the Ershi 貳師 Fort of the Han. To the north-east, [it] adjoins Juzhanti 俱戰提 (Khujand) after 200 *li* (ca. 100 km). To the north [it adjoins] Shi 石 (Chach), to the west Kang 康 (Samarqand), [and] to the north-east Ningyuan 寧遠 (Ferghana), each after about 400 *li* (ca. 200 km). To the south, [one] arrives at Tuhuoluo 吐火羅 (Tokharistan) in 500 *li* (ca. 250 km). There is the Yecha 野叉 Fort, [which] has a large cave locked by a gate. [For] the two offerings made [each] year, the people stand facing the cave. Smoke then comes out of it. [Those who] come first into contact [with it] die.[297] During the Wude 武德 (era, 618–26 CE), [they] sent envoys, together with Kang 康, to come to the court. Their envoy said: "Our state is known as being a vassal with valiant warriors. [We] heard that the king of the Qin became emperor and desire to submit under [your] banner." Gaozu 高祖 greatly rejoiced [over this].

1.14.5 Western Cao 西曹 (Ishitikhan)[298]

西曹者，隋時曹也，南接史及波覽，治瑟底痕城。東北越于底城有得悉神祠，國人事之。有金具器，款其左曰：「漢時天子所賜。」武德中入朝。天寶元年，王哥邏僕羅遣使者獻方物，詔封懷德王，即上言：「祖考以來，奉天可汗，願同唐人受調發，佐天子征討。」十一載，東曹王設阿忽與安王請擊黑衣大食，玄宗尉之，不聽。

Western Cao 曹 (Ishitikhan) was [called] Cao 曹 during the Sui. [It] adjoins Shi 史 (Kesh) and Polan 波覽 (Fārāb?) in the south. [It] is governed from the Sedihen 瑟底痕 Fort (Ishitikhan). North-east [of it] is Yueyudi 越于底 (Kurgantepe?). There is a temple of Dexi 得悉, to which the state's people[299] make offerings. There is a golden object [that] says on its left [side]: "Donated

296 Jiebudanna 劫布呾那 is erroneously correlated to Sutrūshana, Ushrusana, it actually refers to Kapūtānā.

297 This passage seems to tell an incident rather than a ritual, which is how I understand the more detailed account given of it in the *Youyang zazu* 4.32: 蘇都識匿國有夜叉城，城舊有野叉，其窟見在。人近窟住者五百餘家。窟口作舍。設關鑰。一年再祭。人有逼窟口，煙氣出，先觸者死，因以尸擲窟口。其窟不知深淺。" In the state of Jiedushini 蘇都識匿 there is the Yecha 野叉 Fort. In ancient times there was a Yaksha in the fort. Its cave is still there. There are over 500 families who live near the cave. A shelter was made at the entrance of the cave. A locked gate was installed. Offerings are made twice a year. There were people [who came] close to opening of the cave, when smoke [then] came out, those who first came into contact with it died. In consequence, [their] corpses were thrown [into] the opening of the cave. The depth of this cave is unknown."

298 *Xin Tangshu* 221b.6245. The author's translation is based on the translation by Chavannes: Chavannes, *Documents*, 139–40.

299 That may refer to the city community, i.e. the *n'β*.

during the Han by the Son of Heaven."[300] During the Wude 武德 (era, 618–26 CE), [they] came to the court. In Tianbao 天寶 1 (742 CE), King Geluopuluo 哥邏僕羅[301] sent envoys to present local products as gifts. [He was] conferred [the title of] cherishing virtue king. [He] thus sent to the emperor a message: "Since [my] ancestors and my late father, [we] served the heavenly khagan[302] [and] desired to unite with the Tang people to receive the order to assist the Son of Heaven in a punitive expedition." In [Tianbao 天寶] 11 (752 CE), the king of Western Cao 曹, She Ahu 設阿忽,[303] together with the king of An 安, requested to attack the black clothed Arabs (i.e. the Abbasid Caliphate).[304] Xuanzong 玄宗 calmed them [and] did not permit [it].

1.14.6 Middle Cao 中曹 (Kapūtānā)[305]

中曹者，居西曹東，康之北。王治迦底真城。其人長大，工戰鬭[306]。

Middle Cao 曹 (Kapūtānā) is located east of Western Cao 曹 (Ishitikhan) and north of Kang 康 (Samarqand). [Its] king reigns in Jiadizhen 迦底真 Fort.[307] Their people are tall and large, skilled in war and combat.

1.14.7 Shi 石 (Chach)[308]

石，或曰柘支，曰柘折，曰赭時，漢大宛北鄙也。去京師九千里。東北距西突厥，西北波臘，南二百里所抵俱戰提，西南五百里康也。圓千餘里，右涯素葉河。王姓石，治柘折城，故康居小王窳匿城地。西南有藥殺水，入中國謂之真珠河，亦曰質河。東南有大山，生瑟瑟。俗善戰，多良馬。

Shi 石 (Chach), also called Zhezhi 柘支,[309] or Zhezhe 柘折, or Zheshi 赭時. [It] was the northern border of the Dayuan 大宛 of the Han. It is 9,000 *li* (ca. 4,500 km) from the capital. To the north-east, [it] adjoins the Western Tujue 突厥, [and] to the north-west, the Bola 波臘 (Fārāb?). To the south, [one] reaches Juzhanti 俱戰提 (Khujand). To the west, it is 500 *li* (ca. 250 km) from

300 On this, see the analysis below.

301 On the debate about possible identifications, see: Stark, *Transoxanien*, 16–17, fn. 12.

302 Referring to the Chinese emperor.

303 Probably *šyr''γt*, Šir-āγat: Lurje, *Personal*, 380, no. 1205; Stark, *Transoxanien*, 18, fn. 18.

304 Black being the representative colour of their dynasty. Chavannes (Chavannes, *Documents*, 140, fn. 1), *apud:* Abulfeda. *Géographie d'Aboulféda.* Vol. II, 186). On the term *dashi* 大食, see also p. 57 fn. 271.

305 *Xin Tangshu* 221b.6245. The author's translation is based on the translation by Chavannes: Chavannes, *Documents*, 140.

306 A variant of *dou* 鬥.

307 See also the parallel passage in the *Tang hui yao* 98.1754 mentioning Jiabudizhen 迦布底眞.

308 *Xin Tangshu* 221b.6246. The author's translation is based on the translation by Chavannes: Chavannes, *Documents*, 140–43.

309 Also written Zhezhi 赭支 in the *Jing xing ji*. *Tongdian* 193.5275.

Kang 康. [It] has a circumference of over 1,000 *li* (ca. 500 km). [It lies] on the west bank of the Suye 素葉 River (Sūyāb). [Its] king is surnamed Shi 石 [and] reigns in Zhezhe 柘折 Fort, [which is] the former Yuni 窳匿 Fort of a petty king of Kangju 康居.[310] South-west is the Yaosha 藥殺 river (Yaxartes, Syr Darya), [which, when] it [flows] into China, is called Zhenzhu 真珠 (Pearl) River or Zhi 質 River. South-east are large mountains [which] bring forth precious stones. Customarily, [they] do excel in combat [and] have many fine horses.

隋大業初，西突厥殺其王，以特勒匐職統其國。武德、貞觀間，數獻方物。顯慶三年，以瞰羯城為大宛都督府，授其王瞰土屯攝舍提於屈昭穆都督。開元初，封其君莫賀咄吐屯，有功，為石國王。二十八年，又冊順義王。明年，王伊捺吐屯屈勒上言：「今突厥已屬天可汗，惟大食為諸國患，請討之。」天子不許。

At the beginning of the Daye 大業 (era, 605–18 CE), the Eastern Tujue 突厥[311] killed their king, [and] made Fuzhi 匐職[312] Tegin govern their state. During the Wude 武德 and Zhenguan 貞觀 (eras, 618–49 CE), local products were recurrently presented as gifts. In Xianqing 顯慶 3 (658 CE) Kanjie 瞰羯 Fort[313] was [included in the] Dayuan 大宛 Area Command, [and] Kan Tudu Shesheti Yuquzhaomu 瞰土屯攝舍提於屈昭穆[314] was made area commander. At the beginning of the Kaiyuan 開元 (era, 713–41 CE) its lord Moheduo Tutun 莫賀咄吐屯 (Baghatur Tudun),[315] [who] proved meritorious, was enfeoffed as king of the state of Shi 石 (Chach). Further, [in Kaiyuan 開元] 28 (740 CE), [he was] granted [the title of] obedient righteous king.[316] The next year, king Yina[317] Tudun Qule 伊捺吐屯屈勒 sent a message to the emperor: "Now that the Tujue 突厥 are already subject to the heavenly khagan, only the Arabs[318] are a plage for all countries. [I] request that they be punished." The Son of Heaven did not grant [it].

310 See the passage in the *Hanshu* concerning the petty kings of Kangju 康居 p. 16 (1.3.1).

311 Under Heshana Khagan 曷娑那可汗 (d. 619 CE, Turkic: Arslan Khagan). Hesana Khagan 曷薩那可汗 (Arslan Khagan, sometimes also written Heshana 曷娑那) is the title he was given by the Sui, his personal name being Ashina Daman 阿史那達曼 (Ashina Taman), later also known as Nijue chuluo kehan 泥厥處羅可汗.

312 In the *Suishu* written Dianzhi 甸職 (see p. 34; 1.9.4).

313 Mentioned as Danjie 噉羯 Fort in the *Tang hui yao* 99.1771.

314 Shesheti is a Turk tribe name, also written 懾舍提 (*Jiu Tangshu* 83.2778); see: Chavannes, *Documents*, 34, fn. 5. For the relationship between Zhaomu 昭穆 and the Sogdian family name Zhaowu 昭武, see: Yoshida Yutaka, "On the Origin," 50–52.

315 *Baghatur* means "hero", also used as title. Tudun is a title for a commissioner installed by the ruler.

316 For his coalition with the Tang forces, see: Chavannes, *Documents*, 141, fn. 4; and: Beckwith, *Tibetan*, 119–20.

317 Maybe meaning Inäl. For more information, see: Stark, *Alttürkenzeit*, 225–26.

318 See p. 57 fn. 271.

天寶初，封王子那俱車鼻施為懷化王，賜鐵券。久之，安西節度使高仙芝劾其無蕃臣禮，請討之。王約降，仙芝遣使者護送至開遠門，俘以獻，斬闕下，於是西域皆怨。王子走大食乞兵，攻怛邏斯城，敗仙芝軍，自是臣大食。寶應時，遣使朝貢。

At the beginning of the Tianbao 天寶 (era, 742–56 CE), the king's son, Naju Chebishi 那俱車鼻施, was awarded [the title of] embracing transformation king, [and] bestowed an iron certificate. Much later (in 750 CE), the Military Commissioner of Anxi 安西 Gao Xianzhi 高仙芝 accused him of not [following the] rules for foreign ministers [and] requested that he be punished.[319] The king surrendered. Gao Xianzhi 高仙芝 sent envoys to escort [him] to the Kaiyuan 開遠 Gate. [There he was] taken prisoner to present [him to the emperor, and then] beheaded at the palace. Therefore, all of the Western Regions were furious. The son of the king went to ask the Arabs[320] for troops. [He] attacked the Daluosi 怛邏斯 (Talas) Fort [and] defeated the army of Xianzhi 仙芝. From then on, [he] was subject to the Arabs.[321] During the Baoying 寶應 (era, 762–63 CE), [he] sent envoys to present tribute to the court.

1.14.8 Suiye 碎葉 (Sūyāb)[322]

有碎葉者，出安西西北千里所，得勃達嶺，南抵中國，北突騎施南鄙也，西南直葱嶺贏二千里。水南流者經中國入于海，北流者經胡入于海。北三日行度雪海，春夏常雨雪。繇勃達嶺北行贏千里，得細葉川。東曰熱海，地寒不凍；西有碎葉城，天寶七載，北庭節度使王正見伐安西，毀之。川長千里，有異姓突厥兵數萬，耕者皆擐甲，相掠為奴婢。西屬怛邏斯城，石常分兵鎮之。自此抵西海矣。三月訖九月，未嘗雨，人以雪水溉田。

There is Suiye 碎葉 (Sūyāb). Leaving Anxi 安西, [and going] 1,000 *li* (ca. 500 km) north-west [one] reaches the Boda 勃達 Range. [The range] adjoins China in the south [and] the southern border of the Tuqishi 突騎施 (Türgesh) in the north. [From there] south-west, [it is] over 2,000 *li* (ca. 1000 km) to reach the Congling 葱嶺 (Pamirs). The rivers that run south pass through China [and] flow into the sea. [Those] that run north pass through [the territory of the] *hu* 胡 to flow into the sea.[323] Travelling north for three days, [one] crosses the Snow Lake (Xuehai 雪海), [where] in spring and summer snow often falls.

319 Gao Xianzhi 高仙芝 was a famous general of Korean origin. For the events, see: *Jiu Tangshu* 104.3206, *Xin Tangshu* 135.4578, *Zizhi tongjian* 216.6907–8; and: Chavannes, *Documents*, 142–43, fn. 2.

320 See p. 57 fn. 271.

321 Id.

322 *Xin Tangshu* 221b.6246. The author's translation is based on the translation by Chavannes: Chavannes, *Documents*, 143–44.

323 In this case, the "sea" is referring to lakes.

Travelling north for 1,000 *li* (ca. 500 km) from the Boda 勃達 Range, [one] arrives at the Xiye 細葉 (Sūyāb) River. To the east [is the so-] called Warm Lake (Rehai 熱海, Issyk Kul). [Although] the soil is cold it doesn't freeze. To the west is the Suiye 碎葉 Fort (Ak-Beshim Sūyāb). In Tianbao 天寶 7 (748 CE), the Military Commissioner of Beiting 北庭 Wang Zhengjian 王正見 attacked Anxi 安西 [and] destroyed it. The valley is a 1,000 *li* (ca. 500 km) long. [In it] there are several 10,000 Tujue 突厥 troops of different families. The ploughmen all wear armour. [They] pillage each other to make slaves. To the west [it] adjoins the Daluosi 怛邏斯 (Talas) Fort. Shi 石 (Chach) often stations troops there. From here, [one] reaches the Western Sea. [From] the third month to the ninth month, [they] never have rain. People use snowmelt to irrigate [their] fields.

1.14.9 Feihan 怖捍 (Ferghana)[324]

石東南千餘里，有怖捍者，山四環之，地膏腴，多馬羊。西千里距堵利瑟那，東臨葉葉水，水出葱嶺北原，色濁，西北流入大磧。無水草，望大山，尋遺崙，知所指，五百餘里即康也。

Over 1,000 *li* (ca. 500 km) south-east of Shi 石 (Chach) is Feihan 怖捍 (Ferghana). Mountains surround it on four [sides]. The soil is fertile, [and there are] many horses and sheep. A 1,000 *li* (ca. 500 km) to the west [it] adjoins Dulisena 堵利瑟那 (Sutrūshana, Ushrusana). To the east [it] borders on the Yeye 葉葉 River (Jaxartes, Syr Darya). The river emerges from the northern plateau of the Congling 葱嶺 (Pamirs). [Its] colour is turbid. [It] runs north-west into the Great Desert, [where] there is no water and grass. [Only by] looking at the great mountains [and] searching for left over carcasses, [one] knows the direction [to take]. [After] over 500 *li* (ca. 250 km), [one] then reaches Kang 康 (Samarqand).

1.14.10 Mi 米 (Māymurgh)[325]

米，或曰彌末，曰弭秣賀。北百里距康。其君治鉢息德城，永徽時為大食所破。顯慶三年，以其地為南謐州，授其君昭武開拙為刺史，自是朝貢不絕。開元時，獻壁、舞筵、師子、胡旋女。十八年，大首領末野門來朝。天寶初，封其君為恭順王，母可敦郡夫人。

324 *Xin Tangshu* 221b.6247. It is included due to the reference to neighbouring Sogdian countries. The author's translation is based on the translation by Chavannes: Chavannes, *Documents*, 144. Due to another passage about Ningyuan 寧遠 (*Xin Tangshu* 221b.6250), which can be identified as Ferghana, and the distances that do conflict with the content of the *Beishi*, Chavannes still plead to identify Feihan 怖捍 as Ferghana, placing the country described above in its centre or even western part. See the glossary for more information.

325 *Xin Tangshu* 221b.6247. The author's translation is based on the translation by Chavannes: Chavannes, *Documents*, 144–45.

Mi 米 (Māymurgh), also called Mimo 彌末 and Mimohe 弭秣賀. A 100 *li* (ca. 50 km) to the north [it] adjoins Kang 康 (Samarqand). Its ruler governs [from] the Boxide 鉢息德 Fort. [It] was destroyed by the Arabs[326] during the Yonghui 永徽 (era, 650–55, in 654 CE).[327] In Xianqing 顯慶 3 (658 CE), its territory was made Nanmi 南謐 District [and] its ruler, Zhaowu Kaizhuo (Bizhuo[328]) 昭武開拙, appointed prefect. Hereafter, [he] presented tribute to the court without interruption. During the Kaiyuan 開元 (era, 713–41 CE), [he] offered jade,[329] dance carpets,[330] lions,[331] and *hu* 胡 twirl (-dance)[332] women. In [Kaiyuan 開元] 18 (730 CE), the Great Chief Moyemen 末野門[333] came to the court. At the beginning of the Tianbao 天寶 (era, 742–56 CE), their ruler was granted [the title of] respecting obedience king. [His] mother Kedun 可敦[334] [was made] commandery mistress.

1.14.11 He 何 (Kushaniyya)[335]

何，或曰屈霜你迦，曰貴霜匿，即康居小王附墨城故地。城左有重樓，北繪中華古帝，東突厥、婆羅門，西波斯、拂菻等諸王，其君旦詣拜則退。貞觀十五年，遣使者入朝。永徽時上言：「聞唐出師西討，願輸糧于軍。」俄以其地為貴霜州，授其君昭武婆達地刺史。遣使者鉢底失入謝。

He 何 (Kushaniyya), also called Qushuangnijia 屈霜你迦 or Guishuangni 貴霜匿. [It] is the ancient territory of the Fumo 附墨 Fort of a petty king

326 See p. 57 fn. 271.
327 Gibb, *Arab*, 15.
328 It is probably the corrupted form of the name Bizhuo 閉拙, as recorded in the *Suishu* (see p. 35; 1.9.5).
329 I'm not convinced that this is referring to the jade rings named *bi* 璧, as Chavannes proposed (Chavannes, *Documents*, 145).
330 That the Zhonghua shuju edition is right to assume that it were not dancers and carpets (as Chavannes proposed: ibid.), can be gathered from the following quote of the *Jiu Tangshu* 198.5313 (Author's translation): 自開元十年至天寶六載，凡十遣使來朝，并獻方物。……九年四月，獻火毛繡舞筵、長毛繡舞筵、無孔真珠。"From Kaiyuan 開元 10 (722 CE) to Tianbao 天寶 6 (747 CE), overall there were ten envoys sent to the court. All presented local products as gifts. (…) In [Tianbao 天寶] 9/4 (750 CE), [they] presented fire-marten dance carpets, long-furred marten dance carpets, [and] unpierced pearls."
331 Maybe singular.
332 See p. 57 fn. 269.
333 Chavannes pointed out that the *Cefu yuangui* 971.11413a mentioning an individual of the same name (Moyemen 末野門; EMC **matjiamən*) who was apparently being sent as envoy by the king of the state of Kang 康 Duohe 咄褐 (*Tūrγār*; written Duohe 咄曷 in the description of the state of Kang 康 in the *Jiu Tangshu*, p. 50, 1.13.1, and *Xin Tangshu*, p. 54, 1.14.1) in 750 CE is rather odd. Although I agree with Chavannes, I would like to point out that the name of the envoy provided in the *Cefu yuangui* is actually Weiyemen 未野門 (EMC **mujhjiamən*) – who is, however, obviously the same person (Chavannes, *Documents*, 145, fn. 1, 136, fn. 6).
334 See p. 54 fn. 237.
335 *Xin Tangshu* 221b.6247. The author's translation is based on the translation by Chavannes: Chavannes, *Documents*, 145.

of Kangju 康居.[336] In the east of the city stands a storied building. On [its] northern wall are painted the ancient emperors of China; on the eastern [wall], the rulers of the Tujue and Brahmin, and on the western [wall], [the rulers] of Persia (Iranians) and Byzantium. Its lord goes [there] to worship every morning and then retires.[337] In Zhenguan 貞觀 15 (641 CE), [he] sent envoys to come to court. During the Yonghui 永徽 (era, 650–55 CE), [he] sent a message to the emperor: "[As We] heard that the Tang send troops west for an attack [We] desire to supply the army with grain." Shortly after, his country was made Guishuang 貴霜 District [and] their ruler, Zhaowu Podadi 昭武婆達地, was appointed prefect. [He sent] the envoy Bodishi 鉢底失 to court to convey [his] gratitude.

1.14.12 Huoxun 火尋 (Khwārizmik)[338]

火尋，或曰貨利習彌，曰過利，居烏滸水之陽。東南六百里距戊地，西南與波斯接，西北抵突厥曷薩，乃康居小王奥鞬城故地。其君治急多颶遮城。諸胡惟其國有車牛，商賈乘以行諸國。天寶十載，君稍施芬遣使者朝，獻黑鹽。寶應時復入朝。

Huoxun 火尋 (Khwārizmik), also called Huoliximi 貨利習彌 or Guoli 過利, is located on the north bank of the Wuxu 烏滸 River (Amu Darya). Six hundred *li* (ca. 300 km) to the south-east [it] adjoins Wudi 戊地 (Vardana?) [and] touches Persia (Iran) in the south-west.[339] To the north-west, [it] adjoins the Tujue 突厥 Hesa 曷薩 (Khazars). [It was] the ancient territory of the Aojian 奥鞬 Fort of a petty king of Kangju 康居.[340] Its ruler governs [from] the Jiduojuzhe 急多颶遮 Fort. Its state is the only one among all *hu* 胡 [states] to have ox carts. Merchants ride [them] to travel to all countries. In Tianbao 天寶 10 (751 CE), the ruler, Shaoshifen 稍施芬, sent envoys to the court [to] offer black salt.[341] During the Baoying 寶應 (era, 762–63 CE), [envoys] again came to the court.

336 See the passage in the *Hanshu* concerning the petty kings of Kangju 康居 p. 16 (1.3.1).

337 If one follows the now widely accepted interpretation of Marcus Mode, the paintings of the so-called Hall of Ambassadors in Afrasiab may reflect this account, although the only side corresponding to the account is the north side, on which Emperor Taizong 太宗 was apparently to be seen hunting (Mode, *Sogdien*, 77–86).

338 *Xin Tangshu* 221b.6247. The author's translation is based on the translation by Chavannes: Chavannes, *Documents*, 145–46.

339 On the conflicting information, see Fadi 伐地 in the glossary.

340 See the passage in the *Hanshu* concerning the petty kings of Kangju 康居 p. 16 (1.3.1).

341 It is unclear what is meant. Probably some black minerals in the salt made it look black. It was sent with several envoys from Central Asia in the middle of the eighth century. See: Laufer, *Sino-Iranica*, 511; Schafer, *Golden Peaches*, 217.

1.14.13 Shi 史 (Kesh)[342]

史，或曰佉沙，曰羯霜那，居獨莫水南康居小王蘇薤城故地。西百五十里距那色波，北二百里屬米，南四百里吐火羅也。有鐵門山，左右巉峭，石色如鐵，為關以限二國，以金錮闔。城有神祠，每祭必千羊，用兵類先禱乃行。國有城五百。

Shi 史 (Kesh), also called Qusha 佉沙 or Jieshuangna 羯霜那, is located south of the Dumo 獨莫 River (Kashka Darya?). [It is] the ancient territory of the Suxie 蘇薤 Fort of a petty king of Kangju 康居.[343] Five hundred *li* (ca. 250 km) to the west [it] adjoins Nasebo 那色波 (Nakhshab) [and] touches Mi 米 after 200 *li* (ca. 100 km) to the north. Four hundred *li* (ca. 200 km) to the south is Tuhuoluo 吐火羅 (Tokharistan). [There] are the Tiemen 鐵門 (Iron Gates, Dar-i Āhanīn) mountains. On the left and right are steep cliffs [and] the stone's colour is like iron. [It] is a boundary to delimit (the) two countries (of Sogdiana and Tokharistan). The wings are shut with metal [locks]. [In its] city is the temple of a deity [in which] for each sacrifice, a 1,000 sheep must [be offered]. [Before] going to war, [they] first pray [and] only then go. The state has 500 forts.

隋大業中，其君狄遮始通中國，號最彊盛，築乞史城，地方數千里。貞觀十六年，君沙瑟畢獻方物。顯慶時，以其地為佉沙州，授君昭武失阿喝刺史。開元十五年，君忽必多獻舞女、文豹。後君長數死、立，然首領時時入朝。天寶中，詔改史為來威國。

During the Daye 大業 (era, 605–18 CE) of the Sui, their ruler, Dizhe 狄遮,[344] [established] the first communication with China. Known as outstandingly strong and grand,[345] [he] (re?) built the Chishi 乞史 (Kesh) Fort. [His] territory has several 1,000 square *li* (ca. 500 km²). [In] Zhenguan 貞觀 16 (642 CE), [its] ruler, Shasebi 沙瑟畢,[346] offered local products [to the court]. During the Xianqing 顯慶 (era, 656–61 CE), its territory was made [part of the] Qusha 佉沙 District [and] the ruler, Zhaowu Shi'ahe 昭武失阿喝,[347] was appointed prefect. In Kaiyuan 開元 15 (727 CE), the ruler [A]Hubiduo [Yantun] [阿]忽

342 *Xin Tangshu* 221b.6247–48. The author's translation is based on the translation by Chavannes: Chavannes, *Documents*, 146–47.

343 See the passage in the *Hanshu* concerning the petty kings of Kangju 康居 p. 16 (1.3.1).

344 Lurje proposed *δyxcy* (Lurje, *Personal*, 187–88, no. 465).

345 As Chavannes pointed out, this is probably the equivalent of *ming wei qiang guo* 名為強國 ("famous as a mighty state") found in the description of the state of Kang 康 in the *Beishi* 97.3234. It is thus also to be found in the corresponding passages of the *Weishu* 102.2281 and *Suishu* 83.1848.

346 See p. 29 fn. 93.

347 Given as Zhaowu Sha 昭武殺 in the description of the state of Eastern An 安 (Kharghān), see p. 59 fn. 282 (1.14.3). The identification of this individual is unclear. For an overview of the current state of research, see: Stark, *Transoxanien*, 44–45, fn. 144.

必多[延屯][348] sent dancing girls [and] patterned leopards (cheetahs).[349] Thereafter, several rulers died and were enthroned. [Their] leaders still came often to court. During the Tianbao 天寶 (era, 742–56 CE), Shi 史 was changed by decree into state of Laiwei 來威.

1.14.14 Nasebo 那色波 (Nakhshab)[350]

那色波，亦曰小史，蓋為史所役屬。居吐火羅故地，東阨葱嶺，西接波剌斯，南雪山。

Nasebo 那色波 (Nakhshab), also called Lesser Shi 小史 because it is subject to Shi 史 (Kesh), is located at the ancient territory of Tuhuoluo 吐火羅 (Tokharistan).[351] [It] is limited by the Congling 葱嶺 (Pamirs) in the east, [while] in the west, [it] adjoins Bolasi 波剌斯 (Persia, Iran), [and] in the south, [there are] snow mountains.

1.14.15 Dami 呾蜜 (Tirmidh) and others

These accounts continue with the Dami 呾蜜 (Tirmidh), which are not related to Sogdiana, and many other small clans or tribes. The latter are described in the following way:[352]

自呾蜜以下，諸種相與羣聚，華人皆以國名之，故未嘗與唐通，傳記雜詭，不可得而考，然其地與諸國連屬，粗序其名云。

From Dami 呾蜜 (Tirmidh) further down, all the clans (or tribes) settle together. The Chinese use their state to name them. As they did not yet communicate with the Tang, the records are mixed and contradictory. [The information] cannot be obtained and verified, [but] their land is connected, however, to all [the other] countries, [and thus] their names are listed approximately.

348 Mentioned in the in the *Cefu yuangui* 966.11366a and the *Tang hui yao* 99.1777 more completely as Ahubiduo Yantun 阿忽必多延屯. For more on him and how he is related to the *''xwrpt* (Āxwarpat/ Āxurpat) known from coins, see the detailed discussion by: Stark, *Transoxanien*, 45–48, fn. 146.

349 For the leopards, see: Zhang Guangda, "Tangdai".

350 *Xin Tangshu* 221b.6248. The author's translation is based on the translation by Chavannes: Chavannes, *Documents*, 147.

351 Regardless of how unclear the actual definition of "Tokharistan" may be, this is definitely an incorrect attribution. See: *Xin Tangshu* 221b.6252–53; and: *Tongdian* 193.5277.

352 *Xin Tangshu* 221b.6250; author's translation.

1.15 Analysis of the transmitted accounts

The first chapter lists the content of official Chinese sources concerning the foreign regions west of China which geographically refer to Sogdiana. In a next step, the origin of these accounts shall be discussed and the information compared mutually to differentiate between new information and repetition with the goal to establish patterns of narration and the use of *topoi*.

Parenthetically, while most research is focused on the content, i.e. the historical events, the transcription of many foreign names is often ignored, although each transcription reflects a specific choice of characters. This may seem obvious to Sinologists, but I realised that researchers from neighbouring fields mostly read the *pinyin* transcription and are thus are unaware of the connotations. On the other hand, Chinese people, in the unawareness of their mother language, are often too familiar with the terms or the traditional naming habits of foreign individuals or groups. To name only a few, there are the Dashi 大食 (lit. big eating or feeding), the Xiongnu 匈奴 (lit. fierce/brutal slaves), the state of Moshui 沒誰 (lit. "there is nobody"), the elite soldiers *zhejie* 赭羯 (*čākar; lit.* red castrated rams), or personal names as Bizhuo 閉拙 (lit. closed stupid), and Ninieshishi 泥涅師師 (lit. mud black master master). As becomes obvious, certain transcriptions aim at ridiculing these people, and often reduce them to adjectives and nouns, e.g. by referring to the animal world. Quite different naming practices are on the contrary to be observed in more recent and especially colonial times, as e.g., France is transcribed as Faguo 法國 (lit. lawful state), or the United States is called Meiguo 美國 (lit. beautiful state) – manifesting a change of perception, partly due to the shift of power in the world known to the Chinese since coming into the contact with Western nations. By simply reproducing the names without being aware of their inherent mockery, present researchers tend to underestimate the worldview that permeates these accounts.

1.15.1 *Shiji*

Based on the information from Zhang Qian's 張騫 expedition, the *Shiji* provides the blueprint with which the subsequent records of the Western Regions organise their accounts, beginning with Dayuan 大宛:[353]

> 大宛在匈奴西南，在漢正西，去漢可萬里。其俗土著，耕田，田稻麥。有蒲陶酒。多善馬，馬汗血，其先天馬子也。有城郭屋室。其屬邑大小七十餘城，眾可數十萬。其兵弓矛騎射。
>
> Dayuan lies south-west of the territory of the Xiongnu, some 10,000 *li* directly west of China. The people are settled on the land, plowing fields and growing rice and wheat. They also make wine out of grapes. The region has many fine horses which sweat blood;[354] their forebears are supposed to have been foaled

353 *Shiji* 123.3160; translation: Watson, *Records*, 233.
354 See p. 25 fn. 69.

> from heavenly horses. The people live in houses in fortified cities, there being some seventy or more cities of various sizes in the region. The population numbers several hundred thousand. The [soldiers][355] fight with bows and spears and can shoot from horseback.

In the narration, first comes the relative positioning to aforementioned people and the distance to China or the Chinese capital. Next follows their lifestyle, which is sedentary, and their agricultural products as well as livestock. Of particular interest were apparently the horses, to which is added a mythology related to the origin of their people. Then follow more details about their lifestyle. The narrator provides qualitative and quantitative information about their houses and cities, to then state the size of their population. Finally, the "fighting style" of their military is described, which is again related to their horses. These categories will model all later accounts of foreign places.

In the list of countries, Kangju 康居 is described, but as has been laid out, it cannot be successfully related to Sogdiana. However, a state named Suxie 蘇薤 is said to be located east of Dayuan 大宛, but, as has been argued, was probably west of it and may thus refer to a place in Sogdiana or Sogdiana itself. It is said to have sent envoys to China, which is supported by archaeologically excavated bamboo strips. The *Shiji* thus started to record envoys and their gifts which shows the importance given to these events.

In the *Shiji* then follows the description of the regions around Dayuan 大宛, which may have partly included Sogdiana. Particular mention is made of the "heavenly horses" and the wine that doesn't go off for a long time. As the heavenly horses and the wine were desired by the emperor, he imported both of the things that are said to be required to produce them, i.e. grapes and alfalfa and had them planted in China. Moving on to a region that more specifically may have encompassed Sogdiana, i.e. Dayuan 大宛 to Anxi 安息, it is said that the inhabitants had similar customs and spoke different dialects of a same language. Their appearance is defined by deep-set eyes and beards. This description is the first that could be interpreted as discriminatory about Sogdian people. While it reveals that the narrator found this information noteworthy enough to include it, which speaks of the physiognomic difference to himself, or to what was the common understanding and/or knowledge of his expected reader. If interpreted in this way, the accounts can indeed be used as a mirror of the common understanding – and maybe even more importantly, self-understanding – of the narrator, his or her readers, and more broadly, of the Chinese literate upper-class. Keeping this in mind, the following descriptions shall also be viewed under this alternative lens.[356]

Next, their excellency in commerce is pointed out, which is, however, paired with a rhymed statement that is not quite as flattering, namely that they haggle over a

355 Watson translated "people" (ibid.).

356 For a study on the "barbaric" physiognomy, see: Abramson, "Deep Eyes, Physiognomy".

fraction of a cent. While the comment above may have revealed a difference of physiognomy from which we are today unable to extract any aesthetic evaluation – thought it may have been obvious to the contemporaneous reader, i.e. that they did not conform to Chinese beauty standards – this statement quite clearly has a judgemental note to it. This is the first judgement on the character of what may have been Sogdians: They are portrayed as petty and maybe even avaricious. The report continues by telling us that their women were socially esteemed and their advice was sought before making decisions. Like the statement on their physiognomy, this information may have been tainted with judgement, in this case deriding the status of their men in society and criticising a societal order that differs to that of the Han.

What follows is a criticism of their lack of technology, taking two typically Chinese products as point of reference: they were unable to produce silk and lacquer. Moreover, they are depicted as having no knowledge about the cast of coins and generally the casting of objects, which is a skill they were allegedly taught by Chinese envoys and deserters. This clearly reveals the arrogance and ignorance of the narrator. Silk was a highly protected industrial secret, the export of its secrets and commodities like silkworms, moths, and cocoons subject to the death penalty. China virtually had a monopoly on silk production until about the end of the Han. Lacquer is derived from the dried sap of lacquer trees which were mostly cultivated in China. Lacquerware needs a warm and humid atmosphere to dry. Casting coins is a quite peculiar phenomenon unique to China, as coins were minted in other parts of the world. For silk and lacquer, the Chinese author thus describes the Central Asians living in Sogdiana as not knowing how to manufacture products that were famous in China and which at the same time were impossible to have been produced in Central Asia. With regard to lacquerware, the author may have been ill-informed about the technologies and therefore about the requirements of the products, which conceivably is a display of arrogance. To mock these people about their inability to manufacture these products is similar to mocking their sailing skills. The cast of coins is to be seen in the same logic: Instead of, for example, describing how coins were minted in Central Asia – and the rest of the world – and comparing this to the Chinese way of casting coins, casting is perceived as a skill to be taught to Central Asians who were consequently able to produce weapons that were superior to their old ones. Finally, it is said that after having been taught how to cast objects, when the Central Asians subsequently lay hand on Chinese gold and silver, they made it into objects, and not coins. While the Han government installed a state monopoly on ironworking and indeed produced superior quality cast iron and even steel weapons, it is clear that here a narrative technique is employed to frame one's own sense of superiority by positioning oneself in the position of a teacher. This narration is exemplary evidence of Othering techniques. The points of reference used in the comparisons are wittingly chosen so as to establish the Han as superior while the achievements, technology, point of view, and knowledge of the Other are ignored.

Finally, the emperor's thoughts about the report are recorded. The states – although maybe not including Sogdian states but only referring to Dayuan 大宛, Daxia 大夏,

and Anxi 安息 – are qualified as "great". It is further mentioned that they are "rich in unusual products" and are described having a sedentary lifestyle – in opposition to the people inhabiting the steppe – and are thus qualified as generally similar to the Chinese. To continue the comparison with China, they are described as militarily weak and desiring Han goods and wealth.

Besides these *states*, the Kangju 康居 and Yuezhi 月氏 *people* north of these states are then mentioned and contrasted with them as strong in arms. It is said that they could be persuaded through gifts and their prospect of profit (*li* 利). Then, finally, the result of the whole reflection is revealed: The emperor ponders about the proper way to extend his domain, if possible by "righteous" (*yi* 義) means, with the aim to attract people with strange customs to come to China and spread the Han's "might and moral virtue" (*weide* 威德) to the four ends of the world in all languages. In short, he is portrayed as seeking the most efficient way to spread his own might and glory while bribing foreign chiefs. Quite obviously, the foreigners are again one-sidedly portrayed as inherently covetous and attracted by the Han's wealth. Whereas the emperor's desire to gain unusual products, which was stressed at first, is not further emphasised, the dual expansion of their physical realm and their fame as well as the recognition among other people is portrayed as the main motivation to act.

The narration then goes on to reveal that the people of Dayuan 大宛 sought to keep themselves far away, i.e. far enough to be out of reach of the great Chinese army. They thus concluded that they would not trade their horses, which were sought after by the Han in addition to the failed main goal of Zhang Qian 張騫 to forge an alliance against the Xiongnu 匈奴. When the Han envoys then insulted the foreign statesmen on their ground and smashed their golden horse, they were executed and their goods seized. Objectively, one could argue that the ensuing punitive military campaign and occupation of their country was a result of the envoys' scandalous behaviour in a foreign state with the goal to seize the coveted horses. To take an even stronger stance, one could argue that this incident was levied as reason to invade them. The deliberate mention of this behaviour shows, however, that the author wanted to establish another point: He aimed at establishing a narration in which the Han envoys are portrayed as *righteously* desiring their horses and are *wrongfully* denied access to them. And how could these inferior people dare such an offence? A punishment is thus seen as the logical conclusion of such a narration. Finally, while the expansion of the domain achieved through the conquest of Dayuan 大宛 is portrayed as evidence of a successful spread of the Han's might and moral virtue – albeit not in the originally thought out gracious fashion of gifting – another goal is met through sending out of parties west of Dayuan 大宛 to seek for rare objects. The access to the horses, on the other hand, which may have well been the main point of the whole conquest and remained a regularly recurring source of conflicts between Chinese dynasties and their Northern and Western neighbours, is downplayed.

1.15.2 *Hanshu* and *Hou Hanshu*

The *Xiyu zhuan* 西域傳 (Accounts of the Western Regions) of the *Hanshu* is the first of such separate accounts, which became the model for later dynastic histories. In addition to the content, which is also to be found in the *Shiji*, various additional information is provided. The extent of the *Xiyu zhuan* 西域傳 in the *Hanshu*, compared to those of other foreign countries, probably derives from the family background of the editor Ban Biao 班彪. His second son, Ban Chao 班超, was a famous general in charge of the administration of the Western Regions while his first son Ban Gu 班固 and his daughter Ban Zhao 班昭 finalised the edition of the volume he started.

Like the *Shiji*, the *Hanshu* states that starting during the reign of Emperor Wu 武 of the Han, the aim was to spread might and moral virtue (*weide* 威德). In this *mission civilisatrice* they invaded Western countries and created bureaucratic structures by dividing the land in commanderies, and eventually installing a protector-general to supervise and inspect them in 59 CE. We also find for the first time the mention that the rulers of Kangju 康居 – who at this time probably encompassed Sogdiana – sent their sons "to serve the Han", which is a euphemism for a life as hostage at the Chinese court, which in time proved to be an efficient tool for coercion and blackmail. The newly installed officer was, however, said to have been upset at their lack of their etiquette, i.e. the lack of Chinese etiquette, and criticised them as barbaric and arrogant. He surmised that they lied about their intentions, introducing the concept that they were treacherous, and alleged that they only wanted to keep up good relations because of their desire for trade and profit. In a description of another Central Asian state, their envoys were said to be only disguised merchants. Interestingly, while the foreigner's desire for profit was already introduced in the *Shiji* as a fitting method to attract them to China, it was indeed the Chinese who invaded their country partly – or mainly – because of their desire to possess their horses. What seems as an arrogant statement in itself may be explained by the self-righteousness of the Chinese politics, as laid out before, while the lack of etiquette and unfitting behaviour is again a method to position the Han as culturally superior. "Tribute" is also listed, which are gifts that by definition acknowledge the sovereignty of the Chinese emperor. To understate the situation, it is open to debate if this relationship was perceived and acknowledged on both sides in this way. At the same time, the listing of the petty kings of Kangju 康居 and the largely exaggerated distances was shown to be quite revealing of the Han's ignorance of these places. Excavated bamboo strips corroborate that the state of Suxie 蘇薤 may have sent an embassy. It is thus quite likely that at this stage the information was only gathered through the hearsay of the foreign envoys, and that the categories of information such as country, state, and people were mixed.[357]

The *Hou Hanshu* provides another piece of political history relating to the disruption and re-establishment of Han dominion over the Western Regions. Then

357 For more on this, see p. 89 (1.15.13).

follows the first quote on a state that can be distinctively identified as Sogdiana, i.e. Liyi 栗弋. *Li* 栗 is to be understood as *su* 粟, as in the later Suyi 粟弋 and Sute 粟特. This passage first states that it was a dependency of Kangju 康居 and then lists some of the local products, i.e. famous horses, cattle, sheep, grapes, and all sort of fruits. Specifically, the good soil and water are mentioned, which are seen as the reason for their excellent wine. All of this sounds like an expanded version of the description of the countries "around" Dayuan 大宛 of the *Shiji* and *Hanshu*.

1.15.3 *Sanguozhi*

The *Sanguozhi* includes a passage from the now lost *Weilüe* 魏略 in which various hearsay and mythical information is gathered. Among these is a place named Zhuyao 屬繇 which may have been a different transcription of Soghd that was otherwise lost.

1.15.4 *Jinshu*

The *Jinshu* provides somewhat confusing information, as Kangju 康居 is now said to *adjoin* Sogdiana, now referred to as Suyi 粟弋. It is difficult to say if this is to be understood as a political change or derives from a misunderstanding, as Kangju 康居 was before said to *encompass* Sogdiana. Further, Kangju 康居 is now said to be governed from the Suxie 蘇薤 Fort, whereas before, the Fort was said to have been the seat of a petty king of Kangju 康居. It may however be that it being the first in the list of petty kings may have implied this. The mention of paulownias and willows is also new. Seen under this light, this passage may actually have included some otherwise lost material and/or corrections.

1.15.5 *Weishu*

Some centuries later, the *Weishu* includes far more details about Western countries, and even more about Iran and the Byzantine Empire. The compilation process of the volume is, however, problematic to establish, as it was partly lost and eventually reconstructed during the Song by recurring to the later *Zhoushu* and *Beishi*, while the latter relies on the *Suishu*.[358] The additional information is probably a result of the increasing contact between this new Northern Dynasty and the Western Regions, which probably derives from it being more closely interconnected to these regions than the Han of the Central Plains and Southern China. To a greater degree it may also owe to its compilation by Wei Shou 魏收, who was partial in favour for the Northern Xianbei 鮮卑 Tuoba 拓跋 clans that successfully took over Northern China as the first in a row of "conquest dynasties", being followed by the Western and Eastern Wei, the Northern Qi, and the Northern Zhou.

The goals mentioned in the *Shiji* and *Hanshu* are restated, the rulers desired to spread their might and moral virtue and seek precious foreign goods. I suppose, however, that it is no coincidence that the *wei de* 威德 (might and moral virtue) was

358 See: Uchida Gimpo, "Gisho no seriritsu," 19–21, 26. For the compilation history, see also: Dien, "Wei"; Dien, "Historiography," 528–30; and: Chen Yuan, "Huoxianjiao," 113.

spread so that the *Wei de* 魏德 (moral virtue of the Wei) could be heard, which sounds like a historiographer's pun. Whereas in the *Shiji* and *Hanshu*, the rulers of the Western Regions were said to "know themselves far away" and did thus not desire to trade their horses with the Han, in the *Weishu,* the "knowing themselves far away" is said to have resulted in them humbling themselves when in need and otherwise neglecting the emperor's order. Interestingly, while in the *Shiji* and *Hanshu*, this was depicted as a manifestation of the foreigners' greed and desire to access Han goods, the *Weishu* simply states that the emperor thought that there was no benefit (*yi* 益) to be gained and thus had no desire to keep up the coming and going of envoys.

The narration is newly spun in that an official now requested to allow people from the Western Regions to come closer and increase the connections and let them pay their tribute, as they desired to do so with or without Chinese action. The emperor was said to have agreed and the bureaucratic division were changed into four districts and the roads doubled from two to four. The foreigners' general logic in foreign politics was thus taken over from earlier accounts but the assessment and reaction are both completely new. Actually, where the Han failed to do so with peaceful means, the Wei successfully and effectively implemented diplomatic relations to spread their "might and moral virtue". As we read, however, in the remarks of the historiographer following the description of the state of Kang 康, they allegedly were concerned about adapting a loose-reign policy and simply never found time for a conquest after the unification.

While earlier accounts were rather unorganised, the structure of the descriptions of foreign countries in the *Weishu* is far more uniform. The order is relatively rigid and can be differentiated in the following categories:

- capital
  a. name
  b. size
- location
  a. politically
  b. topographically
- older alternative names (referring to previous accounts)
- topography
- products
- fauna and flora
- political history:
  a. in connection with other people
  b. of envoys to China, listing of gifts

There are some notable exceptions to this:

- The name of most of the countries are identical to their capital, which points to these being city-states, or states tightly organised around these cities. Exception to this rule are:[359]

359 Excluding Ferghana, as it does not belong to Sogdiana.

  a. the state of Zheshe 者舌 (Chach), for which no capital is mentioned, but is said to have been part of the ancient state of Kangju 康居,
  b. the state of Kang 康 (Samarqand), with its capital being Aludi 阿魯迪.
- The description of the state of Fuhuo 副貨 (Bukhārā?), which includes a description of the king's palace.
- The description of the state of Kang 康 (Samarqand) is by far the most extensive – especially concerning the products – and includes various additional information:
  a. The political history of the state, including the history of the royal family, their names and their connection to other people (in this case through wedding politics with the Tujue 突厥).[360]
  b. Inner politics, three chancellors handling the politics.
  c. Clothing and hair style of the king and his wife.
  d. Clothing and hair style of the men.
  e. The description as a mighty state and lordship over the surrounding states, counting nine. Among these, however, Amul was quite certainly not under their rule.
  f. Judicial system.
  g. Physiognomy of the people: to the deep-set eyes and beards of the description in the *Shiji* of the people from Dayuan 大宛 to Anxi 安息 are now added high noses.
  h. Commerce is highly valued, being a meeting point of all merchants.
  i. Musical instruments: large and small drums, *pipa* 琵琶, five-stringed lute, harp.
  j. Wedding and mourning ceremonies.
  k. Rituals:
     1. Ancestral temples.
     2. Buddhism.
  l. Script.
  m. Climate.

Some of the new information was amalgamated with older accounts to fit in the legacy. For example, it is stated that the state of Kang 康 is the state of Kangju 康居 from the Han – resembling the effort to conflate the state of An 安 and Anxi 安息 in the Suishu. In consequence, Kangju 康居 may in later sources refer to Kang 康 and Anxi 安息 to An 安.[361] It is also the first time the name of the kings of Kang 康, Wen 溫, is given. For more on this, see below the commentary on Sute 粟特. Then follows his and his people's alleged historical background, which – as just mentioned – is a conflation with the information on Kangju 康居, claiming that he was a Yuezhi 月氏.

Apart from this, it is also the first mention of a Zoroastrian temple in which the law code was deposited. However, we do not know what form this religion exactly

360 For the discussion on the name Zhaowu 昭武, see below.
361 See the glossary.

took in Sogdiana. Parenthetically, as weddings and mournings of Kang 康 are described as being similar to those of the Tujue 突厥, a look at these seems inevitable. As the *Weishu* does not contain a passage about the Tujue 突厥 – which was probably lost – their next description is to be found in the *Suishu*, now listed under the Northern Barbarians (*beidi* 北狄):[362]

> 有死者，停屍帳中，家人親屬多殺牛馬而祭之，遶帳號呼，以刀剺面，血淚交下，七度而止。於是擇日置屍馬上而焚之，取灰而葬。表木為塋，立屋其中，圖畫死者形儀及其生時所經戰陣之狀。嘗殺一人，則立一石，有至千百者。父兄死，子弟妻其羣母及嫂。

> [If] a person dies,[363] the corpse is placed in a tent. The family and relatives slaughter cattle and horses and offer them as sacrifice for the dead. [They] circle around the tent [and] wail, cut [their] faces with knives – blood [and] tears mingle [and run] down. [After proceeding like this for] seven times, they then stop. Then [they] choose a day,[364] place the corpse on a horse and burn them, gather the ashes and bury [them]. A wooden pole is used to demarcate the grave and a room is erected in it, [in which] is painted a portrait of the deceased and depictions of the fights [he] participated in during [his] lifetime. If [he] killed one person, then one stone is placed (at the grave) – sometimes [there are] hundreds, up to thousands. [If] the father [or] elder brother dies, the son [or respectively] cadet brother marries his (step)mothers [365] or [respectively] the elder's brother wives (i.e. the sisters-in-law).

The *Beishi* produces a similar account, but provides additional information:[366]

> 擇日，取亡者所乘馬及經服用之物，并屍俱焚之，收其餘灰，待時而葬。春夏死者，候草木黃落；秋冬死者，候華茂，然後坎而瘞之。葬日，親屬設祭及走馬、剺面如初死之儀。……

> [They] choose a day,[367] get the deceased's horse and commonly used objects, and burn it both [with] the corpse. [They then] collect the remaining ash, wait [for the appropriate] time and bury [it]. [If the person] dies [in] spring [or] summer, [they] wait [for] the grass [and] trees [to turn] yellow [and] fall; [if the person] dies [in] autumn [or] winter, [they] wait [for] the flora [turning] luxuriant, then dig [a grave] and bury it. [On] the day of the burial, the relatives

362 *Suishu* 84.1864; author's translation. See also a translation in German: Liu Mau-tsai, *Chinesischen Nachrichten I*, 42.

363 As can be deduced by the following description, this kind of burial is most likely performed for a warrior.

364 It is unclear what the criteria for the choice are, i.e. if it is based on a calendar or the season. See the passage of the *Beishi* below and: ibid., 463.

365 The *Beishi* (see below) replaces this word by *houmu* 後母 (stepmother), probably to clarify that the son does not marry his consanguine mother.

366 *Beishi* 97. 3288; author's translation.

367 See p. 78 fn. 364.

make offerings, ride horses, [and] cut [their] faces as [they did] in the ritual for his passing. (…)

又以祭之羊、馬頭，盡懸之於標上。是日也，男女咸盛服飾，會於葬所，男有悅愛於女者，歸即遣人聘問，其父母多不違也。父、兄、伯、叔死，子、弟及姪等妻其後母、世叔母、嫂，唯尊者不得下淫。

The offered heads of the sheep and horse finally are hung on top of a pole. On this day, men and women all dress in proper clothing [and] gather at the burial place. [When] a man has feelings for woman, [once] returned home, [he] sends a person to make a [marriage] proposal. Her parents generally agree. [If] a father, an elder brother, an elder [or] cadet brother of the father (i.e. an uncle) dies, the son, [or respectively] the cadet brother, or the nephew marries his stepmother, [respectively] the wife of his father's cadet brother (i.e. his aunts), [or] the elder brother's wives (i.e. the sisters-in-law) – only, [a member of] the older male generation cannot engage in incest with [a member of] the younger [generation].

Whether or not this information reflects the customs of the state of Kang 康, will be reflected on in the following by using later accounts.

Finally, there is some conflicting information that needs to be addressed. Firstly, regarding Niumi 忸密 and Fuhuo 副貨 being both listed. As the *Xin Tangshu* later states that An 安 was also called Buhua 布豁, Buhe 捕喝, and during the Northern Wei 魏 Niumi 忸密, and Niumi 忸密 can be related to Numijkath, we can safely assume that Fuhuo 副貨 indeed refers to Bukhārā. Similarly, Xiwanjin 悉萬斤 and the country of Kang 康 both refer to Samarqand – as the *Xin Tangshu* also rightly concluded. The fact that these are listed as distinctive countries may be explained by the compilers not being quite properly informed. Secondly, regarding Sute 粟特 being listed among the states of Sogdiana and the included information – for the erroneous conflation of Yancai 奄蔡 with Sute 粟特, see the explanations of Shiratori and Enoki.[368] It is quite possible that Sute 粟特 is a new transcription that was recorded when receiving foreign envoys which said to have come from Sogdiana or being Sogdian. This information must have been conflated with the earlier listings that included Suxie 蘇薤 and Suyi 粟弋 and was thus recognised as distinctive state – similar to the misunderstandings about Bukhārā and Samarqand just mentioned.

Based on this logic, by conflating the description of the state of Kang 康 and Sute 粟特, we can conclude that the name of the kings of Kang 康, Wen 溫, is the short version of the name Wennasha 溫那沙, which is erroneously provided as alternative name of the state of Sute 粟特. There is no further information about the country or the products that reinforces this theory. The political history, i.e. their occupation by the Xiongnu 匈奴, and especially the payment of the ransom of the Sogdian merchants of Liangzhou 涼州, is equally to be explained by the lack of understanding of the

368 See p. 25 fn. 71.

compilers. It is nevertheless unclear if it is the king of Kang 康 that is referred to as the one paying the ransom and sending envoys, or some other king. Nevertheless, it is the first time that we read about concrete interaction between a ruler of Sogdiana and the Chinese court, and the first mention in official accounts of a Sogdian merchant colony in a Chinese district.

1.15.6 *Zhoushu*

The *Zhoushu* only includes information about Sute 粟特 without providing new details in its description. The only difference to the *Weishu* is the doubt rightfully cast upon the conflation with Yancai 奄蔡, as mentioned above. According to it, relations were revived after the Eastern Wei, meaning that since the capture of the Sogdian merchants in Liangzhou 涼州, they did not sent envoys, i.e. between 457 CE and 564 CE. In another passage, however concerning the Tujue 突厥, it is recorded that Emperor Wen 文 of the Wei sent An Nuopantuo 安諾槃陀 – a Sogdian, judging by the name[369] – as envoy to communicate with Tumen 土門 of the Tujue in 545 CE (Bumin, later calling himself Yili Kehan 伊利可汗, Illig Qaghan), probably because of his linguistic and intercultural skills.

1.15.7 *Suishu*

The *Suishu*, while reproducing much of the earlier accounts – keeping in mind that the "earlier accounts" were partly produced with its help – provides some additional information but excludes a separate description of Sogdiana. However, information was also collected actively. For example, in the Sui, the cartographer Pei Ju 裴矩 (547–627 CE) was sent by Emperor Yang 煬 to gather information, which resulted in the production of his *Xiyu tuji* 西域圖記 (*Record of the Western Regions*):[370]

> 監知關市，尋討書傳，訪采胡人，或有所疑，即詳衆口。依其本國服飾儀形，王及庶人，各顯容止，即丹青模寫。
>
> [He] inspected frontier markets, searched for written records, inquired among the *hu* 胡, or when there was a doubt, [he would] then thoroughly investigate the public opinion. Based on the country's dress and adornment, [as well as] the features and demeanour of [their] kings and commoners, [he] would then paint [their] likeness.

Nevertheless, as in the *Weishu*, the state of Kang 康 (Samarqand) is said to have been the state succeeding Kangju 康居. Further, the states of Mi 米 (Māymurgh), Shi 史 (Kesh), Cao 曹 (Ishitikhan), and He 何 (Kushaniyya) are now said to have been once part of the ancient territory of Kangju 康居. At the same time, the state of An 安 (Bukhārā) is said to be the state succeeding Anxi 安息 (Parthia). While these states were probably – as has been argued above – once part of Kangju 康居, the statement

369 For the name Nuopantuo 諾槃陀, see also p. 132 fn. 98.
370 *Suishu* 81.1579; author's translation. Pointed out by: Lung, "Interpreters," 207.

that the state of Kang 康 succeeded to the state Kangju 康居 and An 安 to Anxi 安息 is rather obviously a conflation based on their having a similar transcription in Chinese.[371]

Names of kings are newly provided for various states, as well as how they related to each other. If indeed, the cadet sons of the king of Samarqand governed over the surrounding states – as was mentioned in earlier accounts of the state of Kang 康 – Kang 康 and An 安 intermarried among (distant?) cousins. Instead of providing the size of the capital, as in the *Weishu*, the city walls of Kang 康 are described. Further, whereas in the *Weishu* the king is said to have lived in a golden palace under which were seven golden camels of ca. one m in height, he is now described as sitting on a golden camel throne of ca. 2.3 m height. The next two statements seem rather familiar. Firstly, it is said that the king decided upon the governmental affairs with his wife and chancellors. I believe that this is an amalgamation of the *Shiji's* passage on the people between Dayuan 大宛 and Anxi 安息 (that was previously found in the now excluded separate passage on Sogdiana) – saying that women were valued and that husbands sought their wives' advice before making decisions – and of the *Weishu's* passage – noting that three chancellors decided on the matters of state in Kang 康. Through this combination of probable historical information, the *Shiji's* passage – extracted from a judgemental passage – is given the appearance of a fact. Secondly, it is said that their customs were similar to those of the state of Kang 康, apart from the fact that they do marry their sisters and mothers and have intercourse with them – which is metaphorically expressed by "what beasts of the air and ground do". While this is the first explicit slander that we encounter since the *Shiji* and *Hanshu*, this information sounds as if taken from the statement on the wedding customs of the Tujue 突厥 as seen in the *Beishi,* presented above. Whereas the *Weishu* explained that the state of Kang 康 had the same wedding and burial customs as the Tujue 突厥, the state of Kang 康 is now explicitly said to have not practised these – here purposely poorly qualified and thus slandered – customs. Considering firstly this discrepancy, secondly that the *Weishu* mentioning a golden hall on golden camels and the *Suishu* describing a camel throne, and thirdly that no other information matches, the editors of the *Suishu* had conceivably not understood that the state of Fuhuo 副貨 of the *Weishu* refers to Bukhārā, i.e. the state of An 安, which in the *Suishu* is related to Anxi 安息. Some information was probably newly added by help of the accounts of Retainer Commandant Du Xingman 杜行滿, such as the courtesy name of the king – which may, however, have also been misattributed. Nevertheless, most of the description of the country and its customs is a mixture of information taken from other accounts, which is probably due to no envoys of the state of An 安 being mentioned as reaching the Sui.

The state of Bi 畢 – which was proposed to be identified as Paykand – is introduced as having no ruler and thus being governed by the state of An 安. To our knowledge, it is most probably related to envoys arriving in 609 CE and claiming to

371 See also below the commentary on the *Beishi* and the glossary.

have their origins there. The state of Shi 石 (Chach) is also newly introduced, which includes – besides the normal content – two interesting pieces of information. Firstly, a judgement is made about their excellence in fighting, which is repeated for the states of Shi 史, Cao 曹, and He 何, said to have had over 1000 elite soldiers. Secondly, an important piece of political history is recorded in which their conquest by the Tujue 突厥 is mentioned, resulting in it being the Tujue 突厥 ruler that sent envoys to China. The state of Mi 米 and Cao 曹 are introduced as having no king and instead are said to have been respectively ruled by a cadet brother and son of the king of the state of Kang 康. This means that for all of the mentioned Sogdian states in the *Suishu*, only the state of Kang 康, An 安, Shi 史, and He 何 are said to have had kings, which were from the clan of the king of Kang 康, while Shi 石 was governed by the Tujue 突厥. For the state of Cao 曹 are also recorded some of their rituals, including a deity, being represented by a golden statue, and clearly exaggerated amounts of offerings to the deity Dexi 得悉. New is also that the king of He 何 is said to have sat on a golden sheep throne. The rituals at the temple of the "heaven deity" (*tian shen* 天神) – maybe a Zoroastrian deity – of the state of Cao 漕 (Kāpiśī; which was not part of Sogdiana but is included in the list of Kang's 康 vassal states) are further described as obscene.[372]

1.15.8 *Beishi*

The *Beishi* lists Anxi 安息 again in a separate passage, where it is *not* mentioned as the state preceding the state of An 安 (Bukhārā). Instead, its location is given and its king is said to have sent envoys in 567 CE. Confusingly, the description of the state of An 安 does still includes the statement that it was the state succeeding Anxi 安息 from when the Han dynasty ruled. It also includes a description of Mu 穆 (Amul?), in which it is said to have been a vassal state of Kang 康. However, it was not related to what is commonly defined as Sogdiana.

1.15.9 *Da Tang Xiyu ji*

In the *Da Tang Xiyu ji* various new information is added to the older accounts. The structure of the account is slightly different in that it is written in the style of a travel diary, moving from one place to the next. The domestic and foreign politics are therefore left out – only the dominion of the Tujue 突厥 is mentioned for Zheshi 赭時 (Chach) and Sudulisena 窣堵利瑟那 (Sutrūshana, Ushrusana) – as well as the envoys sent to China. Instead, there is a strong focus on the local people and culture, which is owed to Xuanzang 玄奘 being a monk and linguist. Besides providing the location and size of the states like the others, it is the only account that describes the form of the state, e.g. narrow from east to west and broad from south to north. It starts with the Suye 素葉 River Fort (Ak-Beshim Sūyāb) which, together with Taluosi 呾邏私 (Talas) River Fort, is said to have been where "the *hu* 胡 merchants of all countries live together". While this was until then said about the state of Kang 康, the

372 See p. 32 fn. 121.

latter's description now only mentions that Samarqand was considered the centre of all Sogdian countries. Then ensues the first proper definition of Sogdiana in Chinese sources: Suli 窣利 is defined as ranging from the Suye 素葉 River Fort (Ak-Beshim Sūyāb) to the state of Jieshuangna 羯霜那 (Kesh), to then proceed to say that the people and the script are called the same as the state, i.e. Sogdians and Sogdian. Seen from a geographic perspective, this is a rather strange definition, owing to his decision to describe the states from north-east to west, i.e. starting at the Syr Darya from Zheshi 赭時 (Chach) over Feihan 怖捍 (Ferghana) to Sudulisena 窣堵利瑟那 (Sutrūshana/Ushrusana), to then following the course of the Zerafshan, starting from Samojian 颯秣建 (Samarqand) until Huoliximijia 貨利習彌伽 (Khwārizmik) on the bank of the Amu Darya, then jumping back east to the state of Jieshuangna 羯霜那 (Kesh). Xuanzang 玄奘, being linguistically inclined, recorded not only the name of the state of Suli 窣利 but explained in detail how their language functions and that it is read vertically. While being detailed in its descriptions, the account does not lack value judgements, as older judgements are re-combined: Sogdians are described to be of large stature, but cowardly. While the – relatively to the Chinese – large stature is new, the cowardice is added as a contrast to it. Their greediness is also updated, taking the Sogdians' alleged treacherous and covetous nature to the level of not even stopping at the relationship between father and son, in drastic contrast to the Chinese concept of filial piety (*xiao* 孝). Equally reiterated is the judgement about the Sogdians' positive evaluation of seeking wealth in a slightly new fashion. Wealth is said to be highly regarded among poor and rich and although being rich, they are said to clothe themselves in a lowly way. This stands probably in conflict with the narrator's societal rules of status and status symbols, which was strictly defined in a Chinese hierarchical world view. Ironically, the same criticism was applied by the Arabic traveller Ibn Batūtta on the Chinese merchants, which may point to an idiomatic use for a derogatory comment on merchants:[373]

> They are much addicted to the comforts and pleasures of life; but they do not much differ, either in their luxuries or their dress: for you will see one of their merchants, whose wealth is almost immense, clothed in the coarsest cotton.

Finally, it is said that half were farmers and half engaged in trade, which points to the overabundance of merchants.

Contrary to this introduction of the Sogdians as cowardly and greedy, all Sogdian countries are described without a single negative judgement – except Ferghana, which can however be ignored in study on Sogdians. Their craftsmanship and ingenuity is described as outstanding, their virtue and sense for propriety noted, and especially the courage of their king and military qualities are stressed, further stating that although the climate may be moderate, the customs are fierce. A special elite unit of

373 *Ibn Battūta* (trans. Lee), 208; see also: (transl. Gibb), 283.

mercenaries is introduced, the *zhejie* 赭羯 (*čākar*).[374] This greatly reinforces the impression that the preceding description and the negative judgements made on Sogdiana and its people is to be understood as a newly updated edition of many of the statements made about the countries from Dayuan 大宛 to Anxi 安息 in the *Shiji*. In this respect, it is difficult to evaluate if Sogdians were indeed understood as being covetous, greedy, and unfilial at this time or if the information was taken over from older accounts for the sake of tradition.

1.15.10 *Tongdian* and *Jing xing ji*

The accounts of the *Tongdian* on the state of Kang 康 are substantially more detailed and well-informed than earlier accounts, probably relying on a broader range of sources and first-hand information, mostly without added judgement. Their excellency in commerce is stated, furthermore detailing the youth of a Sogdian (male): reaching the age of five, they studied writing and then soon left to learn trade. In stating that larger profits are considered positive, an unformulated value judgement may be included. The sixth month is said to be the beginning of the new year which is the month for which the *Weishu* recorded that ancestral offerings are performed. Their customs and especially the Zoroastrian rites are more detailed than ever before and described without judgemental remarks. Further, a quote from the *Jing xing ji,* contained in the *Tongdian,* may reflect the idea of a Zoroastrian state ritual being performed before going to war. While the *Suishu* and *Da Tang Xiyu ji* seemed to have amended that Sogdiana was indeed not a country to be listed together with other Sogdian states, it is here again mentioned in the list of countries with their own envoys, qualified as a "great state", and thus goes back to closely follow the description of the *Shiji* and *Hanshu*. It is possible, however, that this confusing inclusion is due to the encyclopaedic and traditional character of the work.

1.15.11 *Jiu Tangshu*

The chapter previously entitled *Xiyu zhuan* 西域傳 (*Account of the Western Regions*) is referred to as *Xirong* 西戎 in the *Jiu Tangshu*, which is a general term for the people north-west of China. Oddly, concerning Sogdiana, only the passage on the state of Kang 康 is included, which comprises a comment on the countries of Mi 米 (Māymurgh) and Cao 曹 (Kapūtānā). Apart from reproducing the information provided in earlier historical accounts, the *Jiu Tangshu* presents a new style of recycling various older statements about the state of Kang 康.

Excellency in producing wine and the storing of wine, for example, is changed into the people being bibulous, juxtaposed with them liking to dine and dance in the street. Although the singing and dancing is old, the combination is new. The proficiency in trade of earlier accounts is combined with the comments on their greed and haggling over every cent – taken from the description of the *Shiji* about the people between Dayuan 大宛 and Anxi 安息. I believe that this is owed to the editors

374 See p. 43 fn. 177.

following the logic of the editors of the *Weishu*, who copied from the description of the *Shiji* about the people between Dayuan 大宛 and Anxi 安息 that they had deep-set eyes and profuse beards, and added that they had high noses into the description of the state of Kang 康 – thus pointing to the people of Kang 康 being understood as the ancient people described as living between Dayuan 大宛 and Anxi 安息. Generally writing in a more flowery style, the expression "wherever profit lies they have gone" is further added, which strongly reminds a passage of *Guanzi*.[375] Whereas the *Tongdian* only stated that they learned writing and reading when reaching the age of five and left for trade at a young age, the *Jiu Tangshu* specifies that they left at the age of 20. This entire passage is, however, preceded by a new rather ridiculous fantasy about the new-born Sogdians having their mouth filled with hard honey and their palm smeared with glue, thus when grown up they shall speak sweet talk and stick to money. The metaphor, however, may bring to mind Proverbs 5:3: "For the lips of a loose[376] woman drip honey, and her speech is smoother than oil".[377] For the difference in the description of the women's clothing, see below the description of the *Xin Tangshu*.

The gifts brought to China become more and more exotic, luxurious, and rather fantastic. Clearly established, however, is the alleged direct control over the nobility of their kings by Wu Zetian 武則天 or the Chinese emperor – which leaves no doubt as to actual renewed contact between the two countries. This is also what may have led to new information about the people. Thus, in the *Weishu*, the king is said to have had his hair adorned with a crown, jewellery, and golden flowers, and his wife wore a topknot, veiled with a black cloth. In the *Jiu Tangshu*, however, the king has a felt hat decorated with golden jewellery as crown, and his wife a black cloth on her topknot, but gold flowers are now said to decorate it. These changes either represent updated information, or a mixture of the two accounts. At the same time, instead of having crossed the Pamirs, heading west (*Weishu*), they are said to have moved south along the Pamirs, which is somewhat confusing. For the ritual side, Brahmin are registered as in charge of the astrology/astronomy, Buddhism is described as common, and a rather peculiar ritual, including the splashing of water and praying for cold in winter, is introduced. Interestingly, Zoroastrianism or fire temples are not mentioned, and – unlike in the *Tongdian* – the year is said to begin in the twelfth month.[378]

1.15.12 *Xin Tangshu*

The *Xin Tangshu* provides all earlier information but excludes a separate passage of Sogdiana, which is – like in the *Jiu Tangshu* – partly integrated into the description of the state of Kang 康. While the *Xin Tangshu* aimed to produce a better account than

375 See p. 51 fn. 220.

376 Lit. strange in Hebrew.

377 New Revised Standard Version Bible, 1989, Division of Christian Education of the National Council of the Churches of Christ in the United States of America.

378 For more on this, see p. 87 Table 1 (1.15.12).

the *Jiu Tangshu*, it goes further into providing more alternative names and some new information, e.g. the numbers of fortifications, which do, however, seem like generalising hearsay, or additional imports, such as in the passage concerning the already mentioned embassy of 718 CE, dwarves and dancing girls are added. Some small differences show that the editors thoroughly examined and re-evaluated earlier information. For example, both the *Jiu Tangshu* and *Xin Tangshu* mention that their rulers had the surname Wen 温, but the *Jiu Tangshu* said that they were Yuezhi 月氏, whereas in the *Xin Tangshu*, it is said that they "originally" were Yuezhi 月氏 – however incorrect both statements may be. The "Nine Surnames" represent a quite important difference, which is discussed separately below. Another small alteration was made in the description of the women's clothing. While in the *Jiu Tangshu* (*furen* 婦人) and the *Xin Tangshu* (*nüzi* 女子), women in general are the subject, the *Weishu* (*qi qi* 其妻) – and in consequence also the *Beishi* and *Suishu* – refers to the king's wife. The editors of the *Jiu Tangshu* and *Xin Tangshu* probably choose to understand the *qi qi* 其妻 of the earlier works as "their women" and thus made corrections accordingly. In another example, the account differs to the *Da Tang Xiyu ji*, as the people of Kang 康 are here said to write horizontally. I believe that the authors of the *Xin Tangshu* are not describing the contemporaneous situation, which is probably due to a lack of knowledge, similar to the calendrical problem, which is discussed below. Yoshida proposed that the – gradual – change from horizontal to vertical writing is probably to be dated to the latter half of the fifth century and may have been influenced by the Chinese way of writing. He stressed, however, together with Henning, that the horizontal writing of Sogdian script seems to have been continued, especially in Manichaean and Christian scriptures.[379] In my opinion, the quote from the *Xin Tangshu* – being compiled much later – is either using older information, or, as Yoshida stressed in the mentioned cases, this may be another piece of evidence that Sogdians continued to also write horizontally.

The style of the *Xin Tangshu* also includes direct speech of Emperor Taizong 太宗, famous for his inclusive policies and rhetoric[380] – generally often quoted in this work – instead of narrating the earlier emperors' thoughts. Taizong's 太宗 dissatisfaction with the general situation, is however, quasi identical to the *Weishu*. The only difference is that while the *Weishu's* emperor saw no benefit (*yi* 益) to be gained, the *Xin Tangshu* says that the emperor "despised obtaining empty names and hurt the common people", which is a very literary fashion of self-flattery and alleges that he cared for the common people. Continuing in the same style, the passage on the state of An 安 includes one noteworthy detail – again providing the Emperor Taizong 太宗 the opportunity of direct speech: After defeating the Western Tujue 突厥, he reassured him that *the merchants* were free to travel again. As a result, *all the hu* 胡 were said to have been overjoyed and thus equivocates *hu* 胡 and *merchants*. In this rare case,

379 Henning, "Mitteliranisch," 56; Yoshida Yutaka, "When did Sogdians". Yoshida simply forgot to mention the passage of the *Xin Tangshu* in his article (private communication).

380 See: Abramson, *Ethnic Identity*, 14547.

however, the interest of the emperor for exotics and commerce seems to be combined with the joy of the foreign merchants.

The *Xin Tangshu* omits the Brahmin mentioned in the *Jiu Tangshu*, which are now replaced by the mention of a fire deity temple, where rituals are performed that are qualified as deceitful tricks. Further, the year is said to start in the twelfth month. For clarity, the information concerning the beginning of the year (before the Arab conquest) is combined with the statements about ritual activities in the table below.[381]

Table 1:Chinese sources about ritual activities and the calendar in Sogdian states

Source	*Weishu* (also *Suishu*, *Beishi*, *Tongdian*)	*Suishu* (and *Beishi*, corrupt, *Tongdian*)	*Xifan ji* (*Tongdian*)	*Jiu Tangshu*	*Xin Tangshu*
State	Kangguo 康國	Shiguo 石國	Kangguo 康國	Kangguo 康國	Kangguo 康國
Ritual activities, beliefs	Law books in the Heaven Deity temple		Heaven Deity	Water splashing for winter (11th month)	
			King for a day (at the beginning of the year)		
			Disappearance and search for bones of the deity's son (7th month)		

381 Cristoforetti added further quotes concerning regions further west and after the Arab conquest (Compareti and Cristoforetti, *New Elements*, 621).

	Ancestral sacrifices (6th month)	Ancestral sacrifices, centred around the king's bones (6th day of the 1st month, 15th day of the 7th month)[382]			
	Buddhism			Buddhism	Buddhism
Calendar			Beginning of the year: 1st day of the 6th month	Beginning of the year: 12th month	Beginning of the year: 12th month

As the Sogdian new-year starts in summer, it is probable that the authors and/or editors of the *Jiu Tangshu* and *Xin Tangshu* were misinformed.[383] A new addition is also made in the description of the state of Shi 史 (Kesh): Its city has a temple of a deity in which for each sacrifice, a 1,000 sheep must be offered and that before going to war, they hold a prayer. This does, however, bring to mind the aforementioned quote from the *Jing xing ji* contained in the *Tongdian* in which the idea of a Zoroastrian state ritual before going to war may have been described: It is said there that in the state of Kang 康 (Samarqand), they have a temple of a deity called *xian* 祆 and that all state affairs originate here. While the city is different, the ritual seems to have been the same, which does not exclude that it was copied from one account to the other.

Finally, the passage on Ishitikhan, which is entitled the state of Western Cao 曹, deserves some attention. Firstly, as it starts by saying that "Western Cao 曹 was called Cao 曹 during the Sui", we can affirm that this refers to the *Suishu* – the same as the references to the *Weishu* are introduced as "during the Wei". After a short situation of the state, the deity Dexi 得悉 is introduced in the *Suishu*, while in the *Xin Tangshu* it is further said that its temple was located in north-east, in Yuegandi 越于底 (Kurgantepe?). While the *Suishu* says that the deity was represented by a human gold statue, matched by an extremely large gold *poluo* 破羅 (*piyāla?*) below it, and goes on to exaggeratedly describe the offerings, the *Xin Tangshu* completely alters this part. It says: "There is a golden object, which says on its left side: "Donated during the Han by the Son of Heaven." While I do propose that such a precise information about an

382 The *Beishi* omits the 15th day of the seventh month.

383 Marshak also believed that the beginning of the year in the 12th month is mistakenly attributed to the Sogdians. He proposed that it may refer to the Julian calendar, used by Christians in Sogdiana (Marshak, "Historico-Cultural," 150–51). Cristoforetti proposed that the authors mistook the great celebration of *Nīmhab* for a new-year celebration (Compareti and Cristoforetti, *New Elements*, 621).

inscription relating to the Han may have been newly collected from somewhere, I also firmly believe that it is incorrectly added in this place. Strongly supporting this theory is that the passage is no longer referring to a gold statue and extremely large gold *poluo* 破羅 (*piyāla?*), as in the *Suishu*, but only to a diffuse golden object. This deletion probably due to *poluo* 破羅 being a transcription of a foreign word while the object that was donated by the Han emperor could never have been described by a transcribed term in the *Suishu*. Furthermore, the *poluo* 破羅 (*piyāla?*) was said to have been 4.6 m large, which is probably not an object which could have been transported and offered. It is thus quite clear, that, while there is new information about a donated object, the inscription and a detail of the object of this passage were conceivably amalgamated to make sense with the new information – with the result that the other information on the offerings was sacrificed by the editors of the *Xin Tangshu* in its stead.

1.15.13 Identifying toponyms, surnames, Sogdians, and Sogdiana

While more specific explanations concerning toponyms of single states were organised in the glossary, what has been left out in the analysis above are the various names and surnames, which are best dealt with in a synthetic overview. Traditionally, Sogdians were in academic studies mostly identified through their surnames, which may refer to their place of origin, with the help of the above-mentioned transmitted sources. As we have seen above, the accounts of the *Shiji* and *Hanshu* do not provide a toponym that can be identified with Sogdiana with certainty[384] but describe the customs of the people living in the region. The *Weishu*, reconstructed with the help of the *Suishu*, *Zhoushu* and *Beishi*, provides more information and explain that the newly introduced state of Kang 康 succeeded to Kangju 康居, which is, however, a fictive etymology. It is said that their Kings were surnamed Wen 溫 and stemmed from the Yuezhi 月氏. After being defeated by the Xiongnu 匈奴, they allegedly moved westwards from Zhaowu 昭武, in present-day Gansu Province, crossed the Pamirs, and established a new kingdom in what is commonly defined as Sogdiana, i.e. ca. Transoxania. While this region may in earlier times have been occupied by the Yuezhi 月氏, there is no evidence to support the people's movement from present-day Gansu, and there is no mention of a connection between the city of Zhaowu 昭武 and the Yuezhi 月氏 anywhere.[385] This part is thus to be certainly qualified as a pure construction by the Chinese authors: The Sogdians did not stem from the Yuezhi 月氏 and did not come from Gansu.[386] If not referring to the city located in present-day Gansu, what does Zhaowu 昭武 stand for? As Yoshida proposed in his overview of this 200-year old question, "Zhaowu 昭武" is to be found in the names of some

384 For Suxie 蘇薤, see below.

385 Enoki Kazuo, "Sogdiana," 589; *apud*: Shiratori Kurakichi, "Über den Wu-sun-Stamm," 106 ff.

386 See: Yoshida Yutaka, "On the Origin," 589; *apud*: Shiratori Kurakichi, "Study on Su-t'ê," 102–03. This myth is hard to die in China (although being criticised: Chen Haitao, "Zhaowu," 140), as can be seen by a recent article: Xu Xuya, "Sute".

Sogdian kings in the seventh century and means "jewel".[387] He further supports the idea, proposed by Shiratori, that it can either refer to a title or the name of a legendary hero (Siyāwuš/Siyāwaxš, son of Kai Kawūs).[388] Their origin, as constructed in the Chinese works, is thus either to be seen as a pursuit of ancient Chinese authors to generally trace foreign people back to China, which may have led them to choose Gansu, during their time populated by many Sogdians.

Further, the *Weishu* provides a list of nine countries, said to be subjects to Kang 康. These altogether ten are said to have had the surname Zhaowu 昭武 in order to show that they did not forget their origin. If this is to mean that they thereby remember coming from present-day Gansu, it is certainly incorrect. It could, however, also indicate that they referred to themselves as Zhaowu 昭武, and thereby wanted to remember their stemming from a legendary hero. Later, the *Tongdian* is the first to combine both statements, introducing *the count* of nine: nine countries were of the same clan as Kang 康. The account then provides the same list of countries as the *Weishu*, the *Suishu*, and the *Beishi*. The *Suishu* and *Beishi* did, however, include two countries, Mu 穆 (Amul?) and Cao 漕 (Kāpiśī), in their description of the Western Regions, erroneously saying that these were subject to Kang 康 and part of the Zhaowu 昭武 Clan. Next in line, the *Jiu Tangshu* only provides a description of Kang 康, in which it is laid out how the sons of the ruler of Kang 康 where installed as suzerains of Cao 曹 and Mi 米. Finally, the *Xin Tangshu* provides a new and different listing: Kang 康 is listed together with eight names of countries, which together were called the *Nine Surnames*. While some names of countries used in earlier listings are excluded, new ones are added. Besides that, an extended list of related countries is provided.

As can be observed, there seems to have been some confusion concerning the listing and counting of countries in the Western Regions, especially those related to Kang 康. The number nine first explicitly appeared in the *Tongdian* to describe countries and is then used in the *Xin Tangshu* to list surnames or clan names. It is probable that "Nine Surnames" is a fixed locution, which referred to the countries contemporaneously known or related to Sogdians during the Tang. The description of the Dami 呾蜜 is thus to be applied to all Sogdian states:[389]

> 華人皆以國名之。
>
> The Chinese use their state to name them.

The historiographers thus tried to rationalise *a posteriori* to fit the number. This is corroborated by some of the quoted Nine Surnames, Wudi 戊地 and Huoxun 火尋, for example, not being known as a Sogdian surname (a similar problematic exists for the 16, or 36 countries of the Western Regions). Other surnames which are known to

387 Yoshida Yutaka, "On the Origin".
388 Shiratori Kurakichi, "Study on Su-t'ê," 103.
389 See p. 69 fn. 352 (1.14.15).

have been used by Sogdians, were however not listed: He 賀 (an unclear geographical reference),[390] Xun 尋 (assumed to be the same as Huoxun 火尋, Khwārizmik),[391] Luo 羅 (Tocharistan?),[392] and maybe Xin 辛 (another unclear geographical reference).[393]

As can be further seen in the table below, the number nine was widely used in relation to Sogdians.[394]

Table 2: Counting hu 胡

Name in source		Literal translation
jiu xing	九姓	Nine Surnames[395]
jiu xing hu	九姓胡	Nine Surnames *hu* 胡[396]
liu zhou jiu xing	六州九胡	the Nine *hu* 胡 of the Six Prefectures[397]
jiu xing fu liu hu zhou	九姓府六胡州	the Nine Surnames of the Six *hu* 胡 Prefectures[398]
jiu fu liu hu zhou bu luo	九府六胡州部落	the Nine Surnames (*fu* 府) of the Six *hu* 胡 Prefectures tribes[399]
jiu xing shang hu	九姓商胡	Nine Surnames merchant *hu* 胡[400]
jiu xing guo	九國胡	Nine Countries *hu* 胡[401]
Xiyu jiu guo	西域九國	Nine Countries of the Western Regions[402]

The authors seem to have had some kind of fixation on the number nine, as in other contexts evidenced in the list of nine different countries of the Western Regions in the *Beishi*,[403] or in relationship with Uighurs, which are often referred to as having nine

390 Ikeda On, "Hasseiki chūyō," 601.
391 Luo Feng, "Liuyu Zhongguo," 30.
392 Ikeda On, "Hasseiki chūyō," 601; Yoshida Yutaka, "Sino-Iranica," 378.
393 Ikeda On, "Hasseiki chūyō," 601.
394 The table is based on: Pulleyblank, "Sogdian Colony," 322, 33738; Yoshida Yutaka, "On the Origin," 42; and: Enoki Kazuo, "Gisho," 11–12.
395 Listed together with other people sending their envoys to "present tribute", among them the state of Kang 康 and Mi 米 (altogether not nine): *Cefu yuangui* 972.11415b. Not to be confused with the nine names correlated to the Uighurs and Tujue 突厥.
396 *Zizhi tongjian* 218.6997 (commentary), twice in: 226.7282; and thrice in: 226.7287–88.
397 On the stele of Cang Huailiang 藏懷亮, recorded in the *Quan Tang wen*, in reference to the rebellion of 721 CE: *Quan Tang wen* 265.15a.2693a.
398 *Zizhi tongjian* 218.6986, 6997.
399 *Jiu Tangshu* 120.3451, *Xin Tangshu* 137.4600.
400 A description of An Menwu 安門物 of the Wuwei 武威 Prefecture. *Jiu Tangshu* 10.245; and: *Zizhi tongjian* 219.7015.
401 Used in the account of the victory of Li Siye 李嗣業 in 751 CE over the Tujue 突厥 and Sogdians: *Jiu Tangshu* 109.3298.
402 *Xin Tangshu* 221b.6252.
403 *Beishi* 97.3205–6. 太延中，魏德益以遠聞，西域龜茲、疏勒、烏孫、悅般、渴槃陁、鄯

tribes and names, while sometimes it also refers to Tujue 突厥.[404] In some rare cases the term "*hu* 胡 of the Nine Surnames" *jiu xing hu* 九姓胡, is also synonymous with *zazhong hu* 雜種胡 (mixed *hu* 胡), which, however, conceivably refers to people of mixed foreign background, e.g. of Turk and Sogdian parents.[405]

As to the problem of relating the toponyms with the surnames, Pulleyblank concluded that Mi 米 was the only surname that could help to identify an individual as of strictly Sogdian origin, although An 安 and Kang 康 quite reliably designated Sogdians during the Tang dynasty with their family name referring to their place of origin.[406] This claim has, however, probably been falsified by the epitaph of a self-identified Uighur with the surname Mi 米.[407] It is further important to point out that Uighurs or descendants of Sogdians and Turks demonstrably took Sogdian and Sino-Sogdian names.[408] In the process of identification, it is thus imperative to combine the family name with additional information, such as given names, explicitly stated chrononyms and places of origins in epitaphs, and archaeological context, to safely identify a person as Sogdian or of Sogdian descent.[409]

While it was shown that some of the *content* provided in the separate passage devoted to Sogdiana in earlier works was later integrated in the description of the state of Kang 康, a final question that needs to be addressed are the *terms* that seem to directly refer to Sogdiana and the confusion linked to it. The *Hou Hanshu* qualifies Liyi 栗弋 as a dependency of Kangju 康居. The *Sanguozhi* then lists Kangju 康居 in the countries of the Western Regions, the commentary however also containing the state of Zhuyao 屬繇 (or Juyao), which may be identified as Sogdiana. The *Jinshu* says that Suyi 粟弋 borders on Kangju 康居. The *Weishu* and *Zhoushu* provide the name Sute 粟特, which is also called Wennasha 溫那沙 – actually referring to the surname of the kings of Kang 康 – and is falsely conflated with Yancai 奄蔡 – actually referring to the Alan 阿蘭 and Liao 聊. The *Beishi* reintroduces Sute 粟特. Further, in the *Da Tang Xiyu ji*, Xuanzang 玄奘 uses the name Suli 窣利, and the *Tongdian*

善、焉耆、車師、粟特諸國王始遣使來獻。太武以西域漢世雖通，有求則卑辭而來，無欲則驕慢王命，此其自知絕遠，大兵不可至故也。若報使往來，終無所益，欲不遣使。有司奏：「九國不憚遐險，遠貢方物，當與其進，安可豫抑後來？」乃從之。於是始遣行人王恩生、許綱等西使。恩生出流沙，為蠕蠕所執，竟不果達。又遣散騎侍郎董琬、高明等多賫錦帛，出鄯善，招撫九國，厚賜之。初，琬等受詔：便道之國，可往赴之。琬過九國，北行至烏孫國。

404 There is even a self-defined example: the epitaph of Li Zhonglang 李中郎 (Zhang Xishun, *Sui Tang Wudai muzhi, Shaanxi 1*, 127).

405 Pulleyblank, "Sogdian Colony," 351; against the opinion of Chen Yinke: Chen Yinke, *Tangdai*, 23.

406 Pulleyblank, "Sogdian Colony," 320–23.

407 Apparently a practitioner of Manichaeism: Yang Fuxue, "Da Tang".

408 Tremblay, *Pour une histoire*, 23, fn. 36.

409 For practices concerning the given names, see: Ikeda On, "Hasseiki chūyō"; and: Weber, "Zur sogdischen". For a short overview of the discussion, see also: Yoshida Yutaka, "Personal Names, Sogdian".

reintroduces Suyi 粟弋, which is also said to be called Sute 粟特 (and Tejumeng 特拘夢, which is however erroneous).

As was pointed out before, the lists in several of the accounts include a categorical confusion, as the different countries of Sogdiana are listed together with Sogdiana. To answer the problem of what these terms refer to, Shiratori and Enoki in their magisterial studies disentangled the different factors which may have led to these confusions, which I cannot restate in full length in this paper and thus content myself to paraphrase their conclusions:[410] The terms used in the *Hou Hanshu* (Liyi 栗弋) and *Jinshu* (Suyi 粟弋) refer indeed to Soghd, whereas the *Weishu* (Sute 粟特) refers to Kušānī as the representative of the state of Soghd. All names from the Tang designate an area that approximately corresponded with those of the countries of Kang 康, Mi 米, Cao 曹, An 安, He 何, and Shi 史. Suli 窣利 of Xuanzang 玄奘 represents, however, an exception in the Tang records, as its account neither corresponds to the contemporary description of Soghd nor to the Sogdiana of Western writers. It

> extended on the north as far as the Ču river, comprising the northern foot of the Alexander Mountains, Ferghāna, Taškent, and Xodjend to the north of the Jaxartes;[411] on the other side of the river, it embraced all the basing of the Zarafšān and the Kaška, having its southern limit, however, at the mountain range of Derbend. The space between Derbend and the Oxus, it did not include (…).[412]

Then there is the term Suxie 蘇薤. The *Shiji* and the bamboo slips mention Kangju 康居 and Suxie 蘇薤 as two different polities that both sent envoys to China. The *Shiji* – as was discussed – erroneously locates Suxie 蘇薤 east of Ferghana. The *Hanshu* lists Suxie 蘇薤 as the title of one of the petty kings of Kangju 康居 (subject to the latter), with a dwelling of the same name. The *Jinshu*, most certainly relying on the *Hanshu*, claims that Suxie 蘇薤 was the seat of the king of Kangju 康居, while Kangju 康居 is mentioned as bordering Suyi 粟弋. It is possible that the *Jinshu* mistook one of the petty kings of Kangju 康居 for *the* king of Kangju 康居 because it was mentioned as the first in the list of petty kings in earlier accounts. Finally, the *Xin Tangshu* says that Shi 史 (also said to be alternatively called Qusha 佉沙 or Jieshuangna 羯霜那, which is to be identified as Kesh), is at the ancient location of the Suxie 蘇薤 Fort of a petty king of Kangju 康居 – a claim probably relying on the *Hanshu*. Therefore, besides the confusion of the earlier texts, it seems as if Suxie 蘇薤 and the capital of Shi 史 (Kesh) were *a posteriori* conflated by the editors of the *Xin Tangshu*, trying to attribute to every petty kingdom of the *Hanshu* one Sogdian kingdom of their time.[413]

410 Shiratori Kurakichi, "Study on Su-t'ê"; preceded by the Japanese version: Shiratori Kurakichi, "Sogudo". For a linguistic stance on the Name of Sogdiana, see: Szemerényi, *Four*, 260 (Enoki Kazuo, "Sogdiana," 449, 612). Their studies include far more material, sometimes, however outdated. See also the critical notice by Pelliot: Pelliot, "Les publications," 365.

411 Ču is also written Chu, Shu, Chui, or Chuy, and refers to the Sūyāb river.

412 Shiratori Kurakichi, "Study on Su-t'ê," 143.

413 Yu Taishan tried to rationalise the conflations of the *Xin Tangshu* by correlating the distances given in the *Hanshu* and the Tang polities (Yu Taishan, "Saka History," 106–7) while adding

Marquart provided the Arabic sources to the debate, pointing out that al-Yaʿqūbī (ninth cent.) recorded in his geography a list of cities in the northern part of the province Balkh including Dar-i Āhanīn (Iron Gate, *tie men* 鐵門), Kesh (Shi 史), Nahsaf (Lesser Shi 史), and an unknown city named Soghd, which may have resulted from a misunderstanding.[414] Further, al-Yaʿqūbī included Dabusiya, Kushaniyya (He 何), Kesh (Shi 史), and Nahsaf (Lesser Shi 史) as belonging to Soghd. Ibn al Faqih (tenth cent.) further wrote in a commentary: "Soghd, i.e. Kesh". Marquart therefore proposed that Suxie 蘇薤 may be the Chinese transcription of Soghd, and that these sources point towards Kesh being once considered as capital of Soghd, a suggestion reproduced by Chavannes.[415] Pulleyblank continued this discussion by providing some phonological attempts to connect these two words.[416]

Overall, it becomes clear that since the Han, misunderstandings about the terms Sogdiana and Kesh existed – first in Chinese sources and then in Arabic sources. Partly, this situation was the result of categorical confusions which provoked a conflation of collected misunderstood names and city-states, which was reinforced by the compilation process of editors who desired to correlate sources of different time periods. Although I find Marquart's theory tempting, I doubt that further hypothetical linguistic reconstructions will shed more light in the future on this scene and hope that not yet excavated and/or published texts may provide contemporary pieces of information.

1.15.14 Categories of description and judgement

Patterns of information that can be used to establish categories emerge from the lecture and analysis of the accounts. One possible categorisation is presented in the table below, further differentiating between more descriptive and strongly judgemental content.

Table 3: Information and judgments on Sogdians and Sogdian states in Chinese accounts

Description	Paired Judgments
1. Climate, flora, fauna, agriculture, and products	
1.1 Climate, flora, and agriculture	

linguistic hypotheses. While I do understand that it is tempting to retrace the logic behind the conflation of the *Xin Tangshu*, the arguments he proposed, especially the linguistic ones, are highly speculative, however. I further do not see the necessity to underpin the conflations of the *Xin Tangshu* in the present state of information, as such an argument would be too speculative to build future political, ethnic, or linguistic argumentations on it.

414 Marquart, *Chronologie*, 57; Marquart, *Ērānšahr*, 303–4.

415 Chavannes, *Documents*, 146, fn. 3.

416 Pulleyblank, "Consonantial 2," 219–20.

(Samojian 颯秣建:) climate moderate	customs fierce
(Liyi 栗弋:) mild climate	
(Liyi 栗弋:) water and soil excellent, famous for grape wine	
(Samojian 颯秣建, Kang 康:) fertile soil	
(Samojian 颯秣建:) plentiful harvest	
(Samojian 颯秣建:) forests dense	
(Kangju 康居:) paulownias, willows	
(Samojian 颯秣建:) flowers luxurious	
(Samojian 颯秣建:) luxurious fruits, (Liyi 栗弋:) all sorts of fruits, (Sezhixian 色知顯, Husimi 呼似密:) many of the Five Fruit, (Jiabudan 伽不單:) Five Fruit, (Shi 石:) various fruits	
(Suyi 粟弋:) large grain, over 30 cm high, seeds like broad beans	
(around Dayuan 大宛, Liyi 栗弋, Fuhuo 副貨, Suye 素葉 River Fort, Suyi 粟弋:) grapes	
(Jiabudan 伽不單, Shi 石, Suye 素葉 River Fort:) millet	
(Jiabudan 伽不單, Shi 石, Suye 素葉 River Fort:) wheat	
(Fuhuo 副貨, Kang 康:) Five Crops	
(Kang 康:) vegetable gardens and trees	
(Suli 窣利:) half farmers, half merchants	
(Dayuan 大宛, Daxia 大夏, Anxi 安息, and the other states:) people cultivate land	
1.2 Fauna and agriculture	
(Xiwanjin 悉萬斤, Husimi 呼似密:) lions	
(Fuhuo 副貨, Kang 康, Cao 曹:) camels	
(Fuhuo 副貨, Kang 康:) mules	
(Liyi 栗弋, Suyi 粟弋:) cattle	
(Kang 康:) bumped cattle	
(around Dayuan 大宛:) heavenly horses, (around Dayuan 大宛, Shi 石:) many fine horses, (Liyi 栗弋:) famous horses, (Fuhuo	

副貨, Cao 曹:) horses, (Samojian 颯秣建:) many excellent horses, mighty horses, (Suyi 粟弋, Kang 康:) excellent horses	
(Liyi 栗弋, Cao 曹, Suyi 粟弋, Shi 史:) sheep	
1.3 Products	
(Dayuan 大宛, Daxia 大夏, Anxi 安息, and the other states:) rich in unusual products	
(Mimi 迷密, Kang 康:) gold	
(Mimi 迷密:) jade	
(Mimi 迷密:) much iron	
(Husimi 呼似密:) silver	
(Husimi 呼似密:) amber	
(around Dayuan 大宛, Liyi 栗弋, Kang 康:) wine, (Suyi 粟弋:) choice wine	
(Kang 康:) sal ammoniac	
(Kang 康:) true spikenard scent	
(Kang 康:) *asana* scent	
(Kang 康, Shi 石:) precious stones	
(Kang 康:) roebuck skin	
(Kang 康:) woollen rugs	
(Kang 康:) brocades	
(Kang 康:) cotton	
2. The king and his wife, the palace and throne, inner politics and legislature	
2.1. The king and his wife	
Various names of kings, family history, contact and politics in relation with other people (Tujue 突厥 and Arabs)	
(Kang 康:) brave king	
(Kang 康:) Their king's crown is a felt hat, decorated with gold and jewellery	

(Kang 康:) Their king has plaited hair, a crown with all kind of jewellery and golden flowers, and wears garments of thin silk, silk gaze, brocade, embroidered cloth, and white cotton cloth.	
(Kang 康:) His wife has her hair in a topknot, veiled by a black cloth.	
(Kang 康:) Women/the king's wife (?) wind their hair in a topknot, use a black cloth to cover it, and decorate it with gold flowers.	
2.2 The palace and throne	
(An 安:) City wall with five stories, surrounded by a stream; flat roof	
(Fuhuo 副貨, Bukhārā?) golden palace under which are seven golden camels, each ca. 1 m high	
(An 安:) Golden camel throne, 207–36 cm high	
(He 何:) Golden sheep throne	
Inner politics and legislature	
(Kang 康:) mighty state	
(Kang 康:) small state	
(Kang 康:) Three chancellors handle the politics of the state together	
(An 安:) Every time the king attends to governmental affairs, he sits opposite of his wife, and together with the chancellor(s), they decide on national affairs.	
(Kang 康:) There is a code of law of the *hu* 胡, placed in the Zoroastrian temple. To pass sentence, they retrieve it and decide the penalty. Description of the punishments.	
3. People and customs	
3.1 Women	
(west of Dayuan 大宛 to Anxi 安息:) women held in respect	women held in respect (?)
(west of Dayuan 大宛 to Anxi 安息:) men take decisions on the advice of women (King?)	men take decisions on the advice of women (King?)

3.2 Men

(Suli 窣利:) Clothes made of woollen cloth, upper garments of leather and felt, lower garments short and tight. They adjust their hair so as to reveal the top of the head or shave it all off. They bind a coloured silk band around their foreheads.	
(Kang 康:) Men (envoys?) have their hair cropped short and clothe in brocade robes.	
(Suli 窣利:) traditional teaching method without loss	
(Kang 康:) teaching boys at the age of five to write	
(Kang 康:) sending the boys early off to commerce	
(Kang 康:) when sons turn 20, they come to China	wherever profit lies they have gone
(Kang 康:) usually they learn how to write the *hu* 胡 script	

3.3. Physiognomy (of men)

(between Dayuan 大宛 and Anxi 安息, Kang 康:) deep-set eyes	
(between Dayuan 大宛 and Anxi 安息, Kang 康:) profuse beards	
(Kang 康:) high noses	
(Suli 窣利:) large stature	coward of will

3.4 Military/military abilities

(Middle Cao 中曹:) people tall and large	skilled in war and combat
(Shi 石:) excel in fighting	
(Dayuan 大宛, Daxia 大夏, Anxi 安息, and the others:) militarily weak	
(Mi 米, Shi 史, Cao 曹, He 何:) hundreds or thousands of elite soldiers	
(Samojian 颯秣建:) Soldiers and horses mighty and magnificent, many are *čākar*, fierce elite soldiers that have no fear of death.	
(An 安:) strong and brave are recruited as *čākar*, i.e. warriors	

3.5 Commerce

(Kang 康:) excellent merchants	
(west of Dayuan 大宛 to Anxi 安息, Kang 康:) skilful in commerce, excellent merchants	haggle over a fraction of a cent
(Kangju 康居 of the Han, Sogdiana?:)	lying, disguise their political motives
(Kang 康:) obtaining larger profits is considered positive	
(Kang 康:)	When a son is born, they put hard honey in his mouth for sweet talk and glue on his hand to grasp money in future
prize Han goods and wealth	
(Sogdiana:) half farmers, half merchants	
(Kang 康:) place for commerce among barbarians	
(Kang 康:) sending the boys early off to commerce	
(Kang 康:) when sons turn 20, they go to China	wherever profit lies they have gone

3.6 Agriculture and products

(See above)	

3.7 Technology

(Samojian 飒秣建:) ingenious crafts, highly regarded artisans	
No silk, lacquer, or knowledge of casting	

3.8 Wedding, mourning, and burial

(Kang 康:) Weddings and mourning similar to those of the Tujue 突厥	
(An 安:) Customs similar to those of the state of Kang, but do not marry their older or younger sister, or mother…	…as the beasts of the air and ground do. This is

	considered abnormal.
(Kang 康:) burial practices: specialists outside of the capital, breeding dogs to eat their flesh, collection bones, buried without coffins	
3.9 Other cultural aspects	
(Kang 康:) Fond of music	
(Kang 康:) Fond of wine, like to sing and dance on the street	like to sing and dance on the street (?)
(Kang 康:)	When a son is born, they put hard honey in his mouth for sweet talk and glue on his hand to grasp money in future
(Suli 窣利:)	highly covetous, even between father and son they seek profit
(Suli 窣利:)	highly regarded to possess wealth, among good and lowly alike
(Suli 窣利:)	even when immensely rich, they clothe themselves and eat meanly and lowly
(Suli 窣利:)	treacherous
(Suli 窣利:)	swindle
(Samojian 薩末建:) people are rich	
(Kang 康:) Wine is cherished and stored by rich families over years without going off	
(Kang 康:) Writing direction: horizontal	

(west of Dayuan 大宛 to Anxi 安息:) different languages but mutually understandable	
(Kangju 康居 of the Han, Sogdiana?:)	lack etiquette
(Kangju 康居 of the Han, Sogdiana?:)	barbaric
(Kangju 康居 of the Han, Sogdiana?:)	arrogant
(Suli 窣利:) large stature	cowardly of will
(Kang 康:) The behaviour in virtue and propriety of the people of Samarqand is imitated near and far	
(Kang 康:) All *hu* 胡 countries consider Samarqand as their centre	
3.10 Musical instruments	
(Kang 康:) large drums	
(Kang 康:) small drums	
(Kang 康:) pipa 琵琶	
(Kang 康:) five-stringed lute	
(Kang 康:) harp	
(Kang 康:) drums for rituals	
3.11 Rituals	
(Kang 康:) make offerings to the Heaven Deity	
(Kang 康:) offer to the Zoroastrian Deity	
(Kang 康:) temple with a deity called *xian* 祆 from which all state affairs originate	
(Kang 康:) Ancestral temples, in which they sacrifice to the ancestors in the sixth month, every state contributes to these sacrifices	
(Shi 石:) Southeast of the capital is a house with a seat in it. On two certain dates, the king's parents cremated remains, bones, are placed in a golden urn and then placed on a bed. They have a ritual and then feast together with officials	
(Cao 曹:) In the state there is the deity Dexi 得悉, represented by a human gold statue with a very large golden *poluo* 破羅 (*piyāla*?). Every day, five camels, ten horses, and 100 sheep are	

offered to it. Often there are 1,000 people eating it without being able to finish.	
(He 何:) East of the city stands a storied building, on its northern wall are painted the ancient emperors of China; on the eastern wall, the rulers of the Tujue 突厥 and Brahmin, and on the west wall, of Persia (Iranians) and Byzantium. Its lord goes there to worship every morning and then retires.	
(Shi 史:) In its city is the temple of a deity in which for each sacrifice, 1,000 sheep must be offered. Before going to war, they first pray.	
(Kang 康:) The Buddhist *dharma* is widespread, believe in Buddha	
(Kang 康:) Brahmin study the stars to determine fortune and misfortune	
(Kang 康:) On the 1st day of the 6th month is the beginning of the year, new clothing, cutting of hair and beards, shooting competition, king for one day	
(Kang 康:) in the 7th month, bones of the deity's son are lost and searched	
(Kang 康:) in the 11th month drums and dancing, winter prayers, water splashing	
4. Foreign Affairs	
4.1 General statements	
the rulers of the Western Regions knew themselves far away and out of reach of large armies	humbled themselves when in need, but neglect the orders of the emperor when not in need
nine translations to reach people of strange customs, so that the emperor's might would become known to all the lands within the four seas	
A Sogdian was used by the Western Wei as envoy to the Tujue	
Sogdian rulers send their sons as hostages	
4.2 Gifts foreign envoys bring to court	
(Western Cao 曹, Shi 石, Shi 史:) local products	

(Kang 康:) dwarves	
(Kang 康, Mi 米:) *hu* 胡 twirl (dance) women	
(Suyi 粟弋:) fine horses, (An 安:) excellent horses, (Eastern An 安:) horses	
(Mimi 迷密:) black camel	
(Eastern An 安:) *panthera*	
(Shi 史:) patterned leopard (cheetah)	
(Kang 康, Mi 米:) lion	
(Kang 康:) golden and silver peaches, planted in the imperial garden	
(Kang 康:) ostrich eggs	
(Kang 康:) precious cloth	
(Mi 米:) (fire-marten/long-furred marten) dance carpets	
(Eastern An 安:) two large carpets	
(Eastern An 安:) one embroidered carpet from Zhepi 柘辟 (?)	
(Eastern An 安:) two Persian and one Byzantine embroidered carpets	
(Eastern An 安:) tulip scent	
(Eastern An 安:) hard honey	
(Kang 康:) coats of mail	
(Kang 康:) crystal bowls	
(Kang 康:) agate jars	
(Mi 米:) jade	
4.3 Gifts Chinese envoys bring to court	
(Shi 史:) female dancers	
(Shi 史:) lion skin	
(Shi 史:) fur of the fire-marten	
(An 安:) multicoloured salt	

As already discussed above, the negative judgments made of the people of Sogdiana stem from references to the earliest passages describing the people west of Dayuan 大宛 to Anxi 安息 which were integrated in the separated passages for Sogdiana. These commentaries stand in stark contrast to the positive statements made about the people of various Sogdian states, until the *Jiu Tangshu* and *Xin Tangshu* omitted the passage on Sogdiana and partly integrated these earlier commentaries in the description of the state of Kang 康. These descriptions and judgments *generally* made of Sogdians are thus transmitted from a critique on partly non-sedentary people that are culturally and geographically clearly defined as Others. Due to the compilation process of Chinese writings, which puts emphasis on the classically Chinese referral to ancient literature that is meant to provide authority to one's own writings, they were, however, integrated in later accounts of Sogdian states. It is in this aspect that I differ from Abramson's analysis on the Othering process. On the basis of his reading, Abramson defined groups of stereotypes that were attributed to Western foreigners, which he understood as *hu* 胡.[417] As he showed, by quoting positive as well as negative criticism, the Chinese-centred narration created lines along which the definition of the Other and the Self can be recognised. While inspiring in his refreshing approach on Chinese literature, he did, however, open the door to the very generalisations he criticises by understating some of the problems related to the literary compilation process and confusions occurring in it – such as the just mentioned – and the overestimation of the actual impact of such thoughts on society as well as, inversely, how many of these comments are reflective of the contemporaneous society. Further, the categories he defined do not self-evidently derive from the material but are superimposed on it to fit in his goals and methodology – and therefore strengthen his argument. In contrast, I propose that the categories shown above and the differentiation between more descriptive and judgemental statements emerge rather naturally from the content and thus follow more closely the mindset in which these accounts were redacted. The result is that we can work with categories that do produce less conflicts than would otherwise have arisen, by avoiding as much as possible the danger of an anachronistic conceptualisation, with the downside of being less disruptive and controversial.

417 First the "unarticulated" stereotypes, i.e., *hu* 胡 drinking (17–20), erotic dancers and singers (20–21), illiteracy (21–22), physical strength and warriors (22), merchants and tavern owners (22); then the "articulated" stereotypes, i.e., treachery (23–27, 34–37, 40–41), bestiality, combined with a close relation to and skill with animals (27–33), straightforwardness (38–40), savagery and ignorance (41–43), greed (43–45), credulousness and amazement (45–46), bloodthirstiness, skill in warfare, military prowess (46–49), and courage (51) (Abramson, *Ethnic Identity*). See also: Abramson, "Deep Eyes, Constructing Ethnicity," 132–88.

Chapter 2: Sources about Sogdians in China

2.1 Introduction

After having established how Sogdians in Sogdiana were named and described outside of China, the next step consists in gathering information on their presence in China by combining transmitted and contemporaneous literary sources and excavated material evidence. To clarify the nomenclature used in the following, while a Sogdian in Sogdiana does not need to be further identified as such, the individuals that are called *Sogdian* hereafter are mostly either immigrants or descendants of immigrants and do thus not necessarily share a Sogdian identity.

The first part of this chapter presents a case-study of the graves of the Shi 史 families excavated near Guyuan 固原, Ningxia 寧夏 Province. The second part presents all epitaphs of Sogdians in China from an archaeological context. The third part compiles the information from the first and second parts and combines them with other contemporaneous sources and archaeological evidence.

2.2 Graves of the Shi 史 in Guyuan 固原, Ningxia Province

> Let's talke of Graves, of Worms, and Epitaphs,
> Make Dust our Paper, and with Raynie eyes
> Write Sorrow on the Bosome of the Earth.
> Let's chuse Executors, and talke of Wills :
> And yet not so ; for what can we bequeath,
> Save our deposed bodies to the ground?

Shakespeare
Histories: The life and death of Richard the Second, 35

2.2.1 Introduction

Guyuan 固原, located in present-day Ningxia Province, was part of the administrative area of Yuanzhou 原州 during the fourth to seventh centuries. It was one of the last strongholds in the north, with the Great Wall located directly north of it. At a height of 1300 to 1900 m above the sea, the valley in which it lays, carved by the Qingshui 清水 River into the soil of the arid loess plateau, is one of the main channels between the capital and the northern regions and was an important stage on the Silk Road, as the excavation in recent years have proven.[1]

The graves of the Shi 史 families are located in what then was called the Baida 百達 Plain, used for burials since the Western Zhou (Vol. 2, Appendix 1.1, Figures 1, 2).[2] They belong to a group of large graves dated to Northern Dynasties, Sui, and Tang, that have been discovered there since the 1980': the graves of Yuwen Meng 宇文猛 (d. 565 CE),[3] Li Xian 李賢 (d. 569 CE),[4] Tian Hong 田弘 (d. 575 CE),[5] and the seven graves of the Shi 史,[6] together with the grave of Liang Yuanzhen 梁元珍 (d. 699 CE), and the graves 87M1 and 82M2. These two latter graves are not separately analysed hereafter, as they were found empty, but are taking into consideration in the analysis. Based on their vicinity, they may have been connected to the graves of the Shi 史 families.

According to the epitaphs found in the graves of the Shi 史, the buried individuals could be identified as descendants of Sogdians (see Chapter 2.3). As only six other graves excavated in China can be attributed to Sogdians, they represent an important basis for the archaeological study of Sogdians in China. As was already mentioned in the introduction, most of the articles concerning Sogdians in the past have focused on extraordinary objects found in other graves while some few include quotes from the Shi's 史 epitaphs. Besides the language barrier existing for scholars in the Iranian studies, the graves lack extraordinary finds, such as a richly decorated stone sarcophagus found in other graves, and what is more, the excavations – with the exception of the grave of Shi Daoluo 史道洛, excavated much later by a joint team of Chinese and Japanese archaeologists – were not documented in the detail one would wish for. The relationship between the graves and the deceased is, however, most interesting and still not well studied. The reports are critically presented in the second volume (Appendix 1) – some mistakes were corrected and confusions were resolved as far as possible – and the results are analysed below.

2.2.2 Graves

For the excavation reports of the graves of Shi Shewu 史射勿, Shi Hedan 史訶耽 and his wives lady Kang 康 and Zhang 張, Shi Daoluo 史道洛 and his wife lady Kang 康, Shi Tiebang 史鐵棒, Shi Suoyan 史索嚴 and his wife An Niang 安娘, and Shi Daode 史道德, see Vol. 2 Appendix 1.

1 For more information about the geological context, see: Yuanzhou lianhe kaogudui, *Tang Shi Daoluo mu*, 4–5; for the historic context of this region, see: ibid., 5–6.
2 Guyuan xian wenwu gongzuozhan, "Ningxia Xi Zhou mu". Excavations furthermore show signs of human activity since the Neolithic (Luo Feng, *Guyuan nanjiao Sui Tang mudi*, 3, fn. 4).
3 Ningxia wenwu kaogusuo Guyuan gongzuozhan, "Guyuan Yuwen Meng mu"; and: Ningxia wenwu kaogu yanjiusuo and Geng Zhiqiang, *Ningxia Yuwen Meng mu*).
4 Ningxia huizu zizhiqu bowuguan and Ningxia Guyuan bowuguan, "Ningxia Li Xian fufu mu".
5 Yuanzhou lianhe kaogudui, *Bei Zhou Tian Hong mu.*
6 Luo Feng, *Guyuan nanjiao Sui Tang mudi*; Yuanzhou lianhe kaogudui, *Tang Shi Daoluo mu.*

2.2.3 Analysis

It is impossible to make reliable statements and/or interpretations about sets and composition of the graves in their entirety due to their looted state and the scarcity of the remaining wall paintings. Regarding the size and construction of the graves, they were all built with a dromos, shafts, tunnels, sometimes niches,[7] a corridor built of bricks, one or two bricked walls and/or a stone or wood door, a burial chamber – sometimes built of bricks – and a funerary platform – built of earth, bricks and earth, or stone slabs. On top of the burial chamber was piled a *tumulus*, made of layers of stamped earth. This structure is typical for larger graves in Northern China from the Northern Dynasties to the Tang. Due to their structure and size – and if available, epitaphs – they were attributed to members of the upper society.[8] Among those, an overall length of ca. 27 to 42 m, with what probably were *tumuli* of a diameter of over 20 m, and up to seven shafts and tunnels, the Shi 史 graves are of an impressive size. To properly evaluate the relative size, the graph presented below was made by using information about the tomb construction and measures of contemporaneous local graves, to be found in Table 8 (Volume 2, Appendix 1.8.1).

Three groups were defined geographically, ranging from the Northern Zhou to the Tang (with the great majority of graves in the latter): Group A includes the graves north of the Mayin 馬飲 River – on the then so-called Baida 百達 Plain (including the grave of the Shi 史) – Group B was found on the north foot of the Jiulong 九龍 Mountain, south of the river, and Group C is about 1.5 km north-west of group B and 1.5 km north-east of Group A, also north of the river (Figure 211, Vol. 2, Appendix 1.8.1). The graves in group A were excavated in the course of several campaigns,[9] whereas Group B[10] and C[11] were excavated in 2003 and 2004 in two campaigns, due to the construction of a motorway. To size their importance, axis X represents the "complexity", and the axis Y the overall length on the graph below. The complexity is evaluated on a scale from one to seven, based only on the construction of the tomb, i.e. without considering the grave goods.

7 Already attested in some graves of the Northern Wei (see M2 of Xinji 新集, Pengyang 彭陽: Ningxia Guyuan bowuguan, "Pengyang Xinji mu"), becoming more common during the Northern Zhou.

8 For an overview of tomb structures in graves during the Six Dynasties in Northern China, see: Dien, *Six Dynasties Civilization*, 80–114.

9 The grave of Yuwen Meng 宇文猛 (d. 565 CE; Ningxia wenwu kaogusuo Guyuan gongzuozhan, "Guyuan Yuwen Meng mu"; and: Ningxia wenwu kaogu yanjiusuo and Geng Zhiqiang, *Ningxia Yuwen Meng mu*); the grave of Li Xian 李賢 (d. 569 CE; Ningxia huizu zizhiqu bowuguan and Ningxia Guyuan bowuguan, "Ningxia Li Xian fufu mu; the grave of Tian Hong 田弘 (d. 575 CE; Yuanzhou lianhe kaogudui, *Bei Zhou Tian Hong mu*); the grave of Shi Daoluo 史道洛 (d. 655 CE; Yuanzhou lianhe kaogudui, *Tang Shi Daoluo mu*); the grave of Liang Yuanzhen 梁元珍 (d. 699 CE; Luo Feng, *Guyuan nanjiao Sui Tang mudi*, 112–35); and the graves 87M1 and 82M2 (ibid., 85–86, 96–103).

10 Ningxia wenwu kaogu yanjiusuo, *Guyuan Jiulongshan muzang*.

11 Ningxia wenwu kaogu yanjiusuo, *Guyuan nanyuan mudi*.

Table 4: Factoring grave characteristics

Bricked wall(s), door(s), and other characteristics	Factor
Bricked wall and wood door, two side chambers	7
Two bricked walls and stone door	5
Bricked wall and stone door	4
Wood door	3
Two bricked walls	3
Bricked wall	2
None	1

To this factor is added another factor, measuring if the grave had a funerary platform, and of which kind – as it is considered as part of the construction rather than of the grave goods.

Table 5: Additional factor accounting for the funerary platform

Funerary platform	Added factor
stone slabs	2.5
bricks and earth	2
earth	1
none	0

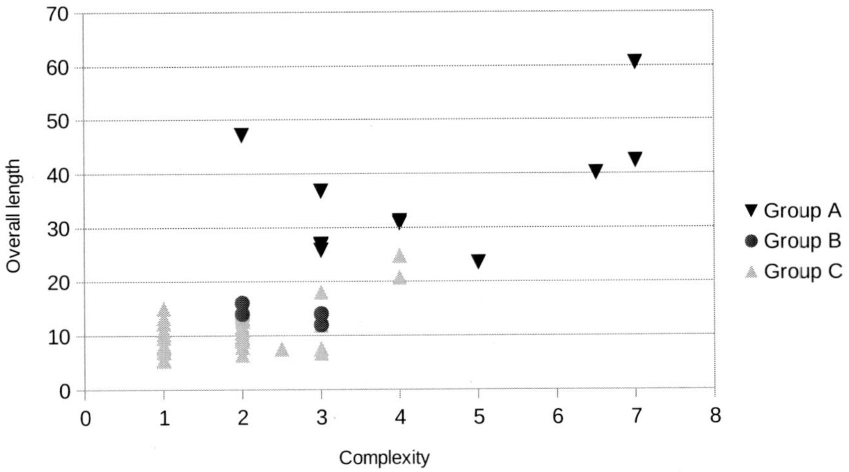

Figure 2: Overall length and complexity of graves west of Guyuan 固原
Source: M. Huber; see Vol.2, Table 8, Appendix 1.8.1

The graves of Group A are generally longer and more complex than those of the other groups. Group B lies in between Group A and C. M34 and M38 of Group C are the exception, although still located on the lower edge of Group A.[12] Based on this data, it can be proposed that Group A – located further away from the city and main valley than the graveyard of Group B – was a cemetery reserved for the largest and most complex graves, while the remaining finds in the graves – not detailed here – further corroborate this conclusion: the Baida 百達 Plain was a cemetery for the well-to-do.[13] This conclusion would have been probably reinforced if all the small graves found during the campaigns of Group C would have been excavated. From 83 identified graves, 71 were excavated. From these, five were dated to the Han, and 66 to the Sui and Tang. Among these Sui and Tang graves, only 40 large graves were analysed in the excavation report, which provide the data Group C.[14]

In archaeological reports in China, structures or finds between the surface and the dromos or burial chamber have been widely neglected – partly a result of the importance of stratigraphy only gradually finding its way into Chinese archaeology, and also due to the lack of information about structures on the surface. The social context in which these graves were constructed remains rarely commented on. Before building such a grave, the family not only needed important sums to finance the construction as well as the order and deposit of objects of value into the deceased's grave, but first required to identify a suitable location that needed to be bought or was already owned, which had to be maintained and reserved for this use. This may have

12 The two upwards pointing triangles in the middle of the graph, attributed a complexity of four.

13 Past comparative research tried to establish a relationship between the rank of the deceased and the number of shafts. It was, however, based on a rather small sample of graves near the capital, and further needs an update and a critical approach to the topic of ranks and their fuzzy relationship to wealth and the concepts of "status", or "elite". Furthermore, the capital and its graves – often taken as point of reference – are not immediately representative for Guyuan 固原, especially if most larger graves of the latter were robbed. See: Filip, "Kulturhistorische Einordnung," 98–100; Jörg, "Grabkultur bei Xi'an"; Sun Binggen, "Xi'an Sui Tang muzang"; Qi Dongfang, "Xi'an diqu Tangdai muzang"; Su Bai, "Xi'an Tang mu xingzhi".
Probably due to the scarcity of finds in Guyuan 固原, Luo Feng tried to establish a connection between the remaining height of the *tumuli* and the rank of the deceased (according to literary regulations), which is, in my opinion, is only acceptable as a last resort, as it is difficult to judge the environmental, human, and other major influences affecting these mounds of rammed earth on the surface in ca. 1,300 years' time (without calling the measurement methods into question: Luo Feng, *Guyuan nanjiao Sui Tang mudi*, 138–39). Wertmann, in his translation of the excavation reports of Luo Feng, went a step further and compared the *tumuli* of Guyuan 固原 with *tumuli* in Taiyuan 太原, to conclude for the case of Shi Hedan 史訶耽: "Comparison with more or less contemporary tombs of high-ranking people of different nationalities suggests that Shi Hedan held a fairly high status in society" (Wertmann, *Sogdians in China*, 40).

14 The exact dating had to be checked individually again, as, e.g., in grave M38 an epitaph was excavated, dated to the Northern Zhou, the excavators however dated the grave into the Tang: Ningxia wenwu kaogu yanjiusuo, *Guyuan Jiulongshan muzang*, 96. Furthermore, one grave was apparently built for the burial of two goats and can be excluded.

represented the major financial burden (and value) – especially near the capital, or in prestigious cemeteries, like this one.

Further, ash pits before the tumulus have often been left uncommented on. These were most probably the result of sacrifices. In front of the tumulus – that is on the south side – of the grave of An Jia 安伽 (d. 579 CE) were many ash pits dated to the Tang, with one large pit on the foot of the tumulus.[15] On the foot of the tumulus of the grave of Shi Daoluo 史道洛 was also an ash pit, in which were found many porcelain pieces dated to the Song. In both cases, we can hypothesise about the continuous maintenance of the grave and/or the performance of rituals.

The orientation of the graves and of the deceased has further rarely been commented on. As can be seen in the Table 9 (Vol.2, Appendix 1.8.2), the great majority of the graves of Sogdians in China are laid out from south to north (entering from the south), while the grave of An Pu 安菩 (An Pusa 安菩薩) represents the exception to the rule. Together with the orientation, the archaeological context of a site is of great importance for its study, but has been noticed only in a side comment for the graves near Chang'an 長安. In their case, the Longshou 龍首 Plain was indeed one of the important burial sites for the high society, east of the city. As can be seen for the case of master Shi 史, the larger graves with a dromos in its vicinity are oriented west, north, and south (Figure 214, Vol. 2, Appendix 1.8.2).

Among the graves near Guyuan 固原 (Figures 211–13, Vol. 2, Table 8, Appendix 1.8.1), all of Group A are entered from the south, whereas in Group B and C, the orientation differs. In Group B, all but grave M4 (and not contemporary M5), further downhill, are oriented uphill, around the foot of the mountain.[16] In Group C, all but grave M5 (and the Han graves M31, and M37), are oriented north. Instead of translating such observations into elements of a *Weltanschauung* or ritual logic – in my opinion – there is a pragmatic explanation to this. If the grave is built on a hill slope, graves are oriented – in the great majority – uphill. This reduces the effort and the digging time, while the dromos does not have to be as steep. In the case of the surrounding of master Shi's 史 grave, the terrain is flat, which may account for the various orientations of the graves and may thus be used as a good starting point for reflections on a possible underlying ritual logic for future studies.

The orientation of the deceased in the graves also defies the archaeological quest for a deeper meaning. Although most of the remains were displaced, the funerary bed or platform shall be considered as a reliable indicator for the orientation of the deceased. As can be seen in Table 9 (Vol. 2, Appendix 1.8.2), no pattern is to be discerned. Quite on the contrary, even in the same family (Shi 史 of Yuanzhou 原州(1)), in a time span from 610 to 671 CE, the deceased laid in their graves oriented in

15 Shaanxi sheng kaogu yanjiusuo, "Xi'an beijiao An Jia mu," 28, 29, fig. 2; or: Shaanxi sheng kaogu yanjiusuo, *Xi'an Bei Zhou An Jia mu*, 6, 7, fig. 2.

16 See: Ningxia wenwu kaogu yanjiusuo, *Guyuan Jiulongshan muzang*, 5, fig. 2. Even M16 and M33, which are both oriented north-west, are oriented uphill, as the foot of the mountain has a bump.

different directions, and there were different types of combinations between the burial chamber and the corridor (*tu* 凸-type and *dao* 刀-type graves). The last descendants of the two Shi 史 families, Shi Tiebang 史鐵棒 and Shi Daode 史道德, had *dao* 刀-type graves, and their bodies were both oriented south-north. Based on this material, a change of burial patterns in such a short time seems unlikeable.

Few wall paintings of the probably richly painted graves remain. In the grave of Shi Shewu 史射勿, some of the paintings in the intersections in between the shafts and tunnels, and the paintings on the side walls of the dromos did not crumble from the walls. The intersections are painted with a building – identified in other graves as a watchtower – floral décors, and in the case of Shi Suoyan 史索嚴, a vermilion bird, looking towards the visitor to the grave. These motifs have been seen in other graves of the well-to-do, as has been shown.

The funeral cortège proceeded from the south entrance of Shi Shewu's 史射勿 grave into the 14-meter-long dromos (for an impression see Figure 4, Vol. 2, Appendix 1.2.5): although some of the individuals have already crumbled to the floor, a row of attendants, holding ceremonial swords, are turned towards the incoming deceased, waiting solemnly. Judging from their facial features, all of them are Central Asians, more exactly – as indicated by the Chinese clothing and ceremonial swords – Central Asians with a military rank in the Chinese bureaucracy. The fourth pair of discernible persons, equally Central Asians with the same red outer garment and white inner garment, are turned towards the entry of the chamber, with a ritual tablet held in front of their chest, in a second step, preparing to enter the burial chamber. The last depicted pair of persons in the row are probably the servants, bowing respectfully in the direction of the people advancing down the dromos towards the burial chamber, one in red, the other one in white clothing. Flanked by these individuals, while going down the dromos, one cannot but notice over the passages the paintings of the watchtower building and further down a floral design.

As mentioned above, one intersection in the grave of Shi Suoyan 史索嚴 is decorated with the vermilion bird, the Chinese cosmological creature representing the direction south, probably also fulfilling an apotropaic function. While it is often depicted on the south side of the burial chamber, in this case, it is to be found on the north side of the intersection, looking south.

Moving into the burial chamber, female servants providing music (or simply instruments?) and gifts are depicted on the west wall of the chamber of Shi Shewu 史射勿. As has already been mentioned, the composition reminds of the painting in the rear burial chamber of the grave of prince Yide 懿德.

Stone carvings were an integral part of the pictorial programme of the graves, mostly painted in bright colours and sometimes even gilt. They decorated the stone door, pillars, the epitaphs, and the burial platforms. The motifs of the stone doors of Shi Hedan 史訶耽 and Shi Suoyan 史索嚴 can be differentiated into five groups, which are combined in different arrangements: vine scrolls, pearl roundels, large flowers, creatures, and humans. Although the leaves of the vine scrolls in sculptures along the Silk Roads have been long debated and variously defined either as acanthus, wine, or half-palmettes (maybe deriving from acanthus leaves), sometimes with honeysuckle, it is generally rather difficult to trace the direction of influences apart from painting in broad strokes. These motifs have been found in variations from the Mediterranean up to China, where they begin to appear as vine scrolls during the Eastern Han, probably influenced by Western motifs.[17] Some hundred years later, the scrolls then became firmly established as part of the artistic vocabulary of the Pingcheng 平城 period of the Northern Wei.[18] The scrolls with large leaves, partly found on the epitaphs and doors of the Shi 史 graves, are typical of the style of the Northern Zhou and Qi. Concerning the pearl roundels, Luo Feng and Compareti proposed that these motifs travelled from the Iranian world to Central Asia in the fifth century CE, then to Sogdiana in the seventh century, and thus via Turfan 吐魯番 and Dunhuang 敦煌 into China.[19] Pearl roundels lined up in a row and arranged symmetrically are, however, a Chinese variation. The finds near Guyuan 固原 are among the few which were found during the Tang, at a time for which the finds of pearl roundels diminish.

All the creatures found on the door of Shi Hedan 史訶耽, in the pearl roundels in the lintel of Shi Suoyan 史索嚴, or in the lunettes of both doors, stem from a Chinese background, except for the prancing horse in the lintel of Shi Hedan 史訶耽. Luo Feng proposed to establish a parallel between the winged horses found in Iranian and Sogdian depictions.[20] However, whereas all the other creatures, i.e., the beast head, the pair of vermilion bird, the beasts, and even the large flowers (see below), are to be located in a symbolical realm, this horse is atypical: it is depicted prancing before a background of small clouds, representing the wind, placed inside a pearl roundel, and has no wings.[21] As much as the famous heavenly horse (*tianma* 天馬) of the west may have been sung about, Western horses in pearl roundels are normally depicted as standing, attacked by a feline, or mounted by a rider performing a Parthian shot, or winged and standing.

The display of large flowers arranged in a row found on the lintel of Shi Hedan's 史訶耽 door can be seen in the contemporary grave of Lou Rui 婁睿 (d. 592 CE), however without pearl roundels and the ornaments being Buddhist in style (Figures 219, 220, Vol. 2, Appendix 1.8.4).[22] Outside of the funerary context, large flowers inside pearl roundels, even with similar triangular spacings, were found in the Mogao

17 Rawson, *Chinese Ornament*, 35. For the Eastern Han, see: See: Gu Sen, *Zhongguo Han hua tudian*, 890.

18 Bush, "Floral Motifs," 75–79.

19 Luo Feng, *Guyuan nanjiao Sui Tang mudi*, 73–77; Matteo Compareti, "The Role of the Sogdian Colonies". See also: Guan Youhui, "Mogaoku Suidai tu'an," 28–34.

20 Luo Feng, *Guyuan nanjiao Sui Tang mudi*, 73–77.

21 No facsimile of the lintel is available, and the drawing itself is inconclusive. If the horse has wings, they are minuscule.

22 Shanxi sheng kaogu yanjiusuo and Taiyuan shi wenwu kaogu yanjiusuo, *Bei Qi Luo Rui mu*, 77, fig. 63.2.

莫高 cave 401, dated to the middle to the end of the Sui (Figure 221, Vol. 2, Appendix 1.8.4).[23] The main difference between the flowers of the cave and the grave of Lou Rui 婁睿 are, however, the number of petals. Whereas Shi Hedan's 史訶耽 flowers have seven petals, the typically Buddhist flowers have eight petals. If the flowers in Shi Hedan's 史訶耽 grave are thus to be qualified as Buddhist, or even only as lotus – as Luo Feng likes to describe it – or should rather be seen as one of the decorative floral motifs to chosen from at the stonemason's shop will however be left open to hypothesises of art historians. The combination of the Western pearl roundels and these motifs is, however, clearly to be traced back to a Western import. Instead, however, of focussing on single details, more weight should be given to its context, as such combinations were flexible in their composition and popular graves of that time. To illustrate how similar compositions in Central China were during the same time, the stone door in the grave of Duan Jianbi 段蕳壁 (d. 651 CE) provides a striking example (Figure 222, Vol. 2, Appendix 1.8.4). Likewise, the guards on the door leaves of Shi Hedan 史訶耽 are widely to be found.

Besides these stone objects, a broken stone base (from Shi Daoluo 史道洛) that may have been on the surface, and an octagonal stone pillar (from Shi Suoyan 史索嚴) have been found. The pillar found in the nearby grave 82M2 is providing excellent comparative material, which, judging from the construction and few remaining finds, can be dated from the Northern Dynasties to the Sui (Figures 223, 224, Vol. 2, Appendix 1.8.4) and may have once contained the remains of a family member. It is an octagonal stone pillar (H 87 cm, Dia 33 cm, each face W 16 cm), made of dark limestone and broken into three pieces. On one end is a square tenon, damaged. Each surface is engraved with a background depicting a large acanthus scroll, in between which figures are placed in symmetrical pairs: foxes, beasts, rams, cranes, and dancing children with a necklace and pendant, having large bangles on wrists and ankles.[24] Although all three graves were disturbed, stone fragments of this size do not move around easily. Judging from the alleged location of the fragments in grave 82M2 (Figure 225, Vol. 2, Appendix 1.8.4), and the missing rest of the stone base found in the grave of Shi Daoluo 史道洛, it is rather safe to advance that these stone fragments were fragments of larger objects, and even sets of objects, of which the rest was stolen. Larger objects were also often broken into pieces in the grave to be transported, and/or sold separately by grave robbers. It is likewise possible that the pillar in grave 82M2 probably broke apart while being dragged to the robber's shaft. Based on similar finds of bases and pillars, they were probably part of a canopy's stand, with a pillar made of stone, or a wood construction, with a cloth, under which probably other burial goods were placed (Figures 226, 227, Vol. 2, Appendix 1.8.4).[25]

23 From: Luo Feng, *Guyuan nanjiao Sui Tang mudi*, 76.

24 See: ibid., 98–103.

25 As seen in: Dien, *Six Dynasties Civilization*, 203–5. See also the articles from which the facsimiles were taken, and: Lu Zhaoyin, "Liang Han Wei Jin de weizhang".

The epitaphs and their cover stones were equally carved. They were placed in the dromos, the corridor leading to the burial chamber, and/or at the entry inside the burial chamber. Covered with beasts and directional symbols, their position in the points of passage was probably apotropaic. As can be seen for the Shi 史 in Guyuan 固原, the epitaph cover stones were decorated with established Chinese elements, that is scrolls of different kinds (as discussed above, these were already imported since the Han), the four directional creatures in front of clouds and mountains, other beasts or beast heads around the sides, the twelve zodiac creatures, two sort of string motifs, and overlapping leaves.

The epitaphs of the Shi 史 can – according to their composition – be divided into three groups: the cover stones of Shi Shewu 史射勿, Shi Daoluo 史道洛, Shi Suoyan 史索嚴, and An Niang 安娘 form the first group, judging by the engraving executed in deep relief on a dark limestone, the scrolls, creatures, clouds, mountains, overlapping leaves, and strings (see Figures 215–18, Vol. 2, Appendix 1.8.3). From this group, the epitaphs of Shi Suoyan 史索嚴 and Shi Daoluo 史道洛, which were both buried in January 659 CE, show a nearly identical composition. The second group include the cover stones of Shi Hedan 史訶耽 and Shi Tiebang 史鐵棒, both buried in January 671 CE. They have also a nearly identical composition, defined by their simple decoration and large leaf scrolls (one with four leaf scrolls, the other with three on each side), equally on dark limestone. Third, Shi Daode's 史道德 epitaph, buried in November 678 CE, is different in all aspects. The cover stone is of a rarely seen reddish limestone, the decoration is engraved in lines and not in deep relief, and the script is entirely different. Further, the epitaph stone is recycled. Based on these few epitaphs, it is reasonable to conclude that the preferences of the motifs and composition were probably the result of the choice and style of a local workshop, as the two families chose nearly identical stones for burials in the same month.

One may come to a similar conclusion when looking at the décor of the cover stone of Lord Yu Hong 虞弘. While it is one of the only three graves containing epitaphs in which was found Zoroastrian imagery (see p. 288; 3.3.11.1), his epitaph cover stone shows rather Buddhist motifs.[26] The side of the epitaph and the cover stone were decorated with large vine scrolls with palmettes. The bevelled side of the cover stone has on its four corners and in the middle of the four sides a lotus with a "diamond". This lotus is on a background of are clouds, representing the domain of heaven. The inscription on top is surrounded by flowers, which, due to their eight petals and axial symmetry, may well be described as lotuses. There are different ways in which this phenomenon could be explained: 1) Yu Hong 虞弘 was besides his Sogdian religious background interested in Buddhist teachings, 2) these motifs were also flexibly used by people of other backgrounds – as the carvings on the few stone funerary beds and

26 Not to mention the four rings that were fixed into the top of it. Some epitaphs were found with these rings, but there is not yet research available on them, besides their alleged function of lowering the cover on the epitaph, and the context.

sarcophagi of Sogdians available to us implement many Buddhist-looking features[27] – or 3) due to his burial in Taiyuan 太原 – being a major centre of Buddhism where those symbols may have become unrelated from the Buddhist teachings – epitaphs were probably engraved with this décor without much Buddhist symbolism and rather to be related to current styles and workshops.

Finally, the length of the inscription, and therefore the size of the epitaph, is however relative to the size of the grave and the official rank recorded on the epitaph. Shi Shewu 史射勿 was in his life a fairly important personality, but had a smaller grave and much shorter epitaph, which is probably related to him being buried in the Sui.

Regarding the finds of ceramics, at least two pots of different sizes were excavated that probably contained food, i.e. grain – as was found in one of the pots of Shi Daode 史道德. The lidded and multi-lugged vessels – in the case of the Shi 史, four in number – the "spittoon", and the long-necked vase were typical for their time. The same goes for the high stemmed *compotes*, rendered in gilt bronze and porcelain.[28] These, and other plates of bronze or porcelain, combined with spoons and ladles of bronze, were equally used to present food.[29]

The singular find of an ink rubbing stone made of porcelain in the grave of Shi Suoyan 史索嚴 is remarkable. Although typical in style for its time, the symbolic importance of the object needs to be emphasised. Rubbing stones are often qualified as the most important – and most resilient in the face of time – of the Four Treasures of the Study (*wenfang si bao* 文房四寶), together with the brush, paper, and ink – tools that are the objectification of the Chinese scholar.

Another very Chinese addition to the grave of Shi Daoluo 史道洛 are the large apotropaic guardian figures. Due to their function, they were placed at the sides of the entrance and are far larger than other figurines and miniatures. The standing warriors are typical in their depiction, wearing cord, plaque armour (*mingguang* 明光), and helmet.[30] They probably once held a spear, halberd, or sword and a shield (now absent), resembling in expression a *lokapala,* although missing the typical pose of the raised arm. The human guardians are accompanied by two beasts, sitting on their haunches. As Dien laid out, these guardian beasts evolved since the Han – resembling unicorns or rhinoceroses – to the later appear as beasts with spikes in the north. There also emerged the doglike creature with a human face. They typically form a pair, one with a beast face, and one with a human face.[31] As can be seen in comparison with counterparts in graves nearby, these examples are masterpieces, well balanced in their

27 Or depictions of Zoroastrian deities in Buddhist conventions.

28 See: Li Zhiyan, "Zhi ciye de chengjiu," 59–60; from, and also for further discussion: Dien, *Six Dynasties Civilization*, 233–51.

29 See also: ibid., 251–56.

30 Dien describes this type as "cuirassiers". See: Dien, "Early Chinese Armor," 33–36, fig. 36. See also: Karg, "Grabkultur der Nördlichen Qi-Zeit," 429.

31 Dien, *Six Dynasties Civilization*, 208–12. See also: Karg, "Grabkultur der Nördlichen Qi-Zeit," 433–36.

composition, sturdy, and fear inducing. In the nearby grave M1 from Nanyuan 南塬 near Guyuan 固原 (Group C), the same set has been found, i.e., two standing armoured human warrior guardians, squatting beasts, one with a human face and the other a beast face (resembling an ape). In detail, quality, and refinement, they are far inferior and the warriors seem malnourished in comparison. They stand on a small flat base and are overall smaller in size.[32] The standing armoured guardian warrior found in grave M36 stands with one foot on a sheep on a large base and shouts out, the most impressive by far, but remains still slender in comparison.[33]

In the grave of Shi Daode 史道德, gilt bronze was used to compose a chin strap, which was combined with a perforated multi-piece face mask. The latter had probably been originally sewn onto a piece of fabric. Very similar chin straps were found just in the vicinity, at the foot of the Jiulong 九龍 mountain (Group C), in the grave M16 (in silver) and M33 (in gold). The use of face masks may be traced back to the movement of an old Han-Chinese custom attested since the eighth or ninth century BCE into cemeteries in Tarim in the third century BCE. Chin straps made of fabric are, however, already attested for the eighth century BCE in present-day Xinjiang Uighur Autonomous Region. The earliest *metal* chin straps were found in the graves of wealthy non-Han Xianbei 鮮卑 of the Northern Wei. Only starting from the Tang, some ethnic Han made use of these in their burials.[34]

Another remarkable feature of these graves are the remains of head-dresses. These were formed by combining hair needles of bronze and/or jade, bronze wires, glass and bronze flowers with glass beads, little animals made of bone (and sometimes amber), and beautifully formed floral patterns made of bronze plates with décor worked in repoussé. The employed techniques came over the Silk Road – partly boosted by the reception of Buddhist prototypes – and gradually developed into an individual Chinese style during the eighth century.[35] An impression of how they may have looked is given by the reconstruction of the head-dress of Li Chui 李倕 (d. 736 CE, Figure 228, Vol. 2, Appendix 1.8.4). The reconstruction did, however, omit the animals and dancers made of bone that were found in the grave.

Other remaining clothing objects include belts, i.e. especially the hooks and some of the rectangular and round plates. They represent an important feature of steppe fashion since the first millennium BCE. How such a belt set may have looked – without the diverse objects that could be attached to it – may be imagined with the help of the better preserved jade and gold belt sets of the grave of Emperor Yang 煬 of the Sui (d. 522 CE),[36] and Ruogan Yun 若干云 (d. 578 CE; Figure 229, Vol. 2,

32 Ningxia wenwu kaogu yanjiusuo, *Guyuan Jiulongshan muzang*, 23, fig. 6A, 24–28, 26–27, figs. 6C, D, colour pls. 9.1–8, 10.1–8.

33 Ibid.: 93, 94, fig. 33B, colour pl. 29.1–3.

34 Müller, "Chin-Straps".

35 Filip, "Kulturhistorische Einordnung," 108–23.

36 See: Nanjing bowuguan, Yanzhou shi wenwu kaogu yanjiusuo and Suzhou shi kaogu yanjiusuo, "Jiangsu Sui Yangdi mu"; and: Liu Sizhe, "Sui Yangdi mu jinyudai".

Appendix 1.8.4).[37] If the bone plates found in the graves were part of a belt (imitating jade?), of a head-dress or crown, or of a pendant, is difficult to say, as they were not perforated.

Besides these and apart from nails and some unidentified rods, one of the other typical metal objects deposited into the grave were iron scissors, a daily life object.[38]

The foreign silver and gold coins, and imitations of coins, present us with more puzzling questions.[39] They clearly stem from a Western background, and went through a life of their own, probably including different uses. The function as *post-mortem* currency is readily proposed by numbers of researchers: as part of the world which once stood under Hellenistic influence, it represented the *obol* to pay Charon in the underworld. It is quite probable that over distance and time, such a payment method would have been altered to pay local deities of the netherworld. Most importantly, as some were imitations and as *bracteate* often perforated, they were taken out of circulation long before they found their way as symbolic currency into the grave – if they ever used as actual currency. The coins may also have been used as lucky charm during lifetime, a sign of recognition, or simply as decorative *bracteates* on clothing or as part of a headdress. Besides these, Chinese coins have also been found in the graves of Sogdians in China and left mostly uncommented on.

To examine possible patterns, all coins in graves of Sogdians were filled in Table 11 (Vol. 2, Appendix 1.8.5). Regarding the situation of the coins in the graves of the Shi 史 families, we know only for Shi Daode 史道德 that the imitation of the Byzantine gold coin was found in his mouth with certainty. In the other graves, it is probable that they were placed in the mouth, given that they laid on the platforms on one end – except for Shi Daoluo 史道洛, were it lay in front of the platform, on one end, the grave being however heavily disturbed. As only some of the coins were perforated, the alternative function as part headdresses seems unlikely, but can still not be dismissed. In four of the graves were discovered *kaiyuan tongbao* 開元通寶 coins, from one to 16 pieces.

To compare these with the nearby Tang graves of Group B, in grave 2004 YKJ M4,[40] a single female individual had a Byzantine silver coin with two perforations located near her head, and in grave 2004 YKJ M33,[41] the male and female held hands,

37 The example is taken from: Dien, *Six Dynasties Civilization*, 328–29; *apud*: Yuan Anzhi and Shaanxi sheng kaogu yanjiusuo, *Zhongguo Beizhou*, 69–70, fig. 149, pl. 173. For a short overview of the history of personal adornments, including belt hooks and plates, see: Dai Junliang, Liu Baoquan and Zou Yilin, *Zhongguo gujin diming - shang*. See also generally the latter for a terminology and history of this sort of belt and further: So, "Belt Ornaments and Fasteners".

38 Dien pointed out that the amount of iron grave goods does not give justice to the role of iron objects in daily life (*apud*: Bronson, "Transition to Iron," 180). Although this comment concerns graves of the Six Dynasties, it equally applies to Sui and Tang graves (Dien, *Six Dynasties Civilization*, 259). For a short discussion of iron in grave goods of the Six Dynasties, see: ibid., 256–60.

39 See also: Lin Ying, "Sogdians".

40 See: Ningxia wenwu kaogu yanjiusuo, *Guyuan Jiulongshan muzang*, 114, figs. 45, 46.1, colour pl. 41.3.

41 See: ibid., 128–29, figs. 51, 52.4, colour pl. 47.3.

in between which was placed a Byzantine gold coin with one perforation – which means that they were probably buried at the same time.[42] Twenty-four of the Sui and Tang graves of group C had coins in them: four graves with only *wuzhu* 五銖 coins (two to three) in the hands of the deceased, 19 graves with *kaiyuan tongbao* 開元通寶 coins (one to seven) – of which 14 probably in the hands of the deceased, two graves with the coins maybe in mouth and/or hand – one grave with one Sasanian silver coin, maybe in the mouth, together with two *kaiyuan tongbao* 開元通寶 coins in the hands, and finally three graves for which it is impossible to determine where the coins were originally deposited.[43]

To further include the other graves of Sogdians in China, in the grave of Kang Ye 康業, a Byzantine gold coin laid in the mouth and one *buquan* 布泉 coin in the right hand. In the grave of An Pu 安菩 (An Pusa 安菩薩), one Byzantine gold coin was found in the right hand of the woman (?),[44] and both individuals each held one *kaiyuan tongbao* 開元通寶 coin in their left hand.

Overall, whether there were one or more individuals, only a single foreign coin (or its imitation) was found per grave. Mostly imitations, only two of these coins were made of silver, the other seven of gold (including the special case of a gold imitation of a silver coin), either intact or perforated once or twice. In most cases, they were placed in the mouth, except for An Pu 安菩 (An Pusa 安菩薩), as mentioned above. Regarding the Chinese coins, either *wuzhu* 五銖,[45] *buquan* 布泉 (worth five *wuzhu* 五銖, 561–76 CE), or after 621 CE *kaiyuan tongbao* 開元通寶, were given into the graves. They were deposited either in small numbers or mostly placed in the hand and sometimes in the mouth of the deceased. Although the data is not extensive enough to confidently call it representative, it is rather safe to say that the Byzantine or Sasanian foreign coin – preferably gold, but also silver – was preferred for the deposition in the mouth.

42 While it does not affect his general argumentation, Selbitschka's erroneous statement concerning the position of the coin in grave M33 – besides this not being the grave of a single female – as well as the omission of the fact that some of the coins in the other graves were not perforated, results in the dismissal of his suggestion that the *solidi* found in the graves near Guyuan 固原 were part of a burial custom in which they were utilised for headdresses instead for the payment of Charon. Further, Sasanian iconography in a headdress is not enough evidence to support that the deceased "retained their native religions", with which he refers to Zoroastrianism and it is unclear to what other "other Zoroastrian imagery he is referring to. Finally, the Shi 史 of Guyuan 固原 were not part of the same family (Selbitschka, "Genuine," 38).

43 This is my enumeration based to the excavation reports (Ningxia wenwu kaogu yanjiusuo, *Guyuan Jiulongshan muzang*, passim). The excavators themselves have a different enumeration: ibid., 129.

44 I propose to identify her as woman, based to the figurines of female servants and tablet with little boxes in her coffin, as for the other individual had figurines of horses with riders in the coffin.

45 They were used in different minting styles from the end of the second century BCE to the Sui, and as the excavation report does not give an analysis and I am not qualified enough in numismatics to propose my interpretation, I will simply propose that these, judging from the graves, are to be dated into the Sui.

Thierry convincingly pointed out the persistence of practices providing the dead with rice and jade (*fanhan* 飯含), cowries, pearls, and depositions of coins in the graves, for different reasons, which may be hypothesised about based on the textual sources.[46] He states, however, that it was only in the graves in the Western Regions, and especially in Astana, that coins were deposited in the mouth of the deceased, and sometimes on the eyes. This seems to have been a Central Asian or even purely local tradition. The placement of coins in the mouth became popular in all of China only since the Song and is according to him unrelated.[47]

Xia Nai proposed a different theory, explaining that after cowries were used since the Neolithic in China,[48] there is ample evidence for their placement the mouth of the deceased since the Zhou.[49] According to him, these were then replaced by copper coins in the Qin and Han, and from then on became established practice. Often, even two coins were placed in the mouth. Why, however, the little jade animals – probably meant to be placed in the mouth to "feed" the deceased – and the jade plugs for various openings of the body were interchangeable with cowry (an object of value or currency) according to him is not self-explanatory. Further, their alleged replacement by metal money seems to be an argumentative stretch, aiming to establish a single tradition.[50]

While there was no tradition of gold or silver coins in China, Sasanian coins were approved as methods of payment in the Hexi 河西 corridor during at least the Sui.[51] The Shi 史 did, however, even resort to the placement of gold and silver imitations and *bracteates* in the mouth in combination with Chinese copper coins, which strongly underpins the symbolic value of the former in this ritual. Assuming that the deposition in the mouth was the more important of the options of deposit, the preferred choice of a foreign gold or silver coin for the mouth may be explained by their scarcity and higher value, which suggests that they were utilised to enhance the prestige of the buried and thus of his and/or her family. To further expand the complexity of these cultural transmissions across thousands of miles and hundreds of years, the point of reference for the Sogdians in China during this time were probably the already culturally hybridised Northern Xianbei 鮮卑 rather than Central Chinese ethnic Han, as for example to be seen in the grave of Tian Hong 田弘 (d. 575 CE), excavated in the vicinity. He was awarded by the emperor the "surname" (*fuxing* 複姓) of Hegan 紇干 and had *five* Byzantine gold coins and ten Chinese copper coins of different sorts in his grave.[52] This Xianbei 鮮卑, the other unidentified individuals buried with foreign coins, and the Shi 史 buried in Northern China may indeed not have perceived a conflict between their own traditions – which may have been influenced by the Hellenistic world and payment in the netherworld – and the traditions of Central

46 Thierry, "Monnaies Sassanides," 100–2. See also: Thierry and Morrison, "Monnaies Byzantines".
47 Thierry, "Monnaies Sassanides," 100–2.
48 See also: Peng Ke and Zhu Yanshi, "Origin of Cowries".
49 See: Xia Nai, "Zongshu Sanshanchao yinbi".
50 This teleological construction of tradition is, however, traditionally Chinese.
51 See p. 224.
52 See: Yuanzhou lianhe kaogudui, *Bei Zhou Tian Hong mu*, 173–76.

China, and while the higher value of the foreign coins was probably important, it is also possible that the Chinese coins served a different ritual and social function.

Also found were finger-rings. One had an inlay with a Pahlavi inscription, whereas for the other, the inlay is lost. Further excavated was a seal stone, which looks like an inlay for a bezel but has no traces of a previous mounting on a ring. Both rings were of Western manufacture. Only four similar rings are known in China, one of which was found in the next vicinity in the grave of Li Xian 李賢 (d. 569 CE), probably belonging to his wife, and further including an exceptional Western glass object.[53] Similar finger rings have apparently been found in Afghanistan, Pakistan, and North-West India, dated to the fourth to sixth century.[54]

The other decorative gilt bronze objects of Western manufacture, inlaid with glass and crystal, of which a pendant looks highly similar to this of multi-piece necklace in the grave of Li Jingxun 李静訓 (d. 608 CE), exemplify the wealth and cultural background of the deceased.[55]

That many of the remaining burial goods – such as the ceramic and bronze dishes and pots, and the coin imitations – were not meant to be used in actual life is underlined by the deposition of other miniatures in the graves. The two remaining ceramic female servants and the small ceramic boots as well as miniature gilt bronze harness pieces were probably once combined in a display of various miniature figurines of riders or other soldiers – probably referring to the military and especially equestrian background of the deceased – servants, and musicians. Additionally, the miniature bronze mirrors were of size fitting the miniature ceramic figurines, having an average diameter of ca. 3–5 cm. Different functions were put forward for such mirrors in graves:[56] the miniaturisation of functional objects – as a range of objects were miniaturised, probably partly due to regulations on tomb furnishings –, apotropaic functions, usage in Daoist meditation, visualisation, and astral travel,[57] not to mention the display of cultural, social, economic, and religious capital and affiliation.[58] Unique until now in its variation are the combination of outwards pointing triangles, or a pearl roundel, together with typically Chinese leaves.

Rarely mentioned, as no complete object of the sort has been excavated to date, are further the regularly perforated slips of bone with bronze push pins, as well as the lacquered and/or painted wood pieces, some of which were decorated with floral decorative elements made of gold. As it seems, these were used for boxes of which

53 Ningxia huizu zizhiqu bowuguan and Ningxia Guyuan bowuguan, "Ningxia Li Xian fufu mu," 12.
54 Juliano and Lerner, *Monks and Merchants*, 259.
55 Tang Jinyu, "Xi'an Li Jingxun mu," 472, fig. 3.7.
56 See: Xu Diankui, "Tang jing fenxi"; Dien, *Six Dynasties Civilization*, 261–66.
57 Cahill, "The Word Made Bronze"; from: Dien, *Six Dynasties Civilization*, 262, fn. 102.
58 See: Fan Shuying, "Sui Tang gujing". It was even proposed that such small mirrors may have been used to ignite fire while travelling, which may be questioned (Sun Ji, *Zhongguo shenghuo*, 1–14; as seen in: Dien, *Six Dynasties Civilization*, 266, fn. 118).

remains were found in the grave around the epitaphs and the coffins, which must have been highly expensive pieces of woodwork, splendid to gaze at. What form the coffins may have taken is impossible to reconstruct with certainty. Although very few examples survive, and considering the finds in the graves, we can suppose that the coffins were trapezoid, made of wood, lacquered in black, and probably even richly painted.[59]

Concerning the glass objects, including the curious miniature semi-globular glass bowls with gilt bronze strips that were perhaps used for the coffin and/or fixed on a cloth, the rarity and high value of glass finds in China should be mentioned.

A final category of finds are the animal skulls. A horse and sheep head were found in the grave of Shi Hedan 史訶耽. Although the excavation report and the drawing of the finds conflict as to their location, the former was probably placed near the east wall of the corridor and the latter near the west wall of the corridor, with the epitaph in between them. The placement of animal skulls was, at least since the Zhou, a long-standing tradition in regions bordering the steppe of present-day China and a marker for non-Han graves.[60] What has also never mentioned in an analysis – although of some interest – is the dog burial in a niche constructed over the grave of Shi Daoluo 史道洛. Both will be considered again in the synthesis.

2.3 Epitaphs of Sogdians from an archaeological context

> 公/幼而明敏，風情爽悟，趫悍蓋世，勇力絕人。……
> 驚飆何迅，崦光遽頹。
>
> The revered ancestor, although only in his youth [was already] intelligent [and of] a bright spirit, agile beyond compare, [and with] unrivalled courage. (…) Why was the storm so fast? The light from Mount Yan 崦 suddenly declined.

Epitaph of Shi Shewu 史射勿[61]

> Les étapes de sa carrière le montrent toujours en avance, toujours plus jeune que ses pairs. La mort, hélas, elle aussi, semble avoir voulu devancer son heure.

59 As for the famous lacquer remains of a coffin of the Northern Wei, also found in Guyuan 固原: Ningxia Guyuan bowuguan, *Guyuan Bei Wei mu*. See also (with caution): Bradford, "The Guyuan Sarcophagus". See also, generally: Dien, *Six Dynasties Civilization*, 194–203.

60 See, e.g. the graves of Maoqinggou 毛慶溝 (Höllmann and Kossack, *Maoqinggou*) from as early as the Spring and Autumn Period, or later, studies on the graves of the Xianbei 鮮卑 (Wei Jian and Neimenggu zizhiqu wenwu kaogu yanjiusuo, *Neimenggu Xianbei muzang*).

61 See Vol. 2, 2.1; author's translation.

> Throughout the stages of his career he was revealed to be always ahead, always younger than his peers. Death too, alas, seemingly wanted to get ahead of its hour.

Obituary for Paul Pélliot (1878–1945) by Jacques Bacot[62]

2.3.1 Introduction

In a fashion akin to ascribing the invention of paper to the single figure of Cai Lun 蔡倫 (d. 121 CE),[63] the *Nan Qishu* informs us that the advent of epitaphs is to be traced back to Yan Yanzhi 顏延之 (384–456 CE).[64] Archaeological records provide us, however, with evidence for antecedents in the Han and some even earlier cases.[65]

The reasons as to why epitaphs were placed inside the graves rather than as steles on the surface remains a matter of debate.[66] We know that Cao Cao 曹操 (155–220 CE) as well as his son Cao Pi 曹丕 (187–226 CE)[67] issued edicts respectively in 206[68] and 222 CE,[69] followed by Sima Yan 司馬炎 (236–290 CE)[70] in 222 CE,[71] to curb the use of lavish burials, including the prohibition of placing stone beasts to guard the spirit path on the surface as well as the erection of mortuary steles. Relying on literary as well as archaeological sources, it is, however, possible to establish that these proscriptions had little influence on actual burial practices.[72] In opposition to the traditional conception that epitaphs stem from Southern China, it was also substantiated that the later standard form found during the Tang – such as was found in the graves of the Shi 史 – actually goes back to the Northern Dynasties, and specifically to the year 499 CE, following movement of the Northern Wei capital to Luoyang 洛陽.[73]

All but one of the below mentioned examples belong to this form, formed by two square stone slabs,[74] one forming a cover or lid and the other the main support for the inscription, laid out flat in the corridor or grave, in front of the coffin. The top stone has vertical sides, bevelled edges,[75] and a flat square upper surface, all polished. The lower surface is mostly roughly polished. The lower epitaph stone is a square slab

62 Bacot, "Paul," 127; author's translation.
63 See: Tsien, *Written on Bamboo and Silk*, 145–74; as seen in: Davis, *Entombed Epigraphy*, 7.
64 Nan Qishu 10.158.
65 Zhao Chao, "Muzhi suyuan," 43–55; Zhao Chao, *Gudai muzhi tonglun*, 32–52.
66 See also: Franz, *Chinesische Innengrabinschrift*, 3–6. The following information is based on: Davis, *Entombed Epigraphy*, 288–306.
67 He established the Wei in 220 CE.
68 *Sanguozhi* 1.27.
69 *Jinshu* 20.634.
70 He established the Jin in 266 CE.
71 *Songshu* 15.407.
72 Davis, *Entombed Epigraphy*, 159.
73 See p. 231 (2.4.4.1) and: Liu Fengjun, "Nanbeichao shike muzhi"; Xu Zhiqiang, *Beijing tushuguan tapian*, 5–6; Müller, "Gräber der Nördlichen Wei-Zeit," 228–32.
74 Made of mostly dark and sometimes brown limestone; in some cases, a brick was inscribed.
75 Dien described it as "four-sided truncated pyramid" (Dien, *Six Dynasties Civilization*, 206).

with vertical sides and the top surface both polished, with the lower side being also roughly polished. The polished tops and vertical sides are mostly engraved with varying combinations of patterns like vine scrolls and leaves, beasts, strings, and the four directional creatures. Some of the earlier lidded epitaphs are very similar to divinatory equipment, showing that there was some metaphysical meaning in their design, probably reproducing the heaven and earth (round and square) in combination with its placement in the burial chamber (with a domed ceiling, sometimes painted with specific stellar constellations), with the four directional creatures included in its cosmological symbolism. If, however, later epitaphs of the Sui and Tang still included such connotations and had an apotropaic function is difficult to establish, as the form became highly standardised.[76] At the same time, the cover stone perceivably served as protection from damage of the lower stone.[77] The cover is inscribed with a few large characters in seal script, or regular script, arranged in a table (2x2, 3x3, 3x4, 4x4, 4x5), whereas the epitaph is mostly written in clerical or regular script. As can be observed through several examples, the epitaphs were first inscribed with a brush and red or gold pigments, to be then mostly carved. In terms of the later epitaphs the length of the inscription stands generally in relation to the individual's importance. The value of the stone itself can be measured by the fact that many older stones were recycled and used for new epitaphs – as is the case with the stone of Shi Daode 史道德 – or for building projects in walls or stairs.[78] Further, they were soon collected, at least since the Song, when antiquarianism was *en vogue*.

Concerning the content, Davis concisely commented that "[biographies] (whether historiographical or commemorative) are not neutral narratives but polemic literary forms. Through carefully edited portrayals of individual lives, the authors (or compilers) of such texts reveal their advocacy of particular moral attributes and ethical principles".[79] "[Muzhiming] were essentially family-focused hagiographies shaping the memory of the progenitor (according to ritual and generic expectations) in a way most useful for conveying identity-securing information to his or her descendants."[80] In his extensive study of epitaphs, Davis crystallised nine characteristics he deemed essential, being unique features of this form of memorialisation.[81] They serve to:

- record marriage alliances and close kin.
- emphasise on choronyms rather than surname origins.
- address multiple audiences.
- de-emphasise patron client-relationships.
- gradually developed into an esteemed genre.
- provided source material for other biographical genres.

76 See: Liu Fengjun, "Nanbeichao shike muzhi," 80; Zhao Chao, "Shi, qionglong ding".
77 See: Tackett, "Transformation of Medieval Chinese Elites," 11.
78 For some examples, see: Tackett, "Transformation of Medieval Chinese Elites," 13–14.
79 Davis, *Entombed Epigraphy*, 254.
80 Ibid., 72.
81 Ibid., 26–33; see also: Franz, *Chinesische Innengrabinschrift*, 2–3. See also generally: Lin Dengshun, *Beichao muzhiwen yanjiu*.

- may have functioned as quasi-legal documents.
- may have been consulted prior to performing graveside sacrifices.[82]
- were believed to have talismanic properties.

Without diving deeper in general theoretical approaches, an impression of how an entire epitaph reads may be gathered through the lecture of the complete transcriptions and translations of the epitaphs of Shi Shewu 史射勿 and Shi Hedan 史訶耽 provided in Vol.2, Appendix 2, listed together with the variant characters found on them.[83] As the content is highly standardised, all available epitaphs of Sogdians found in their archaeological context were directly transcribed, and the informational content extracted and filled into tables, both provided with annotations concerning issues related to characters and narrated information.[84] The typical epitaph of this time is

82 It is however mostly the case that the "detailed descriptions" would not be useful to find a grave, as graves were often built in cemeteries and a stele and/or other markers placed on the surface. When these were lost (or stolen), how would one again find a grave described as two kilometres from such and such a mountain, in the midst of other graves?

83 Although many researchers may want to circumvent the problem of closely looking at the facsimiles and face up to the variant characters and other problems, like the poor readability of earlier Chinese publications, etc., it is as a matter of fact a necessity. Not one of the facsimiles I used for this study was in previous publications transcribed without mistakes, or me having a different opinion – to understate the situation.
Shortly addressing variant characters, they are versions of the standard characters *zhengzi* 正字, called in different dictionaries and compilations, according to the classification, *yitizi* 異體字, *guzi* 古字, *ezi* 訛字, *weizi* 偽字, *biezi* 別字, *caoshu* 草書, *sutizi* 俗體字 or *suzi* 俗字, and *jianhuazi* 簡化字 or *jiantizi* 簡體字. The specific categorisation of the characters is a never-ending debate. Reducing the whole problematic to a minimum, *yitizi* 異體字 encompass all variants, including the *guzi* 古字, *suzi* 俗字, and *jianhuazi* 簡化字, which are determined by the comparison between the character and contemporaneous lists of *zhengtizi* 正體字 (see also: Ou Changjun and Li Haixia, *Liuchao Tang Wudai shike*, 1–33). The authenticity, validity, and authority of the claims of these contemporaneous listings are, however, rarely questioned, which produces conceivably ahistorical claims and a general disregard for the complexity of language (and how it may be defined) as well as cultural change.

84 To help me in this endeavour, I combined all epitaphs available to me in an indexed database (of over. 4,000 pages), which provides material for comparisons which I have drawn on repeatedly. The references to the excavation reports and other relevant articles are to be found in the first footnote of each epitaph. Iwami Kiyohiro also published from 2004 to 2008 in *Shiteki* scrupulous transcriptions in Japanese *kanji* 漢字 of An Jia 安伽, Wirkak (Master Shi 史), Kang Ye 康業, Yu Hong 虞弘, Shi Shewu 史射勿, Shi Hedan 史訶耽, Shi Daoluo 史道洛, Shi Tiebang 史鐵棒, Shi Suoyan 史索嚴, An Niang 安娘, and Shi Daode 史道德 (Iwami Kiyohiro, *Sogudo jin boshi kenkyū*).
Parenthetically, some publications on Sogdians include the grave of An Bei 安備 (buried 589 CE), for which it is only stated that the objects were excavated in 2007 in Henan Province during the laying of the foundation of a building. Even if this were to be true, it remains unclear whether the objects stem from the same grave (see: Ge Chengyong, "Xianjiao shenghuo yishu," 14, fn. 1; Ge Chengyong, "Sui An Bei mu"). At the same time, I believe that the vocabulary used in his choronym (其先/出於安居耶尼國 "His ancestors came from the state of Anjuyeni") refers to the Buddhist continent of Godānīya (also transcribed as 瞿伽尼, 瞿耶尼, 瞿陀尼, 俱助尼, 遇嚩柅, 拘耶尼, and also 西瞿耶尼, that is Aparagodāna, also transcribed as 阿鉢唎瞿陀尼), the western of the four continents into which every world is divided. Furthermore, there is nothing pointing

structured in two parts: first the biography – or biographies, if mentioning a wife or wives, or a son or sons – in prose, followed by the literary repetition of the former in verse, which is generally a four-character verse of which the even lines rhyme. The content is normally structured in the order as follows: [85]

– headline, including the dynasty, sometimes toponym, family name, nobility title(s) or other appellation, office(s), type of epitaph, sometimes mention of an introduction
– prose section:
  a. individual's taboo, courtesy name, choronym, place of residence
  b. ancestry, possibly divided into remote ancestry and origin story, and recent ancestry
  c. personal qualities (youth)
  d. active life, sometimes including the retirement
  e. death
  f. possible biography or biographies for wife or wives
    1. family name, choronym
    2. ancestry
    3. active life, including offices, events and dates
    4. possible transition to death, including a eulogy, and death, including date, circumstances, location, expression of woe (*wuhu aizai* 嗚呼哀哉, "alas!")
  g. burial, including date, location, concluding expression (*li ye* 禮也, "according to ritual protocol")
  h. sons with offices, piety and/or grief, sometimes biography of sons
– verse section, in strophes
– possible dating, including calligraphy, carving, and authorship

The following family trees and biographies are the prose version of the critical analysis of the epitaphs, considering other sources if possible, which was filled into tables in Vol. 2, Appendix 3. The presentation in a prosaic form aims at a comprehensive but not convoluted narration that enables the biography to be embedded in the historical and interpersonal context. Due to these restrictions, the reader interested in the details and the argumentation behind each statement will have to check the corresponding passage in the chronologically organised tables.

to a Zoroastrian affiliation. Mao Yangguang published in 2011 two articles about the epitaph, in the first supporting the Zoroastrian theory of Ge Chengyong, and in the second contradicting exactly this theory, referring to the Buddhist vocabulary mentioned above (Mao Yangguang, "Luoyang chutu (1)"; Mao Yangguang, "Luoyang chutu (2)").

85 For more detailed introduction and examples, see: Franz, *Chinesische Innengrabinschrift*, 21–109.

2.3.2 Biographies

2.3.2.1 Master Shi 史/Wirkak (Sogd. wyrk'k; 494–579 CE) and Lady Kang 康 /Wiyusi (d. 579 CE), epitaph in Chinese and Sogdian

2.3.2.1.1 Family tree[86]

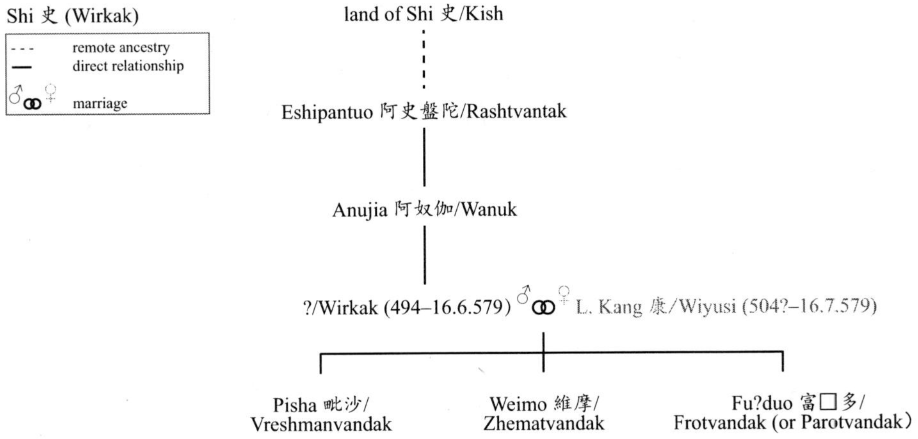

Figure 3: Family tree of Master Shi 史/Wirkak
Source: M. Huber

2.3.2.1.2 Biographies

From the bilingual epitaph, we know that Wirkak's family came from Kesh, which is why they were surnamed Shi 史.[87] There, his grandfather Ashipantuo 阿史盤陀 (EMC* *?a ʂɨ'/ʂi' ban da*, Sogd. Rashtvantak) was *sabao* 薩保, which means that he occupied a position that was similar to the responsibilities of a *sabao* 薩保 in China, i.e. a magistrate.[88] While we don't know anything about his father Anuqie 阿奴伽 (EMC* *?a nɔ gɨa*, Sogd. Wanuk), he or his son, Wirkak, must have moved to Guzang 姑臧 (Sogd. Kachan) in the fifth or early sixth century, which was then under the control of the Northern Wei. Master Shi 史 – as he is introduced in the Chinese epitaph – was born in ca. 494 CE.[89] At the age of 25, on 19.7.519 CE, he married his Sogdian wife Wiyusi[90] in Senpen (Sogd. Synpyn), which may be identified as Xinping 新平. She had been born there and was surnamed Kang 康, which may refer to the fact that

86 The information is divided by a "/" in the table. First Chinese, then Sogdian.
87 Wirkak is "[most] likely to be derived from *wyrk* (wolf)." (Yoshida Yutaka, "The Sogdian Version," 64.)
88 Rashtvantak is a typical Sogdian name combining *ršt* (the goddess of Truth) and *βntk* (slave) (ibid.).
89 Wanuk is a combination of the prefix *wnw* (victorious) and a common suffix (ibid.).
90 Derived from *wy'ws* "dawn" (ibid., 65).

she was originally from Samarqand. Hypothetically, she was around 15 years old at her marriage, about ten years younger than him.

Shortly after the Western Wei took over in 535 CE, Wirkak became chief judge of the *sabao* 薩保 office at the age of ca. 44, most probably in Guzang 姑藏, the administrative centre of Liangzhou 涼州. In 539 CE, at the age of 48, he then was promoted to the office of *sabao* 薩保 of Liangzhou 涼州 in Guzang 姑藏. Sometime during the next forty years, he must have moved to the then capital Chang'an 長安 (Sogd. Khumtan), maybe due to his sons' successful career. It is there that he died on 16.6.579 CE at the age of 85. Only one month later, on 16.7.579 CE, his wife also died at the age of maybe 75 (based on the hypothetical wedding age). Seven months later, on 23.2.580 CE, they were buried together on one of the prestigious burial grounds of the Longshou 龍首 Plain.

They had three sons, Pisha 毗沙 (EMC* *bji ʂaɨ/ʂɛː*)[91]/Vreshmanvandak (Sogd. *βr'yšmnβntk*), Weimo 維摩 (EMC* *jwi maʰ*)[92]/Zhematvandak (Sogd. *δrymtβntk*),[93] and Fu?duo 富□多 (EMC* *puwh…ta*)/Frotvandak (or Parotvandak; Sogd. *pr'wtβntk*),[94] which built the stone sarcophagus – the Sogdian inscription says "house of gods"[95] – with a bilingual epitaph.

91 As Yoshida pointed out, this is a sinicised version (complete: pishamentianwang 毗沙門天王) of Skt. Vaiśravaṇa, Sogd. *βr'yšmn* (ibid., 60–61).

92 As Yoshida pointed out, this is a Chinese version of Skt. Vimalakīrti (ibid., 61).

93 A popular name in Sogdian as well as in its Chinese form (ibid., 68).

94 For more information about the Sogdian name, see: ibid., 68–69.

95 See: ibid., 68, no. 29.

2.3.2.2 Kang Ye 康業 (512–71 CE)

2.3.2.2.1 Family tree

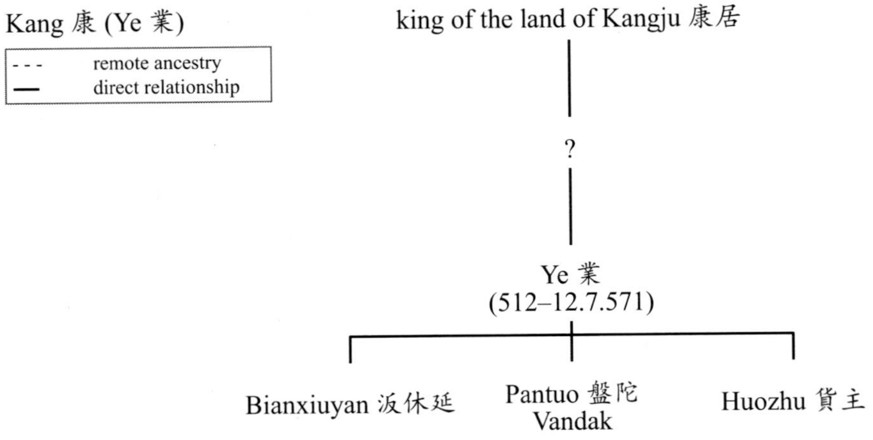

Figure 4: Family tree of Kang Ye 康業
Source: M. Huber

2.3.2.2.2 Biographies

Kang Ye's 康業 (Ye 業, EMC* *ŋiap*) family is said to have descended from the royal house of the land of Kangju 康居, which during this time most probably referred to Kang 康, i.e. Samarqand – his family name underpins such a construction. The choronym given for his father is Luozhou 羅州, which I propose actually referred to the An 安 Fort near Shazhou 沙州, east of which was a Zoroastrian temple. His father must have made a name for himself as a religious specialist, as in 544 CE, the chariot and horse general-in-chief *huyao* 呼藥 officer Di Men 翟門 of the Western Wei capital Yongzhou 雍州 and influential Western families of the Western Regions recommended him as Zoroastrian presider-in-chief, which resulted in his appointment there in 550 CE. After a dozen years in the office, he died in 563 CE, during the Northern Zhou.

Ye 業, who later received the courtesy name Yuanji 元基 (EMC* *ŋuan kɨ/ki*), was born in ca. 512 CE. Three years after his father's death, in 566 CE, his son Kang Ye 康業 was appointed in the office of Zoroastrian presider-in-chief at the age of 54, the office explicitly being mentioned as hereditary.[96] Besides this, we only know that he

96 Frantz Grenet proposed on the conference "Sogdians and their Funerary Monuments in Sixth to Seventh-Century China", held in Venice in December 2018, that the *tianzhu* 天主 might not have been a Zoroastrian specialist but a supervisor of the temple. He based his argument on the depiction of an individual on Kang Ye's 康業 funerary bed as an official, which matches his biography. Instead of identifying the two priests needed for the ritual as *xianzheng* 祆正

died on 12.7.571 CE at the age of 59 and was posthumously promoted to regional inspector of Ganzhou 甘州. As his epitaph was inscribed on 31.12.571 CE, he was probably buried on this day at the prestigious burial grounds of the Longshou 龍首 Plain, Chang'an 長安.

Nothing of his wife is indicated but three sons are mentioned, named Bianxiuyan 汳休延 (EMC* *bian*^{h} *xuw jian*),[97] who ordered the epitaph, Pantuo 盤陀 (EMC* *ban da*),[98] and Huozhu 貨主 (EMC* *xwa*^{h} *tɕuǎ'*).[99]

2.3.2.3 An Jia 安伽 (Sogd. wn'wk; 518–79 CE) [100]

2.3.2.3.1 Family tree

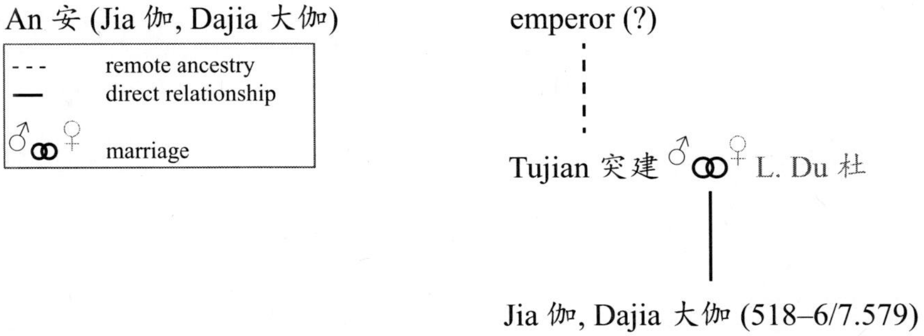

Figure 5: Family tree of An Jia 安伽
Source: M. Huber

2.3.2.3.2 Biographies

An Jia's 安伽 (Jia 伽, EMC* *gia*) epitaph claims that his ancestors were "descendants of the Yellow Emperor", which is a locution to designate the Chinese people. To explain the surname "An 安", the epitaph proceeds to explain that the clan names of these descendants were given according to the place where they settled. The choronym Guzang 姑臧 (in this case the Changsong 昌松 District of Guzang 姑臧) is also to be found on other epitaphs (see, among others, Wirkak's epitaph), and was probably a strategic choice that showed their connection to the powerful An 安 clan of Guzang 姑臧. The latter clan is known through official historical documents and a stele, of

(Zoroastrian regulator) and *xianzhu* 祆主 (Zoroastrian precentor), he believes that both may have been *xianzheng* 祆正. For my proposition, see p. 293 (3.3.11.1).

97 *Yan* 延 is a transcription from the Sogdian word "gift", also bearing the meaning of "honour" and "prosperity" (Xi'an shi wenwu baohu kaogusuo, "Xi'an Bei Zhou Kang Ye," 34).

98 Sogd. vandak (*βntk*) "slave", or "servant", "attested as a personal name among the Upper-Indus inscriptions" (Yoshida Yutaka, "Personal Names, Sogdian", apud: Sims-Williams, *Sogdian*, 47).

99 Literally "goods owner".

100 Dien listed An Jia's 安伽 dates of birth and death 519–79 CE (Dien, "Further Thoughts," 205).

which members claimed to stem from Anxi 安息.[101] His family thus stemmed from either Parthia, or more probably, Bukhārā, which was at this time referred to as Anxi 安息.

His father Tujian 突建 (EMC* *dwət kian*^{h}) was a general commanding the troops and regional inspector of Meizhou 眉州, which apparently was located in present-day Sichuan Province during the Northern Zhou, which – unless another Meizhou 眉州 unknown to us existed – indicates that the title was most probably fictive or of honorary nature. This epitaph is the only one in this study – and a rare example overall – to mention the mother of the deceased, a surnamed Du 杜, said to be district mistress of the Changsong 昌松 District, near Guzang 姑藏. Her surname is quite certainly an indicator that she was an ethnic Han, which is rather rare for the wives of Sogdians we know of.

Jia 伽 was born in 518 CE and later received the courtesy name Dajia 大伽 (EMC* *daj*^{h} *gɨa*). Although the exact dates are not indicated, we know that he became *sabao* 薩保 of Tongzhou 同州, located at present-day Dali 大荔 District, Shaanxi Province (located ca. 100 km north-east of Chang'an 長安). Soon later, he was awarded the honorary title of great commander-in-chief. He probably moved to the capital, as in the summer of 579 CE, he died and was buried on the prestigious Longshou 龍首 Plain east of Chang'an 長安 in November or December of the same year. Nothing of his wife or children is indicated.

2.3.2.4 Lord Yu Hong 虞弘 (534–92 CE) and wife (d. 597 CE)

2.3.2.4.1 Family tree

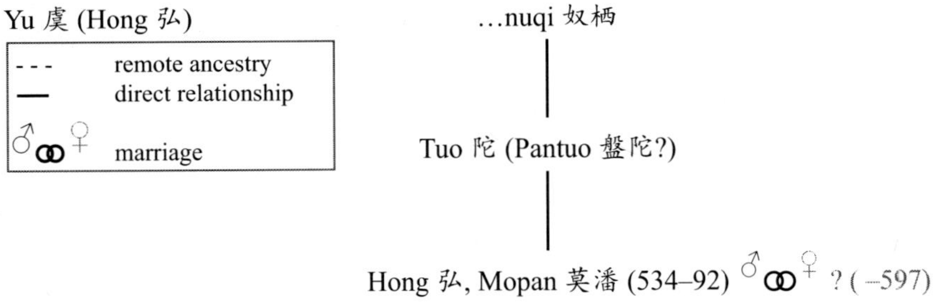

Figure 6: Family tree of Yu Hong 虞弘

Source: M. Huber

2.3.2.4.2 Biographies

Yu Hong's 虞弘 (Hong 弘, EMC* *ɣwəŋ*) epitaph claims that he descended from Yu Shun 虞舜, one of the mythical Chinese emperors. We are then reminded that one of the emperor's family branches went to live in the Western Regions, which is to be

101 See the stele of An Zhongjing 安忠敬 p. 243 (3.2.3.1.7).

understood as an explanation for his foreign – but allegedly Chinese – origin. The choronym Weihelin 尉紇驎 Fort of the state of Yu 魚 is not mentioned in any other historical sources. In context of the biography, it must have been somewhere in a region in or outside of the north-western region of present-day China. Both *yu* 魚 characters in the first and second column of the epitaph, which are both part of the state's name, were changed after the initial carving. As *yu* 魚 and *yu* 虞 are homophonic, and we know from several Sogdian epitaphs that it was common for Sogdians to be named after the place of origin, it is possible that his family was initially called *yu* 魚, or that the country referred to on his epitaph is actually the country of Yu 虞, which is equally unidentified. The last two characters of his grandafther's name are legible, -nuxi 奴栖 (which was maybe pronounced EMC* *nɔ sɛj*). He was said to have been people's commander of the state of Yu 魚. His father was Juntuo 君陀 (EMC* *kun da*), *mohe qufen* 莫賀去汾 (a high ranking official) and Tharkan (?) of the country of the Rouran 柔然.[102]

Hong 弘, who later received the courtesy name Mopan 莫潘 (EMC* *mak pʰan*), was born in ca. 534 CE in the territory of the Rouran 柔然. At the age of 13, in ca. 547 CE, he became *mohe fu* 莫賀弗, a slightly lower ranking official than the one of his father mentioned above, and was sent on a mission to the Sasanian Empire and the Tuyuhun 吐谷渾, possibly to accompany his father. Around this time, his father must have also been sent to the Northern or Eastern Wei.[103] As some characters are missing on the epitaph, we may assume that his father was then appointed as regional inspector of Shuozhou 朔州 (located around present-day Shuozhou 朔州 City, Shanxi Province) at some point in his life, probably an honorary office.[104] As his son started residing on

102 Although this title is unknown for the Rouran 柔然, *daguan* 達官/ *dagan* 達干 is known as a title for high ranking Tujue 突厥 (Luo Feng, *Hu Han zhi jian*, 412–14).

103 Luo Feng already criticised the missing logical connection in the argument of Zhang Qingjie that since Hong 弘 was born in 534 CE, Juntuo 君陀 must have went to the Wei after his birth (ibid., 414; Zhang Qingjie, "Yu Hong muzhi," 104; Zhang Qingjie, "Sui," 214). He then proceeded to argue that according to his identification, Shuozhou 朔州 (Bingzhou 並州) was changed into Yunzhou 雲州 in 532–34 CE. As I explain in the text following this footnote and in the footnote below, I do not see a good reason why his mission to the Wei and his appointment as regional inspector of Shuozhou 朔州 are to be seen as necessarily subsequent, as I propose the appointment was probably honorary or posthumous. As I further explain in the footnote below, I also disagree with the identification of Shuozhou 朔州 by Zhang Qingjie, Luo Feng, and the other identification by Zhou Weizhou. In my opinion, there is no indication as to which of the Wei he was sent, although I believe we can dismiss the Western Wei as quite improbable.

104 I do thus neither agree with the reasoning that this Shuozhou 朔州 was the one changed into Yunzhou 雲州 in 532–34 CE, as proposed by Zhang Qingjie and Luo Feng, or the argument proposed by Zhou Weizhou that it was actually part of Bingzhou 並州 ((Zhang Qingjie, "Yu Hong muzhi," 104; Zhang Qingjie, "Sui," 214; Luo Feng, *Hu Han zhi jian*, 414; Zhou Weizhou, "Sui Yu Hong muzhi," 253). There are two arguments to oppose their hypotheses. First, it is highly improbable that Juntuo 君陀 went to the Wei and stayed there as regional inspector while his son continued to carry out missions for the Rouran 柔然. As I explain in the text following this footnote, I believe this office was honorary or posthumous. Second, because Hong 弘 went to China for the first time during the Northern Qi, probably in 551 CE,

the territory of a Chinese dynasty only after the Northern Qi were installed and then went on to have an impressive career, it is quite possible that Juntuo 君陀 received this title posthumously. It is also clear from this content that Yu Hong 虞弘 – although his sarcophagus is mostly mentioned in line with archaeological evidence of Sogdians – was not of Sogdian descent. Probably in 551 CE, he was promoted to *moyuan* 莫緣 (a higher office) and sent to the Northern Qi. It was the second mission sent by the khagan of the Rouran 柔然 since the dynasty had been newly established in 550 CE by Emperor Wen Xuan 文宣 (r. 550–59 CE), and his goal was possibly to establish treaties or an alliance. Conceivably due to the defeat of the Rouran 柔然 Yujiulü Anagui 郁久閭阿那瓌 Khagan by the Tujue 突厥 Bumin Qhagan[105] in 552 CE, Hong 弘 was captured as eunuch by the Northern Qi and forbidden to return to his country. He probably resided from then on in Jinyang 晉陽, Bingzhou 並州, the secondary capital of the dynasty, stronghold of the first emperor, and centre of his later life.

In 565 CE, the fourth emperor Emperor Wucheng 武成 (and younger brother of the first emperor, r. 561–65) now aged 28, placed his eight year old son on the throne, later known as Emperor Gao Wei 高緯 (r. 565–77 CE) – who was recorded as participating in Zoroastrian sacrifices and thus sympathetic to the *hu* 胡[106] – but kept control of the government until his death in the winter of 568 CE. Under this retired emperor, Yu Hong 虞弘 was appointed as chariot bodyguard in charge of protecting the emperor's carriage. In the following five years, he was promoted thrice. First, he became appointed as general of light chariots, palace bodyguard, and imperial bodyguard. He was next promoted to commandant with extraordinary powers of the military matters of Liangzhou 涼州, regional inspector of Liangzhou 涼州, and skilled bowmen commander. As the Northern Zhou and not the Northern Qi controlled Liangzhou 涼州, the title of regional inspector is probably a fictive title, or a title representing a territorial claim of the Northern Qi. Furthermore, the title of regional inspector of Liangzhou 涼州 is to be found on the epitaph of Shi Fancui 史范粹 of the Northern Qi (d. 575 CE). He was then promoted to honorary commander unequalled in honour and mobile corps commander and rewarded with over 500,000 coins.

When the Northern Qi were invaded and defeated by the Northern Zhou in 577 CE, Hong 弘, now 43 years old, was immediately taken over by Emperor Wu 武, third emperor of the Northern Zhou (r. 561–78 CE), appointed as commandant with extraordinary powers, commander unequalled in honour, as well as made earl of the Guangxing 廣興 District (located in present-day Miyun 密雲 County, Beijing), with a territorial claim of 600 households, and provided with a surrogate office similar to

the Shuozhou 朔州 the epitaph refers to must in any case have been later than 551 CE but earlier than 592 CE, the year in which the epitaph was written. However, as the toponyms used on an epitaph are normally contemporary to the time of composition, the results of the calculations of these authors can thus be dismissed as anachronistic. This in combination with the first argument leave only the Shuozhou 朔州 identified above (among overall four choices, see: Dai Junliang, Liu Baoquan and Zou Yilin, *Zhongguo gujin diming - xia*).

105 Later calling himself Yili Kehan 伊利可汗, Illig Qaghan.

106 See p. 317 fn. 344.

an ambassador, being simultaneously in charge of the local militia. One year later, the emperor died, and his 18-year-old son became Emperor Xuan 宣. The latter had had his first son Yuwen Yan 宇文衍 (later named Yuwen Chan 宇文闡) in 573 CE, at the age of 14, with the concubine Zhu Manyue 朱滿月. In the same year and only nine months later, the emperor married the 12-year-old Yang Lihua 楊麗華, daughter of Yang Jian 楊堅, and made her his crown princess. In 579 CE, after one year as emperor, now aged 20, he decided to make his six-year-old son crown prince, retired one month later, and placed his son on the throne as Emperor Jing 靜, while remaining in power. Unexpectedly, the retired emperor died in 580 CE and Yang Jian 楊堅 became protector of the infant emperor. As prime minister on the left, Yang Jian 楊堅 promoted the then 46 years old Hong 弘 to take charge of the local militia of the three regions of Bingzhou 並州, Daizhou 代州, and Jiezhou 介州, and appointed him as acting *sabao* 薩保, probably holding this office in Jinyang 晉陽, Bingzhou 並州.[107]

One year later, in 581 CE, Yang Jian 楊堅 had the emperor abdicate and installed the Sui Dynasty as Emperor Wen 文. Consequently, Hong 弘 was appointed as commander unequalled in honour, made commandant of the left escort brigade, and placed in control of the Bingzhou 並州 region's army division. Probably in 592 CE, at the age of 58, he died in his private residence in Bingzhou 並州 and was buried nearby on 27.12.592 CE. His wife had an epitaph of her own which unfortunately was broken in many pieces, half of which were lost. I propose that she died five years later in 597 CE and was buried in 598 CE, at which point their grave must have been finally closed. An analysis of her bones indicate that she reached an age of 40 to 60 years and thus must have been born 537–57 CE. No children are mentioned, which is not uncommon, him being a eunuch.

107 To gain popularity, Yang Jian 楊堅 extensively conferred titles and ennobled influential people (Zhang Qingjie, "Sui," 222).

2.3.2.5 Shi 史 of Yuanzhou 原州(1): Family tree[108]

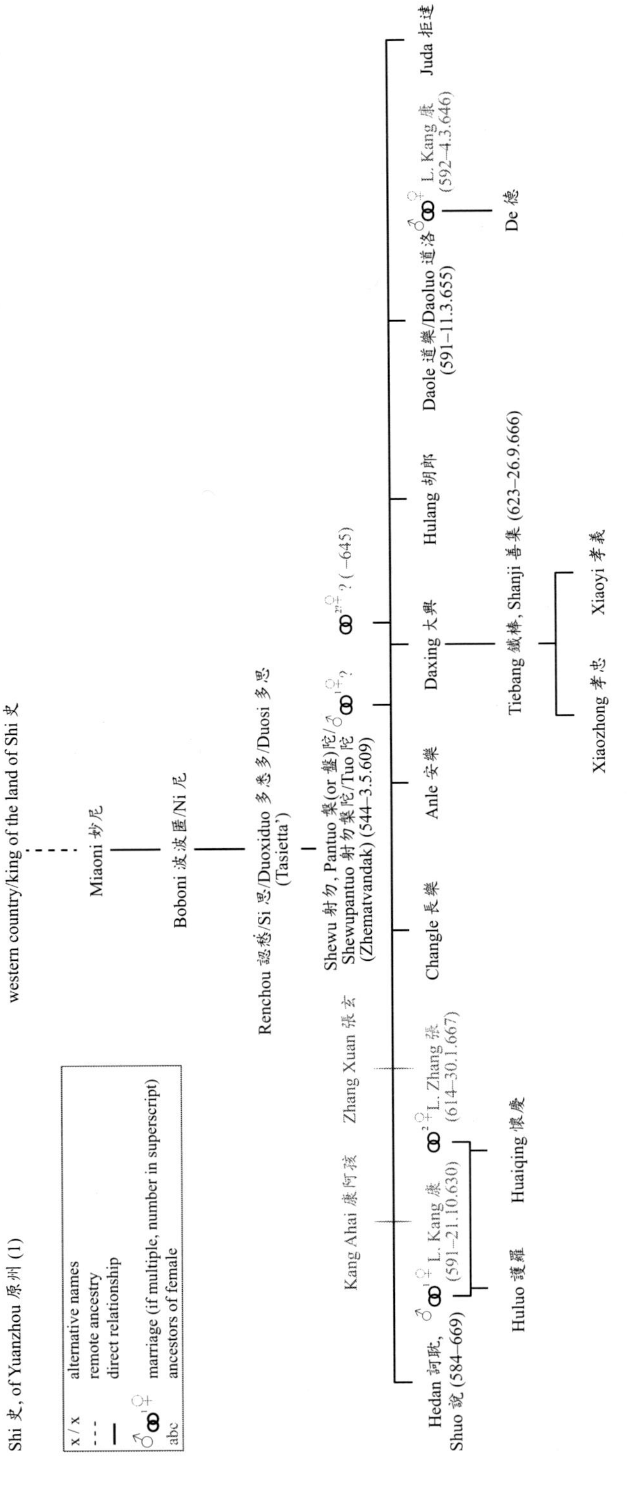

Figure 7: Family tree of the Shi 史 of Yuanzhou 原州 (1)
Source: M. Huber

2.3.2.6 Shi 史 of Yuanzhou 原州(1): Biography of Shi Shewu 史射勿 (544–609 CE)
The full translation of the epitaph is to be found in Vol. 2, Appendix 2.1.

To introduce and contextualise the events and actors, some political background is helpful. Yuwen Tai 宇文泰, the paramount general of the Western Wei, deposed in 554 CE Emperor Fei 廢 and installed the latter's cadet brother as Emperor Gong 恭. Two years later, Yuwen Tai 宇文泰 died and was succeeded by his son Yuwen Jue 宇文覺, with the latter's cousin Yuwen Hu 宇文護 as regent. In 557 CE Yuwen Hu 宇文護 then forced Emperor Gong 恭 off the throne and *de facto* established the Northern Zhou by installing Yuwen Jue 宇文覺 as Emperor Xiaomin 孝閔. His reign did not last long as Yuwen Hu 宇文護 had him executed later that year for plotting. He was replaced by another of his cousins, Xiaomin's 孝閔 cadet brother Yuwen Yu 于文毓, who became Emperor Ming 明. When three years later, in 560 CE, Yuwen Yu 于文毓 was poisoned by Yuwen Hu 宇文護, he still succeeded to appoint his elder brother Yuwen Yong 宇文邕 as Emperor Wu 武 shortly before his death. Emperor Wu 武 then finally succeeded in ridding himself of him in 572 CE.

To return to Sogdians, the family of Shi Shewu 史射勿 (Shewu, EMC* *ẓia*^{h} *mut*) was said to be from a Western state, which was probably Kesh, according to his surname.[109] His great-grandfather Miaoni 妙尼 (EMC* *mjiaw*^{h} *nri*)[110] and grandfather Boboni 波波匿 (EMC* *pa pa nrik*) were *sabao* 薩寶 in Kesh.[111] Concerning his father Renchou 認愁 (EMC* *ŋin*^{h} *dẓuw*), the epitaph says: [112]

> 蹉跎年髮[113]，舛此宦途。
>
> [His time] went by until old age, [and he did] not follow this career path.

On the basis of this epitaph, Luo Feng proposed that his father did not occupy any office.[114] While this statement seems like slander – of which some cases are known – many epitaphs simply omitted the careers of ancestors. To elucidate this problem, instead of "a career", as was previously done, I propose to read "this career" – which

108 Wertmann, Wagner and Tarasov (Wertmann, Wagner and Tarasov, "Sogdian," 127–28) proposed that the two Shi 史 families were actually one. Their argument is based on a row of untenable hypotheses, for which they lay out a list of convincing counter facts and arguments. The article further provides abridged biographies of the Shi 史 families in English which were presented and discussed more extensively in Chinese in: Luo Feng, *Guyuan nanjiao Sui Tang mudi*, 185–220; Luo Feng, *Hu Han zhi jian*, 423–75; Li Jinxiu, "Shi Hedan 1"; and: Li Jinxiu, "Shi Hedan 2".

109 See also his son Hedan's 訶耽 epitaph.

110 According to Yoshida, this is "the male counterpart to *mywn'yh*, the name of the woman who sent Ancient Letters I and III." Yoshida Yutaka, "The Sogdian Version," 65.

111 For the argument behind this statement, see p. 268 fn. 236.

112 Also known as Si 思, Duoxiduo 多悉多, or Duosi 多思 (Tasietta').

113 To be understood as *bin* 鬢.

114 Luo Feng, *Guyuan nanjiao Sui Tang mudi*, 191; Luo Feng, "Sabao: Zai kaocha," 221.

is actually written on the epitaph – and thus refers to the *sabao*, and maybe, even more specifically, to being *sabao* in Kesh. For the discrepancies between these statements and the information from his sons' and grandsons' epitaphs, see below.[115]

Shi Shewu 史射勿, who later received the courtesy name Pantuo 槃陀 (EMC* *ban da*), was born in ca. 544 CE under the Western Wei. The "name Pantuo (< **b'uân d'â*) is a transcription of a Sogdian name Vandak (*βntk*) "slave," which is attested as a personal name among the Upper Indus inscriptions".[116] His taboo, Shewu 射勿 (EMC* *zia^h mut*), and courtesy name, Pantuo 槃陀, are to be read together, i.e. Shewupantuo 射勿槃陀, as it is written on the epitaph of his sixth son Shi Daoluo 史道洛. According to Yoshida Yutaka, this stands for Zhematvandak (Sogd. *δrymtβntk*), which means servant of the deity Zhemat, also known as Demeter.[117] At the age of 20, in 564 CE, he joined his first campaign eastwards under Duke Dang 蕩 of the Jin, i.e. the above-mentioned Yuwen Hu 宇文護. The records state that Yuwen Hu 宇文護 and two generals came to the capital and were ordered to attack the Northern Qi on 28.11.564 CE. Yuwen Hu 宇文護 was dispatched to Tongguan 潼關 and the other two generals to Yuzhou 豫州 and Jiguan 軹關. On 1.12.564 CE, the emperor went to Shayuan 沙苑 to encourage his troops. At this place, a major confrontation between the Western and Eastern Wei had taken place in 537 CE, when Yuwen Tai 宇文泰, the father of the first emperor of the Northern Zhou, defeated Gao Huan 高歡, the father of the first emperor of the Northern Qi. On 7.12.564 CE, they returned to the capital Chang'an 長安. On 28.12.564 CE, an army was dispatched to beleaguer Luoyang 洛陽. One part went to the Mangshan 邙山 but Yuwen Hu 宇文護 moved to camp with his troops in Shanzhou 陝州. On the beginning of the 12th month, one of them then successfully attacked Yuzhou 豫州 of the Northern Qi. On 25.1.565 CE, the army of the Northern Qi retaliated. The troops crossed the Yellow River and arrived in Luoyang 洛陽 in the morning, and all armies of the Northern Zhou allegedly fled in panic – "allegedly" since another account said that the army withdrew, while one army was hit severely at Jiguan 軹關, and Yuzhou 豫州 was lost.

In 566 CE, Shi Shewu 史射勿 then served under the duke of Pinggao 平高 and was stationed in Hedong 河東 (ca. present-day Shanxi Province). This duke was conceivably Li Xun 孝詢, son of Li Xian 李賢, the latter being one of the great generals of the Northern Zhou which happens to be buried in one of the most important tombs near Shewu 射勿. In 567 CE, now aged 23, Shewu 射勿 became appointed as commander-in-chief, and was sent in the same year to the Yubi 玉壁 Fort under the duke of the land of Tan 郯, the latter probably being Wang Gui 王軌, who later conspired with Yuwen Yong 宇文邕, the future Emperor Wu 武. Located

115 See p. 149 (2.3.2.10).

116 Yoshida Yutaka, "Personal Names, Sogdian"; *apud*: Sims-Williams, *Sogdian*, 47.

117 Lin Meicun translated the name Shewupantuo as "slave of Zurvan" instead of slave of Zhemat (Demeter). He proposed that this points towards him being a follower of Zurvanism (Lin Meicun, "Zhongguo jingnei chutu," 202; or as reprint in: Lin Meicun, "Guyuan Sute mu (1998)," 202).

south of present-day Jishan 稷山 County, Shanxi Province, this fort was erected in 538 CE and represented one of the most important defence posts of the Northern Zhou against the Northern Qi, finally dissolved in 577 CE.

As mentioned above, Yuwen Yong 宇文邕 eventually succeeded in killing his cousin Yuwen Hu 宇文護 in 572 CE and assumed full powers. In the same year, Li Mu 李穆, Shi Shewu's 史射勿 former commander during 564 CE, became appointed as area commander-in-chief of Yuanzhou 原州, where Shewu 射勿 came from. Three years later, in 575 CE, Shi Shewu 史射勿, now 31 years old, was sent to serve again under him, together with an army of 30,000 soldiers, to strike back and subjugate Jiguan 軹關. This was probably the first successful campaign he participated in, and like the other soldiers, he was rewarded greatly. Despite their success, the whole campaign was originally aimed at taking Luoyang 洛陽, which after a long siege proved unsuccessful. In 577 CE, the Northern Zhou finally took Ye 鄴, the capital of the Northern Qi, thereby *de facto* ending the dynasty.

One year later, at the age of 34, Shi Shewu 史射勿 engaged in a campaign against the Jihu 稽胡 (a general Chinese term for some Northern foreign tribes) under the Supreme Pillar-of-State King of Qi 齊 Xian 憲. Starting from 578 CE, Emperor Wu 武 engaged in military campaigns against the Tujue 突厥 but fell ill and was succeeded by his eldest son Yuwen Yun 宇文贇. As was already laid out above in more detail in the biography of Yu Hong 虞弘, the latter passed the throne on to his six-year-old son Yuwen Chan 宇文闡 one year later, although he continued to retain power. After Yuwen Yun 宇文贇 fell ill and died in 580 CE, the father-in-law of Yuwen Chan 宇文闡, Yang Jian 楊建, assumed the throne and established the Sui dynasty in 581 CE. Although the epitaph does not mention any appointment, we know from his title mentioned at the beginning of the epitaph that Shewu 射勿 was also grand master for proper consultation, an honorary office which was installed by the Sui. He may thus have been appointed to this office sometime at the start of the new dynasty, probably at the court in Chang'an 長安, where he was conceivably active as a translator for Sogdian. In 582 CE, he then took part in a battle against the Tujue 突厥 north of Liangzhou 涼州 under the Commander Unequalled in Honour Duke of Qizhang 岐章 Li Gui 李軌 (or his brother Li Chong 李崇?), afterwards pursuing the surviving troops under the command of Shi Wansui 史萬歲. One year later, he was again recruited for an expedition north, under the Commander Unequalled in Honour Yao Bian 姚辯. In 583 CE, he was sent to serve under Dou Rongding 竇榮定, who was dispatched on 20.6.583 CE, in command of nine area commanders-in-chief and an army 40,000 men strong, including infantry and cavalry, to go to Liangzhou 涼州 and attack the Tujue 突厥 and Tuyuhun 吐谷渾. They met with the enemy on the Gaoyue 高越 Plain (located in the area stretching over the north-east of present-day Alxa Right Banner of Inner Mongolia Autonomous Region to the north-west of Minqin 民勤 County, Gansu Province). According to the records, when the armies faced each other, there was so little water that thirst compelled the soldiers to drink the horses' blood, and 20 or 30 percent died. As the story continues, when Rongding 榮定 sighed to heaven, it soon started to rain, and the soldiers recovered their spirits. The battle started, the enemy front rows being hit again and again. The Tujue 突厥 eventually asked for a truce and finally retired. Rongding 榮定 was rewarded with 10,000 horses and enfeoffed as lord of the Anfeng 安豐 Commandery with 1,600 households. His son Xian 憲, already mentioned above in the epitaph once, was enfeoffed as lord of the Ankang 安康 Commandery, and rewarded with 5,000 bolts of fine silk (*jian* 縑). As he and his father were greatly rewarded and ennobled, the campaign's success probably reflected beneficially on the future career of Shewu 射勿, as laid out below.

Although there is no mention of a wife on his epitaph, we know that he had seven sons that survived him, of whom we have two epitaphs (see more on these below). According to the epitaph of his eldest son Hedan 訶耽, we can establish that the latter was born one year after this campaign in ca. 584 CE, when Shewu 射勿 was 40 years old. Judging from his age, he may have had other sons born earlier that did not survive him. We do, however, know from the epitaph of Hedan 訶耽 that his mother died in 645 CE. Supposing that she was of the same age as her husband Shewu 射勿, who was born in 544 CE, she would have been 100 years old at the time of her death. He further presumably married a woman younger than him, which makes the hypothetical 100 years the minimal age she would have had attained, which is rather improbable. If one freely hypothesises that she reached the age of 65 – as her husband did – she would have been born in 585 CE and was 40 years younger than her husband. We can thus assume that the mother mentioned on Hedan's 訶耽 epitaph was probably not the first wife of Shewu 射勿, but rather his second or even a later one. His or his sons' epitaph do, however, not provide any information on which of his wives gave birth to the sons that survived him.

His latest success must have opened new perspectives for Shi Shewu 史射勿, as in 590 CE, now 46 years of age, he accompanied the imperial carriage to Bingzhou 並州, where Lord Yu Hong 虞弘 (and Long Run 龍潤?) possibly met with him. One year later, his son Shi Daole 道樂 was born, i.e. his sixth son that survived him.[118] This means that six of his sons were born from ca. 584 to 591 CE, in a time span of ca. eight years – assuming that they were his biological children. In 594 CE, his rank was first "changed" – as this was his first appointment under the Sui – into leading commander-in-chief and three years later he was promoted to great commander-in-chief – both being honorary titles. Honorary or not, in 599 CE, at the age of 55, he participated in his third campaign against the Tujue 突厥. The importance of this campaign for the whole Shi 史 family cannot be underestimated. While the Turkic khaganates were divided in war and the Sui reunited China while playing the Turkish khagans against each other, Tardu (Datou 達頭), the first *khagan* of the Western Turkic Khaganate, made intrusions into China in 599 CE. The Chinese emperor dispatched an army led by his son, the king of Han 漢, Yang Liang 楊諒. Under him, Gao Jiong 高熲, who commanded Wang Cha 王察 and Zhao Zhongqing 趙仲卿, arrived from Shuozhou 朔州, accompanied by Shi Wansui 史萬歲; Yang Su 楊素 – arguably the most prominent general of the Sui – commanded Li Che 李徹 and Han

118 Also known as Daoluo 道洛. See the analysis for a discussion of the naming discrepancies.

Sengshou 韓僧壽 and moved from Lingzhou 靈州; and Yan Rong 燕榮 came from Youzhou 幽州, in order that they successfully fight off the enemy. Shi Shewu 史射勿, who fought under Yang Su 楊素, was rewarded for his outstanding merits and promoted by two ranks – although again honorary. Still, he was appointed as cavalry general in the same year, his first ordinary rank during the Sui. In 600 CE, at the age of 56, he then campaigned north under no less than the king of Qi 齊, that is Yang Jian 楊暕, son of the future second emperor of the Sui Emperor Yang 煬. When the latter was put on the throne in 604 CE, he was sumptuously rewarded with a "piece of the best estate", amongst other things. In 605 CE his title was "changed" to cavalry general on the right (as they were now divided into the left and right), and he was again rewarded. In this year, at the age of 61, he accompanied the imperial carriage (of the new emperor) to Yangzhou 揚州 – as part of the rear guard – and was greatly rewarded. He thus certainly knew Shi Suoyan 史索嚴 of the other Shi 史 family (see below), as the latter had accompanied the imperial carriage of the crown prince one year earlier. During next two years, he conceivably celebrated the marriages of his eldest son Hedan 訶耽 and his sixth son Daole 道樂.[119]

On 3.5.609 CE, at the age of 65, he passed away in his private residence and was buried in the following winter on 20.2.610 CE in the Xianliang 賢良 Hamlet of the Xianyang 咸陽 Town in the Pingliang 平涼 Commandery (south-west of present-day Guyuan 固原, Ningxia Province). The seven sons that survived him were Hedan 訶耽 (EMC* *xa təm/tam*),[120] Changle 長樂 (EMC* *driaŋ*), Anle 安樂 (EMC* *ʔan lak*), who was grandmaster for court audiences and translated at the court as his father did, Daxing 大興 (EMC* *dajʰ xiŋʰ*), Hulang 胡郎 (EMC* *ɣɔ lanŋ*), Daole 道樂 (EMC* *dawʼ lak*),[121] and Juda 拒達 (EMC* *giăʼ dat*). Shi Shewu's 史射勿 life is marked by his solid establishment inside the highest possible ranks for non-Xianbei 鮮卑 and non-Han. His grave's vicinity to other graves of the most eminent generals of the time – among them one of the great generals of the Northern Zhou, Tian Hong 田弘, and Li Xian 李賢, under whose son he campaigned – is therefore only the logical consequence of his life.

2.3.2.7 Shi 史 of Yuanzhou 原州(1): Biography of Shi Hedan 史訶耽 (584–669 CE), Lady Kang 康 (591–630 CE), and Lady Zhang 張 (618–67 CE)

The full translation of the epitaph is to be found in Vol. 2, Appendix 2.3.

119 Also known as Daoluo 道洛. See the analysis for a discussion of the naming discrepancies.

120 His epitaph is listed below. Being born in 583 CE, he was 26 years old at the time of his father's death. Luo Feng states that of the seven sons' offices, only one is named above, which, according to him, may be due to them not having yet occupied the office at this moment, although for his son Hedan 訶耽, who "obviously" had an office, it is not listed. (Luo Feng, *Guyuan nanjiao Sui Tang mudi*, 196). In fact, Hedan 訶耽 was appointed in his first office worth mentioning in 617 CE, that is seven years after the burial (see below). Therefore, there is nothing odd to be seen in the list above.

121 Also known as Daoluo 道洛. See the analysis for a discussion of the naming discrepancies.

While his father's Shi Shewu 史射勿 epitaph stated that he came from a Western state, Hedan's 訶耽 (EMC* *xa təm/tam*) epitaph claims that he descended from the king of Kesh. His great-grandfather Ni 尼 (EMC* *nri*)[122] is said to have been great-grand *sabao* 薩寶 of the Wei and district magistrate of Zhangye 張掖. As is laid out at another place, he was more probably *sabao* 薩寶 in Kesh.[123] Although his grandfather Si 思 (EMC* *si/si*)[124] is said to have been *sabao* 薩寶 of the Northern Zhou capital (Chang'an 長安) and district magistrate of Jiuquan 酒泉, we know that he probably did not occupy these offices.[125] His father Tuo 陀 (EMC* *da*)[126] is said to have been cavalry general on the left of the Sui.[127]

Born under the Sui in ca. 584 CE, Hedan 訶耽, who later received the courtesy name Shuo 說 (EMC* *ɕwiat*), became rectifier of the Pingyuan 平原 Commandery at the age of ca. 11, an office that was in charge of selecting or proposing able people for offices, which seems a bit early. About ten years later he probably married his first wife, Lady Kang 康, him being ca. 21 and her ca. 15 years old. She is said to have come from Zhangye 張掖, Ganzhou 甘州 (present-day Gansu Province) and her family name indicates that her family probably stemmed from Samarqand. Her father Ahai 阿孩 (EMC* *ʔa ɣəj*)[128] was commander unequalled in honour, protective guard on the right, and commandant of the Soaring Hawk garrison of Heli 合黎 of the Sui, which was near Zhangye 張掖. Since he was in the protective guard, he probably met Hedan's 訶耽 father Shewu 射勿 in the capital, who accompanied the emperor during the Sui and was active as translator at the court, which may conceivably resulted in their offspring's marriage.

Only some years later, in 609 CE, his father Shewu 射勿 died and was buried in 610 CE. We can surmise that Hedan 訶耽 retired and mourned for three years, as required, since he was not promoted until the end of the Sui in 617 CE. Meanwhile, Emperor Yang 煬, second emperor of the Sui, campaigned without success against Goguryeo from 611 to 614 CE and faced an increasing number of rebellions. In 616 CE, the emperor finally chose to leave for the southern capital Jiangdu 江都 (Yangzhou 揚州, where Shewu 射勿 had once escorted him once). One of the rebels, General Li Yuan 李淵, then captured Chang'an 長安 in 617 CE, placed Yang You 楊侑, the grandson of the Emperor Yang 煬, as Emperor Gong 恭 on the throne, and made himself regent while declaring Emperor Yang 煬 retired. Installed as Prince of Tang,

122 Also known as Boboni 波波匿. See the analysis for a discussion of the naming discrepancies.

123 For the argument behind this statement, see p. 268 fn. 236.

124 Also known as Renchou 認愁, Duoxiduo 多悉多 (Tasietta'), or Duosi 多思; see the discussion of the discrepancies below.

125 See the discussion of the discrepancies below (p. 149; 2.3.2.10).

126 Also known as Shewu 射勿 (courtesy name Pantuo 槃陀), Shewupantuo 射勿槃陀, or Pantuo 槃陀; see the discussion of the discrepancies below (p. 149; 2.3.2.10).

127 On the epitaph of Shi Shewu 史射勿, he is said to have been cavalry general on the right. See the discussion of the discrepancies below (p. 149; 2.3.2.10).

128 This was also the child name of the son of Emperor Yang 煬 of the Sui, King of Qi 齊 Jian 暕, courtesy name Shiku 世胐 (585–618 CE). *Suishu* 59.1442.

he succeeded to rally some of the country under him. Meanwhile, a certain Xue Ju 薛舉 gathered an army in present-day Gansu and installed himself as emperor of the newly founded Qin in 617 CE.

Zhang Long 張隆, the governor of Pingliang 平涼 – where the Shi 史 family was based – defected to Li Yuan 李淵 on 20.1.618 CE,[129] and the commandant of the Pingliang 平涼 Commandery Shi Suoyan 史索嚴 (who knew Hedan's 訶耽 father Shewu 射勿 and was buried near him, south-west of Guyuan 固原),[130] defected in Yining 義寧 2, which lasted only from 1.2.618 to 29.5.618 CE. As Shi Suoyan 史索嚴 would campaign together with Zhang Long 張隆 against Xue Ju 薛舉 later during the same year, it is quite probable that Suoyan 索嚴 and Hedan 訶耽 (and his cadet brothers Daxing 大興 and Daoluo 道洛) defected together with their superior Zhang Long 張隆 at the end of January 618 CE or slightly later to join the forces of Li Yuan 李淵. The emperor was glad for all the defectors and appointed them in honorary offices or sent them on campaigns. Hedan 訶耽 was thus awarded under the puppet rule of the twelve-year-old Emperor Gong 恭 the honorary office of senior commandant-in-chief of cavalry and appointed grandmaster for court audiences. As is detailed later in his epitaph, this means that he worked as Sogdian translator for the Secretariat. He was also rewarded – supposedly for his defection and to gain his loyalty – with excellent horses and precious cloth. Quite interestingly, not only had his father been grand master for proper consultation under the Sui, but his cadet brother Anle 安樂 also already occupied the office of grandmaster for court audiences under the Sui and was probably at the court at the time. Hedan 訶耽 and his cadet brothers may thus have been appointed at the court due to his father's and brother's recommendation together with Suoyan 索嚴 and the latter's brother – who equally became appointed as grandmaster for court audiences[131] – and/or after getting news of the growing influence of Li Yuan 李淵.

In spring 618 CE, Yuwen Huaji 宇文化及, one of the generals that had moved with the Emperor to Jiangdu 江都, staged a coup and killed Emperor Yang 楊. Hearing of this news, Li Yuan 李淵 disposed of Emperor Gong 恭 in Chang'an 長安 and became the first ruler of the Tang dynasty, known as Emperor Gaozu 高祖. Only some months later, the above-mentioned Xue Ju 薛舉 successfully took Jingzhou 涇州 – where Hedan 訶耽 had allegedly been rectifier – and inflicted a crushing defeat to the Tang forces on the Qianshui 淺水 Plain, forcing Li Shimin 李世民 (the future second emperor of the Tang dynasty) to withdraw to Chang'an 長安. After Xue Ju 薛舉 then unexpectedly died of a sickness and his son Rengao 仁杲 ascended the throne, Tang Gaozu 高祖 sent his son Li Shimin 李世民 again into battle, who eventually succeeded to defeat the Western Qin. It must have been shortly after these events that Hedan 訶耽 was appointed as ceremonial horse groom providing for the North Gate,

129 *Zizhi tongjian* 184.5767.

130 See his biography below (p. 138; 2.3.2.6).

131 See the epitaph of his nephew Shi Daode 史道德.

i.e. the Xuanwu 玄武 Gate of Chang'an 長安.[132] Daxing 大興 and Daoluo 道洛, his cadet brothers, may at this time also have become part of respectively the imperial guard on the right and imperial bodyguard on the right.

It is quite certainly not a coincidence that his next promotion occurred in 626 CE. On the second of July of that year, the above-mentioned famous general Li Shimin 李世民 and second son of the emperor organised a coup at the Xuanwu 宣武 Gate against his older brother, Crown Prince Li Jiancheng 李建成, and his cadet brother, Li Yuanji 李元吉.[133] Fights broke out in the capital between the different imperial troops, among them the soldiers of the North Gate, of which Hedan 訶耽 was part. Li Shimin 李世民 prevailed and killed his brothers. The stamp of approval of the emperor in form of his nomination as crown prince three days later officially ended the conflict. Another sixty days later, the emperor abdicated in favour of Li Shimin 李世民, who became the second emperor of the Tang, known as Tang Taizong 唐太宗. Hedan 訶耽, who presumably was on the side of Li Shimin 李世民, must have proved himself able in his office in the Six Corrals at the palace and was appointed director of the Second Pasturage on the left in the same year. He must also have equally excelled in his new office, as the epitaph mentions that he produced the most outstanding results with his horse breeding skills.[134] However actively he had been involved in the conflict, his war times were over for now.

Under the new emperor, he was then appointed as translator in the Secretariat, followed by a promotion to court gentleman of manifest virtue in 629 CE. One year later, on 21.10.630 CE, his wife died at the age of 39 in their home in Chang'an 長安, located in Yanshou 延壽 Town, him being 46 years old.[135] He probably remarried quickly, but not sooner than three years later, since his second wife was at that time ca. 15 years old. She was named Zhang 張 and conceivably of Chinese descent. She is said to have come from Xi'e 西鄂 of the Nanyang 南陽 Commandery (north of present-day Nanyang 南陽 County, Henan Province), and her father, named Xuan 玄 (EMC* *ɣwɛn*), was district magistrate of the Rencheng 任城 District of Yanzhou 兗州 (in present-day Weishan 微山 County, Shandong Province).

Three years later, Hedan 訶耽 was promoted to gentleman for court audiences in 633 CE, court gentleman for thorough counsel in 635 CE, and gentleman for court discussion in 639 CE, now aged 55. This means that he was promoted ca. every three years since 629 CE, moving up the ranks. During this time, he probably worked together with Long Run 龍潤, who held the office of grand master for closing court and head scribe of the *sabao* 薩寶 office between 618 and 646 CE.

132 For the horses being brought to the Tang from various countries during the Wude 武德 era (618–26 CE), see: *Cefu yuangui* 970.11396a–97a. For calculations of the added benefit, see: Li Jinxiu, "Tangdai de fanshu," 48–49.

133 For an account and more information, see: Bingham, "Li Shih-min's coup I"; Bingham, "Li Shih-min's Coup II"; and: Wechsler, "Founding," 182–87.

134 For more information, see: Li Jinxiu, "Shi Hedan 2," 273.

135 See more about this location below.

His mother's funeral was held in 645 CE, which is the only information we have about her, since she is not mentioned in the epitaph of her husband. The same is true for his father; he must have paused his duties and mourned for three years. It is noteworthy, however, that his father's funeral is not mentioned. This may be due to Hedan 訶耽 occupying an office at the capital at his mother's death, whereas he only had a minor position at his father's death, meaning that his mourning may not have affected his early career. One year later, the wife of his cadet brother Daoluo 道洛 also died.

His nephew Tiebang 鐵棒, son of Hedan's 訶耽 cadet brother Daxing 大興, became appointed merit guard on the right at the imperial palace in 649 CE or early 650 CE. It was in this year that Emperor Taizong 太宗, under which Hedan 訶耽 had served for over 30 years, died, and his son succeeded him, known as Emperor Gaozong 高宗. In the first year of his newly proclaimed era, we read about Hedan 訶耽, written Hedan 訶擔, not on his epitaph, but in the chapter on queries of the *Tang hui yao*, which makes him the only Sogdian individual mentioned on all of the analysed epitaphs in this study to be found in official records:[136]

> 永徽元年十月二十四日，中書令褚遂良抑買中書譯語人史訶擔宅。監察御史韋仁約劾之。大理丞張山壽斷以遂良當徵銅二十斤。少卿張叡冊以為非當，估宜從輕。仁約奏曰：『官市依估，私但兩和耳！園宅及田，不在市肆，豈用應估？叡冊曲憑估買，斷為無罪，大理之職，豈可使斯人處之？』還遂良及叡冊官。
>
> On Yonghui 永徽 1/12/24 (22.11.650 CE),[137] the Secretariat Director Chu Suiliang 褚遂良 forcefully purchased the residence of Secretariat Translator Shi Hedan 史訶擔.[138] The Investigating Censor Wei Renyue 韋仁約[139] queried this. The Grand Judge Aide Zhang Shanshou 張山壽 sentenced that Suiliang 遂良 must be levied 20 *jin* 斤[140] of bronze (as compensation). The Vice Minister [of the Supreme Court] Zhang Ruice 張叡冊 decided [on the contrary] that there was no offence, [as] estimations should conform to the lower [price]. Renyue 仁約 [thus] presented a memorial [to Emperor Gaozong 高宗]: "The official market relies on estimation, but a private [transaction has]

136 *Tang hui yao* 61.1067; author's punctuation, followed by author's translation. It is also to be found in an abridged version in the *Cefui yuangui* 520a.6210a–b and the *Zizhi tongjian* 199.6272–73. These versions do, however, not mention his name.

137 The *Jiu Tangshu* 4.68 and *Xin Tangshu* 3.53 state that Chu Suiliang 褚遂良 was demoted on the Yonghui 永徽 1/12/[*yiwei*] (22.12.650 CE), the *Zizhi tongjian* 199.6272 records that all of these events happened on that same day, and the *Cefui yuangui* 520a.6210a dates all of these events to Yonghui 永徽 1/10 (30.10–28.11.650 CE). The truth lies probably in between.

138 His name is written with another character, i.e. *dan* 擔 (EMC* *tam*) instead of *dan* 耽 (EMC* *tom/tam*).

139 Also known under his courtesy name Siqian 思謙.

140 One *jin* 斤 is about 500 g.

> to satisfy both sides![141] [When] residence and field are not [for sale] on the market, how could the estimation apply? Ruice 叡冊 wrongly used an estimated purchase as evidence [and] decided [that it was] not a crime. The office of the grand judge, how could one permit this person to hold it?" [Thus,] Suiliang 遂良 and Ruice 叡冊 were moved (demoted)[142] to hold office [in the province].[143]

Concerning the location of the residence, as mentioned above, we know that his first wife had died in their private residence in Chang'an 長安 in Yanshou 延壽 Town, another name of the Yanshou 延壽 Quarter. The quarter was south of the Southern Administrative Quarter (*nanbu zhengfang* 南布政坊) – where a Zoroastrian temple had been erected in 621 CE under the first emperor – east of the Western Market – where imported goods were sold – and directly south-west of the imperial palace. It was probably a very lively and apparently desirable quarter, judging from the dispossession of Hedan 訶耽. In the above conflict that occurred between two of the mightiest officials in the empire under the new emperor, Hedan 訶耽 must have been a negligible pawn that happened to own an interesting property. Indeed, it seems that there were no repercussions for him, as shortly after Chu Suiliang 褚遂良 returned and was reappointed at the court on 25.2.652 CE, Hedan 訶耽 was promoted to mobile corps commander for his long and apparently diligent service in 653 CE, now aged 69.

Two years later, his cadet brother Daoluo 道洛 died. In 666 CE, over ten years later and now 82 years old, Hedan 訶耽 also survived his nephew Tiebang 鐵棒. In the same year, he was put in charge of the military matters of Guozhou 虢州 and made prefect of Guozhou 虢州 (located ca. 200 km east of the capital, in present-day Henan Province). Since we know that Li Ming 李明 was prefect of Guozhou 虢州 between 664 and 668 CE, this appointment was either fictive or rather purely honorary, quasi a retirement pension. Indeed, he wrote a memorial later in this year, asking to be dismissed from his duties. It was granted and – according to the epitaph – he was awarded 50 objects of value, which were normally bolts of fine hemp cloth, cloth made of ramie, wool cloth, or floss. He returned to his place of origin in the Quanshan 勸善 Town of the Pinggao 平高 District in Yuanzhou 原州 (present-day Guyuan 固原, Ningxia Province), where, one year later, on 30.1.667 CE, his second wife Lady Zhang 張 died. Eventually, on 23.10.669 CE, he himself died in his hometown at the age of 85. He was buried on 13.1.671 CE, about two weeks earlier than his nephew Tiebang 鐵棒 (who was buried on 29.1.671 CE, ca. 300 m west), in the by far most important grave of his family in the Xianliang 賢良 Hamlet of the Xianyang 咸陽 Town in the Pingliang 平涼 Commandery (south-west of present-day Guyuan 固原)

141 See for another use of the expression *liang he* 兩和 as "to satisfy both sides": *Tang hui yao* 88.1613.

142 That is explicitly stated in the other versions.

143 More specifically, Chu Suiliang 褚遂良 was appointed prefect of Tongzhou 同州 and Zhang Ruice 張叡冊 became prefect of Xunzhou 循州 (see also alternative accounts mentioned in the footnotes above).

together with what conceivably was his second wife – his first wife had been dead for 40 years by then.[144]

The two sons that survived him, Huluo 護羅 (EMC* *ɣɔ la*) and Huaiqing 懷慶 (EMC* *ɣwəɨj/ɣwe:j k^hiajŋ^h*), had probably moved to the capital. We do not know anything about their lives, but another piece of information is indicative of their careers. On the epitaph, their mother-in-law or mother, Lady Zhang 張, is introduced as dame of the Nanyang 南陽 Commandery. As this female nobility title was given to the wives and mothers of officials of rank 4, and her husband attained such a rank (however, honorary) as late as 666 CE, at the age of 82, and we can presume that someone else occupied his alleged office, it may quite well have been one or both of the sons who held such a rank at the time of her death.[145]

2.3.2.8 Shi 史 of Yuanzhou 原州(1): Biography of Shi Daoluo 史道洛 (591–655 CE) and Lady Kang 康 (592–646 CE)

Shi Daoluo's 史道洛 (Daoluo EMC* *dawh lak*) epitaph mentions neither a remote ancestry, nor a great-grandfather, nor does it provide a courtesy name – although he may not have had one – but it states Pinggao 平高 of Yuanzhou 原州 (present-day Guyuan 固原, Ningxia Province) as choronym. Although his grandfather Duoxiduo 多悉多 (Sogd. Tasietta') is said to have been regional inspector of Shanzhou 鄯州 and great *sabao* 薩寶 of the Northern Zhou, we know that he did probably not occupy these offices during his lifetime. His father Shewupantuo 射勿槃陀 (EMC* *ʑiah mut ban da*) is further said to have been cavalry general on the left and commander unequalled in honour of the Sui.

Daoluo 道洛 was born in ca. 591 CE, when his father was 47 years old. From the latter's epitaph, he is known to us as the sixth son who survived his father. He probably married in his teens (possibly in 607 CE) his wife Lady Kang 康, who was of Sogdian descent (judging by her name) and one year younger than him. In 609 CE his father died. As was proposed above in the biography of Hedan 訶耽, he then probably defected to the Tang in 618 CE together with his elder brothers Hedan 訶耽 and Daxing 大興 and became imperial bodyguard on the right. No further appointments are mentioned, which is rather odd, when compared to the impressive career of his elder brother Hedan 訶耽. His mother died in 645 CE, and one year later, his wife, on 4.3.646 CE. His nephew Tiebang 鐵棒, son of his elder brother Daxing 大興, then was appointed at the imperial palace as merit guard on the right in 649 CE or early 650 CE.

On 11.3.655 CE, Daoluo 道洛 died at the age of 64 CE in his home in Quanshan 勸善 Town of the Pinggao 平高 District of Yuanzhou 原州 (present-day Guyuan 固原, Ningxia Province). On 22.1.659 CE, he was buried together with his wife in the Baida 百達 Plain, in the Xianliang 賢良 Hamlet of the Xianyang 咸陽 Town in the Pingliang 平涼 Commandery (south-west of present-day Guyuan 固原), in the same month as Shi

144 This specific name of the location is indicated on his father's epitaph.
145 See the glossary for this mechanism (*jun jun* 郡君).

Suoyan 史索嚴 – who was buried, probably sometime earlier, between 30.12.658–28.1.659 CE. They had one son, named De 德 (EMC* *tək*), who survived them.

2.3.2.9 Shi 史 of Yuanzhou 原州⁽¹⁾: Biography of Shi Tiebang 史鐵棒 (623–66 CE)

Like his uncle, Shi Tiebang's 史鐵棒 (Tiebang EMC* *tʰɛt baɨwŋ'/boeːwŋ'*) epitaph does not mention a remote ancestry but provides as choronym Pinggao 平高 of Yuanzhou 原州 (present-day Guyuan 固原, Ningxia Province). Although his great-grandfather Duosi 多思 (EMC* *sɨ/si ta*)[146] is said to have been great *sabao* 薩寶 of the Northern Zhou capital Chang'an 長安 and district magistrate of Jiuquan 酒泉,[147] we know that he did probably not occupy such offices.[148] His grandfather Pantuo 槃陀 (EMC* *ban da*)[149] was cavalry general on the left of the Sui[150] and his father Daxing 大興 (EMC* *dajʰ xiŋʰ*) imperial senior commandant-in-chief of cavalry of the Tang, part of the imperial guard on the right, and military commander of the Anhua 安化 Garrison (like Shi Daode's 史道德 grandfather Duo 多).[151]

Tiebang 鐵棒, who later received the courtesy name Shanji 善集 (EMC* *dzianʰ dzip*), was born in ca. 623 CE. Following the footsteps of his father and uncles, he became appointed merit guard on the right at the imperial palace in 649 CE or early 650 CE, at the age of 26 or 27. Like his uncle Hedan 訶耽, who had been in charge breeding horses, he became director of the 17th pasturage on the right at the Court of the Imperial Stud in 658 CE. He died on 26.9.666 CE in his residence in the Quanshan 勸善 Town of the Pinggao 平高 District of Yuanzhou 原州 (south-west of present-day Guyuan 固原, Ningxia Province), at the comparatively young age of 43. His sons Xiaozhong 孝忠 (EMC* *xaɨwʰ/xɛːwʰ truwŋ*) and Xiaoyi 孝義 (EMC* *xaɨwʰ/xɛːwʰ ŋiăʰ/ŋiʰ*) reburied him four years later, only some weeks later than his uncle Hedan 史訶耽 (who was buried on 13.1.671 CE). They may have waited for an auspicious date to bury them both, and/or were interrupted with their preparations by the death of Tiebang's 鐵棒 aunt Lady Zhang 張 (Hedan's 訶耽 second wife) in 667 CE. However, it is hardly by chance that he was buried ca. 300 m east of and 16 days after his uncle Hedan 訶耽. Nothing is known of his wife.

146 Also known as Renchou 認愁, Si 思, or Duoxiduo 多悉多; see the discussion of the discrepancies below (p. 149; 2.3.2.10).

147 The title is not mentioned in the epitaph of Shi Shewu 史射勿. The vagueness of the title may point towards a posthumous addition. The next available data concerning this district is from the *Yuanhe junxian tuzhi* 40.438, it is stated that around 713 CE, it counted 2,253 households and eight hamlets, therefore according to *Jiu Tangshu* 43.1825 qualifying as middle district. Despite the considerable time gap between those two dates, his rank may have ranged from 7a2 or 8a2.

148 See the discussion of the discrepancies below.

149 Also known as Shewu 射勿 (courtesy name Pantuo 槃陀), Tuo 陀, or Shewupantuo 射勿槃陀; see the discussion of the discrepancies below.

150 On the epitaph of Shi Shewu 史射勿, he is said to have been cavalry general on the right. See the discussion of the discrepancies below.

151 See below in his biography and in the analysis.

2.3.2.10 Shi 史 of Yuanzhou 原州[1]: Discrepancies

There are several discrepancies between the four epitaphs of the first Shi 史 family which are presented chronologically in the following table – including the information from Suoyan's 索巖 epitaph from the second Shi 史 family is added, as will be explained below. The cell of the epitaph from which the information stems is the lowest:

Table 6: Juxtaposition of the epitaphs' information

Miaoni 妙尼				
office in his land as *sabao* 薩寶				
Boboni 波波匿	Ni 尼			
office in his land as *sabao* 薩寶	great-grand *sabao* 薩寶 of the Wei, district magistrate of Zhangye 張掖			
Renchou 認愁	Si 思	Duoxiduo 多悉多	Duosi 多思	Si 嗣
not this career	*sabao* 薩寶 of the Northern Zhou capital Chang'an 長安, district magistrate of Jiuquan 酒泉	regional inspector of Shanzhou 鄯州, great *sabao* 薩寶 of the Northern Zhou	great *sabao* 薩寶 of the Northern Zhou capital Chang'an 長安, district magistrate of Jiuquan 酒泉	general for securing faraway lands, cavalier attendant-in-ordinary, commandery duke of Xiping 西平, in charge of the military matters of Shanzhou 鄯州 and Kuozhou 廓州, regional inspector of Shanzhou 鄯州 of the Northern Zhou

Shewu 射勿, Pantuo 槃陀 (544–609)	Tuo 陀	Shewupantuo 射勿槃陀	Pantuo 槃陀	Duo 多
commander unequalled in honour, cavalry general on the *right*, grand master for proper consultation	cavalry general on the *left*	cavalry general on the *left*, commander unequalled in honour	cavalry general on the *left*	senior serviceman, outpost general, palace adjutant, part of the imperial guard on the left, cavalry general of the Northern Zhou
	Hedan 訶耽, Shuo 說 (584–669)	Daoluo 道洛 (591–655)	Daxing 大興	Suoyan 索嚴 (579–659)
			imperial senior commandant-in-chief of cavalry, part of the imperial guard on the right, military commander of the Anhua 安化 Garrison	
			Tiebang 鐵棒, Shanji 善集 (623–66)	

The grandfather of Shewu 射勿 and thus great-grandfather of Hedan 訶耽 are respectively called Boboni 波波匿 and Ni 尼. On Shi Hedan's 史訶耽 epitaph the names are merely simplified: for his father Shewu 射勿 from Pantuo 槃陀 to Tuo 陀, and for his grandfather from Boboni 波波匿 to Ni 尼. I further concur with Luo Feng that the exchange of *ni* 匿 and *ni* 尼 is possibly due to the homophony.[152] However, while the epitaph of Shewu 射勿 states that his grandfather Boboni 波波匿 was *sabao* 薩寶 in Kesh, the epitaph of his eldest son Hedan 訶耽 mentions him as great-grand *sabao* 摩訶大薩寶 of the Wei as well as district magistrate of Zhangye 張掖, and the epitaph of his sixth son Daoluo 道洛 does not mention him. The additions of "great-

152 Luo Feng, *Guyuan nanjiao Sui Tang mudi*, 187.

grand" *mahe da* 摩訶大 to *sabao* 薩寶 for Boboni 波波匿, and the claim that he was already in this office during the Wei and district magistrate of Zhangye 張掖 is probably fictive.

Renchou 認愁, Si 思, Duoxiduo 多悉多, and Duosi 多思 are one person. I concur with Luo Feng that the Chinese renderings reflect the meaning of the Sogdian name, which is to be recognised in Duoxiduo 多悉多, Sogd. Tasietta'.[153] The different Chinese names essentially mean "pondering" or "worrying a lot". As was proposed above in the biography of Shewu 射勿, I proposed to read that Renchou 認愁 did not follow "this career", referring to the *sabao*, and maybe, even more specifically, that he was not *sabao* in Kesh. However, the next person to die after Shewu 射勿 was Daoluo 道洛, whose epitaph says that his grandfather was regional inspector of Shanzhou 鄯州 and great *sabao* 薩寶 of the Northern Zhou. The epitaph of his first son, Hedan 訶耽, notes that his grandfather was *sabao* 薩寶 of the Northern Zhou capital Chang'an 長安 and district magistrate of Jiuquan 酒泉. Further, the epitaph of his sixth son Daoluo 道洛 states that his grandfather was regional inspector of Shanzhou 鄯州 and great *sabao* 薩寶 of the Northern Zhou. Finally, the epitaph of his grandson Tiebang 鐵棒, states that his great-grandfather was great *sabao* 薩寶 of the Northern Zhou capital and district magistrate of Jiuquan 酒泉. This is especially remarkable, since Tiebang 鐵棒 was buried only 16 days and 300 m apart from his uncle Hedan 訶耽, with epitaph cover stones that are nearly identical from the composition. However, while the epitaphs of Tiebang 鐵棒 and Daoluo 道洛 – written 12 years apart – accord on calling him great *sabao* 薩寶, the epitaph of Hedan 訶耽 only provides for him the title of *sabao* 薩寶. It is quite astounding that two epitaphs composed at the same time for members of the same family would differ – which does, however, show how flexible they operated with titles, facts, and generally any regulations that might have applied.

That they mention him being *sabao* at all may be explained by revisiting the sentence quoted in the biography of Shewu 射勿: "[His time] went by until old age, [and he did] not follow this career path." The main reason to write such a sentence on the epitaph of Shewu 射勿 was probably to emphasise the grand history of the family and to state how regrettable it was that his father had not been able to follow this career. The quote may also express that being *sabao* in Kesh was usually hereditary and that since he was the one to establish himself in China, he could not follow in the steps of his forefathers and broke with the family tradition. Indeed, neither himself nor his sons or grandsons were *sabao*. In the next generations, the sons' and grandsons' epitaphs reflect the choice to close the gap by claiming that he held the office of *sabao* of the capital and district magistrate of Jiuquan 酒泉 or regional inspector of Shanzhou 鄯州. There is further the possibility, given by the official

153 Ibid., 191. As the excavation report points out (Yuanzhou lianhe kaogudui, *Tang Shi Daoluo mu*, 215, fn. 2), Ikeda On published in 1965 an article studying the settlement of Sogdians in Dunhuang in the eighth century CE which includes a document with the similar name of An Wuxiduo 安烏悉多 (Ikeda On, "Hasseiki chūyō," 65).

system of the Sui and Tang, to apply for a posthumous office for the generation of the grandfather, for example due to the status of Hedan 訶耽.[154] In the case above, these titles were however most probably fictive.

What remains, is the office of regional inspector of Shanzhou 鄯州 for Duoxiduo 多悉多, solely mentioned on the epitaph of Daoluo 道洛. Given that he and Shi Suoyan 史索嚴 were buried only a few weeks and hundred meters apart, and also have epitaph cover stones that are nearly identical from the composition, I propose that the authors of Daoluo's 道洛 epitaph chose to take over the office of Suoyan's 索嚴 grandfather into their own biography, as his own grandfather did not have a career worth mentioning.

Finally, while on Shewu's 射勿 epitaph he is mentioned as cavalry general on the *right* of the Sui, the three other epitaphs state that he was cavalry general on the *left* of the Sui. We can assume that he was cavalry general on the right, as his own epitaph is to be preferred.

154 On such posthumous additions, see: Zhao Heping, "Shi shi jiazu muzhi," 347.

2.3.2.11 Shi 史 of Yuanzhou 原州(2): Family tree

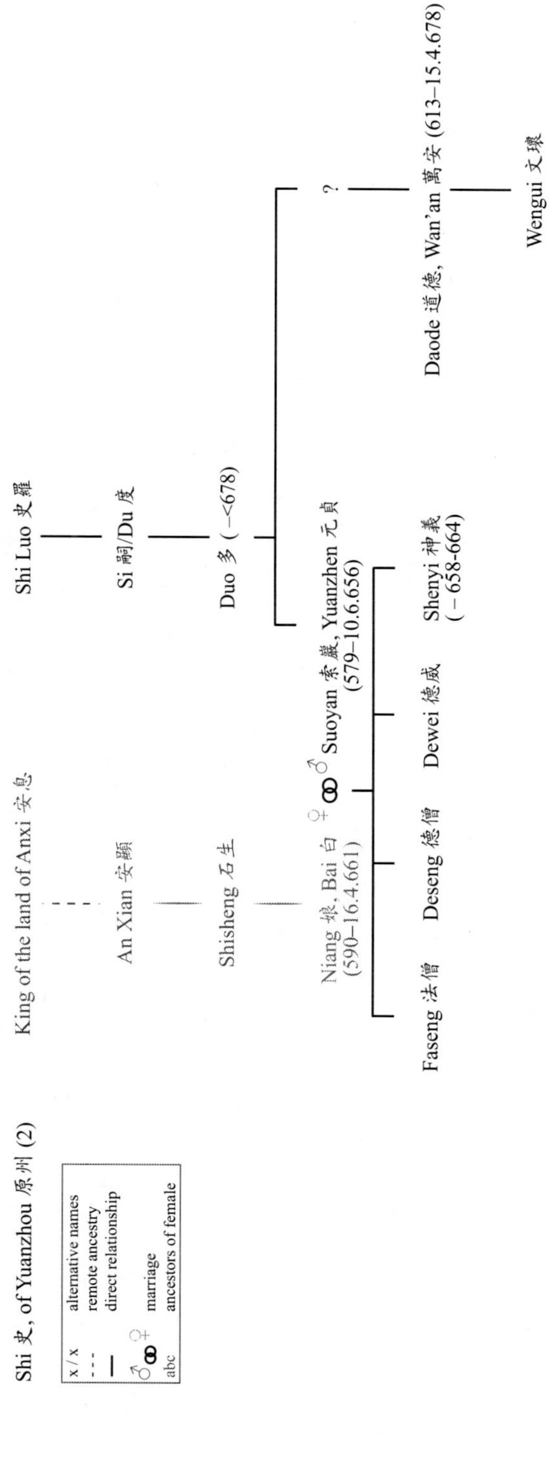

Figure 8: Family tree of the Shi 史 of Yuanzhou 原州(2)
Source: M. Huber

2.3.3.12 Shi 史 of Yuanzhou 原州 (2): Biography of Shi Suoyan 史索巖 (579–656 CE) and An Niang 安娘 (590–661 CE)

Judging from his name, the close relationship to the other Sogdian Shi 史 family, and his burial, Shi Suoyan's 史索嚴 (Suoyan EMC* *sak ŋaim/ŋɛːm*) family probably stemmed from Kesh and immigrated to China maybe as soon as the Northern Wei. When the Northern Wei defeated the Northern Liang in 439 CE and Emperor Taiwu 太武 forced 30,000 families to move to the capital of the Northern Wei (Pingcheng 平城), his family was conceivably afflicted of this resettlement from Liangzhou 涼州, as the epitaph states that one of his ancestors became an official in Yuanzhou 原州 around the Northern Wei. This is probably the reason for the choronym of the epitaph to be Feiqiao 飛橋 of Jiankang 建康 (located in the south-east of present-day Gaotai 高台 County, Gansu Province).[155] His grandfather Luo 羅 (EMC* *la*) was said to have been general for appeasing faraway lands of the Northern Wei and had been ennobled as commandery duke of Xiping 西平 with 800 households (in present-day Huangyuan 湟源 and Ledu 樂都 Counties, Qinghai Province). Under the Northern Zhou, his grandfather Si 嗣 (EMC* *zi^h/zi^h*) was general for securing faraway lands, cavalier attendant-in-ordinary, in charge of the military matters of Shanzhou 鄯州 and Kuozhou 廓州, regional inspector of Shanzhou 鄯州, and, like his father, commandery duke of Xiping 西平 (all located in present-day Qinghai Province). His father Duo 多 (EMC* *ta*) was senior serviceman, outpost general, palace adjutant, part of the imperial guard on the left, and cavalry general under the Northern Zhou.

Suoyan 索嚴, who later received the courtesy name of Yuanzhen 元貞 (EMC* *ŋuan triajŋ*), was born in ca. 579 CE under the Northern Zhou. When the Sui was established two years later, his father must have been employed by the new emperor, as Suoyan 索嚴, following the career path of his father who had been part of the

155 There seems to be a lot of confusion and controversy as to where Shi Suoyan 史索巖 and Shi Daode's 史道德 family came from, as well as where Jiankang 建康 commandery, Jiankang City 建康城, Feiqiao 飛橋 and Lingwu 靈武 are located. See: Zhao Chao, "Shi Daode muzhi"; Ma Chi, "Shi Daode"; Luo Feng, "Ye tan Shi Daode zushu ji xiangguan wenti – da Zhao Chao tongzhi," *Wenwu*, 1988; Luo Feng, *Guyuan nanjiao Sui Tang mudi*, 196–99; Wang Shangshou and Ji Chengjia, *Sichou zhi lu*, 26; Shi Weile, *Zhongguo lishi diming 2*, 1716.
As proposed above, his ancestors were most probably moved during the deportations in Liangzhou 涼州 to Yuanzhou 原州 (其先建康飛橋人事; see p. 231; 2.4.4.1). The epitaph then goes on to propose some other famous examples of people with the same surname. Finally, information that may be more reliable, concerning a closer ancestor, is presented: 遠祖因宦來徙平高，其後子孫家焉，故今為縣人也。"Because a remote ancestor moved to Pinggao 平高 to occupy an office, his sons and grandsons [moved] their family there. From then to now, they lived in this district." The important quality difference is between *qi xian* 其先 (his remote/alleged ancestor, often referring to a famous ancestor, e.g., a king) and *yuan zu* 遠祖 (a remote ancestor, the next being his great-grandfather). I therefore will not dare to rely on the alleged remote ancestors to argument for or against his ethnic affiliation and prefer to rely on the archaeological findings, including golden facial decorations and a chin strap (which came to China during the Northern Wei (See: Müller, "Chin-Straps") and Sasanian coins; the other funerary goods are even less conclusive. He thus perceivably was a Sogdian (from Kesh?) or of some western region and his family came quite early to China, possibly during the Northern Wei.

imperial guard of the Northern Zhou, became appointed as guard attending chariots of the King of Jin 晉 Yang Guang 楊廣 in the Sui. This was none other than the son of the emperor, who was enfeoffed as king of Jin 晉 in 581 CE, at the age of 13. In 600 CE, the emperor deposed his eldest son Yong 勇 and made Guang 廣 crown prince. In the first month of 604 CE, he was then transferred all governmental powers. In the tenth month, the emperor became sick and ordered his heir to come to the palace. It was probably at this occasion that Suoyan 索嚴 escorted the imperial carriage of the crown prince to his residence, the Eastern Palace, and became appointed great commander-in-chief and imperial bodyguard. While the *Suishu* didn't record anything noteworthy, later historians expressed doubts about a harmonious change of power, in which the crown prince played a questionable role. Imperial guards are explicitly mentioned in the related record, as the emperor replaced the guards of his death bed by trusted ones – meaning that 索嚴 could have witnessed the last moments of the emperor.[156] After the emperor died, the epitaph specifically mentions that the new emperor, known as Emperor Yang 煬, first proceeded to appoint his inner retinue and thus made Suoyan 索嚴, aged 26, protective guard on the left and soaring hawk commandant of the Anqiu 安丘 Prefecture.[157] He conceivably met the above-mentioned Shi Shewu 史射勿, as the latter accompanied the imperial carriage one year later.

We know from the epitaph of his wife that in ca. 605 CE, now aged 26, he married An Niang 安娘 (Niang EMC* *nrɨaŋ*), who was 15 years old at that time and later received the courtesy name Bai 白 (EMC* *baɨjk/bɛːjk*, lit. white; maybe referring to her skin colour, white being a sign of beauty – her complexion is mentioned a second time in the third strophe of the epitaph's verse). Judging from her name, her family may have stemmed from Bukhārā in Sogdiana. Her epitaph states that she descended from the king of the land of Anxi 安息, which at the time of the composition of the epitaph probably referred to An 安 (Bukhārā) instead of Parthia.[158] She is said to have come from Qiyang 岐陽 of Qizhou 岐州 (ca. present-day Qishan 岐山 County, Shaanxi Province). Her grandfather Xian 顯 (EMC* *xɛn'*) was said to have been commander unequalled in honour and cavalry general under the Northern Zhou, and her father Shisheng 石生 (EMC* *dʑiajk*) commander unequalled in honour under the Sui.

In 613 CE, Suoyan 索嚴 was then promoted to commandant of the Pingliang 平涼 Commandery, which was where the epitaph says his ancestors had (or were) settled long ago. As was laid out – together with the political events of the following years – in the biography of Hedan 訶耽 above, he probably defected together with Hedan 訶耽, Daxing 大興, Daoluo 道洛, and his superior Zhang Long 張隆 in early 618 CE to the Tang and became grandmaster for court audiences – like his brother[159] – and military

156 See, among others: *Zizhi tongjian* 180.5602–4.

157 Either this title is honorary and it refers to the Anqiu 安丘 District in present-day Shandong province, or there is no other record of it.

158 I.e. in starting from the Xianqing 顯慶 era (656–61 CE). See the glossary.

159 The father of Daode 道德, see below.

commander of the right army. In the same year, he also participated in a campaign with Zhang Long 張隆 against Xue Ju 薛舉 (see also above the epitaph of Hedan 訶耽). Three years later, now aged 42, he was appointed encampment guard on the left and cavalry general. This was his last promotion, as one year after the second emperor took over the throne, he became sick in 627 CE was retired from duty at the age of 48. We may think of this as an act of "inner emigration", defying the second emperor, as he continued to live for another 30 years, eventually dying on the 10.6.656 CE in his private residence in the Wanfu 萬福 Town of Yuanzhou 原州. He was buried in late 658 CE or early 659 CE in the "elevated plain" known to us by the other epitaphs as Baida 百達 Plain (south-west of present-day Guyuan 固原), probably just some days earlier than Shi Daoluo 史道洛 (who was buried on the 22.1.659 CE).

His wife died five years after him on the 16.4.661 CE in the Zhaoyuan 招遠 Town of the Pinggao 平高 District of Yuanzhou 原州, meaning that she had moved in between. As her nephew Daode 道德 (see below) died in the same town, it is possible that she moved in with her brother-in-law or nephew. Her husband's grave was then re-opened and she was buried on the 9.12.664 CE. Whereas his epitaphs mentioned four sons, Faseng 法僧 (EMC* *puap səɲ*), Deseng 德僧 (EMC* *tək səɲ*), Dewei 德威 (EMC* *tək ?uj*), and Shenyi 神義 (EMC* *ʑin ŋiăh/ŋih*), hers lists only Faseng 法僧, Deseng 德僧, and Dewei 德威, leaving out the fourth. Rather peculiar, this conceivably points towards the fourth son having passed away in between the two burials, the first being held in late 658 or early 659 CE, and the second in 664 CE.[160]

2.3.3.13 Shi 史 of Yuanzhou 原州(2): Biography of Shi Daode 史道德 (613–78 CE)

Whereas his uncle Suoyan's 索嚴 epitaph gave Feiqiao 飛橋 of Jiankang 建康 as choronym and recorded that one of his ancestor's became an official in Yuanzhou 原州 during the Northern Wei, Daode's 道德 (EMC* *dawʾ tək*) epitaph gives no choronym and instead recalls historical figures named Shi 史, as Shi Yu 史魚 of the Spring and Autumn Period, and Shi Dan 史丹 of the Han, insinuating that some later members of the family moved to present-day Gansu. Fictive as these figures may be, the same information as found on his uncle's epitaph is produced, i.e. that some ancestor became officials in the Pinggao 平高 District of Yuanzhou 原州.[161] As I already proposed above, his family was conceivably afflicted by this resettlement from Liangzhou 涼州 by Emperor Taiwu 太武 in 439 CE.

His grandfather Du 度 (EMC* *dɔʰ*) is said to have been in charge of the military matters of Hezhou 河州, Weizhou 渭州, and Shanzhou 鄯州 of the Northern Zhou. Suoyan's 索嚴 epitaph says however that this person was called Si 嗣 and had been general for securing faraway lands, cavalier attendant-in-ordinary, in charge of the military matters of Shanzhou 鄯州 and Kuozhou 廓州, regional inspector of Shanzhou 鄯州, and commandery duke of Xiping 西平. While the locations and offices more or less coincide, the names don't seem to do so. Whereas for the other

160 See the analysis below.
161 See p. 156 fn. 155. See also the analysis below.

Shi 史 family, translations and transcriptions from Sogdian or abbreviations led to different names, this conflicting example has not been solved yet. *Si* 嗣 means to inherit, to carry on, to follow, or simply "the next" or "the second". *Du* 度 has a variety of meanings, of which one bears resemblance: it can mean to grant or confer (used in combination with *yu* 與, "to" someone). Although the first expresses the action from the viewpoint of the receiver and the second from the donor, this may be the translation of the meaning of a Sogdian given name, i.e. something close to "conferring" or being "conferred", e.g. "the one who passes on" or "the heir"?

Daode's 道德 grandfather Duo 多 (EMC* *ta*) is said to have been commander unequalled in honour, part of the imperial guard on the left, and cavalry general of the Anhua 安化 Garrison *under the Sui* (like Tiebang's 鐵棒 father Daxing 大興). In comparison, Suoyan's 索嚴 epitaph noted that his father Duo 多 was senior serviceman, outpost general, palace adjutant, part of the imperial guard on the left, and cavalry general *under the Northern Zhou*. As both the name and titles match rather well, is can be assumed that he was employed in these positions under the Northern Zhou and Sui. We don't know his father's name, for which cells were left out, but the character *kao* 考, with which he is introduced, indicates that he already had died at the time of the epitaph's composition in 678 CE. Duo 多 is said to have been imperial grand master for proper consultation – like his brother Suoyan 索嚴 – and had been ennobled as dynasty-founding marquis of the Pingliang 平涼 District.

Daode 道德, who later received the courtesy name Wan'an 萬安 (EMC* *muanh ?an*), was born in ca. 613 CE. Like his grandfather, who had been part of the imperial guard on the left, and his father, who was imperial grand master for proper consultation, he entered the palace as merit guard on the left of the crown prince. Since the next appointment only took place in 663 CE – assuming that he did not become merit guard before the age of 14 – he could have served under four different crown princes: Li Chengqian 李承乾 (crown prince in 627–43 CE), Li Zhi 李治 (crown prince in 643–49 CE), Li Zhong 李忠 (crown prince in 652–56 CE), or Li Hong 李弘 (crown prince in 656–75 CE).[162]

In 663 CE, at the age of 50, he became gentleman attendant at the palace gate, an honorary civil service title, and promoted to pasturage director of Yuting 玉亭.[163] Six years later, he was decreed head pasturage director of Lanchi 蘭池, located approximately in the northern part of present-day Gansu and maybe partly in the Ejin 額濟納 Banner of Inner Mongolia Autonomous Region, and was since long a famous place for horse breeding.[164] Besides historical annals, this is underpinned by poems

162 There was no crown prince 649–52 CE.

163 There is only one Yuting 玉亭 District that I could find, located in present-day Jiangxi Province, which existed 621–24 CE according to the sources. It is however highly improbable that this place was referred to here. Judging from his next office, there must have been a Yuting 玉亭 somewhere north.

164 Among other passages, see the theft of 10,000 horses by Ashina Mochuo 阿史那默啜 (Qapaghan Qaghan) from the Longyou 隴右 region at the beginning of the eighth century: *Jiu Tangshu* 7.143 and 194a.5170; translated in: Liu Mau-tsai, *Chinesischen Nachrichten I*, 164;

from the Southern Chen and Northern Zhou which mention the excellency of these horses.[165] Wang Ji 王績 (585–644 CE), a poet who during the Sui held an office in the imperial library of Chang'an 長安 and then retired after the dynasty collapsed, vividly describes in a poem how in 608 CE, the palace guard cavalry prepared their horses of Lanchi 蘭池, cracked their whips and rode on them until their sweat ran.[166] Daode 道德 did thus provide the horses for the imperial guard, in which he had served.

On the 15.4.678 CE, he died in his private residence in the Zhaoyuan 招遠 Town of the Pinggao 平高 District of Yuanzhou 原州[167] at the age of 65 and was buried on the 27.11.678 CE in the Baida 百達 Plain of Yuanzhou 原州 (south-west of present-day Guyuan 固原, Ningxia Province). Nothing is known about a wife, but one son named Wengui 文瓌 (EMC* *mun kwəj*) is mentioned, who survived him.

2.3.2.14 Cao Yi 曹怡 of the Tang (581–655 CE)

2.3.2.14.1 Family tree

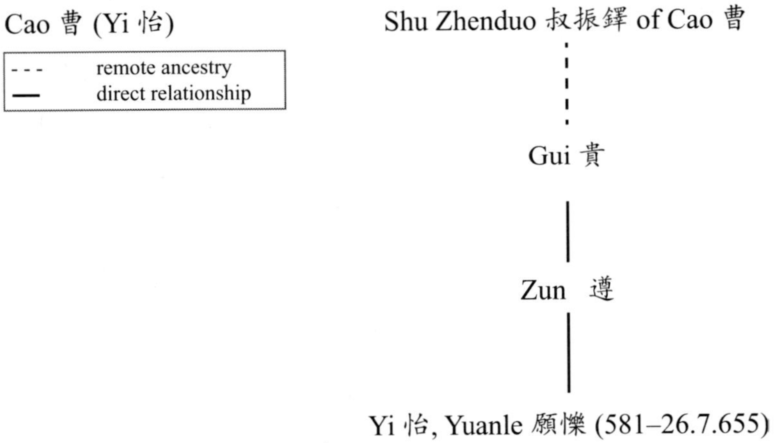

Figure 9: Family tree of Cao Yi 曹怡

Source: M. Huber

also recounted in: *Xin Tangshu* 215a.6047; translated in: Liu Mau-tsai, *Chinesischen Nachrichten I*, 218. The latter account also mentions his theft of 100,000 sheep and horses in Yanzhou 鹽州 and Xiazhou 夏州.

165 *Hou tu kan qima shi* 後園看騎馬詩 (*Liang shi* 梁詩 25.2050; in the *Xian Qin Han Wei Jin Nanbeichao shi*); *Yong hua pinfeng shi ershiwu shou* 詠畫屏風詩二十五首 (*Bei Zhou shi* 北周詩 4.2395); to be found in the *Yiwen leiju* 93.1620.

166 *San ri fu* 三日賦 (*Quan Tang wen* 131.1314b–16a).

167 At the same place as his aunt. See above Shi Suoyan 史索巖 and An Niang 安娘.

2.3.2.14.2 Biography

Cao Yi's 曹怡 (Yi EMC* *ji/ji*) family is said to have descended from the son of King Wen 文 of the Zhou, Shu Zhenduo 叔振鐸 of Cao 曹 – a classical claim to antiquity also employed by other individuals having this family name, such as Cao Cheng 曹澄 (594–673 CE).[168] The Xicheng 隰城 District is given as choronym and corresponds to the location in which the epitaph was found, i.e. present-day Fengyang 汾陽 City, Shanxi Province. His grandfather, Gui 貴 (EMC* *kuj^h*), was said to have been valiant general of the Northern Qi. The Northern Zhou invaded and were eventually themselves replaced by the Sui in 581 CE. Yi 怡 was born in that year. After the Tang were established in 618 CE, his father, Zun 遵 (EMC* *tswin*), was appointed as commandant of cavalry of the *sabao* 薩寶 office of Jiezhou 介州 and stayed in office until at latest 627 CE.

Yi 怡, who later received the courtesy name Yuanle 願懽 (EMC* *ŋuan^h lak (?)*), is said to have been part of the troops helping to establish the Tang and was therefore appointed as commandant of cavalry.[169] It seems as if his father may have been taken over into the Tang army and both him and his son, who was 37 years old in 618 CE, were rewarded similar titles. However, it is difficult to say with certainty if Cao Yi's 曹怡 office was part of the *sabao* 薩寶 office or not. On the 26.7.655 CE, he died in his home at the age of 74 and was buried on the fourth November of the same year, ca. one km north-west of the city wall of Fenyang 汾陽.

Based on his father and maybe even himself being military personnel in the *sabao* 薩寶 office and his family name being Cao 曹, there is a good chance that he was in fact the descendant of Sogdians that once came from the country of Cao 曹, i.e. Kapūtānā. However, there is nothing about or in his grave that provides supportive evidence for this conclusion. If the claim to descend from Chinese rulers is to be interpreted as a possible strategy to cover his foreign descent or if it is simply aiming to increase his prestige, is further impossible to say.

168 叔振鐸之初□，因封命氏；平陽侯/之雅望，纂慶承家。帝子周親，仲尼㪍聖人之後；功臣漢□，茂先/恥王佐之才，由是弈葉傳芳，□□間出，固以載諸史冊，今可略/而言矣。Zhou Shaoliang and Zhao Chao, *Tangdai muzhi*, 574–75.

169 From the epitaph: 起家元從，陪翊[□]義旗。

2.3.2.15 He 何, in Yanchi 鹽池, Ningxia Province

2.3.2.15.1 Family tree

Figure 10: Family tree of He 何
Source: M. Huber

2.3.2.15.2 Introduction: the epitaph of grave M3

In grave M3 was found an epitaph of a surnamed He 何, and two small perforated green glass balls (Dia 3.6 mm, perforation Dia 0.7 mm), probably of a headdress (similar to the ones in Li Chui's 李倕 grave, see Figure 228, Vol. 2, Appendix 1.8.4). Further, in grave M6 was found a stone door with two stone leaves engraved with two dancers performing the swirling Western dance.[170] Although the choronym provided is "Yuezhi 月氏 of Bactria (Daxia 大夏)", He 何 belongs to the few extant Sogdian names. Apart from these few finds, which led to the inclusion in the present study, the connections between the Yuezhi 月氏, Bactria (Daxia 大夏), and the Sogdians remain rather unclear.[171]

2.3.2.15.3 Biography of He 何 ? (616–700 CE)

As just mentioned, the epitaph states that the buried was a Yuezhi 月氏 of Bactria (Daxia 大夏). It does not provide a remote ancestry, although the transcription is admittedly full of *lacunae*. We know at least that it must have been a male, judging from his later office.

His great-grandfather, of which we lack the name, is said to have been majestic general of the Northern Zhou or Sui. His grandfather Yiwei 乙未 (EMC* *?it* muj^h, 575–? CE) is said to have been appointed as supreme pillar-of-state of the Tang and

170 Ningxia huizu zizhiqu bowuguan, "Ningxia Yanchi mu".
171 See: Yoshida Yutaka, "On the Origin".

enfeoffed with some land. His father Panchi 盤池 (EMC* *ban driă/dri*) is mentioned as commandant of some place during the Tang.

He himself, the name lacking, was born in ca. 616 CE. We only know that he became appointed commandant of some place under the Wu Zhou, meaning that he was between 74 and 84 years old at the time of appointment, as he died on the 27.7.700 CE in his private residence in the Rulu 如魯 District of Luzhou 魯州 in some town.[172] Relatively soon later, he was buried 21 days later east of a city in the Shiku 石窟 Plain, in the heat of August, on the 17.8.700 CE, probably due to the climate and soil.

172 As the characters before *duwei* 都尉 (commandant) are illegible, it is possible that he was a *zhechong duwei* 折衝都尉 (assault-resisting commandant) or *guoyi duwei* 果毅都尉 (courageous (vice) commandant), ranging from rank 4a1 to 6b2; alternatively he may have had another office, stated before this one.
According to the *Xin Tangshu* 37.974–75, Luzhou 魯州 was installed in 679 CE to administer the Tujue 突厥, located in present-day Otog Banner and Otog Front Banner of Inner Mongolia Autonomous Region, being part of the Six Foreign Districts (*Liu hu zhou* 六胡州: Luzhou 魯州, Lizhou 麗州, Hanzhou 含州, Saizhou 塞州, Yizhou 依州, Qichou 契州). Due to the grave and epitaph of He 何, it can be established that Luzhou 魯州 stretched also over the northern part of present-day Ningxia Province.

2.3.2.16 An Pu 安菩 (An Pusa 安菩薩, 601–64 CE) and Lady He 何 (622–704 CE)

2.3.2.16.1 Family tree

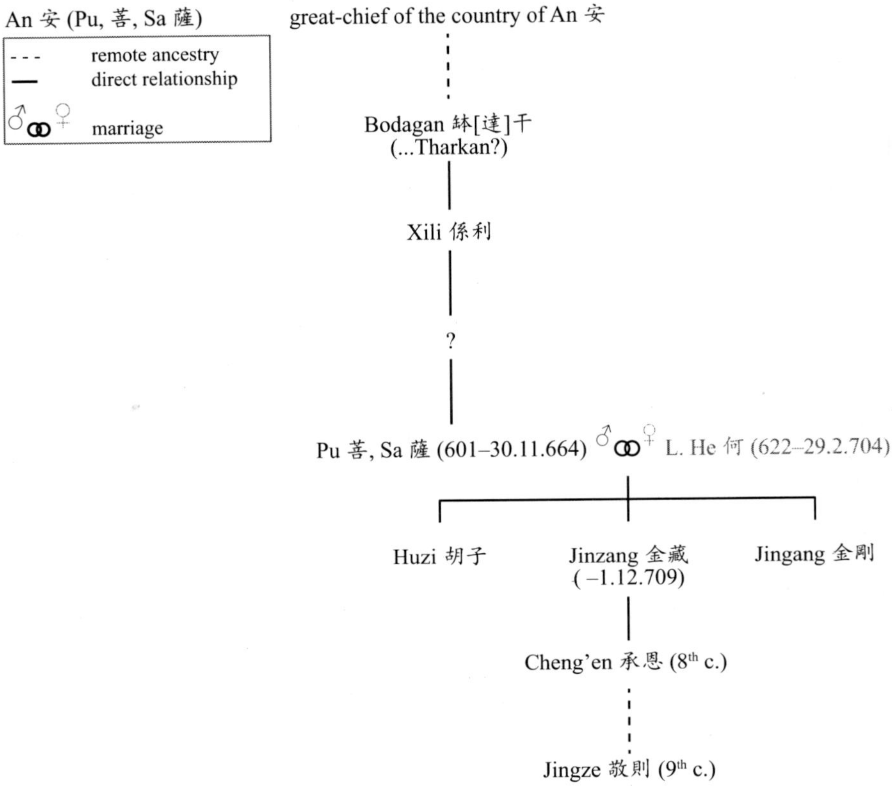

Figure 11: Family tree of An Pu 安菩
Source: M. Huber.

2.3.2.16.2 Biography

Pu's 菩 family is said to have descended from a great chief of Bukhārā – a title that was generically used for foreign leading figures. Regarding his recent ancestors, we only know that his great-grandfather was called Bodagan 缽達干 (EMC* *pat dat kan*), of which "*dagan*" probably stands for Tharkan, which is both a given name and title. His grandfather was called Xili 係利 (EMC* *ɣεj*^{h} *li*^{h}). Nothing is known about his father.

An Pu 安菩, born in ca. 601 CE, had the courtesy name Sa 薩, which was meant to be read with his taboo, resulting in Pusa 菩薩 (EMC* *bɔ sat*), the Chinese translation of *bodhisattva*. The names of his sons were equally clearly Buddhist. After the Eastern Tujue 突厥 were defeated in 630 CE, many were relocated to Northern

China. Pusa 菩薩 may well have been among the Sogdians that were moved to the Bei An 北安 Area Command of the Ordos Region within the loop of the Yellow River.[173] As, like his father, he had been great chief of the Six *hu* 胡 Prefectures, probably in the Turkish army, he was now integrated into the Tang army. While he was appointed general for pacifying faraway lands, he remained great chief, as before. Probably not much later, he married his wife. Born in ca. 622 CE, she was 21 years younger than him, the eldest daughter of a general-in-chief. As her family name was He 何, she conceivably was of Sogdian descent, stemming from Kushaniyya.

The epitaph is rather short and mentions only a single event of his career, probably referring to the campaign against Northern tribes in 646 CE. After Pusa 菩薩 victoriously lead the command and the tribes, he reported the victory to Chang'an 長安:

> 奉敕遄征，一以當千，獨掃蜂飛之衆。領衙帳部落，獻馘西京。

> [He] received instructions to hasten forward on a punitive expedition. Singly he opposed a thousand, by himself swept aside the swarms of flying wasps, and led the headquarters and tribes. He presented the left ears of the slain at the Western Capital.[174]

Although he was Sogdian, the famous lament of the Kül Tigin (684–731 CE) inscription about the alienation of the Turkish people was certainly also directed at people like him:[175]

> (E7) (…) Their sons worthy of becoming lords became slaves, and their daughters worthy of becoming ladies became servants to the Chinese people. (…) (E8) (…) For the benefit of the Chinese emperor they conquered countries. (…) Then the Turkish common people (E9) apparently said as follows: (…) "For whose benefit are we conquering these lands?"

His family must then have moved to the capital, as on the 30.11.664 CE, he died at the age of 63 in his private residence which was in the Jincheng 金城 District of Chang'an 長安. Shortly after his death, on the 32.12.664 CE, he was buried in the famous Longshou 龍首 Plain of Chang'an 長安.

His wife survived him for forty years and died on the 29.2.704 CE, at the age of 82, in her private residence in the Huihe 惠和 District of Luoyang 洛陽, due to her son moving there (see below). Probably due to her sons' office, she also had become commandery mistress of the Jinshan 金山 Commandery, either when he occupied that office, or posthumously.[176] She was then temporarily buried on the 10.3.704 CE east of the Jingshan 敬善 temple, which was erected during the reign of Gaozong 高宗 (649–83 CE), south of Luoyang 洛陽 (located in the northern part of present-day

173 See: Pulleyblank, "Sogdian Colony".

174 After the translation by Dien: Dien, "Sogdian Experience," 123.

175 Tekin, *Grammar*, 264.

176 As this was in any case an honorary title, it may refer to a commandery that once was located in present-day Minle 民樂 District, south of Zhangye 張掖, Gansu Province.

Longmen xishan 龍門西山, south of Luoyang 洛陽 City). Their son Jincang 金藏 eventually had his father exhumed on the 21.10.709 CE in Chang'an 長安 and reburied together with his mother in Luoyang 洛陽 on the 1.12.709 CE. Their eldest son was General of Mobile Cavalry Huzi 胡子 (EMC* *ɣɔ tsɨ'/tsi'*),[177] followed by Jincang 金藏 (EMC* *kim dzaŋ*) and Jingang 金剛 (EMC* *kim kaŋ*).[178]

As Li Jinxiu clarified, Jincang 金藏 was a physician at the court – and not musician.[179] He became a widely known figure due to his memorable display of loyalty. At the end of the seventh century, when Crown Prince Li Dan 李旦, the future Emperor Ruizong 睿宗, was accused of treason against his mother Empress Wu Zetian 武則天, Jincang 金藏 is reported as the only one to loudly protest the alleged charge in front of the investigators:[180]

> 公即不信金藏言，請剖心以明皇嗣不反。
>
> If your excellency does not believe Jincang's 金藏 word, please let me cut open my heart to make it clear that the crown prince did not revolt.

He then cut open his abdomen with a knife to underpin his testimony and the crown prince's innocence, his bowels coming out and blood covering the floor. Eventually, he was stitched together and survived.[181] Wu Zetian 武則天 chose to put an end to the investigation and praised him:[182]

> 吾有子不能自明，不如汝之忠也。
>
> I have a son who cannot clarify himself [and] does not compare to your loyalty.

Besides this episode, the records also provide information about Jincang's 金藏 mother's burial.[183] Contrary to the epitaph – stating that she died on the 29.2.704 CE and was temporarily buried on the 10.3.704 CE to be reburied on the 1.12.709 CE – it is said to have taken place at the beginning of the Shenlong 神龍 era (705–7 CE). The epitaph is however to be preferred as source of information. Her burial is also said to have taken place north of the southern gate of the capital, which also diverges slightly from the epitaph. Jincang 金藏 is said to have erected a hut beside the tomb, as was common practice, but worked without relent to himself make a stone platform and a stone pavilion.

177 Huzi 胡子 means lit. "Westerner's son".

178 We don't know which of them was the elder.

179 See the article for a good overview on the research on An Jincang 安金藏: Li Jinxiu, "'Yuegong' haishi 'yijiang'?".

180 *Da Tang xin yu* 5.73. Other versions are – among others – to be found in the *Jiu Tangshu* 187a.4885, the *Xin Tangshu* 191.5506, and the *Cefu yuangui* 762.9057a and 763.9064b (Li Jinxiu, "'Yuegong' haishi 'yijiang'?" 38–39).

181 As a physician, he probably knew how to cut open his abdomen without risking his life.

182 See footnote above.

183 The following biographical information is to be found in: *Jiu Tangshu* 187a.4885–6, the *Xin Tangshu* 191.5506–7.

The records continue also inform us that he was appointed as commandant of court gentlemen of the militant guard on the right during the Jingyun 景雲 era (710–12 CE).[184] When Xuanzong 玄宗 then claimed the throne in 712 CE, he was made general on the right of the courageous guards and the emperor had scribes organise the account of his deeds.[185] In 732 CE, by imperial decree, he was enfeoffed as duke of the state of Dai 代 and had his name carved into steles on the Taishan 泰山 and Huashan 華山 in his honour. After his death, he was attributed offerings at the palace of Ruizong 睿宗. In the Dali 大曆 era (766–79 CE), he was posthumously appointed as minister of war[186] and received the posthumous title (*shi* 謚) Zhong 忠 (loyal). The popularity of him cutting open his abdomen may be seen in a pottery figurine dated to the Song.[187] In fact, his deed became such a prominent example of loyalty, quoted in various records, that he remained the object of paintings and novels until the Qing Dynasty and even the Republic of China.[188]

His son became appointed as senior scribe of Luzhou 盧州 (in present-day Anhui Province) on the 21.4.782 CE.[189] It is also recorded that one of his descendants, named Jingze 敬則, became appointed as adviser to the crown prince as right proclaimer of virtue during the much later Zhonghe 中和 era (881–85 CE).[190]

2.3.3 Analysis of the Epitaphs

Continuing with the same methodological approach as before, the information from the epitaphs shall be analysed in categories that emerge from them. The result shall then be compared with the findings from the first chapter. Following the epitaph's narration, the following categories can be delineated.

2.3.3.1 Family

2.3.3.1.1 Remote ancestry and origin story

As references to ancestry and choronyms are held to be among the few factors through which we identify Sogdians – or descendants of Sogdians –, they are essential for the construction of further narratives. Whilst all the epitaphs list an ancestry, some relate to a remote ancestry and of these, two claim to be descendants of mythological Chinese emperors. Such claims are not unique – although they do stand out in light of

184 *You wuwei zhongliang jiang* 右武衛中郎將.
185 *You xiao wei jiangjun* 右驍衛將軍.
186 *Bingbu shangshu* 兵部尚書.
187 Du Wen, "Songdai taosu wanju".
188 See the *Wushuang pu* (n.p., Daiguo *gong yuegong* An Jincang 代國公樂工安金藏) that presents 40 figures from the Han to the Tang in painting and commentary, and the novel *Tang shi tongsu bianyi* 33.288–96 (Li Jinxiu, "'Yuegong' haishi 'yijiang'?," 39). For other records, see: ibid., 38–40.
189 *Jiu Tangshu* 12.332.
190 *Xin Tangshu* 191.5507.

the fact that precisely these two individuals' graves, An Jia 安伽, and Yu Hong 虞弘, both entitled *sabao* 薩保, are two of only three graves with epitaphs in which Zoroastrian iconography was found.[191] Other instances of claims to ancient and/or far away royal ancestry were forwarded by Shi Hedan 史訶耽, son of Shi Shewu 史射勿, who amplifies the statement of his father – stemming from a Western state – in professing to descend from the king of the state of Shi 史. And similarly, An Niang 安娘, the wife of Shi Suoyan 史索巖, claims to descend from the king of the state of Anxi 安息.[192] Shi Daode 史道德 recalls in his epitaph historical figures named Shi 史, as Shi Yu 史魚 of the Spring and Autumn Period, and Shi Dan 史丹 of the Han, insinuating that some later members of the family moved to present-day Gansu.

2.3.3.1.2 Choronyms

In respect to the epitaphs of Shi Suoyan 史索巖 and his nephew Shi Daode 史道德, another peculiarity is to be observed. The epitaph of Shi Suoyan 史索巖 claims that his remote ancestor was appointed in Yuanzhou 原州 and subsequently his family moved there, his choronym is given as Feiqiao 飛橋 of Jiankang 建康 (located in the Hexi 河西 corridor, ca. 40 km north-west of Jiuquan 酒泉 and Zhangye 張掖). On the epitaph of his nephew Daode 史道德 no choronym is given; however, his remote ancestor is said to be from Feiqiao 飛橋 of Jiankang 建康, and was appointed in, and therefore moved to, Pinggao 平高 (of Yuanzhou 原州) – the reversed statement of his uncle's epitaph. As mentioned, he does, however, insinuate to descend from a Chinese family since the Han. Due to their close relationship with the other Shi 史 family and the graves which strongly point to a non-Han burial, they conceivably stemmed from the country of Shi 史 (Kesh). As can be seen from their semantic equivalence, the function of recording a choronym and a remote ancestor were nearly identical, which underpins Johnson's conclusion that choronyms were functional markers of ancestry and the status that came with them.[193] Combined with the location of burials, they reveal more about the web of connections in which the Sogdians were involved – a few examples will suffice to demonstrate their analytical utility.

On the epitaph of Master Shi 史, the *sabao* 薩保 of Liangzhou 涼州, the choronym Guzang 姑藏 is recorded. The same choronym is recorded for An Jia 安伽, also *sabao* 薩保, however holding office in Tongzhou 同州. Incidentally, these two *sabao* 薩保 were buried just some hundred meters apart, east of the capital Chang'an 長安, in the Longshou 龍首 Plain – which is at the very same location as Kang Ye 康業, himself a Zoroastrian presider-in-chief of Yongzhou 雍州 (Chang'an 長安), and An Pusa 安菩薩 (later reburied with his wife near Luoyang 洛陽). The epitaph of He 何 is exceptional. Although the choronym provided is Yuezhi 月氏 of Bactria (Daxia 大夏), his name in fact belongs to the few extant Sogdian names. Apart from the few finds[194]

191 Not counting Di Caoming 翟曹明, see p. 310 fn. 312. See also: p. 293 (3.3.11.1).
192 Probably referring to Bukhara; see the glossary.
193 See p. 303 (3.3.7).
194 See p. 162 (2.3.2.15.2).

which led to the inclusion in the present study, the connections to the Yuezhi 月氏, Bactria (Daxia 大夏), and the Sogdians remain rather unclear.[195]

2.3.3.1.3 Given names and cultural identity

Before laying out the different ways in which the people that we believe to have identified as descendants of Sogdians were named, and although it may seem trivial and self-evident, it is first necessary to point out that when reading about a person in Chinese sources, the source is in Chinese language, and therefore the name is written in Chinese characters. There is no alternative method than to render a foreign name as a transcription in Chinese characters. As we will see momentarily, some names are unquestionably transcriptions, whilst others are not wholly evident and are conceivably not transcriptions, being quite typical for Chinese names. Especially Chinese scholars have perceived a development from evident transcriptions to typical Chinese names as evidence for as process of "sinicisation". Regardless of the conclusion reflecting a reality or not, it is most important to be aware of falling into the trap that such an argumentation may hold: a Chinese name lead some scholars to readily conclude that the named individual has become "Chinese", i.e. adapted a Chinese identity. The relationship between Chinese characters, the different languages, dialects, and accents perceived as being part of the Chinese world, and Chinese identity, are, however, today more inclusive and politically charged than they probably were then. In fact, Sogdians that came to live in Northern China were more probably "xianbeicised" than "sinicised", for which the Shi 史 in Guyuan 固原 provide an excellent example.

Engaging with the different overlapping categories of names – but skipping the problematic of the Sogdian family names which was already addressed – it is possible to define three categories of given names.

The first category includes those names that are evidently transcribed. The characters chosen for these do mostly not make any sense in combination nor do they convey any meaning, as for example, Boboni 波波匿 or Pantuo 槃陀. Another indicator of the low importance attached to the characters themselves can be observed in the variation of the characters that comprise personal names within distinct sources. This can be observed in the lists of homophonic variations found in the names of the family trees above, e.g., Pantuo 槃陀 is also written Pantuo 盤陀.[196] Further, some of the names were abbreviated in writing, which is quite typical for Chinese, e.g. Pantuo 槃陀 to Tuo 陀, or Boboni 波波匿 to Ni 尼 – the latter even with another character! By recurring to the knowledge of the pronunciation in the original language, scholars have also convincingly established that for some names, the given name and the courtesy name combined replicate the original name, e.g., Shewu 射勿 (*hui* 諱) Pantuo 槃陀 (*zi* 字) – or Shewupantuo 射勿槃陀 (*hui* 諱), as it is written on the

195 See: Yoshida Yutaka , "On the Origin".

196 And in Turfan also Pantuo 畔陀 (Yoshida Yutaka, "The Sogdian Version," 61, fn. 8).

epitaph of his sixth son – is probably the transcription of Zhematvandak (Sogd. *δrymtβntk*). Pantuo is in Sogdian *vandak* (*βntk*) (slave, or servant), also attested as a personal name among the Upper-Indus inscriptions, and Zhemat stands for Demeter, which combined means "servant of Demeter". Another example is An 安 (*xing* 姓) Pu 普 (*ming* 名 or *hui* 諱) Sa 薩 (*zi* 字). The – obvious – combination of the given name and courtesy name results in the word *pusa* 菩薩, from the Sanskrit (or other Middle Indic or Central Asian cognate) bodhisattva. Using two foreign languages, some even more complex theories have been advanced, as for the son of Master Shi 史, the inscription being bilingual, named in Sogdian *δrymtβntk* (Zhematvandak, as seen above "servant of Demeter") and in Chinese Weimo 維摩, the latter a well-established transcription of the Sanskrit Vimalakīrti; his brother was named *βr'yšmnβntk* (Vreshmanvandak) in Sogdian, and Pisha 毗沙 in Chinese, that is the short version of *pishamentianwang* 毗沙門天王, in Sanskrit *Vaiśravaṇa*.

The second category includes names that are transcriptions using phonetic transcriptions that simultaneously convey meaning.[197] To this belong the names of the father of Shi Shewu 史射勿 found on different epitaphs: Renchou 認愁, Si 思, Duoxiduo 多悉多, and Duosi 多思. As Duoxiduo 多悉多 of the names indicate, it probably refers to the Sogdian Tasietta'. The Chinese names essentially mean "pondering" or "worrying a lot". I also proposed that Si 嗣 and Du 度, which were different names given for the same individual probably are also to be included in this category, which may be translations of the meaning of a Sogdian name, i.e. something close to "conferring" or being "conferred", e.g. "the one who passes on" or "the heir".

The third category is formed by names that appear as typically Chinese, e.g. Xiaozhong 孝忠 (lit. filial piety-loyalty), Daode 道德 (lit. morality-virtue) with the courtesy name Wan'an 萬安 (lit. 10,000-peace), Changle 長樂 (lit. long-joy), etc. The name of Tiebang 鐵棒 (lit. metal-rod) with the courtesy name Shanji 善集 (lit. auspicious-accumulation) does however stick out: the given name, peculiar for a Chinese, has no parallels as a proper name in Chinese history,[198] whereas the courtesy name has other occurrences from the Northern Dynasties up to the Tang.[199] Another of these rather odd examples is Huozhu 貨主 (lit. goods-owner), the name of the son of Kang Ye 康業. Although being a Chinese word attested in literature, it is nowhere near to a "Chinese" proper name. These names probably expressed a wish for a successful career in the military or as merchant, as the others did for virtuous accomplishment. In the latter category are to be counted the Buddhist styled names, e.g., Faseng 法僧 (lit. dharma-monk) and Deseng 德僧 (lit. moral-monk). How "Chinese" such Buddhist styled names are is also debatable, as Buddhism –

197 Similar to present transcription of the brand name Coca-Cola, i.e. *ke kou ke le* 可口可樂, "tasty and making happy".

198 Apart maybe from Kang Tietou 康鐵頭 (metal head). *Jiu Tangshu* 8.182.

199 In the Northern Qi, as the courtesy name of Yuan Bin 元斌, great-grandson of Emperor Wen 文 of the Northern Wei (d. 553 CE; *Bei Qishu* 28.384); as courtesy name of Song Wenju 宋文矩 (d. 646 CE; see: Zhou Shaoliang and Zhao Chao, *Tangdai muzhiming xuji*, 156); and as the name of a donator on a stele (erected in 815 CE; see: Zhou Shaoliang and Zhao Chao, *Tangdai muzhi*, 2004).

coming from India through Central Asia – although advancing across China, conflicted heavily with some traditional perceptions among the Han, besides from being vilified as a foreign religion.

The only names among the Sogdian families presented above that are typically Chinese occur in the two Shi 史 families. Although there is an obvious argument to discern a transition that moves from direct transcriptions towards seemingly Chinese names, three facts must be highlighted. For the first Shi 史 family, among whose forefathers were *sabao*, and in respect to the seven generations for which we have names, we can observe that even by the sixth generation, sons bore recognisably untypical names for Chinese (from Miaoni 妙尼 to Tiebang 鐵棒). How important a "typical" Chinese name may have been for the self-identity is extremely difficult to ascertain but there is fortunately a hiccup in the fifth generation, i.e. Shi Daole 史道樂, which has been ignored or downplayed in previous publications. In fact, on the epitaph of his father, Daole 道樂 being one of the authors, his name was written Daole 道樂, whereas on his own epitaph, his name was written Daoluo 道洛. As can be assessed by checking for old pronunciations of the character, both were homophonic at this time, pronounced EMC* *daw' lak*. What is strikingly evident is that no importance at all was attached to the Chinese characters. If there were any degree of value conferred to the writing of the name, then it would be nigh impossible to imagine the situation that such a drastic oversight would have occurred. From this small irregularity, we can suppose that they were not writing in Chinese, and furthermore, were even probably not able to write Chinese characters, as the lowest threshold for literacy may be considered knowing how to write and recognise your own name and the name of your father. That the writer and carver made a mistake in inscribing the personal names on the epitaphs, and this wouldn't have been noticed, or corrected, is also nearly unthinkable. Of course, not being able to write does not necessarily conflict with the ability to speak Chinese – especially in the case of Chinese – but we can assume with some certainty that their main communication was held in Sogdian. Indeed, it has been convincingly established that even the imperial family of the Tang gave their sons Xianbei 鮮卑 child names, and the use of their language and culture was continued in the family, leading aspiring Han officials to learn their language.[200] In this light, the continuous usage of Sogdian and the subsistence of their non-Han self-identity, whilst bearing the most typical Chinese names, is far from being a far-fetched proposition.

2.3.3.2 Career

2.3.3.2.1 Military offices and sabao

Concerning the offices of the ancestors, be it women or men, all recorded instances are military, and/or *sabao* with but one exception, the father of Kang Ye 康業, who

200 Chen Sanping, "Succession Struggle," 381–82; reproduced in: Chen Sanping, *Multicultural China*, 9; and also: ibid., 183–91.

was appointed as Zoroastrian attendant-in-chief. Indeed, we know of several cases in which individuals simultaneously occupied the *sabao*-office as well as a military station: Several ancestors in the case of the first Shi 史 family, An Jia 安伽 – who was *sabao* 薩保 of Tongzhou 同州 and also occupied a high honorary military office – and Yu Hong 虞弘 – a high ranking military and acting *sabao* 薩保.

For the deceased themselves, the epitaphs provide us generally with far greater detail. The same as for their ancestors, the overwhelming majority of offices – honorary or not – were held in the military. While the names of the office are a great source of information, the exact height of the rank is difficult to determine. This is especially true across dynastic boundaries, since the same rank did not always mean the same relative authority.[201] Yet, in comparing the ranks mentioned before and after such periods of change, many can be assessed relatively well. It is clear, for example, that able men were transferred into the armies of the newly founded dynasty. Every new emperor had a high demand for personnel while at the same time seeking to reward the members of his own army as well as his allies. As too many powerful local generals built up militias and even larger armies during the Northern Dynasties, and not all of them could be employed, they had to be given at least honorary ranks during the Sui, and later in the Tang. The importance of such ranks for the narrated self-identity cannot be underestimated. On some epitaphs, the rank of a foreign office was explicitly specified and the equivalent in the new dynasty given. An Pusa 安菩薩, for example, was great chief of the Six *hu* 胡 Prefectures, which, as the epitaph explicitly explains, was equivalent to an office in the capital of rank five. Consequently, when he was taken into the ranks of the Tang after the defeat of the Eastern Tujue 突厥, he was appointed as general for pacifying faraway lands, but also remained great chief.

After the establishment of the Tang, most of the Sogdians of this study first occupied offices as guards and imperial guards,[202] in the imperial Six Corrals,[203] or as horse breeders,[204] and then progressed to higher military ranks and participated in campaigns, as was detailed before. One notable case in point,[205] is that the official progression of Shi Shewu 史射勿 was achieved exclusively at a time of warfare and instability, whilst under the political stability of the Tang, this kind of career path did not yield many such possibilities for his relatives and descendants.

201 For an article trying to do that, see for example: Su Hang, "Beichao moqi de sabao pinwei".

202 Lord Yu Hong 虞弘, Shi Duo 史多, Kang Ahai 康阿孩, Shi Shewu 史射勿 (was not an imperial guard but accompanied the imperial carriage twice), Shi Suoyan 史索嚴, Shi Daxing 史大興, Shi Daode 史道德, and Shi Tiebang 史鐵棒.

203 Shi Hedan 史訶耽.

204 Shi Hedan 史訶耽, Shi Tiebang 史鐵棒, and Shi Daode 史道德. Hedan's 訶耽 eulogy claims that his family owned 4,000 horses.

205 Although the quantitative minimum is not reached and generalising conclusions may be swiftly challenged.

2.3.3.2.2 Civil offices

Quite exceptional are the few civil service offices held by the studied Sogdians, all of which were honorary in nature, and all related to audiences at the court and to translations. The first we know of, are Shi Shewu 史射勿, grand master for proper consultation, and his third son Anle 安樂, grandmaster for court audiences, as well as An Xun 安巡, who was senior great general unequalled in honour and court gentleman for thorough counsel at the Sui court. After Shewu 射勿 died, his oldest son Hedan 訶耽 came to the Tang court to assume the office of grandmaster for court audiences, concurrently holding the position of senior commandant-in-chief of cavalry, an honorary military office. However, in the same year he was also promoted to a low-ranking ordinary military office, serving as a ceremonial horse groom for the North Gates. In his honorary civil service career, he was then successively promoted to translator in the Secretariat, court gentleman of manifest virtue, gentleman for court audiences, court gentleman for thorough counsel, and gentleman for court discussion. Interestingly, Shi Suoyan 史索嚴, of the other Shi 史 family, was also appointed as grandmaster for court audiences one year later than Shi Hedan 史訶耽, and Suoyan's 索嚴 brother – who we only know from his nephew Daode's 道德 epitaph – also was imperial grand master for proper consultation.

2.3.3.2.3 Nobility and fiefs

Three of these Sogdians even managed to receive a low ranked nobility title, besides Shi Shewu 史射勿, who was rewarded with land: Yu Hong 虞弘 became earl of the Guangxing 廣興 District, with a territorial claim of 600 households; Shi Suoyan's 史索嚴 great-grandfather and grandfather were commandery duke of Xiping 西平, ennobled with 800 households; and the father of Shi Daode 史道德 is stated to have been marquis of the Pingliang 平涼 District. It is reasonable to believe that the nobility status of his father and the wealth that came with it may have been one of the main reasons for the economic and social stability of the two families, as his status probably "contaminated" theirs.[206]

2.3.3.2.4 Paranthesis: Toponyms and offices – connecting the dots

The combination of toponyms and offices inside biographies – in other words, who did what where – provide us with a deep insight into the connections between these individuals.

Although the two Shi 史 families of Yuanzhou 原州, for example, are not directly related per kin – although maybe they were in earlier generations unknown to us – but they are still closely interconnected, and further connected to other Sogdians of which the epitaphs were presented above, as will be shown in chronological order in the following. As the reader may be not be familiar with the family trees of the two Shi 史 families, the members of the two families will be differentiated by the signs "(1)" and "(2)".

206 To use Bourdieu's nomenclature; see p. 325 fn. 7.

During the Wei, An Dan 安但, Wantong's 萬通 great-grandfather, is said to have been great *sabao* 薩寶, the same as Boboni 波波匿, the great-grandfather of Shi Daoluo 史道洛(2).[207] In the next generation, probably under the Western Wei or Northern Zhou, the grandfather of An Wantong 安萬通 was appointed as regional inspector of Shanzhou 鄯州, the same as – among other offices – Shi Si 嗣/Du 度(2), Shi Suoyan's 史索嚴 grandfather (the great-grandfather of Daode 道德(2)).[208] It starts to become even more baffling it that these parallels are also to be seen for the next generation: An Xun 安巡 was senior great general unequalled in honour and court gentleman for thorough counsel during the Sui, Shi Duo 史多(2) was senior serviceman, outpost general, palace adjutant, part of the imperial guard on the left, and cavalry general of the Anhua 安化 Garrison in the Northern Zhou and Sui (Chang'an 長安) while Shi Shewu 史射勿(1) was commander unequalled in honour (which is the same), cavalry general on the right and grand master for proper consultation during the Sui. At the same time, Kang Ahai 康阿孩, father of Lady Kang 康, i.e. father-in-law of Shi Hedan 史訶耽, was imperial bodyguard on the right in Chang'an 長安. This means that the two Shi 史 families and the An 安 family did not only have similar career paths, but worked in the same locations.

During the Sui, Shi Shewu 史射勿(1), father of Shi Hedan 史訶耽, accompanied the imperial carriage of the Sui to Bingzhou 並州 in 590 CE. When Shi Shewu 史射勿 visited Bingzhou 並州, he probably met Yu Hong 虞弘, who was commander unequalled in honour, commandant of the left escort brigade, and in control of the region's army division. In 604 CE, the 33 year old younger Shi Suoyan 史索嚴(2) was then made guard attending chariots of the King of Jin 晉 Yang Guang 楊廣 – in 600 CE, the emperor had made Guang 廣 crown prince. In the same year, the Emperor fell ill. The imperial carriage of the crown prince moved to his residence, the Eastern Palace, to visit his father, escorted by Suoyan 索嚴(2), who became appointed imperial bodyguard in Chang'an 長安. While the *Suishu* did not record anything special, later historians expressed doubts about a harmonious succession, in which the crown prince played a questionable role. Imperial guards are explicitly mentioned in the record, as the emperor replaced the guards of his death bed with trusted ones, with Suoyan 索嚴 maybe being a witness. Sui Wendi 隋文帝 then died and Yang Guang 楊廣 became Emperor, later known as Emperor Yang 煬, and Suoyan 索嚴(2) was appointed as protective guard on the left in Chang'an 長安. One year later, in 605 CE, Shi Shewu 史射勿(1) accompanied the imperial carriage (of the new emperor) to Yangzhou 揚州, forming the rear guard, and was greatly rewarded. In 613 CE, Shi Suoyan 史索嚴(2) became commandant of the Pingliang 平涼 Commandery.

In the Tang, Daxing 大興(1), the father of Shi Tiebang 史鐵棒(1), followed in the footsteps of Shi Duo 史多(2) and became military commander (the same as the office of cavalry general of Duo 多 above, as the name of the office was changed in 618 CE)

207 For the biography of An Wantong 安萬通, see p. 254 (3.2.2.17).

208 As was argued before, Shi Duoxiduo 史多悉多, the grandfather of Daoluo 道洛, was said to have also held this office, which was most probably fictive. See p. 149 (2.3.2.10).

of the Anhua 安化 Garrison militia, while Shi Daoluo 史道洛(1), the sixth son of Shi Shewu 史射勿(1), became imperial bodyguard on the right in Chang'an 長安. Somewhen between 627 and 663 CE Daode 道德(2) was merit guard on the left of the crown prince in Chang'an 長安. In ca. 649 CE, Tiebang 鐵棒(1) became merit guard on the right at the imperial palace in Chang'an 長安. And in 663 CE, Daode 道德(2) first became pasturage director of Yuting 玉亭 and then was appointed as head pasturage director of Lanchi 蘭池, providing the horses for the imperial guard in Chang'an 長安.

All this is to say that the two Shi 史 families and the An 安 family were obviously connected through their careers, maybe met with Lord Yu Hong 虞弘, and that the various members of the Shi 史 supported each other's careers as imperial guards and horse breeders in the capital over generations.

Moving away from the capital, there are still two locations that are mentioned more than once in relationship to offices and career. In Pingliang 平涼, the Shi 史 families were not only based and buried, they were also well connected with other local powerful people. This is for example to be deduced from Shi Shewu's 史射勿 participation in a campaign under the Sui, in 566 CE, in which he served the duke of Pinggao 平高 with the goal "to protect Hedong 河東" (ca. present-day Shanxi Province). This duke was conceivably Li Xun 孝詢, the son of Li Xian 李賢, the latter being one of the great generals of the Northern Zhou, who was buried in one of the most important tombs near Shewu's 射勿 in the Pingliang 平涼 Commandery. Although they do not appear to have had more contact, it is still noteworthy that they were buried in the same area, which – among other indicators – speaks of the high standing their family achieved.[209] The same connection can be seen in the biography of Shi Suoyan 史索嚴, who was appointed as commandant of the Pingliang 平涼 Commandery in 613 CE. Zhang Long 張隆, who was at that time the governor of Pingliang 平涼, defected to Li Yuan 李淵 on the 20.1.618 CE. As was shown, it is quite probable that Suoyan 索嚴(2) and Hedan 訶耽(1) as well as his cadet brothers Daxing 大興(1) and Daoluo 道洛(1) defected together with Zhang Long 張隆 – as he was their superior – at the end of January 618 CE or slightly later to join the forces of Li Yuan 李淵. Suoyan 索嚴 then participated in a campaign of the Tang against Xue Ju 薛舉 in 618 CE, together with Governor of the Pingliang 平涼 Commandery Zhang Long 張隆. Further, the father of Shi Daode 史道德(2) and brother of Suoyan 索嚴(2) – who's name we do not know – is said to have been imperial grand master for proper consultation and dynasty-founding marquis of the Pingliang 平涼 District of the Tang.

Finally, as already mentioned above, the great-grandfather and grandfather of Shi Suoyan 史索嚴 were both commandery dukes of Xiping 西平 and it is most probable that Master Shi 史 and his wife Kang 康 – the latter coming from Senpen – were married in Senpen during this time. If Senpen is to be identified as Xiping 西平,

209 For more information, see the analysis of the graves p. 109 (2.2.3).

instead of the more probable Xinping 新平, they conceivably knew each other, both having an important standing in society.

2.3.3.3 Women and marriage

A detailed study of women and their standing in the biographies and the information that could be deduced by comparing them in detail to other graves would require an own study if taken as focus. While, for example, Davis' study sticks out of the mass by referring to the "men and women" of medieval China, most studies simply ignore women as a topic, or simply extract the information relating to dates and offices, ignoring that they reproduce the narration of antique sources.[210] It is important, however, to point out that the style and content of an epitaph and the burial objects of women were different to a men's and that especially in the cases at hand, they need to be treated in their own right.

From the 15 of epitaphs that were examined, in the following are some of the information that can be gathered. Among these 15, 13 are from men and two are from women. As there were no women buried alone, two of the graves included two epitaphs. Interestingly, in the graves in which an epitaph for both deceased were found, the man's epitaph does not mention a wife. The woman in these cases died respectively six (Lady ?, wife of Yu Hong 虞弘) and five (An Niang 安娘) years later. Among the remaining 11 epitaphs of men, four mention their wife (or wives), and seven do not mention them. From the four that mention their wife (or wives), all four also mention sons. From the seven that do not mention their wife (or wives), only four mention a son or sons. From the two epitaphs of women, one does not mention a son – probably due to her husband being a eunuch – while the other mentions sons – most interestingly, one son less than her husband's epitaph.[211]

Examining those epitaphs that mention the wife or wives and the women's epitaph – with the exception of the broken epitaph of Lady ?, wife of Yu Hong 虞弘, that does not provide much information – and apart from the standardised information about their idealised behaviour as wives and mothers, they include the women's birthplace or choronym, the name and office of the father, their marriage and title (e.g. dame of the Nanyang 南陽 Commandery), and their time and place of death. Further, they mostly married with Sogdians of other family names – meaning that they practised exogamy and thus observed the state regulations. Only Lady Zhang 長 – the second wife of Shi Hedan 史訶耽 – and Du 杜 – the mother of An Jia 安伽 – had a Chinese surname.

One of the factors that may have accounted for the additional epitaph of two of the women is the difference in the time of death. In the four cases that mention wives, Kang 康/Wyusi died only one month later than her husband Master Shi 史, Lady Kang 康, the first wife of Shi Hedan 史訶耽, died 39 years earlier, and Lady Zhang 張, his second wife, died two years earlier than him, Lady Kang 康 died nine years earlier than her husband Shi Daoluo 史道洛, but Lady He 何 died 40 years later than her

210 Davis, *Entombed Epigraphy*, passim.
211 On this discrepancy, see the passage on the dedication p. 182 (2.3.3.4.4).

husband An Pu 安菩. To contrast these with the cases in which we both have an epitaph for man and woman, Lady ? died five years later than her husband Yu Hong 虞弘 and An Niang 安娘 died five years later than her husband Shi Suoyan 史索嚴. Judging from this, the separate epitaph for the woman may have been due to their later joint burial with their husband, except for Lady He 何. In her case, it was, however, explicitly mentioned on her husband's epitaph that their son exhumed him from his grave in Chang'an 長安 and had him transported to Luoyang 洛陽, to be then buried with his wife. We also know that his mother had moved with him to Luoyang 洛陽 as she died there. While it is quite possible that either the epitaph was lost and a new one was made for both, or that it was polished and inscribed anew, most importantly, in the cases in which a second epitaph was made, it was placed in the same grave.

What can also be clearly seen is that the mention of wives is not related to the existence of an aftermath. As to the aftermath, no daughter is mentioned, although the daughters do mention their fathers and their offices, which speaks of the lesser importance attributed to women in this society. An interesting detail to underpin this may be seen in the standardised expression of condolences *ming hu ai zai* 嗚呼哀哉 (alas). While it is included in most epitaphs – in the epitaph of An Niang 安娘 as well – interestingly enough, Shi Hedan's 史訶耽 epitaph uses it twice. Once after mentioning his death, and once after the expression of his sons' pain. His two wives' death do not receive such an "alas".

An interesting exception in the mentions of women is the epitaph of An Jia 安伽, which mentions his mother Du 杜. Her mention does, however, serve the same goal as the mention of fathers, i.e. the epitaph further states that she was district mistress of the Changsong 昌松 District – a title that she most probably gained through the office one of her sons held – to enhance the prestige of the deceased. A good example of how a woman would be understood in her presentation in this context is the beginning of An Niang's 安娘 epitaph. Although she had her own epitaph, she is introduced as "Wife of the Commandant of the Pingliang 平涼 Commandery Lord Shi 史" and even has an own courtesy name, Bai 白 – which may have referred to her skin colour, which is later supplemented by the verse

> [He had] a graceful and kind beauty [as wife], [of a] high official's family, [her] fragrance [was] formed [by] diverse orchids, [her] complexion luxuriant in her youth."

Women's standing in society, as seen through the epitaphs, was thus mostly defined through their relationship with other males in their society, be it in their roles and appearance as ideal mothers (the mourning of his mother is included in Shi Hedan's 史訶耽 epitaph, however, mostly reflecting his own moral quality), wives, or – quasi inexistent in this literature – daughters. Quite importantly, however, is that we can see that Sogdians were probably monogamous – unlike their Chinese peers.

Becoming a wife was thus to form the link between different male groups, which is reflected by the patrilineal kinship system. Seen from the women's perspective, as daughters of Sogdians, one can also imagine that it would have been quite difficult to marry a Chinese man with a higher societal standing than the Sogdian family members. The fact that intermarriage with Chinese was exceptional is further underpinned by the short compilation of Rong Xinjiang.[212] Interestingly all the spouses for whom we know the ancestors' occupation held notable military offices, which were listed on the epitaph to enhance the prestige of the deceased and thus their descendants. Furthermore, even though rates of intermarriage may have increased over time in Dunhuang 敦煌, as was mentioned in the first chapter, Dien states they

> do not necessarily represent a loss of self-identity. Such circumstances bring to mind the Jewish community of Kaifeng that began probably in the eleventh century. A Memorial Book of around 1663 lists a relatively high rate of intermarriage, and yet, even after the community was impoverished by heavy damage to the Kaifeng area from floods and warfare, the remaining members still identified themselves as Jews, and continue to do so to this day.[213]

Although I must point out that this example mentions a diaspora which practices a monotheistic and exclusivist religion, which tends to bind a community together, it nevertheless exemplifies a certain truth concerning the persistence of self-identity.

2.3.3.4 Death and burial

2.3.3.4.1 Age

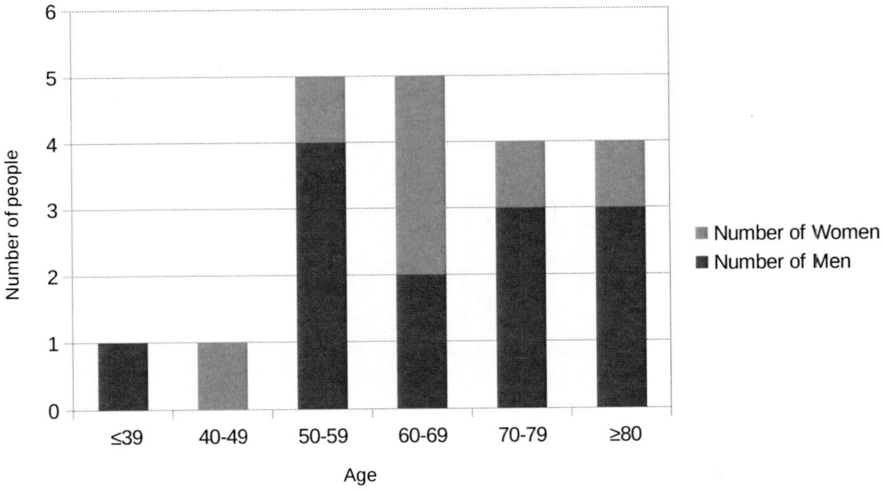

Figure 12: Lifespan of Sogdians with an epitaph from an archaeological context
Source: M. Huber, see Vol. 2, Appendix 3

212 Rong Xinjiang, "Beichao Sui Tang Sute," 133–34.
213 Dien, "Sogdian Experience," 126.

Although the small sample does not lend itself to generalisations and extrapolations, the longevity of these Sogdians needs to be pointed out as remarkable. For the 20 individuals for which we have the living data presented above, the average age is 65.35 and the median age 64.5 years, with eight people among them reaching an age of over 70 and four people reaching an age of over 80. To put these numbers in another context, in the P.R.C., such an average was reached for the life expectancy at birth in the 1970' and at the age of 15 and 20 in the late 1960'.[214] In other words, they became very old.

Obviously, there are several factors typical for the archaeological bias, among others, that epitaphs were found in impressive graves are more likely to be made for more successful and thus older people, that graves of important people included epitaphs were excavated and studied more due to the graves having a tumulus, which was more visible, that graves only including human remains were excluded, or also that this sample does not include epitaphs of Sogdians outside of an archaeological context. This being said, the explanation at hand is that they had the resources to lead a rather healthy and safe life in far above average comfort.

2.3.3.4.2 Burial date

As can be seen below, the burial dates show a clear pattern.

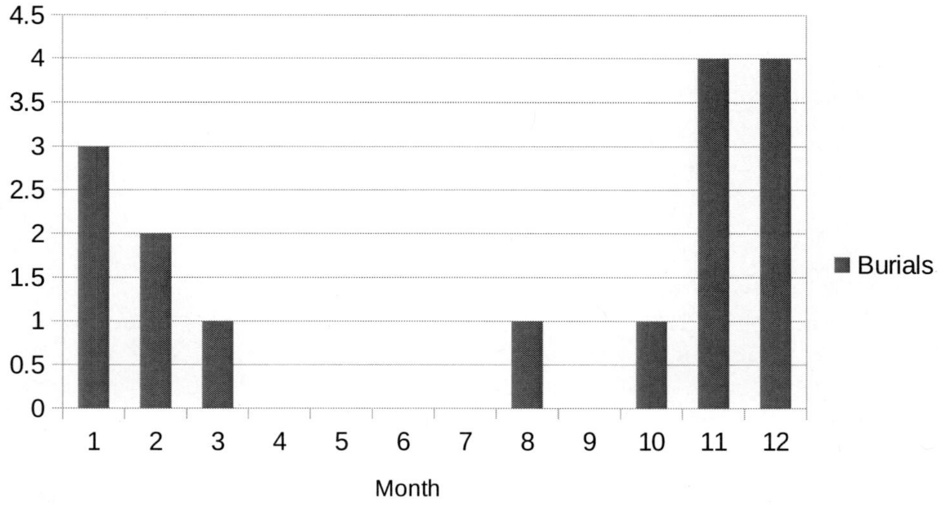

Figure 13: Months in which Sogdians were buried
Source: M. Huber, see Vol. 2, Appendix 3

214 This data was queried at: United Nations DESA / Population Division, "World".

Most burials were made from the tenth to the third month, with only one burial in the eighth month.

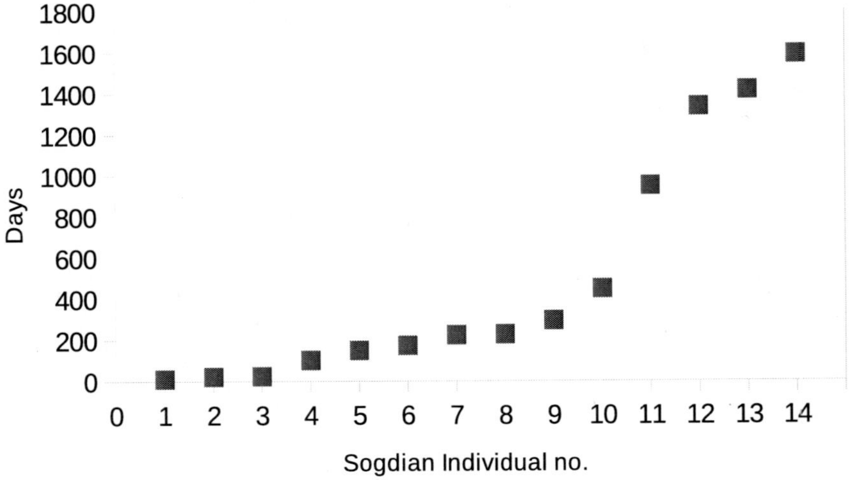

Figure 14: Days between death and burial
Source: M. Huber, see Vol. 2, Appendix 3

The time span between death and (re)burial was on average 497 days whereas the median time span was 225 days. We do know that burial dates were sometimes doctored on epitaphs to fit a certain astrologically auspicious date. However, it must be emphasised that they waited quite long to rebury most of the deceased and that maybe such an auspicious date was either worth waiting for or other requirements had to be met, such as the purchase of a burial ground, the construction of the grave, the burial gifts, etc.

2.3.3.4.3 Burial place

Two burial places recur in the above presented epitaphs of Sogdians. One is the cemetery for elite society near present-day Guyuan 固原 where the Shi 史 were buried, which was discussed in the chapter 2.2.[215] The second is the Longshou 龍首 Plain of Chang'an 長安, equally a burial place for the upper strata of society. Kang Ye 康業, Zoroastrian presider-in-chief during the Northern Wei, died on the 12.7.571 CE and was buried there on the 31.12.571 CE. Next came An Jia 安伽, *sabao* 薩保 of Tongzhou 同州, who died in the in the month 10.6–9.7.579 and was buried in the month 5.11–4.12.579 CE. Wirkak (Master Shi 史), who was *sabao* 薩保 of Liangzhou 涼州 and had moved to Chang'an 長安, died at about the same time on the 16.6.579 CE, and was buried there on the 23.2.580 CE. Finally, we know that An Pusa 安菩薩

215 See p. 123.

died on the 30.11.664 CE in Chang'an 長安, and was buried here on the 23.12.664 CE – before being exhumed on 21.10.709 CE, transported and reburied in Luoyang 洛陽 on the 1.12.709 CE. Besides these, we know about the Sogdian An Wantong 安萬通 who probably died in 653 CE and was buried there on the 22.2.654 CE.[216]

2.3.3.4.4 The dedication

To point out the obvious, only sons of the deceased appear on the epitaph, introduced as those who made the epitaph. Less obvious to us, however, are the differences in nomenclature concerning the eldest son, apparently all refer to the same, i.e.: *zhang zi* 長子, *yin zi* 胤子, *zhou zi* 胄子, *si zi* 嗣子, and *shi zi* 世子. However, as has been laid out in the introduction, standard procedure dictates that after stating the date and place of the burial, the sons are listed along with their titles, descriptions of their virtuous being and behaviour, and that they made an epitaph, containing an eulogy, which ensues thereafter. Although all of the epitaphs respect this custom, four cases present noteworthy exceptions.

- The bilingual epitaph of master Shi 史: the Chinese inscription states that his sons made a stone house (*tang* 堂), whereas the Sogdian part says that a god-house made of stone was constructed. Although the exact connotations of the "stone house" may escape us, it is irregular (as is the whole bilingual stele integrated in the stone house as lintel), for this time, that the epitaph does not include a eulogy.
- The dedication of the epitaph of Kang Ye 康業 is most interesting, for after the information of the burial only his eldest son is listed, who made the ensuing eulogy. The names of his two cadet brothers only follow after the eulogy at the end of the epitaph. Furthermore, judging from the way they are to be found in the last column – after the inscription and before the final statement of the date of engraving of the epitaph – it is quite possible that they were simply appended. This is highly irregular and may indicate the cadet brothers did not participate in the costs of the epitaph, or maybe even the grave.
- Finally, the epitaphs of Shi Suoyan 史索嚴 and his wife An Niang 安娘 differ in respect to the number of sons. Whereas the former states four sons, the latter leaves out the fourth. Rather peculiar, this conceivably points towards the fourth son having passed away in between the two burials, the first being held in late 658 or beginning of 659 CE, and the second in 664 CE. If that is the case, it would underpin the assumption that only alive sons of the deceased are mentioned on the epitaph. As they are mentioned as providers of the epitaph, this seems rather reasonable, but remains a question which needs to be determined by future research.

216 See p. 254 (3.2.2.17).

2.4 Compilation of sources on Sogdians in China, arranged geographically

長安縣人史婆陀家興販，資材臣富，身有勳官驍驍騎尉，其園池屋宇、衣服器玩、家僮侍妾比侯王。	*The family of Shi Potuo from Chang'an was engaged in trade. His wealth was that of a minister and he himself was merit officer of the courageous guards. His garden, pond, and domicile, his clothes and delightful objects, his household's slaves, servants, and maiden did rival those of marquises and kings.*

Wenming panji 文明判集 (P.3813 verso, cols. 114–15)[217]

2.4.1 Introduction

For the following pages I heavily relied on the compilations and research of the articles by Rong Xinjiang. He published seminal articles identifying *settlements* of Sogdians in China and its west border regions, in which include various references to individuals with Sogdian surnames and places through which Sogdians may have passed.[218] The mention of individuals with Sogdian surnames at a certain place and time may be of value for various study purposes but unfortunately remain often inconclusive as to the identification of individuals as Sogdians,[219] while most importantly, *individual* mentions are inconclusive as to the *regular activity* and, indeed, the *settlement* of Sogdians in China.

In consequence, in the following are provided places to which are related either a substantial amount of transmitted information regarding Sogdians, or Sogdian temples

217 Author's punctuation and translation.

218 He divided what can be understood as one study into two articles, which were then updated and translated, resulting in overall 11 papers over the years. The first part, about Sogdians in China, was published in 1999: Rong Xinjiang, "Beichao Suteren"; and republished in: Rong Xinjiang, "Beichao Sui Tang Suteren". It was then partially translated into English: Rong Xinjiang, "Beichao Sui Tang Suteren zhi qianxi jiqi juluo"; and partially updated in Chinese: Rong Xinjiang, "Beichao Sui Tang Suteren bu kao (Ouya xuekan)"; and again partially updated in: Rong Xinjiang, "Beichao Sui Tang Suteren bu kao (Zhonggu Zhongguo)". The second part, concerning Sogdians in the Western Regions (in this case meaning present-day Xinjiang Uighur Autonomous Region), was first published in: Rong Xinjiang, "Xiyu Sute yimin kao"; and republished in: Rong Xinjiang, "Xiyu Sute yimin juluo kao". It was then translated into English: Rong Xinjiang, "Sogdians Around"; and again partially updated in: Rong Xinjiang, "Xiyu Sute yimin juluo bu kao"; which was again translated into English: Rong Xinjiang, "Further Remarks".

219 Methodogically, Rong Xinjiang differentiated between those Sogdians with foreign sounding given names, which are identified as probably Sogdian, and those who bear Chinese sounding names, making them "sinicised" Sogdians.

or leaders of Sogdian settlements (the *safu*/*sabo*/*sabao*)[220] – which presuppose a larger community Sogdians and are therefore among the most reliable indicators of a Sogdian settlement. From the list of places mentioned in the studies of Rong Xinjiang are therefore excluded: Talas and Suiye 碎葉, Gongyue 弓月, Baltistan and Gilgit, Hepantuo 渴槃陀, Jiuquan 酒泉, Zhangye 張掖/Ganzhou 甘州, Xiping 西平 /Shanzhou 鄯州, Lingwu 靈武/Lingzhou 靈州, Xiazhou 夏州, Daizhou 代州, Anbian 安邊/Yuzhou 蔚州/Xingtang 興唐, Youzhou 幽州, Liucheng 柳城/Yingzhou 營州, Changshan 常山/Huolu 獲鹿/Hengzhou 恆州, Xingzhou 邢州, Weizhou 魏州, and the Ji 汲 Commandery/Weizhou 衛州.[221]

Following the example of Rong Xinjiang, the corpus is arranged geographically and chronologically, as an organisation by source would result in a rather confusing compendium. Further, to skip over a geographical presentation in order to directly analyse the content by topic would result in the omission of various mentions and unfitting information. For the sake of orientation, the locations are split into greater spaces, presented in order of their distance from the centres of power in the Central Plains and concluding with the capitals.

220 On these, see p. 238 (3.2).

221 Talas and Suiye 碎葉: Rong Xinjiang, "Xiyu Sute yimin juluo bu kao," 5–7;
Gongyue 弓月: ibid., 7–9;
Baltistan and Gilgit: ibid., 9–10;
Hepantuo 渴槃陀 (also known as Hanpantuo 漢盤陀, Hepantuo 訶盤陀, Hepantuo 喝盤陀, or Jiepantuo 羯盤陀): ibid., 10–11;
Jiuquan 酒泉: Rong Xinjiang, "Beichao Sui Tang Suteren," 62–65;
Zhangye 張掖/Ganzhou 甘州 (to the various individuals that Rong Xinjiang lists that may be related to Sogdians and Ganzhou 甘州 one could add Kang Ye 康業 (see p. 131; 2.3.2.2), and Kang Bada 康拔達 (see p. 253; 3.2.2.16); further, the *Jiu Tangshu* (see p. 50; 1.13.1) mentions the rulers of Kang 康 to stem from north of Zhangye 張掖, which is, however, a fictive construction): ibid., 65–68;
Xiping 西平/Shanzhou 鄯州: Rong Xinjiang, "Beichao Sui Tang Suteren bu kao (Zhonggu Zhongguo)," 28–30;
Lingwu 靈武/Lingzhou 靈州: Rong Xinjiang, "Beichao Sui Tang Suteren," 90–93;
Xiazhou 夏州: Rong Xinjiang, "Beichao Sui Tang Suteren bu kao (Zhonggu Zhongguo)," 30–32;
Daizhou 代州 (not included, among other reasons, because Yu Hong 虞弘 was only in charge of the local militia): ibid., 37; Rong Xinjiang, "Beichao Sui Tang Suteren," 97–98;
Anbian 安邊/Yuzhou 蔚州/Xingtang 興唐: ibid., 98–99;
Youzhou 幽州: ibid., 104–5;
Liucheng 柳城/Yingzhou 營州: ibid., 105–8;
Changshan 常山/Huolu 獲鹿/Hengzhou 恆州: ibid., 102–3;
Xingzhou 邢州: Rong Xinjiang, "Beichao Sui Tang Suteren bu kao (Zhonggu Zhongguo)," 39–40; Rong Xinjiang, "Beichao Sui Tang Suteren," 102;
Weizhou 魏州: Rong Xinjiang, "Beichao Sui Tang Suteren bu kao (Zhonggu Zhongguo)," 38–39; Rong Xinjiang, "Beichao Sui Tang Suteren," 101–2;
Ji 汲 Commandery/Weizhou 衛州: Rong Xinjiang, "Beichao Sui Tang Suteren bu kao (Zhonggu Zhongguo)," 38; Rong Xinjiang, "Beichao Sui Tang Suteren," 99–100.

2.4.2 West of Shazhou 沙州/Dunhuang 敦煌

Coming from Sogdiana, a traveller would have to circumvent the Taklamakan Desert on the so-called Northern or Southern Route. The first space is thus defined ranging from the west edges of present-day Xinjiang Uighur Autonomous Region to Dunhuang 敦煌 (ancient Shazhou 沙州). This was the first major station after the Taklamakan Desert and the Jade Gate Barrier on the way to the Hexi 河西 Corridor. In fact, after General Zhang Qian 張騫 set foot in the regions further west during the Han, they were only temporarily under control, administration, and/or influence of Chinese dynasties between the Han and the Tang. Records of the movement and registrations of caravans in which Sogdians partook, as well as custom registers show that many Sogdians (i.e. registered residents, unregistered travellers, and envoys) were involved in commercial transactions and highly active in the long-distance trade of the region.[222]

2.4.2.1 Northern Route

2.4.2.1.1 Tuojueguan 拓厥關 (Douldour-Āqour) and Kucha

The pass is located 23 km west of Qiuci 龜茲 (Kucha). Some documents were found here that may refer to Sogdians, involved in commercial activities.[223] In Kucha itself, two ossuaries and two lids were found outside the eastern city wall.[224]

2.4.2.1.2 Yanqi 焉耆 (Qarashahr, Argi)

Although there is no conclusive evidence, the excavated objects and fragments of inscriptions combined point towards a Sogdian presence.[225]

222 A useful overview is to be found in: Skaff, "Sogdian Trade Diaspora". Skaff describing the Sogdian activity dominating the long-distance trade based on the snapshot of data accessible at the moment seems however a slight jump to conclusions.

223 That is Chinese business contracts (Yamamoto Tatsuro and Ikeda On, *Tun-huang, Contracts*, 12), and as de la Vaissière pointed out (Vaissière, *Sogdian Traders*, 126), caravan authorisations in Kuchaean: Pinault, "Épigraphie koutchéenne". See also: Vaissière, *Sogdian Traders*, 127, fn. 29; and: Rong Xinjiang, "Xiyu Sute yimin juluo bu kao," 14–17.

224 Two ossuaries and two lids were found at Mazabitam 馬扎不但 County, east of the ancient city wall of Kucha (Huang Wenbi and Zhongguo shehui kexueyuan kaogu yanjiusuo, *Xinjiang kaogu*, 60, fig. 9, pls. 42.6, 43.1, 2; Xinjiang Weiwu'er zizhiqu bowuguan, *Xinjiang chutu wenwu*, 120, pl. 169; Xinjiang Weiwu'er zizhiqu bowuguan, *Xinjiang Weiwu'er zizhiqu bowuguan*, pl. 18), dated to the eighth century (Kageyama Etsuko, "Higashi Turukisutan no ossuari," 80; Kageyama Etsuko, "Sogdians," 365–67.

225 Two archaeological discoveries and one *sūtra* underpin such a conclusion:
The finding of a silver dish with a Sogdian inscription: Lin Meicun, "Zhongguo jingnei chutu". Huang Wenbi found to wooden slips, inscribed in Sogdian (originally mistaken for Uighur): Huang Wenbi and Zhongguo shehui kexueyuan kaogu yanjiusuo, *Xinjiang kaogu*, pl. 27.1–2. Yoshida Yutaka believes these to be related to commercial activities, although the connection is unclear to me: Yoshida Yutaka, "Sogudo go," 83.
The ossuary first attributed to Qarashahr was later thought to have come from the Mazabitam 馬扎不但 County, east of the ancient city wall of Kucha (Huang Wenbi and Zhongguo shehui

2.4.2.1.3 Gaochang 高昌/Xizhou 西州 (Qocho), Turfan 吐魯番 Region

While Chinese influence existed in this region, Gaochang 高昌 was practically an independent polity, vassals of either the Turks or the Chinese until 640 CE, when the Tang invaded and the reign of the Qu 麴 ended. It was established that since the sixth century most of the individuals identified by their names as Sogdians in Gaochang 高昌 were registered as farmers or craftsmen such as weavers, saddlers, goldsmiths, tanners, furriers, brewers, viticulturists,[226] many engaged in some form of trade, and some were even officials.[227]

A *hu* 胡 heaven temple (*hu Tian ci* 胡天祠) is reported east of the city for the year 430 CE.[228] The famous *mogao* 莫高 cave no. 17 (also called "library cave") near Dunhuang 敦煌 was walled up at the beginning of the 11th century and only reopened at the beginning of the 20th century, to find thousands of scrolls.[229] There was found the *Shazhou dudufu tujing* 都督府圖經, only available in fragments, mentions the establishment of Sogdian settlements in several places on the Southern Route.[230] On the first fragment, the table of contents is presented: The first three *juan* 卷 deal with

kexueyuan kaogu yanjiusuo, *Xinjiang kaogu*, 60, fig. 9, pls. 42.6, 43.1, 2; Xinjiang Weiwu'er zizhiqu bowuguan, *Xinjiang chutu wenwu*, 120, pl. 169; or: Xinjiang Weiwu'er zizhiqu bowuguan, *Xinjiang Weiwu'er zizhiqu bowuguan*, pl. 18), dated to the eighth century (Kageyama Etsuko, "Higashi Turukisutan no ossuari," 80; Kageyama Etsuko, "Sogdians," 365–67).

Furthermore, a fragment of a Buddhist sūtra has been edited, which was written in Sogdian, and found in Yanqi 焉耆 (Kōgi Kudara and Sundermann, "Fragmente einer soghdischen Handschrift"; see also: Sundermann, "First Results of Cooperative Work").

226 For this craft, see: Trombert, "La vigne et le vin, deuxième partie," 550–52; and: Trombert, "Un vestige vivant," 267–69.

227 Jiang Boqin, *Dunhuang Tulufan wenshu*, 150–226; Ikeda On, "Shinryō". For a short overview over the importance of Turfan on the Silk Road, see: Hansen, "Introduction: Turfan"; and: Zhang Guangda and Rong Xinjiang, "Concise History of Turfan".

228 As Rong Xinjiang (Rong Xinjiang, "Beichao Sui Tang Suteren bu kao (Zhonggu Zhongguo)," 44–45) pointed out, mentioned in the *Jinguangmingjing* 金光明經 (*Suvarnabhasottama-sūtra*, *Sūtra of Golden Light*), fascicle 2, excavated in Anlecheng 安樂城 in 1965; to be found in: Xinjiang Weiwu'er zizhiqu bowuguan, *Xinjiang Weiwu'er zizhiqu bowuguan*.

229 The International Dunhuang Project, "The International Dunhuang Project". De La Vaissière conveniently listed the related studies (apart from volume IV of the Toyo Bunko project and the supplement; Vaissière, *Sogdian Traders*, 126, fn. 22):
– Sogdian or Turco-Sogdian texts: Sims-Williams and Hamilton, *Documents turco-sogdiens*;
– Uighur texts: Hamilton, *Manuscrits ouïgours*.
Chinese texts:
– legal texts: Yamamoto Tatsuro, Okano Makoto and Ikeda On, *Tun-huang, Legal Texts*.
– census registers: Yamamoto Tatsuro and Dohi Yoshikazu, *Tun-Huang, Census Registers (A)*; Yamamoto Tatsuro and Dohi Yoshikazu, *Tun-Huang, Census Registers (B)*.
– contracts: Yamamoto Tatsuro and Ikeda On, *Tun-huang, Contracts*.
– *She* 社 associations and related documents: Yamamoto Tatsuro, Dohi Yoshikazu and Ishida Yusaku, *Tun-Huang, She Associations*.
Supplement: Yamamoto Tatsuro et al., *Tun-huang, Supplement*.

230 For the different names, references, and editions see the table below.

Shazhou 沙洲, *juan* 卷 four with the Dunhuang 敦煌 District, and *juan* 卷 five with the Shouchang 壽昌 District. The second and fourth *juan* 卷 are lost. It is difficult to establish a reliable time frame for the composition and further edition of the text.[231] The *Tang hui yao* states that Shazhou 沙州 became *dudufu* 都督府 (area command) in 651 CE, which is the earliest *terminus post quem* we can define for the *original composition*.[232] Taboo rules for characters and new characters introduced by Wu Zetian 武則天, as well as some dated anecdotes evidence changes or additions on certain manuscripts during her reign (690–705 CE) and are therefore the best *terminus post quem* for the *excavated manuscripts*.[233] It is, however, impossible to say when the last changes were made, but the fragment S.367 (recto) is inscribed at its end with the date 885 CE.

Table 7: Fragments of the Shazhou dudufu tujing 都督府圖經, arranged by juan 卷, and manuscripts providing additional information[234]

Juan 卷	Sources	Different names
1	S.2593 (verso)	*Shazhou tujing* 沙州圖經, *Shazhou tujing juan di yi* 沙州圖經卷第一
2	lost	–
3	P.2005 (recto)	*Shazhou dudufu tujing* 沙州都督府圖經, *Shazhou zhi can juan* 沙州志殘卷, *Shazhou duduju tujing juan di san* 沙州都督府圖經卷第三
	P.2695 (recto)	*Shazhou dudufu tujing* 沙州都督府圖經
	S.788 (verso)	*Shazhou dizhi* (*can pian*) 沙州地志（殘片）
	P.2691 (recto)	*Shazhou zhi* 沙州志
	S.5448 (verso)	*Dunhuang lu* 敦煌錄

231 For a chronology of articles on the topic, see: Zhu Yuemei and Li Bingcheng, "Shazhou," 61. The most influential recent article is by Ikeda On (Ikeda On, "Sashū zukei ryakkō," 39–46), however making a small mistake with the *terminus post quem* (see the text below).

232 *Tang hui yao* 70.1238.

233 See the Multicoloured Lop Nor (*Puchang hai wu se* 蒲昌海五色; p. 211 fn. 273).

234 After Pelliot brought back the manuscripts of Dunhuang to Beijing, Chinese scholars made photographies that resulted in the first edition, made by Luo Zhenyu 羅振玉, Jiang Fu 蔣斧/蔣黼, and Cao Yuanzhong 曹元忠 in 1910 under the name of *Shazhou zhi* 沙州志 in the first volume of *Dunhuang shishi yi shu* 敦煌石室遺書, which was reproduced, as a facsimile, under the name *Shazhou tujing* 沙州圖經 in the volume *Ming sha shishi yi shu* 鳴沙石室逸書 in 1913 (Chavannes, "Livres"; Halévy, "Société," 627; Pelliot, "Cha tcheou tou fou t'ou king," 112). It was followed by a publication in 1930 by Haneda: Haneda Tōru, "Tō". The first extensive critical edition was made by: Ikeda On, "Sashū zukei ryakkō," 31–101, followed by editions by: Zheng Binglin, *Dunhuang dili wenshu*; Wang Zhongluo, *Duanhuang*; Li Zhengyu, *Guben*; and: Tang Geng'ou and Lu Hongji, *Dunhuang shehui jingji wenxian*, 1–84. A translation of S. 367 is to be found in: Giles, "Chinese Geographical Text". See also a partial translation and commentary in: Pelliot, "Cha tcheou tou fou t'ou king".

4	lost	–
5	P.5034 (verso)	*Shazhou tujing* 沙州圖經, *Shazhou dizhi* 沙州地志, *Shazhou tujing juan di wu* 沙州圖經卷第五
	S.367 (recto)	*Shazhou dizhi* 沙州地志, *Guazhou Yixi can zhi* 瓜沙伊西殘志, *Shazhou Yizhou zhi* 沙州伊州志, *Shazhou Yizhou dizhi* 沙州伊州地志
	S.788 (verso)	Shazhou *tujing* 沙州圖經, *Shazhou zhi duan pian* 沙州志斷片
	Transcription by Xiang Da 向達[235]	*Shouchang xian dijing* 壽昌縣地經
	P.2691 (recto)	*Shazhou dizhi* 沙州地志, *Shazhou cheng tujing* 沙州城土境
	S.5448 (verso)	*Dunhuang lu* 敦煌錄

In it is mentioned a *xianzhu* 祆主 (Zoroastrian presider), named Di Pantuo 翟盤陀 – who may have come from Gaochang 高昌[236] – to have visited the capital before 640 CE and was maybe related to the above-mentioned temple.[237] According to Lin Wushu,[238] the local sky cult is not to be identified as Zoroastrianism, as neither in the accounts of Xuanzang 玄奘 – normally writing in detail about the customs of the places he came by – nor in the passage concerning Gaochang 高昌 in the *Suishu*,[239] a fire cult is mentioned for Gaochang 高昌 "although the literature of China has abundant accounts about the Zoroastrian funerals" – which is, however, unknown to me – speaking about China.[240] Although Lin Wushu is right to point out that these sources do not explicitly talk about the sky burials and the sacred fire, the absence of a mention from Xuanzang 玄奘 and a missing record in the *Suishu* are not enough to conclude that "the majority of the people could not be Zoroastrians. Logically, their principal God could not be the Zoroastrian Deity."[241] As I explain below, I believe that *hu tian* 胡天 and *hu xian* 胡祆 are equivalent and conceivably homonymous in this case.[242] I do not, however, claim to know what specific rituals were performed in Gaochang 高昌, as for example, a local form of Sogdian Zoroastrianism. Archaeological finds further speak against the hypothesis of Lin Wushu, as shown below.

Arakawa Masaharu pointed out that in the middle of the sixth century, a Zoroastrian temple may have stood at the beginning of the Toyuk 吐峪溝 gorge

235 Preserved in Dunhuang 敦煌.

236 It is actually just said that Di Pantuo 翟盤陀 undertook this travel before the conquest of Gaochang 高昌 in 640 CE.

237 See p. 242 (3.2.1.4).

238 Lin Wushu, "Discussion Heaven-God"; Lin Wushu, *Bosi baihuojiao*, 123–38.

239 *Suishu* 83.1846–48.

240 He provides no references for this statement (Lin Wushu, "Discussion Heaven-God," 9). On whether Chinese literature mentions Zoroastrian funerals in China or not, see p. 227 fn. 377.

241 Ibid., 12.

242 See p. 310.

(Dinggutian 丁谷天), based on the passage in a Turfan Manuscript on offering cattle and sheep by an individual surnamed Kang 康. He also proposed that this may have been the same temple as the one located east of the city mentioned above:[243]

> [高昌章和五年]次三月二十四日，康祈羊一口，供祀丁谷天。
>
> [On Gaochang 高昌 Zhanghe 章和 5 (535 CE)]/3/24, Kang 康 offered one sheep for a sacrifice at Dinggutian 丁谷天.

This may be supported by two pottery ossuaries that were found in the graves 81SATM1 and M2 at the Toyuk 吐峪溝 Cemetery, Shanshan 鄯善 District, dated to the second half of the seventh century to the first half of the eighth century.[244] As the bones in the ossuary of M1 were wrapped in a cotton cloth, it may reflect a Zoroastrian local funerary ritual.

Further, papers that were used to clothe the deceased were excavated out of hundreds of graves in Astana and Qarakhoja.[245] Inscribed in different languages and well-preserved, they also include information about Sogdians, as for example a sale contract for a slave in Gaochang 高昌, written in Sogdian (dated 639 CE by the editors). The female slave was born in the Western Regions and sold by a Sogdian of Samarqand for 120 Sasanian drachmas to a monk on the market of Gaochang 高昌, with four Sogdians as witnesses – the anomaly being that slave trade was officially forbidden in Tang China.[246] There are also seven Dunhuang manuscripts of the end of the seventh to the beginning of the eighth century in which translators are mentioned for Gaochang 高昌.[247] They were all locals, who worked as translators in the military, court cases, and business transactions. Among these are one with the family name

243 73 TAM 524: 34 2 (Guojia wenwuju guwenxian yanjiu shi, *Tulufan chutu wenshu 2*, 39, col. 3; Arakawa Masaharu, "'Sappō' no sēkaku," 169; as pointed out, but without reference to the manuscript, in: Rong Xinjiang, *Zhonggu Zhongguo yu wailai wenming*, 47, fn. 4). Rong Xinjiang rejected Arakawa's suggestion. Rong Xinjiang equivocated the temples with Sogdian settlements and believed that these two cannot be the same, as, firstly, the city and the gorge are too far apart, and, secondly, if both refer to the same temple at the gorge, the earlier mention would not have used Gaochang's 高昌 wall as point of reference. In my opinion, however, he is mistaken to understand "Gaochang *cheng dong* 高昌城東" as "east of the city wall of Gaochang 高昌" only to mean in the vicinity of the city wall. It can just as well mean "east of the city of Gaochang 高昌" without any limitations as to the distance.

244 Tulufan diqu wenguansuo, "Xinjiang"; Kageyama Etsuko, "Higashi Turukisutan no ossuari," 78–80.

245 Published in two series: Guojia wenwuju guwenxian yanjiu shi, ed., *Tulufan chutu wenshu*; and, including facsimiles: Tang Changru et al., eds., *Tulufan chutu wenshu*. See also: Vaissière, *Sogdian Traders*, 125–26, fn. 20.

246 69 TAM: 135 1, 2. See, for the most: Yoshida Yutaka, Moriyasu Takao and Xinjiang Uyghur Autonomous Museum, "Sogudo bun baibai monjo"; Arakawa Masaharu, "Turufan"; Lin Meicun, "Sutewen mai bi qi". For the newest translation in English, see: Yoshida Yutaka, "Translation".

247 Li Fang, "Tang".

Kang 康, one named He Deli 何德力,[248] one Di Fuzhi 翟浮知 and one Di Nanipan 翟那你潘 or Ninapan 你那潘. The Kang 康 and He 何 were maybe Sogdians.

Furthermore, Skaff established that in the eighth century, while people with Sogdian names in Chonghua 崇華 Town had more children than the Han and other non-Chinese, almost half of the male Sogdians left their original settlement before the age of 15.[249]

Relying on excavated manuscripts, Grenet and Zhang Guangda collected the information for the end of the ninth to the beginning of the tenth century, concerning the heaven cult and its requirements in paper and alcohol,[250] as well as the names of the cults. They pointed out that some people involved may have been Sogdians or were of Sogdian descent. Although it is rather difficult to explicitly link these practices to specific Zoroastrian rituals, the speculations do overall point towards activities that included Zoroastrian rituals.[251]

2.4.2.1.4 Tingzhou 庭州/Beiting 北庭 (Bešbalik/Panjikath)

Two travel permits were found here.[252] The first dates to 648 CE and was for Mi Xunzhi 米巡職, an individual with a Sogdian surname.[253] The second from 716 CE, was for Li Ciyi 李慈藝, who had a Chinese name, but mentions a location called Donghuxian 東胡祆 which may have derived its name from a fire temple.[254] Additionally, a Zoroastrian ossuary was found here, dated to the second half of the seventh century to the first half of the eighth century.[255] Further, a community of people with Sogdian names is recorded in 728 CE.[256] Combined, this may be considered as sufficient evidence for a Sogdian community.

248 The date is Shenlong 神龍 3/12/11, although the year only lasted until the eighth month. The correct date would thus have been Jinglong 景龍 1/12/11 (8.1.708 CE). 72TAM188: 87(a). Also mentioned in: Guojia wenwuju guwenxian yanjiu shi, *Tulufan chutu wenshu 8*, 87.

249 Skaff, "Sogdian Trade Diaspora," 486–93.

250 Grenet and Zhang Guangda, "Last Refuge".

251 Ibid., 181–83; see also: Zhang Guangda, "Iranian Religious Evidence," 193–96.

252 For travel permits, see: Arakawa Masaharu, "Transit Permit System"; Cheng Xilin, *Tangdai guosuo yanjiu*.

253 Found in the Astana grave no. 221. 73 TAM 221: 5 (Guojia wenwuju guwenxian yanjiu shi, *Tulufan chutu wenshu 7*, 8, col. 2; Tang Changru, *Tulufan chutu wenshu 3*, 306; Jiang Boqin, *Dunhuang Tulufan wenshu*, 187–88).

254 See the decree copied in: (Rong Xinjiang, *Zhonggu Zhongguo yu wailai wenming*, 50); using: Oda Yoshihisa, "Ri Jigei kokushin," 128–29; see also: Oda Yoshihisa, "Tōdai kokushin"; and: Chen Guocan, "Tang Li Ciyi".
The location of the temple is unclear, somewhere west of Tingzhou 庭州 (Rong Xinjiang, *Zhonggu Zhongguo yu wailai wenming*, 50–51; see also: Chen Guocan, "Tang Li Ciyi," 41, 43).

255 See Vol. 2, Appendix 4.1, Figure 250. Found in Jimsar 吉木薩爾 County (ancient Beiting 北庭 and Beshbalik): Kageyama Etsuko, "Higashi Turukisutan no ossuari," 80–81. Kageyama did conclude that the person was Sogdian.

256 In the *Tang Kaiyuan shiliu nian Tingzhou Jinmanxian die* 唐開元十六年庭州金滿縣牒. See: Ikeda On, *Zhongguo gudai jizhang yanjiu*, 354; pointed out by: Rong Xinjiang, *Zhonggu Zhongguo yu wailai wenming*, 49.

2.4.2.1.5 Yiwu 伊吾/Yizhou 伊州 (Hami)

The *Shazhou dudufu tujing* 沙州都督府圖經 (S.367, recto) has the following entry:[257]

> 伊州，下……貞觀四年，首領石萬/年率七城來降。我唐始置伊州.
>
> Yizhou 伊州, 2nd [passage]: (…) In Zhenguan 貞觀 4 (630 CE), chief Shi Wannian 石萬年 led seven forts to come and surrender. At the beginning of the Tang it was changed into Yizhou 伊州.

Shi Wannian 石萬年, probably a Sogdian military leader stemming from the state of Shi 石 (Chach) surrendered to the Tang in 630 CE. Pulleyblank proposed that the above-mentioned seven forts were related to the garrisons of Kang Yandian 康豔典.[258] Further, we know that Di Pantuo 翟槃陀, who was related to Zoroastrian activities in Yiwu 伊吾, visited the capital before 640 CE.[259]

2.4.2.2 Southern Route

2.4.2.2.1 Yutian 于闐/于寘 (Khotan)

Many Chinese and Sogdian documents refer to Sogdians in Khotan, being mostly involved in commercial activities. We can thus assume that there was Sogdian community.[260]

257 Facsimile: (The International Dunhuang Project, "Or.8210/S.367 Recto"). For more information on the manuscript(s), see p. 202 (2.4.2.1.3). For other transcriptions, see: 1) Zheng Binglin, *Dunhuang dili wenshu*, 66–67; *gao* 高, already annotated with a question mark, is actually *wan* 萬, as can be seen on the facsimile; and 2) Tang Geng'ou and Lu Hongji, *Dunhuang shehui jingji wenxian*, 40, cols. 29, 36–37.

258 Pulleyblank, "Sogdian Colony," 347–54. For the forts related to Kang Yandian 康豔典, see p. 208 (2.4.2.2.2).

259 See p. 242 (3.2.1.4).

260 "The existence of Sogdian merchants in Khotan is inferred from a number of Sogdian documents discovered there. They are fragments 12, 15, 16, 23, 27, 30, and 33 published by N. Sims-Williams, *IIJ*, 18, 1976; possibly fragment 36 reproduced by Sims-Williams and Hamilton, *Documents turco-sogdiens du ixe–xe siècle de Touen-houang* (London, 1990), pi. 39; one fragment in the Trinkler collection (cf. G. Gropp, *Archäologische Funde aus Khotan, Chinesisch-Ostturkestan*, Bremen, 1975, 364–7 and Sims-Williams, *BSOAS*, 42/2, 1979, 337, n. 6); one fragment from the Francke collection (cf. Gropp, in W. Skalmowski and A. Van Tongerloo (ed.), *Middle Iranian studies*, Leuven, 1984, 149); and a seal with Sogdian inscription *prn* 'fortune' reproduced by A. Stein, *Serindia,* vol. 4 (London, 1921), pl. V, Khot. 0090.
One also finds some Sogdian names in Chinese documents unearthed from this area, e.g. 羅勃帝分 **pwtyprn* (Maspero, op. cit., 187-8 with an improved reading provided by Professor O. Ikeda), 安芬 **prn* (T. Yamamoto and O. Ikeda, *Tun-huang and Turfan documents*, III, Tokyo, 1987, 77), 石都督 **twtwx*, 康蕓漢 **wnx'n* (both attested in Mazar Tagh 092 published by Guo Feng [sic], *Sitanyin disanci zhongya tanxian suohuo Gansu Xinjiang chutu wenshu,* Lanzhou, 1993, 51), and 野那 **y'n'kk* (cf. Ikeda, op. cit., 349, line 17). *Budävaṃdai* cited above may also be a Sogdian name, i.e. **pwtyβntk*. On this point see also *ṣvặnaka* appearing in SI P 103.52 with which Emmerick compares Sogdian *(')šw'n'kk* or *šw'nkk,* cf. Emmerick, art. Cit., 55.

2.4.2.2.2 Garrisons and Kang Yandian 康豔典: the Shicheng 石城 (Stonewall) Garrison or Dianhe 典合 Fort (Loulan 樓蘭/Shanshan 鄯善), the Xin 新 (New) Fort, the Putao 蒲桃 (Grape-Vine) Fort, the Sapi 薩毗 Fort, and the Boxian 播仙 Fort (Qiemo 且末)

Among various information on the local geography, the *Shazhou dudufu tujing* 都督府圖經 mentions the Sogdian Kang Yandian 康豔典 (from Samarqand), who lived in the seventh century, and several places west of Shazhou 沙州 (Dunhuang 敦煌) that are related to him:[261]

> 石城鎮，東去沙州一千五百八十里，去上都六千一百里。本漢樓/蘭國。漢書西域傳云：地沙滷，少田，出玉。傳介子既殺/其王，漢立其弟，更名鄯善國。隋置鄯善鎮。隋亂，其/城遂廢。貞觀中，康國大首領康豔典東來，居此城，/胡人隨之，因成聚落，亦日典合城。四面皆是沙磧。上元二年/改爲石城鎮，隸沙州。……
>
> The Shicheng 石城 (Stonewall) Garrison. To the east, [one] goes 1,580 *li* (ca. 790 km) to Shazhou 沙州 [and] 6,100 *li* (ca. 3,050 km) to the capital. [It] originally was the Loulan 樓蘭 Kingdom of the Han. The Accounts of the Western Regions of the *Hanshu* say: the soil is sandy, [there are] few fields, [and it] brings forth jade. When Fu Jiezi 傳介子 murdered their king, the Han installed his cadet brother and changed the name [into] the State of Shanshan 鄯善. In the Sui, Shanshan 鄯善 Garrison was installed. [When] the Sui were

On possible Sogdian elements in the Khotanese iconography see M. Mode, 'Sogdian gods in exile–some iconographic evidence from Khotan in the light of recently excavated material from Sogdiana', *Silk Road Art and Archaeology, 2,* 1991/92, 179–214." Yoshida Yutaka, "Corpus Inscriptionum Iranicarum II, Vol. V, Vol. III (review)," 568–69. Besides these, see also the document found in Endere (see p. 211).
The word *srtp'w* (being a later form of *s'rtp'w*) is also mentioned in a document found in Khotan, where it is probably used as a self-identifier, estimated to date from the seventh century (Duan Qing, "Sute"). The important information is actually provided by Yoshida Yutaka's reading of the fragment BH4-136 (115), further estimating the date of the fragment.
See also: Rong Xinjiang, "Xiyu Sute yimin kao," 158–61; updated in: Rong Xinjiang, "Xiyu Sute yimin juluo bu kao," 11–13; or: Compareti, Raffetta and Scarcia, *Ērān ud Anērān*, 514–18.
For an overview of the political history, see: Skjaervo, "Iranians, Indians, Chinese and Tibetans". See also: Rong Xinjiang, "Xiyu Sute yimin juluo bu kao," 13.

261 This is the transcription of: The International Dunhuang Project, "Or.8210/S.367 Recto".
To be found in different versions on the following manuscripts: The International Dunhuang Project, "Pelliot chinois 5034, recto"; The International Dunhuang Project, "Or.8210/S.367 Recto"; and the *Shouchang xian di jing* 壽昌縣地經 (only available as transcription: Li Zhengyu, *Guben*, 445–46, 327–86).
Transcriptions and editions are to be found in: Ikeda On, "Sashū zukei ryakkō," 91–92, cols. 17–39; Tang Geng'ou and Lu Hongji, *Dunhuang shehui jingji wenxian*, 39, cols. 8–22; Zheng Binglin, *Dunhuang dili wenshu*, 65–66; Li Zhengyu, *Guben*; transcribed and translated in: Giles, "Chinese Geographical Text"; translated in: Pelliot, "Cha tcheou tou fou t'ou king," 120–21; published and commented in: Haneda Tōru, "Tō". For more information on the various fragments, see p. 202 (2.4.2.1.3).

> disrupted, their fortification was swiftly destroyed. During the Zhenguan 貞觀 (era, 627–49 CE), the Great Chief of the state of Kang 康, Kang Yandian 康豔典, came east to reside in this fort. Other Sogdians followed him and thus created a settlement, also called Dianhe 典合 Fort. On all sides is desert. In Shangyuan 上元 2 (675 CE), [it was] changed into the Shicheng 石城 Garrison, administrated [by] Shazhou 沙洲. (…)
>
> 新城，東去石城鎮二百卌里。康豔典之居鄯善，先修此城，因名新城，漢名弩支城。/
>
> The Xin 新 (New) Fort. To the east, [one] goes 220 *li* (ca. 110 km) to the Shicheng 石城 Fort. [When] Kang Yandian 康豔典 went to reside in Shanshan 鄯善, [he] first restored this fort, therefore named the Xin 新 (New) Fort, called the Nuzhi 弩支 Fort [during] the Han.
>
> 蒲桃城，南去石城鎮四里，康豔典所築，種蒲桃[於][262]此城中，因號蒲桃城。/
>
> The Putao 蒲桃 (Grape) Fort.[263] To the south, [one] goes four *li* (ca 2 km) to the Shicheng 石城 Garrison. Built by Kang Yandian 康豔典. [As he] planted grapevines in this fort,[264] [it is] therefore called the Putao 蒲桃 (Grape) Fort.
>
> 薩毗城，西北去石城鎮四百八十里，康豔典所築，其城近薩/毗澤，山險阻，恒有吐蕃及吐谷渾來往不絕。/
>
> The Sapi 薩毗 Fort. To the north-west, [one] goes 480 *li* (ca. 240 km) to the Shicheng 石城 Garrison. [It was] built by Kang Yandian 康豔典. The fort [is located] near the Sapi 薩毗 Marshland. The mountain [paths are] difficult. Often there are Tubo 吐蕃 and Tuyuhun 吐谷渾, coming and going without interruption.

The author(s) wanted to ascribe the repopulation of this strip of land to a Sogdian after it was abandoned at the end of the Sui at the beginning of the seventh century. Additionally, the Grape Fort may conceivably point to the (re)introduction of viticulture and generally such activity in the region. Of interest is also the mention of the Tubo 吐蕃 and the Tuhuyun 吐谷渾, coming from the south. It is probable that it was written by someone sympathetic to, or himself being a Sogdian, or an individual

262 The character *yu* 於 is written above the right upper edge of the character *ci* 此 on S.367 (recto), probably a later addition, maybe in reference to P.5034 (verso) that includes the *yu* 於 but not the *ci* 此: 康豔典種蒲桃於城中。

263 Sims-Williams (Sims-Williams, "Sogdian Merchants," 61, fn. 75) proposed to reconstruct the name of the fort as Sogd. **mδwknδ* in parallel to the **nwcknδ* 'New Town' (see p. 210 fn. 266). "Chin. *putao* (EMC *bɔ-daw*, from a form related to Sogd. *mδw* 'wine')" (ibid.) "corresponds to an Iranian **budāwa* or **buδawa*" (Laufer, *Sino-Iranica*, 225).

264 Kang Yandian 康豔典 is the subject of the sentence, as can be seen in another version of the account (The International Dunhuang Project, "Pelliot chinois 5034, recto"). See: Ikeda On, "Sashū zukei ryakkō," 93. On wine and vine see also: Laufer, *Sino-Iranica*, 220–45.

of another Western state, who credits the civilising influence of a Kang 康 on these places. This becomes obvious when reading the differing account of these events in the *Xin Tangshu*:[265]

> 又西八十里至石城鎮，漢樓蘭國也，亦名鄯善，在蒲昌海南三百里，康豔典為鎮使以通西域者。又西二百里至新城，亦謂之弩支城，豔典所築。
>
> Eighty *li* to the west, [one] arrives at the Shicheng 石城 (Stonewall) Garrison. [Known as] the state of Loulan 樓蘭 [during the] Han, [it is] also called Shanshan 鄯善, 30 *li* (ca. 15 km) south of the Puchang 蒲昌 Lake (Lop Nor). Kang Yandian 康豔典 was made commissioner of the garrison to communicate with the people of the Western Regions. Twenty *li* west, [one] arrives at Xin 新 (New) Fort, also called Nuzhi 弩支 Fort,[266] built by Yandian 豔典.

Kang Yandian 康豔典 is introduced as "commissioner of the garrison" in the *Xin Tangshu*. This differs considerably to his above-mentioned title "great chief of the state of Kang 康", which was normally used for foreign dignitaries or generals in this official source from the Tang (edited in the Song), and his record of (re-)establishing civilisation in the named places. Instead, he is styled as communication tool appointed by the Chinese court. By this change, the authority behind the events is shifted and *a posteriori* defined as an action of the Chinese court.

Many individuals that may be identified as Sogdians used Loulan 樓蘭 – the above-mentioned Shicheng 石城 (Stonewall) Garrison – as a commercial hub.[267] The Ancient Sogdian Letter VI (line 5)[268] also mentions *kr'wr'n* (Krōrān) – which was identified as Loulan 樓蘭 and thus refers to the above-mentioned ancient Shanshan 鄯善[269] – as a destination for trade in the early fourth century. Further, Sims-Willians and Bi Bo produced a commented edition of the up-to-date only fragment of a Sogdian letter excavated in a dwelling in Niya 尼雅 (which was at this time also part of Khotan/Shanshan 鄯善) in 1994,[270] which was inhabited from the latter half of the second century to ca. 330 CE (93A27F1:3).[271] Additionally, a Kharoṣṭhī document (Kh.661) found in Endere (which was at this time part of Khotan/Shanshan 鄯善) was

265 *Xin Tangshu* 43b.1151; see also: Pelliot, "Cha tcheou tou fou t'ou king," 116–19.

266 Sims-Williams (Sims-Williams, "Sogdian Merchants," 61, fn. 75) proposed that it "(EMC *nɔ-tɕi(ǎ)*) evidently represents Sogd. **nwcknδ* 'New Town'." Further, simply out of this context, it is to be identified as Nujikath, also referred to as Nuchijian 笯赤建 in another place in the *Xin Tangshu* 221a.6233 and the *Da Tang Xiyu ji*, T51.871b11–14.

267 See: Rong Xinjiang, "Xiyu Sute yimin juluo kao," 26–29; and: Rong Xinjiang, "Xiyu Sute yimin juluo bu kao," 14. See also the Sogdian fragments from Loulan 樓蘭 (as listed in: Sims-Williams, "Sogdian Fragments," 43, no. 10): L.M.II.ii.09 (Or. 8212/1823); L.A.II.x.01 (Or. 8212/1368), L.A.II.x.02 (Or. 8212/1368), L.A.IV.v.028 (Or. 8212/1365); L.A.VI.ii.0104 (Or. 8212/102), and L.L.018 (Or. 8212/1735).

268 For more information on the letters, see p. 214 (2.4.3.1.1).

269 Henning, "Date of the Sogdian Letters," 611; Sims-Williams, "Sogdian Merchants," 49.

270 Sims-Williams and Bi Bo, "Sogdian".

271 Ibid., 91–92.

probably sent from Loulan 樓蘭 and may be dated to the second half of the third century to the beginning of the fourth century and mentions a witness and even maybe a buyer with a Sogdian name.[272]

In the same *Shazhou dudufu tujing* 沙州都督府圖經, a passage recounts an anecdote from 691 CE, entitled "The Multicoloured Lop Nor" (*Puchang hai wu se* 蒲昌海五色),[273] in which is mentioned Kang Dishebo 康地舍撥, a cadet brother of Kang Fudanyan 康拂耽延,[274] was the general in charge of Shicheng 石城 Garrison. It is thinkable that both were related to Kang Yandian 康豔典. The *Shazhou dudufu tujing* 沙州都督府圖經, P.5034 (recto), also mentions after the description of the Shicheng 石城 Garrison "one Zoroastrian building" (*yi suo xian she* 一所祆舍), however, without clear context.[275]

Finally, Chen Guocan pointed out an inscription on a stele in the Tang Qianling 乾陵 Mausoleum, which mentions a further fort:[276]

> 播仙城□河伏帝延。
>
> Boxian 播仙 Fort … He Fudiyan 河伏帝延.

According to similar passages, Chen Guocan proposed that the missing character may be *zhu* 主 "chief", whereas the *He* 河 could be a read as a variant of *He* 何. He thus amended the passage as:

> He Fudiyan 何伏帝延, chief of the Boxian 播仙 Fort.

272 Kharoṣṭhī Inscriptions, 249; Burrow, "Iranian Words," 514–15; Burrow, *Translation*, 137; *apud*: Sims-Williams and Bi Bo, "Sogdian," 99, fn. 75. See also: Vaissière, *Sogdian Traders*, 58.

273 Facsimile: The International Dunhuang Project, "Pelliot chinois 2005, recto"; edition: Ikeda On, "Sashū zukei ryakkō," 81, cols. 449–56; another transcription: Zheng Binglin, *Dunhuang dili wenshu*, 19; for more information on the manuscript, see also p. 202 (2.4.2.1.3).

274 Yamada Nobuo (Yamada Nobuo, "Toruko," 331) and Haneda Tōru (Haneda Tōru, "Baku-hoku," 401–3) propose that the name is interchangeable with Fuduoyan 拂多延, which is Sogdian for *furštadān* meaning "Manichaean priest" (see: Gharib, *Sogdian Dictionary*, 26, no. 679), and thus believe that this fort was managed by a Manichaean priest. In my opinion, this is still a given name, however, maybe meaning "Manichaean priest", such as Sabao 薩保 and Sabao 薩寶 was used as a given name and office title (see p. 278; 3.2.).

275 The International Dunhuang Project, "Pelliot chinois 5034, recto"; transcribed in: Zheng Binglin, *Dunhuang dili wenshu*, 49; Ikeda On, "Sashū zukei ryakkō," 5.97, cols. 123–24; and: Tang Geng'ou and Lu Hongji, *Dunhuang shehui jingji wenxian*, 37, col. 206. To the already hypothetical reconstruction of some of the characters of the next column by Ikeda On, Rong Xinjiang added some further characters in his transcription, which, based on my reading of the fragment, I cannot confirm, unless he reconstructed it from a context that is unknown to me (Rong Xinjiang, *Zhonggu Zhongguo yu wailai wenming*, 42).
Rong Xinjiang wrote that this passage is the end of the description of the Shicheng 石城 Garrison (ibid.). This is, however, not the case, as can be seen on the manuscript, it is clearly an own entry in the list equal to the Shicheng 石城 Garrison, the first character of the passage being elevated.

276 The *you er bei di shi ren* 右二碑第十人 (second stele in the right at the 10th man) (Chen Guocan, "Tang qianling," 197).

According to the *Shazhou Yizhou dizhi* 沙州伊州地志 (S. 367) and the *Shouchang xian dijing* 壽昌縣地經, Qiemo 且末 changed its name to Boxian 播仙 Fort (also written Fanxian 幡仙) in Shangyuan 上元 3 (676 CE).[277] Since Wu Zetian 武則天 was buried in the Mausoleum in 706 CE, the inscription may reference the situation somewhen between 676 and 706 CE.[278] If the amendment is correct, this may be another case of a Sogdian in charge of a Fort, as He 何 may refer to Kushaniyya and Fudiyan 伏帝延 (*EMC *buw*^{h} *tɛj*^{h} *jian*; *Butiyān*)[279] was a name used by Sogdians, meaning "Gift of Buddha".[280]

2.4.2.2.3 Liang xinghu bo 涼興胡泊*, the Moor of the Authorised hu* 胡 *of Liangzhou* 涼州

The *Shazhou tujing* 沙州圖經 (P.2005, recto), contains a passage about the "Moor of the Authorised *hu* 胡":[281]

> 一所興胡泊。東西十九里，南北九里，深五尺。/右[282]在州西北一百一十里。其水鹹苦，唯泉堪食。商胡從玉門關道往還居止，因以為号。
>
> One Moor of the Authorised *hu* 胡. [It is] 19 *li* (ca. 10 km) from east to west, 9 *li* (ca. 4.5 km) from north to south, 5 *chi* (ca. 1.65 m) deep. Again, [located] 110 *li* (ca. 55 km) north-west of [Sha]zhou 沙[州]. Its water [is] salty [and] bitter. [It is] the only potable spring. *Hu* 胡 Merchants [who] come from and go to the Jade Gate Pass halt [here], which is the reason for [its] name.

Also recorded in another fragment, S.788 (verso):[283]

277 Ikeda On, "Sashū zukei ryakkō," 97; Zheng Binglin, *Dunhuang dili wenshu*, 62, 66; Tang Geng'ou and Lu Hongji, *Dunhuang shehui jingji wenxian*, 39, col. 22 p, 53. For more information on the manuscripts, see also p. 202 (2.4.2.1.3).

278 Rong Xinjiang took instead the end of her reign (704 CE) as *terminus ante quem* (Rong Xinjiang, "Beichao Sui Tang Suteren bu kao (Zhonggu Zhongguo)," 40).

279 The etymology was done by Ikeda On, see fn. below.

280 The combination of the surname and given name is the reason why it is included in the present study (Rong Xinjiang, "Beichao Sui Tang Suteren bu kao (Zhonggu Zhongguo)," 40; and: Lurje, *Personal*, 315; *apud*: Weber, "Zur sogdischen," 201; *apud*: Ikeda On, "Hasseiki chūyō," 63).

281 Facsimile: The International Dunhuang Project, "Pelliot chinois 2005, recto"; transcribed in: Ikeda On, "Sashū zukei ryakkō," 3.64, cols. 143–45; Zheng Binglin, *Dunhuang dili wenshu*, 9; and: Tang Geng'ou and Lu Hongji, *Dunhuang shehui jingji wenxian*, 8, cols. 143–45. For more information on the manuscripts, see also p. 202 (2.4.2.1.3).
The Chinese term *xinghu* 興胡 "Authorised Westerners" is an administrative term, paired with *kehu* 客胡, the "Visiting Westerners", the latter being part of an official embassy visiting China.

282 Read *you* 又.

283 Facsimile: The International Dunhuang Project, "Or.8210/S.788"; transcribed in: Ikeda On, "Sashū zukei ryakkō," 64; Zheng Binglin, *Dunhuang dili wenshu*, 56; and: Tang Geng'ou and Lu Hongji, *Dunhuang shehui jingji wenxian*, 42, cols. 6–7.

涼興胡泊。縣西北一百一十里，餘水皆苦，唯此水可飲，商胡從玉門關/往來，皆止於此。

Moor of the Authorised *hu* 胡 of Liang[zhou] 涼[州]. [Located] 110 *li* (ca. 55 km) north-west of the (Shazhou 沙州) district. All the remaining water is bitter. Because this water [is] potable, all Western Foreign Merchants who come from and go to the Jade Gate Pass halt here.

In addition, the fragment P.2691 (recto)[284] mentions it with only one sentence, however, at quite a different distance. It can probably be dismissed as incorrect, as the two other manuscripts concur:

興胡泊，州西北卅五里。

Moor of the Authorised *hu* 胡. [Located] 35 *li* (ca. 18 km) north-west of [Sha]zhou 沙[州].

While these manuscripts provide us with information about this stopover for travellers between Shazhou 沙州 and the Jade Gate Pass, it is noteworthy that S.788 (verso)[285] specifies that the "Authorised *hu* 胡" were from Liangzhou 涼州, which again underlines the importance of Liangzhou 涼州 for what certainly included Sogdian travellers, or more specifically, merchants.

2.4.3 *Neidi* 內地 outside of the capitals

Coming from Dunhuang 敦煌/Shazhou 沙州, a traveller would then enter the Hexi 河西 Corridor, to then move further to the east and south towards Northern China and eventually the Central Plains. Like the above defined space, this was disputed between various Northern Dynasties, tribes of the Rouran 柔然, and the Tujue 突厥. Below, the information related to Sogdians is organised in the five cardinal directions (including the centre) and leaves the capitals for the final section.

2.4.3.1 West

2.4.3.1.1 Shazhou 沙州/Dunhuang 敦煌 and Guazhou 瓜州[286]

The *Sanguozhi* includes an episode recording the deeds of Cang Ci 倉慈, who came from Huainan 淮南 and held an office during the Eastern Han. After the death of Cao Cao 曹操, he moved to Chang'an 長安 and was appointed as commandery governor

284 Facsimile: The International Dunhuang Project, "Pelliot chinois 2691, recto"; transcribed in: Ikeda On, "Sashū zukei ryakkō," 64; Zheng Binglin, *Dunhuang dili wenshu*, 39; and: Tang Geng'ou and Lu Hongji, *Dunhuang shehui jingji wenxian*, 43, cols. 9–10.

285 Rong Xinjiang (Rong Xinjiang, "Beichao Sui Tang Suteren bu kao (Zhonggu Zhongguo)," 54) only mentioned P.2005 (recto) and thus missed out this detail.

286 The toponym changed over time: Installed in 335 CE, it was changed in 619 CE to Guazhou 瓜州, in 622 CE called Western Shazhou 西沙洲, in 742 CE to Dunhuang 敦煌 Commandery, in 758 CE back to Shazhou 沙洲 (Shi Weile, *Zhongguo lishi diming 1*, 1328–29). For more information, see the glossary.

of Dunhuang 敦煌. Although this sounds like a punishment, the account styles his relocation as a Wild West story:[287]

> 太和中，遷燉煌太守。郡在西陲，以喪亂隔絕，曠無太守二十歲，大姓雄張，遂以為俗。前太守尹奉等，循故而已，無所匡革。慈到，抑挫權右，撫恤貧羸，甚得其理。
>
> During the Taihe 太和 era (227–33 CE), [he] was dispatched as [commandery] governor of Dunhuang 敦煌. The commandery is located at the Western border [and] due to the confusion [during the transition after the emperor's] death, [it] was cut off. Left without commander [it was] neglected for 20 years. The [local] great families were at their peak, which subsequently became [the established] norm. The former commander Yin Feng 尹奉 and others accepted the given circumstances and nothing was rectified. When Ci 慈 arrived, [he] suppressed the powers that were, comforted the poor and weak, [and] deeply understood the scheme of it.
>
> 舊大族田地有餘，而小民無立錐之土；慈皆隨口割賦，稍稍使畢其本直。先是屬城獄訟眾猥，縣不能決，多集治下；慈躬往省閱，料簡輕重，自非殊死，但鞭杖遣之，一歲決刑曾不滿十人。
>
> In the past, the big clans had more than enough farmland, but the lower people did not even have [enough] soil to stick an awl. In all these cases, Ci 慈 allocated the land tax according to the population [and thus] gradually perfected the originally due tax. In the past, [because] the judicial cases of local officials [were so] numerous, the districts could not pass sentence, [and] many [cases] accumulated under [their] government. Ci 慈 himself went to inspect [and] determine the severity [of the correction]. Besides death penalties, the [convicted were] castigated with the stick and whip [or] exiled. In one year, not even ten people were sentenced to death.
>
> 又常日西域雜胡欲來貢獻，而諸豪族多逆斷絕；既與貿遷，欺詐侮易，多不得分明。胡常怨望，慈皆勞之。欲詣洛者，為封過所，欲從郡還者，官為平取，輒以府見物與共交市，使吏民護送道路，由是民夷翕然稱其德惠。
>
> Further, often various *hu* 胡 from the Western Regions desired to come [and] present tribute. However, [among] all the great families, many opposed and interrupted [this]. As to the commerce between [the great families] and them, [they were] cheated [and] coerced, [and] many [conflicts] could not be solved. The *hu* 胡 [were] often discontent, [but] Ci 慈 paid all off. The ones that desired to travel to Luoyang 洛陽 were granted a passport, [and from] the ones that desired to go back from the commandery, the government would equitably acquire [their goods], and sell it on the public market as governmental goods.

287 *Sanguozhi* 16.512–13.

[He] sent officials [and] other people to protect them on their way. Therefore, average people [and] barbarians both praised his virtue [and] kindness.

數年卒官，吏民悲感如喪親戚，圖畫其形，思其遺像。及西域諸胡聞慈死，悉共會聚於戊己校尉及長吏治下發哀，或有以刀畫面，以明血誠，又為立祠，遙共祠之。

After many years, he died while in office. Lower officials and common people were sad as if mourning for relatives, painting his portrait, [and] grieving his death portrait. When all the *hu* 胡 of the Western Regions heard [about] Ci's 慈 death, [they] all gathered under the lead of the *wuji* 戊己 commander and higher officials [to] hold a lamenting ceremony. Some cut [their] faces with a knife, to show [their] sincere [affection]. [They] also built a temple [and people from] far away offered sacrifice for him.

Without stating too much of the obvious, instead of a demoted official, this is essentially the account of a righteous Chinese going to the Western Regions to fight corruption and bring justice and help for the suffering ones, befriending the "barbarians". It is unclear, however, if the powerful families in this story were themselves *hu* 胡 or not. More interesting is the information provided on commerce and travel.

While economy was skewed towards the great families, it becomes clear that a part of the local population were farmers. Local government was apparently rather inefficient in upholding the law. Sogdian envoys were in need of passports on their way to Luoyang 洛陽 and depended on officials to provide these, which apparently was sometimes problematic – Cang Ci's 藏慈 actions are meant to contrast with the situation before – because powerful local families interfered with this. These families possibly wanted to control the contact to China and entice the envoys to trade their goods. Thus, Dunhuang 敦煌 represented one of the entry points into Chinese territory. Further, Sogdian merchants encountered difficulties to sell their products on the markets controlled by the families. However, there also existed a market that had officially regulated prizes. Finally, merchants needed protection on their travel. Overall, while the hero of the story excels through his actions, the Chinese government is portrayed as powerless in face of the established local great families. If this is to be seen as differing greatly from the government of the Chinese Central Regions is not entirely clear.

On his famous expedition along the Silk Roads Sir Aurel Stein discovered in 1907 what commonly is referred to as the Sogdian Ancient Letters in an abandoned post-bag in a ruined watchtower, sent from Sogdians in the Western Regions and dated around the years 311–13 CE.[288] It could be established that from the eight letters, one

288 For a discussion of the letters and their dating see: Grenet, Sims-Williams and Vaissière, "Sogdian Ancient Letter V," shortly after 311 CE; and: Grenet and Sims-Williams, "Historical Context".

of them came from Guzang 姑臧 and another from Dunhuang 敦煌. The Sogdian Ancient Letters I and III corroborate a Sogdian presence: a "temple priest"[289] (*βynpt*),[290] "leaders" (*'ypsy'r*),[291] and a "tax councillor" (*β'zkr'm*)[292] are recorded for the Sogdian community in Dunhuang 敦煌. The Sogdian Ancient Letter V, addressed to a chief merchant (*s'rtp'w*)[293] named Aspandhāt[294] in Khotan (?),[295] evidences Sogdian mercantile activity between Samarqand, Dunhuang 敦煌, Guzang 姑臧, and China for the beginning of the fourth century CE.[296] There is no indication as to precisely where it was addressed, although we know that it was at the border or to the west of the Chinese world.[297]

In addition, from a tax register from Dunhuang 敦煌, dating to as early as the sixth century, it can be gathered that registered people bearing Sogdian names were farmers or craftsmen.[298] For the middle of the eighth century, we have further clues of a Sogdian settlement at the An 安 Fort (see below) that may also be interpreted as indicators of an earlier presence. Indeed, Kang Ye's 康業 epitaph gives as his father's

289 This is the earliest mention of a Zoroastrian priest, literally meaning "master of a temple". The term is applied in the Manichaean polemical text M219, as well as in Armenian and Middle Indian sources to a priest serving a temple containing images: Grenet, "Where," 160.

290 Letter I, line 10: Or.8212/92(1)/(T.XII.a.ii.1) (The International Dunhuang Project, "Or.8212/92(1)"; Sims-Williams, "Sogdian Merchants," 48–49; see also: Henning, "Date of the Sogdian Letters," 602, no. 3). The translation of Sims-Williams is to be found on the IDP-Webpage: Silk Road Seattle Website, "Sogdian Ancient Letters". On this and other terms for Magi, see: Grenet, "Where," 160; and: Shenkar, "Rethinking," 484–86.

291 Letter III, lines 8, 12: Or.8212/98/(T.XII.a.ii.3) (The International Dunhuang Project, "Or.8212/98, verso and recto"). The translation of Sims-Williams is to be found on the IDP-Webpage, published in: Whitfield and Sims-Williams, *The Silk Road*, 249; taken from: Silk Road Seattle Website, "Sogdian Ancient Letters". See also: Sims-Williams, "Sogdian Merchants," 49; and: Sims-Williams, *Sogdian*, 45.

292 Letter I, line 4: Or.8212/92(1) (five pieces)/(T.XII.a.ii.1) (The International Dunhuang Project, "Or.8212/92(1)"). The translation of Sims-Williams is to be found on the IDP-Webpage, published in: Whitfield and Sims-Williams, *The Silk Road*, 249; taken from: Silk Road Seattle Website, "Sogdian Ancient Letters". See also: Gershevitch, "Sogdians on a Frogplain," 200, no. 6.

293 On this topic, see p. 278 (3.2.).

294 For other occurrences of this name, see: Lurje, *Personal*, 107, no. 160.

295 The location is purely hypothetical, see below.

296 For the facsimile of the letter, see: The International Dunhuang Project, "Or.8212/100"; for a translation, see: Silk Road Seattle Website, "Sogdian Ancient Letters". See also: Grenet, Sims-Williams and Vaissière, "Sogdian Ancient Letter V".
The letter II also includes a passage mentioning "100 freemen from Samarqand" (The International Dunhuang Project, "Or.8212/95"; for an edition, see: Sims-Williams, "Sogdian Ancient Letter II"; see also: Sims-Williams, "Sogdian Merchants," 48). Grenet and Zhang Guangda believe that it is Sogdian population in Dunhuang: Grenet and Zhang Guangda, "Last Refuge," 183, fn. 2.

297 Grenet, Sims-Williams and Vaissière (Grenet, Sims-Williams and Vaissière, "Sogdian Ancient Letter V," 101) proposed that he lived in Loulan 樓蘭, however without providing an explanation. The letters I and III were destined to Loulan 樓蘭 and Letter II for Samarqand.

298 Vaissière, *Sogdian Traders*, 130; referring to: S.613 (The International Dunhuang Project, "Or.8210/S.613").

choronym Luozhou 羅州, which I propose refers to the An 安 Fort, where he must have been active in the sixth century. According to registers, the majority of the inhabitants were Sogdians, mostly farmers, while some engaged in trade.[299] These documents also reveal that the name giving process gradually changed during this period, as phonetic translations of Sogdian given names decreased over the generations in favour of Chinese names. Among the manuscripts found in the *mogao* 莫高 caves near Dunhuang 敦煌 are also hundreds of local sales contracts:[300] one from the eighth century,[301] and 249 from the ninth and tenth century.[302]

We further know about at least one temple east of the city. Waley[303] listed some related quotes, to which Grenet and Zhang Guangda[304] added a few, which are presented and further expanded below. Including documents from 676 to 979 CE, the documents are provided chronologically together with the original text, a transcription, and a translation (the grey represents the original red colour of the characters):[305]

– The *Shazhou tujing* 沙州圖經 (P.2005, recto), dated to the middle of the eighth century (?),[306] contains a list of four temples dedicated to various deities (*si suo za shen* 四所雜神), i.e. earth, wind, rain, and the *xian* 祆 deity:

299 As Ikeda showed, the percentage of farmers decreased however in the eighth century (Ikeda On, "Hasseiki chūyō"; in Chinese: Ikeda On, "Dunhuang de Suteren juluo," 40–42; see also: Ikeda On, "Marchands sogdiens"; and: Vaissière and Trombert, "Des Chinois et des Hu," 937–38). Tremblay (Tremblay, "Spread," 96, fn. 99) also pointed out the following articles on this topic: Pulleyblank, "Sogdian Colony"; Liu Mau-tsai, *Chinesischen Nachrichten II*, 164, 218f., 255; Sims-Williams, "Sogdian Merchants," 60; Tremblay, *Pour une histoire*, 19, 20, no 30, 99; Trombert, "La vigne et le vin, deuxième partie," 550–54.

300 For more information on the manuscripts, see p. 202 (2.4.2.1.3).

301 Yamamoto Tatsuro and Ikeda On, *Tun-huang, Contracts*, no. 256: vol. A 183 (138), vol. B 77 (1) <162>, S.3877v.

302 See: ibid., 13.

303 Waley, "Some References to Iranian Temples".

304 Grenet and Zhang Guangda, "Last Refuge".

305 The following publications also mention Zoroastrian temples in Dunhuang 敦煌: S.2472 and P.3571. Zhang Guangda, "Une représentation iconographique," 199; Grenet and Zhang Guangda, "Last Refuge," 185, fn. 36; Vaissière, *Sogdian Traders*, 128, fn. 40; *apud*: (Grenet and Zhang Guangda, "Last Refuge," 175). I suppose, however, that de la Vaissière refers to the document P.2690 instead of P.2680, and instead of P.7043 to the document P.5034? Regarding the mentions:
1) In S.2472 there is no mention of a Zoroastrian temple to my knowledge. What may have led them to this conclusion may be the words "*sapo* 薩婆" (col. 4) and "*tian shen* 天神" (col. 6), which are in this case, however, part of Buddhist vocabulary (The International Dunhuang Project, "Or.8210/S.2472").
2) In P.3571 verso, an astrological text, appear in column 2 the characters "*Fo tang xian miao* 佛堂祆廟" (Buddhist and Zoroastrian temples). It is, however, unclear as to whether the text refers to specific temples, and if that was the case, where these would be (The International Dunhuang Project, "Pelliot chinois 3571 verso").

306 See: Chuguevskii, "Novye materialy," 152–53. Facsimile: The International Dunhuang Project, "Pelliot chinois 2005, recto"; transcribed in: Ikeda On, "Sashū zukei ryakkō," 3.70–71; Zheng

祆神。/右在州東一里，立舍畫神主。惣有廿龕、其院周廻/一百步。

[One temple of the] Zoroastrian Deity:
Further, one *li* (ca. 500 m) east of [Sha 沙]zhou 州, [was] erected a building, [and] the main deity painted.[307] There are altogether 20 niches. The circumference of the court is 100 *bu* 步 (paces).

– The poem no. 12 from the *Dunhuang nian yong* 敦煌廿詠 (the famous "Twenty Eulogies of Dunhuang") mentions a Zoroastrian temple. The composition of these poems may be dated to the middle of the eighth century:[308]

安城[祆][309]詠	Eulogy to the Zoroastrian [temple] of the An 安 Fort
板築安城日	On the day the An 安 Fort was built,
神祠與此興	The deity's temple was raised with it.[311]
一州祈景祚	As the whole province make offerings for good fortune,
萬類仰休徵	All beings[312] hope for auspicious omina.
蘋藻來無乏	Endlessly [they] come [with] aquatic weeds,[313]
精靈若有憑	As if the spirit was dependent [on it].[314]
更看雩祭處	And [I] look to the rain's offering site,
朝夕酒如繩[310]	From dawn till dusk alcohol [runs] like a river.[315]

– A dossier concerning Ma Sanniang 馬三娘 and Long Fendui 龍粉堆, official distillers (*guan jiu hu* 官酒戶), dated 887 CE mentions an offering for the Zoroastrian deity (P.3569, verso). Long Fendui 龍粉堆 requested the magistrate

Binglin, *Dunhuang dili wenshu*, 13; and: Tang Geng'ou and Lu Hongji, *Dunhuang shehui jingji wenxian*, cols. 262–64. See also: Pelliot, "Cha tcheou tou fou t'ou king," 113–15.

307 In opposition to Waley's translation, I do not believe that *shenzhu* 神主 is referring to a "spirit-placing" (Waley, "Some References to Iranian Temples," 125, fn. 1).

308 The text is to be found in: P.2748 (verso): The International Dunhuang Project, "Pelliot chinois 2748, verso A"; P.2983 (recto): The International Dunhuang Project, "Pelliot chinois 2983, recto"; P.2690 (verso): The International Dunhuang Project, "Pelliot chinois 2690, verso"; P.3870 (recto): The International Dunhuang Project, "Pelliot chinois 3870, recto"; and: P.3929 (recto): The International Dunhuang Project, "Pelliot chinois 3929, recto"; author's transcription and translation.

309 Originally *yao* 祆, see p. 270 fn. 170.

310 Read *sheng* 澠. A widely quoted expression, probably first to be found in the *Zuozhuan* 45.1491: 有酒如澠，有肉如陵。

311 Instead of "built", Grenet and Zhangda translated it as "appeared" (Grenet and Zhang Guangda, "Last Refuge," 175).

312 Waley translated: "people of every kind" (Waley, "Some References to Iranian Temples," 123).

313 Commonly used for offerings.

314 Waley translates: "And the magic of the Spirit seems to possess the place" (ibid.). I cannot retrace the reasons that brought him to this option. Another possibility is to understand *ping* 憑 as "great": "so the spirit is great".

315 See fn. above.

of Dunhuang 敦煌 to reimburse the millet for an expenditure of alcohol. Alcohol was used for the *sai xian* 賽祆, some kind of Zoroastrian thanksgiving ceremony, conceivably to be identified as the *Āfrīnagān*[316] ritual:[317]

> 四月十四日夏季賽祆用酒肆甕。……光啟三年……
>
> On [Guangqi 光啟 3/]4/14 (10.5.887 CE) four jars of alcohol were used for the summer *sai xian* 賽祆.

– A list of expenditure for the years 899–901 CE (P.4640, verso; *zhi poyong shu* 帋破用數) counts, among others, the amount of paper destined to be painted on, and used in the *sai xian* 賽祆.[318] The expenditures are listed for 899/7/25, 899/10/5, 900/1/13, 900/4/8, 900/4/16, 900/7/9, 900/10/9, 901/1/11, 901/2/21, 901/3/3, and 901/4/13. Each time, 30 sheets of paper (*zhi* 帋) were allocated, with the exception of the 901/3/3, when one coarse (*cu* 麁) sheet of papers was allocated.[319] Exemplary for the allocations of 30 sheets, see the entry for 899/7/25 (3.9.899 CE; col. 90):[320]

> [己未年……七月……廿五日……]又同支賽祆畫帋叁拾張。
>
> [*Jiwei* 己未 … 7th month … 25th day … (3.9.899 CE)] Further, painting paper for the *sai xian* 賽祆, 30 sheets.

And the entry of the 901/3/3 (25.3.901 CE; cols. 249–50) for course sheets:

> [辛酉年……三月……三日]東水池及諸處賽[321]祆用麁帋壹帖。
>
> [*Xinyou* 辛酉 … 3rd month … 3rd day (25.3.901 CE)] one sheet of coarse paper to be used for the *sai xian* 賽祆 at the Eastern Pond and everywhere else.[322]

316 See p. 220 fn. 322. Author's transcription, punctuation, and translation.

317 The International Dunhuang Project, "Pelliot chinois 3569, verso"; see also: Grenet and Zhang Guangda, "Last Refuge," 182.

318 For two articles on the paintings that may have been on them, see: ibid., 181–82; Eliasberg, "À propos".

319 Apart from these, fine paper (*xi zhi* 細帋) and cloth (*bu* 布) is also mentioned. See also p. 220 fn. 322.

320 The International Dunhuang Project, "Pelliot chinois 4640, verso". A transcription is to be found in: Ikeda On, *Chūgoku*, 605–12; and: Lu Xiangqian, "Guanyu guiyijun," 394–414; author's transcription, punctuation, and translation.

321 On 900/4/16, the eight occurrences all have a variant character of *sai* 賽, looking like *han* 寒, which may point to another scribe changing in between the record of 900/4/16 and 900/7/9.

322 Grenet and Zhang Guangda proposed that this paper may have been used for Zoroastrian pictures. While I concur to this possibility, their translation and/or understanding of this passage is slightly erroneous (Grenet and Zhang Guangda, "Last Refuge," 181): "The text specifies when and for what purpose the materials had been allocated. In particular, it mentions the outlay of sheets of paper for painting 'the *xian* (Mazdaean) deities for the occasion of the *saixian*.' The verb *sai*, which is an element of the locution *saxian*, is usually glossed *bao* 'to requite a godsend.' This, in its turn, would perfectly correspond to the Zoroastrian ceremony

- A letter from a "princess" named Jun Zhezhe 君者者[323] (S.2241, recto),[324] dated around 930 CE[325] mentions a Zoroastrian temple. She asks her addressee, Lady Beizhai 北宅 (lit. "Northern Residence"), among other things, to light a light at the Zoroastrian temple(s) (*xian si ran deng* 祆寺燃灯), which either refers to a temple in or near Dunhuang 敦煌 or on the way.[326]
- A list of expenditures of the administration of the gui yi jun 歸義軍 (a military corps),[327] probably from 964 CE,[328] which is now split in three pieces (the quotes are on the first and third piece).[329]

  1st piece: D0038 (F0001):[330]

of the *Āfrīnagān*, 'thanksgiving.'"

First, two different descriptions (as mentioned above) are used in this list. 1) *sai xian hua zhi* 賽祆畫帋 (Painting paper for the *sai xian*), and 2) *sai xian yong cu zhi* (賽)祆用麁帋 (coarse paper to be used for the *sai xian*). There is no mention in this of painting the deities on the paper (the catalogue entry mentions "papier destinées à la fabrication d'images" and does also not provide grounds for such an interpretation; Soymié et al., "Catalogue Pelliot chinois" Cat. no. 4640). I do thus not believe that this list of expenditures is indirectly attesting a painting of deities on the paper (and therefore agree with Eliasberg: Eliasberg, "À propos," 64). On the basis of the other arguments provided in their paper (especially the existence of a string on top of the paper image), I do, however, believe that this theory may well be correct.

As a side note, in my reading (corresponding to the reading of: Lu Xiangqian, "Guanyu guiyijun," 407, cols. 249–50), on the 901/3/3, "one" sheet of paper and not "one hundred" (Grenet and Zhang Guangda, "Last Refuge," 182) were allocated.

323 Waley proposed it could presumably be Uighur, Kün-čäčäk, i.e. Sun-flower (Waley, "Some References to Iranian Temples," 124). He transcribed her name 君闍闍, that is Jun Sheshe or Jun Dudu, for reasons that elude me, as the facsimile is unmistakably clear.

324 The International Dunhuang Project, "Or.8210/S.2241". See also for a summary: Giles, *Six Centuries*, 6.

325 See: Waley, "Some References to Iranian Temples," 124.

326 Waley translates the reason for it as "in order to make blessings for me while I am on my journey" (ibid.), relying on the explanations of Giles 1944. After scrupulous reading of the facsimile, I am still inconclusive as to how interpret the context and the meaning of the letter.

327 Some sort of military corps in charge of the administration. The name of this corps is to be found as a red seal on the document in seal script: *Gui yi jun/jie du shi/xin zhu yin* 歸義軍/節度使/新鑄印.

328 For the date, see: Shi Pingting, "'Jiu zhang' yanjiu," 142–49.

329 The information provided by Grenet and Zhang Guangda (Grenet and Zhang Guangda, "Last Refuge," 182) is not quite complete: The document was broken into three pieces (in reading order): D0038 (F0001), D0784 (F0369), and P.2629. See: Shi Pingting, "'Jiu zhang' yanjiu". In their article are included, among other related questions, a transcription of the first and second part.

The three documents were broken apart, once at the beginning of the 20th century. One (P.2629) fragment was taken away by Pelliot to Paris. Then, in the 40', the middle part, while under the supervision of Dong Xiwen 董希文, then working at the Dunhuang Art Academy (Dunhuang yishu yanjiusuo), was "lost" to Japan. It landed in the hands of the famous Japanese calligrapher Aoyama San'U 青山杉雨. In 1997, his son Aoyama Keiji 青山慶示 donated eight fragments, all from the Dunhuang Mogao caves, including this one, to the Dunhuang Academy (Tai Huili, "Gui").

330 The International Dunhuang Project, "F0001 Recto"; see also: Grenet and Zhang Guangda, "Last Refuge," 182; author's transcription, punctuation, and translation.

（四月……）廿日城東祆神酒壹瓮。

(In the 4th month …) on the 20th day, one jug of alcohol for the Zoroastrian deity [temple] east of the city.

3rd piece: P.2629 (recto):[331]

（七月……）十日城東祆賽神酒两甕。

(In the 7th month …) on the 10th day, two jugs of wine [were used] for the *sai shen* 賽神 [ritual] at the Zoroastrian [temple] east of the city."

In this quote, the "*sai shen* 賽神 [ritual] at the Zoroastrian [temple]" most certainly refers to the *sai xian* 賽祆 ritual mentioned above.

– A register of expenditures of the seat of the central administration of the gui yi jun 歸義軍, S.2474 and S.1366, dated 979/11/2 (24.11.979 CE), also mentions a Zoroastrian temple.[332] In the transcription included in the publication of Tang Geng'ou, it is suggested that S.1366 is the continuation of S.2474, although a piece is missing in between.[333] The author(s) provide two reasons leading to this conclusion: first, the similarity of characters, content, and form, and second, an official in charge of camels (*tuo guan* 駞官), going by the name of Deng Futong 鄧富通, is mentioned once in column 54 of S.1366 and twice at the beginning of the list of S.2474 under the *yi mao* year 11/2 (24.11.979 CE).[334]
S.2474 (verso), cols. 3–4:[335]

城東/祆燈油二升。

Two *sheng* 升 lamp oil [for] the Zoroastrian [temple] east of the city.

S.1366 (recto), cols. 9–12:[336]

331 The International Dunhuang Project, "Pelliot chinois 2629, recto"; see also: Grenet and Zhang Guangda, "Last Refuge," 182; author's transcription, punctuation, and translation.

332 The International Dunhuang Project, "Or.8210/S.2474"; and: The International Dunhuang Project, "Or.8210/S.1366 Recto".

333 Tang Geng'ou and Lu Hongji, *Dunhuang shehui jingji wenxian*, 286.

334 The catalogue (ibid., 281) states that the date is unclear and instead dates it between 980 and 982 CE, although it does state in the commentary (ibid., 286) that S.1366 is the continuation of S.2474 (based on the reasons named above), which mentions the above-mentioned date (979 CE). The commentary of the catalogue does also not mention the specific day and only provide the 11th month of the *jimao* 己卯 year. This is probably because the author(s) did not see that the date is written twice on S.1366, once with the number of the day, and once without.

335 The International Dunhuang Project, "Or.8210/S.2474"; author's transcription, punctuation, and translation.

336 The International Dunhuang Project, "Or.8210/S.1366 Recto"; author's transcription, punctuation, and translation.

十/七日，準舊，城東祆賽神用神（食）[337]五十七分，燈油一升，麨[338]麵/二斗，灌腸九升。

On the 17th day, according to the usual procedure, 57 *fen* 分 of food [for the deity] (ca. 600 g),[339] one *sheng* 升 lamp oil (ca. 600 ml), two *dou* 斗 wheat flour (ca. 12 l), and nine *sheng* 升 of sausages (ca. 5,4 l) were used [for] the *sai shen* 賽神 of the Zoroastrian [temple] east of the city.[340]

– An announcement for the Nuo 儺 festival (P.2569) mentions a Zoroastrian fire-deity.[341] Whereas Naba Toshisada and Lin Wushu believe this manuscript to be a Zoroastrian magic spell, I agree with Chen Sanping that the document is best identified as an announcement of a New Year festival that expels evil spirits and serves to protect the city.[342] However uncertain the exact meaning of the document may be, it is clear that one of the participating deities was the "Zoroastrian fire-[deity] of the An 安 Fort" (*an cheng huo xian* 安城火祆), evincing the inclusion of this deity in a Chinese festival and further underpinning the existence of a Zoroastrian community at this location.

2.4.3.1.2 Liangzhou 涼州 and Guzang 姑藏

On his way into China, a traveller would then enter the Hexi 河西 corridor, which approximately corresponds to present-day Gansu Province. The earliest mention of Sogdian activity here may be found in the *Sanguozhi*, which includes the commentary of Pei Songzhi 裴松之, completed in 429 CE, to the volume concerning the history of the Shu-Han. He records that in the spring of 227 CE people from Liangzhou 涼州 came to support Zhuge Liang 諸葛亮 to move north, towards the old capital. He went on to position his armies at Hanzhong 漢中, near the northern border of Shu-Han:[343]

涼州諸國王各遣月支、康居胡侯支富、康植等二十餘人詣受節度，大軍北出，便欲率將兵馬，奮戈先驅。……

The chiefs of all countries in Liangzhou 涼州 sent the *hu* 胡 noblemen Zhi Fu 支富, of the Yuezhi 月氏, and Kang Zhi 康植, of the Kangju 康居, over 20 men, to receive the military leader [of the Shu-Han]. The large army went north, [the noblemen] vying to lead [their] infantry and cavalry, wielding [their] weapons in the front-line. (…)

337 This addition is made based on the parallel to the next sentence: 南城上偏次賽祆神用神食十九分……

338 A variant of *mai* 麥.

339 Probably referring to grain.

340 For the weights and capacities, see: Wilkinson, *Chinese History*, 554–64.

341 For more information on this festival, see: Li Zhengyu, "Dunhuang"; and: Ren Wei, "Dunhuang".

342 Naba Toshisada 那波利貞, "Senbu," 43–44; Lin Wushu, *Bosi baihuojiao*, 160–61; Chen Sanping, "From Azerbaijan," 184.

343 *Sanguozhi* 33.895–96; author's translation.

It is not entirely clear what the expression *Liangzhou zhu guowang* 涼州諸國王 "the chiefs of all countries of Liangzhou 涼州" refers to. *Wang* 王, literally "king(s)", refers in this context to "chiefs" of various foreign groups in Liangzhou 涼州.[344]

This passage hints at the existence of rather independent forces of the Yuezhi 月氏 and Sogdians being ready to mobilise in Liangzhou 涼州 at a time when the Eastern Han had lost political control. Assuming that this episode is rather distorted in favour of the authors, it may be surmised that Zhuge Liang 諸葛亮 requested the support of powerful military leaders of the north-western realms in a coordinated attack against the Wei. Some of the chiefs probably saw this as an opportunity to attack the Wei and distinguish themselves through military exploits, hoping for advantages with or within the dynasty or the political changes to come.

Written about a hundred years later, the Sogdian Ancient Letter V was sent from Guzang 姑臧.[345] It evinces that Sogdians moved between Liangzhou 涼州 and Dunhuang 敦煌 and engaged in mercantile activity in the early fourth century. For the sixth century, as will be shown below[346] by the combination of information from the *Jiu Tangshu*, three passages of the *Xin Tangshu*, the *Yuanhe Xingzuan*, a stele fragment, the epitaphs of An Yuanshou 安元壽 and his wife Lady Di 翟, and the stele of An Zhongjing 安忠敬, a Sogdian called An Nantuo 安難陀[347] lived in Guzang 姑臧, Liangzhou 涼州, and served as *sabao* 薩寶 during the Northern Wei. Further, the epitaph of Kang Moliangxi Ada 康莫量息阿達 (d. early Tang) records that his grandfather Kang Bada 康拔達 was *sabao* 薩保 of Liangzhou 涼州, which implies the existence of a Sogdian community in the first half of the century.[348] Besides the passage concerning the ransom payment for Sogdian merchants in Liangzhou 涼州 by the king of Sute 粟特 quoted above,[349] the *Weishu* also recounts that Yuan Xian 元暹 was appointed as regional inspector of Liangzhou 涼州 in 531 CE. He extorted, among others, the *hu* 胡 merchants of their wealth, partly by ending their lives.[350] We also know that Wirkak (Master Shi 史) became first appointed as chief judge of the *sabao* 薩保 office and then as *sabao* 薩保 of Liangzhou 涼州/Kachan (Guzang 姑臧) in 539 CE.[351] As Thierry pointed out,[352] the *Suishu* reports that in the sixth century, "silver and gold currency of the Western Regions"[353] (referring to the Sasanian coins

344 "A difficult word to translate, it carries with it the implication of social superiority, but is used to identify a descent group geographically." Johnson, *The Medieval Chinese Oligarchy*, 92.

345 For more information on the letters, see p. 214 (2.4.3.1.1).

346 See p. 261 (3.2.3.1.7).

347 Also known as An Xue Wuzheng 安薛晤徵.

348 See p. 253 (3.2.2.16).

349 See p. 25 (1.7.5).

350 仲景弟暹，字叔照。……普泰元年，除涼州刺史，貪暴無極。欲規府人及商胡富人財物，詐一臺符，誑諸豪等云欲加賞，一時屠戮，所有資財生口，悉沒自入。 *Weishu* 19a.444–45.

351 See p. 129 (2.3.2.1).

352 Thierry, "Monnaies Sassanides," 133; more generally: ibid., 132–35.

353 及武帝保定元年七月，及更鑄布泉之錢，以一當五，與五銖並行。時梁、益之境，又雜用古錢交易。河西諸郡，或用西域金銀之錢，而官不禁。 *Suishu* 24.691.

in circulation) were – besides cloth, silk, and grain – approved as methods of payment in the Hexi 河西 corridor. An Jia's 安伽 (518–79 CE) epitaph gives in the choronym the Changsong 昌松 District of Guzang 姑藏 for himself and his mother, his mother however probably being an ethnic Han.[354] It nevertheless indicates the presence of Sogdian families in the region.

Sogdian merchants continued to travel back and forth between Liangzhou 涼州 and Sogdiana until the seventh century as underpinned by the mention of a moor located north-west of Shazhou 沙州 at which "Authorised *hu* 胡 of Liangzhou 涼州" used to halt for water on their way to the Jade Gate Pass in several manuscripts presented above.[355] Further, when Xuanzang 玄奘 came through Liangzhou 涼州 at that time, he described it as follows:[356]

> 涼州爲河西都會，襟帶西蕃葱/右諸國，商侶往來無有停絶。
>
> Liangzhou 涼州 is the capital of Hexi 河西. [It] watches over all states in the Western Regions east of the Western Cong [ling] 葱[嶺] (Pamirs). Travelling merchants come and go without interruption.

The *Chaoye qianzai*, the content of which precedes the mid of the 7th, also includes an anecdote mentioning a Zoroastrian temple in Liangzhou 涼州 (re-used in the *Guangchuan huaba*).[357] In 1997, the epitaph of Di Sheji 翟舍集 (637–700 CE) and his wife, named An 安 (651–726 CE) was excavated in Wuwei 武威 City.[358] The epitaph states that he came from Guzang 姑藏 and that his wife, a certain An 安, was from an illustrious family, being the granddaughter of the duke of Liangzhou 涼州. Rong Xinjiang proposed that her father was An Yuanshou 安元壽 (607–83 CE), since the latter was the son of the An Xinggui 安興貴.[359] An Yuanshou 安元壽 came from Guzang 姑藏 of Liangzhou 涼州, was duke of Liangzhou 涼州 and married Di Liuniang 翟六娘 (610–98 CE).[360] According to their living dates, she would have been born when her father An Yuanshou 安元壽 was aged 44, and her mother Di Liuniang 翟六娘 41. Whether this assumption is correct or not, the epitaphs show that powerful families of the names An 安 and Di 翟 intermarried over generations.

Finally, a funerary bed dated to the Sui or Tang was found in 1992 in Tianshui 天水, Gansu Province, and included Sogdian iconography.[361] Overall, we can affirm that Liangzhou 涼州 and especially Guzang 姑藏 represented an important hub for Sogdians.[362]

354 See p. 132 (2.3.2.3).
355 See p. 214 (2.4.3.1.1).
356 T50.222c28–29; author's translation.
357 See p. 275 (3.2.4.10).
358 Epitaph: Wang Qiying, *Wuwei*, 46–47. Excavation report: Li Daxiang, "Wuwei".
359 Rong Xinjiang, "Beichao Sui Tang Suteren bu kao (Zhonggu Zhongguo)," 25.
360 On him and his family, see p. 261 (3.2.3.1.7).
361 Tianshui shi bowuguan, "Tianshui shiguan chuang mu".
362 Rong Xinjiang listed other individuals with Sogdian surnames, such as Shi Sili 史思禮 or Shi Yanzhao 石延煦, that came from or held office in Wuwei 武威 in the eighth to tenth century

2.4.3.2 North

2.4.3.2.1 The Six *hu* 胡 Prefectures

An Pusa 安菩薩 (601–64 CE) stemmed from Sogdiana and became great chief of the Six *hu* 胡 Prefectures (*liu hu zhou da shouling* 六胡州大首領), as can be read on is epitaph. [363] However, according to official records, after the Western Turks surrendered to the Tang, the Six *hu* 胡 Prefectures (part of the *jimi zhou* 羈縻州) were only set up in 679 CE in the north.[364] Pulleyblank proposed in his study of this region that there must have been Sogdians among the Turks that migrated or were moved there after their defeat and that the famous rebel An Lushan 安祿山, born of a Sogdian father and a mother from the Turk Ashide 阿史德 clan, probably came from here.[365] Furthermore, people with Sogdian names are mentioned in the prefectures up to the eighth century.[366]

2.4.3.2.2 Yuanzhou 原州

As discussed in the case study above, the two Shi 史 families lived in Yuanzhou 原州 from the Northern Wei to the Tang.[367]

2.4.3.2.3 Jiezhou 介州[368]

The epitaph of Cao Yi 曹怡 (581–655 CE)[369] states that his father Zun 遵 was commandant of cavalry of the *sabao* 薩寶 office of Jiezhou 介州, which points to the existence of a Sogdian community. This may be underpinned by the epitaph of Lord Yu Hong 虞弘 (534–92 CE), which records that he was put in charge of the local militia of Jiezhou 介州 in 580 CE.[370]

2.4.3.3 East

2.4.3.3.1 Dingzhou 定州

The stele of Hui Yu 惠鬱, Xuan Ning 玄凝 and others (585 CE) informs us that He Yongkang 何永康 was record keeper under the *safu* 薩甫 at the time of the inscription, most probably in Dingzhou 定州.[371] Further, there is the epitaph of Kang

to show the importance of what he identifies as Sogdian descendants in this region.

363 See p. 164 (2.3.2.16).

364 For more information, see the glossary.

365 Pulleyblank, "Sogdian Colony".

366 See: Rong Xinjiang, "Beichao Sui Tang Suteren bu kao (Zhonggu Zhongguo)," 93–95.

367 See their graves in chapter 2.2 (p. 123) and their epitaphs in chapter 2.3 (p. 140)

368 Jiang Boqin analysed the iconography of an alleged Zoroastrian temple in Jiexiu 介休, Shanxi Province, dated to the Song, and related literary sources. As doubts may be raised as to the validity of the iconographic identifications and the conclusions he reaches, the temple will not be discussed (Jiang Boqin, "Lun").

369 See p. 161 (2.3.2.14).

370 See p. 133 (2.3.2.4).

371 See p. 259 (3.2.3.1.5).

Po 康婆 (647 CE), which states that the latter stemmed from the king of the state of Kang 康 (although it includes the choronym Boling 博陵 in Shandong), and that his father once served as *sabao* 薩寶 of Dingzhou 定州, probably during the Sui.[372] We can thus infer that there existed a Sogdian community in Dingzhou 定州 in the sixth century.

2.4.3.3.2 Bingzhou 並州, Taiyuan 太原

Lord Yu Hong 虞弘, conceivably coming from the Rouran 柔然, was appointed as acting *sabao* 薩保 near or in Taiyuan 太原 during the Sui.[373]

Besides that, a much-discussed passage, the *liezhuan* 列傳 of Li Gao 李暠 (d. 780 CE) in the *Jiu Tangshu*, contains a famous passage concerning the feeding of human corpses to vultures and dogs in China. Due it being often – mistakenly – quoted in correlation to Zoroastrianism, it shall quickly be addressed:[374]

> 太原舊俗，有僧徒以習禪為業，及死不殮，但以屍送近郊以飼鳥獸。如是積年，土人號其地為「黃坑」，側有餓狗千數，食死人肉，因侵害幼弱，遠近患之，前後官吏不能禁止。暠到官，申明禮憲，期不再犯，發兵捕殺羣狗，其風遂革。

> [There was] an old custom at Taiyuan 太原. Monks and disciples practised *dhyana* (Buddhist meditation) [and] when [they] died, [they] were not clothed [for the coffin] but taken to the outskirts to feed birds and beasts. It was like this for many years. The locals called this place the "yellow pit". At its side, there were a thousand hungry dogs, eating the flesh of the deceased. As [they] assailed the children [and] the weak, [people] near and far suffered from it. The officials then and now were not able to put an end [to it]. When Gao 暠 became official, [he] enlightened [them] on rites and law [and] requested that there would be no more attacks. [He] sent out soldiers to catch and kill the pack of dogs. These practices [were] swiftly changed.

372 See p. 253 (3.2.2.16).

373 See p. 133 (2.3.2.4). Rong Xinjiang also proposed that Di Suo 翟娑, grand great *sabao* 薩寶, father of Di Tusuo 翟突娑 (546–615 CE), was *sabao* 薩保 of Bingzhou 並州 (Rong Xinjiang, "Beichao Sui Tang Suteren bu kao (Zhonggu Zhongguo)," 36). He further chose to call him Di Suomohe 翟娑摩訶. I believe, however, that the *mohe* 摩訶 relates to the next characters, i.e. *sabao* 薩保. Although it is said that Di Tusuo 翟突娑 came from Bingzhou 並州, there is no indication to where his father held office.

374 *Jiu Tangshu* 112.3335; author's translation. Zhang Guangda pointed out that the monk Zhishun 智順 desired to be treated in the same way after his death (Zhang Guangda, "Trois exemples," 204), which is not entirely accurate. The *Gaoseng zhuan* 高僧傳 states that Zhishun 智順, coming from Shandong (Langya Linyi 琅玡临沂, present-day Linyi 临沂, Shandong Province), became monk at the age of 15 in the Yanxian 延賢 monastery on the Zhongshan 鍾山 (in present-day Nanjing 南京 City). Shortly before his death, he uttered his last wish: T50:381b20–21: 遺命露骸空地以施蟲鳥。門人不忍行之。乃窆于寺側。 "[He] ordered that [his] corpse shall be exposed on the open ground to be offered to insects and birds. The disciples did not have the heart to do so. [They] thus buried [him] besides the temple."

Such practices are known for Tibetan Buddhism and for Zoroastrian funerary rituals, but not for China at this time. Who were then these people and what happened here? Maybe it was a form Tibetan Buddhism imported and practised there. As Iranians, and Sogdians were active in China, it may also be possible that such rituals, already engrained in the cultural mainstream of their Zoroastrian background, were then integrated in Buddhist practices on a local level. But then again, there is no mention of the collection of the bones – the ritual accurately recorded in the passage about the state of Kang 康 in the *Tongdian*[375] – which is, however, not strictly necessary for a Zoroastrian ritual.[376] The omission still speaks against this hypothesis.[377] Another – preferable – option is that some information was amalgamated or exaggerated to dramatize Li Gao's 李暠 biography. Lastly, the passage may evidence some form of Buddhist funerary ritual that was not handed down due to, for example, governmental sanctions.

2.4.3.4 South

2.4.3.4.1 Yangzhou 揚州

Hu 胡 merchants, among them probably Sogdians, were established in Yangzhou 揚州 during the Tang.[378] At least one fire temple is mentioned[379] as well as some isolated individuals with Sogdian names.

2.4.3.4.2 Zhenjiang 鎮江 *and Suzhou* 蘇州

The *Mo Zhuang man lu* contains a passage collecting information on Zoroastrian temples that mentions a Zoroastrian temple in Zhenjiang 鎮江:[380]

> 鎮江府。朱方門之東城上乃有祆神祠，不知何人立也。
>
> The Zhenjiang 鎮江 Prefecture. On the east wall of the Zhufang 朱方 Gate there is a Zoroastrian temple. It is not known by whom [it] was built.

375 See p. 47 (1.12.1).

376 Grenet, *Pratiques funéraires*, 36.

377 On this topic Cai Hongsheng also expressed doubts about the relationship to Sogdian customs (Cai Hongsheng, "Tangdai jiuxinghu lisu congkao"). Lin Wushu states that "obviously this situation is the same as that of the Sogdians referred to above" (i.e. the passage on the state of Kang 康 in the *Tongdian*; (Lin Wushu, "Discussion Heaven-God," 9). Rong Xinjiang proposed that this indirectly reflects the influence of Zoroastrian beliefs and customs of the western foreign community of Taiyuan 太原 (Rong Xinjiang, *Zhonggu Zhongguo yu wailai wenming*, 97). De la Vaissière pointed out that the use of dogs is specifically Zoroastrian, particularly attested for Sogdiana, and that the presence of such a custom in the interior of China cannot be explained by chance. However, he did not comment on why Buddhist monks were involved in such Zoroastrian customs (Vaissière, *Sogdian Traders*, 142, fn. 96).

378 Schafer, *Golden Peaches*, 17–19, 18, fn. 101; *apud*: Nakamura Kushirō, "Kanton no shōko," 10.244–48 [92–96].

379 Leslie, "Persian Temples," 289–90, fn. 38.

380 *Mo Zhuang man lu* 4.111 (2b); author's translation.

Additional information on this temple is found in a geographic treatise of the Yuan 元, the *Zhishun Zhenjiang zhi*:[381]

火祆廟

舊在朱方門裏山岡之上。張舜民集：『汴京城北有祆廟。祆神出西域，自秦入中國，俗以火神祠之，在唐已血食宣武矣。』前志引宋祥符圖經：『潤帥周寶婿楊茂實為蘇州刺史，立廟於城南隅。蓋因潤有此廟，而立之也。』

The Zoroastrian temple

Long ago, on the inner side of the Zhufang 朱方 Gate, there was a Zoroastrian temple on a mound.
[Commentary:] The *Records of Zhang Shunmin* 張舜民 [state]: "North of the city of Bianjing 汴京 (Kaifeng 開封) is a Zoroastrian temple. The Zoroastrian Deity comes from the Western Regions, [it] came from the Qin 秦 (Romans) into China. Traditionally, [they] sacrifice to it by [offering to] the fire deity. During the Tang, [they] already performed sacrifices in the Xuanwu 宣武 [Military District] (located in Bianjing 汴京)." The above treatise quotes the *Xiangfu tujing* 祥符圖經 from the Song: "The son-in-law of the Commander of Run[zhou] 潤[州] Zhou Bao 周寶, (814–88 CE), Yang Maoshi 楊茂實 was Prefect of Suzhou 蘇州 [and] erected a temple near the southern city wall. Because Run 潤 had this temple [built] (i.e. the temple of Bianjing 汴京), [Zhou Bao 周寶] erected it."[382] [End of commentary.]

宋嘉定中，遷於山下。郡守趙善湘以此廟高在山岡，於郡庠不便，遂遷於山下，廟門面東，郡守祝板，故有『祆神不致祆』之句。端平閒毀。端平乙未，防江寨中軍作變，有禱於神，其神許之。事定，郡守吳淵毀其廟。

During the Jiading 嘉定 era (1208–24 CE) of the Song, [the Zoroastrian temple of Zhenjiang 鎮江] was moved to the mound's foot.
[Commentary:] Because this temple was high up on the mound and impractical for the commandery's students, the Commandery Governor Zhao Shanxiang 趙善湘 [had it] then moved to the foot of the mountain. The temple's gate faces east. [In it is] a board with the Commandery Governors' prayers. [This is] why there is the phrase 'the Zoroastrian Deity does not reach heaven'. [It] was destroyed during the Duanping 端平 era (1234–36 CE). In Duanping 端平 *yiwei* (1235 CE), the Middle Army defending the stronghold of the Yangtze became mutinous. They prayed to the deity and its (i.e. the temple's) deity permitted it. After the matter was resolved, the Commandery Governor Wu Yuan 吳淵 destroyed its temple. [End of commentary.]

381 *Zhishun Zhenjiang zhi* 8.2728a. Author's punctuation, formatting, and translation.
382 See also the biography of Zhou Bao 周寶, in which Yang Maoshi 楊茂實 is mentioned: *Xin Tangshu* 168.5416.

Besides the erroneous origins of Zoroastrianism also found in other accounts and the important mention of specific dates concerning the existence of Zoroastrian temples in Zhenjiang 鎮江 and Suzhou 蘇州 in the ninth century, two aspects of this account are especially noteworthy. Firstly, we learn that students were offering at the Zoroastrian temple, as they would for example in Buddhist temples or a Confucius Hall, which speaks of the degree of integration into Chinese life and the cosmological efficacy such a sacrifice was attributed. Secondly, the phrase *xian shen bu zhi xian* 祆神不致祆 'the Zoroastrian Deity does not reach heaven' is maybe the best support yet for the theory that *xian* 祆 (Zoroastrian) and *tian* 天 (heaven) were homophonic and pronounced *tian*, and that until the Yuan 元. The passage literally says "the *xian* 祆 (Zoroastrian) deity does not reach *xian* 祆 (Zoroastrian)", which does not make much sense. If one accepts the premise that *xian* 祆 and *tian* 天 were both pronounced *tian*, the passage reads "the *tian* 祆 deity does not reach *tian* 祆", which can be understood as "the *tian* 祆 deity does not reach heaven". Thus, the pun becomes clear: As the temple was moved from the top of the mound to its foot, people derided the Zoroastrian temple to not reach high, contrarily to what its name – sounding like "heaven temple" – indicated.

2.4.3.5 Centre

2.4.3.5.1 Tongzhou 同州

On a stele of the Former Qin (367 CE) of a temple in Tongzhou 同州, the *Dengtai wei ci bei* 鄧太尉祠碑 (cols. 4–5), it is mentioned that there were Sogdians (*Sute* 粟特) living in the region during this time.[383] Additionally, An Jia 安伽, who came from Changsong 昌松 of Guzang 姑臧, was *sabao* 薩保 of Tongzhou 同州 during the Northern Zhou in the sixth century.[384]

2.4.3.5.2 Kaifeng 開封*/Bianjing* 汴京

There are three references to a Zoroastrian temple in Kaifeng 開封. The first is to be found in the *Guangchuan huaba*:[385]

> 書常彥輔[祆][386]神像
>
> 元祐八年七月，常君彥輔就開寶寺之文殊院，遇寒熱疾，大懼不良，及夜禱於[祆][387]神祠。明日良愈，乃祀於庭。又圖像歸事之，屬某書，且使教知神之休也。

383 Rong Xinjiang, "Beichao Sui Tang Suteren bu kao (Zhonggu Zhongguo)," 32. For a facsimile, see: Beijing tushuguan jinshizu, *Beijing tushuguan, San guo etc. (2)*; Rong Xinjiang and Zhang Zhiqing, *Cong Sama'ergan*, 105.

384 See p. 132 (2.3.2.3).

385 *Guangchuan huaba* 4.5b–6a; author's punctuation and translation. See also: Waley, "Some References to Iranian Temples," 127.

386 Originally *yao* 祅, see p. 270, fn. 170.

387 Id.

Chang Yanfu's 常彥輔 Inscription on a Zoroastrian Painting

In Yuanyou 元祐 8/7 (1093 CE), [when] Master Chang Yanfu 常彥輔 [worked] in the Mañjuśrī Court of the Kaibao 開寶 Temple (of Kaifeng 開封), [he] got a fever.[388] Highly afraid of not getting better, [he] prayed at the Zoroastrian Deity's temple in the night. The next day, [he] recovered and sacrificed in the court. [He] drew a portrait [of the deity], returned home and served it. [He] asked for someone to write the inscription to make known the healing [powers] of the deity.

The second mention is to be found in the *Mo Zhuang man lu*:[389]

東京城北有[祆][390]呼煙切廟。[祆][391]神本出西域。蓋胡神也，與大秦穆護同入中國。俗以火神祠之，京師人畏其威靈，甚重之。其廟祝姓史，名世爽，自云：『家世為祝累代矣，藏先世補受之牒凡三：有曰懷恩者，其牒唐咸通三年宣武節度使令狐給。令狐者，丞相綯也。有曰溫者，周顯德三年端明殿學士權知開封府王所給，王乃樸也。有曰貴者，其牒亦周顯德五年樞密使權知開封府王所給，亦樸也。』自唐以來，[祆][392]神已祀於汴矣，而其祝乃能世繼其職，逾二百年，斯亦異矣。

In the eastern capital (Bianjing 汴京) is a Zoroastrian [pronounced] *h(u)* + *(y)an* [= *xian*] temple. The Zoroastrian Deity originally came from the Western Regions. It is a deity of the *hu* 胡 [which] came to China together with the Nestorian Priests. It is [their] custom to offer sacrifice to it by the fire deity. The capital's people fear its spiritual powers [and] respect it deeply. Its temple's precentor has the family name Shi 史 and given name Shishuang 世爽. He said: "For generations, the family line provided the precentors. Of the early ancestors there were three that held the official *insignia*. There was Huai'en 懷恩. In Xiantong 咸通 3 of the Tang (862 CE) he was awarded the official document by the military commissioner Linghu 令狐 of Xuanwu 宣武; Linghu 令狐, [i.e. the] vice director of the Departments of State Affairs [named] Tao 綯. There was Wen 溫. In Xiande 顯得 3 of the [Wu] Zhou (956 CE), [the official *insignia*] was awarded by the Chancellor of the Hanlin 翰林 Academy Probationary (Prefect?) of the Kaifeng 開封 District Wang 王; Wang 王 [was named] Pu 樸. There is Gui 貴. In Xiande 顯得 5 of the [Wu] Zhou (958 CE), he was also awarded the official *insignia* by the Palace Secretary[393] Probationary (Prefect?) of the Kaifeng 開封 District Wang 王; also [Wang 王] Pu 樸." Since the Tang, the Zoroastrian Deity received sacrifices in Bian 汴

388 Literally "hot-cold sickness".

389 *Mo Zhuang man lu* 4.110–11 (1b–2b); author's punctuation and translation.

390 Originally *yao* 祆, see p. 270, fn. 170.

391 Id.

392 Id.

393 Yu Lunian, *Zhongguo guanzhi da cidian 1*, 215–16; Hucker, *Dictionary*, 5450.

and this precentor was still able to pass down the office over generations for over 200 years. This is unusual.[394]

The third reference to a temple is to be found in the above-mentioned *Zhishun Zhenjiang zhi*. According to the account, Zhou Bao 周寶 (814–88 CE), the Prefect of Suzhou 蘇州, erected a temple near the southern city wall.[395]

2.4.4 The capitals

Although borders may be considered as contact zones with foreigners in historical accounts, it is their presence in the capital that will normally be the most extensively documented.

2.4.4.1 Luoyang 洛陽 (also known as Dongdu 東都, lit. eastern capital)

Capital of the	Time
Han	23–190 BCE
Cao Wei	220–65 CE
Western Jin	265–313 CE
destroyed by the Xiongnu 匈奴 in 311 CE	
Northern Wei	493–534 CE
Sui (as Dongdu 東都)	581–618 CE
auxiliary capital of the Tang	657–90 CE
Wu Zhou	690–705 CE
auxiliary capital of the Tang	705–36, and 904–7 CE

The Sogdian Ancient Letter II, dated ca. 311–13 CE, mentions the destruction and famine of Luoyang 洛陽 by the Xiongnu 匈奴 and provides the earliest evidence of a Sogdian and Indian community.[396] Two hundred years later, Emperor Xiaowen 孝文 of the Northern Wei defeated the Northern Liang in 439 CE. From their centre of power in the Hexi 河西 Corridor – in which many Sogdians lived – he deported about 30,000 families to his capital Pingcheng 平城.[397] When he eventually moved the

394 “This” probably refers to the length of the inheritance.

395 See p. 228 (2.4.3.4.2).

396 The International Dunhuang Project, “Or.8212/98, verso and recto”; translation: Silk Road Seattle Website, “Sogdian Ancient Letters”.

397 Mass deportation and movement of people was rather frequent in this unstable time. See: Müller, “Gräber der Nördlichen Wei-Zeit,” 28–31; see also: Luo Feng, *Guyuan nanjiao Sui Tang mudi*, 197.

capital to Luoyang 洛陽 in 493–95 CE with ca. 500,000 people,[398] the city became a vibrant centre of Central Asian mercantile activity, as is recorded in the following self-aggrandising statement of the *Luoyang qielanji*:[399]

> 自葱嶺已西，至於大秦，百國千城，莫不歡附，商胡販客，日奔塞下，所謂盡天地之區已。樂中國土風，因而宅者，不可勝數。是以附化之民，萬有餘家。
>
> From west of the Congling 葱嶺 (Pamirs) to the Roman Empire there are hundreds of states [and] thousands of cities, and all are pleased to rely [on the Central Kingdom]. Daily, Merchant *hu* 胡[400] and traders hurry to come near, "from the regions on the limits of heaven and earth", as they say.[401] [They] are enchanted by the Central Kingdom's customs, which is why those who settle are innumerable. There are over ten thousand families that came to become subjects.

Besides the embassies sent by Sogdian states mentioned in the transmitted records, Rong Xinjiang compiled a table with the names and living dates of individuals with Sogdian surnames that resided or came to Luoyang 洛陽 from 647 to 757 CE, including the quarter in which they resided, which allowed him to make a map: 18 lived in quarters near the Southern Market and three near the Northern Market.[402] To these can be added An Jincang 安金藏, who was a physician at the court in Luoyang 洛陽 that became a widely known figure due to his memorable display of loyalty and reburied his parents here at the beginning of the eighth century.[403]

Four Zoroastrian temples are recorded in the *Tang liangjing chengfang kao*: one in the *Lide fang* 立德坊, near the Northern Market, one on the Southern Market, and two others near it, in the *Xiushan fang* 修善坊 and the *Huijie fang* 會節坊.[404]

Not far away from the capital were the famous Longmen 龍門 Grottoes. From the *Beishi xianghangshe sheren deng zaoxiangji* 北市香行社社人等造像記 (Record of the Manufacturing of a Buddhist Statue by the People of the Business Association of Scents of the Northern Market and others)[405] we know that the Association of Scent

398 Müller, "Gräber der Nördlichen Wei-Zeit," 42–46.

399 *Luoyang qielanji jiaozhu* 3.161.

400 In this case, "*hu* 胡" is rather unclearly referring to foreigners of any Western country, from China to Byzantium.

401 This is the same content, rephrased, of the *Hou Hanshu* 88.2931, in the description of the state of Cheshi 車師: 馳命走驛，馳命走驛，不絕於時月；商胡販客，日款於塞下。

402 Table: Rong Xinjiang, *Zhonggu Zhongguo yu wailai wenming*, 86–87; map: ibid., 88, fig. 6.

403 See the biography of his father An Pu 安菩 p. 164 (2.3.2.16).

404 On the temple in the *Lide fang* 立德坊, see the commentary to the *Guangchuan huaba*, and the *Chaoye qianzai* p. 275 (3.2.4.10).
Rong Xinjiang (Rong Xinjiang, *Zhonggu Zhongguo yu wailai wenming*, 87, 88, fn. 2), *apud*: Li Jianchao, *Tang liangjing chengfang*: 293, 315, 340, 362.

405 For a facsimile, see: Liu Jinglong and Li Yukun, *Longmen shiku beike*, 424. For a low-quality facsimile, see: Rong Xinjiang, *Zhonggu Zhongguo yu wailai wenming*, 89, fig. 7. See also:

Vendors donated on Yongchang 永昌 1/3/8 (3.4.689 CE) for the grotto no. 1410. Among them was the chief of the association An Sengda 安僧達 and four other people with Sogdian names: the scribe Shi Xuance 史玄策, as well as Kang Huideng 康慧登, He Nandi 何難迪, and Kang Jingzhi 康靜智. If these are to be identified as Sogdians based on their names, it shows that they were part of business associations and represented on the Northern Market, and that they were active as donors for Buddhist grottoes. Scents are indeed attested as one of the many import products from Sogdiana in other places.[406]

2.4.4.2 Chang'an 長安 (also known as Daxing 大興, Yongzhou 雍州, or Jingzhao 京兆)

Capital of the	Time
Han	206 BCE – 9 CE, 190–95 CE
Western Jin	313–16 CE
Former Qin	351–85 CE
Later Qin	386–417 CE
Northern Wei	534–35 CE
Western Wei	535–57 CE
Northern Zhou	557–81 CE
Sui (as Daxing 大興)	581–618 CE
Tang	618–90 CE, and 705–904 CE

For the Northern Wei, the epitaph mentions that the father of the Sogdian Kang Ye 康業, and during the Northern Zhou, he himself, were Zoroastrian attendants-in-chief.[407] According to the epitaph of the Sogdians Shi Shewu 史射勿, Shi Hedan 史訶耽, Shi Daoluo 史道洛, and Shi Tiebang 史鐵棒, their ancestor Renchou 認愁[408] was great (grand) *sabao* 摩訶(大)薩寶 during the Northern Zhou – which is, however, most probably fictive.[409] The epitaph of Shi Tiebang 史鐵棒 further states that the office of this ancestor was held in the Northern Zhou capital Chang'an 長安.[410] Wirkak (Master Shi 史), who was *sabao* 薩保 of Liangzhou 涼州, moved to Chang'an

Wen Yucheng, "Longmen zhongwai jiaotong".

406 See: Laufer, *Sino-Iranica*, 455–67; and: Schafer, *Golden Peaches*, 155–75.

407 See p. 131 (2.3.2.2).

408 Also known as Si 思, Duoxiduo 多悉多, or Duosi 多思 (Tasietta').

409 See the discussion p. 149 (2.3.2.10).

410 See p. 149 (2.3.2.9).

長安 at the end of the sixth century (i.e. under the Northern Zhou) and died there.[411] He was buried in the vicinity of other Sogdians on the Longshou 龍首 Plain, east of the capital. The above-mentioned Kang Ye 康業 was buried there several years earlier in 571 CE. An Jia 安伽, *sabao* 薩保 of Tongzhou 同州, was then buried only some hundred meters away in November or December of 579 CE, followed by Wirkak (Master Shi 史), about three months later in 580 CE. Finally, An Wantong 安萬通 was buried there in 654 CE, followed by An Pusa 安菩薩 in 664 CE, who was, however, reburied in Luoyang 洛陽 in 709 CE.

The lists of offices of the Sui in the *Suishu*[412] and the *Tongdian*[413] include a *sabao* 薩保 of Yongzhou 雍州, inside the current (*liu nei* 流内), of the appended rank 7b, in charge of the community of foreigners, among which were Sogdians. The lists of offices of the Tang in the *Tongdian*[414] and the *Jiu Tangshu*[415] include a *sabao* 薩寶 and a Zoroastrian regulator officer in the capital. This is corroborated by the epitaph of Long Run 龍潤 (561–653 CE), which states that he was appointed as head scribe of the *sabao* 薩寶 office during the Tang. The specific location of the office is not specified on the epitaph, but there is enough evidence to conclude that he was appointed in the capital.[416] Further, an anecdote of the *Shazhou dudufu tujing* 沙州都督府圖經 mentions the Zoroastrian attendant Di Pantuo 翟槃陀, saying that he once came to the capital before 640 CE and performed a magic trick while being possessed by the Zoroastrian Deity, an incident probably taking place at one of the capital's temples.[417] Of the five known temples, three were located around the Western Market, in the *Nanbu zheng fang* 南布政坊,[418] *Liquan fang* 醴泉坊, and *Chonghua fang* 崇化坊, one near the Eastern Market, in the *Jinggong fang* 靖恭坊, and one near the north-west corner of the city, in the *Puning fang* 普寧坊.[419]

Rong Xinjiang compiled a table with the known residencies and events related to 28 individuals with Sogdian surnames from 640 to 838 CE and mapped them.[420] To these can be added Shi Hedan 史訶耽, who was a translator at court and once had a residence in the Yanshou 延壽 Quarter.[421] All lived in the northern half of the city,

411 See p. 129 (2.3.2.1).
412 See p. 268 (3.2.4.4).
413 See p. 270 (3.2.4.7).
414 Id.
415 See p. 269 (3.2.4.6)
416 See p. 249 (3.2.2.15).
417 See p. 242 (3.2.1.4).
418 See p. 274 (3.2.4.9)
419 See: Xiang Da, *Tangdai Chang'an*, 89–92; Lin Wushu, *Bosi baihuojiao*, 139; Li Jianchao, *Tang liangjing chengfang*, 182, 207, 219, 227, 149; Rong Xinjiang, *Zhonggu Zhongguo yu wailai wenming*, 84, and 84, fn. 1. See also: Leslie, "Persian Temples".
420 Table: Rong Xinjiang, *Zhonggu Zhongguo yu wailai wenming*, 83–84; map: ibid., 82, fig. 5. Besides these, he added Kang Wentong 康文通 in 2014 (Rong Xinjiang, "Beichao Sui Tang Suteren bu kao (Zhonggu Zhongguo)," 35–36), although only his family name is used to underpin his relationship to Sogdians.
421 For more details, see his biography p. 142 (2.3.2.7).

with three of them near the Western Market which was renowned for exotic imports. Although the relationship between the Sogdians and their commercial activity seems evident, it is important to be aware of our biased source situation: The only Sogdians we know of in the capital came from the well-to-do society and their families were probably involved in commerce, or played an important role in the Sogdian society and/or religious life. It seems therefore standing to reason that they lived near the temples, which were social points of encounter. With a city population of probably over one million at this time, the nearly 30 individuals that may have been related to Sogdians are for a timespan of over 200 years, however, not quantitatively relevant enough to induce general statements about Sogdian activity or settlement patterns in the city. Further, as most of these identifications are based on their family name, it becomes increasingly difficult to discern them from Turks and Uighurs. However, there conceivably were Sogdians among the people protected by Uighurs after the An Lushan 安祿山 Rebellion.[422]

Merchants with Sogdian surnames certainly were active in Chang'an 長安, as three records from Turfan 吐魯番 and one from Dunhuang 敦煌 show. The first group of Turfan 吐魯番 documents records a legal dispute at the court of Gaochang 高昌 between the two merchants Cao Yanyan 曹炎延 (probably Sogdian) and Li Shaojin 李紹謹, probably around 628 CE.[423] Both travelled from Chang'an 長安 to the Gongyue 弓月 Fort in the Western Regions. The former had two guarantors with Sogdian surnames speaking for him, Cao Guoyi 曹果毅 and Cao Bisuo 曹畢娑, both "registered merchants" from Chang'an 長安. Two further documents from Turfan 吐魯番 record the request of a caravan of *hu* 胡 to settle with their families in the capital around the middle of the seventh century.[424] Further, a manuscript from

422 They were referred to as *zazhong hu* 雜種胡 in: *Jiu Tangshu* 127.3573; and as *jiu xing hu* 九姓胡 in: *Xin Tangshu* 217a.6121; and: *Zizhi tongjian* 226.7287–88). *Apud*: Pulleyblank, "Sogdian Colony," 351. See also the discussion p. 89 (1.15.13).

423 It is rather difficult to understand what exactly happened, as the documents are fragmentary and not very detailed (see: Rong Xinjiang, *Zhonggu Zhongguo yu wailai wenming*, 80). The anecdote can be reconstructed by recurring to two documents. The younger one: from Astana 61, dated 665 CE: 66 TAM 61: 17 (b) (一); 23 (b), 27/2, 27/1 (b) (二); 22 (b) (三); 26 (b) (四); 27/5 (b) (五); 24 (b) (六); 16 (b) (七); 25 (八) (Guojia wenwuju guwenxian yanjiu shi, *Tulufan chutu wenshu 6*, 470–79; Tang Changru, *Tulufan chutu wenshu 3*, 242–47).
And the older one: from Astana 135, dated 628 CE: 69 TAM 135: 2, 7 (Guojia wenwuju guwenxian yanjiu shi, *Tulufan chutu wenshu 3*, 242–46; Tang Changru, *Tulufan chutu wenshu 1*, 410–11); 69 TAM 135: 2 is also to be found in: Chutu wenwu zhanlan gongzuozu, *Wenhua da geming*, 112. The latter was excavated together with a contract for a slave sale in Sogdian (69 TAM 135: 1, 2), the Chinese being on the outside. See p. 202 (2.4.2.1.3).

424 From Astana 89: 67 TAM 89: 7/8 (一); 7/1 (二); 7/2 (三); 8/2 (四); 7/6 (五); 7/3 (六); 7/4 (七); 7/5 (八); 7/7 (九); 8/1 (一〇); 8/3 (一一); fragments 8/4–8/7 (Guojia wenwuju guwenxian yanjiu shi, *Tulufan chutu wenshu 3*, 346–54; Tang Changru, *Tulufan chutu wenshu 1*, 462–64). And from Astana 29: 64 TAM 29: 17 (a), 95 (a) (一); 108 (a) (二); 107 (三); 64 TAM 29: 24, 25 (四) (Guojia wenwuju guwenxian yanjiu shi, *Tulufan chutu wenshu 7*, 88–94; Tang Changru, *Tulufan chutu wenshu 3*, 346–50).
The first set of documents is not precisely datable, even though they can be determined to come

Dunhuang 敦煌 tells the story of two brothers in Chang'an 長安, Shi Potuo 史婆陀 and his cadet brother Shi Xieli 史頡利.[425] As the narration goes, the first was a merchant and he and his children allegedly showed off their immense wealth with a residence rivalling those of marquises and kings. The second was poor and did not receive any help from his greedy brother. Potuo 婆陀 was so avaricious that when his neighbour Kang Mobi 康莫鼻 wanted to borrow some clothes, he refused. Thus, the latter accused him in court of illegal indecent behaviour. The exact description of the wealth is most probably an exaggeration, relying on classical *topoi* to amplify the effect. All three individuals have Sogdian names. The account emphasises the three aspects of his status as merchant, his relationship to his brother, and his societal behaviour. It is remarkable that, unlike typical Chinese accounts of officially transmitted sources, it is never insulting, racist, or abusive towards any of the characters. Although being rich, he was said to be low in status, as his honorary office is insinuated as worthless and paid for. The account therefore establishes a contrast between his wealth and his societal standing, which is further exemplified by his moral indecency, as he misses the requirements of an older brother. Its context among the Dunhuang 敦煌 documents hints at its function as an exemplary moral episode to educate about the importance of decent behaviour and reinforce a hierarchical order postulated as natural in society. It is quite possible that a correlation between his indecency and the Confucian disregard for merchants is equally implied.

2.4.4.3 Pingcheng 平城

Capital of the	Time
Northern Wei	386–493 CE

As was just mentioned above, ca. 30,000 families were deported from Guzang 姑藏 of Liangzhou 涼州 to Pingcheng 平城 after the defeat of the Northern Liang in 439 CE, most probably including many Sogdian families.[426] The ancestors of Shi Suoyan 史索嚴 may conceivably have been among them.[427]

from the time the Qu 麴 reigned over Gaochang 高昌 (ca. 501–640 AD). The second set can be dated to around 672–85 AD. See also: Rong Xinjiang, *Zhonggu Zhongguo yu wailai wenming*, 80.

425 *Wenming panji* 文明判集 (P.3813 verso), cols. 114–26 (The International Dunhuang Project, "Pelliot chinois 3813"; Liu Junwen, *Dunhuang Tulufan*, 444–45).

426 See p. 231 (2.4.4.1).

427 See p. 156 (2.3.3.12).

2.4.4.4 Yecheng 鄴城

Capital of the	Time
(Cao Wei, quasi northern capital)	220–66 CE
Later Zhao	335–50 CE
Ran Wei 冉魏	350–52 CE
Former Yan 燕	357–70 CE
Eastern Wei	534–50 CE
Northern Qi	550–57 CE

The Sogdian Ancient Letter II, dated to ca. 311–13 CE includes the lament of a Sogdian on the deplorable situation of Ye 鄴 in the early fourth century after the destruction of Chang'an 長安 by the Xiongnu 匈奴 .[428] Over 200 years later, the epitaph of Kang Yuanjing 康元敬 mentions that his father Kang Wuxiang 康仵相 held the office of *mahe da sabao* 摩訶大薩寶 in what was probably the capital of the Northern Qi and that his ancestors moved there during the Northern Wei, under Emperor Xiaowen 孝文.[429] Further, a funerary bed was excavated in present-day Anyang 安陽, now dispersed in various museums around the world, has iconography reminiscent of other Sogdian funerary beds from this time.[430]

2.4.5 Strange and miraculous stories

Besides the above compiled mentions, there are various references to Zoroastrian temples and priests in literature from the Song to the Qing, which were presented and discussed by several scholars.[431] Some of the sources pertain to strange and miraculous stories and it is in fact difficult to assess with certainty if the Zoroastrian elements are *topoi* or not. I do thus agree with the analyses of Chen Yuan and Liu Mingshu that these references are probably not to be taken as references to real places or events, and in consequence, the passages shall not be re-analysed at this place. The probably most famously cited account related to Sogdiana about the vilified Turko-Sogdian general An Lushan 安祿 who led one of the major rebellions in Chinese history should illustrate these concerns.[432] It was insinuated that he was in a complex relationship with the emperor Xuanzong 玄宗 and the infamous Yang Guifei 楊貴妃.

428 Henning, "Date of the Sogdian Letters," 608–9; The International Dunhuang Project, "Or.8212/95"; translation: Silk Road Seattle Website, "Sogdian Ancient Letters".

429 See p. 255 (3.2.2.18).

430 See: Scaglia, "Central Asians"; Priewe, "Zhangdefu".

431 See: Chen Yuan, "Huoxianjiao," 129–32; Ishida Mikonosuke, "Kanda"; Kanda Kiichirō, "Tenkyō"; Liu Mingshu, "Yuan ren"; and: Lin Wushu, *Zhonggu*, 316–20.

432 See, generally: Pulleyblank, *Rebellion of An Lu-Shan*.

While the main line of narration remains the contrast between the evil foreigner, the consort, and Chinese culture and morals impersonated by a weak or strong emperor, many studies have taken the Chinese accounts as narrations of historical events. For example, although An Lushan 安祿山 is often cited as an agile dancer of the *hu* 胡 Swirl Dance, which may or may not have already been a *topos*, the concerning passage should not be taken to literally, as it is immediately followed by his transformation into a pig with a dragon head:[433]

> 祿山每行，以肩膊左右擡挽其身，方能移步。玄宗每令作胡旋舞，其疾如風。嘗夜晏祿山、祿山醉臥，化為一黑豬而龍首，左右遽言之，玄宗曰：「豬龍也，無能為者。」
>
> Every time Lushan 祿山 walked, [attendants on his] left and right supported his body by [his] shoulders and arms, only then could [he] walk. Every time Xuanzong 玄宗 ordered [him] to do a *hu* 胡 swirl dance, he [was] swift as the wind. One evening [he was] asked to participate at a banquet. Lushan 祿山 laid down drunk [and] turned into a black pig with dragon head. Left and right [people] immediately reported this, [but] Xuanzong 玄宗 said: “A pig-dragon, [he] cannot move”.

That this dance was often associated with an exotic eroticism of the Western prostitutes and servants may furthermore have influenced the record that the *femme fatale* Yang Guifei 楊貴妃 learned it.[434]

433 *An Lushan Shiji* a.5–6; author’s translation. For an annotated translation in French: Rotours, *Histoire de Ngan Lou-Chan*, 48–49.

434 See, among others, Li Bo’s 李白 often quoted poem *Qian you zun jiu xing* 前有樽酒行, in translation: Schafer, *Golden Peaches*, 21. See also: ibid., 50–57; and: Yang Shao-yun, “Reinventing,” 87.

3 Synthesis

3.1 Introduction

While one could argue that a differentiation between information on Sogdians *in Sogdiana* and Sogdians *in China* should not be of import in a study preoccupied with Sogdians in China, it became apparent that the study of Sogdians in China is a prerequisite to understanding how Sogdians were identified by their names in Chinese sources, i.e. these sources are linked methodologically. However, to avoid a conflation of the sources, the first chapter presented only historically transmitted Chinese accounts about Sogdiana. From the analysis of the content and discussion of the identification of toponyms, surnames, Sogdians, and Sogdiana emerged categories that were then used to organise the information. Next, information on Sogdians in China was collected in the second chapter. After the case-study of the Shi 史 in Guyuan 固原, a corpus of biographies was produced from all epitaphs of Sogdians from an archaeological context. As for the first chapter, this corpus was analysed in categories that emerged from the sources itself. Finally, all sources on Sogdians in China were organised geographically – including the previously collected information from the epitaphs.

As was explained in the introduction, the categories of information that emerged in the analysis in the first chapter are used to organise the material. In addition to the corpus presented in the second chapter, other transmitted literary sources and material evidence from outside an archaeological context – that were deliberately left out until this point – shall be integrated in the synthesis. While they were inconclusive or irrelevant for the identification of Sogdian settlements in China or the understanding of the above presented epitaphs, they do supplement the information in these categories. To be able to synthesise without reproducing the entirety of the above-presented information and detailed arguments and to avoid providing again already made references, the reader shall have to look for the reasoning and source of the synthesis' statements in the relevant passage above with help of the table of contents.

- The category "climate, flora, fauna, agriculture, and products" was defined above to keep the local natural conditions and the resulting agricultural activity together. As this is a socio-historical study, the category can be renamed "agriculture and products" and include "technology".
- Due to Sogdians not having ruled over China, the category "the king and his wife, the palace and throne, inner politics and legislature" is changed to "political organisation and legislature".

Further, several sub-categories will be renamed or disappear:
- "Women" and "men", which were meant to describe clothing, youth, and education, are combined into the sub-categories "youth and education" and "family, women, and marrying".
- Consequently, the sub-category "wedding, mourning, and burial" is reduced to "mourning and burial".
- The sub-category "music" is changed to "music and musical instruments".
- As the category "foreign affairs" contained the information about the contact between courts, and Sogdians were not in control of the Chinese court, it is changed to "translators and envoys". The products brought and sent by the court are integrated into the category "people and customs" under the sub-categories "commerce" and "agriculture and products".

3.2 Political organisation and legislature

As was already mentioned in the introduction, the *sabao* is probably what became the first subject of modern scholarly interest in Sogdians in China and is essential to the understanding of their political organisation.[1] The following analysis is based on a presentation given at the International Symposium "Buddhism and the Formation of Authority in East Asia" organised by Martin Lehnert on August 13–14, 2014, which awaits publication in the form of a larger article.[2] To investigate how Sogdians were authorised to administrate their people and religion in China, first, the main Chinese sources related to this topic shall be presented, including manuscripts, epitaphs, steles, and historically transmitted literature, as well as Indic, Sogdian and other sources in various languages. Second, the information shall be compiled and cross-checked to analyse the stages of evolution of the title and office as well as the subordinate offices.

1 To simply lay out the *Forschungsgeschichte* of this topic would require an article of its own; the article of Forte provides a critical and detailed overview of the research until 1999 (Forte, "Sabao 薩寶 Question"). The most important papers on the topic were published by: Pelliot, "Le sa-pao"; Fujita Toyohachi, "Saiiki kenkyū"; Dien, "Sa-Pao Problem"; Luo Feng, "Sabao: Zai kaocha"; Jiang Boqin, "Sabaofu zhidu"; Forte, "Sabao 薩寶 Question"; Rui Chuanming, "Sabao de zai renshi"; Rong Xinjiang, "Sabao yu Sabo: Beichao"; Luo Feng, *Hu Han zhi jian*, 248–79; Dien, "Further Thoughts"; and: Dien, "Consideration".

2 I want to extend my warmest gratitude to Martin Lehnert, Albert Dien, Shing Müller, and Hans van Ess for their exchange and support, Andreas Kaplony for his help with the Arabic sources, and last but not least Henry Albery for his help with the Prakrit sources and the English.

3.2.1 Manuscripts

3.2.1.1 Sogdian Ancient Letters, merchant letters in Sogdian, found near Dunhuang 敦煌, dated ca. 311–13 CE

From these letters, it can be gathered that Sogdians and Indians were engaged in a trading activity between – and in – China and India with caravans, while the Ancient Letter V mentions a merchant leader named Aspandhāt with the title *s'rtp'w* in Khotan (?).[3]

3.2.1.2 Document listing names and titles, found in Astana, in Chinese, dated 550 CE

The last known occurrence of the term *sabo* 薩薄 is to be found in a fragmented document found in Astana, dated 550 CE, col. 9:[4]

虎牙孝怒、薩薄□□ 、虎牙孟義 ……。

Huya 虎牙 Xiao Nu 孝怒, *sabo* 薩薄 □□, *huya* 虎牙 Meng Yi 孟義 (…)

As *huya* 虎牙 is a military title, possibly standing for *huya jiangjun* 虎牙將軍 (*huya* general),[5] and in this case cognates with a personal name, and the two characters after *sabo* 薩薄 are illegible, one can merely deduce that the latter term was used as the title of an office, with a rank possibly similar to, or being related to these military officers, as the individuals listed before also occupy military offices.[6] While trying to establish the history of the office, it is important to keep in mind that this region was part of the then independent Gaochang 高昌 Kingdom, ruled at this time by the Qu 麴 family and was practically an independent polity, vassals of either Turks or Chinese until 640 CE.

A document found in Turfan (60 TAM 331, 12/1–8),[7] dated 619 CE, which lists market transactions, is sometimes provided as further evidence.[8] Apparently, *sabo* 薩薄 is mentioned in col. 13. Based on the facsimile provided by Tang Changru, the transcription of the second character *bo* 薄 is, however, questionable.

3 For more information, see p. 214 (2.4.3.1.1). See also: Sims-Williams, "Sogdian Merchants," 49–51; Forte, "Sabao 薩寶 Question," 92–93.

4 73 TAM 524: 32/2 (Guojia wenwuju guwenxian yanjiu shi, *Tulufan chutu wenshu*, 46, col. 9; Tang Changru, *Tulufan chutu wenshu 1*, 136). In my opinion, Jiang Boqin has drawn a premature conclusion when he affirms that the *sabo* 薩薄 is a specialist for ritual offerings (*zhisiren* 知祀人; Jiang Boqin, *Dunhuang Tulufan wenshu*, 227). I concur with Dien that "each participant has a title such as would be found in the state administration" (Dien, "Further Thoughts," 203).

5 Which is attested for Gaochang 高昌, which we are speaking of (Lü Zongli, *Zhongguo*, 479).

6 Dien, "Further Thoughts," 203; Jiang Boqin, *Dunhuang Tulufan wenshu*, 227–29.

7 Guojia wenwuju guwenxian yanjiu shi, *Tulufan chutu wenshu 3*, 111, col. 13; Tang Changru, *Tulufan chutu wenshu 1*, 355.

8 See, e.g.: Zhang Guangda, "Une représentation iconographique," 200; Vaissière and Trombert, "Des Chinois," 947; Dien, "Consideration," Table 1.2.

3.2.1.3 Document listing names and some personal details, from Dunhuang 敦煌, in Chinese, dated 818 CE

Jiang Boqin pointed out that a document related to a Buddhist monastery from Dunhuang 敦煌 (S.542 verso, dated 818 CE), includes a passage reading:[9]

> 安薩(?)[10]保(注)守囚五日，營田夫五日。
>
> An Sa(?)bao 安薩(?)保. (Commentary:) Kept five days as prisoner, worked five days on the field.

He advanced two possibilities to explain the meaning of the word *sabao* 薩保. Either *An* 安 is the given name of a person of Western origin, maybe a Sogdian, to which the personal name Sabao 薩保 would be added, or it refers to the locality An 安 Fort, just about 500 m east of Shazhou 沙州. In the second case, it would refer to a local official *sabao* 薩保. Given the use of the name Sabao 薩保 as a personal name in several cases, and – fittingly – especially for Buddhists, it is, however, conceivably a personal name.

3.2.1.4 Shazhou dudufu tujing 沙州都督府圖經 (S.367 recto)

The *Shazhou dudufu tujing* 沙州都督府圖經 (S.367 recto) dates from 885 CE but is based on a text of the early Tang (P.5034 verso).[11] Concerning the Yiwu 伊吾 District (Hami) it reads:[12]

> 火/祆廟，中有素畫，[13]形象無數。有祆主翟槃陀者。高昌/未破以前，槃陀因朝入京。即下祆神，以利刀刺腹，左右通過，出腹外，截棄其餘。

9 Jiang Boqin, *Dunhuang Tulufan wenshu*, 234–35; author's translation.
Jiang Boqin quotes S.542 verso (Part 8, col. 177) 戌年六月十八日諸寺丁口車牛役部. He provided an explanation (to be found pp. 34–35 of his book published in 1987; pp. 25–34 of the latter he reproduces the whole passage, col. 177 being p. 32; Jiang Boqin, *Dunhuang sihu zhidu*), based on the poor readability and context, why he replaced the title's *zhuang* 壯 of the original text edition with "口", and argued against Ikeda On, who chose to write *shi* 仕 (Ikeda On, *Zhongguo gudai jizhang yanjiu*, 374, no. 247 (523), 389, no. 80/247 (523)). For the dating, he argumented convincingly for 818 CE (p. 35–40). Their work is based on: Zhongguo kexueyuan lishi yanjiusuo ziliaoshi, *Dunhuang ziliao 1*, 261–74.
In the latter, the quote differs with the edited version above. Instead of An Sabao 安薩保, it reads An Xuebao 安薛保: 安薛保(注)守囚五日。營田夫五日。 As Jiang Boqin only reproduced the beginning of S. 542 verso, in his book from 1987, and I unfortunately have no access to the original, the question of the title and the *sa* 薩/*xue* 薛 cannot be resolved at this point (it will be hopefully be accessible, when digitised: The International Dunhuang Project, "Or.8210/S.542").

10 See fn. above.

11 See p. 202 (2.4.2.1.3).

12 Facsimile: The International Dunhuang Project, "Or.8210/S.367 Recto". See also p. 191 (2.4.2.1.5). For other transcriptions, see: Zheng Binglin, *Dunhuang dili wenshu*, 67–68; and: Tang Geng'ou and Lu Hongji, *Dunhuang shehui jingji wenxian*, 40–41, cols. 55–60.

13 書 Mostly read as *shu* 書, which is rather odd, and in consequence leads to several articles. It is highly doubtable that this character fits in this context. Either there was an editing error by Zheng Binglin, due to misreading or other factors, e.g., by the existence of the word *sushu* 素書 (manuscripts, letters or volumes written on silk), or, rather unlikely, but still not to discard, indeed

以髮系其本。手执刀两頭高/，下絞轉，說國家所舉百事，皆順天心神靈助，無不正驗。/神沒之後，僵仆而倒，氣息奄七曰，即復如舊。有司奏/聞，制授游[擊]將軍。

> [There was] a fire Zoroastrian temple, inside were white (simple?) paintings [in] countless shapes. There was the *xianzhu* 祆主 (Zoroastrian presider) Di Pantuo 翟槃陀.[14] Before the conquest of Gaochang 高昌 (640 CE), Pantuo 槃陀 [once] came to the capital to [report to] the court. Then the Zoroastrian Deity came down [on him]. Taking a sharp knife [he] pierced his belly, going through [from] left to right. Taking out [his] entrails, [he] cut off their ends, [then] used hair to bind together the main [part]. Raising the knife two heads high, [he then] swirled it down, saying "the hundred affairs that are promulgated by the court shall all accord with heaven's will, [and shall obtain the] help of the gods spirits, [and that] all [shall] be truly fruitful". After the deity was gone, [he] dropped dead and collapsed, [his] respiration stopped for seven days. [He] then recovered as if anew. An official presented [to the emperor] this news. [As a result, Pantuo 槃陀 was] appointed as mobile corps commander.[15]

Di Pantuo 翟槃陀, likely Turco-Sogdian or Sogdian judging by the name,[16] is named as *xianzhu* 祆主 (Zoroastrian presider). Similar events are reported in the *Chaoye qianzai* and *Guangchuan huaba*,[17] and it also recalls An Jincang's 安金藏 actions at the court of Wu Zetian 武則天.[18] This story connects Di Pantuo 翟槃陀 to the cutting-tricks and auspicious wishes for the court. He is not otherwise related, either to the temples festivities, nor to temple functions, nor to the *sabao* 薩寶 office.

"books of countless forms" in the temple (Zheng Binglin, *Dunhuang dili wenshu*, 67).
For a hypothesis of the name of the deity the fire temple allegedly was dedicated to, see: Yoshida Yutaka, "Corpus Inscriptionum Iranicarum II, Vol. III, Part II (review)," 392; and: Vaissière, *Sogdian Traders*, 129, fn. 43.
See also: Zhang Xiaogui, *Zhonggu huahua xianjiao kaoshu*, 70–72.

14 It is possible that his given name was "*Zhai*" or "*Ti*" instead of "*Di*", probably pointing to him being Turco-Sogdian. It is a typical name for the Tölös, or Gaoche 高車, or Chile 敕勒. For more information on the state of Di 翟, see the glossary.
As the name Pantuo will be quoted several times, and although this paper will not venture in linguistic debates, the "name Pantuo (< **b'uân d'â*) is a transcription of a Sogdian name vandak (*βntk*) "slave", which is attested as a personal name among the Upper Indus inscriptions. Yoshida Yutaka, "Personal Names, Sogdian". "Slave" can be also understood as "servant". For the Upper Indus inscriptions, see: Sims-Williams, *Sogdian*, 47. It is furthermore often to be found in Buddhist literature – one of the most famous being Shi Pantuo 石槃陀, a guide helping Xuanzang 玄奘 (T50.223b08).

15 An honorary military title.

16 See p. 243 fn. 14.

17 See p. 275 (3.2.4.10).

18 See his father's biography p. 164 (2.3.2.16).

3.2.2 Epitaphs

3.2.2.1 Introductory remarks

In the following, only the epitaphs that are not from a secure archaeological context are provided, as the others were already discussed in detail. A selection of the relevant passages is selected, transcribed (if possible, from the facsimile), translated, and commented on, if necessary.

3.2.2.2 Di Mensheng 翟門生 (d. 538 CE)

Recently, Zhao Chao had the opportunity to have a look at two leaves that were engraved at the front of the side that would have been in the middle of the door, i.e. on the right front side of the left door leaf and the left front side of the right door leaf. The text runs in two columns from top to bottom. After several years, other stone artefacts came into the possession of the same collector, including a bed, screens and the accompanying watch towers, altogether 12 pieces of what seems to have been one grave furnishing set. Among the various scenes and inscriptions on the screens was also the name of Di Mensheng 翟門生. Below is a selection of the relevant passages of the inscription on the door leaves:[19]

> 翟國使主翟門生之墓誌
>
> 君諱育，字門生，翟國東天竺人也。胄藉華方，蟠根萬葉。樹德家邑，為本國薩甫。冠蓋崇勳，美傳弈世，□□二國通好，酬貢往來，因聘使主，遂入皇魏。……以元象元年正月十一日奄致薨背。……以大魏武定元年十一月廿三日……奄葬此土。
>
> Epitaph of Chief Envoy Di Mensheng 翟門生
>
> The master's taboo [was] Yu 育, [his] courtesy name Mensheng 門生, an east Indian of the state of Di 翟. [His] ancestors came to be registered in China [and their family] tree flourished, [being] of established virtue. [He] was *safu* 薩甫 of his home country. [He was] a meritorious official [and] passed [his] good reputation to the next generations, … successfully connected the two countries, bringing gifts and tribute back and forth. Thus, [he] was requested to become chief envoy [and] entered the [Northern] Wei court. (…) On Yuanxiang 元象 1/1/11 (25.2.538 CE) [he] suddenly passed away. (…) On Wuding 武定 1/11/23 of the Great [Eastern] Wei (3.1.544 CE) (…) [he] was swiftly buried.

3.2.2.3 Di Caoming 翟曹明 (480s–578 CE)

The epitaph of Di Caoming 翟曹明 is included because he is said to have been Zoroastrian presider (*tianzhu* 天主). The epitaph has been found out of its original

19 The facsimile doesn't allow for a transcription (Zhao Chao, "Jieshao," 674, figs. 1, 2). The passage above is a selection of the transcription made by Zhao Chao, transcribed by the author from the simplified characters to *zhengzi* 正字: ibid., 673, and 675–76, figs. 3, 4.

archaeological context. Some researchers believe, however, that it should be associated with a grave from the Northern Zhou, excavated 1993 in Jingbian 靖邊 County, Shaanxi Province, which is the ancient location of Xiazhou 夏州; the association is based on interviews with the local population.[20] Judging from the name, he may have been of Turco-Sogdian descent. Below is a selection of the relevant passages:[21]

> 大周大成元年歲次己[亥]三月癸巳朔四日[乙][22]/未。夏州天主儀同翟君墓誌。[□□□□□□□]/君諱曹明，西國人也。祖宗忠烈，令譽家邦。受命/來朝遂居恆夏。……傷魏[國][23]之衰泯，慨臣下之僭凌。是/以慕義從軍，誅除亂逆。巨猾摧峰[24]，六軍振振。□[25]/賞既降，威聲漸著。朝野欽風，臣民敬尚。……七月三日遘疾捐館，春秋[九]……子……
>
> Dacheng 大成 1 [*jihai*]/ 3 [*guiyi*]/ 4 [*yiwei*] (14.3.579 CE) of the Great Zhou. Epitaph of the Zoroastrian Presider Commander Unequalled in Honour Di 翟 of Xiazhou 夏州.
> The master's taboo was Caoming 曹明, he [came from] a Western state. [His] grandfather [and] father, were loyal [and] brave [and had] a good reputation across the country. [He/they] received the order to come to court [and] thus [came to] reside in Hengzhou 恆州 and Xiazhou 夏州. (…) Because [Caoming 曹明] was sorrowed by the decline of the state of Wei 魏 [and] saddened by the excessive encroachments of the officials, [he] enlisted out of admiration and righteousness, [to] punish and wipe out the upheaval. The fighting spirit of the guileful traitors was broken [and] the imperial army grand. … granted a reward [and his] reputation gradually increased. [He was] esteemed in court and country, and ministers and common people respected [him]. (…)
> On [Xuanzheng 宣政 1?] 7/3 (21.8.578 CE)[26] [he] unexpectedly fell ill [and] left office at the age of 9… (…) [His] son(s) [were] (…).

His grandfather and father probably came to reside in the territory of the Northern Wei. It is, however, unclear if the army that Caoming 曹明 joined was of the Western Wei or Northern Zhou. Further, as he was over 90 years old at the time of his death, he was probably born in the 480s. However, the Dacheng 大成 era lasted only several weeks under Emperor Xuan 宣, until it was replaced by the Daxiang 大象 era of the new emperor Jing 靜. The *Zhoushu* states that the change was made on the 2/1 [*guihai*] (14.3.579 CE),[27] but Luo Feng and Rong Xinjiang proposed that it was on the 2/22,

20 Luo Feng and Rong Xinjiang, "Bei Zhou xiguo," 269.
21 Author's transcription from the rubbing, to be found in: ibid., 279.
22 This can be reconstructed as Dacheng 大成 1/3/4 was indeed *yiwei* 乙未.
23 Originally *die* 戜, itself a *zhengzi* 正字 but also a variant (C04049) of *guo* 國. Luo Feng and Rong Xinjiang transcribed it as *die* 戴, which is also a variant of *guo* 國 (ibid., 280).
24 Read *feng* 鋒.
25 Luo Feng and Rong Xinjiang propose to read 寽 (ibid.).
26 He probably died the year before, under Emperor Wu 武. It is, however, possible that he died two or more years before.
27 *Zhoushu* 7.119.

without, however, providing an explanation.[28] Di Caoming 翟曹明 was buried on the 3 [*guiyi*]/ 4 [*yiwei*] (15.4.579 CE) which was in the new era. Luo Feng and Rong Xinjiang proposed that the incorrect era name can be explained by the short period of time in between the change of the era and the burial.[29] According to my calculations, however, there were 33 days in between. The information would conceivably have been transmitted from the capital Chang'an 長安 to Xiazhou 夏州, where he was probably buried.

3.2.2.4 Master Shi 史/Wirkak (Sogd. Wyrk'k) (494–579 CE)

See p. 126 (2.3.2.1).

3.2.2.5 Kang Ye 康業 (512–71 CE)

His epitaph is included due to the mention of the office of Zoroastrian presider-in-chief (*da tianzhu* 大天主). See p. 128 (2.3.2.2).

3.2.2.6 An Jia 安伽 (518–79 CE)

See p. 129 (2.3.2.3).

3.2.2.7 Lord Yu Hong 虞弘 (534–92 CE)

See p. 130 (2.3.2.4).

3.2.2.8 Shi Shewu 史射勿 (544–609 CE)

See p. 135 (2.3.2.6).

3.2.2.9 Cao Yi 曹怡 (581–655 CE)

See p. 156 (2.3.2.14).

3.2.2.10 Shi Hedan 史訶耽 (584–669 CE)

See p. 139 (2.3.2.7).

3.2.2.11 Shi Daoluo 史道洛 (591–655 CE)

See p. 145 (2.3.2.8).

3.2.2.12 Shi Tiebang 史鐵棒 (623–66 CE)

See p. 146 (2.3.2.9).

3.2.2.13 Epitaph of Di Tusuo 翟突娑 (546–615 CE)

Below a selection of the relevant passages:[30]

28 Rong Xinjiang et al., *Suteren zai Zhongguo 1*, 281.

29 Ibid.

30 Author's edition from the rubbing, to be found in: Zhao Wanli, *Han Wei Nanbeichao muzhi*, vol. 5, fig. 484. For a partial edition and commentary, see: ibid., vol. 2, 102.

Cover: Not available

Epitaph: 君諱突娑，字薄賀比多，並州太原人也。父娑，摩訶大薩寶。薄賀比多日月以見勳效，右改宣惠尉，不出/其年，右可除奮武尉、擬通守。祖晉上卿之苗裔翟雄，/漢獻帝尚書令司徒公文海之胤。……春秋七十，大業十一年歲次乙/亥正月十八日疾寢卒於河南郡[洛]陽[31]縣崇[業][32]鄉嘉/善里。葬在芒山北[33]之翟村東南一里。……

The master's taboo was Tusuo 突娑,[34] [his] courtesy name Bohebiduo 薄賀比多, he [came from] 太原 Taiyuan of Bingzhou 並州. [His] father [was] Suo 娑, great grand *sabao* 薩寶. Due to Bohebiduo's 薄賀比多 daily merits, [he] became officer of manifest benevolence, [and] early for his years promoted to officer of vigorous militancy, [and] commandery vice governor. [His] grandfather [was] Di Xiong 翟雄, a descendant of a senior minister of the Jin, a descendant of the Director of the Imperial Secretariat [and] Minister of Education under Emperor Xiandi 獻 of the Han (181–234 CE) Lord Wenhai 文海.[35] (…) At the age of 70, on Daye 大業 11 [*yihai*]/1/18 (21.2.615 CE), [being affected by a] sickness, [he] lied down and passed away in in the hamlet Jiashan 嘉善 of the Chongye 崇業 Town of the Luoyang 洛陽 District of the Henan 河南 Commandery. [He was] buried one *li* south-east of the Di 翟 Village,[36] on the North Mangshan 芒山.[37] (…)

It is probable that Di Suo 翟娑, a great grand *sabao* 薩寶, was born at least 15 years before the birth of his son, meaning in 531 CE. Hypothesising that he was not over 80 when he begot him, he was born at the earliest date of 451 CE. Judging from this date and the fact that his grandfather was a senior minister during the Jin (265–420 CE), it is also highly probable that the latter had this office at the end of the Jin.

3.2.2.14 Kang Moliangxi Ada 康莫量息阿達 (d. early Tang)

Below is a selection of the relevant passages:[38]

31 Originally Luoyang 雒陽, a former name for Luoyang 洛陽.

32 Originally *pu* 菐. A variant of the character *ye* 業.

33 A former name for Bei Mangshan 北邙山.

34 Luo Feng and Yang Junkai erroneously transcribed Di Po 翟婆: Luo Feng, "Guyuan nanjiao Sui Tang Zhongya, 1," 31, no. 35; Luo Feng, *Hu Han zhi jian*, 254; Yang Junkai, "Bei," 54.

35 As Zhao Wanli wrote, he is an unknown figure from the later Han. As the deceased was most certainly of foreign descent – judging from his name and the office of his father – the author fabricated this ancient reference (Zhao Wanli, *Han Wei Nanbeichao muzhi*, vol. 2.102).

36 It does not seem a coincidence that his surname is identical with the village. Maybe a lot of people with his surname lived there and/or it was the choronym of the family (Zhao Chao, "Jieshao," 677–79).

37 An old name for Bei Mangshan 北邙山. One of the most famous burial places of China, a range of hills north of Luoyang 洛陽.

38 The column breaks are not marked in the edited texts. Author's punctuation. Different editions

Cover stone: 康君墓銘

Epitaph: 大唐上儀同故康莫量息阿達墓誌銘。公諱阿達，西域康國人也。其先蓋出自造化之初，藤苗大唐之始，公即皇帝之胄胤也。……祖拔達，梁使持節，驃騎大將軍，開府儀同三司，涼、甘、瓜三州諸軍事，涼州薩保。……詔贈武威太守。父莫量，同葬安樂里。……

Cover stone: Epitaph of master Kang 康

Epitaph: Epitaph of Senior Commander late Kang Moliangxi Ada 康莫量息阿達 of the Great Tang. The master's taboo was Ada 阿達, he [came from] the state of Kang 康 of the Western Regions. His ancestors probably came from the beginning of creation, the descendants [reaching] to the early Tang, the master thus being a descendant of the emperor. (…) [His] grandfather [was] Bada 拔達, commandant with extraordinary powers of the Liang (502–57 CE), cavalry general-in-chief, and commander unequalled in honour, [commandant with extraordinary powers] in charge of the military matters of Liangzhou 涼州, Ganzhou 甘州, and Guazhou 瓜州, and *sabao* 薩保 of Liangzhou 涼州. (…) [He] was posthumously promoted to commandery governor of Wuwei 武威. [Kang Ada 康阿達 and] was buried together with his father Moliang 莫量 in the Anle 安樂 Hamlet (?).

It is possible that characters or parts of the epitaph are missing, yet this unfortunately cannot be confirmed since neither the epitaph nor the rubbing are available.

As Chen Guocan[39] and Dien[40] pointed out, Liangzhou 涼州 (where his grandfather was appointed as *sabao* 薩保), was located outside the jurisdiction of the Southern Liang (502–57 CE). It is furthermore important to mention that no dynasty had stable control over the region. This probably means that he held some kind of societal and military influence independently of the dynasty at this location, the Southern Liang conferring to him flattering titles. However, a change of dynasty is usually mentioned in the epitaphs, either explicitly or reflected through a possible transfer of office under a new dynasty. In this special case, I propose that after the conquest of the Southern Liang by the Northern Zhou in 557 CE, Kang Bada 康拔達 went on to serve under the new rulers and acquired equivalent offices. Thus, probably some of the offices mentioned in the epitaph are of the Northern Zhou and even Sui, and not of the Southern Liang.

of the epitaph are to be found as *Dayun si bei* 大雲寺碑 in: Zhang Wei, *Longyou jinshi lu*, 2.4; or to be found in: Guojia tushuguan shanben jinshi zu, *Sui Tang Wudai shike (4)*, 995; *apud*: Zhou Shaoliang and Zhao Chao, *Tangdai muzhi*, 124.

39 Chen Guocan, "Wei," 205–6.

40 Dien, "Further Thoughts," 208, fn. 21.

3.2.2.15 Long Run 龍潤 *(561–653 CE)*

Below is a selection of the relevant passages:[41]

> Cover stone: 龍君墓誌
>
> Epitaph: 君諱潤，字恆伽，並州晉陽人也。白銀發地，稜崛□□龍/之山。祖先感其譎詭，表靈異而稱族。鑿空鼻始，爰自少/昊之君。實錄采奇，繼以西楚之將。及漢元帝，顯姓名於/史游。馬援之稱伯高，慕其為人，敬之重之。晉中興書特/記隱士子偉，以高邁絕倫。……[□]曾祖康基，高齊青、萊二州刺史。疆[42]埸鄰比，/風化如一。[□]祖盆生，元魏冀州刺史。得綏撫之望，朝廷/嘉美，進號儀同。[□]父求真。周光有天下，舉先巖穴，就拜/儀同三司。……
>
> Cover stone: Epitaph of Master Long 龍
>
> Epitaph: The master's taboo [was] Run 潤, [his] courtesy name Hengjia 恆伽. He [came from] Jinyang 晉陽 of Bingzhou 並州. [There was] a place where silver came out of the ground, projecting … dragon-mountain. [His] ancestors were moved by its strangeness, [it] appeared mysterious and thus named their family (Dragon, *long* 龍). Starting from nothing, [they] turned themselves into gentlemen under Shaohao 少昊.[43] The records collect [their] prodigies continuously until the generals of the Western Chu.[44] During [the reign of] the first emperor of the Han, their name appears related to Shi You 史游.[45] Ma Yuan 馬援 was called [with the courtesy name] Bo Gao 伯高, [he was] admired by the people, respected and valued. In the *Jin zhong xing shu* 晉中興書,[46] the recluse Zi Wei 子偉 is specially recorded as excellent beyond compare. (…) [Master Long's 龍] great-grandfather was Kangji 康基, [during the] Great Qi [he was] regional inspector of both Qingzhou 青州 and Laizhou 萊州. The battlefield was in vicinity, and accordingly were the customs. [His] grandfather [was called] Pensheng 盆生, [during the Northern] Wei [being] regional inspector of Jizhou 冀州. Acquiring a reputation for [successful] appeasement, the court praised [him], promoting [him] to the title of commander unequalled in honour. [His] father [was called] Qiuzhen 求真. [During] the reign of the [Northern] Zhou over the empire, [he] first lived as a recluse, then was awarded [the title of] commander unequalled in honour. (…)

41 Author's transcription from the rubbing, to be found in: Zhang Xishun, *Sui Tang Wudai muzhi, Shanxi*, 8. A transcription of the epitaph is in the *Quan Tangwen buyi* vol. 5.111, and others in: Zhou Shaoliang and Zhao Chao, *Tangdai muzhiming xuji*, 75; and: Rong Xinjiang, "Sui ji Tang," 87.

42 The *Quan Tangwen buyi* erroneously transcribes the epitaph's character *jiang* 畺 as *jiang* 僵.

43 Mythical son of the Yellow Emperor in the 3rd millennium BCE. In this context possibly meaning "integrating into the Chinese elite".

44 A marquisate during the Qin and Han.

45 A eunuch during the reign of the first Han emperor.

46 Traditionally seen to be compiled by He Fasheng 何法盛, of the Song (Southern Dynasties).

唐基締構，草昧區夏。義旗西指，首授朝散大夫，又署/薩[47]寶府長史。貞觀廿年，春秋廖廓，已八十有餘。/[駕]幸晉陽親問耆老詔板授遼州刺史。……盛修第宇，/俊[48]俙南陽樊重之家。子孫就養，仿像西晉安仁之孝。……永徽四年九月十日，薨於安仁坊之第，春/秋九十有三。……永徽六年二月廿日，/……與夫人何氏合葬於並[49]/城北廿里井谷村東義井村北。……

[When] the Tang was established, an initial chaos [found] China. [When the] troops moved west, [Run 潤] was first appointed as grand master for closing court [and] then installed as head scribe[50] of the *sabao* 薩寶 office. In Zhenguan 貞觀 20 (646 CE), [his] years became few,[51] at over 80 [years of age]. The imperial carriage went to Jinyang 晉陽. [The emperor] himself enquired among the elder and issued an imperial edict to promote [Run 潤 to the honorary office of] prefect of Liaozhou 遼州.[52] (…) [He] grandly enlarged [his] private residence, similar to the splendour of Fanzhong's 樊重 Nanyang 南陽 residence.[53] Supported by his son(s) and grandson(s), [they] imitated the filial piety of An Ren 安仁 of the Western Jin.[54] (…) On Yonghui 永徽 4/9/10 (7.10.653 CE), [he] passed away in his private residence in the Anren 安仁 Quarter, at the age of 93.[55] (…) On Yonghui 永徽 6/2/20 (1.4.655 CE), (…) [he was] buried with [his] wife north of the hamlet Yijing 義井, east of the town Jinggu 井谷, 20 *li* north of Bingcheng 並城 (Jinyang 晉陽).

Although the beginning of the epitaph, listing the ancestry, seems of rather mythical content, peppered with some historical quotes, the information concerning his close ancestry and himself may well closely reflect reality. The epitaph does not specifically mention where the *sabao* 薩寶 office was located. While he came from Jinyang 晉陽,

47 The *Quan Tangwen buyi* erroneously transcribes the epitaph's character as *xue* 薛.

48 The *Quan Tangwen buyi* erroneously transcribes the epitaph's character as *ai* 僾.

49 The *Quan Tangwen buyi* includes at this place a *zhou* 州, although it is not written on the epitaph.

50 In connection with the *sabao* 薩寶, the quote of the *Tongdian* 193 may indicate his office to be of rank 5, which coincides with his other office's rank. When the Tang was established, being the earliest date for him to become appointed as scribe of the *sabao* 薩寶 office, he was at least around 58 years old.

51 A metaphor for retirement.

52 This is most certainly an honorary title, as the title was probably at this time held by Li Yun 李惲 (Yu Xianhao, *Tang*, 1268–69).

53 Fanzhong 樊重, maternal grandfather of Emperor Guangwu 光武, was a famous businessman and landowner of Nanyang 南陽 in the first century CE (Zheng Tianting, Wu Ze and Yang Zhijiu, *Zhongguo lishi da cidian 2*, 3174). He became a classical benchmark for residences (Zhao Dexin, *Zhongguo*).

54 Given name of the writer and official Pan Yue 潘岳 (ca. 247–300 CE). He was above all famous for his beauty. Before the Northern Song he was included in the *Ershisi xiao* 二十四孝 (Twenty-four Paragons of Filial Piety) because he left his career and cared for his recovering mother. Later, as his mother was killed in consequence of her sons' conviction and the ensuing three-generations-punishment, he was replaced in the list by Zhu Shouchang 朱壽昌.

55 Per inference he was born around the year 560 CE.

three statements point to the fact that he held this office in the capital Chang'an 長安 and only returned after his retirement. First, the epitaph informs us that he was head scribe of the *sabao* 薩寶 office, without providing more information about the whereabouts of the office, which may point to *the* office, that is in the capital. Second, and more importantly, he was serving as grand master for closing court. Third, he eventually died in the capital in 653 CE, in his private residence in the Anren 安仁 Quarter. He was then, in 655 CE, reburied with his wife in Bingzhou 並州, at his home.

This epitaph was excavated in October 1984 east of the Xiaojingyu 小井峪 Town, located in the northern suburbs of Taiyuan 太原 City, Shanxi Province.[56] It was certainly from a family cemetery, as several other epitaphs of people named Long 龍 were excavated in the same place at the same time: the epitaphs of Long Run's 龍潤 sons Long Yi 龍義 (d. 657–58 CE),[57] Long Deng 龍澄 (596–661),[58] Long Min 龍敏 (604–82 CE),[59] Long Run's 龍潤 grandson Long Shou 龍壽 (627–94 CE),[60] and great-grandson Long Rui 龍叡 (655–741 CE).[61] These epitaphs provide origin stories of different extent which supplement the above-mentioned information. Yi's 義 epitaph says that their clan received the name because they were officers in charge of the imperial horses (*yu long* 御龍). Deng's 澄 epitaph also mentions the Chu in their family's history. Min's 敏 and Shou's 壽 stories are identical, saying that their ancestors held office since Zengchuan 酸川. This is the place that the mythical emperor Shun 舜 gave as a fief to Dong Fu 董父. He is also said to have given him the family name Dong 董 and the clan name Huanlong 豢龍 (lit. raise dragons; dragon is a metaphor for an excellent horse). His aftermath is said to have been the Zengyi 酸夷 (lit. Zeng barbarians) clan, which was then conquered by Xia 夏.[62] The epitaphs then claim that their ancestors continued to hold office during the Liang, a fiefdom during the Han, which includes the Yu 虞 District. Rui's 叡 epitaph, the latest, is the most extensive and the most sensational. It says that their ancestor is the above-mentioned Huanlong 豢龍 of Yu 虞, which is why they received the family name Dong 董. Their great ancestor then was an officer in charge of the imperial horses (*yu long* 御龍) for Xia 夏, which is when they received the family name Long 龍 (dragon). They then assisted the Han and later the Western Chu. Whereas Run 潤 married a wife of the He 何 family, which is a name that was also used by Sogdians or Sogdian descendants stemming from Kushaniyya, Yi 義 married a Lü 旅, Shou 壽 married a Su 粟, and Rui 叡 married a Zhang 張 from Qinghe 清河, which are not used by Sogdians.

The claim of Yi's 義 epitaph that the family was active in the imperial corral is artificially related to their name, which was in other epitaphs used to relate to

56 Zhang Xishun, *Sui Tang Wudai muzhi, Shanxi*, 8.
57 Zhang Xishun, *Sui Tang Wudai muzhi, Shanxi*, 16, *Quan Tang wen bu yi* vol. 6.293.
58 Zhang Xishun, *Sui Tang Wudai muzhi, Shanxi*, 14, *Quan Tang wen bu yi* vol. 6.281–82.
59 Zhang Xishun, *Sui Tang Wudai muzhi, Shanxi*, 37, *Quan Tang wen bu yi* vol. 5.190–91.
60 Zhang Xishun, *Sui Tang Wudai muzhi, Shanxi*, 56, *Quan Tang wen bu yi* vol. 5.216.
61 Zhang Xishun, *Sui Tang Wudai muzhi, Shanxi*, 113, *Quan Tang wen bu yi* vol. 6.430–31.
62 *Guoyu* 16.511.

Huanlong 豢龍. Run's 潤 activity as grand master for closing court and head scribe of the *sabao* 薩寶 office do in my opinion not provide enough information to ascribe to them a foreign identity or ancestry as Zhang Qingjie and Rong Xinjiang believe.[63] They proposed that Long Run 龍潤 actually stemmed from Yanqi 焉耆 (Qarashahr). This is based on an article by Rong Xinjiang in which he tried to relate individuals named Long 龍 who lived in present-day Gansu Province during the late ninth century with the royal Long 龍 clan of Yanqi 焉耆 that held power from the third to the late eighth century.[64] The relation drawn between these various Long 龍 and the family of Long Run 龍潤 is, however, apparently only based on his activity in the *sabao* 薩寶 office and his marriage to a wife named He 何 – and ignores that Long 龍 is a common family name in China since antiquity. According to them, Run 潤 was a Sogdian that concealed his foreign ancestry and first married a Sogdian, while the later generations intermarried with Chinese. Zhang Qingjie further proposed that the place in which he resided, the Anren 安仁 Quarter, has the meaning of "appeasing foreigners" – *an* 安 can mean appease, while *ren* 仁 (humaneness) was apparently ignored.

In my opinion, the epitaph provides information that leads to a somewhat different outlook. Whereas his family background may well be constructed – which is by no means reserved to people of foreign descent – he stemmed from Jinyang 晉陽, Bingzhou 並州, and only came to work in Chang'an 長安 as grand master for closing court and then as head scribe of the *sabao* 薩實 office after the Tang 唐 were established. He was active until 646 CE, when he retired. As he was already 57 years old when he was appointed, it is quite certain that he married his wife He 何 beforehand. If her family name indeed indicates her Sogdian ancestry, it means that he probably was connected to the Sogdian community in Bingzhou 並州. This entails that he may have met Lord Yu Hong 虞弘, who was one of its eminent persons until his death in 592 CE, among others being acting *sabao* 薩保.[65] It is also possible that he then already met Shi Shewu 史射勿, who accompanied the imperial carriage to Bingzhou 並州 in 590 CE. Shewu 射勿 became then grand master for proper consultation at the court of the Sui in Chang'an 長安, who were established when he was 37 years old. This occupation was continued by his son Hedan 訶耽 during the Tang, who was first appointed as gentleman for court audiences in 633 CE at the age of 49, then as gentleman for thorough counsel in 635 CE, and as gentleman for court discussion in 639 CE. This means that Long Run 龍潤 worked together with Shi Hedan 史訶耽 as grand master for closing court and was connected to the Sogdian community in Chang'an 長安 as head scribe of the *sabao* 薩寶 office. Quite to the contrary of the above-mentioned perspective, namely that he was a foreigner who concealed his true ancestry and whose sons intermarried with Chinese and gradually integrated, it seems to me that Long Run 龍潤, whose great-grandfather was said to have held office in present-day Shandong Province, profited greatly from marrying a

63 Rong Xinjiang, "Sui ji Tang," 87; Zhang Qingjie, "Sichou," 561.
64 Rong Xinjiang, "Sui ji Tang," 87; *apud*: Rong Xinjiang, "Long".
65 For more on him, see p. 133 (2.3.2.4).

Sogdian: He used his connections in Bingzhou 並州 and Chang'an 長安 and applied his Chinese skills – which are not simply learned in passing – to become appointed as a head scribe in an office for foreigners while serving in his role as grand master for closing as a mediator between the court and foreign guests.

3.2.2.16 Kang Po 康婆 (573–647 CE)

Below is a selection of the relevant passages:[66]

> Cover stone: 大唐故康府君墓誌銘
>
> Epitaph: 大唐故洛陽康大農墓銘[□□□□□□□□□□□□□□□□□]/君諱婆，字季大，博陵人也。本康國王之裔也。高祖羅，以魏孝文世，/舉國内附，朝於洛陽。因而家焉，故爲洛陽人也。祖陀，齊相府常侍。/父和，隋定州薩寶，又遷奉御。……
>
> Cover stone: Epitaph of the late master Kang 康 of the Great Tang.
>
> Epitaph: Epitaph of the late Minister of Agriculture Kang 康 of Luoyang 洛陽 of the Great Tang. The master's taboo [was] Po 婆, [his] courtesy name Jida 季大[67], he [came from] Boling 博陵. Originally, [he was] a descendant of the king of the state of Kang 康. [His] great-grandfather [was] Luo 羅, [who] lived during the time of (Emperor) Xiaowen 孝文 of the [Northern] Wei. The whole country (region) submitted [to the Wei 魏] and [he] became subject of the emperor in Luoyang 洛陽. Thus [he moved his] family there, which is why [he became] a resident of Luoyang 洛陽. [His] grandfather [was] Tuo 陀, attendant to the office of the chancellor [during the Northern] Qi. [His] father [was] He 和, *sabao* 薩寶 of Dingzhou 定州 [during the] Sui, then promoted head of the services constituting the Palace administration. (…)
>
> 武德中，左僕射裴寂揖君/名義，請署大農。……自裴侯下世，君亦辭位高蹈，閑居養志而已。……[以貞][68]觀廿(一年)[八][69]月十四日終於洛/陽之私第，春秋七十有五。即以其年[九]月一日遷葬於北邙山之/南原也。長子須達……。大唐貞觀廿一年歲次丁未八月乙卯朔十四日戊辰。[□]/[□□□]九月甲申朔一日甲申。……
>
> During the Wude 武德 [era] ([623/3–626/1] CE),[70] the Vice Director on the left of the Imperial Secretariat Pei Ji 裴寂[71] highly praised master [Kang Po's

66 Author's transcription from the rubbing, to be found in: Luoyang shi wenwu gongzuodui, *Luoyang muzhi jisheng*, 126. Another transcription is to be found in: Zhou Shaoliang and Zhao Chao, *Tangdai muzhi*, 96.

67 Erroneously transcribed by de la Vaissière and Trombert as Lida 李大: Vaissière and Trombert, "Des Chinois," 959.

68 This can be reconstructed using the dates below.

69 Id.

70 The Wude 武德 era was 618–26 CE. See fn. below.

71 In the *Xin Tangshu*, his appointment as vice director on the right is dated 618 CE, and vice director

康婆] name [and] requested [to have him] assigned as minister of agriculture. (…) After the Marquis of Pei 裴 passed away (in 629 CE),[72] the master also resigned and [went] to be a recluse, [and] lead his retired life, cherishing his aspirations. (…) On Zhenguan 貞觀 21/8/14 (18.9.647 CE) [he] died in his private residence in Luoyang 洛陽, at the age of 74. In this year's 9/1 (4.10.647 CE) [he was] reburied in the southern plain of Beimang 北邙. [His] eldest son [is] Xuda 須達. (…) [Buried on] Zhenguan 貞觀 21 [*dingwei*]/8 [*yimao*]/14 [*wuchen*] (18.9.647 CE) of the Great Tang. [Inscribed on] (Zhenguan 貞觀 21) 9 [*jiashen*]/1 [*jiashen*] (4.10.647 CE).

3.2.2.17 An Wantong 安萬通 (585–654 CE)

The epitaph is broken into three pieces and various characters are illegible and/or missing. Below is a selection of the relevant information:[73]

Cover stone: missing

Epitaph (1st piece): [□]君姓安名□字萬通，雍州[74]長安/人也。其祖本生西域安息國。……大魏初王，君/高祖但奉使入朝，帝慕其□□□□□□三品，位至摩訶/薩寶。子孫煩讓冠帶。□□□□□□□華陰縣開國公、鄯/州刺史。父巡隋任上開府通議郎。……開皇十六年，枉被/□斂，破家財物，□□□□□□□宅□□公□□納入庫藏/□從配没入官君□沿賤例□□□□絲豪亦不寐群□恨，/利禄未蕩然也。□之□十三至大業三年,□□□□天下/□□真情，遂免思若險□盡安，方得士慮其眷，□不□/□。於時，馳逐存濟。君象□可託，懷得可得。鄉閭用其/量□，衆□□其□首□耳□不隱言□斷終無彼我□歎。……
(2nd piece): ……大唐初建,君受□先□,蒙授五品。……春秋六十九。有妻二，頻潮落□,初割肝腸。……永徽五年十二月一日葬於城/西龍首原。……

Because of the many unreadable fragments, the content is paraphrased below. His given name is illegible, but we know that his courtesy name was Wantong 萬通, said to come from Chang'an 長安 of Yongzhou 雍州. His remote ancestors stemmed from the state of Anxi 安息, which at this time probably referred to Bukhārā.[75] In the early Northern Wei, his great-grandfather Dan 但 was sent as envoy to the court, where he was appointed at an office that is illegible but was of rank 3 and was active as great

on the left in April 623 CE, until February 626 CE. See *Jiu Tangshu* 57.2285–89, *Xin Tangshu* 1.6, 16, 19.

72 *Jiu Tangshu* 57.2289.

73 This is the transcription found in the *Quan Tang wen* buyi vol. 2.129–30.; transcriptions of passages of the epitaph were made by: Luo Feng, "Sabao: Zai kaocha," 217; and: He Zicheng, "Tang muzhiming zhaji," 59. The latter was not used due to disagreement.

74 Luo Feng reads here *Jing tao Chang'an ren ye* "京兆長安人也", without providing a comment. He says, however, that his transcription is based on a facsimile of the epitaph stored in the Shaanxi Province Museum (Luo Feng, "Sabao: Zai kaocha," 217, 242, fn. 13).

75 See the glossary for information.

sabao 薩寶. It is said that many of his sons and grandsons were made officials. His grandfather was appointed as dynasty-founding district duke of Huayin 華陰 and regional inspector of Shanzhou 鄯州, probably under the Western Wei or Northern Zhou. His father, called Xun 巡, held the offices of senior great general unequalled in honour and court gentleman for thorough counsel of the Sui. Wantong 萬通 fell into disgrace in 596 CE and was finally rehabilitated in 607 CE. At the beginning of the Tang, he occupied an office of rank 5. He had two wives and died at the age of 68. He was buried on Yonghui 永徽 5/2/1 (22.2.654 CE), west of Chang'an 長安 on the Longshou 龍首 Plain. If we assume that he died the year before, he was born in ca. 585 CE.

3.2.2.18 Kang Yuanjing 康元敬 (609–73 CE)

Below a selection of the relevant passages:[76]

Cover: Not available

Epitaph: 唐故處士康君墓誌[□□□□□□□□□□□□□□□]/君諱元敬，字留師，相州安陽人也。原夫吹律命氏，其先[肇]自[康]/居畢萬之後。因從孝文，遂居於鄴。祖樂，魏驃騎大將軍，又遷徐/州諸軍事。父仵相，齊九州摩訶大薩寶，尋改授龍驤將軍。……

Epitaph: Epitaph of Privatier[77] late master Kang 康 of the Great Tang. The master's taboo [was] Yuanjing 元敬, [his] courtesy name Liushi 留師, he [came from] Anyang 安陽 of Xiangzhou 相州. Originally flautists, [his forefathers were] bestowed a surname [from the emperor]. [His] ancestors originally came from Kangju 康居 [and were] descendants of Bi Wan 畢萬.[78] [Later, they came to] follow (Emperor) Xiaowen 孝文 and therefore came to reside in Ye 鄴. [His] grandfather [was] Le 樂, cavalry general-in-chief of the Wei,[79] sent to [preside over the] military matters of Xuzhou 徐州. [His] father

76 Author's transcription of the epitaph from the rubbing, to be found in: Luoyang shi wenwu gongzuodui, *Luoyang muzhi jisheng*, 330; and: Beijing tushuguan jinshizu, *Beijing tushuguan, Tang (15)*, 193; another transcription is to be found in: Zhou Shaoliang and Zhao Chao, *Tangdai muzhi*, 571–72. The additions are drawn from the transcription in: ibid.

77 Later in the epitaph, we know that he was awarded the title of *gong shi* 公士 (grandee of the first order). This was the lowest nobility title of the 20 titles that existed since the Qin, awarded for exceptionally meritorious military exploits. Although in most dictionaries it is said that the title was common only in Qin, Han and Song, we know from the *Beishi* 3.110 that it was in use during the Northern Wei. Kang 康 received the title of *chu shi* 處士 (privatier), as mentioned in the first column.

78 After Zhou Gao 周高 (son of a concubine of King Wen 文 of the Zhou) helped King Wu 武 to conquer the Shang, he was enfeoffed with the territory of Bi 畢. In consequence, he and his descendents received the surname Bi 畢, becoming the Duke Gao 高 of Bi 畢. After the fief came to an end, they became commoners again. As the *Shiji* informs us, while some family members stayed in China, others moved to the "barbarians" (*yi di* 夷狄). A famous descendant was the named Bi Wan 畢萬, an important official of the Jin 晉 during the Spring and Autumn period (771–476 BCE). During the Warring States period, he became the founding father of the Wei. See: *Shiji* 44.1835–64; and for a short overview: Zhang Ke, *Shiji*, 27.

79 Which can either mean the Northern Wei or Eastern Wei.

> was Wuxiang 仵相, great grand *sabao* 薩寶 of 'Jiuzhou 九州' of the Qi[80] [and was] soon later appointed as dragon horse general. (…)
>
> 君光應朝命，徙居河洛，即□[81]□土圭之鄉，洛州陽城人也。……授君爲公士。……瘵疾彌留溘先朝/露。春秋六十有□，五月七日壬辰卒於私第陶化里。以咸亨四/年五月景戌朔廿九日甲寅遷厝[於]河南北邙平樂鄉……。子宋生……。
>
> Master (Yuanjing 元敬) followed the order of the (Tang) court and went to reside in [Luoyang 洛陽],[82] … in the hamlet Tugui 土圭, as resident of Yangcheng 陽城 of Luozhou 洛州. (…) [He then was] made grandee of the first order. (…) [Being affected by a] chronic sickness [he] departed too early. At the age of [over] 60,[83] on (Xianheng 咸亨 4)[84]/5/7 [*renchen*] (28.5.673 CE),[85] [he] passed away in [his] private residence in the Taohua 陶化 Hamlet.[86] On Xianheng 咸亨 4/5 [*bing*[87]*xu*]/29 [*jiayin*] (19.6.673 CE) [he was] reburied in the Pingle 平樂 Town, on the Beimang 北邙, Henan 河南. (…) [His] son [is] Songsheng 宋生. (…)

As in the case of Cao Yi 曹怡,[88] due to his name and statement that his ancestors stemmed from Kangju 康居, it is rather safe to say that they were of Sogdian descent. This being the case, the constructed affiliation with Bi Wan 畢萬 – founder of the Wei – alleges that they were part of the descendants of Duke Gao 高 of Bi 畢 of the ancient Zhou dynasty which once resided with the "barbarians" and then "came back" to China.[89] It is thus most probably another example of a historical construction to enhance their prestige.

80 As "*Jiuzhou* 九州" would mean "the whole country", Rong Xinjiang proposed that Kang Yuanjing 康元敬 was great-grand *sabao* (*mahe da sabao* 摩訶大薩寶) of the capital of the Northern Qi, that is Ye 鄴, and at the same time of the whole country. I believe this describes him holding office in the capital (Rong Xinjiang 荣新江, *Zhonggu Zhongguo yu wailai wenming*, 100; Rong Xinjiang, "Beichao Sui Tang Suteren bu kao (Zhonggu Zhongguo)," 37). According to the size of the prefecture his rank may have ranged from 3a to 3b.

81 Zhou Shaoliang proposed that this character is *bian* 编 (Zhou Shaoliang and Zhao Chao, *Tangdai muzhi*, 572).

82 Originally Heluo 河洛, another name for Luoyang 洛陽.

83 At least 60, the character is illegible.

84 See below the date of the burying, assuming he was not buried more than a year later.

85 He was thus born around the year 608 CE (taking 65 as a middle number between 60 and 70).

86 Of Luoyang 洛陽. This can be asserted by a quote from the epitaph *Taipuqing shangzhuguo Huarong xian nan wangfujun muzhiming* 太僕卿上柱國華容縣男王府君墓誌銘, to be found in the *Wenyuan yinghua* Vol.12.940.4a.5878, and in a passage on Zhang Xiucai 張秀才 in the *Taiping guangji* Vol.8.370.2941.

87 *Jing* 景 in the original text is to be read as *bing* 丙, which was tabooed based on its similarity to Li Bing 李昞, father of Tang Gaozu 唐高祖.

88 See p. 161 (2.3.2.14).

89 See p. 256 fn. 78.

3.2.2.19 Mi Sabao 米薩寶 *(678–742 CE)*

This epitaph was excavated in Xi'an 西安 in the 1930s. It is heavily fragmented and is available in the reconstruction of Xiang Da:[90]

> 唐故米國大首領米公墓志銘并序
>
> 公諱薩寶，米國人也。生於西垂，心懷□土。忠（？）志（？）等□□陰陽烈石，剛柔叙（？）德（？）。崇心經律，志行玄（？）門（？）。□苦海以逃名，望愛何而□肩（？）。□□天寶元年二月十一日□長安縣崇化里，春秋六十有五，終於私第。時也天寶三載正[月]廿六日窆於高陵原，禮也。嗣妻（？）子（？）等□喪（？）戚（？）不朽。銘曰：滔滔米君，□□□□，榆（？）楊（？）□□□□□□法心匪固（？），□□沉良。逝川忽逝，长夜永□。
> □维天寶三載正月廿六日。

Mi Sabao 米薩寶 is said to have come from the state of Mi 米 (Māymurgh). He was born in the west border region. He had at least one male child and passed away in his private residence on Tianbao 天寶 1/2/11 (22.3.742 CE) in the Chonghua 崇化 Hamlet in the Chang'an 長安 District, at the age of 64. About two years later, on Tianbao 天寶 3/1/26 (14.2.744 CE), he was reburied in the Gaoling 高陵 Plain.

There is a long-running discussion if the term *sabao* 薩寶 in the inscription is referring to Mi's 米 title, rather than his name, started by comments of Xiang Da in 1932.[91] No strong argument stands in favour of this theory, as *hui* 諱 is most typical for the introduction of the taboo of the deceased. Besides that, Buddhist expressions such as *jinglü* 經律 (*sūtras* and *vinaya*) and *kuhai* 苦海 ("ocean of misery", Skt. *duḥkha-sāgara*) are used, strengthening the assumption that Mi 米 was a Buddhist practitioner, which matches with the Buddhist meaning of the word *sabao* 薩寶, as seen above.[92]

3.2.3 Steles

3.2.3.1 Buddhist donative inscriptions in Prakrit

Buddhist donative inscriptions, composed in various regional Prakrits, provide seven passages in which the title *sārthavāha* is used in combination with the name of a donor.[93] That donors actively defined themselves as such is strong evidence for the

90 I added only the *yue* 月 in square brackets to the version of Xiang Da (Xiang Da, *Tangdai Chang'an*, 84–85).

91 For an article still in favour of understanding it as a name, see: Luo Feng, "Sabao: Zai kaocha," 222–23 (*apud*: He Sui and Xiang Da, "Tang Mi gong").

92 Although one could advance the rather weak argument that these expressions were already of common usage. See also: Dien, "Sa-Pao Problem," 37, fn. 37; Dien, "Further Thoughts," 204.

93 Sarn 192 and 197 (ca. 3–2 c. BC), Math 124 (dated to Kaniṣka 4, 131 CE, taking 127 CE as date of reference the inauguration of Kanishka I, as established by: Falk, "Yuga"), Kuda 25, 28, and 29 (ca. 180–230 CE): Tsukamoto Keisho, *Indo*, 481–82, 688, 931; and: Schopen, "Inscription," 101 (which is a newer edition of Math 79: Tsukamoto Keisho, *Indo*, 666); dated to Huviṣka 26,

exceptional status this group enjoyed. Furthermore, the increase of donations as substantiated by these inscriptions from the early second century CE and the focus on the donors provides evidence of the growing importance of caravans and trade on these roads.

3.2.3.1.1 Stele of Wang Huilüe 王惠略 *and more than 50 others (547 CE)*

As Dien pointed out,[94] the stele that was dedicated on Wuding 武定 5/7/3 (4.8.547 CE) of the Eastern Wei and in catalogues is referred to as "the stele of Wang Huilüe 王惠略 and more than 50 other Buddhist followers",[95] recalls their donation of a Buddha statue or *stūpa*.[96] Among the names of the donors is Wang Sabao 王薩寶, which provides further evidence that Sabao 薩寶 was used as a given name for Buddhists, possibly referring to a *bodhisattva* or *buddha*, as shown above.

3.2.3.1.2 Stele of Qi Faqi 歧法起 *(550 CE)*

On Datong 大統 16/9/1 (27.9.550 CE), the devotee Qi Faqi 歧法起 donated this stele with eight other people – among them a certain Qi Sabao 歧薩保 – to his parents.[97] This provides further evidence for the use of Sabao 薩保 as a given name for Buddhists.

3.2.3.1.3 Stele of Ye Rong 葉容 *and others (554 CE)*[98]

This Buddhist stele was dedicated on Tianbao 天保 5 [*jiawu*], 5 [*bingchen*], 2 [*dingji*] (18.5.554 CE), of the Northern Qi. Among the many names of donors is a certain devotee Gu Sabao 古薩寶. This is another example for the use of this word as a personal name for a Buddhist.

i.e. 153 CE. In the inscription Sarn 197, the name is no longer extant but its declination in the genitive demands that it be understood as an appellation for the donor of the epigraph.

94 Dien, "Further Thoughts," 204, fn. 11.

95 Fifty-one, to be exact.

96 See the Tōyō bunko, where it is referred to as *Wang Huilüe deng si dizi heyi wushi ren zaoxiangji* 王惠略等仏弟子合邑五十人造像記, under the catalogue number II-16-C-1072, accessible here: Tōyō bunko, "Tōyō bunko" http://124.33.215.236/shoshiallsrch/show_detail_allsyoshi.php?targetid=567486.
Or the catalogue of the Shukutoku University 淑徳大学, where it is referred to as *Wang Huilüe deng wushi ren zaotaji* 王惠略等五十人造塔記, under the number s054_8405 or 北図 6-142, accessible with a low-quality facsimile of the rubbing: Shukutoku University 淑徳大学, "Wang Huilüe zaotaji" http://www.shukutoku.ac.jp/shisetsu/takuhon/tougi/s054_8405.jpg.

97 For a transcription, see: Wang Chang, *Jinshi cuibian*, 32.5; and: Yan Kejun, *Quan*, 55.3790a; and for a rubbing of one side: Rong Xinjiang, *Zhonggu Zhongguo yu Sute wenming*, 243, fig. 2.

98 Stored in the Municipal Museum of Xinxiang 新鄉, Henan. See: Yen Chuan-ying, *Selections*, 146–47.

3.2.3.1.4 Stele of Liu 劉 and others (557–58 CE)[99]

This large Buddhist stele was dedicated in the *dingchou* 丁丑 year of the Tianbao 天保 era (557–58 CE) of the Northern Qi. Among the names of the dozens of donors is a certain devotee Liu Sabao 劉薩保. This is an additional example for the use of this word as a personal Buddhist name. Due to the temporal vicinity with the abovementioned steles, it is safe to say that Sabao 薩保 and Sabao 薩寶 were two different ways to write the same name.

3.2.3.1.5 Stele of Hui Yu 惠鬱, Xuan Ning 玄凝 and others (585 CE)

Below a selection of the relevant passages:[100]

> [□□]大隋開皇五年歲次乙巳八月乙酉朔十日己亥，前/[□□]定州沙門都、故魏七帝舊寺主惠鬱、像主玄凝等，以先/師僧暈法，太和十六年敬造三丈八彌勒金像。至後周建德/六年歲次丁酉破滅大象，僧尼還俗。…… 但周將滅/中[101]即禪位。
>
> On Kaihuang 開皇 5 [*yisi*]/8 [*yiyou*]/10 [*jihai*] (9.9.585 CE) of the Great Sui, the former head monk[102] of Dingzhou 定州, Hui Yu 惠鬱, the head of the old 'Seven Emperors Temple' of the Wei, [103] [the temple's] statues director Xuan Ning 玄凝, and others; for the master of an older generation, the monk Yun Fa 暈法, [who] erected a 3 *zhang*, 8 [*chi* high (ca. 1.1 m)] golden Maitreya statue in Taihe 太和 16 (492 CE).[104] In Jiande 建德 6 [*dingyou*] of the [Northern] Zhou (577 CE), the great statue was destroyed [and] monks and nuns were returned to laity. (…) But, the [Northern] Zhou were vanquished and had to abdicate.
>
> 大隋國帝主楊堅建元開皇。…… 佛法/爲首。惠鬱共弟子玄凝等，願欲修理本寺，願[105]復前像。舊處屬/他，悲號無及，黍離之詠，泣誦心口。賴摩訶檀越前定州贊治、/ 並州懋[106]營府戶曹叅軍、博陵人崔子石、前薩甫下司錄商人/何永康二人，同贖得七帝寺院，價等布金，貴餘祇樹，一發□/□，□心俱施，并為俗寺主。

99 Stored in the temple dedicated to this stele in Xi Liu bei 西劉碑 (West Liu Stele) village, Dengfeng 登封, Henan. See: ibid., 159–60.

100 Author's transcription from the rubbing, to be found in: Beijing tushuguan jinshizu, *Beijing tushuguan, Sui (9)*, 25. Rong Xinjiang commented on some of the content, which is, however, unreliable (Rong Xinjiang and Zhang Zhiqing, *Cong Sama'ergan*, 107).

101 I am not quite sure about this character.

102 Emperor Wen 文 of the Sui created a bureaucratic system for the monks in the capital and in the provinces, the *shamendu* 沙門都 being on the provincial level (Tang Jiahong, *Zhongguo gudai dianzhang zhidu*, 663–64). See: Ding Fubao, *Foxue da cidian*, 600.3.

103 Referring to the Emperors Daowu 道武, Wenyuan 明元, Taiwu 太武, Jingmu 景穆, Wencheng 文成, Xianwen 獻文 and Xiaowen 孝文.

104 See p. 37 fn. 140.

105 I am not completely sure about this character.

106 The reading of the character is unclear, it resembles: 懋, 悉 (a variant of it), or 懇.

> Emperor Yang Jian 楊堅 of the Great Sui initiated the Kaihuang 開皇 (era in 581 CE). (…) Buddhism was made the chief [religion]. Hui Yu 惠鬱, together with the disciple Xuan Ning 玄凝 and others, desired to repair the temple [and] restore it to [it's] ancient appearance. The old site belonged to someone else [and thus they] wailed that it was too late, [like] the lament of Shuli 黍離[107] [and] wept and lamented [from their] hearts and mouths. [They] relied on *mahā-dānapatis** (great chief donors): the two men, the former administrative aid[108] of Dingzhou 定州, the bodyguard of the ministry's headquarters general's office of Bingzhou 並州, Cui Zishi 崔子石 from Boling 博陵,[109] and the merchant and former lower record keeper of the *safu* 薩甫,[110] He Yongkang 何永康, [who] together made the expenses for the success of the Seven Emperors Temple, including cloth and gold, in value largely sufficient for the temple, … [their] hearts entirely devoted, both were head laymen.

This episode conflicts with the information of the *Suishu*:[111] according to this stele, there existed a *safu* 薩甫 office during the Sui, whereas the *Suishu* says it was during the Northern Qi. Another novelty is the existence of a junior record keeper (*xia silu* 下司錄). The latter might have been turned into the scribe (*shi* 史 or *zhangshi* 長史, of the same rank) during the Tang.[112] One of the donors, He Yongkang 何永康, is qualified as a merchant, a quite unique statement from the point of view of the official doctrine's stigma on this profession, which on the stele seems however relevant to explain his financial wealth and was part of his appellation. As his Sogdian origin can be deduced from his name (He 何, Kushaniyya) with some probability, it can be established that Sogdians could simultaneously occupy an office in the bureaucracy and act as merchants. Unlike Luo Feng, who affirmed on this basis the religious freedom of the officers, I would rather prefer to observe that a Sogdian merchant, acting in the bureau as record keeper, was supporting Buddhism financially.[113]

107 This chapter of the *Shijing* (*guofeng* 國風) contains pieces grieving the Zhou dynasty. It was later commonly used to refer to the grief about a lost kingdom.

108 Rank 5a, according to the size of Dingzhou 定州.

109 Most probably from the famous Cui 崔 clan of Boling 博陵.

110 Dien wrote: "In 578 He Yongkang 何永康 who had been *sa fu xia silu shangren* (Junior Recorder of Merchants in the *Safu* [Bureau]) during the Northern Qi (…)" (Dien, "Further Thoughts," 204). On the basis of the inscription it seems clear to me that he occupied his office during the Kaihuang 開皇 era of the Sui (581–600 CE), when reconstruction efforts were carried out after the reappraisal of Buddhism. There is, however, the possibility that he occupied the office before.

111 See p. 268 (3.2.4.4).

112 See p. 291 (3.2.5.3.2).

113 Luo Feng, "Sabao: Zai kaocha," 239.

3.2.3.1.6 Fragment of a stele from a family member of the An 安 family, Sui–Tang

As proposed by Yamashita Shōji,[114] a stele known to us from the *Wenguan cilin* and kept in the Tenri Central Library 天理圖書館 provides another occurrence of a person with the *sabao* 薩寶 office. The beginning and end of the inscription are unavailable, but shortly after the missing introduction (which most probably provided the name of the deceased, his titles and offices, choronym, and remote ancestry) it states:[115]

> 祖諱，魏雍州薩寶。父諱，隋開府儀同三司、貴鄉縣開國公、贈石州刺史。
>
> [His] grandfather [was] ?, *sabao* 薩寶 of Yongzhou 雍州 during the Wei. [His] father [was] ?, during the Sui commander unequalled in honour, dynasty-founding district duke[116] of Guixiang 貴鄉, and posthumously [appointed] prefect of Shizhou 石州.

These exact titles can be found for An Luo 安羅 on the epitaph of An Yuanshou 安元壽 (607–83 CE), and for An Luo Fangda 安羅方大 on the stele of An Zhongjing 安忠敬 (661–726 CE), which are two different names for the father of An Xinggui 安興貴. We can therefore safely assume that this is the stele of a member of this An 安 family.[117]

3.2.3.1.7 Parenthesis: The sabao 薩寶 *of the An 安 family*

Based on the information in the *Jiu Tangshu*,[118] the *Xin Tangshu*,[119] and the *Yuanhe Xingzuan*,[120] the stele fragment, the epitaphs of An Yuanshou 安元壽 (ca. 607–83 CE) and his wife Di Liuniang 翟六娘 (ca. 610–98 CE),[121] and the stele of An Zhongjing 安忠敬 (ca. 661–726 CE),[122] a table could be compiled focused on the

114 Yamashita Shōji, “Zui Tō”.

115 *Wenguan cilin* 173–74.

116 Referring to the title of dynasty-founding district duke (*kai guo xian gong* 開國縣公), as the district is specified immediately before the title.

117 For more on this topic, see the parenthesis below.

118 The passage of the *Jiu Tangshu* 132.3645 is not integrated as source in the table, as it doesn’t provide additional information: 李抱玉，武德功臣安興貴之裔。 “Li Baoyu 李抱玉: descendant of the Meritorious Minister of Military Virtue An Xinggui 安興貴.”

119 *Xin Tangshu* 59.1536, *Xin Tangshu* 75b.3445–46 (see above p. 273; 3.2.4.8), and *Xin Tangshu* 138.4619–20.

120 *Yuanhe Xingzuan* vol. 1, 500–3, see p. 269 (3.2.4.5).

121 For an excellent facsimile, see: He Bingwu, *Ashina*, 63–111; the content is also to be found in the *Quan Tang wen bu yi* 1.68; for a discussion of the content of the epitaph, see: Wu Zhigong, “An Yuanshou muzhiming”; for a further discussion on the information provided by both epitaphs, see: Chen Zhijian, “An Yuanshou”; for the excavation report of the grave, in which a partial transcription of her epitaph is also included, see: Zhaoling bowuguan and Chen Zhijian, “Tang An Yuanshou”.

122 This stele was composed by the Great Minister Zhang Yue 張悅 (667–730 CE), whose collected works are available to us only in collections. The inscription of the epitaph is to be found in different works under different titles, e.g. *Hexi jiedu fudashi An gong beiming bingxu* 河西節度副大使安公碑銘並序 (stele inscription with addendum of master An 安, Military

earlier generations of the An 安 family, of whom some were known to have occupied the office of *sabao* 薩寶, presented in Appendix 4.2.[123] There are, however, some inconsistencies and questions that shall be pointed out and corrected to then advance further reflections on the *sabao*.

On the stele and in the *Yuanhe Xingzuan*, it is said that An Xinggui 安興貴 was the grandfather of An Chongjing 安重敬, whereas in the genealogical table of *Xin Tangshu* 75b, he is listed as his great-grandfather. On the stele, in the *Yuanhe Xingzuan*, and in *Xin Tangshu* 75b, it is recorded, on the other hand, that An Chongzhang 安重璋 (Li Baoyu 李抱玉) was the son of An Chongjing 安重敬. Further, on the stele, in the *Yuanhe Xingzuan*, and in the *Xin Tangshu* 138, An Xinggui 安興貴 is recorded as the grandfather of An Chongjing 安重敬, whereas in the genealogical table of *Xin Tangshu* 75b, he is listed as his great-grandfather. Although this already points to a misunderstanding in the genealogical table, another provides further information to solve this inconsistency.

In *Xin Tangshu* 59, An Wencheng 安文成 is recorded as the son of An Xinggui 安興貴, whereas in the genealogical table of *Xin Tangshu* 75b, An Heng'an 安恆安 is recorded as the son, and An Wencheng 安文 as the grandson of An Xinggui 安興貴. Finally, the *Yuanhe Xingzuan* informs us that Heng'an 安恆安 and a certain An Shengcheng 安生成 were the two sons of An Xinggui 安興貴. The name An Shengcheng 安生成 caused probably the confusion: The text of the *Yuanhe Xingzuan* reads: 生恆安、生成 "[He] begot Heng'an 恆安 [and] Shengcheng 生成". However, another reading of the passage would be: 生恆安，生成 "[He] begot Heng'an 恆安. [Heng'an 恆安] begot Cheng 成". The latter reading may have led the compiler of the genealogical table of *Xin Tangshu* 75b to understand the two as being son and grandson, although it is recorded otherwise in *Xin Tangshu* 59. In *Cefu yuangui* 131, Wencheng 文成 is similarly named as Li Baoyu's 李抱玉 grandfather.[124] It is therefore safe to believe that An [Sheng]cheng 安[生]成 is An Wencheng 安文成. Therefore, the following correction can be applied: The three last generations mentioned in the genealogical table of the *Xin Tangshu* 75b can be moved one line upwards in the table of Appendix 4.2, An Wencheng 安文成 being the younger brother of An Heng'an 安恆安.

The next step is to ascertain that the An 安 mentioned in the steles correspond with the An 安 family in the *Xin Tangshu* and the *Yuanhe Xingzuan*. There are three points that underpin this assumption:

Vice Commissioner-in-chief of Hexi 河西): Zhang Yan gong ji 張燕公集, 16.102–3, or in the *Quan Tang wen* 230.2946–47. For a comment on these, see: Forte, *Hostage An Shigao*, 45, fn. 6.

123 This is based Forte's magisterial work: ibid., 17–28, 45–53. There are more sources on this family, which need not be discussed here. For more information see: ibid. In his own article about the *sabao* 薩寶, this information does not resurface, for reasons that I ignore (Forte, "Sabao 薩寶 Question").

124 大曆……四年三月(11.4–10.5.769 CE)……李抱玉祖左武衛郎將文成爲吏部尚書。 *Cefu yuangui* 131.10a.1574b: Wang Qinruo, *Cefu yuangui 2*, 1574–75.
For further discussion, see: Forte, *Hostage An Shigao*, 48, fn. 15.

- An Xinggui 安興貴 is mentioned as the grandfather of An Zhongjing 安忠敬 on his stele, as well as in *Xin Tangshu* 75b (corrected as explained above) and the *Yuanhe Xingzuan*.
- An Chongzhang 安重璋 (Li Baoyu 李抱玉) is mentioned as son of An Zhongjing 安忠敬 on his stele, as well as in *Xin Tangshu* 75b, and as great-grandson of An Xinggui 安興貴 in the *Xin Tangshu* 138 and the *Yuanhe Xingzuan*.
- The titles mentioned for An Chongzhang 安重璋 (Li Baoyu 李抱玉) on the stele of An Zhongjing 安忠敬 correspond to the ones in *Xin Tangshu* 75b almost completely.

Some names can thus be matched:

- An Nantuo 安難陀 = An Xue Wuzheng 安薛晤徵.
  It is possible that the information is corrupted or that the two names may have a similar meaning in Sogdian.
- An He Zangqi 安何藏器 = An Bi 安弼.
- This difference may be due to the character *bi* 弼 representing a corrupted version of *qi* 器, or vice-versa, as they are, in certain variant forms, rather similar.
- An Pansuoluo (Panshaluo?) 安盤娑羅 = An Poluo 安婆羅 = An Luo Fangfa 安羅方大.
  Judging from this name, it seems as if Luo 羅 was the Sogdian part of his name, whereas Fangda 方大 was his Chinese name or a style. As for the difference between *suo* (*sha*?) 娑 and *po* 婆, based on the similarity of the characters, the simplest explanation would be an error during the process of copying, due to poor legibility or writing.
- An Yuanshou 安元壽 = An Heng'an 安恆安?
  This is to be derived from combining the epitaph of An Yuanshou 安元壽, the *Yuanhe Xingzuan*, and *Xin Tangshu* 75b. The table of *Xin Tangshu* 75b, contains, however, obvious corruptions, as An Yongshou 安永壽 – a person with a very similar name – is listed as son of An Xiuren 安脩仁 instead of being listed as son of the latter's cadet brother of An Xinggui 安興貴. The epitaph is to be preferred to the transmitted sources. A last, rather improbable possibility is to match An Yuanshou 安元壽 with An Yuanbiao 安元表.
- An Wencheng 安文成 = An [Sheng]cheng 安[生]成
  See the explanation in the text above.

Finally, the question of the fragmentary stele shall be addressed: Either it is the stele of An Xinggui 安興貴, or of An Xiuren 安修仁, or of another, otherwise unknown, son of An Pansuoluo (Panshaluo?) 安盤娑羅/An Poluo 安婆羅/An Luo Fangfa 安羅方大. As the stele only recounts the career of the deceased until the Sui – in which he had an unfavourable start by serving the fourth son of the emperor that was disgraced in 602 CE – there is no definitive answer to this problem. It is also conceivable that the deceased had an important career during the Tang, as his father was posthumously awarded an honorary title – which is often the result of the career of one of the sons, and, last but not least, because someone erected a stele to remember him.[125]

As can be seen in the above analysis, the often-neglected offices, toponyms, and choronyms, provide us with crucial material for prosopographical research. As the correspondences between these sources have now been established, what remains to be considered are the results for the *sabao* office. Whereas the table of *Xin Tangshu* 75b states that An Pansuoluo (Panshaluo?) 安盤娑羅/An Poluo 安婆羅/An Luo Fangfa 安羅方大 was *sabao* 薩寶 in Wuwei 武威 of Liangzhou 涼州, the *Yuanhe Xingzuan* says that there were three generations of *sabao* 薩寶 in Guzang 姑藏 (Wuwei 武威) of Liangzhou 涼州 of which he would be the last one, and the fragmentary stele informs us that the An 安 of the second generation was *sabao* 薩寶 of Yongzhou 雍州. Again, the far more detailed information found on the stele is to be privileged in the analysis, as the *Yuanhe Xingzuan* was completed in 812 CE and the *Xin Tangshu* was compiled during the Song. The latter two do not provide information for the second generation but maybe relied on a similar source – although the names differ. The passage of the *Yuanhe Xingzuan* – which has been shown to be corrupted – is conceivably mistaken in stating that the three generations from An Nantuo 安難陀 to An Pansuoluo (Panshaluo?) 安盤娑羅 were all *sabao* 薩寶 of Guzang 姑藏, Liangzhou 涼州. The information was probably further corrupted, as the table of the *Xin Tangshu* only mentions An Poluo 安婆羅 as *sabao* 薩寶 of Wuwei 武威, Liangzhou 涼州. It is highly improbable that the fragmentary stele would neglect to mention that the father of the deceased was appointed *sabao* 薩寶, especially since it is mentioned for the grandfather. Furthermore, the stele says that the grandfather was *sabao* 薩寶 of Yongzhou 雍州, indicating that the family moved to the capital no later than during (probably the Western) Wei and possibly they had already moved during the great-grandfather's time.

To conclude, it is conceivable that during the Northern Wei, An Nantuo 安難陀/An Xue Wuzheng 安薛晤徵 lived in Guzang 姑藏, Liangzhou 涼州, and served as *sabao* 薩寶, and his family moved during his or his son's lifetime to Yongzhou 雍州 (the capital), where the son, An He Zangqi 安何藏器/An Bi 安弼 was *sabao* 薩寶 of Yongzhou 雍州 during the Western Wei and possibly even Northern Zhou – as the stele of An Zhongjing 安忠敬 and the epitaph of An Yuanshou 安元壽 probably hint at. His son, An Pansuoluo (Panshaluo?) 安盤娑羅/An Poluo 安婆羅/ An Luo Fangfa 安羅方大 was not *sabao* 薩寶.

3.2.4 Historically transmitted texts

3.2.4.1 Buddhist texts

The first occurrence of *mahasārthavāha* (great caravan leader) as one of the epithets of the Buddha appears around the mid to late first century CE.[126] In Buddhist stories,

125 See p. 153 fn. 154.
126 Hinüber, *Beiträge*, 22, 4b; and: Salomon, "Inscription," 264, 4b.

bodhisattvas are often compared to these caravan leaders, likening the role of these spiritual guides to caravan leaders in directing their disciples along perilous roads to a safe haven.[127] Typically, they refer to actual caravans coming to monasteries to pray for safe travel, with demons being among the typically feared dangers of the road. In Chinese translations of Buddhist texts, the term *sārthavāha* is both variously translated – *daoshi* 導師 (teacher), *guke* 估客 (merchant), *gukezhu* 賈客主 (merchant leader), *shangzhu* 商主 (merchant leader or simply merchant) and *da shangzhu* 大商主 (great merchant leader or simply great merchant), and *shidao* 世導 (leader) – and transcribed – *satuopo* 薩陀婆 (EMC **sat da ba*) and *da* 大 (great) *satuopo* 薩陀婆, *satapo* 薩他婆 (EMC **sat t*^{h}*a ba*) and *da* 大 (great) *satapo* 薩他婆, and *satapohe* 薩他婆訶 (EMC **sat t*^{h}*a ba xa*).[128] Chinese Buddhist texts also started transcribing *sārthavāha* as *sabo* 薩薄 (EMC **sat bak*). The earliest mentions may be found in the *Fo shuo xing qixing jing* 佛說興起行經 (*Sūtra on Causes and Conditions*).[129] Although traditionally the text is attributed to Kang Mengxiang 康孟詳, who was probably Sogdian[130] and lived at end of the second century CE,[131] following Nattier's research,[132] this attribution is now questionable and it is safer to date the earliest known occurrences to texts as late as the fourth century, e.g. in the *Peihua jing* 裴華經 (*Karuṇāpuṇḍarīka sūtra*),[133] attributed to Danwuchan 曇無讖 (Dharmakṣema, 385–433 CE), or the *Fo shuo luomaqie jing* 佛說羅摩伽經 (*Gaṇḍavyūha sūtra*),[134] translated by Shengjian 聖堅 probably between 389 and 406 CE. As for the other translations listed above, one also encounters the prefixed title of *da sabo* 大薩薄 (great *sabo*).[135] The *Xian'yu jing* 賢愚經 (Sūtra *of the Wise and the Fool*),[136] which was rendered into Chinese in 445 CE,[137] provides a good example, including two occurrences of a *sabo* 薩薄 leading a group of 500 merchants over sea.[138] In the

127 Dien, "Sa-Pao Problem," 338, and fn. 33.
See e.g.: T9.548b09/T10.504a15; T25.277b15–18; T8.907b14–16; T10.183b14–25; T10.684c12–13; T16.229b19–c13. In T15.640b14 the term *sabo* 薩薄 is even used as synonym for bodhisattva.

128 A short search in the Chinese Tripitaka will validate this statement. For some examples, see: Rong Xinjiang, "Sabao yu Sabo: Beichao," 137.

129 Thirteen occurrences: T4.169c07–170a19. See: Dien, "Sa-Pao Problem," 336; Dien, "Consideration," table 1.

130 It is said that his forebears came from Kangju 康居. For more information, see: Nattier, *Guide*, 102–9.

131 "(…) [I]t should be noted that prior to Kang Mengxiang, Lokakṣema transcribed sārthavāha, which is part of the name of the bodhisathva Mahāsusārthavāha, as *sahe* 薩和." Forte, "Sabao 薩寶 Question," 86. The Chinese transcription of his name is Mahexusahe 摩訶須薩和.

132 She did not include it in her list of safely attributed texts: Nattier, *Guide*, 104–9, 177.

133 T3.227a20.

134 T10.863c19.

135 T4.422a11; and in four versions of the same story: T4.378b05, T53.189a24, 443a18, and T54.62b20.

136 T202:4.352b19–353b16.

137 See T2145:55.12c15: 宋元嘉二十二年出。 In Yuanqing 元嘉 22 of the (Liu) Song (445 CE)".

138 1) T04:0378b05: 爾時薩薄，欲入大海，貪戀此婦，不能捨離，即將入海，與五百估

Xu gaoseng zhuan 續高僧傳 (*Further Biographies of Eminent Monks*),[139] Xuanzang 玄奘 was also attributed the title *dashangzhu* 大商主 (great merchant-chief) by his 500 companions on his travel home:[140]

> 同伴五百皆共推奘為大商主。
>
> The 500 companions all together promoted him [the title of] "great merchant-chief".

In the *Foguoji* 佛國記, the accounts of the travels of Faxian 法線 in the late fourth century, *sabo shangren* 薩薄商人 is used to describe merchants in Sri Lanka.[141] To add a source of a different kind, the *Fan fanyu* 翻梵語 (*Translated Sanskrit Words*), a dictionary for Sanskrit, possibly compiled by the end of the fifth century, attributed to Baochang 寶唱, also provides an entry for *sabo* 薩薄 that reads:[142]

> 薩薄主。應云薩他婆， 譯日商估。
>
> *Sabo* 薩薄 chief. [One] should read "*sa-ta-po* 薩他婆" (EMC **sat tʰa ba*). The translation is "merchant".

As Forte points out, the translator consciously left out the meaning of "chief" or "leader" in his explanation, which might indicate that at this time, the term was already synonymous. [143] Finally, in two occurrences, Sabo 薩薄 is mentioned as what seems to be a personal name of a merchant in a story. In an *avadāna* of the *Jiu za piyu jing* 舊雜譬喻經 (*The Older Book of Parables*) of Kang Senghui 康僧會 (from 251 to 280 CE), a "merchant" (*shangren* 商人) is "being called" (*hao* 號) Sabo 薩薄;[144] and in the *Tian zun shuo Ayuwang piyu jing* 天尊說阿育王譬喻經 (*Sūtra of the Heavenly Venerated One of the parable of King Aśoka*, translated between 317 and 420 CE), a "great merchant" (*da guke* 大賈客) has the name (*ming* 名) Sabo 薩薄.[145] In both examples, Sabo 薩薄 is given as the name of a merchant (lit. a merchant named caravan leader), evidencing a misunderstanding and/or the necessity for clarification on the part of the translator. In either way, the term needed explanation at this time.

客，上船入海。時婦常以三奇木頭，擎鏡照面，自覩端正，便起憍慢，深生愛著。時有一大龜，以脚蹋船，船破沒海，薩薄及婦、五百估客，一切皆死。
2) T04:0422a26: 當于是時，有眾賈客，勸進薩薄，欲共入海，即答之曰：「為薩薄法，當辦船具；我今窮困，無所復有，何緣得從？」眾人報言：「我等眾人凡有五百，開意出錢，用辦船具。」聞是語已，即便許可。眾人許合，大獲金寶。爾時薩薄，以三千兩金，千兩辦船，千兩辦粮，千兩用俟船上所須，餘故大有給活妻子。
For more information and further references, see: Dien, "Sa-Pao Problem," 336, fn. 9.

139 Traditionally attributed to Dao Xuan 道宣 (596–667 CE).

140 T50:453a22. See also: Dien, "Sa-Pao Problem," 337–38, fn. 34.

141 *Gaoseng Faxian zhuan* 高僧法顯傳, T51.865a15. See: Dien, "Sa-Pao Problem," 336; and: Luo Feng, "Sabao: Zai kaocha," 226–29.

142 T54.1022a23. Author's translation. For more information, see: Forte, "Sabao 薩寶 Question," 86–87, fn. 33.

143 Ibid., 87.

144 T4.510b08, b28, c06, c27, 511a02.

145 T50.170c03, 04, 06, 07, 10.

To summarise, the term *sabo* 薩薄 was not only used as a personal name but often closely linked to merchant activities. If used in the second meaning, *sabo* 薩薄 is the title for a merchant leader, leading large groups of up to several hundred persons (the number 500 is not to be taken literally).[146] He is qualified by his leadership quality, combined with the knowledge of the topography and the ability to plan and provide the necessary means to fulfil the travel requirements. Therefore, the term was used in Buddhist literature in a metaphorical sense for Buddha and the *bodhisattvas*, leading their followers with knowledge and experience, eventually leading the world to enlightenment.

3.2.4.2 Weishu

In the *Weishu*, in the description of the Western Regions, we find that the capital of the state of Kang 康 (Samarqand) was on the Sabao 薩寶 River (Zerafshan).[147] Although the date of composition poses an issue,[148] it shall not be of much consequence for the present argument: Sabao 薩寶 is used as a toponym.

3.2.4.3 Zhoushu and Beishi

In the *Zhoushu*,[149] and the *Beishi*,[150] Sabao 薩保 occurs as the courtesy name of Yuwen Hu 宇文護 (513–72 CE)[151] – the courtesy name being a synonym of his given name (lit. protector). He was of Xianbei 鮮卑 descendance, part of the political and military elite, and very likely a Buddhist.[152] As will be shown later, he was by far not the only one to have such a name, whereas the switch from *bo* 薄 to *bao* 保 (meaning "to protect") might be explained either by changes in the common usage, due to the appealing meaning for the Buddhist context, as shown above, or to likeness with the Sogdian word.[153]

146 As nearly no number is given in Buddhism when counting the numerous qualities, followers etc.

147 See p. 28 (1.7.12).

148 See p. 75 (1.15.5).

149 *Zhoushu* 11.165–72.

150 Six times in: *Beishi* 57.2060–67.

151 See Dien, "Sa-Pao Problem," 341, 52; and Dien, "Further Thoughts," 204. For an annotated translation of the biography of Yuwen Hu 宇文護, see: Dien, *Biography of Yü-wen Hu*.

152 This sort of religious attribution is generally problematic and not highly informative. Today's picture of the theoretical improbable matching of Buddhism and other monotheistic and polytheistic religions – as Manichaeism and Zoroastrianism – might not be accurate. When Buddhism was gaining popularity in China, problematic aspects, like the cremation of the body, were partly circumvented and amalgamated forms as well as new schools of Buddhism emerged.
See: Dien, "Sa-Pao Problem," 342.

153 See also ibid., 343; and Dien, "Further Thoughts," 207.

3.2.4.4 Suishu

In the *Suishu*, in the section that lists the offices of the Northern Qi, *safu* 薩甫 is mentioned for the first time as an official title in a Chinese dynasty: [154]

> 鴻臚寺，掌蕃客朝會，吉凶弔祭。統典客、典寺、司儀等署令、丞。典客署，又有京邑薩甫二人，諸州薩甫一人。
>
> The court of state ceremonial is in charge of foreign guests visiting the court and offerings for auspicious in inauspicious [events]. [It] comprises the directors and aides of the Office of Receptions, the Supervisorate of Monasteries, and the Ceremonial Office. In the Office of Receptions there are further two *safu* 薩甫 for the capital (Ye 鄴) and one *safu* 薩甫 for each prefecture.

This quote suggests that during the Northern Qi, there were apparently two *safu* 薩甫 in the capital and one in every prefecture which were part of the Office of Receptions, which was itself part of the Court of State Ceremonial under the Ministry of Rites.

Further down in the *Suishu*, listing the appended ranks (*shi* 視) at the end of the list of offices of the Sui, we find a listing of two different kinds of *sabao* 薩保:[155]

> 又有流內視品十四等：……雍州薩保，爲視從七品。……諸州胡二百户已上薩保，爲視正九品。
>
> There are 14 appended ranks “inside the current”: the *sabao* 薩保 of Yongzhou 雍州, of the appended rank 7b. The *sabao* 薩保 [in charge of] 200 households or more in the prefectures are of the appended rank 9a.

3.2.4.5 Yuanhe Xingzuan

The *Yuanhe Xingzuan* features a passage on the clan name An 安, mentioning three generations of *sabao* 薩寶:[156]

> 安。……姑藏涼州。出自安[息][157]國，漢代遣子朝，[因][158]居涼土。後魏安難陀至孫盤娑羅，代居涼州，爲薩寶。生興貴，執李軌送京師，以功拜右武衛大將軍、歸國公。生恆安、生成。成生忠敬，右屯兵將軍。忠敬生抱玉，賜姓李氏……

154 *Suishu* 27.756; author’s translation. The “Chineseness” of this dynasty, as well as later ones, is debatable. See: Chen Sanping, *Multicultural China*, Chapter One; and: Abramson, “Deep Eyes, Constructing Ethnicity”.

155 *Suishu* 28.789–91; author’s translation.

156 *Yuanhe Xingzuan* 1.500–3. Author’s punctuation and translation. For a more extensive discussion, see: Forte, *Hostage An Shigao*, 17–22; Wu Yugui, “Liangzhou An shi jiazu”; and: Forte, “Kuwabara’s Misleading Thesis”.

157 The addition of this character is based on the corresponding passage of the *Xin Tangshu* 75b.3445–46 (see below).

158 Originallly *guo* 國. The exchange of characters is based on the corresponding passage of the *Xin Tangshu* 75b.3445–46 (see below).

> The An 安 [clan]. (…) [In] Guzang 姑臧 of Liangzhou 涼州. Stemming from the land of An[xi] 安[息] (Parthia), from which the son was sent to the court during the Han, [from] then [on] residing in the Liang 涼 Area (Liangzhou 涼州). [From] An Nantuo 安難陀 of the Later Wei up to his grandson (An) Pansuoluo (Panshaluo?) 盤娑羅,[159] for generations [they] resided in Liangzhou 涼州 [and] served as *sabao* 薩寶. [The latter] begot Xinggui 興貴. [He] seized Li Gui 李軌 and turned [him] over to the capital,[160] for which [he] was appointed as militant guard general-in-chief on the right and duke of the land of Gui 歸 (?). [He] begot Heng'an 恆安 and Shengcheng 生成. Cheng 成 begot Zhongjing 忠敬, guard general on the right. Zhongjing 忠敬 begot Baoyu 抱玉, who was awarded the surname Li 李 (…).

Kuwabara Jitsuzō calculated that An Nantuo 安難陀 held the office of *sabao* 薩寶 around 526–27 CE.[161] This quote also indicates that the office of a *sabao* 薩寶 might be hereditary, as allegedly at least three generations of the An 安 family held it consecutively. This will later be compared with other sources, and the discrepancies and conflicts discussed.

3.2.4.6 Jiu Tangshu

This information is partly corroborated (the commandant of the office is omitted) by the parallel passage in *Jiu Tangshu*, describing the rank system of the Tang, together with the changes that occurred:[162]

> 流內九品三十階之內，又有視流內起居，五品至從九品。初以薩寶府、親王國官及三師、三公、開府、嗣郡王、上柱國已下護軍已上勳官帶職事者府官等品。開元初，一切罷之。今唯有薩寶、[祆][163]正二官而已。

> In the 30 echelons of the 9 ranks Inside the Current there are further the appended offices inside the current [which range from] rank 5a to rank 9b. Before, [there existed one the one hand those of] the *sabao* 薩寶 office and the officers of Princely Establishments, as well as the three preceptors, the three dukes, the commander, the commandery prince, and the supreme pillar-of-state, and [the offices] below [these], and [on the other hand] the military-protector and [the offices] above [it] – [which] were ranks of the Offices of the Establishment for honorary and concurrent officials. At the beginning of the

159 It is the same person as An Poluo 安婆羅, mentioned as his grandson in the *Xin Tangshu* 75b, for more information, see p. 245 (3.2.3.1.7); see also: Forte, *Hostage An Shigao*, 18, fns. 22, 43, 49.

160 Li Gui 李軌 was the emperor of the Liang 涼 dynasty, which lasted two years from 617 to 619 CE. An Xinggui 安興貴 pretended to submit to him, overthrew him and turned him over to the Tang emperor.

161 Originally published in 1926: Kuwabara Jitsuzō, "Zui Tō jidai"; Reprint: Kuwabara Jitsuzō and Miyazaki Ichisada, *Kuwabara Jitsuzō zenshō 2*, 270–360; see also: Dien, "Sa-Pao Problem," 339, fn. 37, 341, fn. 55.

162 *Jiu Tangshu* 42.1803; author's translation.

163 Originally *yao* 祆, see p. 270, fn. 170.

> Kaiyuan 開元 era (713–41 CE), all [these offices] were dissolved. Now there are only two officers retained, the *sabao* 薩寶 and the Zoroastrian regulator.
>
> 又有流外自勳品以至九品，以為諸司令史、贊者、典謁、亭長、掌固等品。視流外亦自勳品至九品，開元初唯留薩寶[祆][164]祝及府史，餘亦罷之。
>
> There are further the honorary rank to rank 9 Outside the Current. [These] ranks are used for the clerks off various offices, the court herald, receptionist, managing clerk, and [lower] clerk. There are also the Honorary Rank to rank 9 appended Outside the Current. At the beginning of the Kaiyuan 開元 era (713–41 CE), only the Zoroastrian precentor of the *sabao* 薩寶 office and the scribe of the office remained. The rest were also removed.

3.2.4.7 Tongdian

While including in *juan* 卷 39[165] the same content on the Sui dynasty rank system as seen in the *Suishu*,[166] and the geographic information about the river Sabao 薩寶[167] as seen above,[168] the *Tongdian* comprises three more important passages. The first is to be found in *Tongdian* 19, in the rank list of offices of the Tang:[169]

> 大唐自流内以上，並因隋制。又置視正五品、視從七品，以署薩寶及[祆正][170]，謂之視流内。
>
> From the Great Tang [dynasty] on, from inside the current and above, drawing on the system of the Sui, was installed the appended rank 5a and 7b for those that are called the *sabao* 薩寶 and the [Zoroastrian] regulator; these are called inside the current.

We therefore know that in the Sui – its system and codex based on those of the Northern Wei – the *sabao* 薩寶 was integrated in the list of appended ranks in the bureaucratic system of the Chinese Empire. Although "appended" means that the ranks were only vaguely equivalent to the official ones, being listed apart (at the end) to mark the difference, the term is not to be confused with the "honorary" (*xun* 勳) or "prestige/sinecure" (*sanguan* 散官) titles, which do not include a real function. Besides the *sabao* 薩寶 holding the appended rank 5a, a new office is mentioned, a Zoroastrian regulator, of the appended rank 7b2.

164 Id.
165 *Tongdian* 39.1081–82.
166 See p. 268 (3.2.4.4).
167 *Tongdian* 193.5255.
168 See p. 267 (3.2.4.2).
169 *Tongdian* 19.482; author's translation.
170 Originally *zheng ba* "正祓". "Tcheng-ba est doublement fautif ; le second caractère doit se corriger en 祆 *hien*, et les deux mots doivent-être renversés (…)") Pelliot, "Le sa-pao," 669, fn. 2; see also ibid., 666, fn. 3; see likewise: Chen Yuan 陳垣, "Huoxianjiao," 113–14. The character is often erroneously rendered as "*yao* 祆" or "*ba* 祓". For the pronunciation, see p. 310.

The second passage in *Tongdian* includes a rank-listing of the offices of the Tang, rephrasing the same content as in the quote above:[171]

> 視流內
>
> 視正五品：薩寶
> 視從七品：薩寶府祆正。
>
> Appended inside the current:
>
> appended rank 5a: *sabao* 薩寶;
> appended rank 7b: Zoroastrian regulator[172] of the *sabao* 薩寶 office.

Followed by a commentary of Yao Kuan 姚寬 of the Song on the term *xian* 祆:[173]

> 祆，呼煙反。祆者，西域國天神，佛經所謂摩醯首羅也。武德四年，置祆祠及官，常有羣胡奉事，取火呪詛。貞觀二年，置波斯寺。至天寶四年七月，敕：「波斯經教出自大秦，傳習而來，久行中國。爰初建寺，因以為名，將欲示人，必脩其本。其兩京波斯寺宜改為大秦寺。天下諸州郡有者，亦宜准此。」
>
> 祆 *xian* is pronounced 呼 *x*(*u*) + 煙 (*y*)*an* (= *xian*). 祆 *xian:* the heavenly deity of countries of the Western Regions. It is the one called *Moxishouluo* 摩醯首羅 (*Maheśvara*)[174] in the Buddhist *sūtras*. In Wude 武德 4 (621 CE) a Zoroastrian temple and [its] officers were installed. Often there were groups of *hu* 胡 worshipping, gathering [at] the fire [and] making incantations. In Zhenguan 貞觀 2 (628–29, [631 CE]),[175] a Persian (Iranian) temple was erected. In Tianbao 天寶 4/7 (8.745 CE) [it was] decreed [by imperial order]: "The Persian (Iranian) religion of sacred books comes from Rome, through propagation [it] came and since long moved [into] China. [176] Therefore, when initially building temples, they used [it] as a name. To show in the future to people that its origin shall be restored, the two Persian (Iranian) temples in the

171 *Tongdian* 40.1102–3; author's translation.
172 As proposed by: Dien, "Sa-Pao Problem," 339.
173 *Tongdian* 40.1103; author's translation.
174 Possibly copied of an erroneous passage of the *Liang jing xin ji*. See Pelliot, "Le sa-pao," 669.
175 Conceivably in Zhenguan 貞觀 5/1 (7.2–8.3.631 CE), as to be found in the passage narrating the same event in the *Fozu tongji* 佛祖統記 (T49.364a18): 五年正月。詔僧尼道士致敬父母〇詔以慶善宮為穆太后建慈德寺。為皇太子承乾建普光寺。勅沙門法常居之。為太子授菩薩戒〇十一月。化度寺僧邕禪師亡。上敬悼賜帛。勅右庶子李百藥撰碑。更令歐陽詢書初波斯國蘇魯支立末尼火祆(祆; see p. 270, fn. 170)教勅於京師建大秦寺。
And in the *Xixi congyu* 1.42 (*muhu ge*): 至唐貞觀五年，有傳法穆護何祿，將祆教詣闕聞奏，勅令長安崇化坊立祆寺，號大秦寺，又名波斯寺。
Although these works are dated about five centuries later, they seem to have used an independent source, containing more information (Pelliot, "Le sa-pao," 669, fn. 7).
176 According to Manichaeian tradition by the agency of Mar Ammo, the 3rd disciple of the prophet Mani (Asmussen, "Ammō, Mār").

capital shall be changed accordingly to *Daqin* 大秦 (Roman)-temples. In all the prefectures and commanderies of the Empire this shall also be followed."

開元二十年敕：「末摩尼法，本是邪見，妄稱佛教，誑惑黎元，宜嚴加禁斷。以其西胡等既是鄉法，當身自行，不須科罪者。」

In Kaiyuan 開元 20 (732 CE) it was [already] decreed [by imperial order]: "The teaching of Momoni 末摩尼 (Mar Mani)[177] is fundamentally perverted, improperly claims the name of Buddhism, misleads the common people, what shall be strictly prohibited. Because it is the teaching of the native lands of the Western *hu* 胡 and others, and they practice it personally, it shall not be punished as a crime."

The third passage is in *Tongdian* 40, the continuation of the rank-listing of the offices of the Tang (*guanpin* 官品):[178]

視流外。

勳品：薩寶府[祆][179]祝。
四品：薩寶[府率][180]。
五品：薩寶府史。

Appended outside the current:

Honorary Rank (rank 1): Zoroastrian precentor[181] of the *sabao* office;
Rank 4: commandant of the *sabao* office;
Rank 5: scribe[182] of the *sabao* office.

As can be seen, the *Tongdian* mentions a commandant which is not recorded in the *Jiu Tangshu*.

177 Normally "*moni* 摩尼". This alternative is also to be found in the *Laozi hua hu jing* 老子化胡經 (*Laozi Converting the hu* 胡; T54.1267b21). See: Pelliot, "Le sa-pao," 670, fn. 4; and: Pelliot, "Mo-ni et le Houa-hou-king," 321–22, and fn. 5; it probably is a transliteration of Mar Mani, meaning "Lord Mani".
178 *Tongdian* 40.1105–6; author's translation.
179 Originally *yao* 祅, see p. 270, fn. 170.
180 The original text reads *shuaifu* 率府, which is replaced by *fushuai* 府率 in commentary no. 74 of the Zhonghua shuju edition of the *Tongdian*. Whereas *shuaifu* 率府 is the name of an office – *shuai* 率 being used to qualify *fu* 府 (i.e. commander's office) – *fushuai* 府率 means "the commandant of an office". In the case of the *sabao* 薩寶 office, the argument stands in favour of the second option (i.e. commandant of the *sabao* office). *Tongdian* 39.1115; Lü Zongli, *Zhongguo*, 754; some parallel examples are to be found in: Hucker, *Dictionary*, 5476, 5478; 846, 1277, 4258, 5312, 5313, 5834, 7166, 7676, 7821, 8135.
181 As translated by Dien: Dien, "Sa-Pao Problem," 339. *Zhu* 祝 is commonly used for the person in charge of the rite during an offering; *xianzhu* 祆祝 is thus to be seen in parallel to the *miaozhu* 廟祝, in charge of entertaining fires at the temple.
182 Translated by Dien as "archivist" (ibid., 340).

3.2.4.8 Xin Tangshu

In the *Xin Tangshu*, the table of the Genealogies of the Prime Ministers (*zaixiang shixi biao* 宰相世系表) attributes to Zheng Xingchen 鄭行諶 (b. 638 CE)[183] – who was certainly not of Sogdian descent – the office of *guoyi* 果毅 (vice commandant) of the *sabao* 薩寶:[184]

> [鄭]行諶薩寶[府][185]果毅。
>
> [Zheng] Xingchen [鄭]行諶 [was] vice commandant of the *sabao* 薩寶 [office].

In the commentary on the table, we find a passage concerning the genealogy of Li Baoyu 李寶玉,[186] who stems from the An 安 clan referred to above in the *Yuanhe Xingzuan* and was granted a change of his name after the An Lushan 安祿山 rebellion:[187]

> 武威李氏，本安氏，出自姬姓。黄帝生昌意，昌意次子安，居於西方，自號安息國。後漢末，遣子世高入朝，因居洛陽。晉、魏間，家於安定，後徙遼左，以避亂又徙武威。後魏有難陀孫婆羅，周、隋間，居涼州武威爲薩寶。生興貴、修仁。至抱玉賜姓李。……
>
> The Li 李 clan of Wuwei 武威 originally stems from the An 安 clan, which comes from the Ji 姬 family. The emperor begot Changyi 昌意. Chang Yi's 昌意 second son An 安 lived in the West, where [they] referred to themselves as the land of Anxi 安息 (Parthia). At the end of the Later Han, [he] sent [his] son Shigao 世高 to [the Chinese] court and thus resided in Luoyang 洛陽. During the Jin and the Wei, the family [lived] in Anding 安定. Later they moved to Liaozuo 遼左 to avoid turmoil.[188] Again, they moved to Wuwei 武威. During the Later [Northern] Wei there was Nantuo's 難陀 grandson Poluo 婆羅. During the [Northern] Zhou and Sui [he] resided in Wuwei 武威 of Liangzhou 涼州, serving as *sabao* 薩寶. [He] begot Xinggui 興貴 and Xiuren 脩仁. Then Baoyu 抱玉 was conferred the surname of Li 李. (…)

183 This can be deduced from the epitaph of his grandson Zheng Yan 鄭巖. See: Zhao Zhenhua, "Tangdai Zheng Yan," 74.

184 *Xin Tangshu* 75a.3306; author's translation.

185 This character can be added according to the context and parallels in other epitaphs (*fu guoyi* 府果毅). See the epitaphs of Shi Tuo 史陀 (*Shi Tuo ji furen hezang muzhi* 史陀及夫人合葬墓誌, d. 659 CE), and of the wife Shi 史 of master Kang 康君 (*Kang jun qi Shi shi muzhi* 康君妻史氏墓誌, d. 661 CE) (Zhang Xishun, *Sui Tang Wudai muzhi, Luoyang 4*, 17; and: ibid., 72).

186 See: Forte, *Hostage An Shigao*, 22–27. His biography is to be found in: *Xin Tangshu* 138.4619–20.

187 *Xin Tangshu* 75b.3445–46; author's translation.

188 The punctuation of the Zhonghua shuju edition is erroneous in my opinion, as the *you* 又 (again) normally starts a new unit of meaning and should certainly not occur after the construction with *yi* 以. Their desire to avoid turmoil is thus the reason that prompted them to move to Liaozuo 僚佐 and not to Wuwei 武威.

In contrast to the *Yuanhe Xingzuan* (see above), this passage says that only Poluo 婆羅 was *sabao* 薩寶, and not three generations of the An 安 (later Li 李) family. For a discussion, see the parenthesis p. 241 (3.2.3.1.7).[189]

3.2.4.9 Chang'an zhi, including a quote of a passage of the Liang jing xin ji

The *Chang'an zhi* includes a quote of a passage of the now lost *Liang jing xin ji*, recording the building of a foreign temple in the capital in the seventh century.[190] The description of the *nanbu zhengfang* 南布政坊 (Southern Administrative Quarter)[191] reads:[192]

> 西南隅胡[祆][193]祠。
>
> (註:)武德四年立。西域胡祆神也。祠內有薩寶府官，主祠[祆][194]神，亦以胡祝充其職。……
>
> In the south-west corner [is] a *hu* 胡 Zoroastrian temple.
>
> (Commentary:) [It] was erected in Wude 武德 4 (621 CE). [It is of] the Zoroastrian Deity of the *hu* 胡 of the Western Regions. Inside the temple is the *sabao* 薩寶 office, presiding over the offerings to the Zoroastrian Deity. Its task is also fulfilled by the *hu* 胡 precentor.

3.2.4.10 Chaoye qianzai, Guangchuan huaba and Xixi congyu

Zhang Zhuo 張鷟 (658–730 CE) wrote in the *Chaoye qianzai*:[195]

> 河南府立德坊及南市西坊皆有胡祆神廟。每歲商胡祈福，烹豬羊，琵琶鼓笛，酣歌醉舞。酹神之後，募一胡為祆主，看者施錢並與之。其祆主取一橫刀，利同霜雪，吹毛不過，以刀刺腹，刃出於背，仍亂擾腸肚流血。食頃，噴水呪之，平復如故。此蓋西域之幻法也。

189 Forte proposed a different punctuation (後魏有難陀。孫婆羅，周、隋間，居涼州武威爲薩寶。) which leads him to the conclusion that Poluo 婆羅 was living during the Northern Zhou and Sui. He argued: "I think that Lin Bao's text is to be preferred and that the *Xin Tangshu* underwent some changes which altered the original meaning. Accordingly, we have given a different punctuation" (Forte, *Hostage An Shigao*, 27, fn. 52). However, it is entirely possible that he lived during the Northern Wei, Northern Zhou, and Sui; both readings are correct. This problem does, however, not afflict the discussion about the inheritability of the office.

190 The commentary is corroborated by the passage of the commentary on the *Tongdian* 40, as seen above.

191 A quarter of the outer city, ca. 808.5 x 955.5 m, with a door on each of the four sides, with ten large streets. For more information, see: Zhang Yonglu, *Tangdai Chang'an cidian*, 63–64, 170.

192 *Chang'an zhi* 10.2a–b. Author's punctuation.

193 Originally *yao* 祅, see p. 270, fn. 170.

194 Originally *ba* 拔, see p. 270, fn. 170.

195 *Chaoye qianzai* 3.64–65. Altered punctuation. Partly translated in French: Pénélope Riboud, "Réflexions sur *xian* 祆," 81.

> In the *Lide* 立德 Quarter and the Western Quarter of the Southern City of Henan [Luoyang 洛陽],[196] there was a Zoroastrian temple. Every year, merchant *hu* 胡 [held a ceremony to] implore fortune. [They] cooked pig and sheep, [played the] *pipa* 琵琶, drummed and [blew] flutes, and sang and danced drunkenly. After having made libations to the deity, one *hu* 胡 was recruited as Zoroastrian presider. The spectators threw coins at him. Its (the temple's) Zoroastrian presider took a sword, so sharp it shimmered like frost – [it] would have cut a blown hair. [He] cut [his] belly with a sword [so that] the edge came out of [his] back and messily stirred the bowels [while] blood spilled. In a trice,[197] [he] cast a spell and spat water on it, [and] recovered as if anew. This is the magic of the Western Regions.
>
> 涼州祆神祠，至祈禱日，祆主以鐵釘從額上釘之，直洞腋下，即出門，身輕若飛，須臾數百里。至西祆神前，舞一曲，即却，至舊祆所乃拔釘，無所損。臥十餘日，平復如故。莫知其所以然也。
>
> At the Zoroastrian temple of Liangzhou 涼州, when the prayer's day arrived, the Zoroastrian presider took a metal spike, pierced the forehead, [and] nailed it [down] to under the armpits. [He went] then went out of the door, [his] body light like a feather, [and] swiftly [covered] several hundred miles. Arriving in front of the Western Zoroastrian Deity,[198] [he] danced a dance [and] then came back to the place of the old Zoroastrian [temple]. Only then [he] retrieved the spike, [but] nowhere was a wound. [He] then lied down for more than ten days, recovered as if anew. Nobody knew how.

Zhang Zhuo's 張鷟 accounts conceivably are among the source material used for the anecdote in the commentary of Yao Kuan 姚寬 in the Song, or both used similar sources.

Finally, a text of the late 11th to early 12th century, the *Guangchuan huaba* of Dong You 董逌, connects in its description of the Zoroastrian Deity the Zoroastrian temple and the *sabao* 薩寶, and reproduces most of the content of the *Chaoye qianzai* in the commentary:[199]

> [祆][200]祠，世所以奉胡神也。其相希異，即經所謂摩醯首羅。有大神威，普救一切苦，能攝伏四方，以衛佛法。

196 See: Zhao Chao, "Tangdai Luoyang chengfang bukao".

197 Literally "in the time it takes to have a meal".

198 Rong Xinjiang proposed with Chen Guocan that the Western deity, to which the practitioner flies to, actually refers to the Zoroastrian temple in Zhangye 張掖, as it is located 500 *li* (ca. 250 km) to the west. In my opinion, this interpretation takes this passage (and Chinese sources in general) far too literally (Rong Xinjiang, *Zhonggu Zhongguo yu wailai wenming*, 68; Chen Guocan, "Wei," 208).

199 *Guangchuan huaba* 4.5b–6b. Author's punctuation and translation.

200 Originally *yao* 祅, see p. 270, fn. 170.

The Zoroastrian temple is where over generations was worshipped the *hu* 胡 deity. Its appearance is strange, like Moxishouluo 摩醯首羅 (Maheśvara)[201] of the Buddhist *sūtras.* [It] has great spiritual power, equally saving all suffering [ones]. [It] can overthrow the world to protect the Buddhist *dharma.*

當隋之初其法始至中夏。立祠頒政，坊常有羣胡奉事，聚火祝詛，奇幻變怪，至有出腹決腸，吞火蹈刃。故下俚庸人，就以詛誓，取爲信重。唐祠令有薩寶府官主司，又有胡祝以贊於禮事，其制甚重。在當時爲顯祠。

In the early Sui, its teachings first came to China. An edict was issued to erect a temple. In the districts [of the city] often there were groups of *hu* 胡 worshipping. [They] gathered [at] the fire[202] [and] made incantations, performed magic tricks, even [opened and] emptied [their] belly [and] cut [their] bowels, swallowed fire and danced [on] blades. This is why ordinary people from the countryside made oaths [at the temple], [and the temple] earned great respect. During the Tang, the authority over the temple's order was assumed by the *sabao* 薩寶. There was also the *hu* 胡 precentor to assist the ritual affairs. Its protocol was very solemn. In these times [they] were prominent temples.

（注:）河南立德坊及南市西坊有胡[祆][203]神廟。每年商胡祈福。烹宰、鼓樂。酬之神後，募一胡人為[祆][204]主。取一刀，刺腹，刃出背亂攪腹肚流血。食頃，噴水祝之，平復如初。

(Commentary:) In the *Lide* 立德 Quarter and the Western Quarter of the Southern City of Henan 河南 [Luoyang 洛陽],[205] there was a *hu* 胡 Zoroastrian deity temple. Every year, merchant *hu* 胡 [held a ceremony to] implore fortune. Barbarian folk slaughtered and cooked [animals], drummed and [made] music. After having repaid the deity, one *hu* 胡 was made Zoroastrian presider. Taking a knife, [he] cut his belly. The edge came out of [his] back, messily stirred the bowels [while] blood ran. In a trice,[206] [he] spat water and incanted on it (the wound), [and it] recovered as if anew.

涼州[祆][207]主以利刃從額釘之直至腋下。即出神，輕若飛，須臾數百里，至西[祆][208]神前舞一曲，卻至舊祆所，乃為拔釘，一無所損。

201 Possibly copied of an erroneous passage of the *Liang jing xin ji.* See Pelliot, "Le sa-pao," 669.
202 Putting together a fire?
203 Originally *yao* 祆, see p. 270, fn. 170.
204 Id.
205 See: Zhao Chao, "Tangdai Luoyang chengfang bukao".
206 See p. 275 fn. 197.
207 Originally *yao* 祆, see p. 270, fn. 170.
208 Id.

> The Zoroastrian presider of Liangzhou 涼州 took a sharp knife [and] pierced the forehead [down] to under the armpits.[209] [His entranced] spirit then exited [the body], light like a feather, [and] swiftly [covered] several hundred miles. Arriving in front of the Western Zoroastrian Deity, [he] danced a dance [and] then came back to the place of the old Zoroastrian [deity]. Only then [did he] retrieve the knife – [he] was not even injured.

The story about the Zoroastrian presider of Liangzhou 涼州 interestingly differs in the two versions. While the first version includes the unusual fact of him "going out of the door" and includes a miraculous flight. Since "body" (*shen* 身) and "spirit" (*shen* 神) are homophonic, it is quite probable that the story was orally transmitted. Further, the second version does not include the character for "door" (*men* 門) and reads instead of *chu men* 出門 the fixed expression *chu shen* 出神, "being entranced" or literally "exiting spirit". Whereas the *Chaoye qianzai* records that he exited the building, became light as a feather (literally "light like flying"), and flew or ran several hundred miles, the *Guangchuan huaba* records that he became entranced and it was his spirit that was light as a feather and flew several hundred miles. Due to the complicated reconstruction of the *Chaoye qianzai*, it is possible that the *Guangchuan huaba* is closer to the original meaning.

The commentary then goes on to quote a third story about an ominous bronze horse included in Duan Chengshi's 段成式 (803?–63 CE) *Youyang zazu*, which records a Zoroastrian temple in Judejian 俱德建 (Qobadian). Besides a miraculous story involving a gigantic bronze horse, it includes the description of a temple:[210]

> ……內無象，於大屋置立大小爐舍，檐向西，又東祠。……
>
> (…) Inside there was no statue. In the great hall were installed large and small fire altar chambers. The eave faced west and [they] sacrificed [facing] east. (…)

Interestingly, the *Xixi congyu* by Yao Kuan 姚寬 himself also quotes the *Youyang zazu*[211] but differs slightly and further includes a commentary on their calendar:[212]

> ……祠內無象，於大屋下置小爐舍，檐向西，人向東禮。……西域以五月為歲。……
>
> (…) In the temple was no statue. Under the great hall[213] were installed large and small fire altar chambers. The eave faced west and the people conducted ceremonies facing east. (…) The Western Regions have the fifth month as beginning of the year. (…)

209 Likely referring to "swallowing" the blade.
210 *Guangchuan huaba* 4.6b. Author's punctuation and translation.
211 The edition of the *Youyang zazu* is identical. *Youyang zazu* 10.58a.
212 *Xixi congyu* 1.42 (*muhu ge*); author's translation.
213 Maybe meaning in front, below the hall?

3.2.5 Synthesis of sources on *sabao*

The next step consists in further organising and synthesising the material, which shall be started by an introduction into the etymology of the Sanskrit term that stands chronologically at the beginning of the debate: the *sārthavāha*.

3.2.5.1 Sanskrit derivations and the importance of trade

Derivations of the Sanskrit *sārthavāha* (lit. caravan leader) are found in various languages; including, Middle Parthian (*srtw'*), Khotanese E (*sātävāya*), Agnean (*sārthavāk*), Tocharian (*särthavāhe*), and later, Tibetan (*sar-phag*), Mongolian (*sartawaki*), and Manchu (*sartawahi*). The Uighur, Sogdian, and especially Chinese terms shall be dealt with below.[214] That transcriptions of the term are so widespread among the languages of the Silk Roads is quite a remarkable phenomenon and although we can safely assume that people were able to comprehend the meaning of the word, there would have been equally no obstacle to translating the words "caravan" or "leader". Apart from evidencing contact between these groups, the transcription more importantly underlines the eminence of the position of the "caravan leader". Therefore, it is necessary to investigate the distinct qualities manifest in the term and to illuminate the degree to which the caravan leader was officially recognised and thus endowed with legitimacy and official authority. Determining these factors shall ultimately enable us to retrace the history of the office's creation in China.

Most axiomatic of the caravan leader's activities is trade, and thus we may presume that their relevance was awarded foremost priority in recognition of their economic influence. Indeed, this supposition is substantiated by several pieces of epigraphic literary evidence from the Indic context. For instance, the ideal administrative vision of Kauṭilya's *Arthaśāstra* (second century BCE to third century CE),[215] envisions the beneficial effects of their commercial activity for administrators and/or society. In *Arthaśāstra* 2.16, the author advises the superintendent of commodities to support trade by exempting the caravan leaders of the local taxes and jurisdiction:[216]

> He should facilitate the import of commodities from other lands by granting favors. To boat and caravan operators, moreover, he should grant exemptions that would allow them to make a profit, as well as immunity from lawsuits to foreign traders with respects to financial matters, except for those who are members or associates of local corporate bodies.

Although primarily advisory in character, this passage clearly defines "caravan operators" (i.e. caravan leaders) as a distinct group of people who could be and likely were granted special economic and legal status. The exceptional status this group and the growing importance of caravans and trade is further substantiated by the seven Buddhist donative inscriptions in various regional Prakrits provided above. Besides

214 For the sources, see: Dien, "Sa-Pao Problem," 337.

215 Olivelle, *King*, 6–31.

216 Ibid., 139–40; for general comments on the treatise on economy and trade, see also: ibid., 43–46.

the mobilisation of economic capital – their leaders being either wealthy, respected or trusted enough to receive loans – caravans were also large scale operations accompanied by military support in order that they could defend themselves against bandits, and relied on a network of trade posts and an intimate knowledge of the route. Along such trade routes, they supplied local businesses and people with their products and satisfied the exotic palette of society's higher strata.[217] In the same logic, the correlation between economic and social status may offer an explanation as to why the Middle Parthian "greatest caravan leader" was also used as one of the epithets for Mar Zakū (one of the first disciples of Mani) in a eulogy lamenting his death, likely composed shortly thereafter (ca. 300 CE).[218]

We should now turn to the highly debated occurrences of the term in the two languages deliberately omitted at the beginning: *s'rtp'w/srtp'w* in Sogdian, and the later Uighur rendering *sarthavayi*.[219] To date, there are three known occurrences of the term in Sogdian.[220] First, the Sogdian Ancient Letter V, dated to the years 311–13 CE;[221] second, the bilingual epitaph found in the grave of Master Shi 史/Wirkak (494–579 CE), for which the Chinese version gives as equivalent term *sabao* 薩保, in this case referring to the office in the Chinese bureaucracy; and third, the word *srtp'w* (being a later form of *s'rtp'w*) is also mentioned in a document found in Khotan, estimated to date from the seventh century.[222] Due to the problematic suffix *p'w – s'rt,* held to denote "caravan"[223] – the relation between *sārthavāha* in Indic, *s'rtp'w/srtp'w* in Sogdian, and the Chinese titles *sabo* 薩薄, *safu* 薩甫, *sabao* 薩保, and *sabao* 薩寶 has been intensively debated. Three propositions have been forwarded:

- The Chinese titles and the Sogdian *s'rtp'w/srtp'w* derived directly or indirectly from *sārthavāha* and were thus related to the above-mentioned transcriptions.[224] Further, Dien proposed that the above-mentioned addition of the prefix *mahe* 摩訶 (Skt. *maha*) at least shows that there was an awareness of the Sanskrit root of the

217 See: Schafer, *Golden Peaches*.

218 Document M6. See Henning, who himself translated it as "sehr großer Karawanenführer" (Engl. very great caravan leader) although he provided in his translation of the word *wzyšt* as superlative to *wrzg*, i.e. "größt" (Engl. greatest): Andreas and Henning, *Mitteliranische III*, 865, e(20), and 909; also to be found in: Henning, "Mitteliranische Manichaica," [292–94]; see also: Boyce, *Reader*, 139–40. Klimkeit (from which the dating is taken), translated "zealous Caravan leader": Klimkeit, *Gnosis*, 87.

219 See: Dien, "Sa-Pao Problem," 337.

220 A document found in Turfan is sometimes provided as further evidence, see p. 202 (2.4.2.1.3).

221 See p. 214 (2.4.3.1.1).

222 See p. 207 (2.4.2.2.1).

223 Andreas and Henning, *Mitteliranische III*, 865; Sims-Williams, "Indian Elements," 135. See also: Schwartz, "Sārtha".

224 Proposed by: Fujita Toyohachi, "Saiiki kenkyū," 210–11; and supported, among others, by: Kuwabara Jitsuzō, "Zui Tō jidai," 660. Kuwabara proposed that it derived from the Uighur, which would be derived from the Sanskrit. And later supported by: Luo Feng, "Sabao: Zai kaocha," 229; Rui Chuanming, "Sabao de zai renshi"; Forte, "Sabao 薩寶 Question," 81–84; Dien, "Sa-Pao Problem," 337–38.

word *sabao* 薩保 coming from a Buddhist context, but used in a secular sense.[225] To explain how *safu* 薩甫 came to be, Forte proposed that *fu* 甫 may be a variant of *bo* 溥, in an effort to link the terms *safu* 薩甫 and *sabo* 薩溥.[226]

– The Sogdian *s'rtp'w/srtp'w* is an independent hybrid word meaning "protector of the caravan," and thus unrelated to the above-mentioned transcriptions.[227] To support this view, it was proposed that the mention of a *sabo* 薩溥 (EMC **sat bak*) of the Gaochang 高昌 Kingdom in 550 CE was actually equivalent to *sapu* 薩簿 (EMC **sat bɔ*; the second character, *pu* 簿, being used in several office names) and should not be confused with the Buddhist term *sabo* 薩溥.[228] It thus stands as the first piece of recorded evidence for a nexus between the Sogdian and the Chinese titles: *safu* 薩甫 (EMC **sat puǎ'*; the second character, *fu* 甫, is used in several office names), *sabao* 薩保 (EMC **sat paw*) and *sabao* 薩寶 (EMC **sat paw*).
– The Sogdian *s'rtp'w/srtp'w*, although derived from the Sanskrit, may be traced back to the Chinese context rather than the reverse. Dien proposed that 1) the Sogdian *s'rtp'w/srtp'w* only occurs in a Chinese bureaucratic context, which means it refers to an office in China,[229] 2) that a phonetic transition from *sabo* 薩溥 to *sabao* 薩保/薩寶 had already occurred, and 3) that because of the prefix *mahe* 摩訶 (see the first point), it is related to Sanskrit.[230]

To add further confusion to the debate, I would like to point out that in the epitaph of Master Shi 史/Wirkak, the Sogdian reads in the translation of Yoshida Yutaka:[231] "He [obtained?] a [title?] *sabao* of Kachan from the Emperor (and was) a *grandee in the Sogdian land." Taking the commentaries of the edition into consideration, including an important suggestion by Lurje, it is reasonable to read the passage more literally as: "He … *srtp'w* of Kachan from the Emperor, power holder of a Sogdian settlement (in China)."[232] It seems as if the author of the Sogdian text – whose strong suit was

225 Dien, "Further Thoughts," 206.
226 Forte, "Sabao 薩寶 Question," 94.
227 Yoshida Yutaka proposed that the *p'w* may be understood as related to the Persian *xšaçapāvan* "protector of the state": Yoshida Yutaka, "Sogudo," 169–70; this was supported by: Arakawa Masaharu, "'Sappō' no sēkaku," 164–65; and: Rong Xinjiang, "Sabao yu Sabo: Beichao".
228 Wang Su, "Gaochang," 172–74.
229 The three above-mentioned examples of *s'rtp'w/srtp'w* have great bearing on the issue. Dien quoted the hypothesis of Grenet, Sims-Williams and de la Vaissière, i.e. that the addressee of the Sogdian Ancient Letter V resided in Loulan 樓蘭, which is purely hypothetical (see p. 214; 2.4.3.1.1). If the letter was meant for a place in Sogdiana – Letter II was destined for Samarqand – the argument may be falsified. I venture below that the word may have been used differently in Sogdiana and China.
230 Dien, "Consideration"; he already advanced this possibility in: Dien, "Further Thoughts," 206.
231 See Vol. 2., Appendix 3.1.14.
232 "P. Lur'e argued that that *sywδyk-stn* literally means 'Sogdians' place', and that it is not likely to denote Sogdiana itself but a certain place in China where many Sogdians were residents. (…) If one compares the word with Skt. *sthāma* 'power' (cf. also Khotanese *stāma* 'exertion'), *'st'm-δ'r* 'power holder' would be a word denoting a nobleman or landlord, hence my translation 'grandee'." Yoshida Yutaka, "The Sogdian Version," 64, nrs. 7–8.

not Chinese but Sogdian – provided in the second part of the sentence a comment on *srtp'w*, i.e. on the *sabao* 薩保 office in China. It is either 1) a simple paraphrase, 2) an explanation of a perhaps uncommon term that was not quite understood by the typical Sogdian audience, or 3) an explanation of an ambiguous term, i.e. "he was a *caravan leader*, which in the context of a Sogdian settlement in China means that he was the leader of the Sogdian community". The second and especially the third hypotheses underpin Dien's theory that the term occurred only in a Chinese bureaucratic context.

It is obvious that *sārthavāha* and *s'rtp'w/srtp'w* are at least related by the first member of the compound meaning "caravan". Whereas most research has sought to link the *sabo* 薩薄 (EMC **sat bak*) of the Indic sources to the Chinese titles *safu* (EMC **sat puă'*), *sabao* 薩保 (EMC **sat paw*), and *sabao* 薩寶 (EMC **sat paw*), there are the above already mentioned synonymous transcriptions of *sārthavāha*, such as *satuopo* 薩陀婆 (EMC **sat da ba*), *satapo* 薩他婆 (EMC **sat tʰa ba*), and/or *satapohe* 薩他婆訶 (EMC **sat tʰa ba xa*), which are also reasonably close to *sabao* 薩保/*sabao* 薩寶 (EMC **sat paw*). Thus, I do not see why the connection between the terms *sabo* 薩薄 and *sabao* 薩保 should be decisive to the debate. I also find it equally possible that 1) the *sabo* 薩薄 of Gaochang 高昌 may have actually been written *sapu* 薩簿 (EMC **sat bɔ*) and that *pu* 簿 was a suffix for offices, like the suffix *fu* 甫 of *safu* 薩甫, linking these two together, or 2) the *fu* 甫 of *safu* 薩甫 was perhaps a simplification of *bo* 薄, linking those two together. Changing the office to *sabao* 薩保 also sounds rather convincing; it tallies well with the meaning of the Sogdian *s'rtp'w/srtp'w*, which is no argumentative stretch, as they were both written on a bilingual epitaph. At the same time, the rather peculiar sentence in the Sogdian text of Wirkak's epitaph mentioned above may support the idea that the title could have held different meanings in Sogdian and Chinese contexts. It is also a strong argument to propose that the Indic prefix *mahe* 摩訶 is evidence for the connection between *mahe sabao* 摩訶薩寶 and *mahasārthavāha*. Referring to the Sogdian merchant's status to explain why the office was changed from *sabao* 薩保 to *sabao* 薩寶 is actually the weakest link in all these arguments. Furthermore, there were people that we can relate to Buddhism who were named Sabo 薩薄, Sabao 薩保, and Sabao 薩寶, presumably due to the word's relation to the bodhisattva-like "leader of merchants". It is possible, however, that the personal names Sabao 薩保 and Sabao 薩寶 could have been simply chosen for their possessing positive attributes. *Sa* 薩 – not having any meaning in Chinese by itself – is used as an abbreviation for and component of the transcription *pusa* 菩薩 (bodhisattva), in addition to various other terms transcribed from Indic languages. The positively connoted *bao* 保 (lit. protect) and *bao* 寶 (lit. treasure) also commonly occur in Buddhist contexts. The case of a certain Cao Baobao 曹保保, mentioned in a manuscript dated to 703 CE and discovered in the Astana tomb no. 35, who signed the case document himself as Cao Baobao 曹寶寶, clearly shows that the *bao* 保 and *bao* 寶 were – due to their homonymy – objects of confusion in name giving contexts,[233] as has already been observed for the steles of Wang Huilüe 王惠略, Qi Faqi 岐法起,Ye Rong 葉容, and Liu 劉.

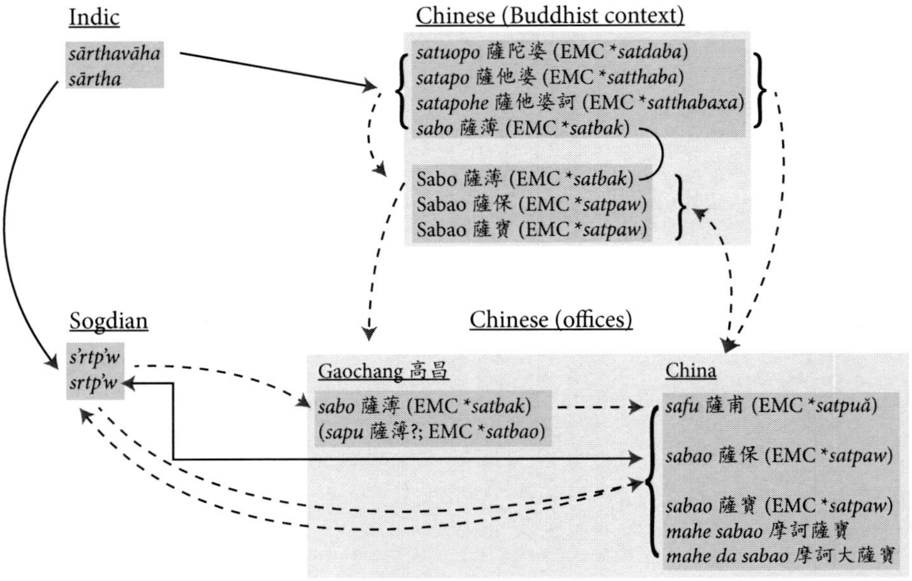

Figure 15: Possible Etymologies
Source: M. Huber

It is important to notice that agreeing with either option has no bearing on the present analysis' results. Thus there is no debate on the great majority of points relevant for the sociological debate: However the words *sārthavāha*, *sabo* 薩薄, *satuopo* 薩陀婆, *satapo* 薩他婆, *satapohe* 薩他婆訶, *safu* 薩甫, *sabao* 薩保, *sabao* 薩寶, *s'rtp'w*/srtp'w, and further words in other languages and dialects mentioned at the beginning may be interrelated, or if not, we can agree that Sabo 薩薄 (as a given name), *sabo* 薩薄, *satuopo* 薩陀婆, *satapo* 薩他婆, and *satapohe* 薩他婆訶 were transcriptions of "caravan leader" in Buddhist texts, that Sabao 薩保 and Sabao 薩寶 were both used as given names for Buddhists in China, and that *sabao* 薩保 was the equivalent of the Sogdian *s'rtp'w*/*srtp'w*, which may have stood for "caravan leader" or "caravan protector," but actually referred to the leader of a Sogdian settlement in the Chinese context, and was later used in Uighur (*sarthavaγi*) and further languages. Additionally, *sabo* 薩薄 (maybe to be read as *sapu* 薩簿) was once a title in Gaochang

233 Astana document 64 TAM 35: 15. Facsimile in: Tang Changru, *Tulufan chutu wenshu 3*, 524; edited in: Guojia wenwuju guwenxian yanjiu shi, *Tulufan chutu wenshu 7*, 453–54, especially 453, col. 10. For more on his case, see: Trombert, "La vigne et le vin, deuxième partie," 524–25, 551.

高昌, and *safu* 薩甫, *sabao* 薩保, and *sabao* 薩寶 came to be used as Chinese offices in charge of Central Asians and especially Sogdians.

3.2.5.2 Excavated material: counter-checking the transmitted evidence

In addition to these historically transmitted sources on the office, another body of excavated materials, including the above quoted epitaphs, steles, letters, and one genealogy, provides further references. These are organised in Table 12 (Vol. 2, Appendix 4.3).[234] Although these documents range from 311 CE to 673 CE and provide first-hand information, they also present their own dating problems, which in turn has implications for our historical analysis of the offices. For even if the date of an epitaph or stele can be ascertained, it is still debatable if the names of the offices and toponyms found thereon pertain to the time at which they were composed or to which they refer. Thus, when the epitaph states that the individual for whom it was made was born in 584 CE and entombed during the Tang in 669 CE, it is not clear whether the reference to the great-grandfather's office as *sabao* 薩寶 therein corresponds to a writing convention and the understanding of 669 CE (Hypothesis A) or to the time the great-grandfather served in this office, which may be over a hundred years earlier and outside of China (Hypothesis B).[235] In the following, both options shall be tested. At first sight, however, the second example seems improbable, as the individual of the above example was *sabao* outside of China.

In the case of Hypothesis A, it can be observed in the few extant examples at hand (organised in Table 13, Vol. 2, Appendix 4.3) that *safu* 薩甫 was used on one epitaph during the Eastern Wei and on one stele during the Sui, *sabao* 薩保 on three epitaphs from the Northern Zhou to the early Tang, and *sabao* 薩寶 on ten epitaphs and one stele from the Sui to the Tang (until 673 CE). Notably, this chronology roughly corroborates the chronology of the official historiography, however, not including the Eastern and Western Wei, i.e. Northern Qi: *safu* 薩甫; Sui: *sabao* 薩保; and Tang: *sabao* 薩寶.

Underpinning Hypothesis B, however, presents far more complications; for it needs to be established when they held office (which will be of interest to us later anyway). Thankfully, the deceased individual's time of appointment is normally provided in the epitaphs. Problematically, most of the individuals who are said to have been *safu* 薩甫 or *sabao* 薩保/薩寶 are the ancestors of the people for whose funeral the epitaph was made, and thus are temporally quite removed. While it is rarely the case that the precise dates for these ancestors' lifetimes are provided, the dynasty in which they held the office is sometimes mentioned. To establish a chronology of the title holders, it is necessary to approximate the dates of their lives and the dates of their office on the basis of the dynasties in which they were active, or the generational relationship to the entombed person. Dedicative steles are generally more informative

234 The Buddhist documents, discussed above, are not integrated (see also: Dien, "Consideration," Table 1.2).

235 Taking the example of the epitaph of Shi Hedan 史訶耽 (Appendix 4.3, Table 12, #5).

in this regard, as they mention the date of dedication and because we can presume that the donors were alive at that time. The resulting chronology, presented in Table 14 (Vol. 2, Appendix 4.3), clearly shows that Hypothesis B is most certainly invalid: if the epitaphs are ordered according to the dates to which they pertain (rather than date of composition), that is, when the individuals are said to have borne the titles, no pattern could be discerned. The notation of office names is thus in accord with contemporaneous naming standards (Hypothesis A, see above), exceptions notwithstanding.

As to the times in which the individuals held office, the following chronology can be outlined, arranged according to dynasties:

- The earliest six examples are said to have been *sabao* (one *sabao* 薩保, five *sabao* 薩寶) during the Northern Wei, although three of them held this title in their home state (of Shi 史, Kesh, in Sogdiana).[236]
- One *safu* 薩甫 is mentioned for the Eastern Wei (in the state of Di 翟);
- one *sabo* 薩薄 is mentioned for the Kingdom of Gaochang 高昌 of the Qu 麴 in 550 CE;
- two *sabao* (one *sabao* 薩保, one *sabao* 薩寶) for the Western Wei (who probably also held this title during the Northern Zhou);

236 All three stem from the country of Shi 史, Kesh, in Sogdiana. Forte (Forte, "Sabao 薩寶 Question," 98) proposed that *benguo* 本國 (lit. home country) referred to the dynasties under which the mentioned individuals lived instead of a country foreign to the Chinese dynasties. Research into comparable examples reveals, however, that this interesting proposition should most probably be dismissed.
A cursory investigation uncovered 23 examples in which *benguo* 本國 is used on an epitaph (Table 15, Vol. 2, Appendix 4.3). Fourteen thereof (Table 15, A); including the three examples named above) occur in the introduction, shortly after a reference to that the buried individual came from a foreign country; the *guo* 國 in these cases refers to their own country of origin.
In the remaining nine epitaphs (Table 15, B), *benguo* 本國 refers to a Chinese dynasty (dating 307–981 CE). Two examples refer to a Chinese dynasty different to that under which the epitaph is written: Table 15, B): E, written in the Eastern Wei, refers to the Northern Wei, but is part of the title of the office of *da zhongzheng* 大中正 (senior rectifier); and Table 15, B): C, as the epitaph is written in the Southern Liang, *benguo* 本國, likely references a Northern Dynasty.
In a further three epitaphs (Table 15, B): D, F–G), the term refers to the Chinese dynasty under which it is written but equally is part of the title *zhongzheng* 中正 or *da zhongzheng* 大中正 (rectifier or senior rectifier).
The remaining four examples (Table 15, B): A–B, H–I) refer to the dynasty under which they were written but are part of the narration and are not included in the description of the individuals.
In the three cases stemming from Shi 史, we may say therefore that when in an epitaph the term *benguo* 本國 is mentioned in the introduction, being part of the description of the deceased's country of origin, it refers to a foreign, non-Chinese country. In the other cases, the term is either used in combination with an office as part of a fixed expression or in reference to a Chinese dynasty; however, here it stands in a narrative context distinct from the introduction in which the deceased and his or her country of origin is introduced. We can thus conclude that the *benguo* 本國 of the epitaphs of the Shi 史 refers to a foreign, non-Chinese country, in this context most probably Kesh.

- one *sabao* 薩寶 for the Northern Qi;
- four for the Northern Zhou (three *sabao* 薩保, one *sabao* 薩寶);
- one *sabao* 薩寶 and one *xia silu* 下司錄 (junior record keeper of the *safu* 薩甫) for the Sui;
- and no *sabao*, one *cheqi qiduwei* 車騎騎都尉 (commandant of cavalry), one *zhangshi* 長史 (head scribe), and one *guoyi* 果毅 (vice commandant) of the *sabao* 薩寶 office for the Tang.

Before proceeding further, a detail in the naming practices needs to be addressed. The title of *sabao* 薩寶 is sometimes mentioned with the prefix *mahe* 摩和 (from Sanskrit *mahā-*, "great")[237] and/or *da* 大:

- The epitaph of Di Tusuo 翟突娑 (546–615 CE) mentions that his father was *mahe da sabao* 摩訶薩寶;
- the epitaph of An Wantong 安萬通 (585–654 CE) mentions that his great-grandfather was *mahe sabao* 摩訶薩寶;
- the epitaph of Shi Hedan 史訶耽 (584–669 CE) mentions that his great-grandfather was also *mahe sabao* 摩訶薩寶, whereas on his father Shi Shewu's 史射勿 (544–609 CE) epitaph, this ancestor is only mentioned as *sabao* 薩寶;
- Shi Hedan's 史訶耽 epitaph also mentions that his grandfather was *mahe da sabao* 摩訶大薩寶, whereas on his father Shi Shewu's 史射勿 epitaph, this ancestor is not mentioned as *sabao*, on his cadet brother Shi Daoluo's 史道洛 (591–655 CE) epitaph, this ancestor is mentioned as *mahe sabao* 摩訶薩寶, and on his nephew Shi Tiebang's 史鐵棒 (623–66 CE) epitaph, this ancestor is also mentioned as *mahe sabao* 摩訶薩寶;
- the epitaph of Kang Yuanjing 康元敬 (609–73 CE) mentions that his father was also *mahe da sabao* 摩訶大薩寶.

However, all occurrences of the latter two cases (*mahe sabao* 摩訶薩寶 and *mahe da sabao* 摩訶大薩寶) are to be found in epitaphs, and they refer to a previous generation at least from the time of the grandfather (if one presumes that the sons of the deceased are normally the authors of the epitaph and not the deceased himself), that is before the Tang. The only *sabao* title attested on an epitaph as being held by the deceased himself was the title *sabao* 薩保 (instead of *sabao* 薩寶 written *sabao* 薩保; to be found in the epitaphs of Master Shi 史/Wirkak and An Jia 安伽). It is therefore conceivable that these prefixes were either posthumous additions of the Tang, the later generations using the official title and its understanding of the time of composition (as was established above), or they are to be understood in the context of Chinese bureaucratic titles, in which *da* 大 is a typical prefix which is to be understood as "senior". In both cases, due to the lack of further evidence, it is still difficult to assert if a hierarchy is to be established between junior and senior *sabao* 薩寶.[238]

237 Dien, "Further Thoughts," 206.
238 Which was proposed in: Luo Feng, "Sabao: Zai kaocha," 219.

3.2.5.3 Further subordinate offices

Besides the mentions of *safu* 薩甫 and *sabao* 薩保/*sabao* 薩寶 listed in Tables 13 and 14 (Vol. 2, Appendix 4.3), there remains four offices occupied by five individuals to be addressed. These are directly or indirectly related to the office and appear only on the steles and epitaphs and not in the transmitted literary sources: 1) the *tianzhu* 天主 or *da tianzhu* 大天主 (Zoroastrian presider and presider-in-chief), 2) the *panshi caozhu* 判事曹主 (chief judge) of the *sabao* 薩保, 3) the *xia silu* 下司錄 (junior record keeper) of the *safu* 薩甫, and 4) the *cheqi qiduwei* 車騎都尉 (commandant of cavalry) of the *sabao* 薩寶 office.

3.2.5.3.1 Jurisdiction

The *tianzhu* 天主 or *da tianzhu* 大天主 (Zoroastrian presider and presider-in-chief fall into the ritual category below (p. 288, 3.3.11). The *panshi caozhu* 判事曹主 (chief judge) of the *sabao* 薩保 (office) is listed as an office in the epitaph of Master Shi 史 /Wirkak (494–579 CE). His grandfather is said to have been *sabao* 薩保 in his own state. He himself was first appointed chief judge of the *sabao* 薩保 office in 535 CE, under the Western Wei. Perhaps in 539 CE, he was then appointed *sabao* 薩保 of Liangzhou 涼州. This provides evidence that the administrative tasks of the *sabao* 薩保 office also included jurisdiction. As was discussed above, merchants may have profited from tax exemption and/or acquired special legal status in certain places along the Silk Roads. The existence of this specialised office may however imply that foreigners were to some extent left to implement legal matters independently. To further complicate the matter, the *Weishu* informs us that the legal texts of Samarqand were deposited in the local temple.[239] Although purely conjecture, it cannot be ruled out that the judge applied foreign law for certain penalties from the temple's law codex. This may be substantiated by the *sabao* 薩保 being in charge of the Zoroastrian temple's activities and the office, including a legal specialist.

Jurisdiction was normally part of the regional inspector/prefect's (*cishi* 刺史) many duties. If, however, there was no legal specialist in certain offices – as this is the only mention of such a chief judge – it may well be that the *sabao* 薩保 himself was in charge of the jurisdiction. This theory is supported by the other offices the *sabao* 薩保/薩寶 and their family members held, as recorded in their biographies. For example, while Kang Ye 康業 and his father were Zoroastrian presider-in-chiefs, he was posthumously promoted to the position of regional inspector. The father of *sabao* 薩保 An Jia 安伽 was a general in command of troops and the regional inspector. The father of the acting *sabao* 薩保 Lord Yu Hong 虞弘 was also regional inspector. Shi Hedan 史訶耽, grandson of a *sabao* 薩寶, was prefect. The great-grandfather and grandfather of the head scribe of the *sabao* 薩寶 office Long Run 龍潤 were regional inspectors, and he himself was later also promoted to the position of prefect. The grandfather of An Wantong 安萬通, descendant of a *sabao* 薩寶, was also regional

239 See the description of the state of Kang 康 p. 28 (1.7.12).

inspector. Finally, An He Zangqi 安何藏器[240] was *sabao* 薩寶 and regional inspector. Although the regional inspector/prefect and *sabao* 薩保/薩寶 were clearly distinct offices, this contextual information supports the idea that in their own community, the *sabao* 薩保/薩寶 or religious specialist was of equal importance and/or entailed similar duties to the former.

An interesting parallel can be made with the foreign headman's office (*fanzhang si* 蕃長司) in charge of Muslims in southern harbours. Chinese sources tell us that the foreign headman (*du fanzhang* 都蕃長, *fanzhang* 蕃長, or *fanshou* 蕃首) was in charge of the Muslim population of Guangzhou's 廣州 and Quanzhou's 泉州 foreign quarters.[241] In the Arabic records of al-Sīrāfī, the traveller Sulaiman records that the Chinese emperor appointed a Muslim to both decide upon the legal disputes between Muslims in accordance with Islamic jurisprudence and to recite the Khutbah and prayer for the Sultan.[242] It seems though as if the foreign headman was in charge of religious and worldly matters. Under the much later and notably more tolerant Yuan, however, Ibn Battūta reported that in Guangzhou's foreign quarter, there was a judge (*Qadi*) and a *Sheikh* in charge of the Muslims' matters.[243]

This case examples the Article 48 of the Tang Code, which states that offences between two foreigners of the same polity shall be judged according to their own law, whereas two foreigners of different polities shall be judged according to Chinese law:[244]

> 諸化外人，同類自相犯者，各依本俗法；異類相犯者，以法律論。疏議曰：化外人，謂蕃夷之國，別立君長者，各有風俗，制法不同。其有同類自相犯者，須問本國之制，依其俗法斷之。異類相犯者，若高麗之與百濟相犯之類，皆以國家法律，論定刑名。
>
> ARTICLE: 48.1–All cases involving foreigners of the same nationality who have committed crimes against each other will be sentenced following their own customary law.
>
> 48.2–Cases involving those of different nationalities who have committed crimes against each other will be sentenced following Chinese law.
> SUB-COMMENTARY: "Foreigners" refers to persons of those barbaric countries who have their own rulers and leaders. They each have their own habits and customs and their regulations, and the laws are not alike. In cases involving those of the same nationality who have committed crimes against

240 Also referred to as An Bi 安弼.

241 As indicated by Dien (Dien, "Sa-Pao Problem," 340, and fns. 46–47), see: Kuwabara Jitsuzō, "On P'u Shou-kêng," 33–34, 40–41. The original footnote no. 5 (p. 40 in the translation) is, however, more extensive in the original; see the five articles originally published from 1915 (no. 26.10) to 1918 (no. 29.10); or the Chinese translation: Kuwabara Jitsuzō, *Pu Shougeng kao*.

242 Sīrāfī, *Voyage*, 38; Sīrāfī, *Relation*, 13; Sīrāfī, *Ancient*, 7–8.

243 *Ibn Battūta* (trans. Lee), 213; (trans. Gibb), 290. For the *jiehaoshi* 結好使 under the Song (that conceivably was established in the Tang), see: Kuwabara Jitsuzō, "On P'u Shou-kêng," 44, no. 10.

244 *Tang lü shuyi* 6.133. For examples of such cases, see: Kuwabara Jitsuzō, "On P'u Shou-kêng," 46–48. Translation: Johnson, *The T'ang Code*, 252.

each other, the court must ask about the regulations in their native country and sentence the offence following their customs and laws.
In all cases involving those of different nationalities who have committed crimes against each other, such as one person from Koryo and another person from Paekche [countries in the Korean peninsula], Chinese law will be used to sentence and decide the punishment.

The *Pingzhou ke tan*, after repeating this law, further provides an interesting detail:[245]

> 廣州蕃坊，海外諸國人聚居，置蕃長一人，管勾蕃坊公事。蕃人有罪，詣廣州，鞫實送蕃坊行遣。縛之木梯上，以藤杖撻之，自踵至頂，每藤杖三下折大杖一下。……徒以上罪則廣州決斷。

> In the foreign quarter of Guangzhou live together all people from the countries beyond the sea. A foreign headman is appointed to manage all public matters of the foreign quarter. (…) When a foreigner commits a crime, [he] is sent to Guangzhou. [If] a charge is proved (by the Chinese authorities), [he] is sent to the foreign quarter. [There he is] tied to a wood ladder [and] whipped with a rattan cane from head to foot; three blows of the rattan cane amount to one of the heavy cane. (…) Penal servitude[246] and more sever punishments [are determined] by [the administration of] Guangzhou.

This indicates that life exile (including forced labour)[247] and capital punishment for Muslims was the prerogative of the Chinese government. It is conceivable that the above regulation equally applied to the Zoroastrians.

3.2.5.3.2 Record Keepers

The *xia silu* 下司錄 (junior record keeper) of the *safu* 薩甫 is mentioned on the stele of Hui Yu 惠鬱, Xuan Ning 玄凝 and others, dedicated on the 9.9.585 CE. The offices of each prefecture had dedicated record keepers. His office is here regarded as junior to the *zhangshi* 長史 (head scribe) and the *sima* 司馬 (adjutant), despite its rank being equal (rank 4 to 6).[248] Although this office is not mentioned in the historically transmitted sources, it is conceivable that it was later amalgamated with the office of scribe (*shi* 史 or *zhangshi* 史長史), mentioned in the official records of the Tang and in the epitaph of Long Run 龍潤 (561–653 CE).

245 *Pingzhou ke tan* 3.3a–b (Zhonghua shuju 2.1–4); author's translation. See: Kuwabara Jitsuzō, "On P'u Shou-kêng," 46; and: Hirth and Rockhill, *Chau Ju-Kua*, 16–17.

246 Kuwabara and Hirth and Rockhill (see the footnote above for the reference) both translated "banishment or more severe punishments". *Tu* 徒 does, however, not refer to banishment, but to penal servitude, i.e. forced labour in a fixed place, with a duration of one to three years. The next most severe punishment was life exile (*liu* 流), at a distance of ca. 1,000–1,500 km, also including forced labour up to four years. The next level of penalty was then capital punishment by strangulation (*jiao* 絞) or decapitation (*zhan* 斬) (Johnson, *The T'ang Code*, 58–59).

247 See the footnote above.

248 See the glossary for more information.

3.2.5.3.3 Military officer

Finally, there is the *cheqi qiduwei* 車騎都尉 (commandant of the cavalry) of the *sabao* 薩保 office, mentioned in the epitaph of Cao Yi 曹怡 (581–655 CE). His father is said to have been commandant of cavalry of the *sabao* 薩寶 office of Jiezhou 介州 during the early Tang. This information corroborates and supplements the details recorded in the historically transmitted sources regarding the existence of a military officer. Moreover, it substantiates the hypothesis proposed above that the *shuai* 率 (commandant) mentioned in the *Tongdian* is to be understood as a generic term.[249]

3.2.5.4 Office or title?

One further problem that must now be addressed concerns the nature of a title mentioned in Chinese manuscripts. As referred to in the beginning of this paper, the term "caravan leader" signified a person of important economic status and it was established in various languages across the Silk Roads as a title. Since Chinese steles and epitaphs in particular were composed in highly standardised modules and phrases, two possible strategies for mentioning that the individual or their ancestor held a title in a foreign state present themselves: Either the title would have been transcribed and used more or less generically,[250] or translated as a generic term for foreign chiefs.[251] The Chinese language inherently causes great difficulties in the process of transcribing the names and titles of foreign peoples and offices. The problem is that it is impossible to decide if these transcriptions and generic terms actually mean that the office holders were included in a ranked bureaucratic system in their respective place of origin or if their title is purely honorific in nature – which does, however, by no means imply that the holders were devoid of power. Chinese records resorted to framing foreign offices in the terms of a Chinese bureaucratic logic, and, on the basis of what is presently known, it appears that no surrounding country had developed a comparable bureaucratic tradition of equal complexity and scope. Since the Chinese record represents the majority of the available sources, our understanding of the administration of surrounding countries is decidedly distorted. Thus, for the cases in which a *safu* 薩甫 or *sabao* 薩保/薩寶 of a foreign state is recorded in an epitaph, in the absence of any extraneous evidence, it is necessary to question the nature of the epitaphs' statement. The question at hand is thus if those epitaphs and steles in China which state, for example, that people were *safu* 薩甫 in the state of Di 翟 and *sabao* 薩寶 in Kesh (in Sogdiana), can be taken as evidence for the existence of such an

249 See p. 270 (3.2.4.7).

250 E.g.: *mohe qufen* 莫賀去汾 (Zhang Qingjie pointed out that the title *mohe qufen* 莫何去汾 is to be found in the *Weishu* and *Beishi*, in the chapter concerning the Ruru 蠕蠕 (Rouran 柔然). It seems that these two homophonic words refer to the same title; namely, an official of considerable rank. For more information, see the glossary; *mohe fu* 莫賀弗 (a title for high ranking officials of the Rouran 柔然, lower than the *mohe qufen* 莫賀去汾) and *moyuan* 莫緣 (another title for high ranking officials, higher than the *mohe fu* 莫賀弗), both to be found in the epitaph of Lord Yu Hong 虞弘 (see Vol. 2, Appendix 3.4).

251 E.g.: *da shouling* 大首領 "great chief" (epitaph of An Pu 安菩, see Vol. 2, Appendix 3.15).

office in these countries, or if, as proposed above, the recorded Chinese office shows the will to translate the office, standing, or the responsibilities of an individual into a Chinese office to make it accessible to the reader at the time of composition.

Previous research on the matter has either offered views in support or opposition, depending respectively on the degree to which the Chinese records or the absence of foreign records acknowledging the office are emphasised. As a result of close reading of the sources, I want to propose a two-phase argument with which I hope to further the debate. The first is founded on an analysis of the combination of toponyms and titles on epitaphs and steles. These sources provide, among other details, the name, title, and stations in the career of the deceased individual, and his or her closest family members and their titles. Ordinarily, a title of nobility is paired with the name of its fief.[252] Similarly, many office titles are related to the administration of a place, which is often stated.[253] Military titles unrelated[254] or implicitly related[255] to a place often occur without a toponym. Appendix 4.3, Table 16, lists the references to the *safu* 薩甫 and *sabao* 薩保/薩寶 and related titles on epitaphs and steles (and one genealogy) according to the time of their office together with their toponym, if applicable. Looking at the pairings of the title with a toponym, we can see that in the twelve mentions of *safu* 薩甫 and *sabao* 薩保/薩寶, three are not paired with a toponym, four are paired with a "home state," and five are paired with a Chinese toponym. Chronologically, those individuals that are either paired with a "home state" or left unpaired were active between the period of the Northern and Eastern Wei, while those paired with a toponym had an active period in office from the Northern Qi, Western Wei to Northern Zhou, Northern Zhou, Sui, up to the Tang.

Before engaging in pure deduction, the second layer of the argument must be briefly laid out, concerning the titles related to the above. Taking the rather extensive list of related titles into account, we can further establish that the following are *directly* mentioned in relation to the *safu* 薩甫 and *sabao* 薩保/薩寶 office (in the table marked with an "X"; hereafter $^{+}$ marks an occurrence in the transmitted written records, * marks an occurrence on steles or epitaphs, including the genealogical mention of Zheng Xingchen 鄭行諶):[256]

– * the *sabao* 薩保 *panshi caozhu* 判事曹主 (chief judge)
– * the acting *sabao* 薩保
– * the junior record keeper of the *safu* 薩甫
– * the *cheqi qiduwei* 車騎都尉 (commandant of the cavalry) of the *sabao* 薩寶

252 E.g.: *Guangxing xian kaiguo bo* 廣興縣開國伯 "earl of the Guangxing 廣興 District" (epitaph of Lord Yu Hong 虞弘, see Vol. 2, Appendix 3.4).

253 E.g.: *Meizhou cishi* 眉州刺史 "regional inspector of Meizhou 眉州" (epitaph of An Jia 安伽, see Vol. 2, Appendix 3.3).

254 E.g.: *youji jiangjun* 游擊將軍 "mobile corps commander" (epitaphs of Lord Yu Hong 虞弘 and Shi Hedan 史訶耽, see Vol. 2, Appendices 3.4 and 3.7).

255 E.g.: *chaoqing dafu* 朝請大夫 "grandmaster for court audiences" (epitaph of Shi Hedan 史訶耽, see Vol. 2, Appendix 3.7), thus referring to the imperial court in the capital.

256 See Vol. 2, Appendix 4.3, Table 12, #56.

- [+] the *huzhu* 胡祝 (*hu* 胡 precentor) related to the *sabao* 薩寶 office
- [+] the *xianzheng* 祆正 (Zoroastrian regulator) of the *sabao* 薩寶 office
- [+] the *xianzhu* 祆祝 (Zoroastrian precentor) of the *sabao* 薩寶 office
- [+] the *shuai* 率 (commandant) of the *sabao* 薩寶 office
- [+] the *shi* 史 and *zhangshi* 長史 (scribe and head scribe) of the *sabao* 薩寶 office
- * the *guoyi* 果毅 (vice commandant) of the *sabao* 薩寶 office

For the *indirectly* related titles (marked in the table with a "Y") – if accepting that Zoroastrian specialists were subordinate to the office even when the office is not mentioned – there are:

- [+] the *xianzhu* 祆主 (Zoroastrian presider), related to the *xian* 祆 deity and performing magic tricks
- one epitaph mentioning two * *da tianzhu* 大天主 (Zoroastrian presider-in-chief) and one epitaph mentioning one * *tianzhu* 天主 (Zoroastrian presider)

Among the above-mentioned offices, not one is to be found with the exact same characters in the transmitted record and on a stele or epitaph, which is one of the reasons behind the complexity of this topic.

Ordering the *directly* related offices chronologically, the chief judge falls into the Western Wei, the Zoroastrian presider and the acting *sabao* 薩保 (*jianjiao sabao* 檢校薩保) offices fall into the Northern Zhou, the junior record keeper of the *safu* 薩甫 falls into the Sui, and the rest of the offices are mentioned for the Tang. Of the two Zoroastrian presiders-in-chief and the one Zoroastrian presider that are *indirectly* related to the office on the two aforementioned epitaphs, one was active during the Western Wei and two during the Northern Zhou.

To recapitulate, the first phases of analysis, concerning instances in which the title is paired with a toponym, revealed that the individuals given as *sabao* 薩保/薩寶 in excavated written sources start to be paired with Chinese toponyms in the Western Wei, Northern Qi, Northern Zhou, Sui, and Tang, while before the Western Wei, they were either only called *sabao* 薩保/薩寶 (i.e. the title alone is given) or related to another state. If subordinates are mentioned, their title mostly refers only to the *sabao* 薩保/薩寶 office, omitting the toponym. The second aspect of the argument – excluding indirect references (perhaps unrelated) to the office, which shall be discussed later – concerns the different offices directly related to the *sabao* 薩保/薩寶 office, demonstrated that subordinates of the office start to appear from the Western Wei, while most are mentioned for the Tang. The existence of surrogates and subordinates are strong indications for the institutionalisation of an office.

Combining these two findings, it can be concluded that individuals *called safu* 薩甫, *sabao* 薩保 or 薩寶 of their own state – or given a *title* of seemingly sufficient significance to their identity or status to be mentioned on an epitaph or stele – arise during the Northern Wei at the earliest. However, the first evidence for the installation of an *office* can be traced to the Western Wei, and the frequency of offices and administrative complexity of the office structure increase dramatically during the Tang, possibly including a *sabo* 薩薄 office in Gaochang 高昌. This conclusion essentially corroborates the dating in the official historiographies, yet the excavated sources push the earliest inclusion of this office into the bureaucracy from the Northern Qi back to the Western Wei and further show that it existed under the Northern Zhou. Collectively, the steles, epitaphs, and a single biography supplement the list of subordinate offices related to this office, and evidence that the office was in charge of various concerns related to the Sogdians, as detailed above.

Following this detailed process of counterchecking, it is apparent that the officially transmitted historiographies do not reflect a bureaucratic reality. Therefore, rather than simply accepting the accounts as regulations that were executed to the letter, I propose – in the light of the afore presented evidence and without disregarding the incontrovertible inconsistencies and discrepancies – that a *safu* 薩甫 was likely not stationed in every prefecture and was not literally in charge of 200 households of Central Asians, but that these listings represent the Chinese authors' portrayal of their idealised state of administration.

3.2.5.5 Further deductions

Adding further nuance to our comprehension of this context, the epitaphs, steles, and archaeological excavation reports provide us with a vast amount of material that can be combined with the transmitted sources to understand the various social aspects of the office. Among these, the background of the officers as well as the inheritability and eligibility of the offices shall be discussed below.

3.2.5.5.1 The backgrounds of the officers

The epitaphs and steles inform us of where the individuals who held these *sabao* or *sabao* related offices came from and, to some degree, how they self-identified in society. Of the 22 individuals[257] related to the title (see Table 16, Vol.2, Appendix 4.3), one is an Eastern Indian from the state of Di 翟, one from somewhere in the Western Regions (Sogdiana and the regions lying adjacent to China's north-west during the Tang, or Rouran 柔然?), two are probably Turco-Sogdian (Di 翟), 13 or 14 of Sogdian descent, two or three of Parthian descent, and two Chinese. Excluding those previously identified as giving a mere title or as being related to their own state, those remaining concern one individual from somewhere in the Western Regions (Rouran 柔然?), two Turco-Sogdians (Di 翟), nine or ten of Sogdian descent, one or two Parthians, and two Chinese.

Before advancing any conclusions, the few Chinese individuals shall be investigated in more detail. Chronologically, the first is Cao Zun 曹遵, father of Cao Yi 曹怡, who is said to have been the commandant of the cavalry of the *sabao* 薩寶 in Jiezhou 介州. Although most people related to the office were from the west and his name is one of the family names used for Sogdians (referring to Kapūtānā), nothing else in his grave or epitaph hint at his being of foreign descent. On the contrary, his ancestry is traced back to the Cao 曹 of the ancient Zhou Dynasty. The

257 Including Zheng Xingchen 鄭行諶.

second is Long Run 龍潤, said to have been *zhangshi* 長史 (head scribe) of the *sabao* 薩寶 office, and again there is no indication of him being of foreign descent. Finally, there is Zheng Xingchen 鄭行諶, said to have been *guoyi* 果毅 (vice commandant) of the office, who can be equally identified as Chinese with fair certainty. In conclusion, most individuals related to the title and office were foreign or of foreign descent, and that the greater majority were Sogdian. That Sogdians are said to have been mostly Zoroastrians explains the presence of Zoroastrian specialists in the office. The one or two identified as Chinese were part of the military branch of the office, which does not contradict anything what is known about its functions.[258] The one Chinese scribe is indeed the only scribe of the office we know of from an epitaph or a stele. It stands to reason that a person trained and proficient in writing Chinese bureaucratic documents, which is not an easy task, would occupy this office.

3.2.5.5.2 Inheritability

In imperial China, offices were granted by imperial decree, which, by definition, is a hindrance to an office being directly hereditary. For the *sabao* himself, we only know of two family members holding the office over a generation. During the Northern Wei, An Nantuo 安難陀[259] lived in Guzang 姑臧, Liangzhou 涼州, and served as *sabao* 薩寶. His family moved during his or his son's time to Yongzhou 雍州 (the capital, later called Chang'an 長安), where the latter, An He Zangqi 安何藏器,[260] was then *sabao* 薩寶 of Yongzhou 雍州 during the Western Wei and possibly even Northern Zhou (as the stele of An Zhongjing 安忠敬 and the epitaph of An Yuanshou 安元壽 probably intimate). His son, the third generation, An Pansuoluo (Panshaluo?) 安盤娑羅[261] was, contrary to what the transmitted record states, most probably not *sabao* 薩寶.[262] The second example is to be found in the epitaphs of one of the Shi 史 families of Guyuan 固原, Ningxia Province, on which it is recorded that two generations of their family were *sabao* 薩寶 during the Northern Wei, but in their state of origin.[263] According to the argument laid out above, this is to be understood as a title and not as a bureaucratic office. Indeed, in the first example, the father held the title but probably not an office – he was living *in* Guzang and was not *sabao* 薩寶 *of* Guzang – and the

258 Their relation to the office led previous researchers to forcefully identify them as Sogdians, allegedly concealing their origin. We can indeed establish that some Sogdians and foreigners "dissimulated" their ancestry, claiming to stem from an illustrious Chinese family. Lord Yu Hong 虞弘 (however, not of Sogdian descent), for example, claims to stem from the legendary emperor Shun 舜, his vita and tomb however speaking of his Western ancestry. The same goes for the Sogdian An Jia 安伽, who claims to descend from the legendary Yellow Emperor. The combination of the literary and archaeological evidence is what leads to such conclusions in these cases.

259 Also referred to as An Xue Wuzheng 安薛晤徵.

260 Also referred to as An Bi 安弼.

261 Also referred to as An Poluo 安婆羅 or An Luo Fangda 安羅方大.

262 See the argumentation p. 245 (3.2.3.1.7).

263 The epitaphs of Shi Shewu 史射勿 (544–609 CE), Shi Hedan 史訶耽 (584–669 CE), and Shi Tiebang 史鐵棒 (623–66 CE), see p. 138 (2.3.2.6), p. 142 (2.3.2.7), and p. 149 (2.3.2.9).

son later occupied the office, but, as the family moved, was now stationed in the capital; and in the second example they held the titles in their own state. Consequently, the question of inheritance of the *sabao* office itself remains inconclusive.

3.2.6 Recapitulation of the political organisation and legislature

Caravan leaders (Skt. *sārthavāha*) were highly respected in several regions along the Silk Roads. As eminent people of great economic and social capital, they formed a separate category with a title transcribed in various languages, among others Chinese. Through a combined analysis of the transmitted literary evidence with the excavated material, it was shown that this title was conceivably linked to the Chinese office in charge of Sogdians, which is to be found in the official records as *safu* 薩甫, *sabao* 薩保, and finally *sabao* 薩寶. Due to the compilation of an up-to-date chronology of their use, including an elucidation of the nomenclature employed in epitaphs and steles, this paper contends that references to individuals active before the Western Wei and/or in a foreign state use *safu* 薩甫, *sabao* 薩保, and *sabao* 薩寶 as *titles* that explain the individual's standing and responsibilities by using a contemporary Chinese term. It is only from this point onwards that we may speak of a Chinese *office*, which possibly required an explanation for the Sogdian reader. While the office was in charge of Sogdians in the capital and provinces and its rank was increased from the Northern Qi to the Tang, the extent of authority and distribution in every district alleged by the official sources should not be taken uncritically. Instead, it was proposed that the officer's function inside of his community was comparable to the authority of a regional inspector/prefect: Probably based in the Zoroastrian temple, the office included various subordinates, showing the extent of its administrative power, of which we know a judge, a scribe, a military officer, and two religious specialists, holding hereditary offices.[264] Although the latter were in charge of Zoroastrian rituals – maybe even before the office itself was installed – the *sabao* office and its officers were not affiliated to one specific religion. Further, the majority of the officers were foreign, most being Sogdians, the Central Asians thus largely being in charge of their own community from the Western Wei to the Song.

Far from being a singular example, the *sabao* office was paralleled by, e.g., the foreign headman (*fanzhang* 藩長) in charge of Muslims in Quanzhou 泉州 and Guangzhou 廣州. Although the *Qadi* and *Sheikh* would later separate the religious and worldly matters, it seems as if during the Tang the headman managed all matters of the foreign quarter. This administration is further to be seen in the historical context of the loosely associated subordinate prefectures, in which local foreign holders of power were "assigned" hereditary offices and titles for military protection during the Qin, Han (*shuguo* 屬國), Tang (*jimi zhou* 羈縻州 or *fanzhou* 番州) and foreign officers in the Yuan (*tuguan* 土官), up to the Ming and Qing (*tusi* 土司), vowing allegiance in return.[265] In the *sabao's* case, besides the service of Sogdians in the

264 On this, see p. 311 (3.3.11.2).
265 See: Wu Yongzhang, *Zhongguo tusi zhidu*.

Chinese military, the economic success and connections of Sogdian traders[266] may be seen as the main reason behind the successful transfer of economic and social capital into political capital.[267] Several Chinese dynasties thus legitimised and endowed Sogdians with authority by the establishment of an office for their community.

3.3 People and customs

3.3.1 Physiognomy

According to the early accounts on what could be identified as Sogdiana in the *Shiji* and various later accounts on Samarqand, Sogdians had deep-set eyes, high noses, profuse beards, and a large stature. While the description fits ancient paintings in Sogdiana itself, they are also match tomb figurines in China and mural paintings in tombs of Sogdians in China. It is also probable that their larger stature may have provided them with an easier access to and success in the army. All four points reflect the discrimination between what may have been characteristic of a typical Chinese person in the eyes of the authors: the Chinese had not as deep-set eyes, low noses, practically no beards, and a smaller stature. The latter statements – besides the relatively smaller stature – can equally be substantiated by contemporary artefacts. Besides these genetic differences, cowardice is added in the *Da Tang Xiyu ji* as a contrast to their large stature. This judgement is probably best understood as a phenomenon of the self-aggrandizing rhetoric of the accounts by contrasting techniques and may further be related to their excellence in commerce, which is qualified as swindling.

3.3.2 Youth and education

In Samarqand, boys were apparently taught how to write and read at the age of five and for the half that did not have to work as peasants it seems that they were sent off to learn the trade of commerce upon reaching the age of 20.

In the eighth century in Chonghua 崇華 Town, more than half of the male people with Sogdian names left the settlement before the age of 15, which may support the idea that a similar habit may have been at work here – be it for trade and/or tax avoidance. If one believes the epitaph of Lord Yu Hong 虞弘 – who, however, was from the Rouran 柔然 – he participated in a mission to Iran and the Tuyuhun 吐谷渾 at the age of 13 as *mohe fu* 莫賀弗. As will be detailed below, several Sogdians were active as translators at the court and sent as envoys to communicate with the Tujue 突厥, which further speaks to their polyglot faculties. In addition, an ink rubbing stone was found in the grave of Shi Suoyan 史索嚴 which points to the importance of his presentation as a scholar at the funeral and conceivably speaks of his ability to write. Finally, a letter written in Chinese from a certain "princess" Jun Zhezhe 君者者,

266 See: Vaissière, *Sogdian Traders*.
267 See: Bourdieu, "Ökonomisches Kapital".

asking her addressee, Lady Beizhai 北宅, among other things, to light a light at the Zoroastrian temple(s) near Dunhuang 敦煌 may further be taken as evidence for Sogdian women – of high standing, at least – learning to read and write in China.[268]

3.3.3 Military

The people of Kapūtānā were described as tall and large and skilled in war and combat, the people of Chach as excellent fighters, and Māymurgh, Kesh, Ishitikhan, and Kušaniyya are said to have been home to thousands of elite soldiers. Further, the soldiers and horses of Samarqand are described as mighty and magnificent and an elite unit of *čākar* is praised as fierce elite soldiers that have no fear of death. Envoys of Samarqand and Sutrūshana also arrived at court during the Wude 武德 era (618–26 CE) and referred to themselves as being known as vassals with valiant warriors. In China, the *Sanguozhi* hints at the existence of rather independent forces of the Yuezhi 月氏 and Sogdians that were ready to mobilise in Liangzhou 涼州 at a time when the Eastern Han had lost political control in the third century. That Sogdians were militarily organised and powerful in the north-west until at least the seventh century can further be seen by the surrender of Shi Wannian 石萬年, a Sogdian military leader from Chach, who in 630 CE led seven forts to surrender in Yizhou 伊州 to the Tang.

While their taller stature – as mentioned above – may have been beneficial for military service, the majority epitaphs of Sogdians due in fact mention them holding offices in the military. How such a Sogdian military official may have looked can be further seen on the walls of the dromos of Shi Shewu's 史射勿 grave (Figure 6–Figure 14, Vol. 2, Appendix 1.2.5). As the biographies further exemplify, they were valued as personal bodyguards by several emperors and employed as horse breeders, even for the corrals of the imperial guards.

3.3.4 Commerce

Sogdians and especially people from Samarqand were in transmitted records praised as excellent merchants who apparently sent their sons to China to trade. Apart from the appreciation of their skill in trade and them travelling everywhere profit is to be made, they are described as having an eye for bargains and a tendency to swindle. Sogdians were demonstrably active in trade between India in China since at least the second half of the third century.[269] More importantly for the present study, Sogdians migrated east along the Silk Roads. Surrounding the Taklamakan Desert, they settled along the Northern Route in Douldour-Āqour and Kucha, Qarashahr, Gaochang 高昌 and the Turfan 吐魯番 Region, Tingzhou 庭州, Hami, and along the Southern Route in Khotan, in several forts in Loulan 樓/Shanshan 鄯善 (including Niya 尼雅, dating to the second century), and Qiemo 且末, and east of the desert in Shazhou 沙州. Among these, Kucha, Gaochang 高昌, Khotan, Loulan 樓蘭 and Shazhou 沙州 can

268 Unless it was written for her, which is possible but improbable.

269 For Sogdian trade with India (*apud*: Tremblay, "Spread," 96, fn. 102), see: Fussman, "Expliquer Shatial," 76 ff.; refuting: Jettmar, "Sogdians"; Jettmar, "Sogdische Händler," 94 ff.

be discerned as commercial hubs. There is even mention of a moor north-west of Shazhou 沙州, were Sogdian merchants halted for water on their way from Liangzhou 涼州. Due to the Sogdian Ancient Letters, it could further be established that long-distance trade between Samarqand, Dunhuang 敦煌, Guzang 姑臧, and the Chinese capitals Chang'an 長安 and Luoyang 洛陽 existed at least as early as the beginning of the fourth century. Among the many mentions of merchants and hundreds of sales contracts found in Dunhuang 敦煌, even one sale contract for a slave in Gaochang 高昌 written in Sogdian and dated 639 CE was found, although slave trade was officially forbidden. On the Southern Route, some of the settlements were, however, deserted and actually re-colonised in the seventh century by Sogdians such as Chief Kang Yandian 康艷典 from Samarqand.

The major settlements of Sogdians must, however, have been in Liangzhou 涼州. Besides the trade activity evinced by the Ancient Sogdian Letters, Chinese records mention Sogdian merchants as mainly travelling to Guzang 姑藏 for trade until the fifth century. When the Wei then invaded, they took Sogdian merchants as prisoners, which had to be ransomed by the king of Sute 粟特 (probably referring to the king of Samarqand). Further, the *Weishu* recounts that Yuan Xian 元暹 was appointed as regional inspector of Liangzhou 涼州 in 531 CE, who extorted, among others, the Sogdian merchants of their wealth, partly by executing them. They must have been dominant in trade because the *Suishu* reports that in the sixth century, Sasanian coins were – besides cloth, silk, and grain – approved as methods of payment in the Hexi 河西 corridor. When in the seventh century, Xuanzang 玄奘 came through Liangzhou 涼州 on his pilgrimage, he recorded that Liangzhou 涼州 was the centre of power and commerce of the Western Regions.

For the main territory of the Chinese dynasties, while Sogdians are recorded mostly settling in the north and in some southern cities, their commercial activities are mainly recorded for the capitals Chang'an 長安 and Luoyang 洛陽. The relative political stability that the Sui and Tang established over long stretches of the Silk Roads were the guarantor of a steady influx of foreigners, their products, and the *exotica* the court and capital craved. The long ranging connections that Sogdians entertained between the Western Regions and the capitals can be inferred form legal disputes in the seventh century between a Sogdian and a Chinese merchant at the court of Gaochang 高昌 recorded in documents from Turfan 吐魯番. The former had two Sogdian guarantors with the same family name that were "registered merchants" in Chang'an 長安 speak for him. Whether or not this is to be taken as evidence of trade between Gaochang 高昌 and the capital, it evidences a functioning Sogdian long-distance network. Further, a caravan of Central Asian people is recorded requesting to settle in the capital in the middle of the seventh century.

While in Chang'an 長安, Western Market was famous for exotic products, Sogdians were part of the Business Association of Scents of the Northern Market in

Luoyang 洛陽.[270] Scents, namely tulip scent from Kharghān, were indeed mentioned as one of the many import products from Sogdiana. Laufer and Schafer made magisterial studies of many of these products, narrating in detail the evolution of the preference for, and eventually tidal wave of Western products and culture in the heart of China.[271] Although it is best understood as a moral episode in the manuscripts of Dunhuang 敦煌, the success of such Sogdian traders may be inferred from the story of the immensely wealthy – and greedy – Sogdian merchant Shi Potuo 史婆陀 and his cadet brother Shi Xieli 史頡利 in Chang'an 長安.

It is, however, important to point out that Sogdians mostly played an intermediary role in these transfers between larger centres of cultural power such as China, Sogdian city-states, and the Sasanian Empire. This being said, specifically "Sogdian" culture, or local variations, are difficult to identify, being overshadowed by Iranian products and culture regulated and defined by the Iranian court such as, for example, Zoroastrianism or the game of polo.[272] To complicate the debate, especially from the middle of the seventh century, it was Turkic culture that dominated the public sphere of exotics.

3.3.5 Translators and envoys

That translations are the tools for any state to communicate with a state of another language and culture seems obvious. However, the alleged motivation to employ translators stated in the *Shiji* is clearly unidirectional: the "nine translations" were meant to reach faraway people and inform the world about the emperor's might. The *Tang Liu dian* 2.35 records that the Honglusi 鴻臚寺 (Court of State Ceremonial) employed 20 interpreters (*yi yu* 譯語) and that ten translators/interpreters (*fan shu yi yu* 翻書譯語, lit. translators of written and spoken language) worked in the Central Secretariat for the Tang. Judging from the office's name, the latter may have had the additional qualification of being able to read and write foreign scripts, although the addition of *fan shu* 翻書 may just be a more complete office title. In the *Xin Tangshu* 47.1212, ten translators, however, are called *fan shu yi yu* 蕃書譯語 (i.e. with another *fan* 蕃, meaning "foreign", lit. *foreign* scripts translators of spoken language).[273]

270 Twitchett provided an overview of the complex market system of the Tang: Twitchett, "T'ang Market".

271 Laufer, *Sino-Iranica*; Schafer, *Golden Peaches*; see also: Cai Hongsheng, *Tangdai*, 46–74.

272 *An Lushan Shiji* A.10: 祿山既移居親仁坊，進表求降墨敕，請宰相至席宴會。是日，玄宗欲於樓下打毬，遂停打毬，命宰相赴焉。"When An Lushan 安祿山 transferred his residence to the Qinren 親仁 District [of Chang'an 長安], [he] sent a request [to the emperor] to issue a hand written decree, asking the ministers to participate in the banquet. On this day, Xuanzong 玄宗 desired to play ball (polo) at the foot of the building. Soon later [he had ordered to stop] playing ball, commanding the ministers to go there." For an annotated translation in French: Rotours, *Histoire de Ngan Lou-Chan*, 87. For a short discussion of the polo game coming to Chang'an 長安, see: Xiang Da, *Tangdai Chang'an*, 74–81.

273 There is an ongoing debate as to the correctness of either option. Based on the standard grammatical structure of Classical Chinese, I propose that the *Xin Tangshu*'s version is probably erroneous. For differing opinions, see: Li Jinxiu, "Tangdai de fanshu," 39, fn. 1.

Sogdians were active at the court as counsels in audiences, which included a function as interpreter and probably translator.[274] There was Shi Shewu 史射勿, grand master for proper consultation, and his third son Anle 安樂, grandmaster for court audiences, as well as An Xun 安巡, who was senior great general unequalled in honour and court gentleman for thorough counsel at the Sui court. During the Tang, Shewu's 射勿 oldest son Hedan 訶耽 came to the court to assume the office of grandmaster for court audiences, concurrently holding military offices. In his honorary civil service career, he was successively promoted to translator in the Secretariat, court gentleman of manifest virtue, gentleman for court audiences, court gentleman for thorough counsel, and gentleman for court discussion. Shi Suoyan 史索嚴, of the other Shi 史 family, was also appointed as grandmaster for court audiences one year later than Shi Hedan 史訶耽, and Suoyan's 索嚴 brother – who we only know from his nephew Daode's 道德 epitaph – was also imperial grand master for proper consultation. Quite interestingly, a commentary to the episode involving the forceful purchase of the property of Shi Hedan 史訶耽 in the version provided in the *Zizhi tongjian* gives a commentary on his office of "Secretariat translator" (*zhongshu yi yu ren* 中書譯語人, translator in the Central Secretariat), showing that at the time of composition, the authors saw it necessary to provide explanations for the existence and/or task of this office:[275]

> 中書掌受四方朝貢及通表疏，故有譯語人。
>
> The Secretariat receives the tribute to the court from everywhere and dispatches reports upwards, which is why there are translators.

Outside the court, translators were also active for local government, which is evidenced by the *Tang hui yao* including the following decree:[276]

> [開元]七年三月敕：胡書進表。並令西蕃所由州府繙訖封進。
>
> [In Kaiyuan 開元] 7/3 (719 CE) it was decreed: to submit *hu* 胡 scripture to the emperor, it shall be translated by the district governments through which the Western Foreigners pass to be [then] sealed and sent to the court.

This is supported by the record in Dunhuang 敦煌 manuscripts of the end of the 7th to the beginning of the eighth century of local translators in the military, court cases, and business transactions in Gaochang 高昌, among which were several Sogdians.

The envoys that came to China or were sent by the Chinese government travelled together with interpreters or knew foreign languages themselves. During the Wei, there is the example of the Sogdian An Nuopantuo 安諾槃陀, who was sent by

274 For a case in which there was suspicion about a Sogdian translator's loyalty in regard to a mission to the Uyghurs, see: Lung, "Sogdian".

275 *Zizhi tongjian* 199.6272–73; author's translation.

276 *Tang hui yao* 26.505; author's translation. Pointed out by: Li Jinxiu, "Tangdai de fanshu," 40.

Emperor Wen 文 to communicate with Tumen 土門 (Bumin, later calling himself Yili Kehan 伊利可汗, Illig Qaghan) of the Tujue 突厥 in 545 CE, conceivably because of his linguistic and intercultural skills. Indeed, Sogdians are famous in historic sources for their role as envoys, such as Sogdian envoys sent by the Tujue 突厥 to Byzantium (as recounted by Menander).[277]

Besides the claims that Chinese rulers such as Wu Zetian 武則天 enthroned Sogdian rulers, envoys present, however, a meagre source of information about the relationship between the Sogdian rulers and the Chinese court. The *Shiji* started to record envoys, the date they arrived and the "gifts" they brought as "tribute" with them, which shows the importance given to these events, and served as example for future records. The Chinese protocol forced the foreigners to recognise in act and word the sovereignty of the Chinese emperor accordingly. How exactly it was observed, is questionable, however.[278] As it is still often the case today, envoys nominally travelled for political motives, but were often either accompanied by merchants, themselves engaging in commerce, or hoping to initiate or uphold a mutually beneficial relationship. The alleged deception of the Chinese court by foreign dignitaries for economic goals was, as already mentioned, a typical topic of complaint and further a manifestation of the conflict between the myth of a sinocentric world order and groups that behaved in an uninformed or incompatible way to this myth.

Political changes did have an important impact on the number of visits. Thus, after the subjugation of the Western Turk Khaganate in 658 CE, envoys from the west, including Sogdians, increased in number, politically reflected by the installation of a system of loosely governed prefectures, the *jimi zhoufu* 羈縻州府, in 679 CE.[279] For the Chinese court, these visitors were not only flattering; rather, the envoys were one of the major sources of the records. Official regulations of the Tang detail that foreign envoys were to be questioned to produce records and it stands to reason that this was practiced more or less systematically in the centuries before. The *Tang liu dian* notes:[280]

> 其外夷每有番官到京，委鴻臚訊其人本國山川、風土，為圖以奏焉，副上於省。其五方之區域，都鄙之廢置，疆埸之爭訟者，舉而正之。
>
> When from the Barbarians a foreign official comes to the capital, the Court of State Ceremonial [shall] enquire about the topography and customs of their country. A map [shall] be made to be submitted to the court [and] copies [shall] be provided to the provincial [governments].

Further, the *Tang Huiyao* describes the importance of this information for the compilation of official histories:[281]

277 Jacoby, *Fragmenta*, IV, 225 ff.; *apud*: Chavannes, *Documents*, 234.

278 For a rather ideal account of these procedures, see: Schafer, *Golden Peaches*, 25–28.

279 For more information, see the glossary.

280 *Tang Liu dian* 5.183.

281 *Tang hui yao* 63.1089. Translation: Twitchett, *Writing*, 27, 29.

蕃國朝貢。每使至。鴻臚勘。問土地風俗。衣服貢獻。道里遠近。並其主名字報。……

Appearance at court of tribute-bearing missions from foreign countries: Whenever such a foreign mission arrives, the Court for Diplomatic Reception [*Hung-lu ssu*][282] should examine them on the natural conditions and customs of their country, on their dress, and the products brought as tribute, and on the distance and route by which they have come. These facts are to be reported together with the names of their leaders. (…)

已上事，并依本条所由，有即勘报史馆，修入国史。如史官访知事由，堪入史者，虽不与前件色同，亦任直牒索，承牒之处，即依状勘，并限一月内报。

All the above matters should be investigated and reported to the Historiographical Office as they occur by the responsible authority specified in the appropriate section. If the Historiographical Office discovers any matter which is appropriate for inclusion in the record, but not analogous with the matters specified above, it may send an official communication directly requesting information about it. Any place receiving such a communication should make enquiries in accordance with the schedule of requests, and make its report within a month.

Besides such accounts, paintings of the envoys (*zhigong tu* 職貢圖) were produced in the Liang and Tang, which would be used for the compilation of the annals.[283] Last but not least, Sogdians were also famously active as translators of Buddhist texts, which is, however, not of greater import for this study.[284]

3.3.6 Agriculture and products

While the *Shiji* mentions that grapes and alfalfa were imported to China by the wish of the Han emperor in order to produce wine and feed horses, there is generally little information on agriculture in transmitted records. Instead, tax registers provide far better insight into the everyday life of settlements. For Gaochang 高昌 in the sixth century, it could thus be established that Sogdians were not only registered as farmers but also in various other crafts, i.e. as weavers, saddlers, goldsmiths, tanners, furriers, brewers, and viticulturists – the latter of which is supported by depictions of viticulture in stone carvings. In Dunhuang 敦煌 in the sixth century, the majority of the population was Sogdian. Most were recorded as farmers, while some engaged in

282 Translated above as Court of State Ceremonial.

283 Lung, "Interpreters," 210–14.

284 Meisterernst and Durkin-Meisterernst, "Buddhist Sogdian Texts"; Meisterernst and Durkin-Meisterernst, "The Buddhist Sogdian P7"; Meisterernst and Durkin-Meisterernst, "Some Remarks"; Zhang Guangda, "Sogdians as Translators"; and, for an important comment on the Buddhist propagation to Sogdiana and China: Tremblay, "Spread," 95–97.

commerce or active as craftsmen. Further, the above-mentioned Kang Yandian 康艷典, who was said to have re-colonised the Southern Route, apparently planted grape vines in one of the Forts, which consequently was called Grape Fort in the seventh century. Finally, Shi Hedan 史訶耽, Shi Tiebang 史鐵棒, and Shi Daode 史道德 were active as horse breeders, in the corrals in the capital and in the periphery. Shi Hedan's 訶耽 eulogy claims that his family owned 4,000 horses and Shi Daode 史道德 was head pasturage director of Lanchi 蘭池, a place famous for horses that were used for the imperial guard – in which he had served.

3.3.7 Family, women and marrying

The major families that held power in China from the collapse of the Han to even after the An Lushan 安祿山 Rebellion of the eighth century, however, stayed essentially the same, i.e. a restricted group of ethnic Han elite families.[285] After the Wei conquered Northern China, the tension between their Northern background Wei and the Han norms and old elites created a tension that threatened their legitimacy as rulers. Xiao Wendi 孝文帝 was one of the Emperors who thought of acculturation and assimilation as necessary steps to maintain his authority, banning Xianbei 鮮卑 clothing and language in the 490s CE, which remained, however, a short-lived and widely challenged endeavour. The imperial clan of the Tang was similarly trapped in a complex tension of different identities:[286] While being themselves of partly foreign descent, the Tang tried, among other strategies, to construct an ancestral myth, relating themselves to the Li 李 clan of which the famous thinker Laozi 老子 (Li Er 李耳) allegedly belonged to.[287]

While the relation to a famous ancestor was one part of the strategy, the toponym related to that famous family represented the other. To describe this phenomenon, Johnson, who worked on social mobility, albeit focusing on the elite, coined the term "choronym" in 1977, and – based on the research of Ikeda On[288] – explained that it "was not necessarily his (the individual's) place of residence or registry, nor the place where he was born [… but rather] his claim to membership in a certain descent group."[289] To support his view, he provided two examples of families that moved south, but after generations continued to use the old northern choronym. In his dissertation of 2006, Tackett worked on the elite – which he chose to call "aristocracy". Since for his project he included in his definition of "elite" every person

285 The Huangchao 黃巢 Rebellion, with the capture of Chang'an 長安 in 881 CE, led to the actual destruction of the old elite. This is the conclusion of the doctoral thesis, and later volume by Tackett. See: Tackett, "Transformation of Medieval Chinese Elites"; and: Tackett, *Destruction of the Medieval Chinese Aristocracy*. This underpins Johnson hypothesis (Johnson, *The Medieval Chinese Oligarchy*) and adds a general and conflicting view to the results of the case-study made by Ebrey (Ebrey, *Aristocratic*).

286 See: Abramson, *Ethnic Identity*, xxi–xxii.

287 See also: Chen Sanping, *Multicultural China*, 4–38; based on: Chen Sanping, "Succession Struggle".

288 Ikeda On, "Tōdai (1)"; Ikeda On, "Tōdai (2)".

289 Johnson, *The Medieval Chinese Oligarchy*, 92–93; see also: ibid., 29–30, 63.

who had an epitaph, he contended that "by the late Tang, any use of a choronym was an aristocratic marker of status".[290] Davis finally wrote in 2015 that choronyms indicated "great clan status".[291] As common foreign immigrants and their descendants immigrants per definition did not stem from the Chinese "aristocracy" and were not part of the "elite", they would, however, have no need for a choronym *on* their epitaph, or even have the need *for* an epitaph, according to Tackett. They did use them, however.

It was shown above that Sogdians produced epitaphs that included choronyms and that since they could not refer to a famous Chinese descent group, they chose instead to present a background story of their family. In distinction to epitaphs of Chinese, they were free to include claims that were then – and are still today – difficult to verify, such as descent from illustrious families or foreign nobility. For example, whereas Shi Shewu's 史射勿 epitaph said to have stemmed from a "Western state", his son Shi Hedan 史訶耽 claimed to descend from the king of the state of Shi 史 (Kesh). An Niang 安娘, the wife of Shi Suoyan 史索嚴, said to have descended from the king of Anxi 安息 (probably referring to Bukhārā) while her nephew Shi Daode 史道德 related his family to Shi Yu 史魚 of the Spring and Autumn Period, and Shi Dan 史丹 of the Han; Cao Yi 曹怡 was allegedly related to the son of King Wen 文 of the Zhou, Shu Zhenduo 叔振鐸 of Cao 曹; and Kang Yuanjing 康元敬 was apparently among the descendants of the Duke Gao 高 of Bi 畢 of the ancient Zhou dynasty, which once lived among the "barbarians" and then "came back" to China. An Jia 安伽 and Yu Hong 虞弘 exaggerated even further and claimed to descend from mythological emperors, which does, however, stand out, since exactly these two held the title of *sabao* 薩保 and represent two of only three graves with epitaphs in which iconography that can explicitly identified as Zoroastrian was found.[292]

Seen through the perspective of previous research, it would not make much sense to provide a choronym such as Pinggao 平高 of Yuanzhou 原州 if it was made explicit that they did not originate from there, but from Sogdiana. The use of choronyms by Sogdians is, however, a reflection of how they understood choronyms. Instead of referring to a Chinese antiquity to which they had no relation, they created their own genesis, hoping that this choronym would be charged with greater meaning in the generations to come. This, however, is telling about the function of choronyms: While recording a certain choronym in paper or stone, with the goal of harvesting its prestige for oneself, the prestige of the choronym gets reinforced, and by its very record is thus prevented from falling into oblivion. Whereas the claim to descend from the famous Cui 崔 Clan of Boling 博陵 seems self-explanatory, the example of the Sogdians' epitaphs exposes the opposite. One does mostly know of the Cui 崔 Clan of Boling's

290 Tackett, "Transformation of Medieval Chinese Elites," 66; see also: Tackett, *Destruction of the Medieval Chinese Aristocracy*.

291 Davis, *Entombed Epigraphy*, 8, fn. 21.

292 Kang Ye's 康業 grave is not included, thus agreeing with the conclusions of Sofukawa (Sofukawa Hiroshi, "Chūgoku shutsudo," 158) and Zheng Yan (Zheng Yan, "Bei Zhou"); although I am not as certain as they are as to whether the depictions refer to his life or are conventional images. See also p. 291 fn. 300.

博陵 prestige because people claimed membership to it. The combination of the choronym and the foreign origin story of the Sogdians' epitaphs makes apparent that the choronym was not only about status, as emphasised by Tackett and Davis. It is an expression of a more complex social construct, what may be described as the "self-identity" of these individuals. Whereas concepts such as status, prestige, elite, or aristocracy propose a two-dimensional view of society, mentioning descent from Sogdian royalty while presenting a Chinese toponym in the choronym paints a far more colourful picture of the deceased's self-identity. The above examples of Northern Chinese families that already moved south and still claimed to be related to a northern toponym after generations conceivably expressed the same complexity of self-identity. It is just that – in comparison to the Sogdians – it is less obvious now.

Concerning women, it was recorded that they were held in respect in Sogdiana and especially at the court in Bukhārā, where the king allegedly conferred with his wife – albeit such statement could have been made by the Chinese authors to mock them. It is difficult to say if there was a difference in social standing or in relationships in Sogdian households in China, but the – for Chinese epitaphs – quite romantic Sogdian part of Master Shi's 史 epitaph and the stone carvings showing him and his wife, demonstrate at least that his wife must have been quite important in his life.

The records further say that mourning and weddings of Samarqand were similar to those of the Tujue 突厥 – implying that they married their mothers or sisters when the male of the household died – but that in Bukhārā they did not allow such practice. While this statement may be related to the contemporary hatred of the Tujue 突厥, on Tang China, exogamy was required by law, and all examples of Sogdians show them marrying accordingly, however mostly among Sogdians or other Western immigrants. In Guzang 姑, for example, powerful families of the names An 安 and Di 翟 intermarried over generations.

Women are recorded in epitaphs as exemplary wives and once even a mother is mentioned, instrumental in raising their status and that of their husbands and allowing for a mention of their male ancestors who held office. Some Sogdian women even had their own epitaph.[293] Finally, the above-mentioned letter of "princess" Jun Zhezhe 君者者, dated around 930 CE, shows that women from the higher society travelled and probably learned to read and write.

3.3.8 Mourning and burial

In the *Weishu*, the burials of Samarqand are described as similar to the Tujue 突厥, which contradicts the description of Zoroastrian burials as seen in the *Tongdian*. Nevertheless, the burial which is described for the Tujue 突厥, includes the placement of a sheep head and a horse head on top of a pole. The placement of animal skulls was, at least since the Zhou, a long-standing tradition in regions bordering the steppe of present-day China and a marker for non-Han graves. Although these burial customs

293 For more details, see p. 176 (2.3.3.3).

related to the steppe might be completely unrelated, it may be one line of explanation for the placement of a sheep and horse in the corridor leading to the burial chamber of Shi Hedan 史訶耽.

In fact, the analysis of the graves showed that the graves of Sogdians were – judging from the structure – typical for the local Xianbei 鮮卑 and/or ethnic Han 漢 traditions. Besides the epitaph, iconographic details – showing Zoroastrian content as well as certain objects such as foreign coins, finger rings of foreign design and with an inscription in a foreign language – provide information regarding the foreign cultural background of the deceased. Besides explicit Zoroastrian iconography in other graves of Sogdians, the only feature that may be related to Zoroastrianism for the Shi 史 in Guyuan 固原 is the burial of a dog in a niche above the burial chamber of Shi Daoluo 史道洛, which has never been mentioned anywhere outside of the excavation report. Very little is known with certainty about the excarnation procedures of Zoroastrianism in Central Asia at this time, although *Dakhmas* have been identified.[294] And, although it is known that dogs received special treatment and were of outstanding importance for the rituals to be performed with a human corpse in official Zoroastrian regulations in the distant Sasanian Empire, the burial of a dog as well as a human, is in direct contradiction to everything else prescribed.[295] Although there may be a connection, and some scholars may be tempted to still forcefully attribute such a unique find to Zoroastrian practices, in light of the burial in a – rather un-Zoroastrian – wood coffin inside a tomb with a dog above it, and without any signs of excarnation or dismemberment, it is rather tempting to propose seeing this dog as being probably the favourite dog of the deceased and/or his wife, which was buried with him, as e.g. Frederick the Great did mandate for his death in 1786.[296] This, altogether, is what raises doubts about the necessity of imposing the Zoroastrian religion on the Shi 史 of Guyuan.[297]

Sogdians, in fact, practised a great diversity of religions and various rituals.[298] Regarding Zoroastrianism, only one Chinese written source mentions Zoroastrian funerary practices, which describes Samarqand, outside of China, and, only a few ossuaries have been found in present-day Xinjiang Uighur Autonomous Region in Kucha, Tingzhou 庭州/Beiting 北庭 (see Vol. 2, Appendix 4.1, Figure 250), and the

294 Grenet, *Pratiques funéraires*, 227–31.

295 See: ibid., 31–41.

296 Although, in accordance with Zoroastrian regulations, it was only carried out in 1991.

297 Lin Meicun arguments that 1) the seal found in his grave, decorated with a Sasanian Zoroastrian imagery and an inscription (see Vol. 2, 1.3.4.1.3) and 2) the name of Shewupantuo, which he translates as "slave of Zurvan" instead of slave of Zhemat (Demeter), point to him being a follower of Zurvanism (Lin Meicun, "Zhongguo jingnei chutu," 202; or reprint in: Lin Meicun, "Guyuan Sute mu (1998)," 202). It seems, however, that he did not take into consideration the wooden coffins of the family and further archaeological information which may oppose such a statement.

298 Grenet, "Religious Diversity".

Toyuk 吐峪溝 Cemetery, Shanshan 鄯善 District.[299] Further only three graves – that of Master Shi 史, An Jia 安伽, and Lord Yu Hong 虞弘 (the latter probably not Sogdian) – were excavated with explicit Zoroastrian imagery.[300] There is no specific indicator that any of the other buried Sogdians were Zoroastrian. The problem with these burials is that Zoroastrian doctrine forbids burial, cremation or being left in the water, as the elements would be polluted. The body should be fed to animals and the bones either left in the open air, or collected.[301] In some of the graves of Sogdians in China, the deceased were placed on a stone platform, on a funerary bed made of stone, or in a stone sarcophagus, which would have served to partially fulfil these requirements, as they would not touch earth. For some researchers, the Northern Chinese style burial points thus to an increasing degree of "sinicisation" of Sogdians in China. This is a typical archaeological bias at work: if the majority of Sogdians were Zoroastrians, and many Sogdians lived in China and if they practised sky burials, nearly nothing of it would possibly be found in the archaeological record, apart from ossuaries, of which a small number has indeed been found. Additionally, the small number of graves of Sogdians do not reach a quantitative minimum that would allow for any inductions concerning cultural changes (neither is the number of epitaphs containing their surname). What can be assertively pointed out is, however, that in the case of the Shi 史 in Guyuan 固原, Sogdians made use of chin straps and face masks. Whereas the combination of these two features may be traced back for non-Han people to the third century BCE in Tarim Basin, the use of metal chin straps – found in the grave of Shi Daode 道德 – is first attest for the Xianbei 鮮卑 in China during the Northern Wei. Sogdians were thus part of the people that imported or practiced this tradition stemming from the oasis states of the Tarim Basin.[302]

Concerning the Zoroastrian burial practices of Sogdians in China, there are thus two possibilities: 1) either the Zoroastrian Sogdians – still supposing that they were

299 See also, for ossuaries outside of an archaeological context: Kageyama Etsuko, "Higashi Turukisutan no ossuari"; Grenet, "Sute naguwen"; Pugachenkova, *Istorii iskusstva*; Pugachenkova, "Sogdian Ossuaries"; Pavchinskaya, "Sogdian Ossuaries".

300 For the exclusion of the grave of Kang Ye 康業 see p. 289 fn. 292.
It is sometimes admittedly difficult to clearly distinguish between Zoroastrian, and for example, Manichaean or Buddhist symbols for the hybridised representations found in the graves or on the ossuaries. See e.g. the stone engravings on the sarcophagus in the grave of master Shi 史/Wirkak (Dien, "Tomb of Master Shi"; Yang Junkai, "Carvings"; Xi'an shi wenwu baohu kaogusuo, "Xi'an Bei Zhou Shijun"; Grenet, Riboud and Yang Junkai, "Zoroastrian Scenes"; Dien, "Tomb of Master Shi"; Yang Junkai, "Ruhua"; Yang Junkai, "Bei Zhou Shi Jun mu"); and: Dien, "Consideration".
The entanglement of pre-Sasanian and later Sasanian Zoroastrianism as well as local forms of Zoroastrianism, such as that found Sogdiana, and Buddhist beliefs, including the worship of Sasan, Bagdana, Nana, and Maitreya as described by Crone makes any attempt at establishing clear iconographical definitions in line with the differing religious backgrounds rather difficult (Crone, *Nativist*, 97–98).

301 See, among others: Grenet, *Pratiques funéraires*, 32–41.

302 See p. 109 (2.2.3).

mainly Zoroastrians – did not practice sky burials on a broad basis in China (as we have *not one single source* telling us so),[303] or 2) they did, and if the supposedly larger Sogdian population in China, and especially in the capitals, would have done it somewhere near, some archaeological evidence of it would probably exist. If these Zoroastrian Sogdians did, however, not perform sky burials, it would have been prohibited by the Chinese government to do so, and there would most probably exist literary evidence of the prohibition. Therefore, if Sogdians supposedly were mainly Zoroastrians (for which there actually is no factual basis, not even mentioning the meagre knowledge of religious practices in Sogdiana) and did practice sky burials, still none of this would be known archaeologically (apart from a few ossuaries). Any of these conclusions are, all in all, based on an argument *ex silentio*, which is not a solid basis for a convincing theory, and it is reasonable to assume that further excavations in China will *not* provide significantly more information about this topic.

3.3.9 Other cultural aspects

The production and consumption of wine was emphasised repeatedly in the accounts of Samarqand. Besides that, their clothing is described as mean and lowly, with clothes made of woollen cloth, upper garments of leather and felt, and lower garments short and tight. They were said to have shaved their heads completely so as to reveal the top of the head with a coloured silk band around their foreheads. While this probably described the common people, on which historiography mostly stays silent, the Sogdians form the high society depicted in graves in China do not match with these descriptions. Their clothing does rather match the description of the Sogdian kings' garbs. What can be said with certainty from the remains in their graves is that they wore pendants, gold finger rings of foreign provenance, and had elaborate headdresses for the women, including glass flowers and miniature parrots and other animals. Besides that, they had wooden boxes with bone slips that were affixed on them with decorative golden push-pins as well as lacquer boxes.

3.3.10 Music and Musical instruments

Chinese sources on Sogdiana repeatedly mention the local population's fondness of music. They were said to sing and dance in the streets and the records even provide several instruments they used: small and large drums, the *pipa* 琵琶, the five-stringed lute, and the harp. *Hu* 胡 twirl (-dance) women and dance carpets made of the fur of the fire-marten were further imported to China. Indeed, the depictions of dancing Sogdians in graves feature a figure dancing on a carpet surrounded by musicians. It may quite well be that increased immigration and thus contact of *hu* 胡 with Chinese in the capitals resulted in the editors linking their personal contact with, or their knowledge of, the Western exotic and erotic male and female servants of taverns, dancers, and highly skilled musicians. These came to be mentioned in contemporaneous poetry and depicted in paintings and represented in the form of the

303 See p. 227 fn. 377.

extremely popular ceramic figurines for tomb furnishing. Indeed, Western music and instruments – especially from Kucha – found their way into China and became so popular at the Chinese court that new classifications for music had to be installed, as well as schools to train new musicians.[304] According to his epitaph, Kang Yuanjing 康元敬 descended from such a family that imported Western music to China. As flautists they came to the court and were honoured by receiving a surname from the emperor himself. Although many anecdotes or poems could be further quoted about just how popular Western music was in the capital and how far it spread, one example may epitomise this *mania*: Emperor Xuanzong 玄宗 once sent flautists and female singers/dancers,[305] described as performers of the famous Kuchaean music, to the southern kingdom of Nanzhao 南詔 as a gift. As only one old flautist and one female singer were left after some time, the emperor received a request to replenish the personnel.[306]

The complexity of these cultural transfers touching the Sogdian world can be observed when looking at the wall paintings excavated in Panjikent, Sogdiana (see Figure 242, Vol. 2, Appendix 4.1), dated to the first half of the eighth century: Female Chinese musicians and dancers were portrayed in a Chinese-Sogdian style – together with other copies of Chinese paintings in the room).[307] As it seems, the (re-)creations of Chinese musicians and dancers, performing originally Western-styled music on originally Western instruments, were revered in paintings – among other aspects, as symbol of status – not only in China, but also back in the region from where the music and instruments were once transferred to China.

3.3.11 Rituals

3.3.11.1 The sabao office, the temple, and its officers

As seen above the *sabao* office was the political broker between Sogdians and the Chinese government and maybe even in charge of certain parts of the jurisdiction, the latter of which was related in Sogdiana to the temple.[308] Beyond that, the mention of a *xianzheng* 祆正 (Zoroastrian regulator), a *xianzhu* 祆祝 (Zoroastrian precentor), and a *huzhu* 胡祝 (*hu* 胡 precentor) in the transmitted record and a *xianzhu* 祆主 (Zoroastrian presider) and a *da xianzhu* 大祆主 (Zoroastrian presider-in-chief) in excavated sources makes evident that the *sabao* office was not only in charge of the

304 For a short English overview of the evolution of Chinese musical institutions, see: Lin Meicun, *Han Tang Xiyu*, 14–40; see further: Kishibe Shigeo, *Tōdai ongaku 1*; and: Kishibe Shigeo, *Tōdai ongaku 2*.

305 They were trained in the newly established *jiguan* 妓館, a school for female singers and entertainers at the court.

306 *Zizhi tongjian* 235.7561–62.

307 The breasts and arms of the females are depicted large, which is atypical in Chinese paintings and the second from the left even has a décolleté, although placed near the throat.

308 See p. 224 (3.2).

administration of the *hu* 胡 but also of the religious affairs of the Zoroastrian community.

It is interesting to notice that while in Sogdiana, priests – unlike their Sasanian counterparts – were not organised hierarchically,[309] and did not constitute a distinctive societal group,[310] their peers in China were integrated in the Chinese bureaucratic system in different ranks. Concerning the different roles that they may have played, de la Vaissière suggested that the Zoroastrian regulator and the Zoroastrian precentor be identified with the two Zoroastrian priests (the *zōt*, the principal priest, and the *raspīg*, the secondary priest) needed for the performance of the *Yasna* ritual, which shall be commented on below.[311] Although these new offices are only mentioned as being part of the bureaucracy since 713 CE, it does not necessarily mean that the *sabao* was only responsible for these affairs from that time. As to the Zoroastrian presider and presider-in-chief, they are mentioned in the epitaphs of Kang Ye 康業 (512–71 CE) and Di Caoming 翟曹明 (buried 579 CE). Kang Ye's 康業 epitaph states that his father was Zoroastrian presider-in-chief during the Northern Wei, while he himself was appointed to the office during the Northern Zhou in 566 CE, at the age of 54. Di Caoming's 翟曹明 epitaph only mentions that he held the office of Zoroastrian presider and some scholars proposed that iconographical elements of the grave doors may be identified with Zoroastrianism.[312] While it is unknown where the epitaph was excavated, Kang Ye 康業 and Di Caoming 翟曹明 were conceivably active together in Chang'an 長安. If that is the case, the prefix *da* 大 (in-chief) supposedly was an indicator for a hierarchy, in which Kang Ye 康業 had the senior office. While de la Vaissière based his above-mentioned comment on the transmitted literary sources, this may well be the fitting epigraphic evidence for his hypothesis, i.e. instead of the Zoroastrian regulator and the *hu* 胡 precentor, the Zoroastrian presider-in-chief and the Zoroastrian presider may be the two Zoroastrian priests (the *zōt* and the *raspīg*) needed for the performance of the *Yasna* ritual – at least until further epigraphic evidence comes to light.[313]

Parenthetically, I opted to translate *tianzhu* 天主 as Zoroastrian presider (lit. heaven presider), as it is most certainly to be equalled with the aforementioned *xianzhu* 祆主 (Zoroastrian presider). To avoid injecting yet further confusion to the debate about

309 Choksy, *Conflict and Cooperation*, 5.

310 Shenkar, "Religion," 206–7.

311 Vaissière, *Sogdian Traders*, 151; *apud*: Duchesne-Guillemin, *Religion*, 71–76. For more information, see: Boyce, *A History of Zoroastrianism*, 147–77; and: Malandra, "Yasna".

312 A short overview of this hypothesis is to be found in: Luo Feng and Rong Xinjiang, "Bei Zhou xiguo," 285–86.

313 Frantz Grenet proposed instead at the conference "Sogdians and their Funerary Monuments in Sixth to Seventh-Century China," held in Venice in December 2018, that the *tianzhu* 天主 might not have been a Zoroastrian specialist but a supervisor of the temple. He based his argument on the depiction of an individual on Kang Ye's 康業 funerary bed as an official, which matches his biography. Instead of identifying the two priests needed for the ritual as *xianzheng* 祆正 and *xianzhu* 祆祝, he believes that both may have been *xianzheng* 祆正.

"Zoroastrianism" and whether *tian* 天 and *xian* 祆 designate different deities, a short comment on the nomenclature follows.[314] In Chinese, Zoroastrianism is now oftenest called *xianjiao* 祆教, *huoxianjiao* 火祆教, or *baihuojiao* 拜火教. The meaning and pronunciation of the character 祆 *xian* at different times is, however, debated. Dien proposed that 天 *tian* was once used to denote Buddhist devas and came to be associated with Zoroastrianism. After being introduced via the north-western routes into China, it was affected by the dialect of what are present-day Shaanxi and Gansu provinces and was eventually pronounced *xian*. The graph *shi* 示 was thus added to *tian* 天 to form the character *xian* 祆 in order to differentiate the two meanings.[315] Further, I found a passage in the *Zhishun Zhenjiang zhi* which was not mentioned by Dien that contains a pun on the word which further underpins that they were once homonymous.[316] These statements and the above-mentioned Zoroastrian iconography, found in at least one grave of a *tianzhu* 天主, lends credence to the conclusion that 天 *tian* may be understood as 祆 *xian* in these cases.

Second, the compilation of all records on religious specialists should allow further conclusions as to the background of specific individuals related to ritual activities (see Table 17, Vol. 2, Appendix 4.3). Two had the surname Kang 康, claiming to descend from the king of Samarqand, while one had the surname Di 翟, claiming to come from a "Western state" (*xi guo* 西國), which cannot be identified with any certainty. A third, Di Pantuo 翟盤陀, described as performing magic tricks in relation to the Zoroastrian Deity, has the same surname, but in all probability was not actually related to the temple.[317] Besides these, two sources mention the *hu* 胡 precentor, the title itself referring to either the temple (*hu* 胡 temple) or the individual's Western background. Although an inference based on such few records must remain hypothetical, it can be proposed that the religious specialists stemmed, or came directly from Western countries themselves, some being Sogdian or of Sogdian descent. Further, three *sabao* graves contained explicit Zoroastrian imagery, i.e. the graves of Master Shi 史/Wirkak, An Jia 安伽, and Lord Yu Hong 虞弘 (see e.g., some of these depictions on Figure 243 – Figure 249, Vol. 2, Appendix 4.1).[318] Regarding the tomb-holders, Master Shi 史/Wirkak came from Kesh, An Jia 安伽 claimed to stem from China but probably came from Bukhārā, and Lord Yu Hong 虞弘 came from the state of Yu 魚, which cannot be identified but may assumed to be in a region in or outside of present-day China's north-western region. The background of the three – religious specialists or not – does therefore reinforce the above statement that the Zoroastrians and Zoroastrian specialists originated from Sogdian or Western countries. In conclusion, the Sogdian communities were administrated in their religious affairs independently,

314 See: Dien, "A Note on Hsien 祆"; Grenet and Zhang Guangda, "Last Refuge," 183, fn. 1; Grenet, "Conférence," 178–79; Pénélope Riboud, "Réflexions sur *xian* 祆"; and a comment concerning the terms "Mazdaism" and "religion of the Avesta": Grenet, *Pratiques funéraires*, 277.

315 Dien, "A Note on Hsien 祆".

316 See p. 310.

317 See p. 242 (3.2.1.4).

318 See p. 291 fn. 300.

while some subordinate administrative offices, such as military or scribal offices, are also known to have been occupied by Chinese individuals.

3.3.11.2 Inheritability and eligibility

Two sources mention that some of the religious specialists of the office held their positions over generations and further that a recommendation played a role in one of the appointments. In the first source, the epitaph of Kang Ye 康業 (512–71 CE), it is recorded that in 544 CE (under the Western Wei), the chariot and horse general-in-chief *huyao* 呼藥 officer[319] Di Men 翟門[320] of Yongzhou 雍州 and some influential *hu* 胡 families of the Western Regions recommended his father to be Zoroastrian presider-in-chief; a request which was granted by imperial decree in 550 CE. As the epitaph states for 566 CE, three years after his father's death:[321]

> 天和元年，蒙[□]詔以君積代蟬聯，門傳忠孝，授世掌大天主。
>
> Since the master (Kang Ye 康業) [was in] the line of descendancy of many generations, [his] family transmitting loyalty and filial piety, [he] was appointed to the hereditary office of *da tianzhu* 大天主 (Zoroastrian presider-in-chief).

This recommendation recalls the patronising function the aristocracy and especially the Sasanian kings occupied in Iranian society, a power which was in the present case exerted by the Chinese emperor and/or his bureaucracy.[322]

From the second source, the *Mo Zhuang man lu*, an account from the Song dynasty, it can be gathered that Zoroastrian rituals were practised in Kaifeng 開封 since the Tang, and a certain Shi 史 family (probably stemming from Kesh) handed down the office of Zoroastrian precentor for over two hundred years since at least the middle of the ninth century.[323] In both cases, it is said that "this" was unusual, although the comment probably refers to the length of the inheritance. Combined, these sources make a strong argument for the inherited succession of this religious office. If the local influential people mentioned in the epitaph really played a role in the appointment or if they were credited here to simply please them is difficult to ascertain. Either way, this information remains an interesting detail in the appointment procedure.

3.3.11.3 Religious "affiliation" of the sabao office

Since the various positions inside the *sabao* office were held by individuals of different backgrounds, it would be unusual if all officers were Zoroastrian. The very question of determining the religious "affiliation" of the officers in a mostly non-monotheistic society is, in my opinion, indicative of a perspective biased by modern categories themselves dominated by monotheism. A good example of the lack of

319 Both high ranking offices.
320 Maybe Turco-Sogdian, judging from his name.
321 Epitaph of Kang Ye 康業, author's translation (see Vol. 2, Appendix 3.2).
322 See: Crone, *Nativist*, 378.
323 See p. 230 (2.4.3.5.2).

affiliation and thus lack of mutual exclusion of, for example, the *sabao* office to Zoroastrianism and Buddhism, is provided by the stele of Hui Yu 惠鬱, Xuan Ning 玄凝 and others (dedicated on 9.9.585 CE).[324] It states that the great Maitreya statue of the Seven Emperors Temple of Dingzhou 定州 was erected in 492 CE and destroyed in 577 CE. After Emperor Yang 煬 of the Sui re-established the status of Buddhism, two laymen – one, a member of the famous Cui 崔 Clan of Boling 博陵, and the other, the above-mentioned merchant and former *xia silu* 下司錄 (junior record keeper) of the *safu* 薩甫, He Yongkang 何永康 – together provided financial support to restore the temple. Judging from his name, He Yongkang 何永康 stemmed from Kušaniyya in Sogdiana. The fact that he was introduced as a "merchant" is unique for such an inscription, as the official status of merchants was rather low in the official Chinese social hierarchy. Most importantly, this stele provides evidence that an individual could be of Sogdian descent, a merchant, an employee in the *safu* 薩甫 office, and at the same time support Buddhism.[325]

Further, due to the information provided by these epitaphs, we can establish that all three excavated graves for which Zoroastrian imagery can be explicitly identified belonged to individuals that were *sabao*.[326] As can be read in their biographies, most *sabao* were high ranking military officials and conceivably were not religious specialists. In light of the archaeological record, it can be ascertained, however, that some *sabao* were Zoroastrian. Further, the possibility that the *sabao* office, in charge of the *hu* 胡, also supervised other religions, cannot be excluded although we only learn of the Zoroastrian specialists of the office. Indeed, the creation of such an office for all *hu* 胡 and their affairs seems more sensible from an administrative point of view. That Sogdians, and thus mostly Zoroastrians, probably comprised the majority of people in the office and administered by the office, combined with the scarcity of information available on other religions, prevents any further hypotheses in this regard.

3.3.11.4 Zoroastrianism and other Western religions in China

Having established that Zoroastrianism was administered by its own devotees, and that religious specialists were in charge of the rituals – maybe even before the existence of the *sabao* office – it is still unclear what Zoroastrianism was *in China*, how it was perceived, and thus how the administration of the religious affairs of the *hu* 胡 by the *sabao* office is to be understood in the Chinese bureaucratic context.

In the Sasanian empire, the king and the aristocracy erected the temples and patronised the clergy. As an ancestral religion into which one was born into, the focus lay on the performance of ritual recitation and sacrifice (*Yasna*) and not on faith or a philosophy. The Zoroastrian temples were thus sacred places where gods were present

324 See p. 259 (3.2.3.1.5).
325 Luo Feng styles this as "religious freedom" of the officers, which seems somewhat of an anachronistic concept (Luo Feng, "Sabao: Zai kaocha," 239).
326 See p. 309 (3.3.11.1).

and had to be satisfied by an invitation to festive meals – and not the space in which a faith-based community held a weekly service. This means that while much of the ritual was effected by priests without the participation of laymen, the latter came to the temple when a ritual had to be performed for them (not by them).[327] When Iranian religious movements then spread to Transoxania, Zoroastrianism in particular rose to prominence and was adapted and transformed in the process. Not much detail is known about religious practices in Sogdiana. It is, however, believed that before the Arab conquest in the eighth century and the ensuing decline of the Zoroastrian faith, Sogdians mostly practised local forms of Zoroastrianism – for the majority of which the practice and not the doctrine can be retraced.[328] Although temples were the centre of the religious life, they probably also served as the most important centre for the civic community.[329] After spreading to Sogdiana and amongst the different peoples of the region, it was only a question of time until the Western religions – however heterogeneous the ideas and removed from their Western form – would be imported further east along the Silk Roads by Iranian and Central Asian migrants.[330] Since Sogdians played an important role in this process, it must be emphasised that Sogdiana

327 Crone, *Nativist*, 375–78.

328 For a short overview of the problematic classification, see: ibid., 97–98; and: Crone, "Buddhism," 219–20.
See further: Shenkar, "Religion"; Grenet, "Zoroastrianism"; Shkoda, *Pyandzhikenstkie*; Marshak, "Sogd"; Shkoda, "The Sogdian Temple," 195; Maršak and Raspopova, "Cultes"; Grenet, *Pratiques funéraires*; Grenet, "L'art Zoroastrien en Sogdiane"; and: Škoda, "Culte du feu".
In the Sasanian empire, regional forms must have also lived on, but slowly disappeared in the highest echelons of Iranian society (Crone, *Nativist*, 385; Crone, "Buddhism," 227–28). Further, "Al-Bīrūnī tells us that one could still find pre-Sasanian forms of Zoroastrianism in his time, partly within Zoroastrianism itself (which he like so many others takes to mean that of the official Sasanian kind) and partly within Buddhism" (in Hind, 10 f./15f. = I, 21; Crone, *Nativist*, 386). Chinese records of Iran do, however, also provide the statement: 西域諸胡事火祅(祆)者，皆詣波斯受法焉。 "The Westerners of the Western Regions who worship the Zoroastrian fire [deity] all go to Persia to receive teachings." *Jiu Tangshu* 198.5311.

329 Shenkar, "Religion," 202–7.

330 The question of Zoroastrianism's time of entry remains an ongoing debate, which will most probably be updated with future archaeological evidence. Among others, Lin Meicun, relying on a quote from the *Hanshu* 漢書 96a.3893, proposed that the earliest influx may have occurred during the reign of Emperor Cheng 成 of the Han (r. 32–7 BCE; Lin Meicun, "Cong kaogu faxian," 102–12); Rong Xinjiang, based on the dating of Sogdian Ancient Letters, proposed 311–13 CE (Rong Xinjiang, *Zhonggu Zhongguo yu wailai wenming*, 277–300); and Chen Yuan proposed ca. 516–19 CE, based on quotes from the *Weishu* 102.2271 and *Liangshu* 54.812 (Chen Yuan, "Huoxianjiao," 110–11).
Whereas al-Bīrūnī (973–1048 CE) reported that "Gushtāsb and his son Isfandiyār adopted Zoroastrianism (Majūsiyya) and spread it by force and by treaty (*qahran wa-ṣulḥan*) in east and west alike (*fī bilād al-mashriq wa'l-maghrib*), setting up fire temples all the way from China to the Byzantine empire (*wa-naṣaba buyūt al-nīrān min al-Ṣīn ilā 'l-Rūm*)" (Hind, 10 f./15f. = I, 21), Kirdīr (late third cent. CE, Mackenzie, "Kerdir," §§14f) boasts that fires and priests were set up throughout the Sasanian Empire and beyond, however, restricting the affected region as to ranging from Syria to India (Crone, *Nativist*, 224–26).

was not a unified state but fairly independent and disparate oasis cities connected under the rule of Samarqand. It is thus most probable that the Western and Eastern Iranians introduced a variety of religious practices to China, according to the local practices they were socialised in.[331] While early Chinese records of regions in the west and foreign countries in general are sometimes confused, confusing, and partly exaggerated or fantastic, the quantity and quality of information concerning Central Asia increased especially since the Northern Wei, paralleling the intensifying contacts between China and its Western neighbours. For example, the *Tongdian*'s description of Samarqand provides detailed information of some Zoroastrian festivities and the funerary ritual.[332] Further, a quote from the *Jing xing ji* contained in the *Tongdian,* may reflect the idea of a Zoroastrian state ritual before to war.[333] The religious offerings are generally exaggerated in their numbers but not criticised, apart from the *Suishu*, where only once the Zoroastrian temples of the state of Cao 漕 are described as obscene, which, however, does in fact not belong to Sogdiana.[334]

For China, literary sources record the erection of Zoroastrian fire temples in the capitals, five being mentioned in Chang'an 長安 and four in Luoyang 洛陽. Further temples are also known to have been founded in different cities: One may have been in Tingzhou 庭州 and at least one temple was located east of Dunhuang's city wall. Indeed, the Sogdian Ancient Letters I and III corroborate Sogdian religious activity in Dunhuang: a "temple priest" *βynpt*, "leaders" *'ypsy'r*, and a "tax councillor" *β'zkr'm,* are mentioned for the Sogdian community. Further, a "*hu* 胡 heaven-temple" (*hu tian ci* 胡天祠) is reported east of Gaochang 高昌 for the year 430 CE. Finally, at least one Zoroastrian temple is mentioned for Kaifeng 開封 and Zhenjiang 鎮江 in the 11th century, and one fire temple is recorded for Yangzhou 揚州, in the south.

Combining three anecdotes found in the *Chaoye qianzai*, *Guangchuan huaba*, *Xixi congyu*, and the *Shazhou dudufu tujing*, which may also be related to the account of An Jincang 安金藏,[335] an obviously etic Chinese idea of the Zoroastrian temple of Luoyang 洛陽 and Liangzhou 涼州 can be outlined. According to these accounts, the temples were very popular places of gathering for *hu* 胡. The temple is related to a fire cult, whose practitioners are described as swearing or performing incantations in

331 The process may be compared to the import of Buddhism: "It must be remarked that even the Chinese monks themselves at this early date were never confronted with Buddhism – of one school or another – as an organic whole, a coherent discipline. (…) The early Chinese monks, forced to be eclectics by the circumstances under which the doctrine was presented to them, had to base their opinions on a bewildering variety of Mahāyāna and Hināyāna sûtras, monastic rules, spells and charms, legends and scholastic treatises of different epochs and schools.
The heterogeneous nature of the doctrine as introduced into China was of course coupled with an all but complete ignorance about the cultural milieu in which the scriptures had originated." Zürcher, *Buddhist*, 2.

332 See p. 47 (1.12.1).

333 Id.

334 See p. 32 fn. 121.

335 See in the biography of An Pu 安菩 p. 164 (2.3.2.16).

the Chinese sources. Their god is said to have been called *xian* 祆, who in these cases is portrayed as appearing and acting like a Buddhist deity. There must indeed have been some misunderstanding and confusion in recounting the activities of the *hu* 胡, variously practising Zoroastrianism, Manichaeism, Nestorianism and other popular Central Asian beliefs and rituals. This confusion becomes apparent through the account of the name of the "Persian temples" being rectified to "Byzantine temples" in an edict of 745 CE,[336] to recall the origin of the Nestorian religion – a misconception that is echoed in the accounts of the *Mo Zhuang man lu*.[337] As an explanation, it is furthermore stated that in 732 CE, Manichaeism – the religion of the then despised Uighurs – was already outlawed among the Chinese due to its alleged attempts at misleading people to confound it with Buddhism.[338]

The aforementioned accounts report that during festivities, the *hu* 胡 gathered at these temples and offered livestock. Women cooking pig and sheep, singing, music, and the performance of magic tricks accompanied the festivities, as well as perhaps the consumption of alcohol. While the cutting tricks mentioned in the *Chaoye qianzai*, *Guangchuan huaba*, and *Xixi congyu*[339] seem mostly related to the Zoroastrian temples, similar stories are mentioned in hagiographies of Buddhist monks and accounts of supernatural events.[340] These practices were, however, forbidden by Emperor Gaozong 高宗 in the first month of 656 CE, with questionable success (see the biography of An Jincang 安金藏, son of An Pusa 安菩薩).[341] While the popularity of the temples is emphasised, the *Mo Zhuang man lu* further states that their deity was feared and respected by the people of Bianjing 汴京 (Kaifeng 開封).[342] The *Xin Tangshu* further mentions that two sacrifices were made each year and that the participation of common people was forbidden in the two capitals and in all provinces west of Dunhuang during the Tang and thus reserved for the religious specialists.[343] The popularity of activities related to the temple is not only to be measured by the account of magic tricks and the temple service of the foreigners: From the time of the

336 See p. 270 (3.2.4.7).
337 See p. 230 (2.4.3.5.2).
338 See p. 270 (3.2.4.7). The *hu* 胡, however, were allowed to continue their practices. For more information about this deception and the resulting confusion, see: Leslie, "Persian Temples". See also: Lieu, Samuel N. C., *Manichaeism in the Later Roman (1985)*, 178–201 (Lieu, Samuel N. C., *Manichaeism in the Later Roman (1992)*, 219–42); Bryder, *Chinese*, 1–33.
339 See p. 275 (3.2.4.10).
340 See the hagiography of Zhu Fotudeng 竺佛圖澄/竺佛圖磴/竺佛圖橙 (232–348 CE), perhaps from the Kingdom of Kucha, who was said to have the ability to pull out his intestines through a hole, wash them, and place them back. T2059.386c27–387a1; translation with short commentary in: Wright, "Fo-t'u-têng," 366. For a discussion of such abilities, their relation to the *Jīvaka Sūtra,* and their situation between medical history and the "anomaly accounts" (*zhi guai* 志怪), see: Salguero, "Buddhist," 198–207.
341 *Taiping Yulan* 737.5b; *Cefu Yuangui* 159.9a.1921a.
342 See p. 230 (2.4.3.5.2).
343 This was in some academic research misunderstood as a prohibition for Chinese people to participate. *Xin Tangshu* 46.1195.

Northern Qi, it is likely that even the highest spheres of society perhaps placed some belief in the effectiveness and power of their gods and participated in the rituals. As can be read in a passage of the *Suishu*, although the rituals related to the *hu* 胡 temples were qualified as perverted, it is said that the emperors of the Northern Qi and Northern Zhou engaged in these rituals themselves:[344]

> 後主末年，祭非其鬼，至於躬自鼓儛，以事胡天 。鄴中遂多淫祀，茲風至今不絕。後周欲招來西域，又有拜胡天制，皇帝親焉。其儀並從夷俗，淫僻不可紀也。
>
> In the last years of the last emperor[345] [Gao Wei 高緯 of the Northern Qi, not only were] the sacrifices not directed to his spirits (i.e. his ancestors),[346] [but] he went as far as to play the drums and dance in person in order to serve the *hu* heaven. As a consequence, there were many obscene sacrifices in the (capital) Ye 鄴. Those customs have not ceased until now. As the Later (Northern) Zhou desired to attract the Western Regions [to their court], [there was] further an order for the worship of the *hu* 胡 heaven, in which the august emperor himself [took part]. Their rituals all followed the barbaric customs – it is impossible to write down [the extent] of the obscenity and malignancy.

It is quite obvious that these comments were made by later dynasties partially in order to vilify these earlier emperors and their allegedly excessive lifestyle. While discrediting the last emperor of a former dynasty is a common *topos*,[347] insinuating a participation in *hu* 胡 and/or Zoroastrian festivities may have been a distortion of information based on events as the one recorded in the *Song hui yao ji gao*:[348]

> 遣官報謝社稷。初，學士院不設配位，及是以問禮官。太常禮院言：「祭必有配，報如常祀，當設配座。又諸神祠，天齊、五龍用中祠例；祆祠、城隍用羊、八籩、八豆。……」

344 *Suishu* 7.149; author's translation.

345 On *hou zhu* 後主: "First used with reference to the Northern Ch'i, the title Hou-chu became the standard epithet of the last ruler of a dynasty regarded by its successor-state as illegitimate. The term was thus applied to the last ruler of the Ch'en, conquered by the Sui in 589, and of Later Shu, Southern Han and Southern T'ang, all conquered by the Sung in the latter part of the tenth century." Jennifer Holmgren, "Politics," 267–68, fn. 1.

346 *Ji fei qi gui* 祭非其鬼 probably referring to the *Lunyu* 2.24: 子曰：非其鬼而祭之，諂也。見義不為，無勇也。 "The Master said, 'for a man to sacrifice to a spirit which does not belong to him is flattery. To see what is right and not do it is want of courage.'" Translation: Legge, *Chinese*, 18.

347 For a longer list of the depravities and excesses of the lifestyle (including being clothed with Western garments and riding without saddle and reigns, to name some of the least offensive criticisms) of the first emperor of the Northern Qi, Gao Yang 高洋 (r. 550–59 CE), specifically for the year 559 CE, see: *Bei Qishu* 4.67–69; reproduced in the *Beishi* 7.259–60; and the *Taiping yulan* 130.761a–b.

348 *Song hui yao ji gao* (*li* 禮) 18.7; author's translation. These regulations are to be understood as programmatic in nature and thus not necessarily reflecting ritual reality.

> An official was sent to return thanks to the deities of soil and millet.[349] Previously, the Institute of Academicians had not installed a representative post,[350] thus they went to ask the Ministry of Rites. The Chamberlain of the Ritual Academy[351] declared: "In sacrificing there is inevitably a representative [to which one should] report just as in any regular sacrifice. [We] shall install an impersonating seat. Further, for all sacrifices to deities, [as well as][352] for [the God] of Heavenly Equality[353] and the Five Dragons,[354] use the capital's sacrifice as rule; for the [deity of the] Zoroastrian temple and the [deity of the] City[355] use lamb, eight *bian* 籩,[356] and eight *dou* 豆.[357] (…)"

The problem of appropriate allocation for this sacrifice does not merely illustrate the importance of the temple and its place in society, but to a greater degree acknowledges the necessity of thanking those gods and thereby recognising their power at a cosmological level. The Zoroastrian temple was located in a foreign context in which it was utilised as part of a Chinese ritual to thank the foreign deities for a good harvest, according to the cosmological regulations of appropriate reciprocation. The religious function this space occupied in the Zoroastrian ritual was, however, likely ignored by the Chinese court and delegated to the *sabao* office. That the foreign practices established themselves in the local calendar can further be seen in the offerings made to a Zoroastrian fire-deity during a New Year festival near Dunhuang 敦煌.[358]

While Crone proposed that "the religion of the Iranians (Ērān) (…) had no communal embodiment apart from whatever social and political organisation the Iranians happened to have at a given time"[359] it is questionable if the Zoroastrian "community" embodied the social and political organisation of the Chinese dynasty under which it operated. In the example above, the Chinese emperor's bureaucracy

349 Standing for all grain.

350 Certain important or legendary personalities were equalled to gods, i.e. representing them. For more information on these mechanisms, see: Ess, *Politik und Gelehrsamkeit*, 186–89; and: Karlgren, "Legends," 239–44. Karlgren choose to describe this phenomenon as "impersonating" gods. It was translated above as "represent," as "impersonating" has a connotation of pretending to be another person, especially for fraudulent purposes.

351 At this time subordinated to the Court of Imperial Sacrifices.

352 The Chinese edition did not place an enumeration comma, thus understanding "the God of Heavenly Equality and the Five Dragons" as explanation of what is meant by "deities," which is rather improbable.

353 Tang Xuanzong 唐玄宗 enfeoffed the deity of Mount Tai 泰 as King of Heavenly Equality (*tian qi wang* 天齊王).

354 Probably referring to the Five Mountains associated with the Five Emperors, or maybe to the Deities of the Five Elements.

355 Lit. of the moat.

356 A sacrificial container made of bamboo and used for fruit.

357 A sacrificial container, mostly pottery, but sometimes made of wood, bamboo, or bronze, used for alcohol and meat.

358 See p. 198 (2.4.3.1.1).

359 Crone, *Nativist*, 376.

did not replace the Sasanian kings or presented themselves as Zoroastrian rulers. The Chinese bureaucrats trespassed into the Zoroastrian space and utilised it for their purposes, simultaneously maintaining the emperor as regulator of the cosmos and acknowledging the efficacy of these foreign deities. Although the Zoroastrian fire was utilised as a tool for the legitimation of the Sasanian dynasty, the erection of fire temples in the Chinese capitals should not be interpreted as symbolising the extent of Sasanian influence,[360] here measured in religious authority. Zoroastrian temples in China should be rather understood as an independent and closed space of religious authority belonging to the Sogdian and Iranian community and managed by the *sabao* office.

3.3.11.5 Collateral damage as "barbaric" religion

As is known from the *Suishu*, the *safu* 薩甫 – later the *sabao* 薩保 and *sabao* 薩寶 – was an office in the Court of State Ceremonial, which itself was in the *li bu* 禮部 (Ministry of Rites). As the Ministry of Rites regulated rituals and offerings, the Court of State Ceremonials was more specifically charged with the proper way to deal with foreigners, among others the receptions of envoys and the etiquette to be followed. That Zoroastrianism was treated under the label of "foreign affairs" was ultimately the reason for its downfall. Due to a series of events unrelated to Zoroastrianism, the following request was made in the seventh month of 845 CE, followed by an edict in the eight month:[361]

> 秋七月……中書門下條疏聞奏：……其大秦穆護等祠，釋教既已釐革，邪法不可獨存。其人並勒還俗，遞歸本貫充稅戶。如外國人，送還本處收管。
>
> 八月，制：……隸僧尼屬主客，顯明外國之教。勒大秦穆護、[祆][362](僧)[363]三千餘人還俗，不雜中華之風。
>
> In the autumn of the seventh month [of 845 CE] (…) the Secretariat-chancellery presented a memorial to the emperor: "(…) As to the temples of

360 As claimed by al-Bīrūnī. See p. 314 fn. 330.

361 *Jiu Tangshu* 18a.604–6; author's translation. It is also to be found in the *Quan Tang wen* 967.10045a; the *Tang hui yao* 47.841; and the *Zizhi tongjian* 248.8016–17.
For a translation of the entire edict, see: Reischauer, *Ennin's Travels*, 225–27; and: Bary and Bloom, *Sources I*, 585–86.

362 Originally *yao* 祆, see p. 270, fn. 170.

363 Added in the *Zizhi tongjian* 248.8017. Reischauer ignored that problem and translated instead: "more than 3,000 Nestorians and Zoroastrians" (Reischauer, *Ennin's Travels*, 227); while Watson translated: "more than 2,000 men of the Nestorian and Mazdean religions" (Bary and Bloom, *Sources I*, 586).
The term *muhu* 穆護 is sometimes used for Zoroastrians and sometimes for Nestorians. The added term *seng* 僧, which is mostly used for Buddhist monks, makes *huan su* 還俗 "return to laity" sensible. In fact, it probably did not make much difference if they were monks or priests, as one of the major points of criticism of Buddhist monks and nuns is their lack of production, which probably equally applied to the priests of the other religions.

> the Roman (Nestorian) priests and others, Buddhism being reformed, [their] perverted teachings cannot be left by themselves. All their people shall return to lay life and be sent back to their birthplace as members of tax paying families; if they are foreigners, [they] should be sent back to their place of origin, to be restrained."
>
> In the eight month it was decreed: "(…) Monks and nuns shall be placed under the jurisdiction of the director of aliens to clearly manifest that [Buddhism] is a foreign teaching. More than 3,000 Roman (Nestorian) and Zoroastrians priests shall return to lay life, [so they may] cease to corrupt China's customs.[364]

The so-called Huichang 會昌 era persecution, instigated by Emperor Wuzong 武宗, "the Imperial nemesis of Buddhism,"[365] is reputed to be the most severe suppression of Buddhism in Chinese history. Economic factors such as the corrupted ordination of monks, the increasing constructions of temples, the tax evasion of monastic communities, as well as the accumulation of land and capital in form of precious metals – direly needed during a monetary deflation – have been identified as the primary reasons behind the persecution.[366] The growing authority of Daoists[367] and Confucian nativists[368] over the emperor, playing on a repertoire of xenophobia, hackneyed Confucian arguments, and popular superstitions, are however important factors leading to the portrayal of Buddhism as foreign and state-endangering creed.[369] Even though the polemic critique may have had a limited impact on overall policy,[370] a consideration of the xenophobic factor is necessary for an understanding of the impact of Wuzong's 武宗 attack on Nestorianism, and Zoroastrianism.

To go back a hundred years, Manichaeism was outlawed among the Chinese beginning in 732 CE.[371] About 20 years later, the An Lushan 安祿山 Rebellion started

364 As Chen Yuan (Chen Yuan, "Huoxianjiao," 129–30) already mentioned, different numbers are provided in other accounts. Chronologically (not going further than the 12th cent.):
– "Over 3,000" in the *Tang hui yao* 47.841;
– "Over 2,000" in the *Zizhi tongjian* 248.8017;
– Id. in the *Xin Tangshu* 52.1361;
– "Over 60" in the *Xixi congyu* 1.42 (*muhu ge*).

365 Reischauer, *Ennin's Travels*, 270.

366 For the persecution, see generally: Weinstein, *Buddhism under the T'ang*, 114–36; Ch'en, *Buddhism*, 226–33; Reischauer, *Ennin's Travels*, 217–71.
For the economic background, see: Ch'en, "Economic"; Twitchett, "Monasteries"; Gernet, *Buddhism*, 3–25, 29–62.

367 Such as e.g. Zhao Guizhen 趙歸真. See also: Nomura Yōshō, *Shūbu*, 371–72.

368 Such as e.g. Li Deyu 李德裕, Fu Yi 傅奕, and Han Yu 韓愈. For Li Deyu 李德裕, see: Feng Chengye, *Li Deyu yanjiu*.

369 For a larger contextualisation of the support, critique, and suppression of Buddhism in China, see: Ch'en, *Chinese*, 65–124; and: Zürcher, *Buddhist*, 254–85, 288–320.

370 Abramson, *Ethnic Identity*, 80–82.

371 See p. 270 (3.2.4.7).

raging in China from 755 CE onwards, leading the Tang government to flee the capital. Meanwhile, in Southern China, "several thousand Arab and Persian merchants" were killed during the pillage of Yangzhou 揚州 by Tian Shengong 天神功 (d. 767 CE) in 760 CE after the defeat of the rebellious general Liu Zhan 劉展.[372] The court eventually resolved to seek help from the powerful Uighurs. Bügü Qaghan responded to the request and attacked the common enemy, resulting in the conquest of Luoyang 洛陽 in 762 CE. It was in this eastern capital of the Tang that the Qaghan was converted to Manichaeism in the same year. To propagate the religion, he dispatched priests to China, resulting in a Manichaean temple being built in Chang'an 長安 in 768 CE, followed by others. After the Kirghiz successfully defeated the Uighurs in 840 CE, the growing unpopularity of the Uighur "occupants" turned into a full-scale persecution. In the second month of 843 CE, Wuzong 武宗 ordered that the Manichaean priests be laicised, their belongings confiscated, and their scriptures and objects burnt in the street. This was followed by an edict in the fourth month, in which it was commanded that the Manichaeans were to shave their heads and be clothed in the fashion of Buddhist monks, to finally be executed.[373] It is only in the light of this xenophobic outburst that the inclusion of Nestorianism and Zoroastrianism in the nativist edict proclaimed two years later can be understood. Although the edict was essentially anti-Buddhist, it was in effect the last step of a larger nativist agenda that also deeply affected the "three barbarian religions" (*san yi jiao* 三夷教), Zoroastrianism, Manichaeism, and Nestorianism.

While Zoroastrianism came from Iran to Sogdiana and finally reached China around the fourth century CE, the Sogdians probably brought their own hybrid version of the religion with them and did not notably proselytise among the Chinese population. The religion, its gods, and the many Zoroastrian temples in the capitals and other districts demonstrably enjoyed great popularity among the people and even the emperors until the Tang. Due to the Arab conquest, Chinese Zoroastrianism was cut off from its state of origin and from Sogdiana while the Huichang 會昌 persecution of 845 CE may have marked the beginning of the end of its most eastern outpost. The persecution may be best used as a lens to understand how Zoroastrianism was dealt with in China. However influential and respected the community of Central Asians and Iranians and their religions may have been at times, the Zoroastrian religion was deemed "barbarian" and "obscene" by Confucian and Daoist nativists. The expulsion during the xenophobic outburst of the Huichang 會昌 era is thus also to be understood as a struggle for authority and political power of concurrent cliques at court. Nevertheless, the Song court was still concerned with the appropriate allocation for the Zoroastrian temple until the 11th century.

372 *Jiu Tangshu* 110.3313, and: *Jiu Tangshu* 124.3532–33.

373 For these events, see: Weinstein, *Buddhism under the T'ang*, 120–21; Lieu, Samuel N. C., *Manichaeism in the Later Roman (1985)*, 189–98.

4 Conclusion and ideas

Having dissected and synthesised the information, I now return to my initial thoughts regarding the artificial separation of different sections of an object and venture five ideas concerning its discursive dimensions. As mentioned in the preface, a study of the material left me with the distinct impression that many of the Chinese and Western publications did not accurately represent the situation of Sogdians in China. It was this ambiguity that ultimately led me to devise another approach. While the materials employed by these publications to ascertain the Sogdian presence in China were concurrently the prerequisite for my own evaluations of their perceived shortcomings as well as the basis for any further experimentation with new perspectives, it is also true that this material corpus had not been comprehensively defined. Therefore, the bulk of this study was concerned with the production of such a corpus. In order to avoid applying a teleological research goal, this study proposed to use the categories that *emerged* from the transmitted literary sources on Sogdians *in Sogdiana* to organise the synthesis of information on Sogdians *in China.*

At the level of discourse (to grossly characterise the present situation), the perspective towards the transmitted literary sources broadly chosen by Chinese scholars was strongly influenced by a traditionalist stance. A general acceptance of the factuality of transmitted literature directed their search for additional contemporary literary and archaeological sources to substantiate the judgements and information of the former – what in the latter field von Falkenhausen called the "historiographical orientation of Chinese archaeology".[1] Thereby, they would – sometimes inadvertently – adopt the transmitted perspectives and judgements that were mainly made on Sogdians in Sogdiana and apply them to the Chinese context. This method led to the creation of research perspectives that fit modern Chinese political and social discourse, giving rise to questions regarding, for example, the cultural inclusiveness of the Chinese Dynasties and the assimilation of minorities into a cosmopolitan and culturally dominant ethnic Han-society inside a Chinese state. To return to the metaphor given in the introduction, for modern Chinese scientists, the shadow that Sogdians in China cast upon the canvas of Chinese historiographers strikingly resembles the one of the *shaoshu minzu* 少數民族 (ethnic minorities) rendered in Chinese academic publications.[2] The resulting narratives of assimilation – e.g. "sinicisation" – are, while being influenced by Marxist historical theory, in

1 Falkenhausen, "Historiographical".

2 How political archaeological studies are in China can be observed by the choice of title of a paper given by Rong Xinjiang in 2014 at Peking University, playing with the agenda announced by President Xi Jinping: Rong Xinjiang, "Suteren de Zhongguomeng".

principle reproductions of the classically imperialistic perspective of Chinese historiography: they construct a "Chinese" continuum as the centre from which cultural power mono-directionally emanates and irradiates, having "the will to dominate and not to be dominated, to impose change whilst remaining unchanged".[3] In fact both temporal and spatial governance of China, presently defined, from the beginning of the Han dynasty until the Republic of China, was evenly shared with foreign people or sovereigns of foreign background. Their organisation into Chinese dynasties within Chinese research stylised their story as the story of a unitary "Chinese" people advancing through different phases of evolution with shrinking or expanding territories, an inclusion more or less of foreign populations, influxes of foreign products and culture, etc. Under this paradigm, the still current scholarly conviction that "foreign" elements were *assimilated* (*ronghe* 融和) eventualised and this notion subsequently transformed into what is sometimes called the snowball of Han culture,[4] or, to use more vague terminology, the premise that foreign elements were "*sinicised*" (*hanhua* 漢化 or *huahua* 華化).[5] Concurrently – to again make sweeping generalisations – Western and Japanese scholars preferred to analyse the material by following categories of Western thought such as politics, economy, society, religion, and arts, which resulted – besides the pitfalls mentioned in the introduction – in perspectives on mercantile activities, the religious affiliation of Sogdians, or the identification of certain examples of Sogdian iconography and their transmission in art historical studies.

The Chinese sources upon which the study of Sogdians in China relies were written for the most part by ethnically and culturally Central Chinese authors whose terms and conceptions provide us with a monolithic narrative of elite families. Political power was framed in terms of such myths as the mandate of heaven, the necessary hierarchical order of family and society, and other influential structuring and controlling methods. Ascertaining how effective such myths and constructs may have been is speculation. However, their usage by new dynasties, especially of foreign (or partly foreign) background – as in the case of the Northern Dynasties, the Sui, and the Tang – resulted in tensions between the ancient narrative and the now altered reality, ultimately precipitating existing or future crises of identity and legitimacy. This tension induced the motivation, even the necessity, to create an identity as new rulers – as in the rulers of "China", or the "Chinese" rulers, or both – and to reformulate a common identity after a period of division against decentralising regional forces.

3 Bush, *Imperialism and Postcolonialism*, 123. Bush states this as a definition of cultural power, *apud*: Laue, *World Revolution of Westernisation*.

4 Xu Jieshun, "Understanding".

5 Dien passed a rather mild judgement on this tendency: "Modern scholars have had much difficulty in finding ways to deal with this large and prominent group of 'outsiders' who came to reside in China. I think the inclination, even necessity, of using the paradigm of assimilation (*ronghe*) is a mistake, for it obscures the experience of the Sogdians in China more than it illuminates it." Dien, "Sogdian Experience," 126.

Among the many ways in which such a definition manifests itself in sources is differentiation and discrimination. Critique is the historical psychograph of the critic rather than the criticised (as was shown in the analysis of the available documents) and thus it is opposition to the *other* that crystallises the self. The descriptions, judgements, and stereotypes of foreigners function therefore as a double-edged sword. On one side, the *othering* of the Sogdians resulted in an assertion of identity on the part of the authors, while on the other, it attributed a distinct identity to loosely related – or even unrelated – individuals. I thus propose as first idea that the *hu* 胡 in China, and among them the Sogdians that defined themselves as stemming from various polities, were created as a group. Returning to Figure 1b of the introduction, different objects cast the same shadow on the transmitted Chinese historiography, whereas the archaeological sources and contemporary literary material provide other shadows that differentiate this identification. Deriving from that, I further venture that the descriptions and judgements simultaneously resulted in discrimination and the projection of abilities, such as martiality and skill in negotiations. Indeed, many Sogdians were associated with certain professional fields, especially commerce and the military, while at the same time thriving in them, possibly by lower competition and/or indigenous disdain for the field, such as for the Jews in Europe.

One of the related aspects that was more thoroughly analysed is the establishment of the *sabao* office. While the Chinese sources lead to the conclusion that it was installed to administer and therefore enhance the control over this part of the foreign population, this is only one part of the picture. As Osterhammel wrote:[6]

> [It] is possible for interactions to transform themselves into networks. In turn, networks gain greater stability through institutions that are often the result of political will, such as a diplomatic alliance or an international trade agreement.

Undoubtedly, self-administration for foreigners and an autonomous supervision of their religious activities were never granted gratuitously and without reason. Hence my second idea is to view these privileges as the fruit of the recognition of their importance and probably the result of negotiations between powerful parties: the Sogdians established their legitimacy out of a certain position of power, and/or out of their already acquired authority in other "fields" in China, such as in the military – to speak after Bourdieu.[7] Thus, the office was the outcome of a successful mobilisation

6 Osterhammel and Petersson, *Globalization*, 23.

7 "In practice, that is, in a particular field, the properties, internalized in dispositions or objectified in economic or cultural goods, which are attached to agents are not all simultaneously operative; the specific logic of the field determines those which are valid in this market, which are pertinent and active in the game in question, and which, in the relationship with this field, function as specific capital – and, consequently, as a factor explaining practices. This means, concretely, that the social rank and specific power which agents are assigned in a particular field depend firstly on the specific capital they can mobilize, whatever their additional wealth in other types of capital (though this may also exert an effect of contamination)." Bourdieu, *Distinction*, 113. See also:

of their accumulated and translated forms of capital, certainly due in part to their growing network on one of the major cultural and economic lines of communication that were the Silk Roads.[8]

The establishment of the *sabao* therefore evidences authority in the shape of a governmentally legitimised office, confirming a powerful individual as "broker", or "mediator"[9] between the government and the community of Central Asian and Iranian people. As Wolf proposed:[10]

> [The] position of [cultural] "brokers" is an "'exposed" one, since, Janus-like, they face in two directions at once. They must serve some of the interests of groups operating on both the community and national level, and they must cope with the conflicts raised by the collision of these interests. They cannot settle them, since by doing so they would abolish their own usefulness to others. Thus they often act as buffers between groups, maintaining the tensions which provide the dynamic of their actions.

Based on his study's insight and the examples of successful Sogdians in this study, I suggest as third idea that the Sogdian's use of stereotypes to their own interest, the practise of exogamous inter-marriage mostly among Sogdians, and the development and upholding of a separate identity in the Chinese society are not to be interpreted as a path to "assimilation" and "acculturation", but rather as the protection of privileges. The institution of the *sabao*, created with the intention to control and encompass, may thus have paradoxically reduced inclusion.

The political unification by the Sui and then Tang provided stability, a consequent strengthening of contacts with foreign polities, and thus exchanges which proved to be a fruitful soil for the growth of larger economical networks. Immigrating foreigners needed to choose among a multitude of strategies with heterogeneous trajectories. As the new field – again in Bourdieu's terms – into which they migrated, had a new set of rules, their position and offices in the old society were not directly translatable. Besides the Sogdians becoming active as farmers, craftsmen, and merchants, the privileged few – judging from the existence of an epitaph and/or an impressive tomb in prestigious burial grounds – often claimed a noble ancestry, mostly of the kings of Sogdiana, espoused the established use of choronyms, and in some rare cases constructed a fictive genealogy to some ancient Han family (a technique commonly used by the Han themselves). To maintain a similar overall volume of capital in the vertical dimension, their already accumulated capital had to be reconverted in a

Bourdieu, "Ökonomisches Kapital".

8 See: Priewe, "Xianghu lianjie de juluo"; and for the network outside of China: Vaissière, *Sogdian Traders*, 95–118, 159–96.

9 The latter is the term chosen by: Skaff, "Sogdian Trade Diaspora," 513.

10 Wolf, "Aspects of Group Relations," 1076. As seen in: Abramson, *Ethnic Identity*, viii–ix.

transverse movement into other types, acting according of the logic of the new field. As a fourth idea, I would like to propose that the military in particular constitutes a field with promising trajectories for individuals with comparatively low social capital. Based on the conclusions reached by Johnson as to the restricted nature of social mobility and access to office from the Northern Dynasties to the Tang, it may actually have been the only means for Sogdians to access an important office.[11] Judging from the trajectories at hand, their accumulation of new capital through military careers, of which the few analysed extraordinary cases may give a glimpse of, led very likely to a "contamination" of their already owned economic and social capital, for example, of their family background. Therefore, a more differentiated picture comes to light: for some extraordinary Sogdians, the economical capital of their allegedly noble family backgrounds and/or the trading networks of their families were mobilised through military careers, a specialised field in which they could also capitalise on their physical difference to Chinese men from the Central Plain and the martial stereotypes that may have been ascribed to them.

Although military careers represented a first step, the accumulation of social capital was nevertheless still a matter of some complexity. As a fifth idea, I propose that for the establishment of a narrative which would secure and potentially increase this capital for future generations, graves, epitaphs, and the establishment of prestigious ancestries offered the effective "tools", while providing for a certain flexibility to preserve the above-mentioned beneficial distinction. Thus, flexible combinations of grave constructions and epitaphs were composed, employing Iranian, Zoroastrian, Buddhist, and typically Chinese structures and symbols. Especially the epitaphs, circulated among the family, were functional for the future prospects of sons, while their advancements could in turn result in the posthumous enhancement of graves and even posthumous appointments of their deceased parents. Parenthetically, the standard approach to graves has been to analyse their size, shafts, finds, etc., and to cross check this information with the content of the epitaph to finally establish the deceased as part of "the elite" – if not directly attributing to them the status of "elite" by virtue of having a grave with an epitaph. Besides being an academic dead-end, the label of "elite" is mostly used as a fuzzy term to obfuscate the inability to determine the precise localisation in society, while coincidentally stating that we have no access to 99 percent of the population. If the core definition of "elite" were used, i.e. a group controlling the main political and economic power in a state, it is absolutely clear that the Sogdians were not part of it.[12] The interpretation of funerary installations as tools thus promises a more fruitful outcome, while being careful not to reduce the individual to a *homo oeconomicus*.

11 Although much of Johnson's pioneering claims can now be challenged and corrected, his remarks on the ceiling under the second rank remain valid (Johnson, *The Medieval Chinese Oligarchy*, 19–31).

12 In opposition, among others, to any "partial elite" such as the "economical elite", "cultural elite", "musical elite", etc. See: Schmoll, *Lob*, 15.

To conclude, the *othering* judgements and stereotypes, combined with the desire and necessity to control Sogdians by the installation of the *sabao* office may actually have coalesced loosely connected individuals, and established them as a community in China. Concurrently, their origin in and contact to the crossroads of the Silk Roads predestined them to capitalise on their social networks for economical means. Their merging into one group in China may thus have enhanced their network and established them even more firmly as important connectors. As the military career in China probably represented one of the most viable trajectories for the efficient accumulation and translation of social capital, some extraordinary Sogdians were able to achieve remarkable careers, while likely also profiting from the stereotypes by means of which they were discriminated. Their existence in an officially sanctioned niche of the Chinese society enhanced their autonomy and boosted the growth of their military and economic network, while their graves and epitaphs provided an effective medium to narrate their self-identity, with the goal of securing and potentially increasing social capital for future generations. Finally, being cut off from their homelands and alienated by the Arab overlords at home, their social and economic relations discontinued while trade on the southern Maritime Silk Road intensified, and with their non-proselytising religion suppressed by the state, the Sogdians' *otherness* must have slowly faded while their culture and deeds – such as for An Jincang 安金藏 – lent wings to the fantastic anecdotes of later dynasties' literature.[13]

13 While after the An Lushan 安祿山 Rebellion, evidence of Sogdians drastically decreases, they are to be found in such stories in the Yuan, Ming, and Qing dynasties. See: Chen Yuan, "Huoxianjiao," 131; Kanda Kiichirō, "Tenkyō"; Ishida Mikonosuke, "Kanda"; Liu Mingshu, "Yuan ren"; and: Lin Wushu, *Zhonggu*, 316–20.

References

Dynasties

Table 8: Conventional list of dynasties[1]

Dynasty, Groups of Dynasties, or Periods	Dates
Shang 商	ca. 1600–1046 BCE
Zhou 周	
Western Zhou 西周	1046–771 BCE
Eastern Zhou 東周	770–256 BCE
Spring and Autumn 春秋	722–403 BCE
Warring States 戰國	403–221 BCE
Qin 秦	221–6 BCE
Han 漢	
Former (Western) Han 前[西]漢	202 BCE–8 CE
Xin 新 (Wang Mang 王莽)	9–23 CE
Later (Easter) Han 後[東]漢	27–220 CE
Three Kingdoms 三國	
Wei 魏	220–65 CE
Shu-Han 蜀漢	221–63 CE
Wu 吳	222–80 CE
Jin 晉	
Western Jin 西晉	265–316 CE
Eastern Jin 東晉	317–420 CE
Sixteen Kingdoms 十六國	304–439 CE
Southern and Northern Dynasties 南北朝	
Southern Dynasties 南朝	420–579 CE
Song 宋	420–79 CE
Qi 齊	479–502 CE
Liang 梁	502–57 CE
Chen 陳	557–89 CE
Northern Dynasties 北朝	386–581 CE
Wei 魏 (Northern Wei 北魏; Hou-Wei 後魏)	386–534 CE
Eastern Wei 東魏	534–50 CE

1 On the basis of: Wilkinson, *Chinese History*, 3–4.

Western Wei 西魏	536–56 CE
Northern Qi 北齊	550–77 CE
Northern Zhou 北周	557–81 CE
Sui 隋	581–618 CE
Tang 唐	618–907 CE
(Wu 武) Zhou 周	690–705 CE
Five Dynasties & Ten Kingdoms 五代十國	
Five Dynasties (Wudai 五代)	902–79 CE
Ten Kingdoms (Shiguo 十國)	907–60 CE
Liao 遼 (Qidan 契丹, Kitan)	916–1125 CE
Song 宋	
Northern Song 北宋	960–1127 CE
Southern Song 南宋	1127–1279 CE
Jin 金 (Nüzhen 女真, Jurchen)	1125–1234 CE
Xia 夏 [Xixia 西夏] (Dangxiang 黨項, Tangut)	1038–1227 CE
Yuan 元 (Menggu 蒙古, Mongol)	1271–1368 CE
Ming 明	1368–1644 CE
Qing 清 (Manzhou 滿洲, Manchu)	1644–1912 CE
Republic of China 中華民國	1912– CE
People's Republic of China 中華人民共和國	1949– CE

Table 9: Short-lived dynasties Northern Dynasties, 4th–5th centuries[2]

Dynasty	Dates (CE)
Cheng-Han 成漢	302–47
Qian-Zhao 前趙	304–29
Hou-Zhao 後趙	319–51
Ran-Wei 冉魏	350–52
Qian-Yan 前燕	337–70
Qian Chouchi 前仇池	296–371
Qian-Liang 前涼	301–76
Dai 代	310–76
Qian-Qin 前秦	351–94
Xi-Yan 西燕	384–94
Hou-Yan 後燕	384–407
Nan-Yan 南燕	398–410
Bei-Yan 北燕	407–36
Zhai-Wei 翟魏	388–92
Hou-Qin 後秦	384–417

2 On the basis of: ibid., 729.

Xi-Qin 西秦	385–431
Xia 夏	407–31
Hou-Liang 後涼	386–403
Nan-Liang 南涼	397–414
Bei-Liang 北涼	397–439
Xi-Liang 西涼	400–21
Hou Chouchi 後仇池	385–442
Bei-Wei 北魏	386–534
Qin 秦 (of Xue Ju 薛舉)	617–18

Primary transmitted Chinese sources

(selection of the main sources, traditional attributions)

An Lushan shiji 安祿山事跡 [Records on An Lushan], edited by Yao Runeng 姚汝能. Shanghai: Guji chubanshe, 1983.

Bai bu congshu [Collection of 100 Collectanea]. In: Lu Xinyuan 陸心源, ed., *Shi wan juan lou cong shu* 十萬卷樓叢書 [Comprehensive Collection of 100,000 *Juan*]. Taipei: Yiwen yinshuguan, 1965.

Bei Qishu 北齊書 [History of the Northern Qi], edited by Li Baiyao 李百藥 in 636 CE. Beijing: Zhonghua shuju, 1983.

Beishi 北史 [History of the Northern Dynasties], by Li Dashi 李大師 (d. 628 CE), completed by his son Li Yanshou 李延壽 in 659 CE. Beijing: Zhonghua shuju, 1974.

Cefu yuangui 冊府元龜 [Models from the Archives], edited by Wang Qinruo 王欽若 (962–1025 CE) and others in 1005–13 CE. Beijing: Zhonghua shuju, 1989.

Chang'an zhi 長安志 [Chronicle of Chang'an], by Song Minqiu 宋敏求 (1019–79 CE). Edited by Bi Yuan 畢沅 in 1784 CE. In the *Bai bu congshu, han* 3.4.

Chaoye qianzai 朝野僉載 [Comprehensive Record of Court and Country], by Zhang Zhuo 張鷟 (d. 730 CE). Beijing: Zhonghua shuju, 1979.

Chunqiu Zuozhuan 春秋左傳, attributed to Zuo Qiuming 左丘明. (*Zhengyi* 正義). 4 vols. Beijing: Beijing daxue chubanshe, 2000.

Da Tang Xiyu ji 大唐西域記 [Records of the Western Regions of the Great Tang], edited by Xuanzang 玄奘, edited in 646 CE. Editions used:

– *Da Tang Xiyu ji jiaozhu* 大唐西域記校注. Beijing: Zhonghua shuju, 2000.

– *Xin yi Da Tang Xiyu ji* 新譯大唐西域記. Taibei: Renmin chubanshe, 2003.

Da Tang xin yu 大唐新語 [A New Account of the Great Tang], edited by Liu Su 劉肅, completed in 807 CE. Beijing: Zhonghua shuju, 2004.

Feng shi wen jian ji jiaozhu 封氏聞見記校注 [Master Feng's records of hearsay and personal experience, annotated], edited by Feng Yan 封演 (end eighth cent.). Beijing: Zhonghua shuju, 2005.

Guanzi 管子, edited by Li Mian 李勉 (717–88 CE). Tabei: Taiwan shangwu yinshuguan 1990.

Guangchuan huaba 廣川畫跋 [Guangchuan's Colophons on Painting], by Dong You 董逌 (active around 1120 CE). In the *Bai bu congshu, han* 8.2.

Guoyu 國語 [Discourses of the States], edited by Zuo Qiuming 左丘明 (fifth cent.). Shanghai: Shanghai guji chubanshe, 1978.

Hanshu 漢書 [Book of the Han], edited by Ban Gu 班固 (32–92 CE). Beijing: Zhonghua shuju, 1979.

Hou Hanshu 後漢書 [Book of the Later Han], edited by Fan Ye 范曄 (398–445 CE). Beijing: Zhonghua shuju, 1979.

Jinshu 晉書 [Book of the Jin], edited by Fang Xuanling 房玄齡 (579–648 CE). Beijing: Zhonghua shuju, 1979.

Jing xing ji 經行記 [Travel Record] by Du Huan 杜环 (late eighth cent.). Lost but partly preserved in the *Tongdian*.

Jiu Tangshu 舊唐書 [Old Book of the Tang], edited in 945 CE under Liu Xu 劉昫. Beijing: Zhonghua shuju, 1974.

Kangxi zidian 康熙字典 [Kangxi character dictionary], ordered by the Kangxi Emperor in 1710 CE. Included in the *Hanyu dazidian* 漢語大字典. Chengdu: Sichuan cishu chubanshe and Hubei cishu chubanshe, 1988.

Liang jing xin ji 兩京新記 [New Notes on the Two Capitals], by Wei Shu 韋述 (d. 757 CE). Known through the *Chang'an zhi* 長安志.

Liangshu 梁書 [Book of the Liang], edited by Yao Sijian 姚思廉 in 636 CE. Beijing: Zhonghua shuju, 1973.

Lunyu 論語 [Analects of Confucius], attributed to the disciples of Confucius. With the most important commentaries in the *Wuyingdian shisan jing zhuliu* 武英殿十三經注疏, edited by Ruan Yuan 阮元 (1764–1849 CE). Beijing: Zhonghua shuju, 1980.

Luoyang qielanji 洛陽伽藍記 (*jiaozhu* 校註) [Record of the Monasteries of Luoyang]. Shanghai: Shanghai guji chubanshe, 1999.

Mo Zhuang man lu 墨莊漫錄 [Diverse Records by Mo Zhuang], by Zhang Bangji 張邦基 (d. ca. 1131 CE). In the *Bai bu congshu, han 8.2*; or: Beijing: Zhonghua shuju, 2004.

Nan Qishu 南齊書 [Book of the Southern Qi], by Xiao Zixian 蕭子顯 (489–537 CE). Beijing: Zhonghua shuju, 1980.

Pingzhou ke tan 萍洲可談 [Talks from Pingzhou], attributed to Zhu Yu 朱彧 in 1119 CE. In *Bai chuan xuehai* 百川学海 edited by Zuo Gui 左圭 in 1273 CE, in the fourth collection (*ding ji* 丁集), under *ke tan* 可談 in the copy of Tao 陶 from 1927 CE; or in the *Siku quanshu* 四庫全書, Taipei: Shangwu yinshuguan, 1981; or: Beijing: Zhonghua shuju, 2007.

Quan Tang wen 全唐文 [Complete Prose of the Tang], by Dong Gao 董誥 (19th cent.). Beijing: Zhonghua shuju, 1987.

Quan Tang wen bu yi 全唐文補遺 [Complete Prose of the Tang, Supplemented], by Dong Gao 董誥 (19th cent.). Xi'an: Sanqin chubanshe, 1995.

Sanguozhi 三國志 [Records of the Three Kingdoms], by Chen Shou 陳壽 (ca. 233–97 CE). Beijing: Zhonghua shuju, 1980.

Shan hai jing 山海經 [Classic of Mountains and Seas], compiled during the Han. Shanghai: Shanghai guji chubanshe, 1980.

Shiji 史記 [Records of the Grand Historian], by Sima Qian 司馬遷, finished in 94 BCE. Beijing: Zhonghua shuju, 1982.

Shijing 詩經 [Book of Odes], traditionally said to be edited by Confucius. In the *Qinding Shijing Yuepu quanshu* 欽定詩經樂譜全書, from the edition *Qing Qianlong chike wuyingdian ju zhenben* 清乾隆敕刻武英殿聚珍本 (edited 1773–1883 CE).

Song hui yao ji gao 宋會要輯稿 [Draft of Documents Pertaining to Matters of State in the Song Dynasty], edited by Xu Song 徐松 (d. 1848 CE; later edited by Chen Yuan 陳垣 in 1935). Beijing: Zhonghua shuju, 1957.

Songshi 宋史 [History of the Song], edited by Tuotuo 脫脫 (Toqtogha, 1314–56 CE). Beijing: Zhonghua shuju, 1979.

Songshu 宋書 [Book of the Song], edited by Shen Yue 沈約 (441–513 CE). Beijing: Zhonghua shuju, 1974.

Suishu 隋書 [Book of the Sui], edited in 636 CE by Wei Zheng 魏徵. Beijing: Zhonghua shuju, 1974.

T: *Taishō shinshū Daizōkyō* 大正新脩大藏經 [The Buddhist Canon, New Compilation of the Taishō Era], edited under Takakusu Junirō 高楠順次郎 and Watanabe Kaikyoku 渡邊海旭 in 1924–29 in Tokyo.

Taiping huanyu ji 太平寰宇記 [Gazetteer of the World During the Taping Era (976–83 CE)], edited by Yue Shi 樂史 (930–1007 CE). Beijing: Zhonghua shuju, 2007.

Taiping sheng'en fang 太平聖惠方 [Taiping Royal Prescriptions], edited by Wang Huaiyin 王懷隱 (925–97 CE). Taibei: Xinwenfeng, 1980.

Taiping Yulan 太平御覽 [Readings of the Taiping Era], edited by Li Fang 李昉 (925–96 CE). Beijing: Zhonghua shuju, 1981.

Tang Da zhaoling ji 唐大詔令集 [Great Collection of Edicts and Commands of the Tang], edited by Song Minqiu 宋敏求 (1019–79 CE). Beijing: Shangwu yinshuguan, 1959.

Tang hui yao 唐會要 [Institutional History of Tang], edited by Wang Pu 王溥 in 961 CE. 3 vols. Beijing: Zhonghua shuju, 1990.

Tang liu dian 唐六典 (*Da Tang liu dian* 大唐六典), by Xuanzong 玄宗. Beijing: Zhonghua shuju, 1992.

Tang lü shuyi 唐律疏議 [The Tang Code], edited by Zhangsun Wuji 長孫無忌 (d. 659 CE). Beijing: Zhonghua shuju, 1983.

Tang shi tongsu bianyi 唐史通俗演義 [Historical Romance of the Tang]. Combined volume (*heding ben* 合訂本). Written 1916–26 CE by Cai Dongfan 蔡東藩. Shanghai: Shanghai wenhua chubanshe, 1982.

Tongdian 通典 [Comprehensive Statutes], edited in 801 CE by Du You 杜佑. Punctuated edition. Beijing: Zhonghua shuju, 1988.

Tongzhi 通志 [Universal Treatise] by Zheng Qiao 鄭樵 in 1161 CE. Beijing: Zhonghua shuju, 2003.

Waitai miyao 外臺秘要 [Medical Secrets of an Official], edited by Wang Dao 王燾 (670–755 CE). Taibei: Zhongguo yiyao yanjiusuo, 1965.

Weisheng jiabao chanke beiyao 衛生家寶產科備要 [Essentials on Obstetrics from the Treasury of the House Hygiene], edited by Zhu Duanzhang 朱端章 in 1184 CE. Beijing: Zhonghua shuju, 1985.

Weishu 魏書 [Book of the Wei], edited in 554 CE by Wei Shou 魏收. Beijing: Zhonghua shuju, 1974.

(Ri cang hong ren ben) Wenguan cilin jiaozheng 日藏弘仁本文館詞林校證 [Annotated Edition of the *Wenguan cilin* from the Hongren Edition Held in Japan]. Edited in 658 CE by Xu Jingzong 許敬宗. Beijing: Zhonghua shuju, 2001.

Wenyuan yinghua 文苑英華 [Blossoms of the Literature Garden], edited by Li Fang 李昉 et al. in 986 CE. Beijing: Zhonghua shuju, 1982.

Wenxuan 文選 [Selections of Refined Literature], edited by Xiao Tong 蕭統 (501–31 CE). Shanghai: Shanghai guji chubanshe, 1986.

Wushuang pu 無雙譜 [List of Unmatched Figures], also known as *Nanling Wushuang pu* 南陵無雙譜, printed in 1694 CE, edited by Jin Guliang 金古良. In *Zhongguo gudai ban hua congkan*, *han* 5. Beijing: Zhonghua shuju, 1961.

Xian Qin Han Wei Jin Nanbeichao shi 先秦漢魏晉南北朝詩 [Poems from the Earlier Qin, Han, Wei, Jin, and Southern and Northern Dynasties], edited by Lu Qinli 逯欽立. Beijing: Zhonghua shuju, 1983.

Xin Tangshu 新唐書 [New Book of the Tang], edited in 1060 CE under Ouyang Xiu 歐陽修. Beijing: Zhonghua shuju, 1974.
Xixi congyu 西溪叢語 [Collected Accounts of Xixi], by Yao Kuan 姚寬 (d. 1162 CE). [1993], 2nd ed. Beijing: Zhonghua shuju, 1997.
Yiwen leiju 藝文類聚 [Anthology of Literary Excerpts Arranged by Categories], edited by Ouyang Xun 歐陽詢 in 624 CE. Beijing: Zhonghua shuju, 1965.
Youyang zazu 酉陽雜俎 [Miscellaneous Morsels from Youyang], edited by Duan Chengshi 段成式 (ca. 803–63 CE). Beijing: Zhonghua shuju, 1981.
Yuanhe Xingzuan 元和姓纂 [Compilation of Clan Names of the Yuanhe Era, 806–20 CE], edited in 812 CE by Lin Bao 林寶. Punctuated edition. Beijing: Zhonghua shuju, 1994.
Yuanhe junxian tuzhi 元和郡縣圖志 [Maps and Gazetteers of Provinces and Districts in the Yuanhe era (806–14 CE)], edited by Li Jifu 李吉甫 in 813 CE. Beijing: Zhonghua shuju, 1983.
Yu Zishan ji 庾子山集 [Collection of Yu Zishan], by Yu Zishan (513–81 CE). Annotated edition. Beijing: Zhonghua shuju,
Zhang Yan gong ji 張燕公集 [Collection of Zhang, Duke of Yan]. Collected works of Zhang Yue 張悅之文集 (d. 730 CE). In the *Si bu congkan chubian suoben* 四部叢刊初編縮本. Taipei: Taiwan shangshu yinshuguan, 1967.
Zhishun Zhenjiang zhi 至順鎮江志 [Gazetteer of Zhenjiang in the Zhishun Era (1330–33 CE)], by Yu Xilu 俞希魯. Beijing: Zhonghua shuju,1990.
Zhouli 周禮 [Rites of the Zhou]. (*Zhengyi* 正義) Beijing: Zhonghua shuju, 1987.
Zhoushu 周書 [Book of the Zhou], edited in 636 CE under Linghu Defen 令狐德棻. Beijing: Zhonghua shuju, 1974.
Zizhi tongjian 資治通鑑 [Comprehensive Mirror in Aid of Governance], edited by Sima Guang 司馬光, finished in 1084 CE. Beijing: Zhonghua shuju, 2004.

Primary sources, other languages

Abulfeda (Abu Al-fida' Isma'il Ibn 'ali ibn Mahmud Al-malik Al-mu'ayyad 'imad Ad-din). *Géographie d'Aboulféda: Traduite de l'arabe en français et accompagnée de notes et d'éclaircissements par M. Reinaud.* 2 vols. Paris: L'Imprimerie Nationale, 1848.
Ibn Battūta, Abū ʿAbdallāh Muhammad. *The Travels of Ibn Batūta: Translated from the Abridged Arabic Manuscript Copies Preserved in the Public Library of Cambridge, With Notes, Illustrative of the History, Geography, Botany, Antiquities, &c. Occurring Throughout the Work.* Translated by Samuel Lee. London: Oriental Translation Committee, 1829.
——. *Ibn Battúta: Travels in Asia and Africa 1325–1354.* Translated and selected by H. A. R. Gibb. London: Routledge & Kegan Paul, 1929.
al-Bīrūnī. *Kitāb fī taḥqīq mā li'l-Hind. Alberuni's India. An Account of the Religion, Philosophy, Literature, Chronology, Astronomy, Customs, Laws and Astrology of India, About A. D. 1030.* Edited by Edward Sachau. London: Trübner, 1887; Hyderabad : Dairatu'l-Ma'arifi'l-Osmania, 1958. Translated by Edward Sachau in: *Alberuni's India. An Account of the Religion, Philosophy, Literature, Chronology, Astronomy, Customs, Laws and Astrology of India, About A. D. 1030.* 2 vols. London: Kegan Paul, Trench, Trübner: 1910. The references are copied from Crone, *Nativist*, 2012; given in the form '41/27 = I, 54', where the first figure stands for the Hyderabad edition and the next two to Sachau's edition and translation.
Shakespeare, William. Comedies, Histories, & Tragedies: Published According to the True

Originall Copies. London: Isaac Iaggard, and Ed. Blount, 1623.
al-Sīrafī, Abū Zayd Ḥasan ibn Yazīd. *Ancient Accounts of India and China, by Two Mohammedan Travellers. Wo Went to Those Parts in the 9th century*. Translated by Eusèbe Renaudot. London: Printed for S. Harding, 1733.
—. *Relation des voyages faits par les Arabes et les Persans dans l'Inde et à la Chine dans le IXe siècle de l'ère chrétienne, texte arabe impr. en 1811 par les soins de feu Langlès: Tome I, introduction et traduction*. Translated by M. Reinaud. Paris: L'imprimerie royale, 1845.
—. *Voyage du marchand arabe Sulaymân en Inde et en Chine, rédigé en 851, suivi de remarques par Abû Zayd Hasan (vers 916)*. Translated by Gabriel Ferrand. Les classiques de l'Orient. Paris: Éditions Bossard, 1922.

Secondary sources

Abramson, Marc S. "Deep Eyes and High Noses: Constructing Ethnicity in Tang China (618–907)." Doctoral Dissertation, East Asian Studies, Princeton University, Last modified June 2001.
—. "Deep Eyes and High Noses: Physiognomy and the Depiction of Barbarians in Tang China." In *Political frontiers, Ethnic Boundaries, and Human Geographies in Chinese History*. Edited by Nicola Di Cosmo, 119–59. London and New York: RoutledgeCurzon, 2003.
—. *Ethnic Identity in Tang China*. Encounters with Asia. Edited by Victor H. Mair. Philadelphia: University of Pennsylvania Press, 2008.
Andreas, Friedrich C., and Walter B. Henning. *Mitteliranische Manichaica aus Chinesisch-Turkestan: III*. Sitzungsberichte der Preußischen Akademie der Wissenschaften, Philosophisch-Historische Klasse Vol. XXVII. Berlin: De Gruyter, 1934.
Arakawa Masaharu 荒川正晴. "Turufan shutsudo 'Kikushi Kōshōkoku jidai no Sogudo bun onna dorei baibai monjo' no rikai o megutte." トゥルファン出土「麹氏高昌国時代のソグド文女奴隷売買文書」の理解をめぐって [A Consideration on the Sogdian Sale Contract of a Female Slave Recently Discovered from Turfan]. *Nairiku ajia gengo no kenkyū*, no. 5 (1990): 137–53. Accessed September 5, 2016. http://hdl.handle.net.cinii.erf.sbb.spk-berlin.de/11094/16358.
—. "Hokuchō Zui Tōdai ni okeru 'Sappō' no sēkaku wo megutte." 北朝隋・唐代における「薩寶」の性格をめぐって [Characteristics of the 'Sabao' (*s'rtp'w*) during the Northern Dynasties, Sui and Tang Periods]. *Tōyō shien*, 50–51 (1998): 164–86.
—. "The Transit Permit System of the Tang Empire and the Passage of Merchants." *Memoirs of the Research Department of the Toyo Bunko (the Oriental Library)*, no. 59 (2001): 1–21.
Asmussen, J. P. "Ammō, Mār: Manichean Apostle, Outstanding Figure in the Missionary History of Manicheism during the 3rd Century CE." *Encyclopaedia Iranica*, I, 9 (1989): 979. Accessed October 20, 2017. http://www.iranicaonline.org/articles/ammo-mar-mid.

Bacot, Jacques. "Paul Pelliot (1878–1945)." *Annales de Géographie*, no. 55 (1946): 127–30.
Bary, Wm. T. de and Irene Bloom, eds. *Sources of Chinese Tradition: Volume I*. 2nd ed. New York: Columbia University Press, 1999.
Beal, Samuel. *Buddhist Records of the Western World: Translated from the Chinese of Hiuen Tsiang (A.D. 629)*. 2 vols. Trübner's Oriental Series. London: Trübner, 1884.
Beckwith. *The Tibetan Empire in Central Asia: A History of the Struggle for Great Power*

among Tibetans, Turks, Arabs, and Chinese during the Early Middle Ages. Princeton: Princeton University Press, 1987.

Beijing tushuguan jinshizu 北京圖書館金石組, ed. *Beijing tushuguan cang Zhongguo lidai shike taben huibian* 北京圖書館藏中國歷代石刻拓本匯編 [Compilation of the Rubbings of Chinese Ancient Dynasties Held at the Beijing Library]. 12 boxes, 101 vols. Zhengzhou: Zhongzhou guji chubanshe, 1989.

Belenitskyi, A. M. "Voprosy ideologii i kul'tov Sogda po materialam pyanjikentskikh khramov." [Problems of Ideology and Worship of Sogd: Based on Materials from the Panjikant Temples]. In *Zhivopis' drevnego Pendzhikenta*. Edited by A. J. Jabukovskij and M. M. D'jakonov, 25–82. Moskva, 1954.

Bernard, Paul. "Marcanda-Afrasiab colonie Grecque." In *La Persia e l'Asia centrale: Da Alessandro al X secolo*. Edited by Accademia Nazionale dei Lincei, 331–65. Atti dei Convegni Lincei 127. Roma: Accademia Nazionale dei Lincei, 1996.

Bi Bo 毕波. *Zhonggu Zhongguo de Sute huren — yi Chang'an wei zhongxin* 中古中国的粟特胡人—以长安为中心 [Sogdians in Medieval China: With Special Reference to the Sogdian Presence in the Capital Chang'an]. Xiyu lishi yuyan yanjiu congshu 西域历史语言研究丛书 [The Monograph Series of Historical and Philological Studies of China's Western Regions]. Beijing: Zhongguo renmin daxue chubanshe, 2011.

Bingham, Woodbridge. "Li Shih-min's Coup in A. D 626. II: Action at the Hsüan-wu Gate." *Journal of the American Oriental Society* 70, no. 4 (1950): 259–71. doi:10.2307/594964.

——. "Li Shih-min's Coup in A. D. 626. I: The Climax of Princely Rivalry." *Journal of the American Oriental Society* 70, no. 2 (1950): 89–95. doi:10.2307/595537.

Bourdieu, Pierre. "Ökonomisches Kapital, kulturelles Kapital, soziales Kapital." In *Soziale Ungleichheiten: Sonderheft 2*. Edited by Reinhard Kreckel, 183–98. Göttingen: Otto Schwartz & Co., 1983.

——. *Distinction: A Social Critique of the Judgement of Taste*. [1979]. Cambridge, Massachusetts: Harvard University Press, 1984.

Boyce, Mary. *A History of Zoroastrianism: Volume One, The Early Period.* Handbuch der Orientalistik Achter Band, Religion, erster Abschnitt, Religionsgeschichte des alten Orients, Lieferung 2, Heft 2a. Leiden, Köln: E. J. Brill, 1975.

——. *A Reader in Manichaean Middle Persian and Parthian: Texts with Notes.* Acta Iranica 9, troisième série: Textes et mémoires Volume II. Leiden: E. J. Brill, 1975.

Bradford, Rosalind E. "The Guyuan Sarcophagus: Motifs and Explication." Doctoral Dissertation, East Asian Languages and Civilizations, University of Pennsylvania, Last modified 2009. Accessed November 4, 2013. http://repository.upenn.edu/dissertations/AAI3363696.

Bronson, Bennet. "The Transition to Iron in Ancient China." In *The Archaeometallurgy of the Asian Old World*. Edited by Vincent C. Pigott, 177–98. Philadelphia: Museum University of Pennsylvania, 1999.

Bryder, Peter. *The Chinese Transformation of Manichaeism: A Study of Chinese Manichaean Terminology*. Bokförlaget Plus Ultra, 1985.

Burrow, Thomas. "Iranian Words in the Kharoṣṭhī Documents from Chinese Turkestan." *Bulletin of the School of Oriental Studies*, no. 7.3 (1934): 509–16.

——. *A Translation of the Kharoṣṭhī Documents from Chinese Turkestan*. London: The Royal Asiatic Society, 1940.

Bush, Barbara. *Imperialism and Postcolonialism*. History: Concepts, Theories and Practice. Harlow: Pearson/Longman, 2006.

Bush, Susan. "Floral Motifs and Vine Scrolls in Chinese Art of the Late Fifth to Early Sixth Centuries A.D." *Artibus Asiae*, no. 38.1 (1976): 49–86.

Cahill, Susan. "The Word Made Bronze: Inscriptions on Medieval Chinese Bronze Mirrors." *Archives of Asian Art*, no. 39 (1986): 62–70.

Cai Hongsheng 蔡鴻生. "Tangdai jiu xing hu lisu congkao." 唐代九姓胡禮俗叢考 [Collected Studies on the Customs of the Hu of the Nine Surnames of the Tang]. *Wenshi*, no. 35 (1992): 109–25.

——. *Tangdai jiu xing hu yu Tujue wenhua* 唐代九姓胡与突厥文化 [The Culture of *Hu* of the Nine Surnames and the Tujue in the Tang]. Beijing: Zhonghua shuju, 1998.

Carter, Martha L. "Notes on Two Chinese Stone Funerary Bed Bases with Zoroastrian Symbolism." In *Iran, questions et connaissances. Actes du congrès européen des études iraniennes organisé par la Societas Iranologica Europaea: Vol.I: La période ancienne*. Edited by Philip Huyse, 263–87. Studia Iranica, Cahier 25. Leuven: Peeters, 2002.

Cen Zhongmian 岑仲勉. *Hanshu Xiyu zhuan dili jiaoshi* 汉书西域传地里校釋 [A Commentary on the Geography of the Account of the Western Regions in the Hanshu]. Beijing: Zhonghua shuju, 1981.

Chavannes, Édouard. "Les pays d'Occident d'après le Wei Lio." *T'oung Pao*, no. 6 (1905): 519–71.

——. "Livres offerts." *Comptes rendus des séances de l'Académie des Inscriptions et Belles-Lettres*, no. 4 (1910): 245–46. Accessed August 26, 2019. https://www.persee.fr/doc/crai_0065-0536_1910_num_54_4_72636.

——. *Documents sur les Tou-kiue (Turcs) occidentaux.* [1903]. Taipei: Ch'eng Wen Publishing, 1969.

Chavannes, Édouard, and Paul Pelliot. "Un traité Manichéen retrouvé en Chine." *Journal Asiatique*, Série 10, Tome 18 (novembre-décembre) (1911): 499–617.

Ch'en, Kenneth. "The Economic Background of the Hui-ch'ang Suppression of Buddhism." *Harvard Journal of Asiatic Studies*, 19.1/2 (1956): 67–105.

——. *Buddhism in China: A Historical Survey*. Princeton: Princeton University Press, 1964.

——. *The Chinese Transformation of Buddhism*. Princeton, New Jersey: Princeton University Press, 1973.

Chen Guocan 陈国灿. "Tang Qianling shi renxiang jiqi xianming de yanjiu." 唐乾陵石人像及其衔名的研究 [A Study of the Stone Statues and Office Titles of the Tang Qianling Mausoleum]. *Wenwu jikan*, no. 2 (1980): 189–203.

——. "Wei Jin zhi Sui Tang Hexiren de juju yu huoxianjiao." 魏晋至隋唐河西人的聚居与火祆教 [The Population and Zoroastrianism of the People in Hexi from the Wei and Jin to the Sui and Tang]. *Xibei minzu yanjiu*, no. 1 (1988): 198.

——. "'Tang Li Ciyi gaoshen' jiqi buque." 《唐李慈艺告身》及其补阙 [The Edict of Appointment of Li Ciyi of the Tang and its Restauration]. *Xiyu yanjiu*, no. 2 (2003): 37–43.

Chen Haitao 陈海涛. "Zhaowu jiu xing zuyuan kao." 昭武九姓族源考 [Study on the Origin of the Nine Surnames of the Zhaowu]. *Xibei minzu yanjiu*, no. 2 (2000): 134–41.

Chen Sanping 陳三平. "Succession Struggle and the Ethnic Identity of the Tang Imperial House." *Journal of the Royal Asiatic Society* [Series 3], no. 6.3 (1996): 379–405.

——. "From Azerbaijan to Dunhuang – A Zoroastrianism Note." *Central Asiatic Journal*, no. 47.2 (2003): 183–97. www.jstor.org/stable/41917644.

——. *Multicultural China in the Early Middle Ages*. Philadelphia: University of Pennsylvania Press, 2012.

Chen Yinke 陳寅恪. *Tangdai zhengzhi shi shu lun gao* 唐代政治史述論稿. [Shangwu yinshu guan 商務印書館, 1947. Shanghai: Shanghai guji chubanshe, 1997.

Chen Yuan 陳垣. "Huoxianjiao ru Zhongguo kao." 火祆教入中國考 [A Study on the Entry of Zoroastrianism into China]. [Beijing daxue guoxue jikan 1.1, 1923]. In *Chen Yuan shixue lunzhu xuan.* 陳垣史學論著選 [Selection of Historiographical Articles by Chen Yuan]. Edited by Chen Yuesu 陳樂素 and Chen Zhichao 陳智超, 109–32. Zhongguo dangdai shixuejia congshu 中國當代史學家叢書 [Chinese Contemporary Historian Collection]. Shanghai: Renmin chubanshe, 1981.

Chen Zhijian 陈志谦. "An Yuanshou ji furen Di shi muzhi kaoshu." 安元寿及夫人翟氏墓志考述. *Wenbo*, no. 2 (1989): 51–56.

Cheng Xilin 程喜霖. *Tangdai guosuo yanjiu* 唐代过所研究 [Research on Tang Period Passports]. Beijing: Zhonghua shuju, 2000.

Chicago University, ed. *The Chicago Manual of Style Online: State-Of-The-Art Recommendations on Editorial Style and Publishing Practices in the Digital Age.* 16th ed. Chicago: University of Chicago Press, 2010. Accessed November 27, 2016. www.chicagomanualofstyle.org/.

Choksy, Jamsheed K. *Conflict and Cooperation: Zoroastrian Subalterns and Muslim Elites in Medieval Iranian Society*. New York: Columbia University Press, 1997.

Chuguevskii, Leonid I. "Novyye materialy k istorii sogdiyskoy kolonii v rayone Dukhovaya." [New Material on the History of the Sogdian Colony in the Dunhuang Area]. *Strany i narody Vostoka*, no. 10 (1971): 147–56.

Chutu wenwu zhanlan gongzuozu 出土文物展览工作组, ed. *Wenhua da geming qijian chutu wenwu, di yi ji* 文化大革命期間出土文物，第一輯 [Artefacts Excavated During the Great Cultural Revolution: 1]. Beijing: Wenwu chubanshe, 1972.

Clauson, Gerard. *An Etymological Dictionary of Pre-Thirteenth Century Turkish.* Oxford: Clarendon Print, 1972.

Compareti, Matteo. "The Role of the Sogdian Colonies in the Diffusion of the Pearl Roundels Pattern." In Compareti; Raffetta; Scarcia, *Ērān ud Anērān*.

Compareti, Matteo, and Simone Cristoforetti. *New Elements on the Chinese Scene in the "Hall of the Ambassadors" at Afrāsyāb along with a reconsideration of "Zoroastrian" Calendar.* Eurasiatica 78. Venezia: Cafoscarina, 2007.

Compareti, Matteo, Paola Raffetta, and Gianroberto Scarcia, eds. *Ērān ud Anērān: Studies Presented to Boris Il'ič Maršak on the Occasion of his 70th Birthday*. Venezia: Cafoscarina, 2006.

Crone, Patricia. *The Nativist Prophets of Early Islamic Iran*. Cambridge: Cambridge University Press, 2012.

——. "Buddhism as Ancient Iranian Paganism." In *The Iranian Reception of Islam: The Non-Traditionalist Strands. Collected Studies in Three Volumes; Volume 2*. Edited by Patricia Crone and Hanna Siurua, 212–32. Islamic History and Civilization 130. Leiden, Boston: Brill, 2016.

Daffinà, Paolo. *L'immigrazione dei Sakā nella Drangiana.* Reports and Memoirs IX. Edited by Giuseppe Tucci. Roma: Instituto Italiano per il Medio ed Estremo Oriente, 1967.

Dai Junliang 戴均良, Liu Baoquan 刘保全, and Zou Yilin 邹逸麟, eds. *Zhongguo gujin diming da cidian - shang* 中国古今地名大词典·上 [Comprehensive Dictionary of Chinese Toponyms from Antiquity to the Present Age, 1]. Shanghai: Shanghai cishu chubanshe, 2010.

——, eds. *Zhongguo gujin diming da cidian - xia* 中国古今地名大词典·下 [Comprehensive Dictionary of Chinese Toponyms from Antiquity to the Present Age, 3]. Shanghai:

Shanghai cishu chubanshe, 2010.
Daryaee, Touraj. *Šahrestānīhā ī Ērānšahr: A Middle Persian Text on Late Antique Geography, Epic, and History. With English and Persian Translations and Commentary*. Costa Mesa, California: Mazda Publishers, 2002.
Davis, Timothy M. *Entombed Epigraphy and Commemorative Culture in Early Medieval China.* Studies in the History of Chinese Texts 6. Leiden: Brill, 2015.
Dien, Albert E. "A Note on *Hsien* 祆'Zoroastrianism'." *Oriens* 10, no. 2 (1957): 284–88. doi:10.2307/1579642.
—. *Biography of Yü-wen Hu: Translated and Annotated by Albert E. Dien.* Chinese Dynastic Histories Translations 9. Berkeley and Los Angeles: University of California Press, 1962.
—. "The *Sa-Pao* Problem Re-examined." *Journal of Asian American Studies*, no. 82.3 (1962): 335–46.
—. "Study of Early Chinese Armor." *Artibus Asiae*, 43.1–2 (1981–82): 5–56.
—, ed. *State and Society in Early Medieval China*. Hong Kong: Hong Kong University Press, 1990.
—. "The Role of the Military in the Western Wei/Northern Chou State." In Dien, *State and Society in Early Medieval China*, 331–67.
—. "Wei Tan and the Historiography of the *Wei shu*." In Studies in Early Medieval Chinese Literature and Cultural History: In Honor of Richard B. Mather and Donald Holzman. Edited by Paul W. Kroll and David R. Knechtges, 399–466. Provo, Utah: T'ang Studies Society, 2003.
—. "Observations Concerning the Tomb of Master Shi." *Bulletin of the Asia Institute*, New Series/Volume 17 (2003): 105–15.
—. "Caravans and Caravan Leaders in Palmyra." In Vaissière; Trombert, *Les Sogdiens en Chine*, 195–206.
—. "Further Thoughts on *Sârthavâha*." In *Tulufan xue yanjiu: Di er jie Tulufan xue guoji xueshu yantaohui lunwenji.* 吐鲁番学研究—第二届吐鲁番学国际学术研讨会论文集 [Research on Turfan - Edited Volume of the Second International Academic Research Forum on Turfan]. Edited by Xinjiang Tulufan diqu wenwuju 新疆吐鲁番地区文物局, 203–10. Shanghai: Shanghai cishu chubanshe, 2006.
—. *Six Dynasties Civilization.* Early Chinese Civilization Series. New Haven and London: Yale University Press, 2007.
—. "The Tomb of the Sogdian Master Shi: Insights into the Life of a *Sabao*." *The Silk Road*, Last modified 7/2009. Accessed October 25, 2013. http://www.silk-road.com/newsletter/vol7/srjournal_v7.pdf.
—. "Historiography of the Six Dynasties Period (220–581)." In *Volume I: Beginnings to AD 600*. Edited by Andrew Feldherr and Grant Hardy, 509–34. The Oxford History of Historical Writing. Edited by Daniel Woolf. Oxford: Oxford University Press, 2011.
—. "The Sogdian Experience in China: Sinicization or Accommodation?" In *China and Beyond in the Mediaeval Period: Cultural Crossings and Inter-Regional Connections*. Edited by Dorothy C. Wong and Gustav Heldt, 117–34. Cambria Sinophone World Series. Delhi and New York: Manohar Publishers & Distributions and Cambria Press, 2014.
—. "Consideration of Some Aspects of the Sogdian Experience in China: From *sabo* to *s'rtp'w*." In Early Medieval North China: Archaeological and Textual Evidence. Edited by Shing Müller, Thomas O. Höllmann and Sonja Filip. Wiesbaden: Harrassowitz, 2019.
Ding Fubao 丁福保, ed. *Foxue da cidian* 佛學大辭典 [Comprehensive Dictionary of Buddhism]. Beijing: Wenwu chubanshe, 2005.

Du Wen 杜文. "Songdai taosu wanju shang suo jian 'qi sheng dao' huanshu." 宋代陶塑玩具上所见'七圣刀'幻术 ["Seven Knives" Magic as Evidenced by a Ceramic Toy from the Song]. *Zhongyuan wenwu*, no. 3 (2009): 106–8.

Duan Qing 段晴. "Sute shangdui dao Yutian." 粟特商队到于阗 [Accounts in Khotanese with Signature of the Leader of a Sogdian Caravan]. In Rong Xinjiang 荣新江; Luo Feng 罗丰; Ningxia wenwu kaogu yanjiusuo 宁夏文物考古研究所; Beijing daxue zhongguo gudaishi yanjiu zhongxin 北京大学中国古代史研究中心, *Suteren zai Zhongguo II*, 96–115.

Duchesne-Guillemin, Jacques. *La religion de l'Iran ancien*. Paris: Presses universitaires de France, 1962.

Ebrey, Patricia B. *The Aristocratic Families of Early Imperial China: A Case Study of the Po-ling Ts'ui Family*. Cambridge: Cambridge University Press, 1978.

Eichhorn, Werner. "Materialien zum Auftreten iranischer Kulte in China." In *Die Welt des Orients. Wissenschaftliche Beiträge zur Kunst des Morgenlandes*. Band 2, Heft 5/6. Edited by Michel Ernst, 531–41. Göttingen: Vandenhoeck & Ruprecht, 1959.

Einstein, Albert, and Hirsch L. Gordon. "My Opinion About the Origin of New Ideas and New Understanding." Accessed December 1, 2019. http://alberteinstein.info/vufind1/Record/EAR000032496.

Eliasberg, Danielle. "À propos d'images disparues." In *Études de Dunhuang et Turfan*. Edited by Jean-Pierre Drège, 53–70. II Hautes Études Orientales 41 Extrême-Orient 6. Genève: Librairie Droz, 2007.

Enoki Kazuo 榎一雄. "Sogdiana and the Hsiung-nu." *Central Asiatic Journal*, no. 1 (1955): 43–62. http://www.jstor.org/stable/41926300.

——. "Gisho Zokudo kuni den to kyōdo-Fun dōzoku mondai." 魏書粟特国伝と匈奴・フン同族問題 [The Statement of the Wêi-shu on Su-t'ê and the Hsiung-nu- and Huns Identity]. *Tōyō-gakuhō*, no. 37.4 (1955): 1–48.

Epstein, H. *Domestic Animals of China*. Farnham Royal: Commonwealth Agricultural Bureau, 1969.

Ess, Hans van. *Politik und Gelehrsamkeit in der Zeit der Han (202 v. Chr.–220 n. Chr.): Die Alttext / Neutext-Kontroverse*. Wiesbaden: Harrassowitz, 1993.

"Faguo Hanxue" congshu bianji weiyuanhui 《法国汉学》丛书编辑委员会, ed. *Suteren zai Zhongguo, lishi, kaogu, yuyan de xin tansuo* 粟特人在中国 —历史、考古、语言的新探索 [Les Sogdiens en Chine: nouvelles recherches historiques, archéologiques et philologiques]. With the assistance of Rong Xinjiang 荣新江, Hua Lan 华澜, and Zhang Qingjie 张庆捷. Faguo hanxue 法国汉学 [Sinologie française] 10. Beijing: Zhonghua shuju, 2005.

Falk, Harry. "The Yuga of Sphujiddhvaja and the Era of the Kuṣâṇas." *Silk Road Art and Archaeology*, no. 7 (2001): 121–36.

——. "The Five Yabghus of the Yuezhi." *Bulletin of the Asia Institute*, New Series/Volume 28 (2014): 1–43.

Falkenhausen, Lothar v. "On the Historiographical Orientation of Chinese Archaeology." *Antiquity*, no. 67 (1993): 839–49. doi:10.1017/S0003598X00063821.

Fan Shuying 范淑英. "Sui Tang mu chutu de 'gujing': Jianlun Sui Tang tongjing tuwen de fugu wenti." 隋唐墓出土的'古镜'—兼论隋唐铜镜图文的复古问题 [On "Ancient Mirrors" Excavated from the Sui & Tang Periods' Tombs: with Exploration into the Retro-style Bronze Mirrors of the Sui & Tang Dynasties]. *Gugong bowuyuan yuankan*, no. 6 (2010):

104–25, 161.
Feng Chengye 馮承業. *Li Deyu yanjiu 李德裕研究* [A Study of Li Deyu]. Taipei: Taiwan xuesheng shuju, 1974.
Filchner, W. *Ein Ritt über den Pamir*. Berlin: Mittler, 1903.
Filip, Sonja. "Kulturhistorische Einordnung der Befunde und Funde aus dem Grab der Li Chui." In *Das Grab der Li Chui: Interdisziplinäre Detailstudien zu einem Tang-zeitlichen Fundkomplex*. Edited by Susanne Greiff et al., 97–148. Monographien des Römisch-Germanisches Zentralmuseums 111. Mainz: Verlag des Römisch-Germanischen Zentralmuseums, 2013.
Forte, Antonino. *The Hostage An Shigao and his Offspring: An Iranian Family in China*. Kyoto: Istituto Italiano du Cultura Scuola di Studi sull'Asia Orientale, 1995.
—. "Kuwabara's Misleading Thesis on Bukhara and the Family Name An 安." *Journal of the American Oriental Society*, Vol. 116, No. 4 (1996): 645–52. Accessed October 20, 2013. http://www.jstor.org/stable/605437.
—. "The Sabao 薩寶 Question." In *The Silk Roads Nara International Symposium: 1997 Nara-shi, Japan; Silk Roads of Sanzō-hōshi · Xuanzang*, 80–106. Nara, 1999.
Frankl, Victor E. "Die Revolutionierung der Wissenschaften und das Menschliche im Menschen." In *Das neue Menschenbild: Ein internationales Symposium*. Edited by Arthur Koestler and J. R. Smythies, 374–85. Wien, München, Zürich: Molden, 1970.
—, ed. *Der Mensch vor der Frage nach dem Sinn: Eine Auswahl aus dem Gesamtwerk*. München: R. Piper & Co., 1979.
Franz, Rainer v. *Die chinesische Innengrabinschrift für Beamte und Privatiers des 7. Jahrhunderts*. Münchener ostasiatische Studien Bd. 74. Stuttgart: Franz Steiner, 1996.
Fujita Toyohachi 藤田豊八. "Saiiki kenkyū (dai nikai): 4. Sappō ni tsukite." 西域研究（第二回):（四）薩寶につきて [Western Regions Studies (2nd): (4) Regarding Sappō]. *Shigaku zasshi*, no. 36.3 (1925): 195–215.
—. *Xiyu yanjiu* 西域研究 [Western Regions Studies]. Translated by Yang Lian 楊鍊. Hanyi shijie mingzhu 漢譯世界名著 117. Taiwan shangwu yinshuguan, 1966 [1925].
Fukushima Megumi 福島恵. *Tōbu Yuurasia no Sogudo jin: Sogudojin kanbun bashi no kenkyū* 東部ユーラシアのソグド人 ソグド人漢文墓誌の研究 [The Sogdians in the Eastern Eurasia: A Study of Sogdian Epitaphs in Chinese]. Kyūko sōsho 汲古叢書 [Kyūko Collectanea] 140. Tōkyō: Kyūko Shoin, 2017.
Fussman, Gérard. "Expliquer Shatial." In Fussman; König, *Die Felsbildstation von Shatial*, 73–84.
Fussman, Gérard and Ditte König, eds. *Die Felsbildstation von Shatial.* Materialien zur Archäologie der Nordgebiete Pakistans 2. Mainz: Philipp von Zabern, 1997.

Gansu sheng wenwu kaogu yanjiusuo 甘肃省文物考古研究所. "Dunhuang Xuanquan Han jian shiwen xuan." 敦煌悬泉汉简释文选 [A Selected Edition of Han Slips of Xuanquan, Dunhuang]. *Wenwu*, no. 5 (2000): 27–45.
Ge Chengyong 葛承雍. "Sui An Bei mu xin chutu shike tuxiang de Sute yishu." 隋安備墓新出土石刻圖像的粟特藝術 [Sogdian Art in the Stone Carving Images Recently Excavated from the Tomb of An Bei of the Sui Dynasty]. *Yishushi yanjiu*, no. 12 (2010): 1–13.
Gernet, Jacques. *Buddhism in Chinese Society: An Economic History from the Fifths to the Tenth Centuries.* Translated by Franciscus Verellen. [Les aspects économiques du bouddhisme dans la société chinoise du Ve au Xe siècle. Saigon: EFEO, 1956. New York: Columbia University Press, 1995.
Gershevitch, I. "Sogdians on a Frogplain." In *Mélanges linguistiques offerts à Émile*

Benveniste. Edited by Françoise Bader, 195–211. Louvain: Peeters, 1975.
Gharib, B. *Sogdian Dictionary: Sogdian-Persian-English*. Tehran: Farhangan Publications, 1995.
Gibb, H. A. R. *The Arab Conquest in Central Asia*. James G. Forlong Fund Vol. II. London: The Royal Asiatic Society, 1923.
Giles, Lionel. "A Chinese Geographical Text of the Ninth Century." *Bulletin of the School of Oriental Studies, University of London*, no. 6.4 (1932): 825–46. Accessed August 9, 2017. http://www.jstor.org/stable/606896.
——. *Six Centuries at Tunhuang: A Short Account of the Stein Collection of Chinese Mss. in the British Museum*. London: The China Society, 1944.
Goldin, Paul R. "On the Meaning of the Name Xi wangmu, Spirit-Mother of the West." *Journal of the American Oriental Society*, no. 122.1 (2002): 83–85. doi:10.2307/3087655.
Grenet, Frantz. *Les pratiques funéraires dans l'Asie centrale sédentaire de la conquête grecque à l'islamisation*. Publication de l'U.R.A. 29, mémoire no 1. Paris: Éditions du Centre national de la recherche scientifique, 1984.
——. "L'art Zoroastrien en Sogdiane: Études d'iconographie funéraire." *Mesopotamia, Rivista di Archeologia, Epigrafia e Storia Orientale Antica* 21 (1986): 97–131.
——. "Conférence de M. Frantz Grenet." *École pratique des hautes études, Section des sciences religieuses*, no. 108 (1999 (1999–2000)): 175–80. http://www.persee.fr/doc/ephe_0000-0002_1999_num_112_108_13021.
——. "Beichao Sute bentu naguweng shang de xianjiao zhuti." 北朝粟特本土纳骨瓮上的祆教主题 [Zoroastrian Themes on Early Medieval Sogdian Ossuaries]. In *4–6 shiji de Beichao Zhongguo yu Yazhou dalu*. 4–6 世纪的北朝中国与亚洲大陆 [The Northern Dynasties of China and Continental Asia in the 4th to 6th century BC]. Edited by Shanxi sheng Beichao wenhua yanjiu zhongxin 山西省北朝文化研究中心, 190–98. Beijing: Kexue chubanshe, 2006. ['Zoroastrian Themes on Early Medieval Sogdian Ossuaries.' In: J. Godrej und F. P. Mistree, eds., A Zoroastrian Tapestry: Art, Religion and Culture. Ahmedabad: Mapin Publishing Pvt. Ltd., 2002].
——. "Religious Diversity among Sogdian Merchants in Sixth-Century China: Zoroastrianism, Buddhism, Manichaeism, and Hinduism." *Comparative Studies of South Asia, Africa and the Middle East* 27, no. 2 (2007): 463–78. Accessed October 25, 2013. http://cssaame.dukejournals.org/content/27/2/463.
——. "Where Are the Sogdian Magi?" With the assistance of Samra Azarnouche. *Bulletin of the Asia Institute*, no. 21 (2007): 159–77.
——. "Zoroastrianism in Central Asia." In *The Wiley Blackwell Companion to Zoroastrianism*. Edited by Michael Stausberg and Yuhan S. D. Vevaina, 129–46. Chichester: Wiley Blackwell, 2015.
Grenet, Frantz, Pénélope Riboud, and Yang Junkai 杨军凯. "Zoroastrian Scenes on a Newly Discovered Sogdian Tomb in Xi;an, Northern China." *Studia Iranica*, Last modified 2004. Accessed August 27, 2011. http://poj.peeters-leuven.be/content.php?url=issue&journal_code=SI&issue=2&vol=33.
Grenet, Frantz, and Nicholas Sims-Williams. "The Historical Context of the Sogdian Ancient Letters: Actes du symposium de Fribourg-en-Brisgau (22–24 mai 1985)." *Studia Iranica*, Cahier 5, Transition Periods in Iranian History (1987): 101–22.
Grenet, Frantz, Nicholas Sims-Williams, and Étienne de la Vaissière. "The Sogdian Ancient Letter V." *Bulletin of the Asia Institute*, New Series, 12 (1998): 91–104.
Grenet, Frantz, and Zhang Guangda. "The Last Refuge of the Sogdian Religion: Dunhuang in

the Ninth and Tenth Centuries." *Bulletin of the Asia Institute*, New Series/Volume 10 (1996): 175–86.

Gu Sen 顾森, ed. *Zhongguo Han hua tudian* 中国汉画图典 [Pictorial Dictionary of Han Painting]. Hangzhou: Zhejiang sheying chubanshe, 1997.

Guan Youhui 关友惠. "Mogaoku Suidai tu'an chutan." 莫高窟隋代图案初探 [Discussion of the Motifs from the Sui in the Mogao Caves]. *Dunhuang yanjiu*, no. 00 (1983): 26–38.

Guojia tushuguan shanben jinshi zu 國家圖書館善本金石組, ed. *Sui Tang Wudai shike wenxian quanbian* 隋唐五代石刻文獻全編 [Complete Collection of Stone Inscriptions of the Sui, Tang, and Five Dynasties]. 4 vols. Beijing: Beijing tushuguan chubanshe, 2003.

Guojia wenwuju guwenxian yanjiu shi 国家文物局古文献研究室, ed. *Tulufan chutu wenshu* 吐鲁番出土文书 [Excavated Documents of Turfan]. 6 vols. Beijing: Wenwu chubanshe, 1981–91.

Guyuan xian wenwu gongzuozhan 固原县文物工作站. "Ningxia Guyuan xian Xi Zhou mu qingli jianbao." 宁夏固原县西周墓清理简报 [Brief Excavation Report of a Grave from the Western Zhou in the Guyuan District, Ningxia]. *Kaogu*, no. 11 (1983): 982–84.

Halévy, J. "Société asiatique: Séance du 11 Novembre 1910." *Journal Asiatique*, no. 16 (1910): 625–30.

Haloun, Gustav. *Seit wann kannten die Chinesen die Tocharer oder Indogermanen überhaupt*. Leipzig: Asia Major, 1926.

——. "Zur Üe-tṣï-Frage." *Zeitschrift der Deutschen Morgenländischen Gesellschaft*, Vol. 91/ Neue Folge Bd. 16 (1937): 243–328.

Hamilton, James. *Manuscrits ouïgours du IXe-Xe siècle de Touen-Houang*. 2 vols. Paris: Peeters, 1986.

Haneda Tōru 羽田亨. "Tō Kōkei gannen shosha Sashū - Yishū chishi zankan ni tsuite." 唐光啟元年書寫沙州·伊州地志殘卷について [Regarding the Fragments of the Yizhou-Shazhou Local Chronical Manuscripts of the First Year of the Tang Guangqi Era (885 CE)]. In *Shigaku chirigaku ronsō: Ogawa hakushi kanreki kinen.* 史學地理學論叢: 小川博士還曆記念. Edited by Ishibashi Gorō 石橋五郎, 131–52. Tōkyō: Kobundo Shobo, 1930.

——. "Baku-hoku no chi Kankoku-jin." 漠北の地と康國人 [La Mongolie et les Sogdiens; originally published in Shinagaku 支那学 3.5 (1924)]. In *Haneda hakushi shigaku ronbunshū: shū kan (kireshi hen).* 羽田博士史學論文集—上卷(歷史篇) [Recueil des œuvres posthumes de Tôru Haneda, I, Études historiques]. Edited by Haneda Tōru 羽田亨, 395–405. Kyōto: Tōyōshi Kenkyūkai, 1975.

Hansen, Valerie. "Introduction: Turfan as a Silk Road Community." *Asia Major/Third Series*, no. 11 (1998.2): 1–11.

Hao Shusheng 郝樹聲, and Zhang Defang 張德芳. *Xuanquan Han jian yanjiu* 懸泉漢簡研究 [A Study of the Han Bamboo Slips from Xuanquan]. Lanzhou: Gansu wenhua chubanshe.

Haussig, H. W. "Theophylakts Exkurs über die skythischen Völker." *Byzantion*, no. 23 (1953): 275–462.

He Bingwu 何炳武, ed. *Ashina Zhong, An Yuanshou muzhi* 阿史那忠、安元寿墓志 [The Epitaphs of Ashina Zhong and An Yuanshou]. Da Tang muzhi shufa jingxuan 大唐墓志书法精选 [Selected Calligraphy of Tang Epitaphs]. Xi'an: Shijie tushu chubanshe Xi'an you xian gongsi, 2011.

He Sui 何遂, and Xiang Da 向達. "Tang gu Miguo dashouling Mi gong muzhiming kao." 唐故米國大首領米公墓志銘考 [Research on the Epitaph of the Late Great Supervisor of the State of Mi Lord Mi of the Tang]. *Guoli Beiping tushuguan guankan*, no. 6.2 (1932): 141–44.

He Zicheng 贺梓城. "Tang Wangchao yu bianjiang minzu he linguo de youhao guanxi - Tang muzhiming zhaji zhi yi." 唐王朝与边疆民族和邻国的友好关系—唐墓志铭扎记之一 [The Friendly Relations of the Tang Dynasty with Bordering Ethnicities and Neighbouring Countries – Notices on Epitaphs of the Tang]. *Wenbo*, no. 1 (1984): 59.

Henning, W. B. "The Date of the Sogdian Letters." *Bulletin of the School of Oriental and African Studies*, no. 12.3 (1948): 601–15.

——. "Mitteliranisch." In *Linguistik*. Edited by Bertold Spuler, 20–129. Handbuch der Orientalistik Abt. 1 Der Nahe und der Mittlere Osten, Bd. 4 Iranistik, Abschn. 1. Leiden: Brill, 1958.

——. "A Sogdian God." *Bulletin of the School of Oriental and African Studies*, no. 28.2 (1965): 242–54. doi:10.1017/S0041977X00075091.

——. "Mitteliranische Manichaica aus Chinesisch-Turkestan II." In *W. B. Henning Selected Papers I*. Edited by J. Guillemin-Duchhesne, 191–273. Acta Iranica 14, deuxième série: Hommages et Opera Minora Volume V. Leiden: E. J. Brill, 1977.

Hill, John E., ed. *Through the Jade Gate - China to Rome: A Study of the Silk Routes during the Later Han Dynasty 1st to 2nd Centuries CE An annotated translation from the Hou Hanshu 'The Chronicle on the Western Regions' Updated and Expanded.* 2nd edition in Two Volumes. 2015.

Hinüber, Oskar von. *Beiträge zur Erklärung der Senavarma-Inschrift.* Abhandlungen der Geistes- und Sozialwissenschaftlichen Klasse 1. Stuttgart: Franz Steiner, 2003.

Hirth, Friedrich. *China and the Roman Orient: Researches into Their Ancient and Mediæval Relations as Represented in Old Chinese Records*. Leipzig, München: Georg Hirth, 1885.

——. *Ueber fremde Einflüsse in der chinesischen Kunst*. München und Leipzig, 1896.

——. "Mr. Kingsmill and the Hiung-nu." *Journal of the American Oriental Society*, no. 30.1 (1909): 32–45.

Hirth, Friedrich, and W. W. Rockhill. *Chau Ju-Kua: His Work on the Chinese and Arab Trade in the twelfth and thirteenth Centuries, entitled Chu-fan-chï*. St. Petersburg: Imperial Academy of Sciences, 1911.

Höllmann, Thomas O. and Georg W. Kossack, eds. *Maoqinggou: Ein eisenzeitliches Gräberfeld in der Ordos-Region (Innere Mongolei), nach der Veröffentlichung von Tian Guangjin und Guo Suxin*. With the assistance of Karl Jettmar et al. Mainz am Rhein: Philipp von Zabern, 1992.

Holmgren, Jennifer. "Politics of the Inner Court under the Hou-chu (Last Lord) of Northern Ch'i (ca. 565–73)." In Dien, *State and Society in Early Medieval China*, 267–330.

Holzman, Donald. "Les débuts du système médiéval de choix et de classement des fonctionnaires: Les Neuf Catégories et l'Impartial et Juste." In *Mélanges publiés par l'Institut des hautes études chinoises*. Vol. 1. Edited by Bibliothèque de l'Institut des hautes études chinoises, 387–414. Paris, 1957.

Hu Pingsheng 胡平生, and Zhang Defang 張德芳. *Dunhuang Xuanquan Han jian shicui* 敦煌懸泉漢簡釋粹 [Essential Edition of the Han Slips from Xuanquan, Dunhuang]. Shanghai: Shanghai guji chubanshe, 2001.

Huang Wenbi 黄文弼 and Zhongguo shehui kexueyuan kaogu yanjiusuo 中国社会科学院考古研究所, eds. *Xinjiang kaogu fajue baogao (1957–1958)* 新疆考古發掘報告 *(1957–1958)* [An Archaeological Tour of Xinjiang *(1957–1958)*]. Zhongguo tianye kaogu baogao ji 中国田野考古报告集 [Chinese Field Archaeology Reports Collection] 25. Beijing: Wenwu chubanshe, 1983.

Hucker, Charles O. *A Dictionary of Official Titles in Imperial China.* Stanford, California:

Stanford University Press, 1985.
Hulsewé, A. F. P., and M. A. N. Loewe. *China in Central Asia: The Early Stage: 123 B.C.–A.D. 23: An Annotated Translation of Chapters 61 and 96 of the History of the Former Han Dynasty*. Sinica Leidensia: Institutum Sinologicum Lugduno Batavum 14. Leiden: Brill, 1979.
Humbach, Helmut, ed. *Baktrische Sprachdenkmäler: Teil 1*. With the assistance of Adolf Grohmann. Wiesbaden: Otto Harrassowitz, 1966.

Ikeda On 池田温. "Tōdai no gumbōhyō: Ku, jusseiki no Tonkō shahon o chūshin to shite - shō -." 唐代の郡望表：九十世紀の敦煌寫本を中心として-上- [The Junwang Biao of the Tang: With a Focus on Dunhuang Manuscripts from the 9th and 10th Century (1)]. *Tōyō gakuhō*, no. 42.3 (1959): 293–331 (57–95).
——. "Tōdai no gumbōhyō: Ku, jusseiki no Tonkō shahon o chūshin to shite - ge -." 唐代の郡望表：九十世紀の敦煌寫本を中心として-下- [The Junwang Biao of the Tang: With a Focus on Dunhuang Manuscripts from the 9th and 10th Century (2)]. *Tōyō gakuhō*, no. 42.4 (1960): 412–30 (40–58).
——. "Hasseiki chūyō ni okeru Tonkō no Sogudojin juraku." 8世紀中葉における敦煌のソグド人聚落 [A Sogdian Settlement in Dunhuang in the Mid-Eight Century]. *Yūrashia bunka kenyū*, no. 1 (1965): 49–92.
——. "Sashū zukei ryakkō." 沙州圖經略考 [A Study of the Shazhou Tujing]. In *Tōyōshi ronsō: Enoki Hakushi kanreki kinen.* 東洋史論叢：榎博士還歷記念 [Collectanea of Research on East Asian History: Festschrift for the 60th Birthday of Dr. Enoki]. Edited by Enoki Hakushi Kanreki Kinen Tōyōshi Ronsō Hensan Iinkai 榎博士還歷記念東洋史論叢編纂委員会, 31–101. Tōkyō: Yamakawa Shuppansha, 1975.
——. *Chūgoku kodai sekichō kenkyū: gaikan, rokubun* 中国古代籍帳研究：概観，錄文 [A Study of Ancient Chinese Household Registers and Related Documents: General Introduction and Collected Documents]. Tōkyō: Daigaku Tōyō Bunka Kenkyūjo, 1979.
——. "Les marchands sogdiens dans les documents de Dunhuang et de Turfan." *Journal Asiatique*, no. 269 (1981): 77–79.
——. *Zhongguo gudai jizhang yanjiu* 中國古代籍帳研究 [Research on Ancient Chinese Records]. Beijing: Zhonghua shuju, 1984.
——. "Shinryō sannen Kōshōken Sūkakyō tensekiyō ni tsuite." 神竜三年高昌県崇化郷点籍様について [Regarding the Household Register Inspection of the Chonghua Town, Gaochang District, of 707 CE]. In *Chūgoku kodai no hō to shakai: Kurihara Masuo sensei koki kinen ronshū.* 中国古代の法と社会：栗原益男先生古稀記念論集 [Law and Society of Ancient China: Festschrift for Mr. Kurihara Masua's 70th Birthday]. Edited by Kurihara Masuo sensei koki kinen ronshū henshō iinkai 栗原益男先生古稀記念論集編集委員会, 245–70. Tōkyō: Kyūko Shoin, 1988.
——. "Ba shiji zhongye Dunhuang de Suteren juluo." 八世纪中叶敦煌的粟特人聚落 [The Settlements of Sogdians in Dunhuang in the Eight Century]. In *Tang yanjiu lunwen xuanji.* 唐研究論文選集 [Selection of Papers on Tang Studies]. Edited by Ikeda On 池田温, 3–67. Tang yanjiu jijinhui congshu. 唐研究基金会丛书. Beijing: Zhongguo shehui kexue chubanshe, 1999.
Ishida Mikonosuke 石田幹之助. "Kanda gakushi no 'Tenkyō zakkō' o yomite." 神田学士の'祆教雑考'を読みて [Reading Mr. Kanda's "Miscellaneous Notes on Zoroastrianism"]. *Shigaku zasshi*, no. 39.6 (1928).
Iwami Kiyohiro 石見清裕, ed. *Sogudo jin boshi kenkyū* ソグド人墓誌研究 [A Study of Sogdian Epitaphs]. Tōkyō: Kyūko Shoin, 2016.

Jacoby, Felix, ed. *Fragmenta historicorum Graecorum: Collegit, disposuit, notis et prolegomenis illustravit, indicibus instruxit Carolus Müllerus*. 5 vols. Scriptorum graecorum bibliotheca. Paris: Ambroise Firmin-Didot, 1841–73. Accessed December 1, 2019. http://www.dfhg-project.org/.

Jettmar, Karl. "Sogdians in the Upper Indus Valley." In *Histoire et Cultes de l'Asie Centrale Préislamique: Sources écrites et documents archéologiques, Actes du colloque international du C.N.R.S. (Paris, 22–28 novembre 1988)*. Edited by Paul Bernard and Frantz Grenet, 251–53. Paris: CNRS, 1991.

——. "Sogdische Händler und ein Maitreya-Heiligtum." In Fussman; König, *Die Felsbildstation von Shatial*, 85–91.

Jiang Boqin 姜伯勤. *Tang Wudai Dunhuang sihu zhidu* 唐五代敦煌寺戶制度 [The Temple System of Dunhuang in the Tang and Five Dynasties]. Zhonghua lishi congshu 中華歷史叢書 [Chinese History Collectanea]. Beijing: Zhonghua shuju, 1987.

——. *Dunhuang Tulufan wenshu yu sichou zhi lu* 敦煌吐鲁番文书与丝绸之路 [Documents of Dunhuang and Turfan and the Silk Road]. Beijing: Wenwu chubanshe, 1994.

——. "Sabaofu zhidu yuanliu lunlüe: Hanwen Suteren muzhi kaoshi zhi yi." 薩寶府制度源流論略—漢文粟特人墓誌考釋之一 [A Discussion of the Evolution of the Sabao-System – with a Focus on the Close Reading of Epitaphs of Sogdians in Chinese Language]. *Huaxue*, no. 3 (1998/11): 290–308.

——. "Lun Song Yuan Ming shiqi Shanxi Jiexiu de Xianshen lou." 论宋元明时期山西介休的祆神楼 [A Discussion of the Zoroastrian Building of Jiexiu in Shanxi from the Song, Yuan, and Ming]. In *Zhongguo Xianjiao yishushi yanjiu.* 中国祆教艺术史研究. Edited by Jiang Boqin 姜伯勤, 271–84. Beijing: San lian shudian, 2004.

Jin Yijiu 金宜久, ed. *Yisilanjiao cidian* 伊斯兰教辞典 [Islam Dictionary]. Shanghai: Shanghai cishu chubanshe, 1997.

Johnson, David G. *The Medieval Chinese Oligarchy*. Boulder: Westview Press, 1977.

Johnson, Wallace S. *The T'ang Code: Volume I, General Principles.* Translated by Wallace Johnson. Studies in East Asian law 10,1. Princeton, New Jersey: Princeton University Press, 1979.

Jörg, Ulrich. "Die Grabkultur bei Xi'an in der späten mittleren Tang-Zeit: Exemplarisch aufgezeigt anhand der Gräber von Prinzessin Tang'an (dat. 784 n.Chr.) und von Kronprinz Huizhao (dat. 811 n.Chr.)." Doctoral Dissertation, Ludwigs-Maximillians-Universität München, Last modified 1999.

Juliano, Annette L. and Judith A. Lerner, eds. *Monks and Merchants, Silk Road Treasures from Northeast China: Gansu and Ningxia, 4th–7th Century*. With the assistance of Michael Alram et al. New York: Harry N. Abrams, Inc., 2001.

Kageyama Etsuko 影山悦子. "Higashi Turukisutan shutsudo no ossuari (zoroasutā kyōto nōkotsuki) ni tsuite." 東トルキスタン出土のオッスアリ(ゾロアスター教徒の納骨器)について [The Ossuaries (Bone-receptacles of Zoroastrians) Unearthed in Chinese Turkestan]. *Oriento*, no. 40.1 (1997): 73–89.

——. "Sogdians in Kucha: A Study from Archaeological and Iconographical Material." In Vaissière; Trombert, *Les Sogdiens en Chine*, 363–75.

Kanda Kiichirō 神田喜一郎. "Tenkyō zakkō." 祆教雜考 [Miscellaneous Notes on Zoroastrianism]. *Shigaku zasshi*, no. 39.4 (1928): 381–94.

Karg, Christine U. "Die Grabkultur der Nördlichen Qi-Zeit (550–577): Blüte einer neuen Epoche in der chinesischen Grabkunst dargestellt am archäologischen Material neuerer

Ausgrabungen." Doctoral Dissertation, Ludwigs-Maximillians-Universität München, Last modified 2001.

Karlgren, Bernhard. "Legends and Cults in Ancient China." *Bulletin of the Museum of Far Eastern Antiquities*, no. 18 (1946): 199–365.

Kishibe Shigeo 岸邊成雄. *Tōdai ongaku no rekishiteki kenkyū: Gakusei hen jōkan 唐代音樂の歷史的研究, 乐制篇* [A Historical Study of Music in the T'ang Dynasty, Music Organization in the Court]. 2 Volumes. Tōkyō: University of Tokyo Press, 1961.

Klimkeit, Hans-Joachim. *Gnosis on the Silk Road: Gnostic texts from Central Asia.* San Francisco: Harper, 1993.

Kljaštornyj, S. G., and V. A. Livšic. "Sogdijskaja nadpis' iz Buguta." [The Sogdian Inscription of Bugut]. *Strany i narody Vostoka*, no. 10 (1971): 121–46.

Kōgi Kudara, and Werner Sundermann. "Fragmente einer soghdischen Handschrift des Viśeṣacinti -brahma-paripṛcchā-sūtra." *Altorientalische Forschungen*, no. 18.2 (1991): 246–63.

Kuwabara Jitsuzō 桑原隲藏. "Zui Tō jidai ni shina ni raijū shita sai-ikijin ni tsuite." 隋唐時代に支那に来住した西域人に就いて [Regarding the Immigration of People of the Western Regions to China during the Sui and Tang Periods]. In *Naitō hakushi kanreki shukuga shinagaku ronzō. 内藤博士還暦祝賀支那学論叢* [Sinological Festschrift for Dr. Naitō]. Edited by Naitō hakushi kanreki shuguka kaihen 内藤博士還暦祝賀会編, 565–660. Kyōto: Hirofumihiro shobō, 1926.

——. "On P'u Shou-kêng 蒲壽庚." *Memoirs of the Research Department of the Toyo Bunko (the Oriental Library)*, no. 2 (1928): 1–79.

——. *Pu Shougeng kao 蒲壽庚考* [On Pu Shougeng]. Translated by Chen Yujing 陳裕菁. [1929]. Beijing: Zhonghua shuju, 1954.

Kuwabara Jitsuzō 桑原隲藏, and Miyazaki Ichisada 宮崎市定. *Kuwabara Jitsuzō zenshō: 2 桑原隲蔵全集, 2* [Complete Collection of Kuwabara Jitsuzō, 2]. Tōkyō: Iwanami shoten, 1968.

Laue, Theodore H. von. *The World Revolution of Westernisation: The Twentieth Century in Global Perspective*. London: Oxford University Press, 1989.

Laufer, Berthold. *Sino-Iranica: Chinese Contributions to the History of Civilization in Ancient Iran. With Special Reference to the History of Cultivated Plants and Products.* Anthropological Series Vol. 15, No. 3. Chicago: Field Museum of Natural History, 1919.

Legge, James. *The Chinese Classics: With a Translation, Critical and Exegetical Notes, Prolegomena, and Copious Indexes. Vol. I, Containing: Confucian Analects, The Great Learning, and The Doctrine of the Mean.* Hongkong, London: At the Author's, Trübner, 1861.

Lerner, Judith A. "Aspects of Assimilation: The Funerary Practices and Furnishings of Central Asians in China." *Sino-Platonic Papers*, no. 168 (2005/12).

Leslie, D. D., and K. H. J. Gardiner. "Chinese Knowledge of Western Asia during the Han." *T'oung Pao*, no. 88 (1982): 254–308.

Leslie, Donald D. "Persian Temples in T'ang China." *Monumenta Serica* XXXV (1981–83): 275–303.

Li Daxiang 黎大祥. "Wuwei Da Tang shang zhu guo Di gong mu qingli jianbao." 武威大唐上柱国翟公墓清理简报 [Brief Excavation Rreport on the Grave of Commander Unequalled in Honour Lord Di of the Tang]. *Longyou wenwu*, no. 1 (1998).

Li Fang 李方. "Tang Xizhou de yiyu ren." 唐西州的译语人 [Translators of Xizhou of the Tang]. *Wenwu*, no. 2 (1994): 45–51.

Li Jianchao 李健超. *Zengding Tang liangjing chengfang kao* 增訂唐兩京城坊考 [Enhanced

Study of the Quarters in the Two Capitals of the Tang]. Xi'an: San qin chubanshe, 1996.

Li Jinxiu 李锦绣. "Shi Hedan yu Sui mo Tang chu zhengzhi: Guyuan chutu Shi Hedan muzhi yanjiu zhi yi." 史诃耽与隋末唐初政治—固原出土史诃耽墓志研究之一 [Shi Hedan and the Politics of the End of the Sui and the Beginning of the Tang: A Study on the Epitaph of Shi Hedan, Excavated in Guyuan]. In *Sichou zhi lu shang de kaogu, zongjiao yu lishi.* 丝绸之路上的考古、宗教与历史 [Archaeology, Religion and History on the Silk Road]. Edited by Luo Feng 罗丰 and Ningxia wenwu kaogu yanjiusuo 宁夏文物考古研究所, 49–60. Beijing: Wenwu chubanshe, 2011.

——. "Shi Hedan yu Tang chu mazheng: Guyuan chutu Shi Hedan muzhi yanjiu zhi er." 史诃耽与唐初马政—固原出土史诃耽墓志研究之二 [Shi Hedan and the Administration of Horse Raising in the Beginning of Tang Dynasty]. *Ouya xuekan*, no. 10 (2012): 261–76.

——. "'Yuegong' haishi 'yijiang'? An Jincang yanjiu." '乐工'还是'医匠'?—安金藏研究 [Was An Jincang a 'Musician' or a 'Physician'?]. *Jinyang xuekan*, no. 3 (2015): 37–44.

——. "Tangdai de fanshu yiyu zhiguan: Cong Shi Hedan muzhi tan qi." 唐代的翻书译语直官：从史诃耽墓志谈起 [Auxiliary Officials for Translation and Interpreting of the Tang: Discussing the Epitaph of Shi Hedan]. *Jinyang xuekan*, no. 5 (2016): 35–57, 135.

Li Ruizhe 李瑞哲. "Wei Jin Nanbeichao Sui Tang shiqi lulu sichou zhi lu shang de hushang." 魏晋南北朝隋唐时期陆路丝绸之路上的胡商 [The Ethnic Merchant Along The Silk Road From The Wei To The Tang Dynasty]. Doctoral Dissertation, Sichuan daxue 四川大学, Last modified 2007.

Li Zhengyu 李正宇. "Dunhuang nuo san lun." 敦煌傩散论 [Discussing Some Aspects of the Nuo Festival of Dunhuang]. *Dunhuang yanjiu*, no. 2 (1993): 111–22.

——. *Guben Dunhuang xiangtuzhi ba zhong jianzheng* 古本敦煌鄉土志八種箋證 [Eight Annotated Ancient Local Records of Dunhuang]. Dunhuang congkan 敦煌叢刊 [Dunhuang Collectanea] 2.11. Taibei: Xinwenfeng, 1997.

Li Zhiyan 李知宴. "San guo, liang Jin, Nanbeichao zhi ciye de chengjiu." 三国、两晋、南北朝制瓷业的成就 [The Achievements of the Porcelain Producing Industry of the Three Kigndoms, two Jin, and Southern and Northern Dynasties]. *Wenwu*, no. 2 (1979): 49–54.

Lieu, Samuel N. C. *Manichaeism in the Later Roman Empire and Medieval China: A Historical Survey*. Manchester and Dover, New Hampshire: Manchester University Press, 1985.

——. *Manichaeism in the Later Roman Empire and Medieval China.* [1985]. 2nd edition, revised and expanded. Tübingen: J. C. B. Mohr (Paul Siebeck), 1992.

——. *Manichaeism in Central Asia and China.* Nag Hammadi and Manichaean Studies 45. Leiden, Boston, Köln: Brill, 1998.

Lin Dengshun 林登順. *Beichao muzhiwen yanjiu* 北朝墓誌文研究 [Research on Epitaph Inscriptions of the Northern Dynasties]. Taibei: Liwen wenhua, 2009.

Lin Meicun 林梅村. "Sutewen mai bi qi yu sichou zhi lu shang de nünu maoyi." 粟特文买婢契与丝绸之路上的女奴贸易 [The Sogdian Female Slave Sales Contract and Female Slave Commerce on the Silk Road]. *Wenwu*, no. 9 (1992): 49–54.

——. "Zhongguo jingnei chutu dai mingwen de bosi he zhongya yinqi." 中国境内出土带铭文的波斯和中亚银器 [Silverware from Persia and Central Asia with Inscriptions, Excavated in China]. *Wenwu*, no. 9 (1997): 55–65.

——. "Cong kaogu faxian kan huoxianjiao zai Zhongguo de chu chuan." 从考古发现看火祆教在中国的初传 In Lin Meicun 林梅村, *Han Tang Xiyu yu Zhongguo wenming*, 102–12.

——. "Guyuan Sute mu suo chu zhonggu Bosi wen yinzhang jiqi xiangguan wenti." 固原粟特墓所出中古波斯文印章极其相关问题 [Concerning a Middle-Age Persian Seal Inscription in a Sogdian Grave in Guyuan and Related Questions]. In Lin Meicun 林梅村,

Han Tang Xiyu yu Zhongguo wenming, 198–208 [*Kaogu yu wenwu* 1997.1].
—–, ed. *Han Tang Xiyu yu Zhongguo wenming* 汉唐西域与中国文明 [The Western Regions during the Han to Tang Dynasties and Chinese Civilization]. Beijing: Wenwu chubanshe, 1998.
Lin Wushu 林悟殊. "A Discussion About the Difference Between the Heaven-God in the Qočo Kingdom and the High Deity of Zoroastrianism." *Zentralasiatische Studien des Seminars für Spach- und Kulturwissenschaft Zentralasians der Universität Bonn*, no. 23 (1992/1993): 7–12.
—–. *Bosi baihuojiao yu gudai Zhongguo* 波斯拜火教與古代中國 [Zorastrianism & Ancient China]. Taipei: Xinwenfeng, 1995.
—–. *Zhonggu san yi jiao bian zheng* 中古三夷教辯證 [Debate and Research on the Three Persian Religions: Manichaeism, Nestorianism, and Zoroastrianism in Mediaeval Times]. Beijing: Zhonghua shuju, 2005.
Lin Ying. "Sogdians and the Imitations of Byzantine Gold Coins Unearthed from the Heartland of China." In Compareti; Raffetta; Scarcia, *Ērān ud Anērān*, 387–401.
Liu Fengjun 刘凤君. "Nanbeichao shike muzhi xingzhi tanyuan." 南北朝石刻墓志形制探源 [Tracing the Origins of the Form of Inscribed Stone Epitaphs of the Northern and Southern Dynasties]. *Zhongyuan wenwu*, no. 2 (1988).
Liu Jinglong 刘景龙 and Li Yukun 李玉昆, eds. *Longmen shiku beike tiji huilu* 龙门石窟碑刻题记汇录 [Record of Inscriptions on Stelae in the Longmen Grottoes]. Beijing: Zhongguo dabaike quanshu chubanshe, 1998.
Liu Junwen 劉俊文. *Dunhuang Tulufan Tangdai fazhi wenshu kaoshi* 敦煌吐魯番唐代法制文書考釋 [A Philological Study on the Legal Documents of Dunhuang and Turfan of the Tang]. Beijing: Zhonghua shuju, 1989.
Liu Mau-tsai. *Die Chinesischen Nachrichten zur Geschichte der Ost-Türken (T'u-küe)*. 2 vols. Göttinger Asiatische Forschungen 10. Wiesbaden: Otto Harrassowitz, 1958.
Liu Mingshu 刘铭恕. "Yuan ren zaju zhong suo jian zhi huoxian jiao." 元人雜劇中所見之火祆教 [The Zoroastrian Fire Religion as Evidenced in Plays of the Yuan]. *Jinling xuebao*, no. 11.1 (1941): 35–50.
Liu Sizhe 刘思哲. "Sui Yangdi mu faxian de shisan huan diexie jinyudai ji xiangguan wenti yanjiu." 隋炀帝墓发现的十三环蹀躞金玉带及相关问题研究 [Research on the Thirteen Ring Multi-Piece Gold and Silver Belt Excavated from the Grave of Sui Yangdi and Related Questions]. *Kaogu yu wenwu*, no. 5 (2015): 69–73.
Livshits, Vladimir Aronovich. *Iuridicheskie dokumenty i pis'ma: Chtenie, perevod i kommentarii* [Legal Documents and Letters: Lecture, Translation and Comments] Sogdiyskiye dokumenty s gory Mug. Chteniye [Sogdian Documents from Mount Mugh] 2. Moskva: Izdatel'stvo vostochnoy literatury, 1962.
—–. "The Sogdian Wall Inscriptions on the Site of Afrasiab." *Rivista degli Studi Orientali*, Nuova Serie, Vol. 78, Supplemento No. 1: Royal Naurūz in Samarkand: Proceedings of the Conference Held in Venice on the Pre-Islamic Paintings at Afrasiab (2006): 59–74.
Lu Xiangqian 盧向前. "Guanyu guiyijun shiqi yi fen bu zhi poyongli de yanjiu: Shi yi P.4640 beimian wenshu." 关于归义军時期一份布纸破用历的研究—试譯伯四六四〇背面文書 [A Study of the History of Expenses of Cloth and Paper During the Guiyijun Period: A Tentative Translation of the Inscription P.4640 Verso]. In *Dunhuang Tulufan wenxian yanjiu lunji.* 敦煌吐鲁番文献研究论集 [Collection of Research Concerning Documents from Dunhuang and Turfan 3]. Edited by Beijing Daxue Zhongguo gushi yanjiu zhongxin 北京大学中国古史研究中心, 394–466. Beijing: Beijing daxue chubanshe, 1986.
Lu Zhaoyin 卢兆荫. "Lue lun Liang Han Wei Jin de weizhang." 略论两汉魏晋的帷帐 [A Brief Discussion of the Canopies from the Two Han, Wei, and Jin]. *Kaogu*, no. 5 (1984): 454–67.

Lü Zongli 吕宗力, ed. *Zhongguo lidai guanzhi da cidian* 中国历代官制大辞典 [Comprehensive Dictionary of the Historical System of Officials]. Beijing: Beijing chubanshe, 1994.

Lung, Rachel. "Interpreters and the Writing of History in China." *Meta*, 54 (2) (2009): 201–17. doi:10.7202/037676ar.

——. "Sogdian Translators in Tang China An Issue of Loyalty." *Ritsumeikan Studies in Language and Culture*, Vol. 22, No. 1 (2010/09): 95–105. Accessed March 16, 2015. http://r-cube.ritsumei.ac.jp/bitstream/10367/4136/1/LCS_22_1pp95-105_LUNG.pdf.

Luo Feng 罗丰. "Ye tan Shi Daode zushu ji xiangguan wenti - da Zhao Chao tongzhi." 也谈史道德族属及相关问题—答赵超同志 [Also Discussing the Ethnic Affiliation of Shi Daode and Related Questions: Answering Comrade Zhao Chao]. *Wenwu*, 1988, 92–94.

——. "Guyuan nanjiao Sui Tang Zhongya Shi shi muzhi kaoshi: shang." 固原南郊隋唐中亞史氏墓志考釋—上 [A Study on the Epitaphs of the Central Asian Shi Families of the Sui and Tang in the Southern Suburbs of Guyuan, 1]. *Dalu zazhi*, no. 90.5 (1995): 13–33 (205–225).

——. *Guyuan nanjiao Sui Tang mudi* 固原南郊隋唐墓地 [Graveyard of Sui & Tang Dynasties of the South Suburbs of Guyuan]. Beijing: Wenwu chubanshe, 1996.

——. "Sabao: Yi ge Tangchao weiyi wailai guanzhi de zai kaocha." 薩寶：一個唐朝唯一外來官職的再考察 [Re-Examining the Sabao: a Unique Foreign Official Position in the Tang Dynasty]. *Tang yanjiu*, no. 4 (1998): 215–49.

——, ed. *Hu Han zhi jian: 'Sichou zhi lu' yu xibei lishi kaogu* 胡漢之間：'絲綢之路'與西北歷史考古 [Between Hu and Han: History and Archaeology of the North-West and the 'Silk Road']. Beijing: Wenwu chubanshe, 2004.

——. "Bei Zhou Shi jun mu chutu de Baizhanting jinbi fangzhipin xi." 北周史君墓出土的拜占庭金币仿制品析. *Wenwu*, no. 3 (2005): 57–65.

——. "Liuyu Zhongguo de Zhongya Shiguo ren." 流寓中国的中亚史国人 [The Central Asians of the Country of Shi Migrating to China]. *Guoxue yanjiu*, no. 7 (2000): 235–78.

Luo Feng 罗丰, and Rong Xinjiang 荣新江. "Bei Zhou xiguo huren Di Caoming muzhi ji muzang yiwu." 北周西国胡人翟曹明墓志及墓葬遗物 [The Epitaph and Relics Found in the Tomb of Di Caoming from the Western Kingdoms' Hu people of the Northern Zhou]. In *Suteren zai Zhongguo I: Kaogu faxian yu chutu wenxian de xin yinzheng.* 粟特人在中国—考古发现与出土文献的新印证(上册) [Sogdians in China: New Evidence in Archaeological Finds and Unearthed Texts (I)]. Edited by Rong Xinjiang 荣新江 et al., 269–99. Ningxian wenwu kaogu yanjiusuo congkan 宁夏文物考古研究所丛刊 [Collectanea of the Ningxia Institute for Cultural Relics and Archaeology] 31. Beijing: Kexue chubanshe, 2016.

Luo Feng 羅丰, Zheng Kexiang 郑克祥, Geng Zhiqiang 耿志强, Ningxia wenwu kaogu yanjiusuo 宁夏文物考古研究所, and Ningxia Guyuan bowuguan 宁夏固原博物馆. "Ningxia Guyuan Sui Shi Shewu mu fajue jianbao." 宁夏固原隋史射勿墓发掘简报 [Brief Excavation Report on the Grave of Shi Shewu of the Sui in Guyuan, Ningxia]. *Wenwu*, no. 10 (1992): 15–22.

Luoyang shi wenwu gongzuodui 洛陽市文物工作隊, ed. *Luoyang chutu lidai muzhi jisheng* 洛陽出土歷代墓誌輯繩 [Collection of Epitaphs of Ancient Dynasties Excavated in Luoyang]. Beijing: Zhongguo shehui kexue chubanshe, 1991.

Lurje, Pavel B. *Personal Names in Sogdian Texts: Iranisches Personennamenbuch, Band II Mitteliranische Personennamen, Faszikel 8.* Österreichische Akademie der Wissenschaften. Philosophisch-Historische Klasse, Sitzungsberichte, 808. Band. Iranische Onomastik Nr. 8. Wien: Verlag der Österreichischen Akademie der Wissenschaften, 2010.

Ma Chi 馬馳. "Shi Daode de zushu, jiguan ji houren." 史道德的族属、籍贯及后人 [The Ethnic Affiliation, Place of Ancestry and Descendants of Shi Daode]. *Wenwu*, no. 5 (1991): 38–41.
Ma Xiaohe 馬小鶴. "Suoluoyaside jiao Sadeweisi shen yu Monji jiao Dianguang fo." 琐罗亚斯德教萨德维斯神与摩尼教电光佛 [Sadwēs in Zoroastrianism and the Buddha of Lightning in Manichaeism]. *Wenshi*, no. 4 (2013): 23–41.
Ma Yong. "The Chinese Inscription of the 'Da Wei' Envoy of the 'Sacred Rock of Hunza'." In *Antiquities of Northern Pakistan: Reports and Studies, Vol. 1, Rock Inscriptions in the Indus Valley, Text*. Edited by Karl Jettmar, 139–57. Mainz: Philipp von Zabern, 1989.
Mackenzie, D. N. "Kerdir's Inscription." In *The Sasanian Rock Reliefs at Naqsh-i Rustam*. Edited by G. Hermann, 35–72 Naqsh-i Rustam 6. Iranische Denkmäler, Reihe II: Iranische Felsreliefs I. Berlin: 1989.
Mair, Victor H. "The North(west)ern Peoples and the Recurrent Origins of the 'Chinese' State." In *The Teleology of the Modern Nation-State: Japan and China*. Edited by Joshua A. Fogel, 46–84. Encounters with Asia. Edited by Victor H. Mair. Philadelphia: University of Pennsylvania Press, 2005.
Malandra, William W. "Yasna: The Name for the Central Ritual in Zoroastrianism and for the Long Liturgical Text Recited during the Daily Performance of the Ritual." *Encyclopædia Iranica, online edition*, Last modified August 15, 2006. Accessed October 20, 2017. http://www.iranicaonline.org/articles/yasna.
Mao Yangguang 毛阳光. "Luoyang chutu Sui 'An Bei muzhi' kao shi." 洛阳新出土隋《安备墓志》考释 [Textual Research on the Newly Discovered Epitaph of An Bei of the Sui in Luoyang]. *Kaogu yu wenwu*, no. 5 (2011): 84–88.
—. "Luoyang xin chutu Sui 'An Bei muzhi' kaoshi." 洛阳新出土隋《安备墓志》考释 [Textual Research on the Newly Discovered "Epitaph of An Bei" of the Sui in Luoyang]. Last modified October 31, 2011. Accessed August 17, 2017. http://bmzy.lynu.edu.cn:88/hlwhweb/hlarcheology/2011-10-26-01.html#_ftn1.
Marquart, J. *Die Chronologie der alttürkischen Inschriften: Mit einem Vorwort und Anhang von Prof. W. Bang in Löwen*. Leipzig: Dieterich, 1898.
—. *Ērānšahr nach der Geographie des Ps. Moses Xorenac'i: Mit historisch-kritischem Kommentar und historischen und topographischen Excursen*. Abhandlungen der Gesellschaft der Wissenschaften zu Göttingen, Philologisch-Historische Klasse Neue Folge Band III.2. Berlin: Weidmannsche Buchhandlung, 1901.
Marshak, Boris I., and Valentina I. Raspopova. "Cultes communautaires et cultes privés en Sogdiane." In *Histoire et cultes de l'Asie centrale préislamique: Sources écrites et documents archéologiques; actes du colloque international du CNRS (Paris, 22–28 novembre 1988)*. Edited by Paul Bernard, 187–201. Paris: Centre National de la Recherche Scientifique, 1991.
Marshak, Boris I. "The Historico-Cultural Significance of the Sogdian Calendar." *Iran*, no. 30 (1992): 145–54. doi:10.2307/4299877.
—. "Sogd V-VIII vv. Ideologiya po pamyatnikam iskusstva." [Sogd in the 5th–8th Centuries According to the Monuments of Art]. In *Srednjaja Azija i Dal'nij Vostok v ėpochu srednevekov'ja, Srednjaja Azija v rannem srednevekov'e* [Central Asia in the Early Middle Ages]. Edited by Galina A. Brykina, 175–91. Moskva [Москва]: Nauka [Наука], 1999.
—. "Panjikant." *Encyclopædia Iranica*, online edition, Last modified July 20, 2002. Accessed March 13, 2018. http://www.iranicaonline.org/articles/panjikant.
Matsuda Hisao 松田寿男. *Kodai Tenzan no rekishi-chirigakuteki kenkyū* 古代天山の歴史地

理学的研究 [Geo-Historical Studies on the Ancient T'ien-shan Region]. Tōkyō: Waseda Daigaku Shuppanbu, 1970.

Meisterernst, Barbara, and Desmond Durkin-Meisterernst. "Some Remarks on the Chinese and Sogdian 'Sūtra of the Causes and Effects'." In *Languages of Iran: Past and Present. Iranian Studies in memoriam David Neil MacKenzie*. Edited by Dieter Weber, 109–27. Wiesbaden: Harrassowitz, 2005.

—. "The Buddhist Sogdian P7 and Its Chinese Source." In Sundermann; Hintze; Blois, *Exegisti monumenta*, 313–24.

—. "The Buddhist Sogdian Texts in Relation to Their Chinese Sources." In *Shoujie Zhongguo shaoshu minzhu guji wenxian guoji xueshu yantaohui lunwenji.* 首届中国少数民族古籍文献国际学术研讨会论文集 [Proceedings of the 1st International Colloquium on Ancient Manuscripts and Literatures of the Minorities in China]. Edited by Huang Jianming 黄建明, Nie Hongyin 聂鸿音 and Ma Lan 马兰, 410–25. Beijing: Minzu chubanshe, 2012.

Miller, Roy A. *Accounts of Western Nations in the History of the Northern Chou Dynasty.* Translated and Annotated by Roy Andrew Miller. East Asia Studies. Institute of International Studies of California. Chinese Dynastic Histories Translations 6. Berkeley: University of California Press, 1959.

Miyakawa Hisayuki 宮川尚志. *Rikuchō shi kenkyū Seiji, shakai hen* 六朝史研究 政治・社会篇 [Research on the History of the Six Dynasties: Politics and Society Section]. Tōkyō: Nippon Gakujutsu Shinkokai, 1956.

Miyazaki Ichisada 宮崎市定. *Kyūhin kanjin hō no kenkyū: kakyo zenshi* 九品官人法の研究：科挙前史 [A Study of the Nine Grade Official System: On the Prehistory of the Civil Service System]. Kyōto: Tōyōshi Kenkyūkai, 1956.

Mode, Markus. *Sogdien und die Herrscher der Welt: Türken, Sasaniden und Chinesen in Historiengemälden des 7. Jh. n Chr. aus Alt-Samarqand.* Europäische Hochschulschriften Reihe 28, Kunstgeschichte, Bd. 162. Frankfurt am Main, Berlin, Bern, New York, Paris, Wien: Peter Lang, 1993.

Moribe Yutaka. "Military officers of Sogdian origin from the late Tang Dynasty to the period of Five Dynasties." In Vaissière; Trombert, *Les Sogdiens en Chine*, 243–54.

Müller, Shing (Soong Shing 宋馨). "Die Gräber der Nördlichen Wei-Zeit (386–534)." Doctoral Dissertation, Ludwigs-Maximillians-Universität München, Last modified 2000.

—. "Chin straps of the Early Northern Wei: New Perspectives on the Trans-Asiatic Diffusion of Funerary Practices." *Journal of East Asian Archaeology*, Volume 5, Issue 1 (2003): 27–71. doi:10.1163/156852303776172971.

—. "Zhongguo jingnei jinshu xia'etuo de yuanliu yu yanbian: jian tan xia'etuo yu liuyu Zhongguo Suteren de guanxi." 中国境内金属下颚托的源流与演变—兼谈下颚托与流寓中国粟特人的关系 [The Origin and Development of the Metal Chin straps in China: Its Relations with Sogdians in China]. In Rong Xinjiang 荣新江; Luo Feng 罗丰; Ningxia wenwu kaogu yanjiusuo 宁夏文物考古研究所; Beijing daxue zhongguo gudaishi yanjiu zhongxin 北京大学中国古代史研究中心, *Suteren zai Zhongguo II*, 501–31.

—. "Sogdier in China um 600 n. Chr.: Archäologische Zeugnisse eines Lebens zwischen Assimilation und Identitätsbewahrung." *Nachrichten der Gesellschaft für Natur- und Völkerkunde Ostasiens*, 183–184 (2008): 117–48.

Naba Toshisada 那波利貞. "Senbu Iwao Bakkoukutsu to Tonkō bunsho." 千佛巖莫高窟と敦煌文書 [Chinese Manuscripts from Tunhuang Cave Temples]. In *Seiiki bunka kenkyū dai ni : Tonkō Toroban shakai keizai shiryō (shū).* 西域文化研究第二：敦煌吐魯番社會經

濟資料（上） [Monumenta Serindica Volume II, Chinese Fragmentary Manuscripts on Social and Economical System in the T'ang Era Unearthed from Tunhuang and Turfan/Introduction and Monographical Remarks on Social and Economical System in the T'ang Era Based Upon Chinese Fragmentary Manuscripts from Tunhuang and Turfan Facs. 1]. Edited by Seiiki Bunka Kenkyūkai 西域文化研究會, Japanese: 11–68; English: 1–16. Kyōto: Hōzōkan, 1959.

Nakamura Kushirō 中村久四郎. "Kanton no shōko oyobi Kanton Chōan o renketsu suru suiro shūru no kōtsu." 廣東の商胡及び廣東長安を連結する水路舟運の交通 [Foreign Traders in Canton and the Communication by Water Between Canton and Chang'an]. *Tōyō-gakuhō*, no. 10.2 (1920): 244–266 [92–114].

Nanjing bowuguan 南京博物館, Yanzhou shi wenwu kaogu yanjiusuo 揚州市文物考古研究所, and Suzhou shi kaogu yanjiusuo 苏州市考古研究所. "Jiangsu Yangzhou shi Caozhuang Sui Yangdi mu." 江苏扬州市曹庄隋炀帝墓 [The Grave of Sui Yangdi in Caozhuang of Yangzhou City, Jiangsu]. *Kaogu*, no. 7 (2014): 71–77 [695–701].

Nattier, Jan. *A Guide to the Earliest Chinese Buddhist Translations: Texts from the Eastern Han* 東漢 *and Three Kingdoms Periods* 三國. Bibliotheca Philologica et Philosophica Buddhica Vol. X. Tōkyō: The International Research Institute for Advanced Buddhology, 2008.

Naymark, Aleksandr. "O date monet Keshskogo tsarya Akhurpata." [On the Date of the Ccoins of Akhurpat, King of Kesh]. *Transoxania. History and Culture*, no. 60 (2004): 215–24.

Ningxia Guyuan bowuguan 宁夏固原博物馆. "Ningxia Guyuan Tang Shi Daode mu qingli jianbao." 宁夏固原唐史道德墓清理简报 [Brief Excavation Report of the Grave of Shi Daode from the Tang in Guyuan, Ningxia]. *Wenwu*, no. 11 (1985): 21.

——, ed. *Guyuan Bei Wei mu qiguanhua* 固原北魏墓漆棺画 [The Paintings on the Lacquer Coffin of the Northern Wei of Guyuan]. Yinchuan: Ningxia renmin chubanshe, 1988.

——. "Pengyang Xinji Bei Wei mu." 彭阳新集北魏墓 [Graves from the Northern Wei in Xinji, Pengyang]. *Wenwu*, no. 9 (1989): 26–42.

Ningxia huizu zizhiqu bowuguan 宁夏回族自治区博物馆. "Ningxia Yanchi Tang mu fajue jianbao." 宁夏盐池唐墓发掘简报 [Brief Excavation Report on a Tang Grave in Ningxia, Yanchi]. *Wenwu*, no. 9 (1988): 43–56.

Ningxia huizu zizhiqu bowuguan 宁夏回族自治区博物馆, and Ningxia Guyuan bowuguan 宁夏固原博物馆. "Ningxia Guyuan Bei Zhou Li Xian fufu mu fajue jianbao." 宁夏固原北周李贤夫妇墓发掘简报 [Brief Excavation Report on the Tomb of Li Xian and His Wife of the Bei Zhou in Guyuan, Ningxia]. *Wenwu*, no. 11 (1985): 1–20.

Ningxia wenwu kaogu yanjiusuo 宁夏文物考古研究所, ed. *Guyuan nanyuan Han Tang mudi* 固原南塬汉唐墓地 [Han and Tang Tombs at Nanyuan of Guyuan]. Ningxian wenwu kaogu yanjiusuo congkan 宁夏文物考古研究所丛刊 [Collectanea of the Ningxia Institute for Cultural Relics and Archaeology] 12. Beijing: Wenwu chubanshe, 2009.

——, ed. *Guyuan Jiulongshan Han Tang muzang* 固原九龙山汉唐墓葬 [Han and Tang Graves at the Juliongshan in Guyuan]. Ningxian wenwu kaogu yanjiusuo congkan 宁夏文物考古研究所丛刊 [Collectanea of the Ningxia Institute for Cultural Relics and Archaeology] 18. Beijing: Kexue chubanshe, 2012.

Ningxia wenwu kaogu yanjiusuo 宁夏文物考古研究所 and Geng Zhiqiang 耿志强, eds. *Ningxia Bei Zhou Yuwen Meng mu fajue baogao yu yanjiu* 宁夏北周宇文猛墓发掘报告与研究 [Excavation and Research on the Grave of Yuwen Meng of the Beizhou in Ningxia]. Beijing: Yangguang chubanshe, 2014.

Ningxia wenwu kaogusuo Guyuan gongzuozhan 宁夏文物考古所固原工作站. "Guyuan Bei

Zhou Yuwen Meng mu fajue jianbao." 固原北周宇文猛墓发掘简报 [Brief Excavation Report of the Grave of Yuwen Meng of the Bei Zhou in Guyuan]. In *Ningxia kaogu wenji.* 宁夏考古文集 [Collectanea of Archaeological Articles in Ningxia]. Edited by Xu Cheng 许成, 134. Yinchuan: Ningxia renmin chubanshe, 1994.

Nomura Yōshō 野村耀昌. *Shūbu hōnan no kenkyū* 周武法難の研究 [Research on the Wu Zhou Persecution of Buddhism]. Tōkyō: Azuma shuppan, 1968.

Oda Yoshihisa 小田義久. "Tōdai kokushin no ichi kōsa: Ōtani tankentai shorairijigei oyobichokaijaku no kokushin o chushin to shite." 唐代告身の一考察: 大谷探検隊将来李慈藝及び張懐寂の告身を中心として [A Study of Appointment Decrees in the Tang Period]. *Tōyō shien*, no. 56 (2000): 1–27.

——. "Tokutomi Sōhō kinenkan zō 'Ri Jigei kokushin' no shashin no tsuite." 德富蘇峰記念館蔵<李慈藝告身>の寫眞について [On the Facsimile of the Appointment Decree of Li Ciyi of the Tokutomi Sōhō Museum]. *Ryokokū daigaiku ronshū*, no. 456 (2000): 122–41.

Okamoto Takashi 岡本孝. "Sogudo-ō tōkō: O•I•Sumirunwa mise hiban o chūshin toshite." ソグド王統攷: オ＝イ＝スミルノワ説批判を中心として [Chronology of the Sogdian Kings: A Critique on O. I. Smirnova's Theories]. *Tōyō-gakuhō*, no. 65 (1985): 71–104. Accessed November 2, 2017. http://www.i-repository.net/il/meta_pub/G0000171kenkyu_1691.

Olivelle, Patrick. *King, Governance, and Law in Ancient India: Kauṭilya's Arthaśāstra*. New York: Oxford University Press, 2013.

Osterhammel, Jürgen, and Niels P. Petersson. *Globalization: A Short History.* Translated by Dona Geyer. [2003. Princeton and Oxford: Princeton University Press, 2005.

Ou Changjun 歐昌俊, and Li Haixia 李海霞. *Liuchao Tang Wudai shike suzi yanjiu* 六朝唐五代石刻俗字研究 [A Study of the Variant Characters in Stone Inscriptions of the Six Dynasties, Tang, and Five Dynasties]. Chengdu: Bashu shushe, 2004.

Panaino, Antonio. "Tištrya." *Encyclopædia Iranica, online edition*, Last modified July 20, 2005. Accessed August 19, 2016. http://www.iranicaonline.org/articles/tistrya-2.

Pavchinskaya, L. V. "Sogdian Ossuaries." *Bulletin of the Asia Institute*, no. 8 (1994): 209–25.

Pelliot, Paul. "Le sa-pao." *Bulletin de l'École Française d'Extrême-Orient*, no. 3 (1903): 665–72.

——. "Les Mo-ni et le Houa-hou-king." *Bulletin de l'École Française d'Extrême-Orient*, no. 3 (1903): 318–27.

——. "Le 'cha tcheou tou fou t'ou king' et la colonie Sogdienne de la région du Lob Nor." *Journal Asiatique*, no. 7 (1916): 111–23.

——. "Les publications du Tōyō Bunko." *T'oung Pao*, no. 26.1 (1929): 357–66.

Peng Ke, and Zhu Yanshi. "New Research on the Origin of Cowries Used in Ancient China." *Sino-Platonic Papers*, no. 68 (1995): 1–21.

Pinault, Georges-Jean. "Épigraphie koutchéenne." In *Sites divers de la région de Koutcha: épigraphie koutchéenne*. Edited by Chao Huashan et al., 59–196. Mission Paul Pelliot – Documents archéologiques 8. Paris: Collège de France, Institut d'Asie, Centre de Recherche sur l'Asie Centrale et la Haute Asie, 1987.

Priewe, Sascha. "Das Zhangdefu-Sargbett – Grundlegende Fragen erneut gestellt." *Ostasiatische Zeitschrift*, no. 17 (2009): 15–24.

——. "Xianghu lianjie de juluo: Bei Qi, Bei Zhou yu Suichao shiqi Zhongguo beibu diqu de Suteren jiqi xiazang fangshi." 相互联结的聚落—北齐、北周与隋朝时期中国北部地区的粟特人及其下葬方式 [Networked Communities: Sogdians and their Burials in North-

Central China during the Northern Qi, Northern Zhou and Sui Periods]. In *Gudai muzang meishu yanjiu.* 古代墓葬美术研究 [Studies on Ancient Tomb Art]. Vol. 2. Edited by Wu Hung 巫鴻, Zhu Qingsheng 朱青生 and Zheng Yan 郑岩, 215–31. Changsha: Hunan meishu chubanshe, 2013.

Pugachenkova, Galina A., ed. *Iz istorii iskusstva velikogo goroda: (K 2500-letiyu Samarkanda)* [From the History of Art of the Great City (On the 2500th Anniversary of Samarkand)]. With the assistance of L. I. Rempel. Tashkent: Literatury i Iskusstva Imeni Gafura Gulâma, 1972.

——. "The Form and Style of Sogdian Ossuaries." *Bulletin of the Asia Institute – The Archaeology and Art of Central Asia. Studies from the Former Soviet Union*, no. 8 (1994): 227–43.

Pulleyblank, Edwin G. "A Sogdian Colony in Inner Mongolia." *T'oung Pao*, no. 41 (1952): 317–56.

——. *The Background of the Rebellion of An Lu-Shan.* London Oriental Series 4. London, New York: Oxford University Press, 1955.

——. "The Consonantal System of Old Chinese: Part II." *Asia Major/New Series*, no. 9.2 (1962): 206–65.

——. "The Wusun and Sakas and the Yüeh-chih Migration." *Bulletin of the School of Oriental and African Studies*, no. 33 (1970): 154–60. doi:10.1017/S0041977X00145227.

——. "Han China in Central Asia: (Review of) A. F. P. Hulsewé. *China in Central Asia, the Early Stage: 125 B.C.-A.D. 23. An Annotated Translation of Chapters 61 and 96 of the History of the Former Han Dynasty, with an Introduction by M. A. N. Loewe.*" International History Review, no. 3.2 (1981): 278–86.

——. *Lexicon of Reconstructed Pronunciation in Early Middle Chinese, Late Middle Chinese, and Early Mandarin.* Vancouver: UBC Press, 1991.

——. "Review: *The Roman Empire as Known to Han China* by D. D. Leslie, K. H. J. Gardiner. Studi Orientali, vol. 15. Rome: Department of Oriental Studies, University of Rome, 1996. Pp. xxvi + 422 + map." *Journal of the American Oriental Society*, no. 119.1 (1999): 71–79. doi:10.2307/605541.

Qi Dongfang 齐东方. "Shilun Xi'an diqu Tangdai muzang de dengji zhidu." 试论西安地区唐代墓葬的等级制度 [On the Hierarchy of Graves of Tang Dynasty in the Xi'an Area]. In *Jinian Beijing daxue kaogu zhuanye sanshi zhounian lunwenji. 1952–1982.* 纪念北京大学考古专业三十周年论文集—1952–1982 [Collected Works for the Thirtieth Anniversary of the Archaeology Specialty of Peking University (1952–1982)]. Edited by Beijing daxue kaoguxi 北京大学考古系, 286–310. Beijing: Wenwu chubanshe, 1990.

Qiu Guangming 丘光明. *Zhongguo gudai jiliang shi* 中国古代计量史 [The History of Ancient Chinese Measures and Weights]. Hefei: Anhui kexue jishu chubanshe, 2012.

Rawson, Jessica. *The Ornament on Chinese Silver of the Tang Dynasty (A.D. 618–906).* London: British Museum, 1982.

——. *Chinese Ornament: The Lotus and the Dragon.* London: British Museum, 1984.

——. "Creating Universes: Cultural Exchange as Seen in Tombs in Northern China between the Han and Tang Periods." In *Between Han and Tang: Cultural and Artistic Interaction in a Transformative Period.* 漢唐之間文化藝術的互動與交融. Edited by Wu Hung 巫鴻, 113–49. Beijing: Wenwu chubanshe, 2001.

Reichelt, Hans. *Die soghdischen Handschriftenreste des Britischen Museums: in Umschrift und mit Übersetzung. II. Teil: die nicht-buddhistischen Texte mit 9 Tafeln und Nachtrag zu den buddhistischen Texten.* Heidelberg: Carl Winters Universitätsbuchhandlung, 1931.

Reischauer, Edwin O. *Ennin's Travels in T'ang China.* New York: The Ronald Press Company, 1955.

Ren Wei 任伟. "Dunhuang Nuo wenhua yanjiu." 敦煌傩文化研究 [A Study of Dunhuang Nuo Culture]. Doctoral thesis, Zhongguo shi, lishi wenxian xue 中国史·历史文献学, Lanzhou daxue 兰州大学, Last modified 2017.

Riboud, Pénélope. "Réflexions sur les pratiques religieuses désignées sous le nom de *xian* 祆." In Vaissière; Trombert, *Les Sogdiens en Chine*, 73–91.

Rickett, Allyn W. *Guanzi* 管子*: Political, Economic, and Philosophical Essays from Early China. A Study and Translation. Volume Two.* Translated by W. Allyn Rickett. Princeton, New Jersey: Princeton University Press, 1998.

Rong Xinjiang. "Sogdians Around the Ancient Tarim Basin." In Compareti; Raffetta; Scarcia, *Ērān ud Anērān*, 513–24.

——. "Further Remarks on Sogdians in the Western Regions." In Sundermann; Hintze; Blois, *Exegisti monumenta*, 399–416.

Rong Xinjiang 荣新江. "Xiyu Sute yimin kao." 西域粟特移民考 [Research on the Migration of Sogdians in the Western Regions]. In *Xiyu kaocha yu yanjiu* 西域考察与研究 [Investigation and Research of the Western Regions]. Edited by Ma Dezheng 马大正, Wang Rong 王嵘 and Yang Lian 杨镰, 157–72. Wulumuqi: Xinjiang renmin chubanshe, 1994.

——. "Long jia kao." 龙家考 [On the Tribe of Longjia]. *Zhongya xuekan*, no. 4 (1995): 144–61.

——. "Beichao Suteren zhi qianxi jiqi juluo." 北朝粟特人之遷徙及其聚落 [The Sogdian Migration and Colonies in pre-Tang and Tang China]. *Guoxue yanjiu*, no. 6 (1999): 27–86.

——. "Beichao Sui Tang Suteren zhi qianxi jiqi juluo." 北朝隋唐粟特人之遷徙及其聚落 [The Migrations and Settlements of the Sogdians in the Northern Dynasties, Sui and Tang]. *China Archaeology and Art Digest*, Volume 4, Number 1: Zoroastrianism in China (December 2000 [1999]): 117–63.

——. "Beichao Sui Tang Sute juluo de neirong xingtai." 北朝隋唐粟特聚落的内容形态 In Rong Xinjiang 荣新江, *Zhonggu Zhongguo yu wailai wenming*, 111–68.

——. "Beichao Sui Tang Suteren zhi qianxi jiqi juluo." 北朝粟特人之迁徙及其聚落 [The Migration and Settlements of Sogdians during the Northern Dynasties, Sui, and Tang]. In Rong Xinjiang 荣新江, *Zhonggu Zhongguo yu wailai wenming*, 37–110.

——. "Sui ji Tang chu Bingzhou de *sabao* fu yu Sute juluo." 隋及唐初并州的萨保府与粟特聚落 [The Sabao Office and the Sogdian Settlement in Bingzhou in the Sui and Early Tang]. *Wenwu*, no. 4 (2001): 84–89.

——. "Xiyu Sute yimin juluo kao." 西域粟特移民聚落考 [Study on the Migration and Settlement of Sogdians in the Western Regions]. In Rong Xinjiang 荣新江, *Zhonggu Zhongguo yu wailai wenming*, 19–36.

——, ed. *Zhonggu Zhongguo yu wailai wenming* 中古中国与外来文明 [Medieval China and Foreign Civilizations]. Beijing: San lian shudian, 2001.

——. "An Shi zhi luan hou Sute huren de dongxiang." 安史之乱后粟特胡人的动向 [The Movement of Sogdians after the An Lushan Rebellion]. *Jinan shixue*, no. 2 (2003): 102–23.

——. "Beichao Sui Tang huren juluo de zongjiao xinyang yu xianci de shehui gongneng." 北朝隋唐胡人聚落的宗教信仰与祆祠的社会功能 [The Religious Beliefs in the Settlements of Hu and the Social Function of Xian Temples during the Northern Dynasties, Sui, and Tang]. In *Tangdai zongjiao xinyang yu shehui.* 唐代宗教信仰与社会. Edited by Rong Xinjiang 荣新江, 385–412. Beijing daxue shengtang yanjiu congshu 北京大学盛唐研究丛书 [Collectanea on Studies on the High Tang of Beijing University]. Shanghai: Shanghai cishu chubanshe, 2003.

——. "Sabao yu Sabo: Beichao Sui Tang huren juluo shouling wenti de zhenglun yu bianxi." 萨保与萨薄：北朝隋唐胡人聚落首领问题的争论与辨析 [Sabao and Sabo: a Discussion and Differentiation of Questions Concerning the Settlement Leaders of the Westerners during the Northern Dynasties, Sui and Tang]. In *Yilangxue zai Zhongguo lunwenji* 伊朗学在中国论文集 [Collection of Papers on Iranian Studies in China]. Vol. 3. Edited by Ye Yilang 叶奕良, 128–43. Beijing daxue chubanshe, 2003.

—. "*Sabao* or *Sabo*: Sogdian Caravan Leaders in the Wall-Paintings in Buddhist Caves." In Vaissière; Trombert, *Les Sogdiens en Chine*, 207–30.

—. "Sabao yu Sabo: fojiao shiku bihua zhong de Sute shangdui shouling." 萨保与萨薄：佛教石窟壁画中的粟特商队首领 [Sabao and Sabo: The Sogdian Merchant Leader in Buddhist Grotto Wall Paintings]. In 'Faguo Hanxue' congshu bianji weiyuanhui 《法国汉学》丛书编辑委员会, *Suteren zai Zhongguo, lishi, kaogu, yuyan de xin tansuo*, 49–71.

—. "Beichao Sui Tang Suteren zhi qianxi jiqi juluo bu kao." 北朝隋唐粟特人之迁徙及其聚落补考 [Migration and Settlements of the Sogdians in the Northern Dynasties, Sui, and Tang Periods]. *Ouya xuekan* 6 (2007): 165–78.

—. "Beichao Sui Tang Suteren zhi qianxi jiqi juluo bu kao." 北朝隋唐粟特人之迁徙及其聚落补考 [Additional Research on the Migration and Settlements of Sogdians during the Northern Dynasties, Sui, and Tang]. In Rong Xinjiang 荣新江, *Zhonggu Zhongguo yu Sute wenming*, 22–41.

—. "Xiyu Sute yimin juluo bu kao." 西域粟特移民聚落补考 [Additional Research on the Emigration of Sogdians from the Western Regions]. In Rong Xinjiang 荣新江, *Zhonggu Zhongguo yu Sute wenming*, 3–21.

—, ed. *Zhonggu Zhongguo yu Sute wenming* 中古中国与粟特文明 [Medieval China and Sogdian Culture]. Beijing: San lian shudian, 2014.

—. "Suteren de Zhongguomeng: Han Tang shiqi de Sute shangdui, jing sizhou zhi lu lianjie Ouya dalu de jingji wanglai, Suteren jiang Tangchao xihua, ye bei Tangchao hanhua." 粟特人的中国梦—汉唐时期的粟特商队，经丝绸之路连接欧亚大陆的经济往来，粟特人将唐朝西化，也被唐朝汉化 [The Chinese Dream of the Sogdians: Sogdian Merchant Groups of the Han to the Tang, Who through Travelling on the Silk Road Connected the Economical Contacts of the Eurasian Continent, Westernised the Tang Dynasty, and Were Sinicised by the Tang]. Last modified August 29, 2014. Accessed September 10, 2016. http://cul.qq.com/zt2014/shuyuan065/#are9.

Rong Xinjiang 荣新江, Luo Feng 罗丰, Ningxia wenwu kaogu yanjiusuo 宁夏文物考古研究所, and Beijing daxue zhongguo gudaishi yanjiu zhongxin 北京大学中国古代史研究中心, eds. *Suteren zai Zhongguo I: Kaogu faxian yu chutu wenxian de xin yinzheng* 粟特人在中国—考古发现与出土文献的新印证(上册) [Sogdians in China: New Evidence in Archaeological Finds and Unearthed Texts]. 2 vols. Ningxian wenwu kaogu yanjiusuo congkan 宁夏文物考古研究所丛刊 [Collectanea of the Ningxia Institute for Cultural Relics and Archaeology] 31. Beijing: Kexue chubanshe, 2016.

Rong Xinjiang 荣新江 and Zhang Zhiqing 张志清, eds. *Cong Sama'ergan dao Chang'an: Suteren zai Zhongguo de wenhua yiji* 從薩馬爾干到長安，粟特人在中國的文化遺迹 [From Samarkand to Chang'an: Cultural Traces of the Sogdians in China]. Beijing: Zhongguo guojia tushuguan chubanshe, 2004.

Rong Xinjiang 荣新江 and Li Xiaocong 李孝聪, eds. *Zhongwai guanxi shi: xin shiliao yu xin wenti* 中外关系史：新史料与新问题 [History of Chinese Foreign Relations: New Historical Material and New Questions]. Beijing: Kexue chubanshe, 2004.

Rotours, Robert des. *Histoire de Ngan Lou-Chan (Ngan Lou-Chan che tsi).* Bibliothèque de l'Institut des hautes études chinoises 18. Paris: Presses universitaires de France, 1962.

Rui Chuanming 芮传明. "'Sabao' de zai renshi." '萨宝'的再认识 [New Discussion of the

'Sabao']. *Shilin*, no. 3 (2000): 23–39.

Rybatzki, Volker. "Titles of Türk and Uigur Rulers in the Old Turkic Inscriptions." *Central Asiatic Journal*, no. 44.2 (2000): 205–92.

Sachau, C. E., ed. *Chronologie orientalischer Völker von Albêrûnî.* Annotated and Translated by Sachau, Eduard C. [1878]. Leipzig: Harrassowitz [Brockhaus], 1923.

Salguero, C. P. "The Buddhist Medicine King in Literary Context: Reconsidering an Early Medieval Example of Indian Influence on Chinese Medicine and Surgery." *History of Religions*, no. 48.3 (2009): 183–210. doi:10.1086/598230.

Salomon, Richard. "The Inscription of Senavarma, King of Oḍi." *Indo-Iranian Journal*, no. 29 (1986): 261–93.

Scaglia, Gustina. "Central Asians on a Northern Ch'i Gate Shrine." *Artibus Asiae*, no. 21 (1958): 2–28.

Schafer, Edward H. *The Golden Peaches of Samarkand: A Study of T'ang Exotics*. Berkeley: University of California Press, 1963.

Schmoll, Heike. *Lob der Elite: Warum wir sie brauchen*. München: C. H. Beck, 2008.

Schopen, Gregory. "The Inscription on the Kuṣān Image of Amitābha and the Character of Early Mahāyāna in India." *Journal of the International Association of Buddhist Studies*, no. 10 (1987): 99–137.

Schwartz, Martin. "*Sārtha-* and Other Caravan Words." *Bulletin of the Asia Institute*, New Series/Vol. 23 (2009): 179–80.

Selbitschka, Armin. "Genuine Prestige Goods in Mortuary Contexts: Emulation in Polychrome Silk and Byzantine *Solidi* from Northern China." *Asian Perspectives*, Vol. 57, No. 1 (2018): 2–50.

Shaanxi sheng kaogu yanjiusuo 陕西省考古研究所. "Xi'an beijiao Bei Zhou An Jia mu fajue jianbao." 西安北郊北周安伽墓发掘简报 [Brief Excavation Report on the Grave of An Jia of the Northern Zhou in the Northern Suburbs of Xi'an]. *Kaogu yu wenwu*, no. 6 (2000): 28–35.

——. "Xi'an faxian de Bei Zhou An Jia mu." 西安发现的北周安伽墓 [Excavation of the Tomb of An Jia of the Northern Zhou from Xi'an]. *Wenwu*, no. 1 (2001): 4–26.

——, ed. *Xi'an Bei Zhou An Jia mu* 西安北周安伽墓 [The Tomb of An Jia of the Northern Zhou from Xi'an]. Shaanxi sheng kaogu yanjiusuo tianye kaogu baogao 陕西省考古研究所田野考古报告 [Field Archeology Excavation Reports of the Shaanxi Province Archaeological Institute] 21. Beijing: Wenwu chubanshe, 2003.

Shanxi sheng kaogu yanjiusuo 山西省考古研究所 and Taiyuan shi wenwu kaogu yanjiusuo 太原市文物考古研究所, eds. *Bei Qi Dong'an wang Lou Rui mu* 北齐东安王娄睿墓 [The Grave of Lou Rui, Prince of Dong'an from the Northern Qi]. Beijing: Wenwu chubanshe, 2006.

Shanxi sheng kaogu yanjiusuo 山西省考古研究所, Taiyuan shi wenwu kaogu yanjiusuo 太原市文物考古研究所, and Taiyuan shi Jinyuan qu wenwu lüyouju 太原市晋源区文物旅游局. "Taiyuan Suidai Yu Hong mu qingli jianbao." 太原隋代虞弘墓清理简报 [Brief Excavation Report of the Tomb of Yu Hong of the Sui Dynasty from Taiyuan]. *Wenwu*, no. 1 (2001): 27–51.

Shenkar, Michael. "Rethinking Sasanian Iconoclasm." *Journal of the American Oriental Society*, no. 135.3 (2015): 471–98. doi:10.7817/jameroriesoci.135.3.471.

——. "The Religion and Pantheon of the Sogdians (5th–8th Centuries CE) in Light of Their Sociopolitical Structures." *Journal Asiatique*, no. 305.2 (2017): 191–209. doi:10.2143/JA.305.2.3262803.

Shi Pingting 施萍亭. "Ben suo cang 'jiu zhang' yanjiu." 本所藏《酒帐》研究 [Research on the Originally Stored 'Alcohol Expenditure List']. *Dunhuang yanjiu*, no. 3 (1983): 142–55.

Shi Weile 史为乐, ed. *Zhongguo lishi diming da cidian: shang* 中国历史地名大辞典 [Comprehensive Historical Geography Dictionary of China]. 2 vols. Beijing: Zhongguo shehui kexue chubanshe, 2005.

Shiratori Kurakichi. "Über den Wu-sun-Stamm in Centralasien." *Keleti Szemle*, III.2–3 (1902): 1–38.

——. "A Study on Su-t'ê (粟特), or Sogdiana." *Memoirs of the Research Department of the Toyo Bunko (the Oriental Library)*, no. 2 (1928): 81–145.

Shiratori Kurakichi 白鳥庫吉. "Sogudo kuni koū." 粟特国考 [A Study on Sogdiana]. *Tōyō-gakuhō*, no. 14.4 (1924): 453–545.

Shkoda, V. G. "The Sogdian Temple: Structure and Rituals." *Bulletin of the Asia Institute*, New Series/Vol. 10 (1996): 195–206.

——. *Pyandzhikenstkie khramy i problemy religii Sogda (V-VIII vv)* [The Temples of Pendjikent and the Problems of Sogdian Religion (5th to 8th Centuries)]. St. Petersburg: The State Hermitage, 2009.

Shukutoku University 淑徳大学. "Wang Huilüe deng wushi ren zaotaji." 王惠略等五十人造塔記 [Wang Huilüe and More Than 50 People's Stela Commemorating the Construction of a Stupa]. Last modified November 16, 2015. Accessed November 17, 2015. http://www.shukutoku.ac.jp/shisetsu/takuhon/tougi/s054_8405.html.

Sichou zhi lu da cidian bianweihui 丝绸之路大辞典编委会, Zhou Weizhou 周伟洲, Ding Jingtai 丁景泰, ed. *Sichou zhi lu da cidian* 丝绸之路大辞典 [Comprehensive Dictionary of the Silk Road]. Xi'an: Shaanxi renmin chubanshe, 2006.

Silk Road Seattle Website. "Sogdian Ancient Letters 1, 2, 3, and 5: Translated by Nicholas Sims-Williams." Introduction by Daniel C. Waugh, Last modified October 1, 2004. Accessed September 8, 2016. http://depts.washington.edu/silkroad/texts/sogdlet.html.

Sims-Williams, Nicholas. "The Sogdian Fragments of the British Library." *Indo-Iranian Journal*, no. 18: 43–82.

——. "Indian Elements in Parthian and Sogdian." In *Sprachen des Buddhismus in Zentralasien: Vorträge des Hamburger Symposions vom 2. Juli bis 5. Juli 1981*. Edited by Klaus Röhrborn and Wolfgang Veenker, 132–41. Veröffentlichungen der Societas Uralo-Altaica 16. Wiesbaden: O. Harrassowitz, 1983.

——. *Sogdian and other Iranian inscriptions of the upper Indus I. and II.* Corpus Inscriptionum Iranicarum 2,3,2,1; 2,3,2,2. London, 1989/1992.

——. "The Sogdian Merchants in China and India." In *Cina e Iran: Da Alessandro Magno alla Dinastia Tang*. Edited by Alfredo Cadonna and Lionello Lanciotti, 45–67. Orientalia venetiana 5. Firenze: Leo S. Olschki, 1996.

——. "The Sogdian Ancient Letter II." In *Philologica et Linguistica, Historia, Pluralitas, Universitas: Festschrift für Helmut Humbach zum 80. Geburtstag am 4. Dezember 2001*. Edited by Maria G. Schmidt and Walter Bisang, 267–80. Trier: Wissenschaftlicher Verlag Trier, 2001.

Sims-Williams, Nicholas, and Bi Bo. "A Sogdian Fragment from Niya." In *Great Journeys across the Pamir Mountains: A Festschrift in Honor of Zhang Guangda on his Eighty-Fifth Birthday*. Edited by Chen Huaiyu and Rong Xinjiang, 83–104. Leiden, Boston: Brill, 2018.

Sims-Williams, Nicholas, and James Hamilton. *Documents turco-sogdiens du IXe-Xe siècle de Touen-houang*. Corpus Inscriptionum Iranicarum Pt. 2: Inscriptions of the Seleucid and Parthian Periods and of Eastern Iran and Central Asia. Vol. 3: Sogdian, 3. London: Corpus Inscriptionum Iranicum, 1990.

Sinor, Denis. "'Pray to God on my behalf that he give me such intelligence that I can learn fast and well your languages.' Medieval Interpreters and Inner Asia." *The Journal of Popular*

Culture, no. 16.1 (1982): 176–84. doi:10.1111/j.0022-3840.1982.00176.x.

Skaff, Jonathan K. "The Sogdian Trade Diaspora in East Turkestan during the Seventh and Eight Centuries." *Journal of the Economic and Social History of the Orient*, Vol. 46, no. 4 (2003): 475–524.

——. "La documentation sur la communauté sogdienne à Turfan aux VIIe et VIIIe siècles: les registres de population comme témoin des différences et des changements culturels." In 'Faguo Hanxue' congshu bianji weiyuanhui 《法国汉学》丛书编辑委员会, *Suteren zai Zhongguo, lishi, kaogu, yuyan de xin tansuo*, 141–77.

Skjaervo, Prods O. "Iranians, Indians, Chinese and Tibetans: The Rulers and Ruled of Khotan in the First Millennium." In *The Silk Road: Trade, Travel, War and Faith*. Edited by Susan Whitfield and Ursula Sims-Williams, 34–42. London: British Library, 2004.

Škoda, V. G. "Le culte du feu dans les sanctuaires de Pendžikent." In *Cultes et monuments religieux dans l'Asie centrale préislamique*. Edited by Frantz Grenet, 63–72. Paris: Éditions du Centre national de la recherche scientifique, 1987.

Small, Ian, ed. *De Profundis, 'Epistola: in Carcere et Vinculis'*. The Complete Works of Oscar Wilde Volume 2. Oxford: Oxford University Press, 2005.

Smirnova, Olga I. *Svodnyi katalog sogdiiskikh monet: bronza* [Complete Catalogue of Sogdian Coins: Bronze]. Moscow: Nauka, 1981.

So, Jenny F. "Belt Ornaments and Fasteners." In *Traders and Raiders on China's Northern Frontier*. Edited by Jenny F. So and Emma C. Bunker, 77–85. Seattle: Arthur M. Sackler Gallery, Smithsonian Institution, in association with University of Washington Press, 1995.

Sofukawa Hiroshi 曽布川寛. "Chūgoku shutsudo no Sogudo sekkoku gazō shiron." 中国出土のソグド石刻画像試論 [A Discussion of the Sogdian Stone Carved Images Excavated in China]. In *Chūgoku bijutsu no zuzō to yōshiki: kenkyūhen*. 中国美術の図像と様式·研究篇 [The Iconography and Style of Chinese Art: Research Edition]. Edited by Sofukawa Hiroshi 曽布川寛, 97–182. Tōkyō: Chūō Kōron Bijutsu Shuppan, 2006.

Soymié, Michel, Jean-Pierre Drège, Danielle Eliasberg, Richard Schneider, Éric Trombert, Paul Magnin, Christine Mollier, and Françoise Wang-Toutain. "Catalogue des manuscrits Pelliot chinois 4001-6040: Volume V (édition électronique)." Last modified 1995. Accessed August 2, 2017.
http://idp.bl.uk/database/oo_cat.a4d?shortref=PelliotChinois_V.

Spiegel, Friedrich v. *Erânische Altertumskunde: Zweiter Band. Religion. Geschichte bis zum Tode Alexanders der Grossen*. Leipzig: Wilhelm Engelmann, 1873.

Stark, Sören. *Die Alttürkenzeit in Mittel- und Zentralasien. Archäologische und historische Studien: Archäologische und historische Studien*. Nomaden und Sesshafte 6. Wiesbaden: Dr. Ludwig Reichert, 2008.

——. *Transoxanien nach dem Tang Huiyao des Wang Pu: Übersetzung und Kommentar*. Norderstedt: Books on Demand GmbH, 2009.

Su Bai 宿白. "Xi'an diqu de Tang mu xingzhi." 西安地区的唐墓形制 [Structure of the Tang Tombs in the Xi'an Area]. *Wenwu*, no. 12 (1995): 41–50.

Su Hang 苏航. "Beichao moqi de *sabao* pinwei." 北朝末期的萨保品位 [The Official Rank and Political Status of the Sabao in the Late Period of the Northern Dynasties]. *Xiyu yanjiu*, no. 2 (2005): 12–24.

Sun Binggen 孫秉根. "Xi'an Sui Tang muzang de xingzhi." 西安隋唐墓葬的形制 [The Form of Tombs of the Sui and Tang Dynasties in Xi'an]. In *Zhongguo kaoguxue yanjiu: Xia Nai xiansheng kaogu wushi nian jinian lunwenji, er*. 中国考古学研究—夏鼐先生考古五十年纪念论文集[二] [Archaeological Researches in China: A Collection of Papers in

Commemoration of the Fiftieth Year of Prof. Xia Nai's Work in Archaeology. Vol. 2]. Edited by Xu Yuanbang 徐元邦 and Kaoguxue yanjiu weiyuanhui 考古学研究委员会, 151–90. Beijing: Kexue chubanshe, 1986.

Sun Ji 孫機. *Zhongguo shenghuo: Zhongguo guwenwu yu Dong Xi wenhua jiaoliu zhong de ruogan wenti* 中国圣火：中国古文物与东西文化交流中的若干问题 [Chinese Sacred Fire: General Questions on Ancient Chinese Cultural Relics and East-West Cultural Exchange]. Shenyang: Liaoning jiaoyu chubanshe, 1996.

Sun Wujun 孫武軍. "Beichao Sui Tang ruhua Suteren muzang tuxiang de wenhua yu shenmei yanjiu." 北朝隋唐入华粟特人墓葬图像的文化与审美研究 [A Study of the Culture and Aesthetics of the Funerary Decoration of Sogdians Coming to China during the Northern Dynasties, Sui, and Tang]. Doctoral Dissertation, Xibei Daxue 西北大学, Last modified 2012.

——. *Ruhua Suteren muzang tuxiang de sangzang yu zongjiao wenhua* 入华粟特人墓葬图像的丧葬与宗教文化 [The Burial and Religious Culture of the Funerary Paintings of Sogdians Coming to China]. Beijing: Zhongguo shehui kexue chubanshe, 2014.

Sundermann, Werner. "First Results of Cooperative Work Between Ryukoku University and the Academy of Sciences of the GDR on Buddhist Sogdian Turfan Texts." *The Annual of the Buddhist Cultural Institute, Ryukoku University*, no. 12 (1989): 12–18.

Sundermann, Werner, Almut Hintze, and François de Blois, eds. *Exegisti monumenta: Festschrift in Honour of Nicholas Sims-Williams.* Iranica 17. Wiesbaden: Harrassowitz, 2009.

Szemerényi, Oswald. *Four Old Iranian Ethnic Names: Scythian - Skudra - Sogdian - Saka.* Österreichische Akademie der Wissenschaften. Philosophisch-Historische Klasse, Sitzungsberichte 371. Band; Veröffentlichungen der Iranischen Kommission, Band 9. Wien: Verlag der Österreichischen Akademie der Wissenschaften, 1980.

Tackett, Nicolas O. *The Destruction of the Medieval Chinese Aristocracy.* Harvard-Yenching Institute Monograph Series 93. Cambridge, Massachusetts: Harvard University Asia Center, 2014.

——. "The Transformation of Medieval Chinese Elites: (850–1000 C.E.)." Dissertation, Columbia University, Last modified 2006. Accessed December 6, 2015. http://history.berkeley.edu/sites/default/files/slides/Dissertation.pdf.

Tai Huili 邰惠莉. "Gui yi jun ya fu jiu po li." 归义军衙府酒破历 [The Fragmented Alcohol Record of the Gui yi jun ya fu]. Accessed August 2, 2017. Last modified? http://public.dha.ac.cn/content.aspx?id=418223473108.

Tang Changru 唐長孺 et al., eds., *Tulufan chutu wenshu* 吐魯番出土文書 [Excavated Documents of Turfan]. With the assistance of Zhongguo wenwu yanjiusuo 中國文物研究所, Xinjiang Weiwu'er zizhiqu bowuguan 新疆維吾爾自治區博物館, and Wuhan daxue lishixi 武漢大學歷史系. 4 vols. Beijing: Wenwu chubanshe, 1992–96.

Tang Geng'ou 唐耕耦 and Lu Hongji 陆宏基, eds. *Dunhuang shehui jingji wenxian zhenji shilu* 敦煌社会经济文献真迹释录 (Annotated Collection of Manuscripts on the Society and Economy of Dunhuang]. Zhongguo wenxian zhenben congshu 中国文献珍本丛书 [Collectanea of Rare Chinese Documents]. 5 vols. Beijing: Quanguo tushuguan wenxian suowei fuzhi zhongxin, 2008 [1986–90].

Tang Jiahong 唐嘉弘, ed. *Zhongguo gudai dianzhang zhidu da cidian* 中国古代典章制度大辞典. [Dictionary of the Bureaucratic System of Ancient China]. Zhengzhou: Zhongzhou guji chubanshe, 1998.

Tang Jinyu 唐金裕. "Xi'an xijiao Sui Li Jingxun mu fajue jianbao." 西安西郊隋李靜訓墓發掘簡報 [Brief Excavation Report of the Grave of Li Jingxun of the Sui in the Western

Suburb of Xi'an]. *Kaogu*, no. 7 (1959): 471–72.
Tekin, Talât. *A Grammar of Orkhon Turkic*. Bloomington: Indiana University, 1968.
The International Dunhuang Project. "The International Dunhuang Project: The Silk Road Online." Accessed August 29, 2016. http://idp.bl.uk/.
——. "F0001 Recto: Dunhuang mogao / Dunhuang Academy." Accessed August 2, 2016. http://idp.bl.uk:80/database/oo_loader.a4d?pm=F0001;img=1.
——. "Or.8210/S.1366 Recto: R.1 accounts of goods." Dunhuang mogao / British Library. Accessed August 8, 2017. http://idp.bl.uk:80/database/oo_loader.a4d?pm=Or.8210/S.1366;img=10.
——. "Or.8210/S.2241: R.1 letter/letter model." Dunhuang mogao / British Library. Accessed October 10, 2016. http://idp.bl.uk:80/database/oo_loader.a4d?pm=Or.8210/S.2241;img=1.
——. "Or.8210/S.2472." Dunhuang mogao / British Library. Accessed August 10, 2017. http://idp.bl.uk:80/database/oo_loader.a4d?pm=Or.8210/S.2472;img=22.
——. "Or.8210/S.2474 verso, V.2 title not entered/not known: Dunhuang mogao (Ch.76.II.18) / British Library." Accessed August 8, 2016. http://idp.bl.uk:80/database/oo_loader.a4d?pm=Or.8210/S.2474;img=14.
——. "Or.8210/S.367 Recto: (*Shazhou Yizhou dizhi* 沙州伊州地誌)." Dunhuang mogao / British Library. Accessed October 10, 2016. http://idp.bl.uk:80/database/oo_loader.a4d?pm=Or.8210/S.367;img=1.
——. "Or.8210/S.542." Dunhuang mogao / British Library. Accessed October 10, 2016. http://idp.bl.uk:80/database/oo_loader.a4d?pm=Or.8210/S.542;img=1.
——. "Or.8210/S.613: (Tax Register)." Dunhuang mogao / British Library. Accessed October 10, 2016. http://idp.bl.uk:80/database/oo_loader.a4d?pm=Or.8210/S.613;img=1.
——. "Or.8210/S.788: (*Shazhou tujing* 沙州圖經), Dunhuang Mogao (Ch.76.III.18)." Accessed January 8, 2019. http://idp.bl.uk/database/oo_scroll_h.a4d?uid=60633385715;recnum=787;index=1.
——. "Or.8212/100: (Sogdian Ancient Letter V)." Dunhuang Limes (T.XII.a.ii.6) / British Library. Accessed October 10, 2016. http://idp.bl.uk:80/database/oo_loader.a4d?pm=Or.8212/100;img=1.
——. "Or.8212/92(1): (Sogdian Ancient Letter I)." Dunhuang Limes (T.XII.a.ii.1) / British Library. Accessed October 10, 2016. http://idp.bl.uk:80/database/oo_loader.a4d?pm=Or.8212/92(1);img=1.
——. "Or.8212/95: (Sogdian Ancient Letter II)." Dunhuang Limes (T.XII.a.ii.2) / British Library. Accessed October 10, 2016. http://idp.bl.uk:80/database/oo_loader.a4d?pm=Or.8212/95;img=1.
——. "Or.8212/98, verso and recto: (Sogdian Ancient Letter III)." Dunhuang Limes (T.XII.a.ii.3) / British Library. Accessed October 10, 2016. http://idp.bl.uk:80/database/oo_loader.a4d?pm=Or.8212/98;img=1.
——. "Pelliot chinois 2005, recto: (*Sha zhou du du fu tu jing* 沙州都督府圖經)." Dunhuang mogao / Bibliothèque nationale de France. Accessed August 9, 2017. http://idp.bl.uk:80/database/oo_loader.a4d?pm=Pelliot chinois 2005;img=25.
——. "Pelliot chinois 2629, recto: (Comptes des dépenses en alcool par l'administration du Gui yi jun 歸義軍)." Dunhuang mogao / Bibliothèque nationale de France. Accessed October 10, 2016. http://idp.bl.uk:80/database/oo_loader.a4d?pm=Pelliot chinois 2629;img=1.
——. "Pelliot chinois 2690, verso: (Exercices d'écriture et copies diverses)." Dunhuang mogao / Bibliothèque nationale de France. Accessed October 10, 2016.

http://idp.bl.uk:80/database/oo_loader.a4d?pm=Pelliot chinois 2690;img=1.
——. "Pelliot chinois 2691, recto." Dunhuang mogao / Bibliothèque nationale de France. Accessed January 8, 2019. http://idp.bl.uk/database/oo_scroll_h.a4d?uid=6057156959;recnum=59842;index=1.
——. "Pelliot chinois 2748, verso A: (IV. *Sha zhou dun huang er shi yong, bing xu* 沙州燉煌二十詠并序)." Dunhuang mogao / Bibliothèque nationale de France. Accessed October 10, 2016. http://idp.bl.uk:80/database/oo_loader.a4d?pm=Pelliot chinois 2748;img=12.
——. "Pelliot chinois 2983, recto: (*[Cha zhou] Dun huang [gu ji] nian yong [bing xu]* [沙州]燉煌[古跡]廿詠[並序])." Dunhuang mogao / Bibliothèque nationale de France. Accessed October 10, 2016. http://idp.bl.uk:80/database/oo_loader.a4d?pm=Pelliot chinois 2983;img=1.
——. "Pelliot chinois 3569, verso: (Dossier concernant Ma San niang et Long Fen dui, distillateurs officiels, *guan jiu hu* 官酒戶馬三娘龍粉堆)." Dunhuang mogao / Bibliothèque nationale de France. Accessed October 10, 2016. http://idp.bl.uk:80/database/oo_loader.a4d?pm=Pelliot chinois 3569;img=1.
——. "Pelliot chinois 3571 verso: 1. Clef des songes; 2. Texte d'astrologie bouddhique." Dunhuang mogao / Bibliothèque nationale de France. Accessed August 10, 2017. http://idp.bl.uk:80/database/oo_loader.a4d?pm=Pelliot chinois 3571;img=1.
——. "Pelliot chinois 3813: (recto: [*Jin shu* 晉書 par Fang Xuan ling 房玄齡; verso: recueil de sentences judiciaires)." Dunhuang mogao / Bibliothèque nationale de France. Accessed October 10, 2016. http://idp.bl.uk:80/database/oo_loader.a4d?pm=Pelliot chinois 3813;img=1.
——. "Pelliot chinois 3870, recto: (*Dun huang nian yong* 燉煌廿詠, *Ti yin shi yong* 提隱士詠, col. 60)." Dunhuang mogao / Bibliothèque nationale de France. Accessed August 1, 2017. http://idp.bl.uk:80/database/oo_loader.a4d?pm=Pelliot chinois 3870;img=1.
——. "Pelliot chinois 3929, recto: (*Sha zhou Dun huang gu ji nian yong* 沙州燉煌古跡廿詠; *Gu xian ji* 古賢集)." Dunhuang mogao / Bibliothèque nationale de France. Accessed August 1, 2017. http://idp.bl.uk:80/database/oo_loader.a4d?pm=Pelliot chinois 3929;img=1.
——. "Pelliot chinois 4640, verso: (Compte de dépenses de pièces de toile et de quantités de papier distribuées par l'administration)." Dunhuang mogao / Bibliothèque nationale de France. Accessed October 10, 2016. http://idp.bl.uk:80/database/oo_loader.a4d?pm=Pelliot chinois 4640;img=1.
——. "Pelliot chinois 5034, recto: (Traité géographique; *Shazhou tujing* 沙州圖經)." Dunhuang mogao / Bibliothèque nationale de France. Accessed October 10, 2016. http://idp.bl.uk:80/database/oo_loader.a4d?pm=Pelliot chinois 5034;img=1.
Thierry, François. "Sur les monnaies Sassanides trouvées en Chine." In *Circulation des monnaies, des marchandises et des biens*. Edited by Michael Alram and Rika Gyselen, 89–139. Res Orientales 5. Leuven: Peeters Press, 1993.
——. "La monétarisation de la société türke (VIe-IXe siècle) - Influence chinoise, influence sogdienne." In 'Faguo Hanxue' congshu bianji weiyuanhui 《法国汉学》丛书编辑委员会, *Suteren zai Zhongguo, lishi, kaogu, yuyan de xin tansuo*, 241–58.
Thierry, François, and Cécile Morrison. "Sur les monnaies Byzantines trouvées en Chine." *Revue numismatique* 6e série, no. 36 (1994): 109–45.
Tianshui shi bowuguan 天水市博物馆. "Tianshui shi faxian Sui Tang pingfeng shiguan chuang mu." 天水市发现隋唐屏风石棺床墓 [A Tomb of the Sui–Tang Period with Panels and a

Funerary Couch Excavated in Tianshui]. *Kaogu*, no. 1 (1992): 46–54.

Tomaschek, Wilhelm. *Centralasiatische Studien: I. Sogdiana*. Wien: In Commission bei Karl Gerold's Sohn, 1877.

Tōyō bunko 東洋文庫. "Tōyō bunko." 東洋文庫 [The Oriental Library]. Accessed November 17, 2015. http://www.toyo-bunko.or.jp/.

Tremblay, Xavier. *Pour une histoire de la Sérinde: Le manichéisme parmi les peuples et religions d'Asie Centrale d'après les sources primaires.* Veröffentlichungen der Kommission für Iranistik 28. Wien: Verlag der Österreichischen Akademie der Wissenschaften, 2001.

——. "The Spread of Buddhism in Serindia: Buddhism Among Iranians, Tocharians and Turks Before the 13th Century." In *The Spread of Buddhism*. Edited by Ann Heirman and Stephan P. Bumbacher, 75–129. Handbuch der Orientalistik Section Eight: Central Asia, Vol. 16. Leiden, Boston: Brill, 2007.

Trombert, Éric. "La vigne et le vin en Chine. Misères et succès d'une tradition allogène. Deuxième partie: Vins, vignes et vignerons de Tourfan." *Journal Asiatique*, no. 290.2 (2002): 485–563.

——. "Un vestige vivant de la présence sogdienne en Chine du Nord : le vignoble du Shanxi." In Vaissière; Trombert, *Les Sogdiens en Chine*, 261–82.

Tsien, Tsuen-hsuin. *Written on Bamboo and Silk: The Beginnings of Chinese Books and Inscriptions.* [1962]. 2nd ed. Chicago: University of Chicago Press, 2004.

Tsukamoto Keisho 塚本啓祥. *Indo Bukkyō himei no kenkyū I: Text, Note, wayaku* インド仏教碑銘の研究：Text, Note, 和訳 [A Comprehensice Study of the Indian Buddhist Inscriptions, Part I: Text, Notes, and Japanese Translation]. Kyōto: Heirakuji Shoten, 1998.

Tulufan diqu wenguansuo 吐鲁番地区文管所. "Xinjiang Shanshan xian Tuyugou faxian taoguan zang." 新疆鄯善县吐峪沟发现陶棺葬 [Discovery of an Ossuary Burial in Tuyugou, Shanshan County, Xinjiang]. *Kaogu*, no. 1 (1986): 87–89.

Twitchett, Denis C. "The Monasteries and China's Economy in Medieval Times." *Bulletin of the School of Oriental and African Studies*, no. 19.3 (1957): 526–49. doi:10.1017/S0041977X00133610.

——. "The T'ang Market System." *Asia Major/New Series*, no. 12 (1966): 202–48.

——. *The Writing of Official History under the Tang*. Cambridge: Cambridge University Press, 1992.

Uchida Gimpo 内田吟風. "Gisho no seriritsu ni tsuite." 魏書の成立に就いて [Considerations on the Formation of the Weishu]. *Tōyoshi Kenkyū*, no. 2.6 (1937): 513–41. doi:10.14989/138769.

United Nations DESA / Population Division. "World Population Prospects 2019." Accessed September 6, 2019. https://population.un.org/wpp/.

Vaissière, Étienne de la. *Histoire des marchands sogdiens*. Paris: Collège de France, Institut des Hautes Études Chinoises, 2002.

——. "Sogdians in China: A Short History and Some New Discoveries." *The Silk Road* 1, no. 2 (2003-10): 23–27. Accessed October 25, 2013. http://www.silkroadfoundation.org/newsletter/december/new_discoveries.htm.

——. "Čākar sogdiens en Chine." In Vaissière; Trombert, *Les Sogdiens en Chine*, 255–60.

——. *Sogdian Traders: A History.* Translated by James Ward. Handbuch der Orientalistik Section Eight, Volume Ten. Leiden und Boston: Brill, 2005.

——. "Sute zhejie jun zai Zhongguo." 粟特柘羯军在中国 [Châkars sogdiens en Chine]. In

'Faguo Hanxue' congshu bianji weiyuanhui 《法国汉学》丛书编辑委员会, *Suteren zai Zhongguo, lishi, kaogu, yuyan de xin tansuo*, 235–40.

Vaissière, Étienne de la, and Éric Trombert. "Des Chinois et des Hu: Migration et intégration des Iraniens orientaux en milieu chinois durant le haut Moyen Âge." *Annales. Histoire, Sciences Sociales*, 2004, 931–69.

—–, eds. *Les Sogdiens en Chine.* Etudes thématiques 17. Paris: École française d'Extrême-Orient, 2005.

Vovin, Alexander, Edward Vajda, and Étienne de la Vaissière. "Who Were the *Kjet (羯) and What Language Did They Speak?" *Journal Asiatique*, no. 304.1 (2016): 125–44.

Waley, Arthur. "Some References to Iranian Temples in the Tun-huang Region." In *Qingzhu Hu Shi xiansheng liushiwu sui lunwenji.* 慶祝胡適先生六十五歲論文集 [Festschrift for the Celebration of the 65th Birthday of Mr. Hu Shi]. Edited by Zhongyang yanjiuyuan 中央研究院, 123–28. Lishi yuyan yanjiusuo jikan 歷史語言研究所集刊 [Bulletin of the Academy for History and Language] 28. Taipei: Jinghua yinshuguan chubanshe, 1957.

Wang Chang 王昶, ed. *Jinshi cuibian* 金石萃編 [Exquisite of Metal and Stone Inscriptions]. Shanghai: Zui liu tang, 1893.

Wang Qiying 王其英, ed. *Wuwei jinshi lu* [Metal and Stone Inscriptions of Wuwei]. Lanzhou: Lanzhou daxue chubanshe, 2001.

Wang Rui 王睿. "Zai lun Zhongguo de Sute zhejie jun." 再论中国的粟特柘羯军 [Discussing Again the Sogdian *Zhejie* Armies of China]. *Xiyu yanjiu*, no. 3 (2011): 14–25.

Wang Shangshou 王尚寿 and Ji Chengjia 季成家, eds. *Sichou zhi lu wenhua da cidian* 丝绸之路文化大辞典 [Dictionary of Silk Road Culture]. Lanzhou: Hongqi chubanshe, 1995.

Wang Su 王素. "Gaochang huoxianjiao lungao." 高昌火祆教论稿 [A Preliminary Discussion of the Fire Xian Cult of Gaochang]. *Lishi yanjiu*, no. 3 (1986): 168–77.

—–. "Xuanquan Han jian suo jian Kangju shiliao kaoshi." 悬泉汉简所见康居史料考释 [Edition of the Historical Material Concerning Kangju on the Han Bamboo Slips of Xuanquan]. In Rong Xinjiang 荣新江; Li Xiaocong 李孝聪, *Zhongwai guanxi shi: xin shiliao yu xin wenti*, 149–61.

Wang Zhongluo 王仲犖. *Duanhuang shishi dizhi canjuan kaoshi* 敦煌石室地志殘卷考釋 [Annotated Edition of the Fragments of Geographical Treaties in the Stone Caves of Dunhuang]. With the assistance of Zheng Yixiu 鄭宜秀. Zhonghua xueshu congshu 中華學術叢書 [Chinese Academia Collectanea]. Shanghai: Shanghai guji chubanshe, 1993.

Wang Zijin 王子今. "'Chongyi': Handai minzu shi yu waijiao shi zhong de yi zhong wenhua xianxiang." "重译": 汉代民族史与外交史中的一种文化现象 ['Multiple Translations': A Cultural Phenomenon in the History of Foreign Affairs and the History of the Han Dynasty]. *Hebei xuekan*, no. 4 (2010).

Watson, Burton. *Records of the Grand Historian: Han Dynasty I. By Sima Qian (Revised Edition).* [1961]. Hong Kong, New York: Columbia University Press, 1993.

Waugh, Daniel C. "Richthofen's 'Silk Roads': Toward the Archaeology of a Concept." *The Silk Road* 5, no. 1 (Summer 2007): 1–10.

Weber, Dieter. "Zur sogdischen Personennamengebung." *Indogermanische Forschungen*, no. 77 (1972): 191–208.

Wechsler, Howard J. "The Founding of the T'ang Dynasty: Kao-tsu (Reign 618–26)." In *The Cambridge History of China: Volume 3: Sui and T'ang China, 589–906, Part I.* Edited by Denis C. Twitchett, 150–87. Cambridge: Cambridge University Press, 2008.

Wei Jian 魏坚 and Neimenggu zizhiqu wenwu kaogu yanjiusuo 内蒙古自治区文物考古研究所,

eds. *Neimenggu diqu Xianbei muzang de faxian yu yanjiu* 内蒙古地区鲜卑墓葬的发现与研究 [Discovery and Study of the Graves of the Xianbei in the Region of Inner Mongolia]. Beijing: Kexue chubanshe, 2004.

Weinstein, Stanley. *Buddhism under the T'ang*. Cambridge, London, New York, New Rochelle, Melbourne, Sydney: Cambridge University Press, 1987.

Wen Yucheng 溫玉成. "Longmen suo jian zhongwai jiaotong shiliao chutan." 龍門所見中外交通史料初探 [Preliminary Study of the Historical Material on Chinese-Foreign Communication Seen in Longmen]. *Xibei shidi*, no. 1 (1983): 61–68.

Wertmann, Patrick. *Sogdians in China: Archaeological and art historical analyses of tombs and texts from the 3rd to the 10th century AD.* Archaeology in China and East Asia 5. Darmstadt: Philipp von Zabern, 2015.

Wertmann, Patrick, Mayke Wagner, and Pavel Tarasov. "Sogdian Careers and Families in Sixth- to Seventh-Century Northern China: A Case Study of the Shi family Based on Archaeological Finds and Epitaph Inscriptions." *The History of the Family*, no. 22.1 (2017): 103–35. doi:10.1080/1081602X.2016.1243484.

Whitfield, Susan and Ursula Sims-Williams, eds. *The Silk Road: Trade, Travel, War and Faith*. London: British Library, 2004.

Wilkinson, Endymion. *Chinese History: A New Manual*. Third, revised printing. Cambridge, MA: Harvard University Press, 2013.

Wolf, Eric R. "Aspects of Group Relations in a Complex Society: Mexico." *American Anthropologist*, no. 58 (1956): 1065–78.

Wright, Arthur F. "Fo-t'u-têng: A Biography." *Harvard Journal of Asiatic Studies* 11, 3/4 (1948): 321–71. doi:10.2307/2718153.

Wu Hung 巫鴻. "A Case of Cultural Interaction: House-shaped Sarcophagi of the Northern Dynasties." *Orientations*, no. 5 (2002): 34–41.

Wu Rengzhou 吴礽骧. "Dunhuang Xuanquan yizhi jian du zhengli jianjie." 敦煌悬泉遺址简牍整理简介 [A Preliminary Reading and Organisation of the Slips from the Remains of Quanxuan, Dunhuang]. *Dunhuang yanjiu*, no. 4 (1994): 98–106, 188.

Wu Yongzhang 吳永章. *Zhongguo tusi zhidu yuanyuan yu fazhan shi* 中國土司制度淵源与發展史 [The Origin and Evolution of the *Tusi*-System of China]. Chengdu: Sichuan minzu chubanshe, 1988.

Wu Yugui 吴玉贵. "Liangzhou Sute huren An shi jiazu yanjiu." 凉州粟特胡人安氏家族研究 [Research on the Sogdian An Clan of Liangzhou]. *Tang yanjiu*, no. 3: 295–338.

Wu Zhigong 牛致功. "'An Yuanshou muzhiming' zhong de ji ge wenti." 《安元寿墓志铭》中的几个问题 [Several Questions Concerning the 'Epitaph of An Yuanshou']. *Shixue yuekan*, no. 3 (1999): 37–40.

Xia Nai 夏鼐. "Zongshu Zhongguo chutu de bosi Sashanchao yinbi." 综述中国出土的波斯萨珊朝银币 [Summary of the Sasanian Silver Coins Excavated in China]. *Kaogu xuebao*, no. 1 (1974): 91–110.

Xi'an shi wenwu baohu kaogusuo 西安市文物保护考古所. "Xi'an Bei Zhou Liangzhou *sabao* Shijun mu fajue jianbao." 西安北周凉州萨保史君墓发掘简报 [Brief Excavation Report on the Tomb of the *Sabao* Master Shi of Liangzhou of the Northern Zhou from Xi'an]. *Wenwu*, no. 3 (2005): 4–33.

——. "Xi'an Bei Zhou Kang Ye mu fajue jianbao." 西安北周康业墓发掘简报 [Brief Excavation Report on the Grave of Kang Ye of the Northern Zhou in Xi'an]. *Wenwu*, no. 6 (2008): 14–35.

Xiang Da 向達. *Tangdai Chang'an yu Xiyu wenming* 唐代長安與西域文明 [Chang'an during the Tang Dynasty and the Civilisation of the Western Regions]. Yanjing xuebao zhuanhao 燕京學報專號 [Special Issue of the Yanjing Academic Journal] 2. Beijing: Hafo-Yanjing she, 1933.

Xinjiang Weiwu'er zizhiqu bowuguan 新疆維吾爾自治區博物館, ed. *Xinjiang chutu wenwu* 新疆出土文物 [Cultural Relics Unearthed in Sinkiang]. Beijing: Wenwu chubanshe, 1975.

——, ed. *Xinjiang Weiwu'er zizhiqu bowuguan* 新疆維吾爾自治區博物館 [Museum of the Xinjiang Uyghur Autonomous Region]. Beijing: Wenwu chubanshe, 1991.

Xu Diankui 徐殿魁. "Tang jing fenqi de kaoguxue tantao." 唐镜分期的考古学探讨 [An Archaeological Study of the Periodization of the Tang Mirror]. *Kaogu xuebao*, no. 3 (1994): 299–342.

Xu Jieshun. "Understanding the Snowball Theory of the Han Nationality." In *Critical Han Studies: The History, Representation, and Identity of China's Majority*. Edited by Thomas S. Mullaney et al., 113–27. Berkeley, Los Angeles, London: University of California Press, 2012.

Xu Xuya 许序雅. "Sute, Suteren yu jiu xing hu kaobian." 粟特、粟特人与九姓胡考辨 [Verification of Soghd, Soghdian and Jiu Xing Hu]. *Xiyu yanjiu*, no. 2 (2007): 8–15.

Xu Zhiqiang 徐自強. *Beijing tushuguan cang muzhi tapian mulu* 北京圖書館藏墓誌拓片目錄 [Inventory of the Epitaph Rubbings in the Beijing Library]. Beijing, 1990.

Yamada Nobuo 山田信夫. "Toruko zoku to Sogudo Shōnin." トルコ族とソグド商人 [The Turkish People and Sogdian Merchants]. In *Perusha to Tō*. ペルシアと唐 [Persia and the Tang]. Edited by Yamada Nobuo 山田信夫, 276–335. Tōzai bunmei no kōryū 2. Tōkyō: Heibonsha, 1971.

Yamamoto Tatsuro, and Dohi Yoshikazu. *Tun-Huang and Turfan Documents Concerning Social and Economic History, II Census Registers, (B) Plates*. Tōkyō: The Toyo Bunko, 1984.

——. *Tun-Huang and Turfan Documents Concerning Social and Economic History, II Census Registers, (A) Introduction & Texts*. Tōkyō: The Toyo Bunko, 1985.

Yamamoto Tatsuro, Dohi Yoshikazu, and Ishida Yusaku. *Tun-Huang and Turfan Documents Concerning Social and Economic History, IV She Associations and Related Documents*. Tōkyō: The Toyo Bunko, 1988, 1989.

Yamamoto Tatsuro, and Ikeda On. *Tun-Huang and Turfan Documents Concerning Social and Economic History, III Contracts*. 2 vols. Tōkyō: The Toyo Bunko, 1986, 1987.

Yamamoto Tatsuro, Ikeda On, Dohi Yoshikazu, Kegasawa Yasunori, Okano Makoto, Ishida Yusaku, and Seo Tatsuhiko. *Tun-Huang and Turfan Documents Concerning Social and Economic History, Supplement*. Tōkyō: The Toyo Bunko, 2001.

Yamamoto Tatsuro, Okano Makoto, and Ikeda On. *Tun-Huang and Turfan Documents Concerning Social and Economic History, I Legal Texts*. 2 vols. Tōkyō: The Toyo Bunko, 1978, 1980.

Yamashita Shōji 山下将司. "Zui Tō sho no kasei Sogudojin gundan Tenri toshokanzo *bunkan shirin* 'An Shujin bohimei' zankan o megutte." 隋–唐初の河西ソグド人軍團--天理圖書館藏『文館詞林』「安修仁墓碑銘」殘巻をめぐって [The Sogdian Army Corps in Ho-hsi during the Sui and Early T'ang: A Section of the Epitaph of An Hsiu-jen in the Wen-kuan tz'u-lin Held by the Tenri Central Library]. *Tōhōgaku*, no. 110 (2005): 65–78.

Yan Kejun 嚴可均, ed. *Quan shang gu san dai Qin Han San Guo Liu Chao wen* 全上古三代秦漢三國六朝文 [Complete Prose of High Antiquity, the Three Dynasties, Qin Han, Three Kingdoms, and Six Dynasties]. [1894]. Beijing: Zhonghua shuju, 1991.

Yang Fuxue 杨富学. "Da Tang Xishi bowuguan cang 'huihe Mi fuhou muzhi' kaoshi." 大唐西市博物馆藏《回鹘米副侯墓志》考释 [A Study on *Epitaph of Uighur Sub-Marquess*

Mi Kept in Tang West Market Museum, Xi'an]. *Minzu yanjiu*, no. 2 (2015): 78–86.

Yang Junkai 杨军凯. "Bei Zhou Shi jun mu shiguo dongbi fudiao tuxiang chutan." 北周史君墓石椁東壁浮雕圖像初探 [Preliminary Study on the Images from the Eastern Wall of the Stone Coffin of Master Shi of the Northern Zhou]. *Yishushi yanjiu*, no. 5 (2003): 189–98.

——. "Ruhua Sute juluo shouling muzang de xin faxian: Bei Zhou Liangzhou *sabao* Shi jun mu shiguo tuxiang chushi." 入華粟特聚落首領墓葬的新發現……北周涼州薩保史君墓石椁圖像初釋 [Newly Discovered Burials of Sogdian Community Leaders in China: A Preliminary Decoding of the Illustrations on the Stone Sarcophagus of the *Sabao* Shi of Liangzhou Dating from the Northern Zhou Dynasty]. In *Cong Sama'ergan dao Chang'an: Suteren zai Zhongguo de wenhua yiji.* 從薩馬爾干到長安, 粟特人在中國的文化遺迹 [From Samarkand to Chang'an: Cultural Traces of the Sogdians in China]. Edited by Rong Xinjiang 荣新江 and Zhang Zhiqing 张志清, 17–26. Beijing: Zhongguo guojia tushuguan chubanshe, 2004.

——. "Carvings on the Stone Outer Coffin of Lord Shi of the Northern Zhou." In Vaissière; Trombert, *Les Sogdiens en Chine*, 21–45.

——. "Bei Zhou Shi jun mu shuangyu mingwen ji xiangguan wenti." 北周史君墓双语铭文及相关问题 [The Bilingual Epitaph of the Grave of Master Shi of the Northern Zhou and Related Questions]. *Wenwu*, no. 8 (2013): 49–58.

Yang Shao-yun. "Reinventing the Barbarian: Rhetorical and Philosophical Uses of the Yi-Di in Mid-Imperial China, 600–1300." Doctoral Dissertation, University of California, Last modified 2014. Accessed February 11, 2019. https://escholarship.org/uc/item/2z57382p.

Yang Yunru 楊筠如. *Jiu pin zhongzheng yu Liu chao menfa* 九品中正與六朝門閥 [The Nine Ranks of Impartial and Just and the Six Dynasties' Great Families]. Shanghai: Shangwu yinshu guan, 1930.

Yao Kuan 姚寬 and Lu You 陸遊, eds. *Xixi congyu; Jia shi jiu wen* 西溪叢語; 家世舊聞. [1993]. 2nd ed. Beijing: Zhonghua shuju, 1997.

Ye Wa. "Mortuary Practice in Medieval China A Study of the Xingyuan Tang Cemetery." Doctoral Dissertation, University of California, Last modified 2005.

Yen Chuan-ying 顏娟英, ed. *Selections of Buddhist Stone Rubbings from the Northern Dynasties.* Zhongyang yanjiuyuan lishi yuyan yanjiusuo zhencang shiliao ji dianji xilie 中央研究院歷史語言研究所珍藏史料暨典籍系列 [The Institute of History and Philology, Academia Sinica, Special Collections of Historical Materials] 3. Taipei: Institute of History and Philology, 2008.

Yoshida Yutaka. "Review of: Nicholas Sims-Williams, *Sogdian and other Iranian inscriptions of the Upper Indus* I, (Corpus Inscriptionum Iranicarum. Part II, Volume III/II), 36pp., 170 plates. London, School of Oriental and African Studies, 1989." *Indo-Iranian Journal*, no. 36.3 (1993): 252–56.

——. "Translation of the Contract for the Purchase of a Slave Girl Found at Turfan and Dated 639." *T'oung Pao*, no. 89 (2003): 159–61.

——. "When did Sogdians begin to write vertically?" *Tokyo University Linguistic Papers*, no. 33 (2013): 375–94.

Yoshida Yutaka 吉田豊. "Sogudo go kenkyū bunkan mokuroku." ソグド語研究文献目録 (1979–1984) [Bibliography of Studies on the Sogdian Language (1979–1984)]. *Sēnan ajia kenkyū*, no. 23 (1984).

——. "Sogudo-go zatsuroku (ni)." ソグド語雑録 (II) [Miscellaneous Sogdian Records (II)]. *Oriento*, no. 31.2 (1988): 165–72.

——. "Corpus Inscriptionum Iranicarum. Part II: Inscriptions of the Seleucid and Parthian periods and of Eastern Iran and Central Asia. Vol. III: Sogdian. Part II: Sogdian and other Iranian inscriptions of the Upper Indus. By Nicholas Sims-Williams. 94 pp., plates 171–265, 3 maps. London: School of Oriental and African Studies, 1992. £50." *Bulletin of the School of Oriental and African Studies*, no. 57 (1994): 391–92. doi:10.1017/S0041977X00025155.

—. "*Review: Corpus Inscriptionum Iranicarum. Part II: Inscriptions of the Seleucid and Parthian Periods and of Eastern Iran and Central Asia. Vol. V: Saka Documents Text Vol. III: The St. Petersburg Collections. By Ronald E. Emmerick and Margarita I. Vorob'ëva-Desjatovskaja.* 256 pp., Plates 160–198. London: School of Oriental and African Studies, University of London, 1995. £53." *Bulletin of the School of Oriental and African Studies*, no. 60.3 (1997): 567–69.

—. "Sino-Iranica." *Seinan ajia kenkyū*, no. 48 (1998): 33–51.

—. "On the Origin of the Sogdian Surname Zhaowu 昭武 and Related Problems." *Journal Asiatique*, 291.1–2 (2003): 35–67.

—. "The Sogdian Version of the New Xi'an Inscription." In Vaissière; Trombert, *Les Sogdiens en Chine*, 57–72.

—. "Personal Names, Sogdian: I. In Chinese Sources." *Encyclopædia Iranica, online edition*, Last modified August 15, 2006. Accessed October 20, 2017. http://www.iranicaonline.org/articles/personal-names-sogdian-1-in-chinese-sources.

Yoshida Yutaka 吉田豊, Moriyasu Takao 森安孝夫, and Xinjiang Uyghur Autonomous Museum 新疆ウィグル自治区博物館. "Kikushi Kōshōkoku jidai Sogudo bun onna dorei baibai monjo." 麹氏高昌国時代ソグド文女奴隷売買文書 [A Sogdian Sale Contract of a Female Slave from the Period of the Gaochang 高昌 Kingdom under the Rule of Qu 麹 Clan]. *Nairiku ajia gengo no kenkyū*, no. 4 (1989): 1–50. Accessed September 5, 2016. http://hdl.handle.net/11094/18715.

Yu Lunian 俞鹿年, ed. *Zhongguo guanzhi da cidian* 中国官制大辞典 [Comprehensive Dictionary of the Bureaucratic System of China]. 2 vols. Harbin: Heilongjiang renmin chubanshe, 1992.

Yu Taishan. "A Study of Saka History." *Sino-Platonic Papers*, no. 80 (1998): 1–225.

—. "The Sui Dynasty and the Western Regions." *Sino-Platonic Papers*, no. 247 (2014): 1–24. Accessed September 10, 2016.

Yu Xianhao 郁賢皓, ed. *Tang cishi kao quanbian: er* 唐刺史考全編：二 [Complete Edition of Studies on the Magistrate of the Tang, 2]. Hefei: Anhui daxue chubanshe, 2000.

Yuan Anzhi 員安志 and Shaanxi sheng kaogu yanjiusuo 陝西省考古研究所, eds. *Zhongguo Bei Zhou zhengui wenwu: Bei Zhou muzang fajue baogao* 中國北周珍貴文物：北周墓葬發掘報告 [Exquisite Relics of the Northern Zhou from China: Funerary Excavation Reports from the Northern Zhou]. Xi'an: Shaanxi renmin meishu chubanshe, 1992.

Yuanzhou lianhe kaogudui 原州联合考古队, ed. *Bei Zhou Tian Hong mu* 北周田弘墓 [The Grave of Tian Hong of the Northern Zhou]. Beijing: Wenwu chubanshe, 2009.

—, ed. *Tang Shi Daoluo mu* 唐史道洛墓 [The Tomb of Shi Daoluo of the Tang]. Beijing: Wenwu chubanshe, 2014.

Zhang Guangda 张广达. "Trois exemples d'influences mazdéennes dans la Chine des Tang." *Études chinoises*, 13.1–2 (1994): 203–19.

—. "Une représentation iconographique de la Daēnā et de la Daēva? Quelques pistes de réflexion sur les religions venues d'Asie centrale en Chine." In *La Sérinde, terre d'échanges: Art, religion, commerce du Ier au Xe siècle*. Edited by Jean-Pierre Drège, 191–

218. XIVes Rencontres de l'École du Louvre. Paris: La Documentation française, 2000.
——. "Iranian Religious Evidence in Turfan Chinese Texts 吐魯番出土漢語文書中所見伊朗語地區宗教的踪迹." *China Archaeology and Art Digest*, no. 1 (2000): 193–206.
——. "Tangdai de bao lie: Wenhua chuanbo de yi ge shili." 唐代的豹猎—文化传播的一个实例 [Cheetah in Hunting Game in Early Tang Dynasty of China]. *Tang yanjiu*, no. 7 (2001): 177–204.
——. "The Role of the Sogdians as Translators of Buddhist Texts." In *Nomads, Traders and Holy Men Along China's Silk Road: Papers Presented at a Symposium Held at the Asia Society in New York, November 9–10, 2001*. Edited by Annette L. Juliano and Judith A. Lerner, 75–78. Silk Road studies 7. Turnhout: Brepols, 2002.
Zhang Guangda, and Rong Xinjiang. "A Concise History of the Turfan Oasis and Its Exploration." *Asia Major/Third Series*, no. 11 (1998.2): 13–36.
Zhang Ke 张克. *Shiji renwu cidian* 史记人物辞典 [Shiji Biographical Dictionary]. Nanning: Guangxi renmin chubanshe, 1991.
Zhang Naizhu 张乃翥. "The Luoyang Nestorian Pillar and the Gande Township: A Settlement of Foreigners in the Luoyang Area during the Tang Dynasty." In *From the Oxus River to the Chinese Shores: Studies on East Syriac Christianity in China and Central Asia*. Edited by Li Tang and Dietmar W. Winkler, 177–202. Orientalia-Patristica-Oecumenica 5. Zürich: LIT, 2013.
Zhang Qingjie 张庆捷. "'Yu Hong muzhi' zhong de ji ge wenti." 《虞弘墓誌》中的几个问题中的几个问题 [Some Problems in the "Epitaph of Yu Hong"]. *Wenwu*, no. 1 (2001): 102–9.
——. "Sui Yu Hong mu kao shi." 隋虞弘墓考釋 [A Study of the Grave of Yu Hong of the Sui]. In *Taiyuan Sui Yu Hong mu.* 太原隋虞弘墓 [The Tomb of Yu Hong of the Sui from Taiyuan]. Edited by Shanxi sheng kaogu yanjiusuo 山西省考古研究所, Taiyuan shi wenwu kaogu yanjiusuo 太原市文物考古研究所 and Taiyuan shi Jinyuan qu wenwu lüyouju 太原市晋源区文物旅游局, 209–34. Beijing: Wenwu chubanshe, 2005.
——. "*Hutengwu* and *Huxuanwu* Sogdian dances in the Northern, Sui and Tang Dynasties." In Vaissière; Trombert, *Les Sogdiens en Chine*, 93–106.
——. "Sichou zhi lu yu Beichao Jinyang." 丝绸之路与北朝晋阳 [The Silk Road and Jinyang in the Northern Dynasties]. In *Zhongguo Wei Jin Nanbeichao shixuehui: Di shi jie nianhui ji guoji xueshu yantao lunwenji.* 中国魏晋南北朝史学会第十届年会暨国际学术研讨会论文集 [Collection of Papers of China's 10th History Conference on the Wei, Jin, Northern and Southern Dynasties and International Academic Discussion Forum]. Edited by Zhongguo Wei Jin Nanbeichao shixuehui 中国魏晋南北朝史学会 and Shanxi daxue lishi wenhua xueyuan 山西大学历史文化学院, 551–66. Taiyuan 太原 : Beiyue wenyi chubanshe, 2012.
Zhang Wei 張維, ed. *Longyou jinshi lu* 隴右金石錄 [Inscriptions on Metal and Stone of Longyou]. [Lanzhou: Gansu sheng wenxian weiji weiyuanhui, 1943]. Xian Qin, Qin, Han, Wei Ji, Nanbeichao shike wenxian quanbian 先秦秦漢魏晋南北朝石刻文獻全編 [Complete Collection of Stone Inscriptions from the Former Qin, Qin, Han, Wei, Jin, and Northern and Southern Dynasties]. Beijing: Beijing tushuguan chubanshe, 2003.
Zhang Xiaogui 张小贵. *Zhonggu huahua xianjiao kaoshu* [A Study on the Sinicisation of Zoroastrianism in Medieval Times]. 中古华化祆教考述. Beijing: Wenwu chubanshe, 2010.
Zhang Xishun 張希舜, ed. *Sui Tang Wudai muzhi huibian* 隋唐五代墓誌彙編 [Compilation of the Epitaphs of the Sui, Tang and Five Dynasties]. 1st ed. 30 vols. Tianjin: Tianjin guji chubanshe, 1991.
Zhang Yi 張毅 and Zhang Yichun 張一純, eds. *Wang wu Tianzhu guo zhuan jianshi/ [Tang];*

Jing xing ji jiangzhu/[Tang] 往五天竺國傳箋釋/[唐]; 經行記箋注/[唐] [A Commented Edition of the *Travel Account to the Five Indian Kingdoms* from the Tang; A Commented Edition of the *Travel Record* from the Tang]. Zhongwai jiaotong shiji congkan 中外交通史籍叢刊 [Collectanea of Historical Records on Chinese-foreign Exchange] 9. Beijing: Zhonghua shuju, 2000.

Zhang Yonglu 张永禄, ed. *Tangdai Chang'an cidian* 唐代长安词典 [Dictionary of Tang Chang'an]. Xi'an: Shaanxi renmin chubanshe, 1990.

Zhao Chao 赵超. "Muzhi suyuan." 墓誌溯源 [Investigating the Origin of Epitaphs]. *Wenshi*, no. 10 (1983): 43–55.

——. "Dui Shi Daode muzhi jiqi zushu de yi dian kanfa." 对史道德墓志及其族属的一点看法 [A Comment on the Epitaph and Ethnic Affiliation of Shi Daode]. *Wenwu*, no. 12 (1986): 87–89.

——. "Tangdai Luoyang chengfang bukao." 唐代洛阳城坊补考 [An Additional Study on the City Quarters of Luoyang during the Tang Dynasty]. *Kaogu*, no. 9 (1987): 835–41.

——. "Shi, qionglong ding mushi yu fudou xingshi muzhi: jiantan gudai muzang zhong 'xiang tian di' de sixiang." 式、穹窿顶墓室与覆斗形墓志—兼谈古代墓葬中'象天地'的思想 [Shi-Plate, the Domed Tomb Chamber and the Epitaph with a Pyramidal Top]. *Wenwu*, no. 5 (1999): 72–82.

——. *Gudai muzhi tonglun* 古代墓志通论 [Introduction to Ancient Epitaphs]. Zhongguo kaogu wenwu tonglun congshu 中国考古文物通论丛书 [Collectanea of General Introductions on the Archaeology and Cultural Relics of China]. Edited by Li Xueqin 李学勤 and Sun Guangen 孙关根. Beijing: Zijincheng chubanshe, 2002.

——. "Jieshao huke Di Mensheng mumen zhiming ji shi pingfeng." 介绍胡客翟门生墓门志铭及石屏风 [An Introduction to the Epitaph of Di Mensheng 翟門生 Inscribed on a Pair of Stone Tomb Gates and the Related Stone Funerary Panels]. In Rong Xinjiang 荣新江; Luo Feng 罗丰; Ningxia wenwu kaogu yanjiusuo 宁夏文物考古研究所; Beijing daxue zhongguo gudaishi yanjiu zhongxin 北京大学中国古代史研究中心, *Suteren zai Zhongguo II*, 673–84.

Zhao Dexin 赵德馨, ed. *Zhongguo jingji shi cidian* 中国经济史辞典. Wuhan: Hubei cishu chubanshe, 1990.

Zhao Heping 趙和平. "Du Guyuan nanjiao Sui Tang Shi shi jiazu muzhi zhaji." 讀固原南郊隋唐史氏家族墓誌劄記 [Notes on the Epitaphs of the Shi Families of the Sui and Tang from the Southern Suburbs of Guyuan]. *Tang yanjiu*, 16 (2010): 343–57.

Zhao Wanli 趙萬里, ed. *Han Wei Nanbeichao muzhi jishi* 漢魏南北朝墓誌集釋 [Annotated Compilation of Epitaphs of the Han, Wei, and Southern and Northern Dynasties]. [1953]. Guilin 桂林: Guangxi shifan daxue chubanshe, 2008.

Zhao Zhenhua 赵振华. "Tangdai shaofujian Zheng Yan jiqi Suteren zuxian." 唐代少府监郑岩及其粟特人祖先 [The Tang Dynasty Director of Imperial Workshops Zheng Yan and his Sogdian Ancestors]. *Zhongguo guojia bowuguan guan kan*, no. 5 (2012): 69–76.

Zhaoling bowuguan 昭陵博物馆, and Chen Zhijian 陈志谦. "Tang An Yuanshou fufu mu fajue jianbao." 唐安元寿夫妇墓发掘简报 [Brief Excavation Report of the Grave of An Yuanshou and Wife of the Tang]. *Wenwu*, no. 12 (1988): 37–49.

Zheng Binglin 鄭炳林, ed. *Dunhuang dili wenshu huiji jiaozhu* 敦煌地理文書匯輯校注 [An Annotated Collection of Geographic Literature on Dunhuang]. Lanzhou: Gansu jiaoyu chubanshe, 1989.

Zheng Tianting 郑天挺, Wu Ze 吴泽, and Yang Zhijiu 杨志玖, eds. *Zhongguo lishi da cidian: xia juan* 中国历史大辞典 [Comprehensive Dictionary of Chinese History]. 2 vols.

Shanghai: Shanghai cishu chubanshe, 2000.

Zheng Yan 郑岩. "Bei Zhou Kang Ye mu shita huaxiang zhaji." 北周康业墓石塌画像札记 [Notes on the Stone Panel Portraits of the Grave of Kang Ye from the Northern Zhou]. *Wenwu*, no. 11 (2008): 67–76.

Zhongguo kexueyuan lishi yanjiusuo ziliaoshi 中國科學院歷史研究所資料室, ed. *Dunhuang ziliao: di yi ji* 敦煌資料—第一輯 [Dunhuang Material, 1]. [1961. Beijing: Zhonghua shuju, 1964.

Zhou Shaoliang 周紹良 and Zhao Chao 趙超, eds. *Tangdai muzhi huibian* 唐代墓誌彙編 [Collectanea of Epitaphs from the Tang Dynasty]. 2 vols. Shanghai: Shanghai guji chubanshe, 1992.

——. *Tangdai muzhiming huibian xuji* 唐代墓誌銘彙編續集 [Collectanea of Epitaphs from the Tang Dynasty, Sequel]. Shanghai: Shanghai guji chubanshe, 2001.

Zhou Weizhou 周伟洲. "Sui Yu Hong muzhi shizheng." 隋虞弘墓志释证 [Close Reading of the Epitaph of Yu Hong of the Sui]. In Rong Xinjiang 荣新江; Li Xiaocong 李孝聪, *Zhongwai guanxi shi: xin shiliao yu xin wenti*, 247–57.

Zhu Yuemei 朱悦梅, and Li Bingcheng 李并成. "'Shazhou dudufu tujing' zuanxiu niandai jiqi xiangguan wenti kao." 《沙州都督府图经》纂修年代及其相关问题考 [Questions Concerning the Editing Date of the 'Shazhou Dudufu Tujing']. *Dunhuang yanjiu*, no. 5 (2003): 61–65.

Zürcher, E. "The Yüeh-chih and Kaniṣka in the Chinese Sources." In *Papers on the Date of Kaniṣka: Submitted to the Conference on the Date of Kaniṣka. London, 20–22 April, 1960.* Edited by A. L. Basham, 346–90. Leiden: Brill, 1968.

——. *The Buddhist Conquest of China: The Spread and Adaptation of Buddhism in Early Medieval China.* [1959]. 3rd ed. Leiden: E. J. Brill, 2007.